DIGITAL COMPUTER FUNDAMENTALS

DIGITAL COMPUTER FUNDAMENTALS

Fourth Edition

Thomas C. Bartee
Harvard University

McGraw-Hill Book Company

New York   St. Louis   San Francisco
Auckland   Bogotá   Düsseldorf
Johannesburg   London   Madrid
Mexico   Montreal   New Delhi
Panama   Paris   São Paulo   Singapore
Sydney   Tokyo   Toronto

DIGITAL
COMPUTER
FUNDAMENTALS

Copyright © 1977, 1972, 1966, 1960 by McGraw-Hill, Inc. All rights reserved.
Printed in the United States of America. No part of this publication may be
reproduced, stored in a retrieval system, or transmitted, in any form or by any
means, electronic, mechanical, photocopying, recording, or otherwise, without the
prior written permission of the publisher.

1 2 3 4 5 6 7 8 9 0   DODO   7 8 3 2 1 0 9 8 7

This book was set in Helvetica Light by Ruttle, Shaw & Wetherill, Inc.
The editors were Peter D. Nalle and Matthew Cahill;
the designer was Jo Jones;
the production supervisor was Leroy A. Young.
New drawings were done by J & R Services, Inc.
R. R. Donnelley & Sons Company was printer and binder.

Library of Congress Cataloging in Publication Data

Bartee, Thomas C
    Digital computer fundamentals.

    Bibliography: p.
    Includes index.
    1.   Electronic digital computers.   I.   Title.
QA76.5.B297   1977   001.6'4   76-43336
ISBN 0-07-003892-9

CONTENTS

PREFACE
xi

1 COMPUTER OPERATION   1

  1·1   Calculators and Computers   2
  1·2   Differences between Desk Calculators and Computers   4
  1·3   Electronic Digital Computers   4
  1·4   Application of Computers to Problems   6
  1·5   Applications of Computers in Business   8
  1·6   Scientific Applications   9
  1·7   Some Different Types of Computer Systems   11
  1·8   The Use of Digital Computers in Control Systems   14
  1·9   Special-Purpose and General-Purpose Computers   16
  1·10   Time-shared Computer Systems   17
  1·11   Basic Components of a Digital Computer   18
  1·12   Construction of Memory   20
  1·13   Instructions   20
  1·14   Multiplication Instruction   23
  1·15   BRANCH, SKIP, or JUMP Instructions   25
  1·16   Reading the Program into the Computer   26
  1·17   Programming Systems   33
  1·18   Assembly Languages   34
  1·19   Compiler Languages   37
  1·20   A Short Introduction to PL/1   38
  Questions   42

v

2   NUMBER SYSTEMS   47

2·1   The Decimal System   48
2·2   The Binary System   49
2·3   Counting in the Binary System   49
2·4   Binary Addition and Subtraction   51
2·5   Binary Multiplication and Division   51
2·6   Converting Decimal Numbers to Binary   53
2·7   Negative Numbers   54
2·8   The Use of Complements to Represent Negative Numbers   56
2·9   Complements in Other Number Systems   57
2·10   Binary Number Complements   57
2·11   Binary-coded-decimal Number Representation   58
2·12   Octal and Hexadecimal Number Systems   61
       Questions   65

3   BOOLEAN ALGEBRA AND GATE NETWORKS   73

3·1   Fundamental Concepts of Boolean Algebra   74
3·2   Logical Multiplication   75
3·3   OR Gates and AND Gates   76
3·4   Complementation and Inverters   78
3·5   Evaluation of Logical Expressions   79
3·6   Evaluation of an Expression Containing Parentheses   80
3·7   Basic Laws of Boolean Algebra   82
3·8   Proof by Perfect Induction   84
3·9   Simplification of Expressions   86
3·10   De Morgan's Theorems   86
3·11   Basic Duality of Boolean Algebra   87
3·12   Derivation of a Boolean Expression   87
3·13   Combination of Gates   91
3·14   Sum-of-Products and Product-of-Sums   92
3·15   Derivation of Product-of-Sums Expressions   94
3·16   Derivation of a Three-Input-Variable Expression   95
3·17   NAND Gates and NOR Gates   97
3·18   The Map Method for Simplifying Expressions   100
3·19   Subcubes and Covering   103
3·20   Product-of-Sums Expressions—Don't-cares   108
       Questions   110

4   LOGICAL DESIGN   124

4·1   The Flip-Flop   125
4·2   The Transfer   127

4·3   The Clock   128
4·4   The Shift Register   131
4·5   The Binary Counter   132
4·6   BCD Counters   138
4·7   Integrated Circuits   139
4·8   Medium- and Large-Scale Integration   148
4·9   Gated Flip-Flop Designs   152
4·10   The Gated Flip-Flop   152
4·11   The Master-Slave Flip-Flop   154
4·12   Counter Design   157
Questions   161

5   **DIGITAL CIRCUITS**   168

5·1   Computer Circuits   169
5·2   Characteristics of Diodes and Transistors Used in
       Switching Circuits   169
5·3   The Emitter Follower   177
5·4   The AND Gate   178
5·5   The Diode AND Circuit   179
5·6   The OR Gate   180
5·7   The Inverter Circuit   181
5·8   NOR Gates   184
5·9   The Transistor Flip-Flop   186
5·10   Resistor-Transistor Logic   187
5·11   Diode-Transistor Logic   189
5·12   Transistor-Transistor Logic   191
5·13   Emitter-coupled Logic   198
5·14   Metal-Oxide Semiconductor Circuits   202
5·15   CMOS Logic Circuits   206
Questions   209

6   **THE ARITHMETIC-LOGIC UNIT**   219

6·1   Construction of the ALU   220
6·2   Integer Representation   221
6·3   The Binary Half Adder   222
6·4   The Full Adder   223
6·5   A Parallel Binary Adder   224
6·6   Positive and Negative Numbers   227
6·7   Addition in the 1s Complement System   228
6·8   Addition in the 2s Complement System   229
6·9   Addition and Subtraction in a Parallel Arithmetic Element   231
6·10   The Full Adder   234

6·11   The Binary-Coded-Decimal (BCD) Adder   237
6·12   Positive and Negative BCD Numbers   239
6·13   Addition and Subtraction in the 9s Complement System   241
6·14   The SHIFT Operation   245
6·15   Basic Operations   246
6·16   Binary Multiplication   250
6·17   Decimal Multiplication   253
6·18   Division   254
6·19   Logical Operations   260
6·20   Floating-Point Number Systems   262
6·21   Performing Arithmetic
       Operations with Floating-Point Numbers   267
       Questions   268

7   **THE MEMORY ELEMENT**   274

7·1   Random-Access Memories   276
7·2   Magnetic Core Storage   278
7·3   Storage of Information in Magnetic Cores in a
       Two-dimensional Array   281
7·4   Assembly of Core Planes into a Core Memory   285
7·5   Timing Sequence   287
7·6   Characteristics of Core-Memory Array   289
7·7   Memory Address and Memory Buffer Registers   289
7·8   Driving the X- and Y-Selection Lines   290
7·9   Memory Buffer Register and Associated Circuitry   292
7·10   Characteristics of Core Memory   294
7·11   Decoders   295
7·12   Core-Memory Organization and Wiring Schemes   300
7·13   Random-Access Semiconductor Memories   304
7·14   Bipolar IC Memories   305
7·15   Static MOS Memories   308
7·16   Dynamic Memories   314
7·17   Read-only Memories   316
7·18   Magnetic Drum Storage   321
7·19   Parallel and Serial Operation of a Magnetic Drum   325
7·20   Magnetic Disk Memories   327
7·21   Flexible Disk Storage Systems—The Floppy Disk   332
7·22   Magnetic Tape   336
7·23   Tape Cassettes and Cartridges   340
7·24   Digital Recording Techniques   346
7·25   Return-to-Zero and Return-to-Bias Recording Techniques   346
7·26   Non–Return-to-Zero Recording Techniques   349
       Questions   351

8 INPUT-OUTPUT DEVICES 357

8·1 Differences in Business and Scientific Uses 358
8·2 Perforated Tape 359
8·3 Tape Readers 362
8·4 Punched Cards 365
8·5 Card Readers 367
8·6 Alphanumeric Codes 369
8·7 Data Preparation 373
8·8 Character Recognition 374
8·9 Output Equipment 376
8·10 Printers 377
8·11 Cathode-Ray-Tube Output Devices 382
8·12 Other Output Devices 384
8·13 Error-detecting and Error-correcting Codes 385
8·14 Terminals 387
8·15 Input-Output Devices for Systems with Analog Components 391
8·16 Analog-to-Digital Converters — Shaft Encoders 392
8·17 Digital-to-Analog Converters 394
8·18 Electronic High-Speed Analog-to-Digital Converters 395
Questions 399

9 THE CONTROL UNIT 405

9·1 Construction of Instruction Word 406
9·2 Instruction-Cycle and Execution-Cycle Organization of Control Registers 412
9·3 Sequence of Operation of Control Registers 415
9·4 Controlling Arithmetic Operations 417
9·5 Typical Sequence of Operations 424
9·6 BRANCH, SKIP, or JUMP Instructions 426
9·7 SHIFT Instructions 429
9·8 Microprogramming 432
9·9 Variations in Microprogramming Configurations 438
Questions 440

10 COMPUTER ORGANIZATION 443

10·1 Instruction Word Formats — Number of Addresses 444
10·2 Representation of Instructions and Data 448
10·3 Addressing Techniques 449
10·4 Index Registers 449
10·5 Paging and Indirect Addressing 451
10·6 Interconnecting System Components 455
10·7 Interfacing — Buses 463

10·8   Microprocessors and Microcomputers   470
10·9   Single-Address Computer Organization   481
10·10   A Single-Address Microprocessor   488
10·11   Two-Address Computers   500
10·12   IBM 360/370 Computer Series   506
Questions   513

BIBLIOGRAPHY   521

ANSWERS TO SELECTED ODD-NUMBERED QUESTIONS   527

INDEX   552

PREFACE

The purpose of this book is to present, as clearly as possible, the principles of modern digital computers. Many questions are included in a separate section of each chapter, and answers to selected odd-numbered questions are given at the end of the book.

This edition of the book includes major recent computer developments such as microprocessors, floppy disk memories, large-scale integrated circuits, and microprogramming. As a result, a considerable amount of the book has been rewritten, and consequently there are also many new questions. Further, I have received a number of suggestions and comments from users of the book and these have been used to improve the presentation and coverage.

Chapter 1 describes the uses of the computer in business, industry, and science, and it also presents a brief introduction to programming. Some historical material is also included, as are some basic concepts relating to computer usage.

Chapters 2 through 5 introduce some of the basic ideas and principles which are used in all digital computers and also in digital instruments, digital communications systems, digital control systems, and in fact in all digital devices. These chapters describe number systems, Boolean algebra, logic design, and the major digital circuit lines. The sections on counters and, in general, logic design using flip-flops have been expanded into a complete chapter. The material on digital circuits has been updated, and the major new circuit advances have been included.

Chapters 6, 7, and 8 treat arithmetic operations, memories, and input-output devices. The material on arithmetic operations first explains how arithmetic is performed in computers and then how arithmetic-logic units in computers are organized. The chapter on memories presents magnetic core and integrated circuit memories followed by drum, disk, tape, and other mass storage devices. The latest developments in this area, such as tape cartridges, floppy disks, dynamic integrated circuit memories, etc., are included here. The chapter on input and output describes the major input-output devices and also includes some material on analog-to-digital converters, digital-to-analog converters, terminals, modems, and acoustic couplers.

The final two chapters, 9 and 10, first discuss the control unit in modern computers, including a description of both conventional logic design of control circuitry and microprogramming for computer control. The overall organization of computers is then discussed, as are the major topics in computer architecture—addressing techniques, bus organization, interrupt servicing, etc. Existing computers are used as examples of the ideas presented. There is some emphasis on microcomputers and minicomputers, but the basic ideas in large systems, such as multiprocessors, pipeline computers, multiprogramming, etc., are also discussed.

The book is arranged so that the material on electronic circuits can be skipped over. There are several reasons for this. In some schools, circuits are covered in a separate course. Other schools wish to treat circuit material lightly, since an understanding of circuit details is not essential to comprehending the functions performed by the circuits. Also, the widespread use of integrated circuits makes it possible to study the operation of a computer from a module, or block, viewpoint, as in Chapters 3 and 4, so that computer operation can be understood by considering flip-flops and gates from a functional, or operational, viewpoint.

The block diagram symbols in this book are those which have been adopted by the American National Standards Institute and also as Military Standards.

I have had considerable help and advice during the preparation of the various editions of this book. The first edition was written at MIT Lincoln Laboratory, and I will always be indebted to MIT and the laboratory members for the considerable support provided me.

Many friends and users of the book have contributed to later editions. I regret that I cannot name them all. Certainly Professors Glen Goff, W. W. Peterson, Robert Carroll, Irving Reed, and Irwin Lebow should be singled out. I must also thank the teaching assistants in my courses for their many suggestions.

Ms. E. M. Vadeboncoeur prepared the manuscript for this edition, and I am permanently indebted to her for her work on both this and prior editions.

Thomas C. Bartee

COMPUTER OPERATION

The computer industry continues to be the fastest-growing major industry. The sales of large computers increase every year, and the size of the overall computer industry has been further supplemented by the booming minicomputer market and the introduction of microcomputers to the market.

Minicomputers and microcomputers make possible exciting new application areas for computers because of their low cost, reliability, small size, and low weight. These small computers are able to calculate at a rate of hundreds of thousands to millions of operations per second and offer computing power which was available in only the larger computers as recently as 10 years ago. The places where small computers can be used appear endless: such areas as process control; medical monitoring; production testing; scientific instrument recording; store checkout systems; and automobile test and evaluation systems were among the first to appear.

Well over a million people now work in the computer industry, and this does not include the millions who work with computers indirectly, such as bank clerks who put all their transactions into computers, airline and motel employees who work with computers to make reservations, and machinists who use computer-controlled power tools.

In fact, computers now route our long-distance telephone calls, process and issue the checks in our banks, schedule our planes and trains, make our weather forecasts, predict and process our elections, and figure in so many things that entire books will be (and have been) written just documenting the types of applications.

Computers now use the major share of the electronics components being manufactured, and this share will continue to rise. The need for computer personnel in all areas continues pressing: over a quarter of a million new programmers are needed each year; the federal government's Department of Labor continues to maintain business machine service personnel and electronic computer operating personnel in first and second place in a list of five "fastest-growing employment areas."

1•1 CALCULATORS AND COMPUTERS

From the time individuals first started using arithmetic, they have been inventing devices to aid in handling numbers. One of the earliest and most ingenious examples of an aid to computation is the abacus. This primitive (4000 to 3000 B.C.) predecessor of modern computers consists of a rectangular frame carrying several parallel wires. Each wire supports a number of beads which are free to slide along the length of the wire. The Romans called these beads *calculi,* the plural of *calculus,* meaning pebble. This Latin root gave rise to our word "calculate." By manipulating the beads, a skillful operator can add, subtract, multiply, and divide with amazing speed. In a contest between a Japanese proponent of this ancient invention and the trained operator of a modern manually operated calculating machine, the abacus won easily. Science will have the last word, however, for the computers described in this book perform operations several million times faster than the best of the abacus experts.

Calculating machines, including such familiar devices as adding machines, desk calculators, and cash registers, were invented more recently. The first successful mechanical calculator was constructed by Blaise Pascal in the seventeenth century. It was completed in 1642, and authentic models are still in existence. The primary conception which this machine introduced was the mechanization of the carry. The machine consists of a series of numbered wheels, or dials, each numbered from 0 to 9 and arranged to be read from left to right. When one of the dials passes from 9 to 0, a ratchet causes the wheel on its left to be moved one unit forward. The machine adds and subtracts directly, but multiplication and division are accomplished by repeated additions and subtractions.

In 1671, Leibniz constructed a calculating machine which could not only add and subtract but also multiply. Addition and subtraction were accomplished in the same manner as in Pascal's machine, but additional gears were included which enabled the machine to multiply directly.

Leibniz commented that although the device was not completely automatic, the slight effort involved in using it was certainly preferable to the tedious and often erroneous procedures required in manual arithmetic. The calculator designed by Leibniz was the model for most later machines and embodied almost all the principles now used in the design of calculators.

As business techniques and science progressed, the need for the mechanization of simple arithmetic operations increased. The amount of arithmetic done by business concerns increased vastly and became far more complex, and bookkeepers increased in number, as did all types of white-collar workers. The paper work required to manage government functions efficiently also reached staggering proportions. For instance, it took so long to process the data gathered during the United States government census that the information was not available in a convenient summary form until after it had lost its timeliness. The problems of the Bureau of the Census are so acute that it became the developer of the punched card, using punched cards for its tabulating as early as the 1890s.†

In the fields of science and engineering, many problems were being reduced to mathematical expressions which were so complex that it took a prohibitive amount of time to perform the arithmetic necessary to evaluate them for the various sets of parameters. For example, when the mathematical formulas describing the flight of an artillery shell along a ballistics trajectory were first known with considerable accuracy, the solution of these formulas (involving many different gun-elevation angles, distances, etc.) required the services of a large staff of human computers for long periods of time. Further, the tables had to be recalculated for new types of shells and weapons. This often introduced a lag from the time weapons became available until they could be accurately used.

Fortunately, the calculator was progressing also. Improvements in design and construction increased the speed and the number and variety of operations which could be performed by these devices, and at the same time improved manufacturing techniques made them more readily available. In early models, hand cranks were replaced by electric motors, and the speed of calculation was increased. Numerous aids to the operator were also introduced, thus increasing the speed of computation and decreasing the chances of error. Various types of desk calculating machines were common, and most business arithmetic was performed by these devices.

The final step in calculator development came with the introduction of electronic calculators. The speed of these devices is electronic — not mechanical — and in the larger models, there are even small electronic memories or sometimes tape strips or metal cards which can store short "programs" containing instructions to the calculator. The calculator can then perform these short programs at electronic speeds at the will of the operator.

The fact remains that the data (generally numbers) operated on must be inserted by the human operating the calculator. The remarkable functions provided by electronic calculators greatly help but do not remove the need for computers.

For instance, many computers operate on large files of data which are stored in computer memory devices, such as magnetic tape or disks. These data would occupy many filing cabinets and it would take human operators long periods of time to find items in these files. The computer, however, can search these files, often in fractions of a second but occasionally in seconds, and find and update records automatically. For instance, the larger banking computers contain millions of records relating to customers' accounts. All transactions made in the branches of a large bank must be recorded and the

---

† Herman Hollerith, who developed the punched card for the Census Bureau, later formed his own company, which still later was incorporated into IBM.

appropriate records updated at the end of each day. The computer can accomplish this automatically, and banks and insurance companies are large users of computers as are businesses which use computers to maintain their inventories, such as large grocery chains which use computers to order automatically, to bookkeep their operations, etc.

Computers are used to control production devices in industry, monitor the operation of industrial processes, and help set type for newspapers and books; they perform many functions automatically and often at speeds and with accuracy and precision not possible for humans.

For scientific applications, some calculations are extremely complicated and long, requiring hundreds of millions of calculations. The speed and lack of errors in computer calculations make computers ideal for performing these calculations. Often scientific calculation involves large amounts of test data (from satellites or nuclear experiments or from medical laboratories, for instance). These data must be analyzed using mathematical techniques which require many calculations. While such calculations could be performed on electronic calculators, the amount of human effort and time required would make the cost of such calculations prohibitive.

1•2 DIFFERENCES BETWEEN DESK CALCULATORS AND COMPUTERS

The basic difference between the automatic digital computer and the electromechanical and electronic calculator is that the computer performs *long* sequences of computations without human intervention and generally has a memory of some size. Also, the input data are generally read automatically. The computer can also make certain logical decisions and alter its future actions as a result of these decisions, sometimes changing the way it proceeds through the input data.

The sequence of instructions which tells the computer how to solve a particular problem is called a *program*. The program tells the machine what to do, step by step, including all decisions which are to be made. It is apparent from this that the computer does not plan for itself, but that all planning must be done in advance. The growth of the computer industry created the need for trained personnel who do nothing but prepare the programs, or sequences of instructions, which direct the computer. The preparation of the list of instructions to the computer is called *programming,* and the personnel who perform this function are called *programmers*.

1•3 ELECTRONIC DIGITAL COMPUTERS

The history of attempts to make machines which would perform long sequences of calculations automatically is fairly long. The best known early attempt was made in the nineteenth century by Charles Babbage, an English scientist and mathematician. Babbage attempted to mechanize sequences of calculations, eliminating the operator and designing a machine so that it would perform all the necessary operations in a predetermined sequence. The machine designed by Babbage used cardboard cards with holes punched in them to introduce both instructions and the necessary data (numbers) into the machine. The machine was to perform the instructions dictated by the cards automatically, not stopping until an entire sequence of instructions had been completed. The punched cards used to control the machine had already been used to control the operation of weaving machines. Surprisingly enough, Babbage obtained some money for his project from the English government and started construction. Although he was severely limited by the technology of his time and the machine was never completed, Babbage succeeded in establishing the basic principles upon which modern computers are constructed. There is even some speculation that if he had not run short of money, he might have constructed a successful machine. Although Babbage died without realizing his dream, he had established the fundamental concepts which were used to construct machines elaborated beyond even his expectations.

By the 1930s punched cards were in wide use in large businesses, and various types of punched-card-handling machines were available. In 1937 Howard Aiken, at Harvard, proposed to IBM that a machine could be constructed (using some of the parts and techniques from the punched-card machines) which would automatically sequence the operations and calculations performed. This machine used a combination of electromechanical devices, including many relays. The machine was in operation for some time, generating many tables of mathematical functions (particularly Bessel functions), and was used for trajectory calculations in World War II.

Aiken's machine was remarkable for its time, but limited in speed by its use of relays rather than electronic devices, and by its use of punched cards for sequencing the operations. In 1943, S. P. Eckert and J. W. Mauchly, of the Moore School of Engineering of the University of Pennsylvania, started the Eniac, which used electronic components (primarily vacuum tubes) and was therefore faster, but which also used switches and a wired plug board to implement the programming of operations. Later, Eckert and Mauchly built the Edvac, which had its program stored in the computer's memory, not depending on external sequencing. This was an important innovation, and a computer which stores its list of operations, or program, internally is called a *stored-program computer.* Actually, the Edsac, at the University of Manchester, started later but completed before Edvac, was the first operational stored-program computer.

A year or so later, John Von Neumann, at the Institute for Advanced Study in Princeton, started the IAS in conjunction with the Moore School of Engineering, and this machine incorporated most of the general concepts of parallel binary stored-program computers.

The Univac I was the first commercially available electronic digital computer and was designed by Eckert and Mauchly at their own company, which was later bought by Sperry Rand. The U.S. Bureau of the Census bought the first Univac. (Later Univac and half of Aiken's machine were placed in the

Smithsonian Institution, where they may now be seen.) IBM entered the competition with the IBM 701, a large machine, in 1953, and in 1954 with the IBM 650, a much smaller machine which was very successful. The IBM 701 was the forerunner of the 704–709–7094 series of IBM machines, the first "big winners" in the large-machine category.

There were quite a few vacuum-tube electronic computers available and in use by the late 1950s, but at this time an important innovation in electronics appeared — the transistor. The replacement of large, expensive (hot) vacuum tubes with small, inexpensive, reliable, comparatively low heat-dissipating transistors led to what are called "second-generation computers," and the size and importance of the computer industry grew at amazing rates, while the costs of individual computers dropped substantially.

By 1965 a third generation of computers was introduced. (The IBM Corporation, in introducing their 360 series, used the term "third-generation" as a key phrase in their advertising, and it remains as a catch word in describing all machines of this era.) The machines of this period began making heavy use of *integrated circuits* in which many transistors and other components are fabricated and packaged together in a single small container. The low prices and high packing densities of these circuits plus lessons learned from prior machines led to some differences in computer-system design, and these machines proliferated and expanded the computer industry to its present multibillion-dollar size.

Fourth-generation machines are less easily distinguished from earlier generations. There are some striking and important differences, however. The manufacture of integrated circuits has become so advanced as to incorporate thousands of active components in volumes of a fraction of an inch, leading to what is called medium-scale integration (MSI) and large-scale integration (LSI). This has led to small-size, lower-cost, large-memory, ultrafast computers. Large computers have become increasingly complex; medium-sized computers now perform as large computers of the near past did; and there is a new breed of computers called microcomputers and minicomputers which are small and inexpensive, are manufactured by many different companies, and are proliferating at a surprising rate.

1•4 APPLICATION OF COMPUTERS TO PROBLEMS

Large office forces have for many years been employed in the accounting departments of business firms. The clerks employed by these businesses spend most of their time performing arithmetic computations and then entering their results into company books and on paychecks, invoices, order forms, etc. Most of the arithmetic consists of repetitious sequences of simple calculations which the clerks perform over and over on different sets of figures. Few decisions are required, rules having usually been defined covering almost all problems which might arise.

A typical task in a payroll office is the processing of paychecks for company employees who work at an hourly rate.† This job involves calculating total earnings by multiplying each employee's hourly wage rate by the number of hours worked, taking into consideration any overtime; figuring and then deducting taxes, insurance, contributions to charity, etc.; then making out the necessary check and entering a record of all figures. Figure 1 · 1 is a flow-chart of a possible procedure. Flowcharts such as this are standard tools of business and are often used by the computing industry. Such flowcharts are very useful when reducing problems to the necessary steps required and are an invaluable aid in the field of programming. The example given deliberately omits overtime rates, irregular taxes such as FICA, and other such complicating features. The procedure followed by a clerk in performing this sequence of computations might be as follows:

1. The clerk looks up the employee's daily work record, and adds the number of hours worked each day, obtaining the total number of hours worked during the week.
2. The total number of hours worked is multiplied by the pay rate, and the total earnings for the week are obtained.
3. The total earnings are multiplied by tax rate for the employee, and the amount of withholding tax is found.
4. Withholding tax is subtracted from the total earnings.
5. Any regular deductions such as insurance are subtracted.
6. A record of each of the above operations is entered in the company books, and a check is made out for the correct amount.

It can be seen that almost all of the above procedure can be mechanized by a machine which can be caused to add, multiply, and subtract in the correct sequence. The machine must also have the following less obvious features:

1. The ability to remember the intermediate results which have been obtained. For instance, the total amount earned must be remembered while the tax is being figured. It is also convenient to keep the employee's pay rate, rate of withholding tax, insurance rates, and the amount regularly given to charity in the machine.
2. The ability to accept information. The records of time worked, changes in pay rates, deduction amounts, etc., must be entered into the machine.
3. The ability to print out the results obtained.

The widespread acceptance of digital computing machines in payroll offices is largely due to the repetitious type of work which is normally done in such offices. Mechanization of such tasks is straightforward, although often complicated; but the additional accuracy and speed, as well as the lower operating costs, which electronic business machines make possible have made their use especially popular in this field. Most large companies now

---

† It is interesting to note that 95 percent of the checks issued by the federal government are made out by computers.

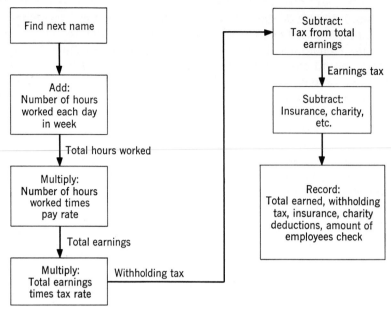

FIG. 1•1 Flowchart of paycheck calculation.

use special time clocks which enter the time each employee arrives and leaves by punching holes in time cards. The time cards are "read into" a computer which interprets the holes in the cards, then automatically performs all the necessary arithmetic operations and prints a record of all totals, subtotals, etc., for the company books. The computer also keeps a record of the total amount paid each week and each year to the employee, as well as a record of the various deductions, such as withholding tax. The computer can determine the total number of hours worked by all employees during any given week, the average pay for all workers during any selected period, the number of people contributing to various charities, and practically any other type of payroll information.

1•5 APPLICATIONS OF COMPUTERS IN BUSINESS

It can be readily seen that the use of computers is not restricted to the area of scientific calculation. In fact, far more machines are produced for business than for laboratory or scientific use. The main difference between the use of digital machines in business and in scientific work lies in the ratio of operations performed to total data processed. While the business machine performs only a few calculations using each datum, a great volume of data must be processed. The scientific problem generally starts with fewer data, but a great many calculations are performed using each datum. Both types of machines still fall under the heading of automatic digital computers, and either type of work may be done on all computers, although some machines may be better adapted to one or the other type of problem.

One of the first uses for the digital computer has been in the mechanizing of the more routine and clerical aspects of management. The description of the use of a computer in figuring payrolls (Sec. 1 · 4) is an example of a business application and illustrates the similarity in programming the operation of a computer and figuring out employee office procedures. First, the problem to be solved is reduced to a series of simple operations: finding the name of the next employee whose wages are to be computed, figuring how many hours she has worked, and multiplying this figure by hourly rate of pay. After the procedure to be used has been worked out and explained to the clerk, the clerk is provided with the necessary numerical information, such as pay rates, insurance rates, etc. If the operations are further simplified, each step in Fig. 1 · 1 may be performed by a different clerk. For instance, the first clerk may find the employee's record and send it to the second clerk, who computes the total number of hours worked and presents this to the next clerk, who multiplies by the wage rate; and so on until all the operations have been performed. It may be seen from this that the breaking down of business procedures into basic steps is a very old practice indeed.

The procedure for preparing a list of instructions for a digital computer is basically the same. All the operations the computer is to perform are written in flowchart form (Fig. 1 · 1). The problem is then broken down into a list of instructions to the machine which specify exactly how the solution is to be obtained. After the problem has been programmed, the list of instructions is transferred onto some medium which the machine can "read" (punched cards, for instance) and is then read into the machine. The machine automatically performs the required steps. Notice that once the procedure has been established and the programmed steps have been read in, the programming is finished until a change in procedure is desired. Changes in rates, for instance, can be inserted by simply reading the new pay rates into the machine. This does not affect the procedure.

1•6 SCIENTIFIC APPLICATIONS

Modern science and engineering use mathematics as a language for expressing physical laws in precise terms. The electronic digital computer is a valuable tool for studying the consequences of these laws. Often the exact procedure for solving a problem has been found, but the time required to perform the necessary calculations manually is prohibitive. Sometimes it is necessary to solve the same problem many times using different sets of parameters, and the computer is especially useful for solving problems of this type. The computer is not only able to evaluate types of mathematical expressions at high speeds, but if a set of calculations is performed repeatedly on different sets of numerical values, the computer is able to compare the results and determine the optimum values which were used.

An algebraic formula is an expression of a mathematical relationship. Many of the laws of physics, electronics, chemistry, etc., are expressed in this form, in which case digital computers may be easily used, because algebraic formulas may be directly changed to the basic steps they represent. Figure 1·2 is a flowchart illustrating the steps necessary to evaluate the expression $ax^3 + bx^2 + cx + d$, given numerical values for a, b, c, d, and x. The required steps are as follows:

1. Multiply a times x, yielding ax.
2. Add b, yielding $ax + b$.
3. Multiply this by x, forming $ax^2 + bx$.
4. Add c, yielding $ax^2 + bx + c$.
5. Multiply this by x; $x(ax^2 + bx + c)$ or $ax^3 + bx^2 + cx$.
6. Add d, obtaining $ax^3 + bx^2 + cx + d$.

It would take several minutes to perform the calculations necessary to evaluate this algebraic expression for a single set of values using manually operated calculators, but practically any computer could perform this series of operations several thousand times per second. While the algebraic expression shown is certainly much simpler than many formulas encountered

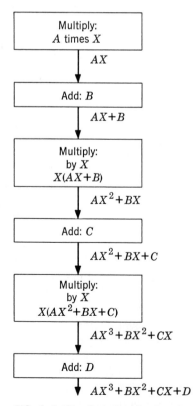

FIG. 1•2 Flowchart of evaluation of expression.

by members of the engineering and scientific professions, the value of using a computer for certain types of problems may be readily seen.

1•7 SOME DIFFERENT TYPES OF COMPUTER SYSTEMS

The most familiar use of computers is in operating programs punched into cards (or perhaps recorded on paper or magnetic tape) and run by a computer which then prepares printouts, checks, or some form of data presentation recording the results. This is an example of what is called *batch processing*. When a computer is used in this way, the input data (and often the program) are introduced into the computer and processed automatically, generally without operator intervention. Often many different jobs (or sets of data) are processed, one right after the other, or even at the same time, but without any interaction from the system's user during program operation. For instance, the keypunch operators may punch many decks of punched cards containing data on customers and claims. These cards are then stacked together and transported to a large computer which processes the cards, issuing checks, sending out bills, printing records for the company, etc. This is batch processing.

Similarly, the user of a computer in a scientific laboratory may submit program cards and data cards as a *job,* with the familiar elastic band around these, along with any notes to the operators of the machine. A number of these decks of cards are collected and then stacked together, and finally run by the machine. Later the results are printed out and, perhaps even the next day, delivered to the individual users. This is also batch processing.

In other types of systems, users interact with the computer directly, inserting and receiving the data as desired. For instance, an airline ticket agent wishes to make a reservation. The agent types the desired aircraft flight number and passenger identification on a special typewriter which communicates, via the telephone lines, with a computer. The computer looks in its memory, sees if the flight is full, and if not, enters the passenger's name on its list for the flight, and then communicates this fact back to the airline ticket agent. If no seats are available, the computer sends this information to the ticket agent, who attempts to interest the passenger in another flight. In this way an airline connects all its ticket agents together, keeping a constant record of flights, passengers, and payments and doing all the bookkeeping. The terminals where the ticket agents are located are scattered throughout the world, but communicate with the computer via telephone lines. Motels, hotels, stockbrokers, and many other businesses have similar systems for reservations, information transferral, and bookkeeping.

All these are called *online interactive* systems, for the users of the system communicate directly with the computer, and the computer responds directly. The development of these systems has progressed in parallel with the development of keyboard input devices, as well as output devices for users of various types, including television displays, printers, and other data display devices.

FIG. 1·3 Teletype Model 33 KSR. (Courtesy of AT&T.)

Online systems are also widely used in scientific applications where users operate their programs at a terminal connected to the computer, perhaps by telephone lines, trying changes and variations at will. Experimenters can try a set of inputs and study the results, then try other inputs and study these results. The technique of online interactive computing is used by circuit designers, architects, and chemists, and in almost any area, including medical systems for hospital use.

A widely used input-output device is the *teletype,* shown in Fig. 1·3. This is an example of a keyboard which is "typewriterlike," generating a printed record when used, but also generating electrical signals which can be used as computer input. Similarly, electronic signals from a computer can be used to control the teletype, and the teletype will type, under the computer's control, the results of calculations.

The teletype is often used in systems where the console (in this case the teletype) is some distance from the computer. A special attachment called a *modem* is used which makes it possible to transmit the electrical signals generated by the teletype to the computer and receive the computer's response back over telephone lines. At the computer another modem is located which can also transmit or receive, and this pair of modems allows communication in both directions over telephone lines. The user of the teletype simply dials the number at which the computer is located, establishes a connection and the user's identity and right to use the computer (the computer generally checks a password), and then proceeds to use the computer.

Since teletypes are fairly well standardized, the same teletype console can use several different computers, when available. There are now many companies which provide computer service to users who have teletypes at their disposal. The users simply dial the computer they prefer.

The teletype is only one of many kinds of *computer terminals* currently in use. (There are many competitors to the teletype in Fig. 1·3.) Figure 1·4 shows a keyboard similar to a typewriter for data entry, but the computer

FIG. 1•4 Portable computer terminal with cathode-ray-tube display. (Courtesy of Logitron, Inc.)

responses are sent to an oscilloscope display which is similar to a television, thus providing a temporary display (instead of "hard copy," which is the printed page). (Sometimes some means for making a copy of what is displayed, at the user's convenience, is provided.) This type of output device is called a *display device* and enables the computer to draw pictures or make graphs as well as use printed characters.

The computer terminal in Fig. 1 · 4 is portable. An attachment which holds a telephone hand set is provided so that when the telephone hand set is placed in the attachment, a computer can be dialed, and once the connection is made, the terminal then generates audio tones into the hand set when keys are depressed on the keyboard. The terminal receiver also decodes coded tones representing characters generated by the computer, displaying the information received on the oscilloscope display device. In this way the user of a terminal can "converse," or communicate, with any compatible computer connected to the telephone system.

When a number of users share a computer, using the computer, often via telephone lines, at the same time, the computer is said to be *time shared*. By time sharing is meant that the computer is able to alternate and interleave the running of its programs so that several jobs or users can be on at the same time. This makes for more efficient use, and the airline, motel, and hotel reservation systems and most online systems use time sharing. We shall return to these systems in Sec. 1 · 10.

1 • 8 THE USE OF DIGITAL COMPUTERS IN CONTROL SYSTEMS

The ability of digital computers to make precise calculations and decisions at high speeds has made it possible to use them as parts of control systems. The first example of the use of a computer in a large control system was the SAGE Air Defense System. In this system, data from a network of radar stations, which are used to detect the positions of all aircraft in the area, are fed via communication links into a high-speed computer. The computer stores all the incoming positional information from the radar stations, and from this calculates the future positions of the aircraft, their speed and altitude, and all other pertinent information. A number of other types of information are also relayed into the computer, including information from picket ships, AEW aircraft, Ground Observer Corps aircraft spotters, flight plans for both military and civilian aircraft, and weather information.

A single computer receives all this information and from it calculates a composite picture of the complete air situation. The computer then generates displays on special oscilloscopes which are used by members of the military services to make tactical decisions. The computer further aids these operators by calculating the most effective use of the interceptor aircraft, antiaircraft guns, and also antiaircraft missiles. By means of radio links, the computer automatically guides both interceptor aircraft and missiles to their targets.

It may be seen that the computer in this system is truly a high-speed data processing machine. The computer receives data from many sources, processes these data, and then "controls" the defending air power.

A system of this sort is called a *real-time control system* because information must be processed and decisions must be made in real time. When a computer is used to process business data or to perform most scientific calculations, time is not as critical a factor. In real-time systems, the computer must "keep up," processing all data at high speeds in order to be effective.†

Other examples of real-time control applications include oil refineries and other manufacturing areas which use the computer to control the manufacturing processes automatically. Digital computers are also used to guide machine tools which perform precision-machining operations automatically, as shown in Fig. 1·5. Further, both manned and unmanned space vehicles carry digital computers which perform the necessary guidance functions,

FIG. 1•5 Computer used in industrial online control system.

† Most reservation systems would be considered real-time systems by their operators, since delays of any consequence would be detrimental to business.

while a network of computers on the ground monitor and direct the progress of the flight.

Most real-time control systems require an important device known as an *analog-to-digital converter*. The inputs to these systems in many cases are in the form of *analog quantities* such as mechanical displacements (for instance, shaft positions) or temperatures, voltages, pressures, etc. Since the digital computer operates on digital rather than analog data, a fundamental "language" problem arises which requires the conversion of the analog quantities into digital representations. The analog-to-digital converter does this.

The same problem occurs at the computer output, where it is often necessary to convert numerical output data from the computer into mechanical displacements or analog-type electrical signals. For instance, a "number" output from the computer might be used to rotate a shaft through the number of revolutions indicated by the output number. A device which converts digital-type information into analog quantities is called a *digital-to-analog converter*. A description of both analog-to-digital and digital-to-analog converters will be found in Chap. 8.

The basic elements of a control system using a digital computer consist of (1) the data-gathering devices which perform measurements on the external environment and, if necessary, also perform analog-to-digital conversion on the data from the system which is to be controlled; (2) the digital computer itself, which performs calculations on the data supplied and makes the necessary decisions; and (3) the means of communication with, or control over, certain of the elements in the external environment. If no person aids the computer in its calculations or decisions, the system is considered to be fully automatic; if a human being also enters the control loop, the system is defined as semiautomatic.

Figure 1·5 shows a computer being used in a manufacturing application. Because of their high speed, computers can measure, test, analyze, and control manufacturing functions as they occur, often operating unattended. Computers can handle shop floor control, quality-control testing, materials handling, and production monitoring. The typewriterlike station to the left of the computer in Fig. 1·5 is used to communicate with the system.

1•9 SPECIAL-PURPOSE AND GENERAL-PURPOSE COMPUTERS

In general, there are two types of digital computers. The first is the *special-purpose digital computer,* which performs a fixed and preset sequence of calculations. This type of computer may be constructed more efficiently in that it can be lighter and smaller and may consume less power, etc., than the general-purpose computer. Because of the advantages in construction, small special-purpose computers are used where such factors as weight, power consumption, etc., are critical, as in aircraft control systems, missile guidance systems, special checkout equipment for military devices used in the field, etc.

The second type of computer is defined as a *general-purpose digital computer*. The sequence of instructions which the machine follows is generally read into this type of machine and stored in the memory of the machine. The machine can be made to follow another sequence of instructions by simply reading in the desired set of instructions. Since the sequence of operations performed by the general-purpose digital computer may be easily changed, the machine possesses great flexibility, and this is the type of machine generally used in business and for scientific computations. The general-purpose computer can process a stack of payroll cards, and then, after another program has been read into it, can perform an inventory of a company's stock. In scientific applications, a general-purpose computer can calculate the orbit of a satellite, and then, after a new program has been read in, design a set of lenses for a movie projector. The general-purpose computer may be used to solve a wide variety of problems, the details of which may have been unknown when the machine was designed. The special-purpose computer is generally only capable of solving a special type of problem.

1•10 TIME-SHARED COMPUTER SYSTEMS

Among the more important real-time computer systems are those designed to aid research operations, businesses, and military decision making. These systems provide users with a large file of information and a computational facility using which they can communicate in a direct manner. As has been mentioned, the user of the system is able to introduce instructions to the computer by utilizing some device such as a teletype keyboard or a set of push buttons at a console. The computer responds by either printing the results or displaying them on an oscilloscope. The interaction between the user and the computer is direct; the computer is made to respond immediately. In general, the time elapsing from when a command is given to a computer to when results are obtained is called *turnaround* time. The designer of a time-shared online system tries to minimize turnaround time.

These systems are used in many ways. Computer-aided design systems have consoles and displays such that a designer can work out the details of a design by using the computer to perform all calculations and to display the effects of changes in the design. The designer then attempts to optimize the design by changing the parameters and noting the effects of those changes in the design.

The business manager or military leader uses large digital systems in a manner which relies heavily on the enormous number of records which can be stored in the memory of a digital machine. The business systems are called *management control systems,* and the military systems are called *command and control systems*. The business systems contain the files and records for the business, as well as any other pertinent data, and the military systems store the military information required by officers to make critical decisions. In either case, the information is continually updated, using communications facilities. When a category of data is requested, the computer locates it in its memory and provides selected features upon request. For instance, the computer might store the types of aircraft available at each airport in the world, along with the range and ability of each aircraft to carry bombs. If aircraft were flown from one place to another, or if they were in the air or had been lost, this information would be entered into the computer. If Air Force personnel then wanted to design a bombing raid, they would ask the computer for the data and then try to use aircraft which were favorably placed and suited for their tasks. The computer could also supply data concerning the fuel and ammunition available at each place, to further facilitate decision making.

Similarly, an executive in a business would have access to all the company's sales records, salaries, current stock levels, overhead figures, and any other data he or she might wish to calculate, using the company records.

In the above systems, the computer is liable to be *time shared,* since it has many input and output information channels, each with different users, and these users share the main computer.

1•11 BASIC COMPONENTS OF A DIGITAL COMPUTER

The block diagram in Fig. 1·6 illustrates the five major operational divisions of an electronic digital computer. Although presently available machines vary greatly in the construction details of various components, the overall system concepts remain roughly the same. It is interesting to note that

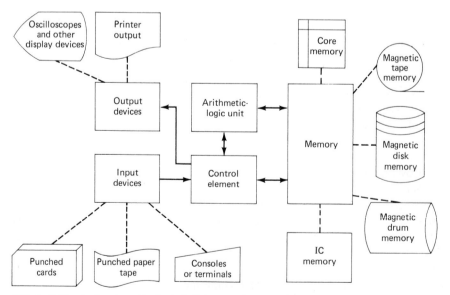

FIG. 1•6 Block diagram of typical digital computer.

present-day machines are basically designed according to the precepts which Charles Babbage proposed for his "analytic engine." Although Babbage's machine was of mechanical construction whereas present-day computers are electronic, the functions which the various sections of the machines perform are much the same.

Perhaps the outstanding conceptual difference lies in the ability of the modern computer's memory to store either instructions or the data to be used in the same location. This permits more efficient use of the memory and also enables the computer to alter the instructions which constitute the program while the computer is operating.

A digital computer may be divided into the following fundamental units:

1. *Input*   The input devices read the necessary data into the machine. In most general-purpose computers, the instructions which constitute the program must be read into the machine along with all the data to be used in the computations. Some of the more common input devices are punched-card and punched-paper-tape readers, magnetic-tape readers, and various manual input devices such as toggle switches and push buttons.

2. *Control*   The control section of a computer sequences the operation of the computer, controlling the actions of all other units. The control circuitry interprets the instructions which constitute the program and then directs the rest of the machine in its operation.

3. *Memory*   The memory, or storage, section of the computer consists of the devices used to store the information which will be used during the computations. The memory section of the computer is also used to hold both intermediate and final results as the computer proceeds through the program. The principal or high-speed memory devices for a computer are divided into pieces of equal size, each of which is then identified with what is called an *address,* or *location in memory.* If the control unit is looking for a specific piece of information or an instruction located in the memory section, it calls for it by means of its address. Memory devices are constructed so that it is possible for control to obtain the information contained at any address. The length of time required to obtain information may vary somewhat, however, and is determined by the type of device used to store the information. Common storage devices are magnetic cores, integrated circuit memories, magnetic drums, magnetic tape, and magnetic disks.

4. *Arithmetic-logic unit*   The arithmetic-logic units of most computers are capable of performing the operations of addition, subtraction, division, and multiplication, as well as some "logical operations" which will be described. The control unit tells the arithmetic-logic unit which of these operations to perform and then sees that the necessary numbers are supplied. The arithmetic element can be compared to the calculating machines described previously, in that the numbers to be used are inserted and it is then directed to perform the necessary operations.

5. *Output*   The output devices are used to record the results obtained by the

computer and present them to the "outside world." Most output devices are directed by the control element, which also causes the necessary information to be supplied to them. Common output devices are card-punching machines, magnetic-tape machines, special electromechanical typewriters, cathode-ray tubes, and high-speed printing devices. There are also many unusual types of output devices, such as lights, buzzers, and loudspeakers.

1•12 CONSTRUCTION OF MEMORY

It has been mentioned that the inner or high-speed memory is broken into a number of addresses, or locations. At each of these addresses a group of digits is stored and is handled by the computer as a unit. The group of digits stored at each address in memory is generally referred to as a "word."† Each address in memory is assigned a number, and the address is then referred to by that number. We say that address 100 contains the value 300, or that address 50 contains an instruction word. In most computers, instruction words may be stored in the same locations as number or data words, which makes the memory more flexible. Notice also that instruction words consist of a group of digits when stored in the computer.

The time it takes to obtain a word from a storage device is called the *access time*. The access time of the storage devices used in a machine has a profound effect on the speed of the computer. One of the factors which for a long time impeded the construction of high-speed computers was the lack of reliable storage devices with short access times. The development of storage devices (such as magnetic cores) with very short access times plus the ability to store information for an indefinite time was a great forward step.

1•13 INSTRUCTIONS

It has been mentioned that computers can make simple logical decisions. Many of these decisions are based on numbers and are therefore quantitative rather than qualitative decisions. The sort of decision the computer might make is whether one number is larger than another, or whether the result of some series of calculations is positive or negative. However, most of the decisions made by clerical workers and scientists are also based on figures. For instance, once physical phenomena have been expressed in formulas, the solutions to specific problems are expressed by means of numbers. Perhaps

---

† There are actually two ways of organizing a memory now in general use. One way is to store a *character* at each address (a character is a 1 or 2, an *A* or *B*, etc.). These systems are called *character addressable* systems. The second way is to store a complete *operand* or instruction word at each address. These systems are called *word addressable* systems. As might be guessed, character addressable systems have smaller amounts of information at each address than word addressable systems. There are, quite naturally, pros and cons for each type of system. We shall simplify the description by assuming that each successive address contains a word, as in word addressable systems, but we will describe other systems later.

the following remark, made by Lord Kelvin, is relevant: "When you can measure what you are speaking about, and express it in numbers, you know something about it. But when you cannot measure it or express it in numbers, your knowledge is of a meager and unsatisfactory kind."

The digital computer does not figure out its own solution to problems, but must be told exactly how to solve any given problem, as well as how to make all decisions. As mentioned, preparing a list of instructions which tells the computer how to perform its calculations is called programming. The procedure for programming a problem generally consists of two separate steps. The first step, planning the program, involves determining the sequence of operations required to solve the problem. It consists, generally, in breaking the problem down into flow diagrams such as those illustrated in the preceding chapter. Once the problem has been reduced to this form, it is ready to be *coded;* this is the second step. *Coding* consists in writing the steps outlined in the flowchart in a special language which can be interpreted by the machine. The final coded program consists of a list of instructions to the computer, written in a special format which details the operations the computer is to perform.

The instruction words which direct the computer are stored in the machine in numerical form. The programmer rarely writes instructions in numerical form, however; instead, each instruction to the computer is written using a letter code to designate the operation to be performed, plus the address in memory of the number to be used in this step of the calculation.† Later, the alphabetic section of the instruction word is converted to numerical form by a computer program called an *assembler.* This will be described in a later section.

An instruction word as written by the programmer consists of two parts: (1) the *operation-code* part which designates the operation (addition, subtraction, multiplication, etc.) to be performed, and (2) the *address* of the number to be used. A typical instruction word written by the programmer is

ADD 535

This instruction word is divided into two main parts: first, the operation-code part, consisting of the letters ADD, which directs the computer to perform the arithmetic operation of addition; and second, the address part, which tells the computer the address in storage of the number to be used.

It is important to notice that the second section of the instruction word gives only the location (address) in storage of the number to be added. The number 535 in the instruction shown is not the actual number to be added, but

---

† The instructions described are typical instructions for a *single-address computer.* Computers are also constructed which use two, three, and four addresses in each computer instruction word. These computers are called *multiple-address* computers, and will be described in Chap. 9. The single-address type of instruction is very straightforward, and will be used in the illustrations in this chapter. The two-address computer is equally popular and equally easy to learn, and will be discussed later in the book. Learning two-address coding after single-address coding has been mastered is very simple indeed.

only tells the computer where to find the desired number. To what is the number at address 535 added? It is to be added to the number which is already in the arithmetic-logic unit in a storage device or register called an *accumulator*. If the accumulator contains zero before the instruction is executed, the accumulator will contain the number which is stored at address 535 after the instruction has been performed. If the accumulator contains the number 500 before the instruction is performed, and the number stored at address 535 is 200, the number stored in the accumulator after the ADD operation will be 700. To illustrate this principle more fully, several more instructions are explained in Table 1·1.

TABLE 1·1

INSTRUCTION WORD		
OPERATION CODE	ADDRESS PART	FUNCTION PERFORMED BY INSTRUCTION
CLA	430	The accumulator is emptied of all previous numbers and the number at address 430 is added into it. After the instruction is performed the accumulator contains the number in storage at address 430. CLA is a mnemonic code for "clear and add."
ADD	530	The number located at address 530 is added to the number in the accumulator. After the instruction, the accumulator contains the sum of the number it previously contained and the number in address 530.
SUB	235	Subtracts the number located at address 235 in the memory from the number in the accumulator and places the difference in the accumulator.
STO	433	The number in the accumulator is stored at address 433. Any information previously in this address is destroyed. The number which was in the accumulator before the instruction was performed remains in the accumulator. This is generally referred to as a STORE instruction.
HLT	000	The machine is ordered to stop. The number in the accumulator remains.

TABLE 1·2

ADDRESS IN MEMORY	INSTRUCTION WORD		CONTENTS OF ARITHMETIC ELEMENT AFTER INSTRUCTION IS PERFORMED
	OPERATION CODE	ADDRESS PART	
1	CLA	6	200
2	ADD	7	500
3	ADD	8	900
4	STO	9	900
5	HLT	0	900
6 contains the number 200			
7 contains the number 300			
8 contains the number 400			

A short program which adds three numbers together using these instructions is shown in Table 1·2.

The program operates as follows: The control section starts with the instruction word at address 1, which clears the accumulator and then adds the number at address 6 into it. The instruction at address 2 adds the number at address 7 to the number already in the accumulator. This produces the sum of 200 + 300, or 500. The third instruction adds the contents of address 8 to this sum, giving 900 in the accumulator. This number is then stored in memory at location 9 in the memory. The machine is then ordered to halt. Notice that the machine is stopped before it reaches the data. This is to prevent the control element from picking up the data, for instance, the number 200, which is at address 6, and trying to use it as an instruction.

There is no difference between a number and an instruction as far as storage is concerned. Both are stored in the same basic form. From this it can be seen that the instructions are generally placed in a different section of the memory than the data to be used. The computer progresses through the instructions and is stopped before it reaches the data. The fact that either instructions or data may be stored at all addresses makes the machine more flexible. It may be seen that either a large amount of data and a few instructions, or many instructions and few data, can be used as long as the total amount of storage available is not exceeded.

1•14 MULTIPLICATION INSTRUCTION

By adding another instruction, that of multiplication, it will be possible to write more sophisticated programs (see Table 1·3).

The program in Table 1·4 evaluates the expression $ax^3 + bx^2 + cx + d$. The actual quantities for a, b, c, d, and x are stored in memory at locations 22, 23, 24, 25, and 26, respectively. It is important to notice that the program shown evaluates the expression for any values which might be read into these locations. The expression could be evaluated for any number of values for x by

TABLE 1·3

INSTRUCTION WORD		
OPERATION CODE	ADDRESS PART	FUNCTION
MUL	400	The number at address 400 is multiplied by the number already in the accumulator and the product placed in the accumulator.

running the program for one value of x, then substituting the succeeding values of x into register 26 and rerunning the program for each value. In actual practice it is possible to have the program automatically repeat itself by means of special instructions. All the various desired values for x can then be stored and the equation solved for each x without stopping the computer.

It can be seen from Table 1·4 that very complicated algebraic functions can be evaluated using only a very few instructions. The program shown can be performed by a high-speed computer in less than $1/10,000$ s. The value of such speed in the solution of the more complex problems encountered in engineering and science may readily be seen. Computers are making possible engineering techniques which were previously unusable because of the high costs in time and money of lengthy computations.

TABLE 1·4

ADDRESS IN MEMORY	INSTRUCTION WORD		CONTENTS OF ACCUMULATOR AFTER INSTRUCTION IS PERFORMED
	OPERATION CODE	ADDRESS PART	
1	CLA	22	a
2	MUL	26	ax
3	ADD	23	$ax + b$
4	MUL	26	$x(ax + b)$ or $ax^2 + bx$
5	ADD	24	$ax^2 + bx + c$
6	MUL	26	$x(ax^2 + bx + c)$ or $ax^3 + bx^2 + cx$
7	ADD	25	$ax^3 + bx^2 + cx + d$
8	STO	27	$ax^3 + bx^2 + cx + d$
9	HLT	000	$ax^3 + bx^2 + cx + d$

22 contains a
23 contains b
24 contains c
25 contains d
26 contains x
27 contains 0

1•15 BRANCH, SKIP, OR JUMP INSTRUCTIONS

All the instructions explained so far have been used to perform problems in simple arithmetic. It has been pointed out, however, that the computer is able to repeat the same sequence of instructions without being stopped and re-started. This facility is provided by a group of instructions referred to as *branch, skip,* or *jump* instructions. These instructions tell the computer not to perform the instruction at the address following that of the instruction being performed, but to skip to some other instruction. Some branch instructions are *unconditional* in nature and cause the computer to skip regardless of what the conditions may be. Other branch instructions are *conditional* and tell the computer to skip only if certain things are true. Branch instructions enable the computer to make logical choices which alter its future actions.

Two typical instructions are shown in Table 1·5.

The short program shown in Table 1·6 illustrates several very important principles. The purpose of the program is to add all the even integers from 2 to 100. The program is of the repetitious sort where a few short orders are used to generate a program which runs for some time by repeating the same sequence of instructions. The program illustrates how the ability to branch on a negative number can be used to form a counter which will determine how many times a part of a program is repeated.

The number stored in location 39 increases by 2 each time the program runs through. The total of these numbers is stored in address 43, which, after the program has halted, contains the total of all the numbers which have been in location 39. The number stored at address 40 decreases in magnitude by 1 each time the program runs through, until the number stored at 40 is no longer negative. When the program "falls through" the BRANCH WHEN MINUS (BRM) instruction, it then performs the next instruction in sequence, which is a HALT instruction. Zero is considered to be a positive number, al-

TABLE 1·5

OPERATION CODE	ADDRESS PART	FUNCTION
BRA	420	This instruction tells the computer to perform the instruction at address 420 next. The computer will skip or branch from the instruction it would have performed and perform instruction 420 instead. The computer will then perform instruction 421, followed by 422, etc.
BRM	420	The computer will branch to instruction 420 only if the number in the accumulator is negative. If the number is positive or zero, the computer will not branch, but will perform the instruction stored at the next address in memory. BRM is a mnemonic code for "branch on minus."

TABLE 1·6

| ADDRESS | INSTRUCTION WORD | | CONTENTS OF ACCUMULATOR | | |
	OPERATION CODE	ADDRESS PART	1ST TIME	2D TIME	LAST TIME
1	CLA	39	0	2	98
2	ADD	41	2	4	100
3	STO	39	2	4	100
4	ADD	43	2	6	$2 + 4 + 6 + \cdots + 100$
5	STO	43	2	6	$2 + 4 + 6 + \cdots + 100$
6	CLA	40	-50	-49	-1
7	ADD	42	-49	-48	$+0$
8	STO	40	-49	-48	$+0$
9	BRM	1	-49	-48	$+0$
10	HLT	000			

39 contains 000
40 contains -50
41 contains 2
42 contains 1
43 contains 0

though this varies with different machines. Notice that the first section of the program will cycle a number of times equal to the negative number stored in register 40. A simulated counter is formed by the -50 stored at address 40, the 1 stored in location 41, and the instructions at addresses 6 through 9. Any sequence of instructions which precedes a counter of this sort will be run through the number of times determined by the counter. This is an especially useful device for iterative schemes when the number of iterations required is known.

1•16 READING THE PROGRAM INTO THE COMPUTER

After the programmer has written the list of instructions which the computer is to perform, another step must be taken before the written program can be read into the machine. This generally consists in recording the program in some medium, such as punched cards or punched paper tape, which the computer's input devices can read. If the input medium is perforated paper tape, the written program will be given to an operator of a paper-tape-punching machine. The tape-punching machine has a keyboard resembling a typewriter which contains both alphabetic and numeric characters. A long strip of paper tape is fed through the punching section of the machine as the operator of the machine operates the keyboard. Each time the operator depresses a key of the keyboard, several holes are punched into the paper tape. The keyboard mechanism is arranged so that a different combination of holes is punched into the tape for each key which is depressed. The operator of the tape-punching machine types the program just as a secretary types a letter. The result is a strip of paper tape which has been perforated with coded groups of holes.

A paper-tape reader connected to the digital computer is used to read this tape into the computer. The paper-tape reader "senses" the holes perforated into the tape and delivers the locations of these holes in the tape to the computer in the form of electrical signals. The computer then stores this information. A description of paper-tape readers, punches, and the way the paper tape is coded will be presented in Chap. 8.

Figure 1 · 7 shows a teletype that can punch or read paper tape with a keyboard which can also be attached to telephone lines (notice the dial on the lower right corner). A small section of tape can be seen extending from the tape-punching device. After a tape is punched, the tape can be read by a high-speed computer tape reader. Often, however, a teletype is connected directly to a computer, and its tape reader is used to read the tape into the computer.

Paper for "hard copy"

Telephone dial for dialing computer when teletype is used at a remote location

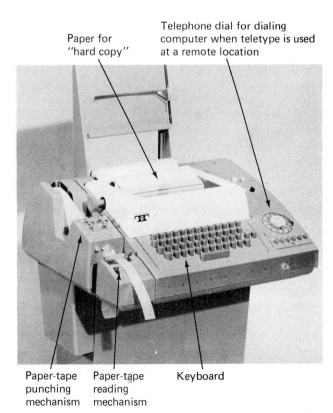

Paper-tape punching mechanism   Paper-tape reading mechanism   Keyboard

FIG. 1 • 7 Teletype console with tape punch. (Courtesy of AT&T.)

Card   Column   Printing   Card
stacker   indicator   mechanism   hopper

Read   Backspace   Punch   Keyboard
station   key   station

FIG. 1·8 Card punch.

The preparation of punched cards is similar. The operator of a card punch (refer to Fig. 1·8) depresses keys of a keyboard which punches holes into succeeding columns of a rectangular "punched card." The set of cards thus punched is then assembled in order into a "deck" of cards which can be read by a punched-card reader.

The general procedure for punched cards is for the programmer to write the program on a special coding form such as that shown in Fig. 1·9. A keyboard is then used to type (or *keyboard*) the program written on the form. Figure 1·9 also shows a punched card containing the first line of page 2 of the program. In general, one line of writing on a coding form is entered into a single card.†

There are a number of other techniques for data and program entry into computers. Figure 1·10 shows a special card on which data can be entered by simply marking boxes on the card with a soft lead pencil. A special "mark sense" reading device can sense the position of the boxes which have been marked and transmit their location on the card to a computer.‡

Another mode of program entry is in *online* systems, where the operator of

---

† The program on the coding form in Fig. 1·9 is a section of a business data processing program written in a "higher-level" programming language called PL/1 (see Sec. 1·20). Notice that the language is similar to that used by accountants. (In this, PL/1 resembles an earlier business language called Cobol.)

‡ The particular card shown has a single statement from a programming language called Basic written on it.

IBM FORTRAN Coding Form — GX28-7327-6 U/M 050** Printed in U.S.A.

PROGRAM: RECORD-ORIENTED DATA TRANSMISSION
PROGRAMMER: R.L. TONN

```
UPDATE: PROCEDURE OPTIONS (MAIN);
DECLARE INFILE FILE RECORD INPUT;
DECLARE WAGES  FILE RECORD OUTPUT;
DECLARE 1 PAYROLL,
          2 NAME,
            3 LAST CHARACTER (12),
            3 FIRST CHARACTER (8),
            3 MIDDLE CHARACTER (1),
          2 PAY-NO CHARACTER (S),
          2 RATE
            (3 REGULAR,
             3 OVERTIME)
            FIXED DECIMAL (3,2);
AGAIN: READ FILE (INFILE) INTO (PAYROLL);
DECLARE 1 PAY-RECORD,
          2 NAME,
            3 LAST CHARACTER (12),
            3 FIRST CHARACTER (8),
            3 MIDDLE CHARACTER (1),
          2 HOURS,
            (3 REGULAR, 3 OVERTIME) FIXED DECIMAL (2),
          2 PAY,
            (3 REGULAR, 3 OVERTIME) FIXED DECIMAL (S,2);
GET LIST (PAY-RECORD.NAME, PAY-RECORD.HOURS);
```

FIG. 1•9 Coding forms and a punch card.

29

FIG. 1·9 *(Continued.)*

30

Notes: BASIC language statements have three elements: <u>statement number</u>, <u>statement type</u>, and <u>operands</u>. The card below is marked for the statement: $15\emptyset$ LET $\overline{A = B + C - 5}$

The statement number ($15\emptyset$) is indicated in the STATEMENT NUMBER field by a single pencil mark in the boxes labeled 1, 5, and $\emptyset$.

The statement type (LET) is indicated in the STATEMENT field by a single mark in the box labeled LET.

The operand ($A = B + C - 5$) is indicated in the FORMULA field.

FIG. 1•10 Card with pencil marks which can be read by a mark sense reader.

a keyboard types the program directly into the computer. In this case the keyboard contains electrical circuitry which generates signals to the computer each time a key is depressed. Generally, a printing mechanism also types or prints the characters the operator keyboards on paper. The computer generally has the ability to write responses using the same printing mechanism that was used to record the program and data entered, or sometimes the computer gives the responses by means of an oscilloscope display or some other graphic device. Such systems enable the computer and its user to communicate directly instead of using some intermediate medium such as cards or tape.

Figure 1•11 shows a keyboard and oscilloscope display in a system where the information keyboarded at the console is recorded on paper (notice the roll of paper in the printer above the keyboard) as well as displayed on the oscilloscope. Both the printer and oscilloscope are also used to print or display computer output information.

Most of the data entered into computers are still in the form of punched cards. (There are over 500,000 card punches now in active use.) The use of online systems and other input media is growing, however, and represents a substantial portion of the overall usage of computers.

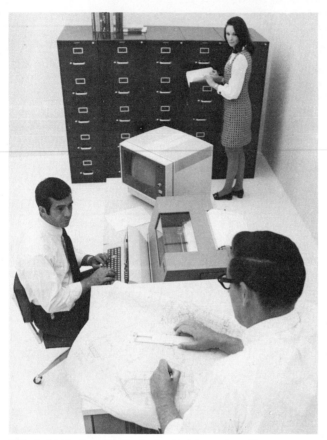

FIG. 1•11 Keyboard with attached printer and oscilloscope display.

The preceding description of the steps in preparing a program should make it apparent that it is not always economical to use a large digital computer to perform very simple sequences of calculations which need be performed only once or twice. The computer is valuable when very repetitious sets of calculations must be performed.

Consider the payroll accounting procedure described earlier. Once a program has been written which will calculate the weekly gross earnings, taxes, deductions, etc., for the employees of a large manufacturer, the same program can be used to compute each of thousands of employees' checks. If a combined clock and card-punching device is used to punch the time an employee enters a factory and the time the employee leaves into a time card which also records, in punched form, an identifying number for the employee, the entire operation can be made automatic. The time cards can then be "read" by the computer, which will compute the amount of time worked, total weekly earnings, etc., and will actually print the paycheck, and then record in printed form all the data required by the bookkeeping system.

Figure 1·12 shows a system where ledger cards are used to record printed data from the computer (and keyboarded data, if desired). Ledger cards are widely used in accounting systems for billing, bookkeeping, and general record handling. The ledger cards are dropped into the feed slot in the center just above the keyboard. Different sizes of ledger cards can be used for different applications. This type of printer is typical of those used in many business applications.

1•17 PROGRAMMING SYSTEMS

The preceding discussion showed a basic procedure for writing a program and introducing it into the computer. There are, however, various types of *programming languages* which greatly facilitate the actual writing of programs. One of the first things the programming profession discovered was that the greatest aid to programming was the computer itself; it was found to

FIG. 1•12 Keyboard and ledger-card printer.

be capable of translating written programs from a language which was straightforward and natural for the programmer into computer, or machine, language.

As a result, programs were written whose purpose was to read other programs written in a language natural for the programmer and translate them into the machine's language. The program systems now in use are primarily of two types: *assemblers* and *compilers.*† The assembler and the compiler are intended for the same basic purpose; each is a program designed to read a program written in a programming language and translate it. The assembler or compiler is read into the machine first, and is then followed by the program to be translated. After translation, the assembler or compiler stores the machine-language program on punched cards or on magnetic or paper tape or in some large memory, so that it can be performed when desired.

The purpose of this procedure is to enable programmers to write the operations they want the computer to perform in a manner which is simpler than machine language. The language which the programmer writes is called a *programming language,* and a program written in such a language is called a *source program.* The translated program in machine (or some intermediate) language is called an *object program.*

To return to the subject of the translator programs, an assembly language differs from a compiler language in that most assembly language closely resembles machine language, primarily because each instruction to the computer in assembly language is translated into a single computer word. In compiler systems, a single instruction to the computer may be converted into many computer words.

1•18 ASSEMBLY LANGUAGES

Each instruction to the computer in an artificial programming language is called a *statement.* The basic characteristic which most distinguishes an assembly language is that each statement is translated by the assembly program into a single machine instruction word.‡ As a result, an assembly language somewhat resembles machine language. The facilities offered the programmer are substantial, however, and generally include:

1. *Mnemonic operation codes* The programmer can write instructions to the computer using letters instead of binary numbers, and the letters which designate a given operation are arranged into a mnemonic code which conveys the "sense" of the instruction. In our preceding example of coding, the mnemonic codes ADD, MUL, CLA, etc., were used. The assembler would translate these mnemonic codes into the correct machine

---

† There is also a translator type of program which translates one line or statement at a time called an *interpreter* used with such programming languages as Basic.

‡ This is not, of course, strictly the case (sometimes a single statement may be translated into several words), but is generally true.

binary or binary-coded-decimal numbers and "package" these into the instruction words constituting the object program.

2. *Symbolic referencing of storage addresses*   One of the greatest facilities offered the programmer is the ability to name the different pieces of data used in the program and to have the assembler automatically assign addresses to each name.

If we wish to evaluate the algebraic expression $y = ax^3 + bx^2 + cx + d$ as in Sec. 1·14, the program can appear as shown in Table 1·7.

Notice that the address of the first instruction was simply given a name FST, consisting of three letters, and that no further addresses in memory were specified. If we tell the assembler that FST = 1, the assembler then will see that the instructions are placed in memory as in the program in Sec. 1·14. Notice also that the operands were simply given the variable names X, A, B, C, and D, as in the equation, instead of assigning addresses in memory to them. The assembly program will assign addresses to these names of variables, and if it assigns A to 22, B to 23, C to 24, etc., the final program will look as in Sec. 1·14.

The assembler will also see that actual arithmetic values for X, A, B, C, and D are placed in the correct locations in memory when the data are read into the computer.

3. *Convenient data representation*   This simply means that the programmer can write input data as, for instance, decimal numbers or letters, or perhaps in some form specific to the problem, and that the assembly program will convert the data from this form into the form required for machine computation.

4. *Program listings*   An important feature of most assemblers is their ability to print for the programmer a listing of the source program and also a listing of the object program which is in machine language. A study of these listings will greatly help the programmer in finding any errors made in writing the program and also in modifying the program when this is required.

TABLE 1·7

ADDRESS IN MEMORY	INSTRUCTION WORD	
	OPERATION	OPERAND
FST	CLA	A
	MUL	X
	ADD	B
	MUL	X
	ADD	C
	MUL	X
	ADD	D
	STO	Y
	HLT	

5. *Error detection* An assembler program will also notify the programmer if an error has been made in the usage of the assembly language. For example, the programmer may use the same variable name, for instance X, twice, and then give X two different values, or the programmer may write illegal operation codes, etc. This sort of diagnosis of a program's errors is very useful during the checking out of a new program.

Assemblers provide many other facilities which help the programmer, such as the ability to use programs which have already been written as part of a new program and the ability to use routines from these programs as part of a new program. Often programmers have a set of different programs which they will run together in different combinations. This is made possible simply by specifying to the assembler the variable names in the different programs which are to be the same variable, the entry and exit points for the programs, etc. This means that programs written in an assembly language can be linked together in various ways.

Let us consider the short program in Table 1·6 which sums the even integers from 0 to 100. This will illustrate the use of symbolic names for addresses when a branch instruction is used. The assembly-language program is shown in Table 1·8.

Notice that the values of the variables were specified before the program was begun; the DEC's indicate that the values given for A, B, C, D, and E are in decimal. This enables the assembler to locate the variables in the memory and assign values to them.† Also, note that the transfer instruction BRM was to the symbolic address N.

TABLE 1·8

ADDRESS	INSTRUCTION WORDS		COMMENTS
	OPERATION	OPERAND	
A	DEC	0	
B	DEC	−50	
C	DEC	2	
D	DEC	1	
E	DEC	0	
N	CLA	A	last value of integer
	ADD	C	
	STO	A	stores sum for next time
	ADD	E	
	STO	E	
	CLA	B	
	ADD	D	
	STO	B	
	BRM	N	
	HLT		

† In a sense, the operation code DEC says "assign the decimal value in the operational column to the variable name in the address column."

If the assembler was told to start the program at address 1 in the memory, conversion into object or machine language would make it look similar to the one in Sec. 1 · 15, provided the assembler decided to store A, B, C, D, and E in locations 39 through 43. Also, the operation codes of CLA, MUL, etc., would be converted to numerical or machine form, if this were necessary.

1 • 19 COMPILER LANGUAGES

More advanced types of programming languages are called *compiler languages, high-level languages,* or *problem-oriented languages.* These are the simplest languages to use for most problems and are also the simplest to learn. These languages reveal very little about the digital machines on which they are run, however. The designer of the language generally concentrates on specifying a programming language which is simple enough for the casual user of a digital computer and yet which has enough facilities to make the language and its associated compiler valuable to professional programmers. In fact, many languages are almost completely computer-independent, and programs written in one of these languages may be run on any computer which has a compiler or translator for the language in its program library.

Certain languages have been very successful and have found extremely wide usage in the computer industry. The most famous language is Fortran, which is the earliest of the languages and has been regularly updated. A program written in Fortran can be run on most commercial computers which have a memory size large enough to accommodate a Fortran compiler, because most manufacturers will prepare a Fortran compiler for their computer.

There are a number of other languages in active use. Algol, a language which was designed for international use, is widely used in describing algorithms in technical journals and has had moderate success in actual practice; Cobol is a language especially for business systems; Mad and several other languages have been developed by universities for educational purposes; Formac does symbolic manipulation; Jovial is a language for real-time systems; Basic is a very simple, easy-to-use language which is often used in online systems and which has become quite popular; etc. About all that can be said is that there is no truly universal programming language but that there are several good languages. Fortunately, there is no staggering difference in these languages from a conceptual viewpoint, and when one of the languages has been learned, learning another presents no great problem.

A popular programming language is called Programming Language One (abbreviated PL/1). Some of the features of this language will suffice for illustrating the general appearance of compiler languages. PL/1 has been chosen because of its simplicity for algebraic equations and because of the very elementary format for reading in data and printing results. Also, PL/1 at this level looks almost like Fortran except that we need not worry about mixing real variables with integer variables, nor about format statements for printing or reading, provided we are willing to use the standard PL/1 format (in this we adopt the attitude of Basic, and our programs will be quite similar). Finally, several simple versions of PL/1 have been developed by microprocessor and microprogrammed computer manufacturers.

Since the following section gives an introduction to a specific compiler language, those who are familiar with compiler languages such as Fortran or Cobol may omit it. Others may wish to skip over this material until later. The text is arranged so that subsequent material in the book does not depend on the following section and this section can be omitted or studied at a later time. The material is introduced at this point because many believe it is a good idea to look at a compiler language fairly early in studying computers (or else there may be a misconception that computer programmers must actually write their programs in computer or machine language, which would greatly limit the use of computers). Merely a reading of this material will be sufficient in many cases. For those who wish to study it in more depth, quite a few questions have been provided at the end of the chapter which call for a study of some additional features of PL/1, and these can be used as a supplement.

* 1•20 A SHORT INTRODUCTION TO PL/1

As has been mentioned, the distinguishing feature of compilers and their programming languages is that a single statement which the programmer writes may be converted by the compiler into a number of machine-language instructions. In PL/1, for instance, a single statement to the computer can generate quite a number of instructions in object or machine language. As a result, the language is not particularly dependent on the structure of the computer on which the program is run, and the following programs may be run on any computer with a PL/1 compiler.

The PL/1 compiler is written in machine language, of course, and a PL/1 program is ultimately run in machine language. For this reason, knowledge of the machine and its organization can be of great use to those writing and checking out programs. Further, for the systems programmers (those who maintain, modify, and prepare the compilers, assemblers, load programs, etc.), a knowledge of the machine on which the program is operated is indispensable. The fact that compilers are backed up by an army of technical personnel, from systems programmers through design and maintenance engineers, technicians, and computer operators, is often overlooked by the user of the machine whose program is miraculously debugged and operated by professionals in the computer field. Like most electronic devices, digital computers are not as independent and self-supporting as they may appear to casual users.

Thus forewarned, let us examine the structure of PL/1 in a little detail, leaving a more complete exposition to one of the references.

The first thing to be learned in writing statements is the use of the $=$ symbol. This is treated somewhat as a command to the computer, for when we write $Y = A + B$, what is meant is "replace the current value of Y with that of $A + B$." So therefore, if we write

```
A = 50;
B = 20;
Y = A + B;
END;
```

we find that after this is run, A will be equal to 50, B to 20, and Y to 70. Notice that each statement is followed by a semicolon. As a further example, we can increase, decrease, or otherwise change the current value of Y by adding or subtracting from it. Consider

```
Y = 30;
A = 40;
Y = Y + A;
END;
```

After these four statements are operated, Y will have the value of 70; that is, the location in memory which has been used to store Y will have the value 70 in it. Notice that the statements above took the form of algebraic equations. Here is one further example:

```
Y = 20;
Z = 50;
W = Y + Z;
M = W − 30;
END;
```

After this is run, W will have the value 70 and M the value 40.

In PL/1, the addition symbol is the familiar + and the subtraction symbol is the usual −, but multiplication is indicated by an asterisk (*), and exponentiation (raising to a power) by two asterisks. Thus A * B means "multiply A by B" and A ** B means A^B or "raise A to the Bth power." Therefore the program statements

```
A = 20;
B = 30;
C = A * B;
END;
```

give a value of 600 for C, and the program

```
A = 20;
B = 2;
C = A ** B;
END;
```

gives a value of 400 to C.

Division is indicated by a / symbol. Thus

$$A = 20;$$
$$B = 2;$$
$$Y = 20/2;$$
$$END;$$

will place the value 10 in the location in memory delegated to Y.

Let us examine one simple way to form a loop in the program, that is, to repeat a sequence of instructions until we desire to stop. Here are two PL/1 statements:

LOOP. DO WHILE X LE Y;

and

END LOOP;

The first of these says "do the following set of statements up to the END LOOP, while X is less than or equal to Y." In other words, "repeat the following instructions until Y is greater than X." If we write the following statements:

$$T = 0;$$
$$M = 4;$$
$$N = 2;$$
$$P = 6;$$
LOOP. DO WHILE N LE M;
$$S = P * N;$$
$$T = T + S;$$
$$N = N + 1;$$
END LOOP;
$$Y = T * 2;$$
END;

then the statements between the LOOP and END LOOP will be repeated until N is greater than M. Since N starts with the value 2 (and as 1 is added each time) while M starts with the value 4, N will take the values 2, 3, 4, 5. But when N equals 5, it will be greater than M and the program will proceed with the instruction Y = T * 2; and then END. The LOOP statements will therefore be repeated three times. The first time, S will equal P times N, or 12, T will be equal to 0 + S, or 12, and N will then be increased from 2 to 3. The second time, S will equal P times N, or 6 times 3, which is 18; T will be equal to 12 + 18, or 30; and N will be increased to 4. The third and last time through the loop, S will equal 6 times 4, or 24, T will take the value 30 + 24, or 54, and N will be increased to 5. N will then be greater than M, and the END LOOP statement will be operated. T, which has the value 54, will then be multiplied by 2, giving 108, and the program will stop with Y equal to 108.

Let us examine two other features. To read data we simply write

$$READ \ (X, \ Y, \ Z);$$

and this will tell the compiler to arrange for reading the value of X, Y, and Z from cards and continue with the values read as the current values of X, Y, and Z. We must therefore supply values of X, Y, and Z on punched cards. The advantage of this is that we can change the values of X, Y, and Z by simply replacing our data cards with cards containing new values. If we write

$$READ \ (X, \ Y, \ Z);$$
$$M = X + (Y * Z);$$
$$END;$$

and attach cards with the values X = 20, Y = 30, and Z = 2, we shall have M = 80. If we change our data cards to read X = 5, Y = 3, and Z = 4, we shall then have M = 17 after we run the program.

To print out data, we write the statement

$$WRITE \ (X, \ Y, \ Z, \ A),$$

and the computer will print out the current values of X, Y, Z, and A.

It should be noted that the READ and WRITE statements assume that the programmer will be satisfied with the standard format for the input data and print statements. Assuming that this is the case, we can write the following program, which will first evaluate the equation $Y = AX^3 + BX^2 + CX + D$ for values of A, B, D, and X which are read in on data cards or tape and for C = 1. If the value of Y for these particular values is greater than 2,000, the program will print the value of Y as calculated and also the value C = 1. If, however, Y is less than or equal to 2,000, the program will calculate the smallest positive integer which, when substituted into C, will make $AX^3 + BX^2 + CX + D$ greater than 2,000. The program will then print this value of C and the value of $AX^3 + BX^2 + CX + D$ associated with the value of C.

```
READ (A, B, D, X);
    C = 0;
    Y = 0;
LOOP. DO WHILE Y LE 2000;
    C = C + 1;
    Y = A * X ** 3 + B * X ** 2 + C * X + D;
END LOOP;
PRINT (C, Y);
END;
```

We have only touched on the power of this language. It is not possible in a short exposition to do more than show several statements and give a general idea of how such a language operates. Nevertheless, a clever programmer could do quite a lot with the limited vocabulary we have introduced.

One thing which should become apparent from this brief introduction is that, once the statement types and details of the language are learned, the job of programming a given problem is greatly facilitated.

QUESTIONS

1. Discuss batch processing and give several examples of businesses and industries that might use batch processing.
2. Discuss online computer systems and give examples of businesses and industries that might use online systems.
3. Give examples of industries that might use real-time control systems for manufacturing.
4. Sometimes the same computer is used by several different companies during the day and the computer is time-shared between these companies. Discuss problems which might arise in billing the companies for the computer's services.
5. Values for X, Y, and Z are stored at memory addresses 40, 41, and 42, respectively. Using the instructions for the generalized single-address computer described in Secs. $1 \cdot 13$ to $1 \cdot 15$ write a program which will form the sum $X + Y + Z$ and store it at memory address 43.
6. Explain the difference between the *address* of a word in memory and the *word* itself.
7. Given that values for X, Y, and Z are stored in locations 20, 21, and 22, respectively, use the instructions for the computer given in Secs. $1 \cdot 13$ to $1 \cdot 15$ to write a program which will form $X^2 + Y^2 + Z^2$ and store this at memory address 40.
8. The program in Table $1 \cdot 4$ is run with the following values when the program is started: 4 in address 22, 3 in address 23, 4 in address 24, 5 in address 25, and 2 in address 26. What value will be in address 27 after the program has been run?
9. Convert the flowchart in Fig. $1 \cdot 2$ into a computer assembly-language program using the instructions described in the chapter.
10. If the program in Table $1 \cdot 4$ is started with location 22 containing 5, location 23 containing 4, location 24 containing 3, location 25 containing 1, and location 26 containing 2, what number will be stored in location 27 after the program is run?
11. Write a program that will store $X^5 + X$ in register 40, using the assembly language in Secs. $1 \cdot 13$ to $1 \cdot 15$ given that X is in register 20. Use less than 20 instructions. Now rewrite this program using the assembly language in Sec. $1 \cdot 18$.
12. If the program in Table $1 \cdot 6$ were operated but the number at address 40 were -20 instead of -50 when the program was started, the number

at address 43 would be the sum of all even integers from 2 to — instead of 2 to 100.

13. Draw a flowchart for the program in Sec. 1 · 15.

14. Given that a value for X is stored at address 39, write a program which will form X^4 and store it at address 42, using the assembly language in Secs. 1 · 13 through 1 · 15.

15. Draw a flowchart showing how to find the largest number in a set of five numbers stored at locations 20, 21, 22, 23, and 24 in memory.

16. Values for X and Y are stored at addresses 30 and 31. Write a program which will store the larger of the two values at address 50, using the assembly language in Secs. 1 · 13 to 1 · 15.

17. Given three different numbers, determine whether they are in ascending or descending order. Draw a flowchart for the problem, and write a program using the assembly language in Secs. 1 · 13 to 1 · 15. Assume that the numbers are stored in memory locations 30, 31, and 32.

18. A value for Y is stored at location 55 and a value for A at location 57. Write an assembly-language program to store AY^2 at location 30.

19. Write a program to find $AX^2 + BY + CZ^2$, with A in location 20, B in location 21, C in location 22, X in location 23, Y in location 24, and Z in location 25. Store your result in location 30.

20. A value for X is stored at address 40. Write a program which will store X^8 at address 45, using less than 10 instruction words.

21. Using the assembly language described in Secs. 1 · 13 to 1 · 15, write a program which will branch to location 300 if the number stored in memory register 25 is larger than the number stored in register 26, and which will transfer or branch to location 400 if the number at address 26 is equal to or larger than the number at address 25.

22. Write a program which will produce the value $X - Y$ or X, whichever is larger, in both the assembly language in Secs. 1 · 13 to 1 · 15 and the compiler language in Sec. 1 · 20. Store this value in location 300 for the assembly program and assign the variable B to this value for the program written in the compiler language. For the assembly program, assume that X is in location 100 and Y in 101.

23. Calculate the largest of the three numbers A, B, and C and assign the largest of the numbers to the variable X, using the assembly language in Sec. 1 · 18 to write the program.

24. Write a PL/1 program that will assign the value 50 to variable B and the value 60 to variable C.

25. Write a program in PL/1 that will assign the value of 10 to A, 20 to B, and 5 to C and which will then calculate the value $(A \times B)^C$ and assign this value to a variable D.

26. In PL/1 what will be the value of D if we execute the statement $D = X + (Y ** Z)$ when X has value 5, Y has value 2, and Z has value 3?

27. If the PL/1 program which was used to illustrate the LOOP command is run with P having value 4 but with T, M, and N as in the program in the text, what will be the value of Y after the program is run?

28. Suppose the final PL/1 program in the text is run with values of 4 for A, 3 for B, 2 for C, and 2 for X. What values of C and Y will the program cause to be printed?

29. Using the compiler language in Sec. 1·20, write a program which will determine which of $X - Y$ or $Y - X$ is positive or equal to 0 and which will print the value of this positive number or 0, assigning the variable Z to this number.

30. Modify the program in Sec. 1·15 so that it will sum all the odd numbers from 1 through 77.

31. We have 30 numbers stored in successive registers in our memory, starting at location 300. Write a program which will convert any negative numbers in the 30 to positive form. That is, write a program which will take the 30 numbers, convert each number to its positive value without changing its magnitude, and restore it in the same location. Use assembly language.

32. Write a program, using the assembly language in Secs. 1·13 to 1·15, which will rearrange five numbers stored in addresses 300 through 304 so that they are in descending order (for example, 10, 3, 0, −5, −7).

Additional Questions on PL/1

33. In a nonparenthesized section of a given statement, the PL/1 language, like Fortran and Algol, first performs exponentiation, or raising to a power, then multiplication and division, and then addition and subtraction. Within this hierarchy, statements are evaluated from left to right. Thus the statement $A = ((B/C) - (D * E))/(C ** D)$ can be written as $A = (B/C - D * E)/(C ** D)$. The following are four more examples of the way in which the compiler evaluates arithmetic statements:

(a) $A^B + C \cdot D + E/F$ can be written A ** B + C * D + E/F.

(b) $(A \cdot B \cdot C)E^F + (G/H)$ can be written A * B * C * E ** F + G/H.

(c) $\dfrac{A \cdot B \cdot C}{D \cdot E}$ must be written (A * B * C)/(D * E).

(d) $A \cdot B + (C/D) + EF$ is written A * B + C/D + E * F.

Find the value of X in the following statements if $A = 5, B = 2, C = 20$, and $D = 15$:

(a) X = A ** B + C   (b) X = A * C ** B

(c) X = C + D * B + A (d) X = C + D ** B/A + A

34. Using the compiler language in Sec. 1·20, assume we have read in values for the variables X, Y, and Z. Assign the largest of these values to the variable A, the second largest to the variable B, and the third largest to the variable C. For instance, if X is read in as 29, Y as 31, and Z as 23, after the program operates we would like the value $A = 33, B = 29$, and $C = 21$.

35. Write PL/I statements which correspond to the following algebraic formulas written in conventional mathematical notation:

(a) $\dfrac{a^c}{b^d}$ (b) $a^2 + b + cd$ (c) $\left(\dfrac{a}{b}\right) + \left(\dfrac{c}{d}\right)^e$ (d) $(a \cdot b)^e + \dfrac{bd}{e}$

36. In PL/1 it is possible to write mathematical statements with subscripted variables, which are called array variables. That is, if we have a set of variables X_1, X_2, X_3, and X_4, we can write these as in PL/1 as X(1), X(2), X(3), and X(4). Notice that the parentheses do not indicate multiplication, but rather the fact that the variable is an array variable or a subscripted variable. Now, if we write in a program X(K), whether this indicates X(1) or X(2) or X(3) or X(4), for instance, depends upon the value of the variable K at that particular time. What are the values of X in each of the following statements if A(1) = 3, A(2) = 4, A(3) = 5, and K = 1:
   (a) X = A(1) + A(2) (b) Y = A(2) ** A(1) + A(3)
   (c) X = A(K) + A(2) * A(3) (d) Y = A(K + 2) + A(K)

37. There is a class of statements in PL/1 called *control statements*. These statements make it possible to iterate many times through a given set of instructions, providing indexing facilities during these iterations. The general form of the most important one of these statements, which is the DO statement, is DO N K = P, Q. Here N is the statement number or location of some executable statement, K is a simple variable, and P and Q are either constants or nonarray variables. A typical DO statement might therefore appear as DO 30 K = 1, 25. This statement in a program will cause the instructions or statements following the DO statement up to statement 30 to be repeated, with the variable K equal to 1 through 25. That is, the loop from the DO statement to statement 30 in the program is repeated 25 times, the first time with the variable K equal to 1, the second time with the variable K equal to 2, the third time with the variable K equal to 3, etc., until K = 25. This time the program will pass through statement 30 to the next statement. If we therefore write

$$
\begin{aligned}
&X = 2\\
&B(1) = 5\\
&B(2) = 6\\
&B(3) = 7\\
&B(4) = 8\\
&DO\ 19\ K = 1,\ 4\\
&A(K) = B(K) + 6\\
19\quad &X = X\ **\ 2
\end{aligned}
$$

After this program has been run, A(1) will equal 11, A(2) will equal 12, A(3) will equal 13, and A(4) will equal 14, while X = 65,536.

Using the DO statement in PL/1, write a program which will rearrange a set of 20 numbers which are stored in successive registers. These variables are A(1) through A(20), where each value is assumed to be positive. Assign these values to a set of variables B(1) through B(20) so that B(1) is equal to the smallest of the values of A, B(2) is equal to the second smallest of the values of A, and, finally, B(20) is equal to the largest value of the A variables.

38. Using the DO statement explained in Question 37, write a program which will examine and form an average of the values of a set of variables A(1) through A(10), where A(1) through A(10) are assumed to be already stored in the memory of the computer when the program begins. Call this average of the 10 values the *mean* of these values, and give a variable named M this value when the program has operated.

NUMBER SYSTEMS

It is India that gave us the ingenious method of expressing all numbers by means of ten symbols, each symbol receiving a value of position as well as an absolute value; a profound and important idea which appears so simple to us now that we ignore its true merit.

Marquis de Laplace

As a mathematician, Laplace could well appreciate the decimal number system. He was fully aware of the centuries of mental effort and sheer good luck which had gone into the development of the number system we use, and was in a position to appreciate its advantages. Our present number system provides modern mathematicians and scientists with a great advantage over those of previous civilizations and is an important factor in our rapid advancement.

Since hands are the most convenient tools nature has provided, human beings have always tended to use them in counting. It is both natural and fortunate that our number system is based on the number of digits we possess. It was quite some time after we learned to count, however, that we attempted to represent numbers graphically. The earliest numerals which have been found consist of either vertical or horizontal marks. Our 1 is an example of this sort of symbol, and it is interesting to note that the symbol for 2 consists of two horizontal marks with a connecting line, and 3 consists of three horizontal lines with connections. Roman numerals are good examples of lines used as the basis for numerals.

The decimal system for counting has been so widely adopted throughout our present civilization that we rarely consider the possibilities of other number systems. Nevertheless, it is not reasonable to expect a system based on the number of fingers we possess to be the most efficient number system for machine construction. The fact is that a little-used but very simple system, the binary number system, has proved the most natural and efficient system for machine use.

2•1 THE DECIMAL SYSTEM

Our present system of numbers has 10 separate symbols: 0, 1, 2, 3, . . . , 9, which are called Arabic numerals. We would be forced to stop at 9 or to invent more symbols if it were not for the use of *positional notation*. An example of earlier types of notation can be found in Roman numerals, which are essentially additive: III = I + I + I, XXV = X + X + V. New symbols (X, C, M, etc.) were used as the numbers increased in value. Thus V rather than IIIII = 5. The only importance of position in Roman numerals lies in whether a symbol precedes or follows another symbol (IV = 4, while VI = 6). The clumsiness of this system can easily be seen if we try to multiply XII by XIV. Calculating with Roman numerals was so difficult that early mathematicians were forced to perform arithmetic operations almost entirely on abaci, or counting boards, translating their results back into Roman-number form. Pencil-and-paper computations are unbelievably intricate and difficult in such systems. In fact, the ability to perform such operations as addition and multiplication was considered a great accomplishment in earlier civilizations.

The great beauty and simplicity of our number system can now be seen. It is necessary to learn only the 10 basic numerals and the *positional notation system* in order to count to any desired figure. After memorizing the addition and multiplication tables and learning a few simple rules, it is possible to perform all arithmetic operations. Notice the simplicity of multiplying 12 × 14 using the present system:

$$
\begin{array}{r}
1\,4 \\
1\,2 \\
\hline
2\,8 \\
1\,4 \\
\hline
1\,6\,8
\end{array}
$$

The actual meaning of the number 168 can be seen more clearly if we notice that it is spoken as "one hundred and sixty-eight." Basically, the number is a contraction of $(1 \times 100) + (6 \times 10) + 8$. The important point is that the value of each digit is determined by its position. For example, the 2 in 2,000 has a different value than the 2 in 20. We show this verbally by saying "two thousand" and "twenty." Different verbal representations have been invented for numbers from 10 to 20 (eleven, twelve . . .), but from 20 upward we break only at powers of 10 (hundreds, thousands, millions, billions). Written numbers are always contracted, however, and only the basic 10 numerals are used regardless of the size of the integer written. The general rule for representing numbers in the decimal system using positional notation is as follows: $a_1 10^{n-1} + a_2 10^{n-2} + \ldots + a_n$ is expressed as $a_1 a_2 \ldots a_n$, where n is the number of digits to the left of the decimal point.

The *base*, or *radix*, of a number system is defined as the number of different digits which can occur in each position in the number system. The decimal number system has a base, or radix, of 10. This means that the system has 10 different digits (0, 1, 2, . . . , 9), any one of which may be used in each position in a number. History records the use of several other number systems. The quinary system, which has 5 for its base, was prevalent among Eskimos and North American Indians. Examples of the duodecimal system (base 12) may be seen in clocks, inches and feet, and in dozens or grosses.

2•2 THE BINARY SYSTEM

A seventeenth-century German mathematician, Gottfried Wilhelm von Leibniz, was an advocate of the binary number system which has 2 for a base, using only the symbols 0 and 1. If it seems strange for an eminent mathematician to advocate such a simple number system, it should be noted that he was also a philosopher. Leibniz's reasons for advocating the binary system seem to have been mystical. He felt there was great beauty in the analogy between zero, representing the void, and one, representing the Deity.

Regardless of how good Leibniz's reasons for advocating it were, the binary system has become very popular in the last decade. Present-day digital computers are constructed to operate in binary or binary-coded number systems, and present indications are that future machines will also be constructed to operate in these systems.

The basic elements in early computers were relays and switches. The operation of a switch, or relay, can be seen to be essentially binary in nature. That is, the switch is either on (1) or off (0). The principal circuit elements in more modern computers are transistors similar to those used in radios and television sets. The desire for reliability led designers to use these devices so that they were essentially in one of two states, fully conducting or non-conducting. A simple analogy may be made between this type of circuit and an electric light. At any given time the light (or transistor) is either on (conducting) or off (not conducting). Even after a bulb is old and weak, it is generally easy to tell if it is on or off. The same sort of thing may be seen in radios. As a radio ages the volume generally decreases, and we compensate by turning the volume control up. Even when the radio becomes very weak, however, it is still possible to tell easily whether it is on or off.

Because of the large number of electronic parts used in computers, it is highly desirable to utilize them in such a manner that slight changes in their characteristics will not affect their performance. The best way of accomplishing this is using circuits which are basically *bistable* (having two possible states).

2•3 COUNTING IN THE BINARY SYSTEM

The same type of positional notation is used in the binary number system as in the decimal system. Table 2·1 lists the first 20 binary numbers.

While the same positional notation system is used, the decimal system

TABLE 2·1

DECIMAL		BINARY	DECIMAL		BINARY
1	=	1	11	=	1011
2	=	10	12	=	1100
3	=	11	13	=	1101
4	=	100	14	=	1110
5	=	101	15	=	1111
6	=	110	16	=	10000
7	=	111	17	=	10001
8	=	1000	18	=	10010
9	=	1001	19	=	10011
10	=	1010	20	=	10100

uses powers of 10, and the binary system powers of 2. As was previously explained, the number 125 actually means $(1 \times 10^2) + (2 \times 10^1) + (5 \times 10^0)$. In the binary system, the same number (125) is represented as 1111101, meaning $(1 \times 2^6) + (1 \times 2^5) + (1 \times 2^4) + (1 \times 2^3) + (1 \times 2^2) + (0 \times 2^1) + (1 \times 2^0)$.

To express the value of a binary number, therefore, $a_1 2^{n-1} + a_2 2^{n-2} + \ldots + a_n$ is represented as $a_1 a_2 \ldots a_n$, where a is either 1 or 0, and n is the number of digits to the left of the binary (radix) point.

The following examples illustrate the conversion of binary numbers to the decimal system:

$$101 = (1 \times 2^{3-1}) + (0 \times 2^{3-2}) + (1 \times 2^{3-3})$$
$$= (1 \times 2^2) + (0 \times 2^1) + (1 \times 2^0)$$
$$= 4 + 1 = 5$$

$$1001 = (1 \times 2^{4-1}) + (0 \times 2^{4-2}) + (0 \times 2^{4-3}) + (1 \times 2^{4-4})$$
$$= (1 \times 2^3) + (0 \times 2^2) + (0 \times 2^1) + (1 \times 2^0)$$
$$= 8 + 1 = 9$$

$$11.011 = (1 \times 2^{2-1}) + (1 \times 2^{2-2}) + (0 \times 2^{2-3}) + (1 \times 2^{2-4}) + (1 \times 2^{2-5})$$
$$= (1 \times 2^1) + (1 \times 2^0) + (0 \times 2^{-1}) + (1 \times 2^{-2}) + (1 \times 2^{-3})$$
$$= 2 + 1 + \tfrac{1}{4} + \tfrac{1}{8}$$
$$= 3\tfrac{3}{8}$$

Notice that fractional numbers are formed in the same general way as in the decimal system. Just as

$$0.123 = (1 \times 10^{-1}) + (2 \times 10^{-2}) + (3 \times 10^{-3})$$

in the decimal system,

$$0.101 = (1 \times 2^{-1}) + (0 \times 2^{-2}) + (1 \times 2^{-3})$$

in the binary system.

2•4 BINARY ADDITION AND SUBTRACTION

Binary addition is performed in the same manner as decimal addition. Actually, binary arithmetic is much simpler to learn. The complete table for binary addition is as follows:

$$0 + 0 = 0$$
$$0 + 1 = 1$$
$$1 + 0 = 1$$
$$1 + 1 = 0 \quad \text{plus a carry-over of 1}$$

"Carry-overs" are performed in the same manner as in decimal arithmetic. Since 1 is the largest digit in the binary system, any sum greater than 1 requires that a digit be carried over. For instance, 100 plus 100 binary requires the addition of the two ones in the third position to the left, with a carry-over. Since $1 + 1 = 0$ plus a carry-over of 1, the sum of 100 and 100 is 1000. Here are three more examples of binary addition:

DECIMAL	BINARY	DECIMAL	BINARY	DECIMAL	BINARY
5	101	15	1111	$3\frac{1}{4}$	11.01
6	110	20	10100	$5\frac{3}{4}$	101.11
11	1011	35	100011	9	1001.00

Subtraction is the inverse operation of addition. To subtract, it is necessary to establish a procedure for subtracting a larger from a smaller digit. The only case in which this occurs using binary numbers is when 1 is subtracted from 0. The remainder is 1, but it is necessary to borrow 1 from the next column to the left. This is the binary subtraction table:

$$0 - 0 = 0$$
$$1 - 0 = 1$$
$$1 - 1 = 0$$
$$0 - 1 = 1 \quad \text{with a borrow of 1}$$

A few examples will make the procedure for binary subtraction clear.

DECIMAL	BINARY	DECIMAL	BINARY	DECIMAL	BINARY
9	1001	16	10000	$6\frac{1}{4}$	110.01
−5	−101	−3	−11	$-4\frac{1}{2}$	−100.1
4	100	13	1101	$1\frac{3}{4}$	1.11

2•5 BINARY MULTIPLICATION AND DIVISION

The table for binary multiplication is very short, with only four entries instead of the 100 necessary for decimal multiplication. The binary multiplication table is

$$0 \times 0 = 0$$
$$1 \times 0 = 0$$
$$0 \times 1 = 0$$
$$1 \times 1 = 1$$

The following three examples of binary multiplication illustrate the simplicity of each operation. It is only necessary to copy the multiplicand if the digit in the multiplier is 1, and to copy all 0s if the digit in the multiplier is a 0. The ease with which each step of the operation is performed is apparent.

DECIMAL	BINARY	DECIMAL	BINARY	DECIMAL	BINARY
1 2	1 1 0 0	1 0 2	1 1 0 0 1 1 0	1 . 2 5	1 . 0 1
× 1 0	× 1 0 1 0	× 8	× 1 0 0 0	× 2 . 5	× 1 0 . 1
1 2 0	0 0 0 0	8 1 6	1 1 0 0 1 1 0 0 0 0	6 2 5	1 0 1
	1 1 0 0			2 5 0	1 0 1 0
	0 0 0 0			3 . 1 2 5	1 1 . 0 0 1
	1 1 0 0				
	1 1 1 1 0 0 0				

Binary division is, again, very simple. As in the decimal system (or in any other), division by zero is meaningless. The complete table is

$$0 \div 1 = 0$$
$$1 \div 1 = 1$$

Here are two examples of division:

```
        DECIMAL                         BINARY
              5                              1 0 1
        5 ) 2 5                  1 0 1 ) 1 1 0 0 1
                                          1 0 1
                                          1 0 1
                                          1 0 1
```

```
        DECIMAL                         BINARY
          2 . 4 1 6 ···              1 0 . 0 1 1 0 1 0 1 0 1 ···
    1 2 ) 2 9 . 0 0 0 0      1 1 0 0 ) 1 1 1 0 1 . 0 0
          2 4                          1 1 0 0
            5 0                        1 0 1 0 0
            4 8                        1 1 0 0
              2 0                      1 0 0 0 0
              1 2                        1 1 0 0
                8 0                    1 0 0 0 0
                7 2                      1 1 0 0
                  8                    ······
```

Converting the quotient obtained in the second example from binary to decimal would proceed as follows:

$$
\begin{aligned}
10.0110101 = 1 \times 2^1 &= 2.0 \\
0 \times 2^0 &= 0.0 \\
0 \times 2^{-1} &= 0.0 \\
1 \times 2^{-2} &= 0.25 \\
1 \times 2^{-3} &= 0.125 \\
0 \times 2^{-4} &= 0.0 \\
1 \times 2^{-5} &= 0.03125 \\
0 \times 2^{-6} &= 0.0 \\
1 \times 2^{-7} &= 0.0078125 \\
0 \times 2^{-8} &= 0.0 \\
1 \times 2^{-9} &= \underline{0.001953125} \\
&\ 2.416015625
\end{aligned}
$$

Therefore 10.0110101 binary equals approximately 2.416 decimal.

2•6 CONVERTING DECIMAL NUMBERS TO BINARY

There are several methods for converting a decimal number to a binary number. The first and most obvious method is simply to subtract all powers of 2 which can be subtracted from the decimal number until nothing remains. The highest power of 2 is subtracted first, then the second highest, etc. To convert the decimal integer 25 into the binary number system, first the highest power of 2 which can be subtracted from 25 is found. This is $2^4 = 16$. Then $25 - 16 = 9$. The highest power of 2 which can be subtracted from 9 is 2^3, or 8. The remainder after subtraction is 1, or 2^0. The binary representation for 25 is therefore 11001.

This is a laborious method for converting numbers. It is convenient for small numbers when it can be performed mentally, but is less used for larger numbers. Instead, the decimal number is repeatedly divided by 2, and the remainder after each division is used to indicate the coefficients of the binary number to be formed. Notice that the binary number derived is written from the bottom up.

$$
\begin{aligned}
125 \div 2 &= 62 + \text{remainder of } 1 \\
62 \div 2 &= 31 + \text{remainder of } 0 \\
31 \div 2 &= 15 + \text{remainder of } 1 \\
15 \div 2 &= 7 + \text{remainder of } 1 \\
7 \div 2 &= 3 + \text{remainder of } 1 \\
3 \div 2 &= 1 + \text{remainder of } 1 \\
1 \div 2 &= 0 + \text{remainder of } 1
\end{aligned}
$$

The binary representation of 125 is therefore 1111101. Checking this result gives

$$
\begin{aligned}
1 \times 2^6 &= 6\,4 \\
1 \times 2^5 &= 3\,2 \\
1 \times 2^4 &= 1\,6 \\
1 \times 2^3 &= 8 \\
1 \times 2^2 &= 4 \\
0 \times 2^1 &= 0 \\
1 \times 2^0 &= \underline{1} \\
& 1\,2\,5
\end{aligned}
$$

This method will not work for mixed numbers. If similar methods are to be used, it is necessary first to divide the number into its whole and fractional parts. That is, 102.247 would be divided into 102 and 0.247, and the binary representation for each part found, and then the two parts added together.

The conversion of decimal fractions to binary fractions may be accomplished using several techniques. Again, the most obvious method is to subtract the highest negative power of 2 which may be subtracted from the decimal fraction. The next highest negative power of 2 is then subtracted from the remainder of the first subtraction, and this process is continued until there is no remainder, or to the desired precision.

$$
\begin{aligned}
0.875 - (1 \times 2^{-1}) &= 0.875 - 0.5 = 0.375 \\
0.375 - (1 \times 2^{-2}) &= 0.375 - 0.25 = 0.125 \\
0.125 - (1 \times 2^{-3}) &= 0.125 - 0.125 = 0
\end{aligned}
$$

Therefore 0.875 decimal is represented by 0.111 binary. A much simpler method for longer fractions consists of repeatedly "doubling" the decimal fraction. If a 1 appears to the left of the decimal point after a multiplication by 2 is performed, a 1 is added to the right of the binary fraction being formed. If after a multiplication by 2, a 0 remains to the left of the decimal point of the decimal number, a 0 is added to the right of the binary number. The following example illustrates the use of this technique in converting 0.4375 decimal to the binary system:

	BINARY REPRESENTATION
$2 \times 0.4375 = 0.8750$	0.0
$2 \times 0.875 = 1.750$	0.01
$2 \times 0.75 = 1.50$	0.011
$2 \times 0.5 = 1.0$	0.0111

The binary representation of 0.4375 is therefore 0.0111.

2•7 NEGATIVE NUMBERS

A standard convention adopted for writing negative numbers consists in placing a "sign symbol" before a number which is negative. For instance, negative 39 is written as -39. If -39 is to be added to $+70$, we write

$$+70 + (-39) = 31$$

When a negative number is subtracted from a positive number, we write $+70 - (-39) = +70 + 39 = 109$. The rules for handling negative numbers are well known and will not be repeated here, but since negative numbers constitute an important part of our number system, the techniques used to represent negative numbers in digital machines will be described.

In binary machines, numbers are represented by a set of bistable storage devices, each of which represents one binary digit. As an example, given a set of five switches, any number from 00000 to 11111 may be represented by the switches, if we define a switch with its contacts closed as representing a 1 and a switch with open contacts as representing a 0. If we desire to increase the total range of numbers which we can represent so that it will include the negative numbers from 00000 to -11111, another bit (or switch) will be required. We then treat this bit as a *sign bit* and place it before the magnitude of the number to be represented.

Generally, the convention is adopted that when the sign bit is a 0, the number represented is positive, and when the sign bit is a 1, the number is negative. If the previous situation, where five switches are used to store the magnitude of a number, is extended so that both positive and negative numbers may be stored, a sixth switch will be required. When the contacts of this switch are open, the number will be a positive number equal to the magnitude of the number stored in the other five switches, and if the switch for the sign bit is closed, the number represented by the six switches will be a negative number with a magnitude determined by the other five switches. An example is shown in Fig. 2·1.

Sets of storage devices which represent a number or are handled as an entity are referred to as *registers*, and they are given names such as register A, register B, register C, etc. We can then write that register A contains -12 and register B contains $+22$. In writing a signed number in binary form,

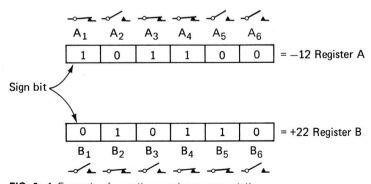

FIG. 2•1 Example of negative number representation.

the sign bit is generally set apart from the magnitude of the number by means of a period, so that 0.0111 represents positive 0111, or positive 7 decimal, and 1.0111 represents −0111, or negative 7 decimal.

The confusion which arises from separating the sign bit from the magnitude of the number with a period which can also be a radix (binary or decimal) point is compensated for when negative numbers are handled in what is known as the "complemented form," as we shall see in the following section. It should be emphasized that a symbol other than the period could be used to separate the sign and magnitude bits, such as a hyphen or a star. Then −1011 (negative 11 decimal) could be written 1-1011 or 1*1011, and +1100 as 0-1100 or 0*1100. There is no particular objection to these conventions, but the use of a period to separate the sign bit from the magnitude is fairly well established and will be adhered to in this text.

2•8 THE USE OF COMPLEMENTS TO REPRESENT NEGATIVE NUMBERS

The convention of using a sign bit to indicate whether a stored number is negative or positive has been described. The magnitude of the number stored is not always represented in normal form, however, but quite often negative numbers are stored in "complemented form." By using this technique, a machine can be made to both add and subtract, using only circuitry for adding. The actual technique involved will be described in Chap. 6.

There are two basic types of complements which are useful in the binary and also in the decimal number systems. In the decimal system the two types are referred to as the 10s *complement* and the 9s *complement.*

The 10s complement of any number may be formed by subtracting each digit of the number from 9 and then adding 1 to the least significant digit of the number thus formed. For instance, the 10s complement of 87 is 13, and the 10s complement of 23 is 77. Subtraction may be performed by simply adding the 10s complement of the subtrahend to the minuend and discarding the final carry, if any. For instance:

NORMAL SUBTRACTION	10s COMPLEMENT SUBTRACTION
$\begin{array}{r} 89 \\ -23 \\ \hline 66 \end{array}$	$\begin{array}{r} 89 \\ -23 = +77 \\ \hline \end{array} \quad \begin{array}{r} 89 \\ +77 \\ \hline \boxed{1}\,66 \end{array}$ └→ the carry is dropped
$\begin{array}{r} 98 \\ -87 \\ \hline 11 \end{array}$	$\begin{array}{r} 98 \\ -87 = +13 \\ \hline \end{array} \quad \begin{array}{r} 98 \\ +13 \\ \hline \boxed{1}\,11 \end{array}$ └→ the carry is dropped

The 9s complement of a decimal number is formed by subtracting each digit of the number from 9. For instance, the 9s complement of 23 is 76, and the 9s complement of 87 is 12. When subtraction is performed using the 9s complement, the complement of the subtrahend is added as before, but any carry generated must be added to the rightmost digit of the result.

```
   NORMAL SUBTRACTION          9s COMPLEMENT SUBTRACTION
          8 9                      8 9        8 9
        − 2 3                    − 2 3 =      7 6
        ———                                ——————
          6 6                              ⌐ 1 6 5
                                           └→     1
                                               ————
                                                6 6


                                        9 8        9 8
           9 8                         − 8 7 =      1 2
         − 8 7                                    ——————
         ———                                     ⌐ 1 1 0
           1 1                                    └→     1
                                                     ————
                                                      1 1
```

The rules for handling signs during the subtraction process and for handling all combinations of positive and negative numbers will be explained in Chap. 6. If this seems, at first, to be an unwieldy technique, it should be noted that the majority of machines now being constructed subtract using a complemented number.

2•9 COMPLEMENTS IN OTHER NUMBER SYSTEMS

There are two types of complements for each number system. Since only binary and binary-coded-decimal machines are now being constructed in quantity, only these number systems will be explained in any detail. The two types of complements and the rules for obtaining them are:

1. *True complement*   This is formed by subtracting each digit of the number from the radix-minus-one of the number system and then adding 1 to the least significant digit of the number formed. The true complement of a number in the decimal system is referred to as the 10s complement, and in the binary system as the 2s complement.
2. *Radix-minus-one complement*   The radix-minus-one is 9 for the decimal system and 1 for the binary system. The complement in each system is formed by subtracting each digit of the number from the radix-minus-one. For instance, the radix-minus-one complement of decimal 72 is 27.

2•10 BINARY NUMBER COMPLEMENTS

According to the rule in the preceding section, the 2s complement of a binary number is formed by simply subtracting each digit (bit) of the number from the radix-minus-one and adding a 1 to the least significant bit. Since the radix in the binary number system is 2, each bit of the binary number is subtracted from 1. The application of this rule is actually very simple; every 1 in the number is changed to a 0 and every 0 to a 1. A 1 is then added to the least significant bit of the number formed. For instance, the 2s complement of 10110 is 01010, and the 2s complement of 11010 is 00110. Subtraction using the 2s complement system involves forming the 2s complement of the subtrahend and then adding this "true complement" to the minuend. For instance:

$$
\begin{array}{r} 1\ 1\ 0\ 1\ 1 \\ -1\ 0\ 1\ 0\ 0 \\ \hline 0\ 0\ 1\ 1\ 1 \end{array}
=
\begin{array}{r} 1\ 1\ 0\ 1\ 1 \\ +0\ 1\ 1\ 0\ 0 \\ \hline 1\ \ 0\ 0\ 1\ 1\ 1 \end{array}
\quad \text{and} \quad
\begin{array}{r} 1\ 1\ 1\ 0\ 0 \\ 0\ 0\ 1\ 0\ 0 \\ \hline 1\ 1\ 0\ 0\ 0 \end{array}
=
\begin{array}{r} 1\ 1\ 1\ 0\ 0 \\ 1\ 1\ 1\ 0\ 0 \\ \hline 1\ \ 1\ 1\ 0\ 0\ 0 \end{array}
$$

         └→ the carry is dropped   └→ dropped

Subtraction using the 1s complement system is also straightforward. The 1s complement of a binary number is formed by changing each 1 in the number to a 0 and each 0 in the number to a 1. For instance, the 1s complement of 10111 is 01000, and the 1s complement of 11000 is 00111.

When subtraction is performed in the 1s complement system, any end-around carry is added to the least significant bit. For instance:

$$
\begin{array}{r} 1\ 1\ 0\ 0\ 1 \\ -1\ 0\ 1\ 1\ 0 \\ \hline 0\ 0\ 0\ 1\ 1 \end{array}
=
\begin{array}{r} 1\ 1\ 0\ 0\ 1 \\ +0\ 1\ 0\ 0\ 1 \\ \hline 1\ \ 0\ 0\ 0\ 1\ 0 \\ \qquad \longrightarrow 1 \\ \hline 0\ 0\ 0\ 1\ 1 \end{array}
\quad \text{and} \quad
\begin{array}{r} 1\ 1\ 1\ 1\ 0 \\ -0\ 1\ 1\ 0\ 1 \\ \hline 1\ 0\ 0\ 0\ 1 \end{array}
=
\begin{array}{r} 1\ 1\ 1\ 1\ 0 \\ 1\ 0\ 0\ 1\ 0 \\ \hline 1\ \ 0\ 0\ 0\ 0 \\ \qquad \longrightarrow 1 \\ \hline 1\ 0\ 0\ 0\ 1 \end{array}
$$

2•11 BINARY-CODED-DECIMAL NUMBER REPRESENTATION

Since most of the electronic circuit elements used to construct digital computers are inherently binary in operation, the binary number system is the most natural number system for a computer. Also, computers constructed using the binary number system require a smaller amount of circuitry and are therefore more efficient than machines operating in other number systems. On the other hand, the decimal system has been used for a long time, and there is a natural reaction to performing calculations in a binary number system. Also, since checks, bills, tax rates, prices, etc., are all figured in the decimal system, the values of most things must be converted from decimal to binary before computations can begin. For these and other reasons most of the early machines operated in binary-coded-decimal number systems. In such systens a coded group of binary bits is used to represent each of the 10 decimal digits. For instance, an obvious and natural code is a simple "weighted binary code," as shown in Table 2·2.

This is known as a *binary-coded-decimal 8, 4, 2, 1 code*, or simply BCD.

TABLE 2·2

BINARY CODE	DECIMAL DIGIT
0000	0
0001	1
0010	2
0011	3
0100	4
0101	5
0110	6
0111	7
1000	8
1001	9

Notice that 4 binary bits are required for each decimal digit, and each bit is assigned a weight; for instance, the rightmost bit has a weight of 1 and the leftmost bit in each code group has a weight of 8. By adding the weights of the positions in which 1s appear, the decimal digit represented by a code group may be derived. This is somewhat uneconomical since $2^4 = 16$ and therefore the 4 bits could actually represent 15 different values; but the next lesser choice, 3 bits, gives only 2^3, or 8, values, which are insufficient. If the decimal number 214 is to be represented in this type of code, 12 binary bits are required as follows: 0010 0001 0100. For the decimal number 1246 to be represented, 16 bits are required: 0001 0010 0100 0110.

This is a very useful code and has been much used. One difficulty with the code, however, lies in forming the complements of numbers in this system. It is common practice to perform subtraction in a computer by adding the complement of the subtrahend; however, when the BCD 8, 4, 2, 1 system is used, the most natural complement of the number stored is not useful because the most direct way for a computer to complement a number is simply to change each 0 to a 1 and each 1 to a 0. However, the natural complement of 0010 (2 decimal) is 1101, which is 13, and not an acceptable BCD character in this system. To get around this difficulty, several other codes have been used. One of the first, a code which was used in the early Mark machines built at Harvard and has been used a good deal since, is known as the *excess 3* code, and is formed by adding 3 to the decimal number and then forming the binary-coded number in the normal weighted binary code. For instance, to form the excess 3 representation for 4, first 3 is added, yielding 7, and then the "normal" BCD is used, which is 0111. Therefore 0111 is the excess 3 code for the decimal digit 4. Table 2·3 shows all 10 decimal digits and the code for each.

By complementing each digit of the binary code representing a decimal digit, the 9s complement of that digit may be formed. For instance, the complement of 0100 (1 decimal) is 1011, which is 8 decimal.

The decimal number 243 coded in the excess 3 system would be 0101

TABLE 2·3

EXCESS 3 CODE	
DECIMAL	BINARY CODE
0	0011
1	0100
2	0101
3	0110
4	0111
5	1000
6	1001
7	1010
8	1011
9	1100

0111 0110, and the decimal number 347 would be 0110 0111 1010. The 9s complement of 243 is 756 decimal, or 1010 1000 1001 binary. Table 2·4 lists the excess 3 code representation for each of the 10 decimal digits along with the 9s complements listed below. It may be seen that the 9s complement of each code group may be formed by changing each 0 to a 1 and each 1 to a 0 in the code group.

The excess 3 code is not a weighted code, however, because weights cannot be assigned to the bits so that their sum equals the decimal digits represented.

A weighted code in which the 9s complement may be formed by complementing each binary digit is the 2, 4, 2, 1 code (see Table 2·5). If each bit of a code group is complemented, the 9s complement of the decimal digit represented is formed. For instance, 0010 (2 decimal) complemented is 1101 (7 decimal), and 1011 (5 decimal) complemented is 0100 (4 decimal). This code is widely used in instruments and electronic calculators.

TABLE 2·4

DECIMAL DIGIT	EXCESS 3 CODE	9s COMPLEMENT
0	0011	1100
1	0100	1011
2	0101	1010
3	0110	1001
4	0111	1000
5	1000	0111
6	1001	0110
7	1010	0101
8	1011	0100
9	1100	0011

TABLE 2·5

	2, 4, 2, 1 CODE			
	CODED BINARY			
	WEIGHT OF BIT			
DECIMAL	2	4	2	1
0	0	0	0	0
1	0	0	0	1
2	0	0	1	0
3	0	0	1	1
4	0	1	0	0
5	1	0	1	1
6	1	1	0	0
7	1	1	0	1
8	1	1	1	0
9	1	1	1	1

The following convention is generally adopted to distinguish binary from decimal. A binary number is identified by a subscript of 2 placed at the end of the number (00110_2), and a decimal number by the subscript 10 (for instance, decimal 948 may be written 948_{10}). We may then write 0111_2 as 7_{10}. This convention will be used when necessary.

2•12 OCTAL AND HEXADECIMAL NUMBER SYSTEMS

There are two other number systems which are very useful in the computer industry: the octal number system and the hexadecimal number system.

The octal number system has a base, or radix, of 8; eight different symbols are used to represent numbers. These are commonly 0, 1, 2, 3, 4, 5, 6, and 7. Using positional notation, the first few octal numbers and their decimal equivalents are as shown in Table 2·6.

TABLE 2·6

OCTAL	DECIMAL	OCTAL	DECIMAL
0	0	11	9
1	1	12	10
2	2	13	11
3	3	14	12
4	4	15	13
5	5	16	14
6	6	17	15
7	7	20	16
10	8	21	17

To convert an octal number to a decimal number, we use the same sort of polynomial as was used in the binary case, except that we now have a radix of 8 instead of 2. Therefore 1213 in octal is $(1 \times 8^3) + (2 \times 8^2) + (1 \times 8^1) + (3 \times 8^0) = 512 + 128 + 8 + 3 = 651$ in decimal. Also, 1.123 in octal is $(1 \times 8^0) + (1 \times 8^{-1}) + (2 - 8^{-2}) + (3 \times 8^{-3})$, or $1 + \frac{1}{8} + \frac{2}{64} + \frac{3}{512} = 1\frac{83}{512}$ in decimal.

There is a simple trick for converting a binary number to an octal number. Simply group the binary digits into groups of threes, starting at the octal point, and read each set of three binary digits according to Table 2·7.

Let us convert the binary number 011101. First we break it into 3s (thus 011 101), and then, converting each group of three binary digits, we get 35 in octal. Therefore 011101 binary = 35 octal. Here are several more examples:

$$111110111_2 = 767_8$$
$$110110101_2 = 665_8$$
$$11011_2 = 33_8$$
$$1001_2 = 11_8$$
$$10101.11_2 = 25.6_8$$
$$1100.111_2 = 14.7_8$$
$$1011.1111_2 = 13.74_8$$

Conversion from decimal to octal can be performed by repeatedly dividing the decimal number by 8 and using each remainder as a digit in the octal number being formed. For instance, to convert 200_{10} to an octal representation, we divide as follows:

$$200 \div 8 = 25 \qquad \text{remainder is } 0$$
$$25 \div 8 = 3 \qquad \text{remainder is } 1$$
$$3 \div 8 = 0 \qquad \text{remainder is } 3$$

Therefore $200_{10} = 310_8$.

Notice that when the number to be divided is less than 8, we use 0 as the quotient and the number as the remainder. Let us check this:

$$310_8 = (3_{10} \times 8^2_{10}) + (1_{10} \times 8^1_{10}) + (0_{10} \times 8^0_{10}) = 192_{10} + 8_{10} = 200_{10}$$

TABLE 2·7

THREE BINARY DIGITS	OCTAL DIGIT
000	0
001	1
010	2
011	3
100	4
101	5
110	6
111	7

Here is another example. We wish to convert 3964_{10} to octal.

$$
\begin{aligned}
3964 \div 8 &= 495 \qquad \text{with a remainder of 4}\\
495 \div 8 &= 61 \qquad \text{with a remainder of 7}\\
61 \div 8 &= 7 \qquad \text{with a remainder of 5}\\
7 \div 8 &= 0 \qquad \text{with a remainder of 7}
\end{aligned}
$$

Therefore $7574_8 = 3964_{10}$. Checking,

$$
\begin{aligned}
7574_8 &= (7_{10} \times 8_{10}^3) + (5_{10} \times 8_{10}^2) + (7_{10} \times 8_{10}) + 4_{10}\\
&= (7_{10} \times 512_{10}) + (5_{10} \times 64_{10}) + (7_{10} \times 8_{10}) + (4_{10} \times 1_{10})\\
&= 3584_{10} + 320_{10} + 56_{10} + 4_{10}\\
&= 3964_{10}
\end{aligned}
$$

There are several other techniques for converting octal to decimal and decimal to octal, but they are not used very frequently manually, and tables prove to be of about as much value as anything in this process. Octal-to-decimal and decimal-to-octal tables are readily available in a number of places, including the manuals distributed by manufacturers of binary machines.

An important use for octal is in listings of programs and for memory "dumps" for binary machines, thus making the printouts more compact. The manuals for several of the largest manufacturers use octal numbers to represent binary numbers because of ease of conversion and compactness.

The hexadecimal number system is useful for a similar reason. All the IBM 360 series of computers, the RCA Spectra 70, the NOVA, the PDP-II, and a great many other computers, in particular most minicomputers, have their memories organized into sets of *bytes,* each consisting of eight binary digits. Each byte either is used as a single entity to represent a single alphanumeric character or is broken into two 4-bit pieces. (We shall examine the coding of alphanumeric characters using bytes in Chap. 8.) When the bytes are handled in two 4-bit pieces, the programmer is given the option of declaring each 4-bit character as a piece of a binary number or as two binary-coded-decimal numbers. For instance, the byte 00011000 can be declared a binary number, in which case it is equal to 24 decimal, or as two binary-coded-decimal characters, in which case it represents the decimal number 18.

When the machine is handling numbers in binary, but in groups of four digits, it is convenient to have a code for representing each of these sets of four digits. Since there are 16 possible different numbers which can be represented, the digits 0 through 9 will not suffice; so the letters A, B, C, D, E, and F are also used (see Table 2·8).

To convert binary to hexadecimal we simply break a binary number into groups of four digits and convert each group of four digits according to the preceding code. Thus $10111011_2 = BB_{16}$, $10010101_2 = 95_{16}$, $11000111_2 = C7_{16}$, and $10001011_2 = 8B_{16}$. The mixture of letters and decimal digits may seem

TABLE 2·8

BINARY	HEXADECIMAL	DECIMAL
0000	0	0
0001	1	1
0010	2	2
0011	3	3
0100	4	4
0101	5	5
0110	6	6
0111	7	7
1000	8	8
1001	9	9
1010	A	10
1011	B	11
1100	C	12
1101	D	13
1110	E	14
1111	F	15

strange at first, but these are simply convenient symbols, just as decimal digits are.

The conversion of hexadecimal to decimal is straightforward but time-consuming. For instance, BB represents $(B \times 16^1) + (B \times 16^0) = (11 \times 16) + (11 \times 1) = 176 + 11 = 187$. Similarly,

$$
\begin{aligned}
AB6_{16} &= (10_{10} \times 16^2_{10}) + (11_{10} \times 16_{10}) + 6_{10} \\
&= (10_{10} \times 256_{10}) + 176_{10} + 6_{10} \\
&= 2560_{10} + 176_{10} + 6_{10} \\
&= 2742_{10}
\end{aligned}
$$

To convert, for instance, $3A6_{16}$ to decimal:

$$
\begin{aligned}
3A6_{16} &= (3_{10} \times 16^2_{10}) + (10_{10} \times 16_{10}) + 6_{10} \\
&= (3_{10} \times 256_{10}) + (10_{10} \times 16_{10}) + 6_{10} \\
&= 768_{10} + 160_{10} + 6_{10} \\
&= 934_{10}
\end{aligned}
$$

Again, tables are convenient for converting hexadecimal to decimal and decimal to hexadecimal. Table 2·9 is useful for converting in either direction.

The chief use of the hexadecimal system is in connection with byte-organized machines. Users of these computers become amazingly adept, with experience, at handling the hexadecimal system.

Quite a large number of questions have been included below for this chapter. For those desiring to study octal and hexadecimal number systems further, Questions 60 through 69 contain information and exercises on octal

TABLE 2·9 HEXADECIMAL-TO-DECIMAL CONVERSION TABLE

A. INTEGER CONVERSION

EXAMPLE: 2322_{16} is
$8192_{10} + 768_{10} + 32_{10} + 2_{10}$
$= 8994.0.$

HEX	DEC	HEX	DEC	HEX	DEC	HEX	DEC
0	0	0	0	0	0	0	0
1	4,096	1	256	1	16	1	1
2	8,192	2	512	2	32	2	2
3	12,288	3	768	3	48	3	3
4	16,384	4	1,024	4	64	4	4
5	20,480	5	1,280	5	80	5	5
6	24,576	6	1,536	6	96	6	6
7	28,672	7	1,792	7	112	7	7
8	32,768	8	2,048	8	128	8	8
9	36,864	9	2,304	9	144	9	9
A	40,960	A	2,560	A	160	A	10
B	45,056	B	2,816	B	176	B	11
C	49,152	C	3,072	C	192	C	12
D	53,248	D	3,328	D	208	D	13
E	57,344	E	3,584	E	224	E	14
F	61,440	F	3,840	F	240	F	15

Hexadecimal Positions: 4, 3, 2, 1

B. FRACTIONAL CONVERSION

HEX	DEC (0123)	HEX	DECIMAL (4567)	HEX	DECIMAL (0 1 2 3)	HEX	DECIMAL EQUIVALENT (4 5 6 7)
.0	.0000	.00	.0000 0000	.000	.0000 0000 0000	.0000	.0000 0000 0000 0000
.1	.0625	.01	.0039 0625	.001	.0002 4414 0625	.0001	.0000 1525 8789 0625
.2	.1250	.02	.0078 1250	.002	.0004 8828 1250	.0002	.0000 3051 7578 1250
.3	.1875	.03	.0117 1875	.003	.0007 3242 1875	.0003	.0000 4577 6367 1875
.4	.2500	.04	.0156 2500	.004	.0009 7656 2500	.0004	.0000 6103 5156 2500
.5	.3125	.05	.0195 3125	.005	.0012 2070 3125	.0005	.0000 7629 3945 3125
.6	.3750	.06	.0234 3750	.006	.0014 6484 3750	.0006	.0000 9155 2734 3750
.7	.4375	.07	.0273 4375	.007	.0017 0898 4375	.0007	.0001 0681 1523 4375
.8	.5000	.08	.0312 5000	.008	.0019 5312 5000	.0008	.0001 2207 0312 5000
.9	.5625	.09	.0351 5625	.009	.0021 9726 5625	.0009	.0001 3732 9101 5625
.A	.6250	.0A	.0390 6250	.00A	.0024 4140 6250	.000A	.0001 5258 7890 6250
.B	.6875	.0B	.0429 6875	.00B	.0026 8554 6875	.000B	.0001 6784 6679 6875
.C	.7500	.0C	.0468 7500	.00C	.0029 2968 7500	.000C	.0001 8310 5468 7500
.D	.8125	.0D	.0507 8125	.00D	.0031 7382 8125	.000D	.0001 9836 4257 8125
.E	.8750	.0E	.0546 8750	.00E	.0034 1796 8750	.000E	.0002 1362 3046 8750
.F	.9375	.0F	.0585 9375	.00F	.0036 6210 9375	.000F	.0002 2888 1835 9375

Hexadecimal Positions: 1, 2, 3, 4

addition and multiplication, and Questions 70 through 74 can be used to supplement the study of the hexadecimal system.

QUESTIONS

1. Convert the following decimal numbers to equivalent binary numbers.
(a) 39   (b) 59   (c) 512

(d) 0.4475   *(e)* $\frac{25}{32}$ *(f)* 0.796875
(g) 256.75   *(h)* 129.5625   *(i)* 4096.90625

2. Convert the following decimal numbers to the equivalent binary numbers.
   (a) 14   *(b)* 13   *(c)* 15
   (d) 6   *(e)* 21   *(f)* 19
   (g) 63   *(h)* 103   *(i)* 256

3. Convert the following decimal numbers to equivalent binary numbers.
   (a) 43   *(b)* 64   *(c)* 4096
   (d) 0.375   *(e)* $\frac{27}{32}$ *(f)* 0.4375
   (g) 512.5   *(h)* 131.5625   *(i)* 2048.0625

4. Convert the following numbers to the equivalent binary numbers.
   (a) 11   *(b)* 0.125   *(c)* $2\frac{7}{16}$
   (d) 4.62   *(e)* $3\frac{5}{8}$ *(f)* 0.775

5. Convert the following binary numbers to equivalent decimal numbers.
   (a) 1101   *(b)* 11011   *(c)* 1011
   (d) 0.1011   *(e)* 0.001101   *(f)* 0.001101101
   (g) 111011.1011   *(h)* 1011011.001101   *(i)* 10110.0101011101

6. Convert the following binary numbers to equivalent decimal numbers.
   (a) 1101   *(b)* 1001   *(c)* 10111
   (d) 1011   *(e)* 11011   *(f)* 10101

7. Convert the following binary numbers to equivalent decimal numbers.
   (a) 1011   *(b)* 100100   *(c)* 10011
   (d) 0.1101   *(e)* 0.1001 ·   *(f)* 0.0101
   (g) 1011.0011   *(h)* 1001.1001   *(i)* 101.011

8. Convert the following binary numbers to equivalent decimal numbers.
   (a) 0.01   *(b)* 0.0111   *(c)* 1.110
   (d) 111.101   *(e)* 0110.011   *(f)* 1101.0011

9. Perform the following additions and check by converting the binary numbers to decimal.
   (a) 1001.1 + 1011.01   *(b)* 100101 + 100101
   (c) 0.1011 + 0.1101   *(d)* 1011.01 + 1001.11

10. Perform the following additions and check by converting the binary numbers to decimal and adding.
   (a) 1011 + 1101   *(b)* 1110 + 1111   *(c)* 11.11 + 10.011
   (d) 1101.11 + 1.01   *(e)* 11101.1 + 10010.1 *(f)* 111.1 + 111.11

11. Perform the following additions and check by converting the binary numbers to decimal.
   (a) 1101.1 + 1011.1   *(b)* 101101 + 1101101
   (c) 0.0011 + 0.1110   *(d)* 1100.011 + 1011.011

12. Perform the following subtractions in binary and check by converting the numbers to decimal and subtracting.
   (a) 1111 − 1000   *(b)* 1101 − 1011   *(c)* 1011.1 − 111.1
   (d) 1111.01 − 1011.1   *(e)* 111.11 − 111.1   *(f)* 1101.1 − 1110.01

13. Perform the following subtractions in the binary number system.
   (a) 64 − 32   *(b)* 127 − 63
   (c) 93.5 − 42.75   *(d)* $84\frac{9}{32} - 48\frac{5}{16}$

14. Perform the following subtractions in the binary number system.
(a) $128 - 32$ (b) $\frac{1}{8} - \frac{1}{16}$ (c) $2\frac{1}{8} - 4\frac{3}{32}$
(d) $31 - \frac{5}{8}$ (e) $62 - 31\frac{1}{16}$ (f) $129 - 35$

15. Perform the following subtractions in the binary number system.
(a) $37 - 35$ (b) $128 - 64$ (c) $94.5 - 43.75$ (d) $255 - 127$

16. Perform the following multiplications and divisions in the binary number system.
(a) 16×6 (b) 31×8 (c) 23×2.525
(d) 15×7.625 (e) $6 \div 3$ (f) $16 \div 6$

17. Perform the following multiplications and divisions in the binary number system.
(a) 24×12 (b) 18×14 (c) $32 \div 8$
(d) $27 \div 18$ (e) 49.5×51.75 (f) $58.75 \div 23.5$

18. Perform the following multiplications and divisions in the binary number system.
(a) 15×2.75 (b) $18 \div 6$ (c) $256\frac{1}{2} \div 128\frac{1}{4}$
(d) $31.5 \div 15.75$ (e) $3 \div \frac{3}{8}$ (f) $2\frac{2}{8}$

19. Perform the following multiplications and divisions in the binary number system.
(a) 15×13 (b) 10×15 (c) $44 \div 11$
(d) $42 \div 12$ (e) 7.75×2.5 (f) $22.5 \div 4.75$

20. Convert the following decimal numbers into both their 9s and 10s complements.
(a) 8   (b) 18   (c) 7
(d) 23   (e) 24   (f) 98

21. Convert the following decimal numbers into both their 9s and 10s complements.
(a) 5436   (b) 1932   (c) 45.15   (d) 18.293

22. Convert the following decimal numbers into both their 9s and 10s complements.
(a) 98   (b) 78   (c) 0.81
(d) 0.15   (e) 297.64   (f) 332.51

23. Convert the following decimal numbers into both their 9s and 10s complements.
(a) 3654   (b) 2122   (c) 54.19   (d) 37.263

24. Convert the following binary numbers into both their 1s and 2s complements.
(a) 1101   (b) 1010   (c) 1111
(d) 1110   (e) 1011   (f) 1001

25. Convert the following binary numbers into both their 1s and 2s complements.
(a) 1011   (b) 11011   (c) 1011.01   (d) 11011.01

26. Convert the following binary numbers into both their 1s and 2s complements.
(a) 1011   (b) 1101   (c) 0.0111
(d) 0.101   (e) 11.101   (f) 101.011

27. Convert the following binary numbers into both their 1s and 2s complements.
(a) 101111   (b) 100100   (c) 10111.10   (d) 10011.11

28. Perform the following subtractions using both 9s and 10s complements.
(a) 8 − 4   (b) 16 − 8   (c) 198 − 124
(d) 28.5 − 23.4   (e) 27.6 − 23.4   (f) 0.55 − 0.42

29. Perform the following subtractions using both 9s and 10s complements.
(a) 948 − 234   (b) 347 − 263   (c) 349.5 − 245.3   (d) 412.7 − 409.2

30. Perform the following subtractions using both 9s and 10s complements.
(a) 14 − 8   (b) 15 − 8   (c) 0.5 − 25
(d) 0.41 − 0.2   (e) 0.434 − 0.23   (f) 1.2 − 0.35

31. Perform the following subtractions using both 9s and 10s complements.
(a) 1024 − 913   (b) 249 − 137   (c) 24.1 − 13.4   (d) 239.3 − 119.4

32. Perform the following subtractions of binary numbers using both 1s and 2s complements.
(a) 1010 − 1001   (b) 110 − 11   (c) 110 − 0.11
(d) 0.111 − 0.101   (e) 0.1111 − 0.11   (f) 11.11 − 10.11

33. Perform the following subtractions using both 1s and 2s complements:
(a) 1011 − 101   (b) 11011 − 11001
(c) 10111.1 − 10011.1   (d) 11011 − 10011.11

34. How many different numbers can be stored in a set of four switches, each having three different positions (4 three-position switches)?

35. How many different binary numbers can be stored in a register consisting of six switches?

36. How many different BCD numbers can be stored in 12 switches? (Assume 2 position or ON-OFF switches.)

37. How many different BCD numbers can be stored in a register containing 12 switches using an 8, 4, 2, 1 code? Using an excess 3 code?

38. Write the first 12 numbers in the base 5 (or quinary) number system.

39. Write the first 10 numbers in the quaternary number system, which has a base, or radix, of 4. Use the digits 0, 1, 2, and 3 to express these numbers.

40. Write the first 20 numbers in the base 12 (or *duodecimal*) number system. Use A for 10 and B for 11.

41. Write the first 25 numbers in a base 11 number system, using the digits 0, 1, 2, 3, 4, 5, 6, 7, 8, 9, and A to express the 25 numbers that you write. (Decimal 10 = A, for instance.)

42. Perform the following subtractions in the binary number system using 1s complements.
(a) 1011 − 1001   (b) 1110 − 1001
(c) 101.11 − 101.01   (d) 111.1 − 110.1

43. Using the 1s complement number system, perform the following subtractions:
(a) 0.1001 − 0.0110   (b) 0.1110 − 0.0110   (c) 0.01111 − 0.01001
(d) 11011 − 11001   (e) 1110101 − 1010010

44. Perform the following subtractions in the binary number system using 2s complements.

(a) 1111 − 1101   (b) 1110 − 1101
(c) 1011.11 − 101.01   (d) 111.1 − 110.1
45. Using the 2s complement number system, perform the following subtractions and also represent the answers as decimal fractions.
(a) 0.101010 − 0.010101   (b) 0.11001 − 0.00100
(c) 0.111000 − 0.000111   (d) 0.101100 − 0.010011
46. Convert the following hexadecimal numbers to decimal numbers.
(a) 15   (b) B9   (c) AA4
(d) 9.A   (e) 9.1A
47. Convert the following hexadecimal numbers to decimal.
(a) B6C7 (b) 64AC (c) A492 (d) D2763
48. Convert the following octal numbers to decimal.
(a) 14   (b) 124   (c) 105
(d) 123   (e) 156   (f) 15.5
49. Convert the following octal numbers to decimal.
(a) 2376 (b) 2483 (c) 286431 (d) 22632
50. Convert the following binary numbers to octal.
(a) 111   (b) 111011   (c) 101.111
(d) 0.11101   (e) 11.11   (f) 1101.1101
51. Convert the following binary numbers to octal.
(a) 101101   (b) 101101110   (c) 10110111
(d) 110110.011   (e) 011.1011011
52. Convert the following octal numbers to binary.
(a) 56   (b) 43   (c) 231.2
(d) 231.4   (e) 454.45   (f) 32.234
53. Convert the following octal numbers to binary.
(a) 7423 (b) 3364 (c) 33962 (d) 3232.14 (e) 3146.52
54. Convert the following decimal numbers to octal.
(a) 15   (b) 9   (c) 19
(d) 0.54   (e) 0.625   (f) 2.125
55. Convert the following decimal numbers to octal.
(a) 932 (b) 332 (c) 545.375 (d) 632.97 (e) 4429.625
56. Convert the following hexadecimal numbers to binary.
(a) 9   (b) 1A   (c) 0.A1
(d) 0.AB   (e) A.A   (f) 12.A
57. Convert the following hexadecimal numbers to binary.
(a) CD (b) 649 (c) A13 (d) AA.1A (e) AB2.234
58. Convert the following binary numbers to hexadecimal.
(a) 1101.0110   (b) 11011110   (c) 1111
(d) 11101   (e) 11110.01011   (f) 1011.11010
59. Convert the following binary numbers to hexadecimal.
(a) 10110111   (b) 10011100   (c) 1011111
(d) 0.01111110   (e) 0.10110111101
60. A simple rule for multiplying two digits in any radix is simply to multiply
the two digits in decimal. If the product is less than the radix, take it; if
greater, divide (in decimal) by the radix and use the remainder as the

first, or least significant, position and the quotient as the carry, or most significant, digit. Thus, in base 6, $2 \times 2 = 4$, $3 \times 1 = 3$, etc.; however, $2 \times 4 = 8$, and

$$
\begin{array}{r}
1 \\
6\overline{)\,8}
\end{array}
$$

So $2_6 \times 4_6 = 12_6$. Similarly, in base 7, $3 \times 4 = 12$ and

$$
\begin{array}{r}
1 \\
7\overline{)\,12} \\
\underline{7} \\
5
\end{array}
$$

So $3_7 \times 4_7 = 15_7$. Using this rule perform, in base 7:
(a) $2_7 \times 3_7 =$ (b) $2_7 \times 2_7 =$
(c) $4_7 \times 4_7 =$ (d) $4_7 \times 3_7 =$

61. Using the rule in Question 60 perform:
(a) $3_6 \times 4_6$ (b) $3_6 \times 3_6$ (c) $3_9 \times 4_9$
(d) $4_9 \times 5_9$ (e) $5_9 \times 15_9$

62. An addition table for octal is as follows:

+	0	1	2	3	5	5	6	7
0	0	1	2	3	4	5	6	7
1	1	2	3	4	5	6	7	10
2	2	3	4	5	6	7	10	11
3	3	4	5	6	7	10	11	12
4	4	5	6	7	10	11	12	13
5	5	6	7	10	11	12	13	14
6	6	7	10	11	12	13	14	15
7	7	10	11	12	13	14	15	16

$$
\begin{array}{r}
1\ 1 \longleftarrow \text{carries} \\
\text{Using this table, we add in octal} \quad 1\ 2\ 6 \\
3\ 5\ 7 \\
\hline
5\ 0\ 5
\end{array}
$$

Perform the following additions:

(a) $7_8 + 6_8 =$ (b) $6_8 + 6_8 =$ (c) $6_8 + 16_8 =$
(d) $5_8 + 4_8 =$ (e) $5_8 + 14_8 =$

63. Using the table in Question 62, perform:
   (a) $15_8 + 14_8 =$ (b) $24_8 + 36_8 =$ (c) $126_8 + 347_8 =$
   (d) $67_8 + 45_8 =$ (e) $136_8 + 636_8 =$

64. Make up a hexadecimal addition table.

65. Using the table in Question 64, perform:
   (a) $6_{16} + Al_{16}$ (b) $7_{16} + 17_{16}$ (c) $8_{16} + 28_{16}$
   (d) $A16A_{16} + B16A_{16}$ (e) $A84_{16} + A83_{16}$

66. Perform the additions in Question 65 in binary and convert back to hexa-decimal.

67. Perform the additions in Question 63 in binary convert back to octal.

68. To multiply two numbers in octal we use the rule given in Question 60 and then proceed as follows:

$$6 \times 27 = 6 \times 20 = (6 \times 20) + (6 \times 7)$$
$$= 140 + 52 = 212$$

Multiply the following in octal.
   (a) $6 \times 7 =$ (b) $6 \times 10 =$ (c) $5 \times 14 =$

69. To multiply numbers of more than one digit, proceed as in Question 68, then add in octal.

$$
\begin{array}{r}
23 \\
\underline{23} \\
70 \\
\underline{46} \\
550
\end{array}
$$

Multiply the following octal numbers.
   (a) 3×14 (b) 23×12 (c) 11×22
   (d) 22×44 (e) 13×13 (f) 14×15

70. Perform the following multiplications of hexadecimal numbers.
   (a) $A \times 7$ (b) 9×15 (c) $A1 \times 8$
   (d) $A11 \times 7$ (e) $A12 \times 7$ (f) $A13 \times 2B$

71. Using the rule in Question 60, perform the following multiplications of hexadecimal numbers.
   (a) $15 \times B$ (b) $14 \times B$ (c) $14 \times B$
   (d) $142 \times A$ (e) 13×14

72. Perform the multiplications in Question 70 in binary, then convert back to hexadecimal.

73. Perform the multiplications in Question 71 in binary, then convert back to hexadecimal.

74. In converting decimal numbers to hexadecimal, it is convenient to go first to octal, then to binary, then to hexadecimal. For instance, to convert 412_{10} to hexadecimal, we go first to octal.

```
      51                    6
   8)412               8)51
      40                  48
      12                   3
       8
       4                         ↖2d digit        6 ← 1st digit
         ↖3d digit
```

Now $412_{10} = 634_8$; converting this to binary, $634_8 = \underbrace{110}_{6}\ \underbrace{011}_{3}\ \underbrace{100}_{4}$; then

regrouping, $\underbrace{1}_{1}\ \underbrace{1001}_{9}\ \underbrace{1100}_{C}$; so $412_{10} = 19C$.

Convert the following decimal numbers to hexadecimal.

(a) 25   (b) 396   (c) 1342

(d) 512   (e) 261

BOOLEAN ALGEBRA AND GATE NETWORKS

3

Modern digital computers are designed, maintained, and their operation analyzed using techniques and symbology from a field of mathematics called *modern algebra.* Algebraists have studied for a period of over a hundred years mathematical systems called *Boolean algebras.* Nothing could be more simple and normal to human reasoning than the rules of a Boolean algebra, for these originated in studies of how we reason, what lines of reasoning are valid, what constitutes proof, and other allied subjects.

The name Boolean algebra honors a fascinating† English mathematician, George Boole, who in 1854 published a classic book, *An Investigation of the Laws of Thought, on Which Are Founded the Mathematical Theories of Logic and Probabilities.* Boole's stated intention was to perform a mathematical analysis of logic. The work of Boole is perhaps best introduced by the following quotation from the first chapter:

> The design of the following treatise is to investigate the fundamental laws of those operations of the mind by which reasoning is performed; to give expression to them in the symbolical language of a Calculus, and upon this foundation to establish the science of Logic and construct its method; to make that method itself the basis of a general method for the application of the mathematical doctrine of Probabilities; and, finally, to collect from the various elements of truth brought to view in the course of these inquiries some probable intimations concerning the nature and constitution of the human mind.

Starting with his investigation of the laws of thought, Boole constructed a

---

† George Boole was the son of a shoemaker. His formal education ended in the third grade. Despite this, he was a brilliant scholar, teaching Greek and Latin in his own school, and an accepted mathematician who made lasting contributions in the areas of differential and difference equations as well as in algebra.

"logical algebra." This investigation into the nature of logic and ultimately of mathematics led subsequent mathematicians and logicians into several new fields of mathematics. Two of these, known as "the calculus of propositions" and "the algebra of sets," were based principally on Boole's work. This book will designate the algebra now used in the design and maintenance of logical circuitry as *Boolean algebra*.†

Boolean algebra was first brought to bear on problems which had arisen in the design of relay switching circuits in 1938 by Claude E. Shannon, a research assistant in the department of electrical engineering at the Massachusetts Institute of Technology. A version of Shannon's thesis, written at MIT for the degree of Master of Science, was published under the title, "A Symbolic Analysis of Relay and Switching Circuits." This paper presented a method for representing any circuit consisting of combinations of switches and relays by a set of mathematical expressions, and a calculus was developed for manipulating these expressions. The calculus used was shown to be based on the rules of Boolean algebra. The basic techniques described by Shannon were adopted almost universally for the design and analysis of switching circuits. Because of the analogous relationship between the actions of relays and of modern electronic circuits, the same techniques which were developed for the design of relay circuits are still being used in the design of modern high-speed computers.

There are several advantages in having a mathematical technique for the description of the internal workings of a computer. For one thing, it is often far more convenient to calculate with expressions used to represent switching circuits than it is to use schematic or even logical diagrams. Further, just as an ordinary algebraic expression may be simplified by means of the basic theorems, the expression describing a given switching circuit network may also be reduced or simplified. This enables the logical designer to simplify the circuitry used, achieving economy of construction and reliability of operation. Boolean algebra also provides an economical and straightforward way of describing the circuitry used in computers. In all, a knowledge of Boolean algebra is indispensable in the computing field.

3•1 FUNDAMENTAL CONCEPTS OF BOOLEAN ALGEBRA

When a variable is used in an algebraic formula, it is generally assumed that the variable may take any numerical value. For instance, in the formula $2X + 5Y = Z$, we assume that X, Y, and Z may range through the entire field of real numbers.

The variables used in Boolean equations have a unique characteristic,

---

† This algebra is sometimes called *switching algebra*. It is, in fact, only one of several realizations of what modern algebraists call Boolean algebra.

however; they may assume only one of two possible values. These two values may be represented by the symbols 0 and 1.† If an equation describing logical circuitry has several variables, it is still understood that each of the variables can assume only the value 0 or 1. For instance, in the equation $X + Y = Z$ each of the variables X, Y, and Z may have only the values 0 or 1.

This concept will become clearer if another symbol is defined, the $+$, or *logical addition,* symbol. When the $+$ symbol is placed between two variables, say X and Y, since both X and Y can take only the role 0 or 1, we can define the $+$ symbol by listing all possible combinations for X and Y and the resulting value of $X + Y$.

The possible input and output combinations may be arranged as follows:

$$0 + 0 = 0$$
$$0 + 1 = 1$$
$$1 + 0 = 1$$
$$1 + 1 = 1$$

This is a logical addition table and could represent a standard binary addition table except for the last entry. When both X and Y represent 1s, the value of $X + Y$ is 1. The $+$ symbol therefore does not have the "normal" meaning, but is a logical addition symbol. The equation $X + Y = Z$ can be read "X or Y equals Z" or "X plus Y equals Z." This concept may be extended to any number of variables; for instance, in the equation $A + B + C + D = E$, even if A, B, C, and D all had the value of 1, the sum of the values, or E, would represent only a 1.

To avoid ambiguity, a number of other symbols have been recommended as replacements for the $+$ sign. Some of these are U,‡ v, and V. The majority of computer people still use the $+$ sign, however, which was the symbol originally proposed by Boole.

3•2 LOGICAL MULTIPLICATION

A second important operation in Boolean algebra is the operation which we will call *logical multiplication.* The rules for logical multiplication can again be given by simply listing all values which might occur. These are

$$0 \cdot 0 = 0$$
$$0 \cdot 1 = 0$$
$$1 \cdot 0 = 0$$
$$1 \cdot 1 = 1$$

---

† Or T and F or $+$ and $-$, etc. 0 and 1 are almost universally used in computer work, however.
‡ The preceding equation might then be written $A \cup B \cup C \cup D = E$.

Thus, for instance, if we write $Z = X \cdot Y$, and find $X = 0$ and $Y = 1$, then $Z = 0$. Only when X and Y are both 1s would Z be a 1.

Both $+$ and $\cdot$ obey a mathematical rule called the *associative law*. This law says, for $+$, that $(X + Y) + Z = X + (Y + Z)$, and for $\cdot$, that $X \cdot (Y \cdot Z) = (X \cdot Y) \cdot Z$. What this means is that, for instance, we can write $X + Y + Z$ without ambiguity, for no matter in what order the logical addition is performed, the result is the same; i.e., adding X to Y and then adding Z gives the same result as adding Y to Z and then adding this to X. We can test this for both $+$ and $\cdot$ by again trying all combinations.

Note that while either $+$'s and $\cdot$'s can be used freely, the two cannot be "mixed" without ambiguity in the absence of further rules. For instance, does $A \cdot B + C$ mean $(A \cdot B) + C$ or $A \cdot (B + C)$? The two form different values for $A = 0$, $B = 0$, and $C = 1$, for then we have $(0 \cdot 0) + 1 = 1$ and $0 \cdot (0 + 1) = 0$, which differ. (Always operating from left to right will alleviate this, and is used in some programming languages but not usually by algebraists or computer designers or maintenance personnel.) The rule which is used is that $\cdot$ is always performed before $+$. Thus, $X \cdot Y + Z$ is $(X \cdot Y) + Z$, and $X \cdot Y + X \cdot Z$ means $(X \cdot Y) + (X \cdot Z)$.

3•3 OR GATES & AND GATES

The $+$ and $\cdot$ operations are physically realized by two types of electronic circuits called OR gates and AND gates. We shall treat these as "black boxes," deferring until later any discussion of how the actual circuitry operates.

A *gate* is simply an electronic circuit which operates on one or more input signals to produce an output signal. One of the simplest and most frequently used gates is called the OR gate, and the block diagram symbol for the OR gate is shown in Fig. 3·1, as is the table of combinations for the inputs and outputs for the OR gate. Since the inputs X and Y are signals with values either

INPUT		OUTPUT
X	Y	Z
0	0	0
0	1	1
1	0	1
1	1	1

FIG. 3·1 The OR gate.

$$X \quad\quad\fbox{AG}\quad Z = X \cdot Y$$
$$Y$$

INPUT		OUTPUT	
X	Y	Z	
0	0	0	$0 \cdot 0 = 0$
0	1	0	$0 \cdot 1 = 0$
1	0	0	$1 \cdot 0 = 0$
1	1	1	$1 \cdot 1 = 1$

FIG. 3·2 The AND gate.

0 or 1 at any given time, the output signal Z can be described by simply listing all values for X and Y and the resulting value for Z. A study of the table in Fig. 3·1 indicates that the OR gate performs logical addition on its inputs.

   Similarly, the AND gate in Fig. 3·2 performs logical multiplication on input values, yielding an output Z with value $X \cdot Y$, so that Z is a 1 only when both X and Y are 1s.

   Just as the $+$ and $\cdot$ operations could be extended to several variables using the associative law, OR gates and AND gates can have more than two inputs. Figure 3·3 shows three input OR and AND gates and the table of all input combinations for each. As might be hoped, the OR gates with input X, Y,

INPUT	OUTPUT
X Y Z	W
0 0 0	0
0 0 1	1
0 1 0	1
0 1 1	1
1 0 0	1
1 0 1	1
1 1 0	1
1 1 1	1

INPUT	OUTPUT
X Y Z	W
0 0 0	0
0 0 1	0
0 1 0	0
0 1 1	0
1 0 0	0
1 0 1	0
1 1 0	0
1 1 1	1

FIG. 3·3 Three-input OR and AND gates.

and Z has a 1 output if X OR Y OR Z is a 1, so that we can write $X + Y + Z$ for its output. Also, the output of the AND gate with inputs X, Y, and Z is a 1 only when all three of the inputs are 1s, so that we can write the output as $X \cdot Y \cdot Z$.

The above argument can be extended. A four-input OR gate has a 1 output when any of its inputs is a 1, and a four-input AND gate has a 1 output only when all four inputs are 1s.

It is often convenient to shorten $X \cdot Y \cdot Z$ to XYZ, and we will sometimes use this convention.

3•4 COMPLEMENTATION AND INVERTERS

The two operations defined so far have been what algebraists would call *binary operations* in that they define an operation on two variables. There are also *singulary,* or *unary, operations,* which define an operation on a single variable. A familiar example of unary operation is −, for we can write −5 or −10 or −X, meaning that we are to take the negative of these values. (− is also used as a binary operation symbol for subtraction, which makes it a familiar but ambiguous example.)

In Boolean algebra we have an operation called *complementation,* and the symbol we shall use is ‾. Thus we write $\overline{X}$, meaning "take the complement of X," or $\overline{(X + Y)}$, meaning "take the complement of $X + Y$." The complement operation can be defined quite simply:

$$\overline{0} = 1$$
$$\overline{1} = 0$$

The complement of a value can be taken repeatedly. For instance, we can find $\overline{\overline{\overline{X}}}$; for $X = 0$ it is $\overline{\overline{\overline{0}}} = \overline{\overline{1}} = \overline{0} = 1$. For $X = 1$ it is $\overline{\overline{\overline{1}}} = \overline{\overline{0}} = \overline{1} = 0$.

A useful rule is based on the fact that $\overline{\overline{X}} = X$; checking, we find that $\overline{\overline{0}} = \overline{1} = 0$ and $\overline{\overline{1}} = \overline{0} = 1$. [This rule, that double complementation gives the original value, is an important characteristic of a Boolean algebra which does not generally hold for most unary operations. For instance, notice that for the operation of squaring a real number, the rule does not hold: $(3^2)^2 = 81$, not 3.]

The complementation operation is physically realized by a gate or circuit called the *inverter.* Figure $3 \cdot 4(a)$ shows an inverter and the table of combinations for its input and output. Figure $3 \cdot 4(b)$ shows also that connecting two inverters in series gives an output equal to the input, and this is the gating counterpart to the law of double complementation, $\overline{\overline{X}} = X$.

Several other symbols have been used for the complementation symbol. For instance, the $\sim$ is often used by logicians, who write $\sim X$ and read this "the negation of X." The $'$ symbol has been used by mathematicians and computer people; thus X' is the complement of X in these systems. The overbar symbol is now used by the American National Standards Institute and Military Standards, as well as most journals and manufacturers, however, and we will use it.

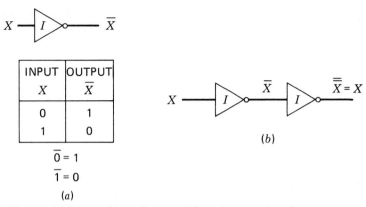

FIG. 3·4 (a) Inverter block diagram; (b) two inverters in series.

3•5 EVALUATION OF LOGICAL EXPRESSIONS

The tables of values for the three operations which have been explained are sometimes called *truth tables,* or *tables of combinations.* To study a logical expression it is very useful to construct a table of values for the variables and then to evaluate the expression for each of the possible combinations of variables in turn. Consider the expression $X + Y\bar{Z}$. There are three variables in this expression, X, Y, and Z, each of which can assume the value 0 or 1. The possible combinations of values may be arranged in ascending order,† as in Table 3·1.

One of the variables, Z, is complemented in the expression $X + Y\bar{Z}$; so a column is now added to the table listing values of $\bar{Z}$ (see Table 3·2).

TABLE 3·1

X	Y	Z
0	0	0
0	0	1
0	1	0
0	1	1
1	0	0
1	0	1
1	1	0
1	1	1

TABLE 3·2

X	Y	Z	$\bar{Z}$
0	0	0	1
0	0	1	0
0	1	0	1
0	1	1	0
1	0	0	1
1	0	1	0
1	1	0	1
1	1	1	0

† Notice that the variables in each row of this table may be combined into a binary number. The binary numbers will then count from 000 to 111 in binary, or from 0 to 7 decimal. Sometimes each row is numbered in decimal according to the number represented. Reference may then be made to the row by using the decimal number. For instance, row 0 has values of 0, 0, 0 for X, Y, and Z, row 6 has values of 1, 1, 0, and row 7 has values of 1, 1, 1.

TABLE 3·3

X	Y	Z	$\overline{Z}$	$Y\overline{Z}$
0	0	0	1	0
0	0	1	0	0
0	1	0	1	1
0	1	1	0	0
1	0	0	1	0
1	0	1	0	0
1	1	0	1	1
1	1	1	0	0

TABLE 3·4

X	Y	Z	$\overline{Z}$	$Y\overline{Z}$	$X + Y\overline{Z}$
0	0	0	1	0	0
0	0	1	0	0	0
0	1	0	1	1	1
0	1	1	0	0	0
1	0	0	1	0	1
1	0	1	0	0	1
1	1	0	1	1	1
1	1	1	0	0	1

A column is now added listing the values that $Y\overline{Z}$ assumes for each value of X, Y, and Z. This column will contain the value 1 only when both Y is a 1 and $\overline{Z}$ is a 1 (see Table 3·3).

Now the logical addition of the values of X to the values which have been calculated for $Y\overline{Z}$ is performed in a final column (see Table 3·4).

The final column contains the value of $X + Y\overline{Z}$ for each set of input values which X, Y, and Z may take. For instance, when $X = 1$, $Y = 0$, and $Z = 1$, the expression has the value of 1.

3·6 EVALUATION OF AN
EXPRESSION CONTAINING PARENTHESES

The following example illustrates the procedure for constructing a truth table for the expression $X + Y(\overline{X} + \overline{Y})$. There are only two variables in the expression, X and Y. First a table of the values which X and Y may assume is constructed (see Table 3·5).

Now, since the expression contains both $\overline{X}$ and $\overline{Y}$, two columns are added listing complements of the original values of the variables (see Table 3·6).

TABLE 3·5

X	Y
0	0
0	1
1	0
1	1

TABLE 3·6

X	Y	$\bar{X}$	$\bar{Y}$
0	0	1	1
0	1	1	0
1	0	0	1
1	1	0	0

The various values which the term inside parentheses, $(\bar{X} + \bar{Y})$, assumes are now calculated (see Table 3·7).

The values for $\bar{X} + \bar{Y}$ are now multiplied by the values of Y in the table, forming another column representing $Y(\bar{X} + \bar{Y})$ (see Table 3·8).

Finally, the values for $Y(\bar{X} + \bar{Y})$ are added to the values for X which are listed, forming the final column and completing the table (see Table 3·9).

Inspection of the final column of the table indicates that the values taken

TABLE 3·7

X	Y	$\bar{X}$	$\bar{Y}$	$(\bar{X} + \bar{Y})$
0	0	1	1	1
0	1	1	0	1
1	0	0	1	1
1	1	0	0	0

TABLE 3·8

X	Y	$\bar{X}$	$\bar{Y}$	$\bar{X} + \bar{Y}$	$Y(\bar{X} + \bar{Y})$
0	0	1	1	1	0
0	1	1	0	1	1
1	0	0	1	1	0
1	1	0	0	0	0

TABLE 3·9

X	Y	$\bar{X}$	$\bar{Y}$	$\bar{X} + \bar{Y}$	$Y(\bar{X} + \bar{Y})$	$X + Y(\bar{X} + \bar{Y})$
0	0	1	1	1	0	0
0	1	1	0	1	1	1
1	0	0	1	1	0	1
1	1	0	0	0	0	1

by the function $X + Y(\overline{X} + \overline{Y})$ are identical with the values found in the logical addition table. This indicates that the function $X + Y(\overline{X} + \overline{Y})$ is equivalent to the function $X + Y$. This equivalence has been established by the *proof by perfect induction*. If a logical circuit were constructed for each of the two expressions, one circuit would require two inverters, two OR circuits, and an AND circuit, while the other circuit would require only an OR circuit. Both circuits would perform the same function, yielding identical outputs for each combination of inputs.

3•7 BASIC LAWS OF BOOLEAN ALGEBRA

Some fundamental relations of Boolean algebra have been presented. A complete set of the basic operations is listed below.† Although simple in appearance, these rules may be used to construct a Boolean algebra,‡ determining all the relations which follow:

$$\text{If } X \neq 0, \text{ then } X = 1$$

and

$$\text{If } X \neq 1, \text{ then } X = 0$$

LOGICAL ADDITION	LOGICAL MULTIPLICATION	COMPLEMENT RULES
$0 + 0 = 0$	$0 \cdot 0 = 0$	$\overline{0} = 1$
$0 + 1 = 1$	$0 \cdot 0 = 0$	$\overline{1} = 0$
$1 + 0 = 1$	$1 \cdot 0 = 0$	
$1 + 1 = 1$	$1 \cdot 1 = 1$	

A list of useful relations is presented in Table 3 · 10. Most of the basic rules by which Boolean algebra expressions may be manipulated are contained in this table. Each of these rules may be proved using the "proof by perfect induction." An example of this proof for rule 3 in Table 3 · 10 is as follows: The variable X can have only the value 0 or 1; if X has the value 0, then $0 + 0 = 0$; if X has the value 1, then $1 + 1 = 1$. Therefore $X + X = X$.

The same basic technique may be used to prove the remainder of the rules. Rule 9 states that double complementation of a variable results in the

---

† There are, actually, a number of possible sets of postulates which may be used to define the algebra. The particular treatment of Boolean algebra given here is derived from that of E. V. Huntington and M. H. Stone. The author would also like to acknowledge the influence of I. S. Reed and S. H. Caldwell on this development of the concepts of the algebra.

‡ Notice that these rules are used to construct an *example*, or *realization*, of a Boolean algebra. We note that, strictly speaking, this Boolean algebra consists of a set B of two elements which we call 0 and 1, an addition operation +, a multiplication operation ·, and a complement operation ⁻. There are other Boolean algebras (an infinite number), but this was Boole's original algebra. This algebra is sometimes called *switching algebra* to identify it more closely, but it is the same as "propositional calculus," for instance.

TABLE 3·10 BOOLEAN ALGEBRA RULES

1. $0 + X = X$
2. $1 + X = 1$
3. $X + X = X$
4. $X + \overline{X} = 1$
5. $0 \cdot X = 0$
6. $1 \cdot X = X$
7. $X \cdot X = X$
8. $X \cdot \overline{X} = 0$
9. $\overline{\overline{X}} = X$
10. $X + Y = Y + X$
11. $X \cdot Y = Y \cdot X$
12. $X + (Y + Z) = (X + Y) + Z$
13. $X(YZ) = (XY)Z$
14. $X(Y + Z) = XY + XZ$
15. $X + XZ = X$
16. $X(X + Y) = X$
17. $(X + Y)(X + Z) = X + YZ$
18. $X + \overline{X}Y = X + Y$
19. $XY + YZ + \overline{Y}Z = XY + Z$

original variable. If X equals 0, then the first complement is 1 and the second will be 0, the original value. If the original value for X is 1, then the first complement will be 0 and the second 1, the original value. Therefore $\overline{\overline{X}} = X$.

Rules 10 and 11, which are known as the *commutative* laws, express the fact that the order in which a combination of terms is performed does not affect the result of the combination. Rule 10 is the commutative law of addition, which states that the order of addition does not affect the sum ($X + Y = Y + X$). Rule 11 is the commutative law of multiplication ($XY = YX$), which states that the order of multiplication does not affect the product.

Rules 12 and 13 are the *associative laws*. Rule 12 states that in the addition of several terms, the sum which will be obtained if the first term is added to the second and then the third term is added will be the same as the sum obtained if the second term is added to the third and then the first term is added [$X + (Y + Z) = (X + Y) + Z$]. Rule 13 is the associative law of multiplication, stating that in a product with three factors, *any* two may be multiplied together, followed by the third, $X(YZ) = (XY)Z$.

Rule 14, the *distributive law,* states that the product of a monomial (X) multiplied by a polynomial ($Y + Z$) is equal to the sum of the products of the monomial multiplied by each term of the polynomial, $X(Y + Z) = XY + XZ$.

The three laws, commutative, associative, and distributive, may be extended to include any number of terms. For instance, the commutative law for addition states that $X + Y = Y + X$. This may be extended to

$$X + Y + Z + A = A + Y + Z + X$$

The commutative law for multiplication may also be extended: $XYZ = YZX$. These two laws are useful in rearranging the terms of an equation.

The laws may also be combined:

$$(X + Y) + (Z + A) = (A + Y) + (X + Z)$$

and $(XY)(ZA) = (XA)(ZY)$. These two laws are useful in regrouping the terms of an equation.

The distributive law may be extended in several ways:

$$X(Y + Z + A) = XY + XZ + XA$$

If two polynomials, such as $(W + X)$ and $(Y + Z)$, are to be multiplied together, one of the polynomials is treated as a monomial and multiplied by the individual terms of the other polynomial. The results are then multiplied out according to the distributive law. For instance,

$$(W + X)(Y + Z) = W(Y + Z) + X(Y + Z) = WY + WZ + XY + XZ$$

3•8 PROOF BY PERFECT INDUCTION

Notice that, among others, rule 17 does not apply to "normal" algebra. The rule may be obtained from the preceding rules as follows:

$$
\begin{aligned}
(X + Y)(X + Z) &= XX + XZ + XY + YZ && \text{where } XX = X, \text{ rule 7, so} \\
&= X + XZ + XY + YZ \\
&= X + XY + XZ + YZ \\
&= X(1 + Y) + Z(X + Y) && \text{where } (1 + Y) = 1, \text{ rule 2, so} \\
&= X + Z(X + Y) \\
&= X + XZ + YZ \\
&= X(1 + Z) + YZ && \text{where } (1 + Z) = 1, \text{ rule 2, so} \\
&= X + YZ
\end{aligned}
$$

Therefore

$$(X + Y)(X + Z) = X + YZ$$

Since rule 17 does not apply to normal algebra, it is interesting to test the rule using the proof by perfect induction. It will therefore be necessary to construct truth tables for the right-hand $(X + YZ)$ and left-hand $(X + Y)(X + Z)$ members of the equation and compare the results (see Tables 3•11 and 3•12).

The last column of the table for the function $X + YZ$ is identical with the last column of the table for $(X + Y)(X + Z)$. This proves (by means of the proof by perfect induction) that the expressions are equivalent.

TABLE 3·11

X	Y	Z	ZY	X + YZ
0	0	0	0	0
0	0	1	0	0
0	1	0	0	0
0	1	1	1	1
1	0	0	0	1
1	0	1	0	1
1	1	0	0	1
1	1	1	1	1

TABLE 3·12

X	Y	Z	X + Y	X + Z	(X + Y)(X + Z)
0	0	0	0	0	0
0	0	1	0	1	0
0	1	0	1	0	0
0	1	1	1	1	1
1	0	0	1	1	1
1	0	1	1	1	1
1	1	0	1	1	1
1	1	1	1	1	1

Rules 15 and 16 are also not rules in "normal" algebra. The following is a proof of rule 15 using preceding rules:

$$X + XZ = X(1 + Z) \quad \text{distributive law, and since}$$
$$(1 + Z) = 1 \quad \text{by rule 2}$$
$$X + XZ = X(1) \quad \text{and} \quad X(1) = X \quad \text{by rule 6}$$

Therefore

$$X + XZ = X$$

It is worthwhile to try and prove rule 15 using the proof by perfect induction at this point. Here is a proof of rule 16 using rules which precede it.

$$X(X + Y) = XX + XY \quad \text{distributive law, and since } XX = X$$
$$= X + XY$$
$$= X (1 + Y) \quad \text{where } 1 + Y = 1, \text{ rule 2, so}$$
$$= X$$

It is instructive to prove this rule also by perfect induction at this point.

3•9 SIMPLIFICATION OF EXPRESSIONS

The rules given may be used to simplify Boolean expressions, just as the rules of normal algebra may be used to simplify expressions. Consider the expression

$$(X + Y)(X + \overline{Y})(\overline{X} + Z)$$

The first two terms consist of $(X + Y)(X + \overline{Y})$; these terms may be multiplied together and, since $X + X\overline{Y} + XY = X$ and $Y\overline{Y} = 0$, reduced to X.

The expression has now been reduced to $X(\overline{X} + Z)$, which may be expressed as $X\overline{X} + XZ$ (rule 14), and since $X\overline{X}$ is equal to 0, the entire expression $(X + Y(X + \overline{Y})(\overline{X} + Z)$ may be reduced to XZ.

Another expression which may be simplified is $XYZ + X\overline{Y}Z + XY\overline{Z}$. First the three terms $XYZ + X\overline{Y}Z + XY\overline{Z}$ may be written $X(YZ + \overline{Y}Z + Y\overline{Z})$, using rule 14. Then, using rule 14 again: $X[Y(Z + \overline{Z}) + Y\overline{Z}]$; and since $Z + \overline{Z}$ equals 1, we have $X(Y + \overline{Y}Z)$.

The expression $X(Y + \overline{Y}Z)$ may be further reduced to $X(Y + Z)$ by using rule 18. The final expression can be written in two ways: $X(Y + Z)$ *or* $XY + XZ$. The first expression is generally preferable if the equation is to be constructed as an electronic circuit, because it requires only one AND circuit and one OR circuit.

3•10 De MORGAN'S THEOREMS

The following two rules are known as De Morgan's theorems.

$$\overline{(X + Y)} = \overline{X} \cdot \overline{Y}$$
$$\overline{(X \cdot Y)} = \overline{X} + \overline{Y}$$

The complement of any Boolean expression, or a part of any expression, may be found by means of these theorems. In these rules, two steps are used to form a complement:

1. Addition symbols are replaced with multiplication symbols or multiplication symbols with addition symbols.
2. Each of the terms in the expression is complemented.

The use of De Morgan's theorem may be demonstrated by finding the complement of the expression $(X + YZ)$. First, it is important to notice that a multiplication sign has been omitted and the expression could be written $X + (Y \cdot Z)$. To complement this, the addition symbol is replaced with a multiplication symbol and the two terms are complemented, giving $\overline{X} \cdot \overline{(Y \cdot Z)}$; then the remaining term is complemented, $\overline{X}(\overline{Y} + \overline{Z})$. The following equivalence has been found: $\overline{(X + YZ)} = \overline{X}(\overline{Y} + \overline{Z})$.

The complement of $(\overline{W}X + Y\overline{Z})$ may be formed by two steps:

1. The addition symbol is changed.
2. The complement of each term is formed.

$$\overline{(\overline{W} \cdot X)}\,\overline{(Y \quad \cdot \overline{Z})}$$

becomes $(W + \overline{X})(\overline{Y} + Z)$. Notice that since W and Z were already complemented, they become uncomplemented by the theorem $\overline{\overline{X}} = X$.

It is sometimes necessary to complement both sides of an equation. This may be done in the same way as before:

Complementing both sides,
$$\begin{aligned} WX + YZ &= 0 \\ \overline{(WX + YZ)} &= \overline{0} \\ (\overline{W} + \overline{X})(\overline{Y} + \overline{Z}) &= 1 \end{aligned}$$

3•11 BASIC DUALITY OF BOOLEAN ALGEBRA

De Morgan's theorem expresses a basic duality which underlies all Boolean algebra. The postulates and theorems which have been presented can all be divided into pairs. For example, $(X + Y) + Z = X + (Y + Z)$ is the "dual" of $(XY)Z = X(YZ)$, and $X + 0 = X$ is the dual of $X \cdot 1 = X$.

Often the rules or theorems are listed in an order which illustrates the duality of the algebra. In proving the theorems or rules of the algebra, it is then necessary only to prove one theorem, and the "dual" of the theorem follows necessarily. For instance, if you prove that $X + XY = X$, you can immediately add the theorem $X(X + Y) = X$ to the list of theorems as the "dual" of the first expression.† In effect, all Boolean algebra is predicated on this "two-for-one" basis.

3•12 DERIVATION OF A BOOLEAN EXPRESSION

When designing a logical circuit, the logical designer works from two sets of known values: (1) the various states which the inputs to the logical network can take, and (2) the desired outputs for each input condition. The logical expression is derived from these sets of values.

Consider a specific problem. A logical network has two inputs, X and Y, and an output Z. The relationship between inputs and outputs is to be as follows:

1. When both X and Y are 0s, the output Z is to be 1.

---

† When the first expression, $X + XY = X$, has been complemented, $\overline{X}(\overline{X} + \overline{Y}) = \overline{X}$ is obtained. Uncomplemented variables may then be substituted on both sides of the equation without changing the basic equivalence of the expression.

2. When X is 0 and Y is 1, the output Z is to be 0.
3. When X is 1 and Y is 0, the output Z is to be 1.
4. When X is 1 and Y is 1, the output Z is to be 1.

These relations may be expressed in tabular form as shown in Table 3·13.

It is now necessary to add another column to the table. This column will consist of a list of *product terms* obtained from the values of the input variables. The new column will contain each of the input variables listed in each row of the table, with the letter representing the respective input complemented when the input value for this variable is 0, and not complemented when the input value is 1. The terms obtained in this manner are designated as product terms. With two input variables X and Y, each row of the table will contain a product term consisting of X and Y, with X or Y complemented or not, depending on the input values for that row (see Table 3·14).

Whenever Z is equal to 1, the X and Y product term from the same row is removed and formed into a *sum-of-products*. Therefore the product terms from the first, third, and fourth rows are selected. These are $\overline{X}\overline{Y}$, $X\overline{Y}$, and XY.

There are now three terms, each the product of two variables. The sum of these products is equal to the expression desired. This type of expression is often referred to as a *canonical expansion* for the function. The complete expression in normal form is

$$\overline{X}\overline{Y} + X\overline{Y} + XY = Z$$

The left-hand side of this expression may be simplified as follows:

$$\overline{X}\overline{Y} + X\overline{Y} + XY = Z$$
$$\overline{X}\overline{Y} + X(\overline{Y} + Y) = Z$$
$$\overline{X}\overline{Y} + X = Z$$

and finally, by rule 18 in Table 3·10, $\qquad\qquad X + \overline{Y} = Z$

The truth table may then be constructed to check the function which has been derived (see Table 3·15).

The last row of this column agrees with the last row of the truth table of the desired function, showing that the expressions are equivalent.

TABLE 3·13

INPUTS		OUTPUT
X	Y	Z
0	0	1
0	1	0
1	0	1
1	1	1

TABLE 3·14

INPUTS		OUTPUT	PRODUCT TERMS
X	Y	Z	
0	0	1	$\overline{X}\overline{Y}$
0	1	0	$\overline{X}Y$
1	0	1	$X\overline{Y}$
1	1	1	XY

TABLE 3·15

X	Y	$\overline{Y}$	$X + \overline{Y}$
0	0	1	1
0	1	0	0
1	0	1	1
1	1	0	1

TABLE 3·16

INPUTS			OUTPUT
When: $X = 0,\ Y = 0,\ Z = 0$			1
$X = 0,\ Y = 0,\ Z = 1$			0
$X = 0,\ Y = 1,\ Z = 0$			1
0	1	1	0
1	0	0	1
1	0	1	0
1	1	0	1
1	1	1	0

The expression $X + \overline{Y}$ may be constructed in one of two ways. If only the inputs X and Y are available, as might be the case if the inputs to the circuit were from another logical network or from certain types of storage devices, an inverter would be required to form $\overline{Y}$. The circuit would then require an inverter plus an OR gate. Generally, the complement of the Y input would be available, however, and only one OR gate would be required for the second way the expression would be constructed.

Another expression, with three inputs (designated as X, Y, and Z), will be derived. Assume that the desired relationships between the inputs and the output have been determined, as shown in Table 3·16.

1. A truth table is formed (see Table 3·17).
2. A column is added listing the inputs X, Y, and Z according to their value in the input columns (see Table 3·18).
3. The product terms from each row in which the output is a 1 are collected $(\overline{X}\overline{Y}\overline{Z},\ \overline{X}Y\overline{Z},\ X\overline{Y}\overline{Z},$ and $XY\overline{Z})$, and the desired expression is the sum of these products $(\overline{X}\overline{Y}\overline{Z} + \overline{X}Y\overline{Z} + X\overline{Y}\overline{Z} + XY\overline{Z})$. Therefore the complete expression in standard form for the desired network is

$$\overline{X}\overline{Y}\overline{Z} + \overline{X}Y\overline{Z} + X\overline{Y}\overline{Z} + XY\overline{Z} = A$$

TABLE 3·17

INPUTS			OUTPUT
X	Y	Z	A
0	0	0	1
0	0	1	0
0	1	0	1
0	1	1	0
1	0	0	1
1	0	1	0
1	1	0	1
1	1	1	0

TABLE 3·18

INPUTS			OUTPUT	PRODUCT TERMS
X	Y	Z	A	
0	0	0	1	$\overline{X}\overline{Y}\overline{Z}$
0	0	1	0	$\overline{X}\overline{Y}Z$
0	1	0	1	$\overline{X}Y\overline{Z}$
0	1	1	0	$\overline{X}YZ$
1	0	0	1	$X\overline{Y}\overline{Z}$
1	0	1	0	$X\overline{Y}Z$
1	1	0	1	$XY\overline{Z}$
1	1	1	0	XYZ

This expression may be simplified as shown below:

$$\overline{X}\overline{Y}\overline{Z} + \overline{X}Y\overline{Z} + X\overline{Y}\overline{Z} + XY\overline{Z} = A$$
$$\overline{X}(\overline{Y}\overline{Z} + Y\overline{Z}) + X(\overline{Y}\overline{Z} + Y\overline{Z}) = A$$
$$\overline{X}[\overline{Z}(\overline{Y} + Y)] + X[\overline{Z}(\overline{Y} + Y)] = A$$
$$\overline{X}\overline{Z} + X\overline{Z} = A$$
$$\overline{Z} = A$$

The function can therefore be performed by a single inverter connected to the Z input. Inspection of the truth table will indicate that the output A is always equal to the complement of the input variable Z.

(a)

(b)

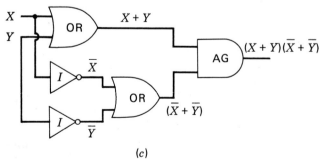

(c)

FIG. 3·5 Three gating networks.

3·13 COMBINATION OF GATES

The OR gates, AND gates, and inverters described in Secs. 3·3 and 3·4 can be interconnected to form *gating*, or *logic*, *networks*. (Those who study switching theory would also call these *combinational networks*.) The Boolean algebra expression corresponding to a given gating network can be derived by systematically progressing from input to output on the gates. Figure 3·5(a) shows a gating network with three inputs X, Y, and $\overline{Z}$ and an output expression $(X \cdot Y) + \overline{Z}$. A network which forms $(X \cdot Y) + (\overline{X} \cdot \overline{Y})$ and another network which forms $(X + Y) \cdot (\overline{X} + \overline{Y})$ are shown in Fig. 3.5(b) and (c).

We can analyze the operation of these gating networks using the Boolean algebra expressions, and can, for instance, in troubleshooting a computer, determine which gates have failed by examining the inputs to the gating network and the outputs and seeing if the Boolean operations are properly performed. The bookkeeping for computer circuitry is done by means of block diagrams, as in Fig. 3·6, which shows a typical print. The use of Boolean algebra is spread completely throughout the computer industry.

FIG. 3·6 Block diagram from a computer.

3 • 14 SUM-OF-PRODUCTS AND PRODUCT-OF-SUMS

An important consideration in dealing with gating circuits and their algebraic counterparts is the *form* of the Boolean algebra expression and the resulting form of the gating network. Certain types of Boolean algebra expressions lead to gating networks which are more desirable from most implementation viewpoints. We will now define the two most used and usable forms for Boolean expressions.

First let us define terms:

1. *Product term*   A product term is a single variable or the logical product of several variables. The variables may or may not be complemented.
2. *Sum term*   A sum term is a single variable or the sum of several variables. The variables may or may not be complemented.

For example, the term $X \cdot Y \cdot Z$ is a product term; $X + Y$ is a sum term; X is both a product term and a sum term; $X + Y \cdot Z$ is neither a product term nor a sum term; $X + \overline{Y}$ is a sum term; $X \cdot \overline{Y} \cdot \overline{Z}$ is a product term; $\overline{Y}$ is both a sum term and a product term. (*Comment:* Calling single variables sum terms and product terms is disagreeable but necessary. Since we must suffer with it, remember that some apples are red, round, and shiny, i.e., more than one thing.)

We now define two most important forms:

1. *Sum-of-products expression*   A sum-of-products expression is a product term or several product terms logically added together.
2. *Product-of-sums expression*   A product-of-sums expression is a sum term or several sum terms logically multiplied together.

For example, the expression $\overline{X} \cdot Y + X \cdot \overline{Y}$ is a sum-of-products expression; $(X + Y)(\overline{X} + \overline{Y})$ is a product-of-sums expression. The following are all sum-of-products expressions:

$$X$$
$$X \cdot Y + Z$$
$$\overline{X} \cdot \overline{Y} + X \cdot \overline{Y} \cdot \overline{Z}$$
$$X + Y$$

The following are product-of-sums expressions:

$$(X + Y) \cdot (X + \overline{Y}) \cdot (\overline{X} + \overline{Y})$$
$$(X + Y + Z) \cdot (X + \overline{Y}) \cdot (\overline{X} + \overline{Y})$$
$$(\overline{X} + Z)$$
$$\overline{X}$$
$$(X + Y)X$$

One prime reason for liking sum-of-products or product-of-sums expressions is their straightforward conversion to very nice gating networks.

In their purest, nicest form they go into *two-level networks*, which are networks for which the longest path through which a signal must pass from input to output is two gates.

Note: In the following discussion it will be assumed that when a signal is available, its complement $\overline{X}$ is also available. That is, no inverters are required to complement inputs. This is quite important and quite realistic, since most signals come from flip-flops, which we shall study later, and which provide both an output and its complement.

Figure 3·7 shows several gating networks. Section (a) of the figure shows sum-of-products networks, and section (b) shows product-of-sums networks. The gating networks for sum-of-products expressions in "conventional" form, i.e., expressions with at least two product terms and with at least two variables in each product term, go directly into and AND-to-OR gate network, while

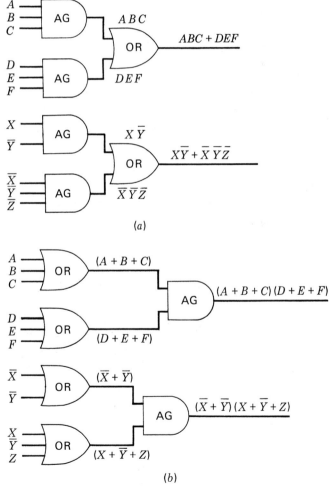

(a)

(b)

FIG. 3·7 (a) AND-to-OR gate networks; (b) OR-to-AND gate networks.

"conventional" product-of-sums expressions go directly into OR-to-AND gate networks as shown in the figure.

3•15 DERIVATION OF PRODUCT-OF-SUMS EXPRESSIONS

The sequence of steps described in Sec. 3·12 derived a sum-of-products expression for a given circuit. Another technique, really a dual of the first, forms the required expression as a product-of-sums. The expression derived in this manner is made up, before simplification, of terms each consisting of sums of variables such as $(X+Y+Z)$ ···. The final expression is the product of these sum terms and has the form $(X+Y+Z)(X+Y+\overline{Z})$ ··· $(\overline{X}+\overline{Y}+\overline{Z})$.

The method for arriving at the desired expression is as follows:

1. Construct a table of the input and output values.
2. Construct an additional column of sum terms containing complemented and uncomplemented variables (depending on the values in the input columns) for each row of the table. In each row of the table, a sum term is formed; however, in this case, if the input value for a given variable is 1, the variable will be complemented, and if 0, not complemented.
3. The desired expression is the product of the sum terms from the rows in which the output is 0.

The use of these rules will be illustrated by working examples in this and the following sections.

Table 3·19 contains the input and output values which describe a function to be realized by a logical network.

A column containing the input variables in sum-term form is now added in each row. A given variable is complemented if the input value for the variable is 1 in the same row, and not complemented if the value is 0 (see Table 3·20). Each sum term is therefore simply the complement of the product term which occurs in the same row in the previous table for sum-of-products expressions. Notice that the sum term $(\overline{X} + Y)$ in the third row of Table 3·20 is the complement of the product term $X\overline{Y}$ used in the sum-of-products derivation.

A product-of-sums expression is now formed by selecting those sum terms for which the output is 0 and multiplying them together. In this case 0s appear in the second and third rows, showing that the desired expression is

TABLE 3·19

INPUTS		OUTPUT
X	Y	Z
0	0	1
0	1	0
1	0	0
1	1	1

TABLE 3·20

INPUTS		OUTPUT	SUM TERMS
X	Y	Z	
0	0	1	$(X + Y)$
0	1	0	$(X + \overline{Y})$
1	0	0	$(\overline{X} + Y)$
1	1	1	$(\overline{X} + \overline{Y})$

$(X + \bar{Y})(\bar{X} + Y)$. A sum-of-products expression may be found by multiplying the two terms of this expression together, yielding $XY + \bar{X}\bar{Y}$. In this case, the same number of gates would be required to construct circuits corresponding to both the sum-of-products and the product-of-sums expressions.

3•16 DERIVATION OF A THREE-INPUT-VARIABLE EXPRESSION

Consider Table 3·21, expressing an input-to-output relationship for which an expression is to be derived.

Two columns will be added this time, one containing the sum-of-products terms and the other the product-of-sums terms (see Table 3·22).

The two expressions may now be written in the following way:

Sum-of-products: $$(\bar{X}Y\bar{Z}) + (\bar{X}YZ) + (XY\bar{Z}) = A$$

Product-of-sums: $$(X + Y + Z)(X + Y + \bar{Z})(\bar{X} + Y + Z)$$
$$(\bar{X} + Y + \bar{Z})(\bar{X} + \bar{Y} + \bar{Z}) = A$$

TABLE 3·21

	INPUTS		OUTPUT
X	Y	Z	A
0	0	0	0
0	0	1	0
0	1	0	1
0	1	1	1
1	0	0	0
1	0	1	0
1	1	0	1
1	1	1	0

TABLE 3·22

	INPUTS		OUTPUT	PRODUCT TERMS	SUM TERMS
X	Y	Z	A		
0	0	0	0	$\bar{X}\bar{Y}\bar{Z}$	$X + Y + Z$
0	0	1	0	$\bar{X}\bar{Y}Z$	$X + Y + \bar{Z}$
0	1	0	1	$\bar{X}Y\bar{Z}$	$X + \bar{Y} + Z$
0	1	1	1	$\bar{X}YZ$	$X + \bar{Y} + \bar{Z}$
1	0	0	0	$X\bar{Y}\bar{Z}$	$\bar{X} + Y + Z$
1	0	1	0	$X\bar{Y}Z$	$\bar{X} + Y + \bar{Z}$
1	1	0	1	$XY\bar{Z}$	$\bar{X} + \bar{Y} + Z$
1	1	1	0	XYZ	$\bar{X} + \bar{Y} + \bar{Z}$

The two expressions may be simplified as shown below:

SUM-OF-PRODUCTS

$$(\overline{X}Y\overline{Z}) + (\overline{X}YZ) + (XY\overline{Z}) = A$$
$$\overline{X}(Y\overline{Z} + YZ) + (XY\overline{Z}) = A$$
$$\overline{X}Y + XY\overline{Z} = A$$
$$Y(\overline{X} + X\overline{Z}) = A$$
$$\overline{X}Y + Y\overline{Z} = A$$

PRODUCT-OF-SUMS

$$(X + Y + Z)(X + Y + \overline{Z})(\overline{X} + Y + Z)(\overline{X} + \underline{Y} + \overline{Z})(\overline{X} + Y + \overline{Z})(\overline{X} + \overline{Y} + \overline{Z}) = A$$
$$(X + Y)(\overline{X} + Y)(\overline{X} + \overline{Z}) = A$$
$$Y(\overline{X} + \overline{Z}) = A$$

The two final expressions can clearly be seen to be equivalent. Notice, however, that the shortest sum-of-products expression, which is $\overline{X}Y + Y\overline{Z}$, requires two AND gates and an OR gate, as is shown in Fig. 3·8, while the shortest product-of-sums expression, $Y(\overline{X} + \overline{Z})$, requires only a single AND gate and a single OR gate. In some cases, the minimal sum-of-products expression will require fewer logical elements to construct, and in other instances the construction of the minimal product-of-sums will require fewer elements. If the sole criterion is the number of logical elements, it is necessary to obtain both a minimal sum-of-products expression and also a minimal product-of-sums expression to compare the two. It is possible to derive the canonical expansion expression for the network to be designed in one of the forms—for instance, product-of-sums—to simplify the expression, and then to convert the simplified expression to the other form, using the distributive laws. Any additional simplification which is required can then be performed. In this way, minimal expressions in each form may be obtained without deriving both canonical expansions, although this may be desirable.

The simplification techniques which have been described are algebraic and depend on judicious use of the theorems which have been presented. The problem of simplifying Boolean expressions so that the shortest expression is always found is quite complex; however, it is possible, by means of the repeated use of certain algorithms, to derive minimal sum-of-products and

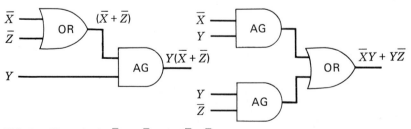

FIG. 3·8 Networks for $\overline{X}Y + Y\overline{Z}$ and $Y(\overline{X} + \overline{Z})$.

product-of-sums expressions. We shall examine this problem in following sections.

3•17 NAND GATES AND NOR GATES

Two other types of gates, NAND gates and NOR gates, are often used in computers. It is fortunate that the Boolean algebra which has been described can be easily made to analyze the operation of these gates.

A NAND gate is shown in Fig. $3 \cdot 9$. The inputs are A, B, and C, and the output from the gate is written $\overline{A} + \overline{B} + \overline{C}$. The output will therefore be a 1 if A is a 0 or B is a 0 or C is a 0, and the output will be a 0 only if A AND B AND C are all 1s.

The operation of the gate can be analyzed using the equivalent block diagram circuit shown in Fig. $3 \cdot 9$, which has an AND gate followed by an inverter. If the inputs are A, B, and C, the output of the AND gate will be $A \cdot B \cdot C$, and the complement of this is $\overline{(A \cdot B \cdot C)} = \overline{A} + \overline{B} + \overline{C}$, as shown in the figure.

The NOR gate can be analyzed in a similar manner. Figure $3 \cdot 10$ shows the NOR gate block diagram symbol with inputs A, B, C, and output $\overline{AB}\overline{C}$. This says the NOR gate's output will be a 1 only when all three inputs are 0s. If any input represents a 1, the output of a NOR gate will therefore be a 0.

Below the NOR gate block diagram symbol in Fig. $3 \cdot 10$ is an equivalent circuit showing an OR gate and an inverter.† The inputs A, B, and C are ORed by the OR gate, giving $A + B + C$, which is complemented by the inverter, giving $\overline{(A + B + C)} = \overline{A}\overline{B}\overline{C}$.

Multiple-input NAND gates can be analyzed similarly. A four-input NAND gate with inputs A, B, C, and D has an output $\overline{A} + \overline{B} + \overline{C} + \overline{D}$, which says that the output will be a 1 if any one of the inputs is a 0 and will be a 0 only when all four inputs are 1s.

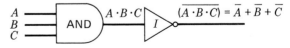

FIG. $3 \cdot 9$ The NAND gate.

---

† The "bubble," or small circle, on the output of the NAND and NOR gate represents complementation. The NAND can then be seen to be an AND symbol followed by a complementer, and the NOR can be analyzed similarly.

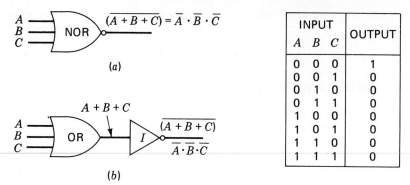

INPUT			OUTPUT
A	B	C	
0	0	0	1
0	0	1	0
0	1	0	0
0	1	1	0
1	0	0	0
1	0	1	0
1	1	0	0
1	1	1	0

(a)

(b)

FIG. 3·10 (a) Block diagram symbol for NOR gate; (b) OR gate and inverter equivalent circuit to NOR gate.

Similar reasoning will show that the output of a four-input NOR gate with inputs A, B, C, and D can be represented by the Boolean algebra expression $\overline{ABCD}$, which will be equal to 1 only when A, B, C, and D are all 0s.

If one of the two input lines to a two-input NAND gate contained the inputs $A + B$ and the other contained $C + D$, as shown in Fig. 3·11(a), the output from the NAND gate would be

$$\overline{[(A + B)(C + D)]} = \overline{A}\overline{B} + \overline{C}\overline{D}$$

We can show this by noting that the NAND gate first ANDs the inputs (in this case $A + B$ and $C + D$) and then complements this.

If one of the input lines to a two-input NOR gate contained the signal $A \cdot B$ and the other input line contained the signal $C \cdot D$, the output from the NOR gate would be $\overline{(A \cdot B + C \cdot D)} = (\overline{A} + \overline{B})(\overline{C} + \overline{D})$, as shown in Fig. 3·11(b).

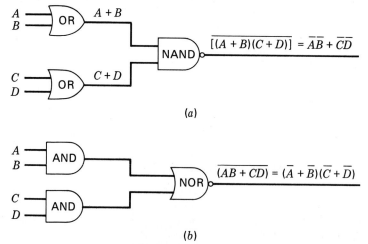

(a)

(b)

FIG. 3·11 Two types of gating networks. (a) OR-to-NAND gate networks; (b) AND-to-OR gate networks.

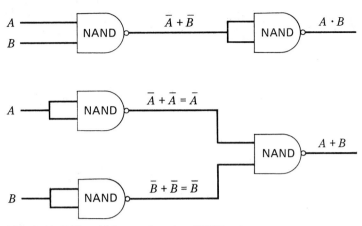

FIG. 3·12 AND and OR operations from NAND gates.

Notice that we can make an AND gate from two NAND gates, using the trick shown in Fig. 3·12, and a two-input OR gate from three NAND gates, as is also shown in the figure. A set of NAND gates can therefore be used to make any combinational network by substituting the block diagrams shown in Fig. 3·12 for the AND and OR blocks. (Complementation of a variable, when needed, can be obtained from a single NAND gate by connecting the variable to all inputs.)

The NOR gate can also be used to form any Boolean function which is desired, and the fundamental tricks are shown in Fig. 3·13.

Actually, it is not necessary to use the boxes shown in Figs. 3·12 and 3·13 to replace AND and OR gates singly, for a two-level NAND gate network yields the same function as a two-level AND-to-OR gate network, and a two-level NOR gate network yields the same function as a two-level OR-to-AND gate network. This is shown in Fig 3·14. Compare the output of the NAND gate network with that in Fig. 3·7, for example.

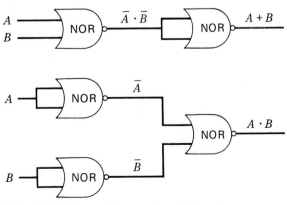

FIG. 3·13 AND and OR gates from NOR gates.

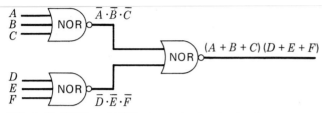

FIG. 3·14 NAND and NOR gates in two-level networks.

*3•18 THE MAP METHOD FOR SIMPLIFYING EXPRESSIONS

We have examined the derivation of a Boolean algebra expression for a given function using a table of combinations to list the desired function values. To derive a sum-of-products expression for the function, a set of product terms were listed, and those for which the function was to have value 1 were selected and logically added together to form the desired expression.

The table of combinations provides a nice natural way to list all values of a Boolean function. There are several other ways to represent or list function values, and the use of certain kinds of maps, which we will examine, will also permit minimization of the expression formed in a nice graphic way.

The particular type of map we will use is called the *Karnaugh map* after its originator.† Figure 3·15 shows the layouts for Karnaugh maps of from two to four variables. The diagram in each case lists the 2^n different product terms which can be formed in exactly n variables, each in a different square. For a function of n variables, a product term in exactly these n variables is called a *minterm*. Thus, for three variables X, Y and Z, there are 2^3, or 8 different minterms, which are $\bar{X}\bar{Y}\bar{Z}$, $\bar{X}\bar{Y}Z$, $\bar{X}Y\bar{Z}$, $\bar{X}YZ$, $X\bar{Y}\bar{Z}$, $X\bar{Y}Z$, $XY\bar{Z}$, and XYZ. For four variables there are 2^4, or 16 terms, for five variables there are 32 terms, etc. As a result, a map of n variables will have 2^n squares, each representing a single minterm. The minterm in each box, or cell, of the map is the product of the variables listed at the abscissa and ordinate of the cell. Thus $\bar{X}YZ$ is at the intersection of $\bar{X}Y$ and Z.

---

* This and following sections are optional. Subsequent chapters can be read without this material.
† Similar maps are sometimes called *Veitch diagrams*.

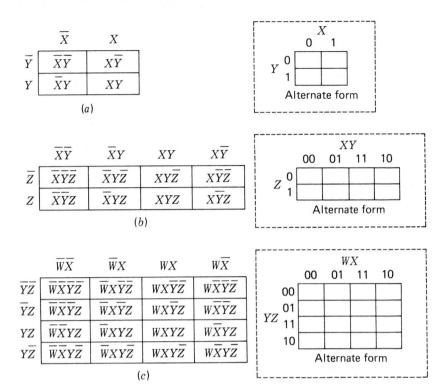

FIG. 3·15 Karnaugh maps for (a) two variables, (b) three variables, and (c) four variables.

Given a Karnaugh map form, the map is filled in by placing 1s in the squares, or cells, for each term which leads to a 1 output.

As an example, consider a function of three variables which for the following input values are to be 1:

$$X = 0, Y = 1, Z = 0$$
$$X = 0, Y = 1, Z = 1$$
$$X = 1, Y = 1, Z = 0$$
$$X = 1, Y = 1, Z = 1$$

This function is shown in Fig. 3·16(a) in both table-of-combinations and Karnaugh map form. Another function of four variables is shown in Fig. 3·16(b).

As a means for displaying the values of a function, the Karnaugh map is convenient, and provides some "feeling" for the function because of its graphic presentation. Its chief use, however, is due to the arrangement of cells. Each cell differs from its adjacent cell by having exactly one variable complemented in the minterm in one cell which is not complemented in the minterm in the adjacent cell.

As an example of this, consider the four-variable map in Fig. 3·16 and the

X Y Z	FUNCTION VALUES
0 0 0	0
0 0 1	0
0 1 0	1
0 1 1	1
1 0 0	0
1 0 1	0
1 1 0	1
1 1 1	1

	$\overline{X}\overline{Y}$	$\overline{X}Y$	XY	$X\overline{Y}$
$\overline{Z}$	0	1	1	0
Z	0	1	1	0

(a)

W X Y Z	FUNCTION VALUES
0 0 0 0	1
0 0 0 1	1
0 0 1 0	0
0 0 1 1	0
0 1 0 0	0
0 1 0 1	1
0 1 1 0	1
0 1 1 1	0
1 0 0 0	0
1 0 0 1	1
1 0 1 0	1
1 0 1 1	0
1 1 0 0	0
1 1 0 1	0
1 1 1 0	0
1 1 1 1	1

	$\overline{W}\overline{X}$	$\overline{W}X$	WX	$W\overline{X}$
$\overline{Y}\overline{Z}$	1	0	0	0
$\overline{Y}Z$	1	1	0	1
YZ	0	0	1	0
$Y\overline{Z}$	0	1	0	1

(b)

FIG. 3·16 Two Karnaugh maps. (a) Map of Boolean expression $\overline{X}Y\overline{Z} + \overline{X}YZ + XY\overline{Z} + XYZ$; (b) map of four-variable function.

minterm $\overline{W}X\overline{Y}Z$. There are four cells adjacent to the cell containing $\overline{W}X\overline{Y}Z$. These contain (1) $WX\overline{Y}Z$, which differs in the variable W; (2) $\overline{W}\overline{X}\overline{Y}Z$, which differs from $\overline{W}X\overline{Y}Z$ in X; (3) $\overline{W}XYZ$, which differs from $\overline{W}X\overline{Y}Z$ in Y; and (4) $\overline{W}X\overline{Y}\overline{Z}$, which differs from $\overline{W}X\overline{Y}Z$ in Z.

One trick should be noted at this point. The maps are considered to be "rolled," or continuous, so that top and bottom edges or left and right side edges are touching. For the three-variable map, consider the left side edge and right side edge to be touching, so that the map is considered to be rolled like a hoop horizontally on the page. This places the cell containing $\overline{X}\overline{Y}Z$ next to $X\overline{Y}\overline{Z}$, as well as to $\overline{X}\overline{Y}Z$ and $\overline{X}Y\overline{Z}$. Also, for this map, it places $\overline{X}Y\overline{Z}$ next to $\overline{X}\overline{Y}\overline{Z}$, which touches because of the rolling, as well as to $\overline{X}YZ$ and $X\overline{Y}\overline{Z}$.

For the four-variable map, the map is rolled so that the top edge touches the bottom edge and the left side touches the right side. The touching of top and bottom places $\overline{W}X\overline{Y}\overline{Z}$ next to $\overline{W}XY\overline{Z}$, and the left side to right side edges touching places $W\overline{X}YZ$ next to $\overline{W}\overline{X}YZ$.

A good rule to remember is that there are two minterms adjacent to a given minterm in a two-variable map; there are three minterms next to a given minterm in a three-variable map; there are four minterms next to a given minterm in a four-variable map; etc.

3•19 SUBCUBES AND COVERING

A *subcube* is defined as a set of exactly 2^m adjacent cells containing 1s. For $m = 0$ the subcube consists of a single cell (and thus of a single minterm). For $m = 1$ a subcube consists of two adjacent cells; for instance, the cells containing $\overline{X}\overline{Y}Z$ and $\overline{X}YZ$ form a subcube as shown in Fig. 3·17(a), as do $X\overline{Y}\overline{Z}$ and $\overline{X}\overline{Y}\overline{Z}$ (since the map is rolled).

For $m = 2$, the subcube has four adjacent cells, and several such subcubes are shown in Fig. 3·17(c). Notice that we have here omitted 0s for clarity, and filled in only the 1s for the function. This policy will be continued.

Finally, a subcube containing eight cells (for $m = 3$) is shown in Fig. 3·17(d).

(It is sometimes convenient to call a subcube containing two cells a 2-cube, a subcube of four cells a 4-cube, a subcube of eight cells an 8-cube, etc., and this will be often used.)

To demonstrate the use of maps and subcubes in minimizing Boolean algebra expressions we need to examine a rule of Boolean algebra:

$$AX + A\overline{X} = A$$

In the above equation, the variable A can stand for more than one variable. For instance, let $A = WY$; we then have

$$(WY)X + (WY)\overline{X} = (WY)$$

Or let $A = W\overline{Y}\overline{Z}$; we then have

$$W\overline{Y}\overline{Z}X + W\overline{Y}\overline{Z}\overline{X} = W\overline{Y}\overline{Z}$$

The basic rule can be proved by factoring

$$AX + A\overline{X} = A(X + \overline{X})$$

Then, since $X + \overline{X} = 1$, we have

$$AX + A\overline{X} = A(X + \overline{X}) = A \cdot 1 = A$$

Each of the examples given can be checked similarly; for instance,

$$W\overline{Y}\overline{Z}\overline{X} + W\overline{Y}\overline{Z}X = W\overline{Y}\overline{Z}(\overline{X} + X) = W\overline{Y}\overline{Z} \cdot 1 = W\overline{Y}\overline{Z}$$

This rule can be extended. Consider

$$WX\overline{Y}\overline{Z} + WX\overline{Y}Z + WXY\overline{Z} + WXYZ$$

There are four terms here, each with two variables WX constant while the other two variables Y and Z take all possible values. The term WX is then equal to the sum of the other terms, for

$$\begin{aligned}
WX\overline{Y}\overline{Z} + WX\overline{Y}Z + WXY\overline{Z} + WXYZ &= WX\overline{Y}(\overline{Z} + Z) + WXY(Z + \overline{Z}) \\
&= WX\overline{Y} + WXY \\
&= WX(\overline{Y} + Y) \\
&= WX
\end{aligned}$$

Thus WX could be substituted for the other four terms in an expression without changing the values the expression takes for any input values to the variables, that is, $WX = WX\overline{Y}\overline{Z} + WX\overline{Y}Z + WXY\overline{Z} + WXYZ$.

On a map, the above algebraic moves may be performed easily. Since a subcube of two cells has both cells with a single variable differing, a product term in just those variables which do not differ will cover (can be substituted for) the two minterms in the two cells.

Consider the subcube of two cells for $\overline{X}\overline{Y}Z$ and $\overline{X}YZ$ on the three-variable map in Fig. 3·17(a). The single product term $\overline{X}Z$ is equal to the sum of these two minterms; i.e.,

$$\overline{X}\overline{Y}Z + \overline{X}YZ = \overline{X}Z$$

Similarly, the two cells containing minterms $\overline{X}\overline{Y}\overline{Z}$ and $X\overline{Y}\overline{Z}$ form a subcube of two cells, as shown in Fig. 3 · 17 (a), from which we form $\overline{Y}\overline{Z}$, which can be substituted for $\overline{X}\overline{Y}\overline{Z} + X\overline{Y}\overline{Z}$ in an expression.

Similarly, the subcube of four cells in a three-variable map [Fig. 3·17(b)] with terms $\overline{X}\overline{Y}\overline{Z}$, $\overline{X}\overline{Y}Z$, $X\overline{Y}\overline{Z}$, $X\overline{Y}Z$ has a single-variable constant $\overline{Y}$; and we find $\overline{Y} = \overline{X}\overline{Y}\overline{Z} + \overline{X}\overline{Y}Z + X\overline{Y}\overline{Z} + X\overline{Y}Z$.

In general, a subcube with 2^m cells in an n-variable map will have $n - m$ variables, which are the same in all the minterms, and m variables, which take all possible combinations of being complemented or not complemented. Thus, for a four-variable map for $m = 3$, any eight adjacent cells which form a subcube will have $4 - 3 = 1$ variable constant and three variables which change complementation from cell to cell. Then a subcube of eight cells in a

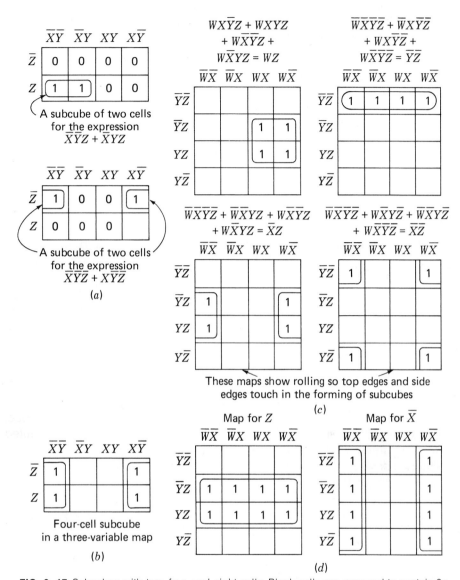

FIG. 3·17 Subcubes with two, four, and eight cells. Blank cells are assumed to contain 0s.

four-variable map can be used to determine a single variable which can be substituted for the sum of the minterm in all eight cells.

As an example in Fig. 3·17(d) we find a subcube of eight cells with the minterms $\overline{W}\overline{X}\overline{Y}\overline{Z}$, $\overline{W}\overline{X}Y\overline{Z}$, $\overline{W}X\overline{Y}\overline{Z}$, $\overline{W}XY\overline{Z}$, $W\overline{X}\overline{Y}\overline{Z}$, $W\overline{X}Y\overline{Z}$, $WX\overline{Y}\overline{Z}$, and $WXY\overline{Z}$, and the sum of these will be found to be equivalent to Z.

The set of minterms in an expression do not necessarily form a single subcube, however, and there are two cases to be dealt with. Call a *maximal subcube* the largest subcube which can be found around a given minterm. Then the two cases are:

1. All maximal subcubes are nonintersecting; i.e., no cell in a maximal subcube is a part of another maximal subcube. Several examples are shown in Fig. 3·18.
2. The maximal subcubes intersect; i.e., cells in one maximal subcube are also in other maximal subcubes. Figure 3·19 shows examples of this.

Case 1 is the more easily dealt with. In this case the product terms corresponding to the maximal subcubes are selected and the sum of these forms a minimal sum-of-products expression.

(In switching theory, the product term corresponding to a maximal subcube is called a *prime implicant*.)

Figure 3·18 shows an example of this in four variables; there is a subcube of two cells containing $WX\overline{Y}Z$ and $WX\overline{Y}\overline{Z}$ which can be covered by the product term $WX\overline{Z}$. There is also a subcube of four cells containing $\overline{W}XYZ$, $\overline{W}X\overline{Y}Z$, $\overline{W}X\overline{Y}\overline{Z}$, and $\overline{W}XY\overline{Z}$ which can be covered by $\overline{W}X$. The minimal expression is therefore $\overline{W}X + WX\overline{Z}$.

Two other examples are shown in Fig. 3·18(b) and (c). In each case the subcubes do not intersect or share cells, and so the product term (prime implicant) which corresponds to a given maximal subcube can be readily derived, and the sum of these for a given map forms the minimal expression.

When the subcubes intersect, the situation can be more complicated. The first principle to note is: *Each cell containing a 1 (i.e., each 1-cell) must be contained in some subcube which is selected.*

Figure 3·19(a) shows a map with an intersecting pair of subcubes plus another subcube. The minimal expression is, in this case, formed by simply adding together the three product terms associated with the three maximal subcubes. Notice that a single term, $\overline{W}XYZ$, is shared between two subcubes, and because of this is effectively in the minimal expression twice. This is permissible because of the idempotent rule of Boolean algebra, $A + A = A$, which states that repetition of terms does not change functional equivalence.

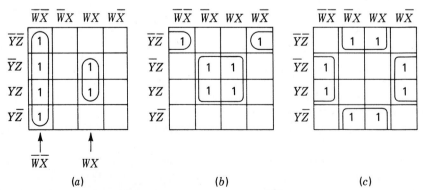

FIG. 3·18 Maps with disjoint subcubes. (a) Map for $\overline{W}X + WX\overline{Z}$; (b) map for $X\overline{Z} + \overline{X}Y\overline{Z}$; (c) map for $X\overline{Z} + \overline{X}Z$.

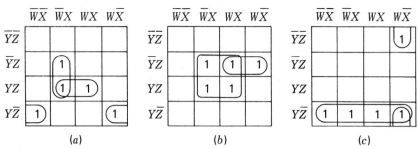

FIG. 3•19 Intersecting subcubes. (a) $\overline{W}XZ + XYZ + \overline{X}Y\overline{Z}$; (b) $XZ + W\overline{Y}Z$; (c) $\overline{Y}\overline{Z} + W\overline{X}\overline{Z}$.

Two other examples of intersecting maximal subcubes are shown in Fig. 3·19(b) and (c).

As long as the maximal subcubes can be readily found and there are no options in subcube selection, the minimization problem is straightforward. In some cases the problem is more complicated. Figure 3·20 shows an expression with a subcube of four cells in the center of the map, which is maximal. The selection of this maximal subcube does not lead to a minimal expression, however, because the four cells with 1s around this subcube must also be covered. In each case these 1-cells can be found to have a single adjacent cell and therefore to be part of maximal subcubes consisting of 2-cells. In Fig. 3·20(a), $\overline{W}XYZ$ is in a cell adjacent to only $\overline{W}X\overline{Y}Z$, and so forms part of a 2-cell. Figure 3·20(b) shows another way to form subcubes for the map, and this leads to the minimal expression $WX\overline{Y} + WYZ + \overline{W}XY + \overline{W}\overline{Y}Z$.

The finding of minimal expressions for such maps is not direct. The rules to be followed are:

1. Begin with cells which are adjacent to no other cells. The minterms in these cells cannot be shortened and must be used as is.
2. Find all cells which are adjacent to only one other cell. These form subcubes of two cells each.
3. Find those cells which lead to maximal subcubes of four cells. Then find subcubes of eight cells, etc.

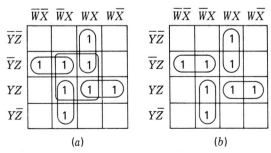

FIG. 3·20 Intersecting subcubes and solution. (a) $XZ + W\overline{Y}Z + \overline{W}\overline{Y}Z + \overline{W}XY + WX\overline{Y}$; (b) $WX\overline{Y} + WYZ + \overline{W}XY + \overline{W}\overline{Y}Z$.

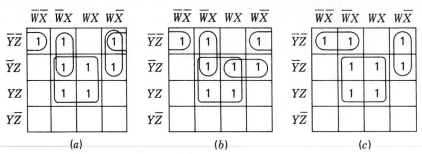

FIG. 3·21 Three coverings of the same map. (a) $XZ + \overline{X}\overline{Y}\overline{Z} + W\overline{X}\overline{Y} + \overline{W}X\overline{Y}$; (b) $XZ + \overline{X}\overline{Y}\overline{Z} + \overline{W}X\overline{Y} + W\overline{Y}Z$; (c) $XZ + \overline{W}\overline{Y}\overline{Z} + W\overline{X}\overline{Y}$.

4. The minimal expression is formed from a collection of as few cubes as possible, each of which is as large as possible, i.e., each of which is a maximal subcube.

Figure 3·21 shows an example of a difficult map. The maximal subcubes can be selected in several ways so that all cells are covered. The figure shows three maps, of which only one leads to a minimal expression. Practice with various maps will lead to skill in finding minimal expressions. For difficult cases there are algebraic techniques which guarantee a minimal expression, and these may be found in Bartee, Lebow, and Reed, Birkhoff and Bartee, McCluskey, and others in the Bibliography.

3•20 PRODUCT-OF-SUMS EXPRESSIONS – DON'T-CARES

The technique for product-of-sums expressions is almost identical with the design procedure using sum-of-products expressions. The basic rule can be stated quite simply: *Solve for 0s, then complement the resulting expression.*

Let us examine an example. Figure 3·22(a) shows table combinations and Karnaugh map for a four-variable problem. In Fig. 3·22(a) the sum-of-products expression is derived, and in minimal form is found to be $\overline{X}Y + YZ + WY$.

In Fig. 3·22(b) the same problem is solved for the 0s, which gives $X\overline{Y} + \overline{W}\overline{Y}\overline{Z}$. Since we have solved for 0s, we have solved for the complement of the desired problem. If the output is called F, then we have solved for $\overline{F}$. We then write $\overline{F} = X\overline{Y} + \overline{W}\overline{Y}\overline{Z}$.

Now, what is wanted is F; so both sides of this expression are complemented, and we have

$$F = (\overline{X} + Y)(W + \overline{Y} + Z)$$

This expression is in product-of-sums form and is somewhat simpler than the sum-of-products expression.

If sum-of-products and product-of-sums expressions are equally easy to implement, then a given problem must be solved in both forms and the simpler solution chosen. There is no way to determine which will be simpler other than a complete working of the problem.

There is another frequently encountered situation where certain outputs are not specified in a problem. Such outputs are called *don't-care* outputs, for the designer does not care what the outputs are for these particular inputs.

Figure 3·23(*a*) shows such a problem with 6 of the possible 16 output values listed as d's (don't-cares). This is a part of a BCD translator, and so these particular six input combinations are never used.

Since d output values are of no importance, they may be filled in with 1s and 0s in any way that is advantageous. Figure 3·23(*a*) shows a Karnaugh map of the table of combinations in the figure, with d's in the appropriate places. In solving this table, a d may be used as either a 1 or a 0; so the d's are used to enlarge or complete a subcube whenever possible, but are otherwise ignored (i.e., made 0). *The d's need not be covered by the subcubes selected, but are used only to enlarge subcubes containing 1s, which must be covered.*

In Fig. 3·23(*a*), the vertical string of four d's in the *WX* column are of use twice, once in filling out, or completing, the top row of 1s and once in completing the third row. These subcubes give the terms $\overline{Y}\overline{Z}$ and YZ; so the minimal sum-of-products expression is $\overline{Y}\overline{Z} + YZ$. Notice that if all the d's were made 0s, the solution would require more terms.

Another problem is worked in Fig. 3·23(*b*). For this problem the solution

INPUTS	FUNCTION VALUES
W X Y Z	
0 0 0 0	1
0 0 0 1	1
0 0 1 0	0
0 0 1 1	1
0 1 0 0	0
0 1 0 1	0
0 1 1 0	0
0 1 1 1	1
1 0 0 0	1
1 0 0 1	1
1 0 1 0	1
1 0 1 1	1
1 1 0 0	0
1 1 0 1	0
1 1 1 0	1
1 1 1 1	1

(*a*)

(*b*)

FIG. 3·22 Solving for product of sums. (*a*) $\overline{X}\overline{Y} + YZ + WY$; (*b*) $(\overline{X} + Y)(W + \overline{Y} + Z)$.

W	X	Y	Z	
0	0	0	0	1
0	0	0	1	0
0	0	1	0	0
0	0	1	1	1
0	1	0	0	1
0	1	0	1	0
0	1	1	0	0
0	1	1	1	1
1	0	0	0	1
1	0	0	1	0
1	0	1	0	d
1	0	0	1	d
1	1	0	0	d
1	1	0	1	d
1	1	1	0	d
1	1	1	1	d

(a)

	$\overline{W}\overline{X}$	$\overline{W}X$	WX	$W\overline{X}$
$\overline{Y}\overline{Z}$	1	1	d	1
$\overline{Y}Z$			d	
YZ	1	1	d	d
$Y\overline{Z}$			d	d

$\overline{Y}\overline{Z} + YZ$

(b)

	$\overline{W}\overline{X}$	$\overline{W}X$	WX	$W\overline{X}$
$\overline{Y}\overline{Z}$			1	1
$\overline{Y}Z$			1	d
YZ	d	d		
$Y\overline{Z}$			1	d

$W\overline{Z} + W\overline{Y}$

FIG. 3·23 Don't-care conditions. (a) Map for table with don't-cares; (b) solving another map with don't-cares.

is $W\overline{Z} + W\overline{Y}$. Notice that two of the d's are made 0's. In effect, the d's are chosen so that they lead to the best solution.

QUESTIONS

1. Prepare a table of combinations for the following Boolean algebra expressions:
   $\overline{X}\overline{Y} + XY$ (b) $X\overline{Y}Z + \overline{Y}Z$
2. Prepare a table of combinations (truth table) for the following Boolean
   (a) $\overline{X} + Y$ (b) $A \cdot \overline{B} \cdot C$ (c) $A + \overline{B} + \overline{C}$
   (d) $\overline{A} \cdot \overline{B}$ (e) $\overline{AB} + A\overline{B}$ (f) $A + \overline{AB}$
3. Prepare a truth table for the following Boolean expressions:
   (a) $XYZ + \overline{X}\overline{Y}\overline{Z}$ (b) $ABC + A\overline{B}C + \overline{A}\overline{B}C$
   (c) $A(\overline{B}C + B\overline{C})$ (d) $(A + B)(A + C)(\overline{A} + \overline{B})$
4. Prepare a table of combinations for the following Boolean algebra expressions:
   (a) $\overline{X}\overline{Y} + XY$ (b) $XYZ + \overline{X}\overline{Y}\overline{Z}$
   (c) $\overline{X}YZ + \overline{X}\overline{Y}$ (d) $\overline{X}\overline{Y}\overline{Z} + XYZ + \overline{X}Y\overline{Z}$
   (e) $X\overline{Z} + \overline{Y}Z$ (f) $AB(\overline{A}\overline{B}C + \overline{B}C)$
5. Prepare a truth table for the following Boolean expressions:
   (a) $A\overline{B} + \overline{A}B$ (b) $A\overline{B} + BC$
   (c) $A\overline{C} + AC$ (d) $\overline{A}\overline{B}C + AB\overline{C} + \overline{A}BC$
   (e) $AB(A\overline{B}C + A\overline{B}\overline{C} + ABC)$
6. Prepare a table of combinations for the following Boolean algebra expressions:

(a) $X(\overline{Y}+\overline{Z})+XY$

(b) $X\overline{Y}(Z+YZ)+\overline{Z}$

(c) $[X(Y+\overline{Y})+\overline{X}(Y+\overline{Y})]\cdot Z$

(d) $AB(\overline{AB}+\overline{A}B)$

(e) $A((B+C)+\overline{C})$

(f) $\overline{ABC}(\overline{ABC}+\overline{ABC})$

7. Simplify the following expressions and draw a block diagram of the circuit for each simplified expression, using AND and OR gates. Assume the inputs are from flip-flops.

(a) $A\overline{BC}+\overline{ABC}+\overline{AB}C+\overline{ABC}$

(b) $ABC+\overline{ABC}+A\overline{BC}+AB\overline{C}+\overline{AB}C+\overline{ABC}+\overline{ABC}$

(c) $A(A+B+C)(\overline{A}+B+C)(A+\overline{B}+C)(A+B+\overline{C})$

(d) $(A+B+C)(A+\overline{B}+\overline{C})(A+B+\overline{C})(A+\overline{B}+C)$

8. Simplify the expressions in Question 4 and draw block diagrams of gating networks for your simplified expressions, using AND gates, OR gates, and inverters.

9. Simplify the following expressions:

(a) $ABC(A\overline{BC}+\overline{AB}C+\overline{ABC})$

(b) $AB+A\overline{B}+\overline{AC}+\overline{AC}$

(c) $XY+XYZ+XY\overline{Z}+\overline{XY}Z$

(d) $XY(\overline{XY}Z+X\overline{Y}Z+XY\overline{Z})$

10. Simplify the expressions in Question 6 and draw block diagrams of gating networks for your simplified expressions, using AND gates, OR gates, and inverters.

11. Form the complements of the following expressions. For instance, the complement of $(XY+XZ)$ is equal to

$$(\overline{XY+XZ})=(\overline{X}+\overline{Y})(\overline{X}+\overline{Z})=\overline{X}+\overline{YZ}$$

(a) $(A+BC+AB)$

(b) $(A+B)(B+C)(A+C)$

(c) $AB+\overline{BC}+C\overline{D}$

(d) $AB(\overline{CD}+\overline{BC})$

(e) $A(B+C)(\overline{C}+\overline{D})$

12. Complement the following expressions (as in Question 11).

(a) $\overline{XY}+XY$

(b) $XYZ+\overline{XY}$

(c) $X(\overline{Y}+\overline{Z})$

(d) $X(YZ+\overline{YZ})$

(e) $XY(\overline{YZ}+XZ)$

(f) $XY+\overline{XY}(YZ+\overline{XY})$

13. Prove the two basic De Morgan theorems using the proof by perfect induction.

14. Prove the following rules using the proof by perfect induction.

(a) $X\overline{Y}+XY=X$

(b) $X+\overline{X}Y=X+Y$

15. Convert the following expressions to sum-of-products form.

(a) $(A+B)(\overline{B}+C)(\overline{A}+C)$

(b) $(\overline{A}+C)(\overline{A}+\overline{B}+\overline{C})(A+\overline{B})$

(c) $(A+C)(A\overline{B}+AC)(\overline{AC}+B)$

16. Convert the following expressions to sum-of-product form.

(a) $(\overline{A}+B)(\overline{C}+\overline{B})$

(b) $\overline{AB}(\overline{BC}+\overline{BC})$

(c) $(A+\overline{BC})(\overline{AB}+\overline{AB})$

(d) $AB(\overline{ABC}+\overline{AC})$

(e) $(\overline{A}+B)(\overline{AC}+(B+C))$

(f) $(\overline{A}+C)(AB+\overline{AB}+AC)$

17. Which rule is the dual of rule 12 in Table $3\cdot10$?

18. Give a dual of the rule $X+\overline{X}Y=X+Y$.

19. Multiply the following sum terms together, forming a sum-of-products expression in each case. Simplify while multiplying when possible.

(a) $(A+C)(B+D)$

    (b) $(A + C + D)(B + D + C)$
    (c) $(AB + C + DC)(AC + BC + D)$
    (d) $(A\overline{B} + \overline{A}B + A\overline{C})(\overline{A}B + AB + A\overline{C})$

20. Convert the following expressions to product-of-sums form.
    (a) $A + AB + \overline{A}C$ *(b)* $BC + \overline{A}B$
    (c) $AB(\overline{B} + \overline{C})$ *(d)* $\overline{AB}(\overline{BC} + \overline{BC})$
    (e) $(A + B + C)(AB + AC)$ *(f)* $(\overline{A} + \overline{B})A\overline{B}C$

21. Write the Boolean expression (in sum-of-products form) for a logical circuit which will have a 1 output when $X = 0$, $Y = 0$, $Z = 1$, and $X = 1$, $Y = 1$, $Z = 0$; and a 0 output for all other input states. Draw the block diagram for this circuit, assuming the inputs are from flip-flops.

22. Derive a Boolean algebra expression and draw a block diagram for a gating network which will have output 1 only when $X = 1$, $Y = 1$, $Z = 0$; $X = 0$, $Y = 0$, $Z = 0$.

23. Prove rule 17 in Table 3·10 by multiplying out the left side and using rule 15 to simplify.

24. Prove the following theorem using the rules in Table 3·10.

$$(X + Y)(X + \overline{Y}) = X$$

25. Write the Boolean expression (in sum-of-products form) for a logical network which will have a 1 output when $X = 0$, $Y = 1$, $Z = 1$; $X = 1$, $Y = 1$, $Z = 0$; $X = 1$, $Y = 1$, $Z = 0$; and $X = 1$, $Y = 1$, $Z = 1$. The circuit will have a 0 output for all other sets of input values. Simplify the expression derived and draw a block diagram for the simplified expression.

26. Derive the Boolean algebra expression for a gating network which will have outputs 0 only when $X = 1$, $Y = 1$, $Z = 0$; $X = 0$, $Y = 0$, $Z = 0$; $X = 1$, $Y = 0$, $Z = 0$. The outputs are to be 1 for all other cases.

27. Prove rule 18 in Table 3·10 using the proof by perfect induction.

28. Develop sum-of-products and product-of-sums expressions for F_1, F_2, and F_3 in Table 3·23.

29. Develop both the sum-of-products and product-of-sums expressions which describe Table 3·24, and then simplify both expressions. Draw a

TABLE 3·23

INPUTS			OUTPUT	OUTPUT	OUTPUT
X	Y	Z	F_1	F_2	F_3
0	0	0	0	0	1
0	0	1	0	1	1
0	1	0	1	1	1
0	1	1	1	0	0
1	0	0	0	0	0
1	0	1	0	1	1
1	1	0	1	1	1
1	1	1	1	0	1

TABLE 3·24

INPUTS			OUTPUT
X	Y	Z	A
0	0	0	0
0	0	1	1
0	1	0	1
0	1	1	0
1	0	0	0
1	0	1	1
1	1	0	1
1	1	1	0

block diagram for logical circuitry which corresponds to the simplified expressions, using only NAND gates for sum-of-products and NOR gates for product-of-sums.

30. Draw block diagrams for the F_1, F_2, and F_3 in Question 28 using only NAND gates.

31. Write the Boolean algebra expressions for Tables 3·25 to 3·27, showing combinations in sum-of-products form; then simplify the expressions and draw a block diagram of the circuit corresponding to each expression.

TABLE 3·25

INPUTS			OUTPUT
A	B	C	Z
0	0	0	0
0	0	1	1
0	1	0	1
0	1	1	0
1	0	0	1
1	0	1	1
1	1	0	0
1	1	1	0

TABLE 3·26

INPUTS			OUTPUT
A	B	C	Z
0	0	0	1
0	0	1	0
0	1	0	0
0	1	1	1
1	0	0	1
1	0	1	0
1	1	0	0
1	1	1	1

TABLE 3·27

INPUTS			OUTPUT
X	Y	Z	P
0	0	0	1
0	0	1	1
0	1	0	1
0	1	1	1
1	0	0	1
1	0	1	0
1	1	0	0
1	1	1	0

32. Draw block diagrams for the F_1, F_2, and F_3 in Question 28, using only NOR gates.

33. Draw a block diagram for F_1, F_2, and F_3 in Question 28 using OR-to-NAND networks.

34. Draw block diagrams for F_1, F_2, and F_3 in Question 28 using AND-to-NOR gate networks.

35. Draw Karnaugh maps for the expression in Question 4.

36. Draw Karnaugh maps for the expression in Question 2.

37. For a four-variable map in W, X, Y, and Z draw the subcubes for:
   (a) $WX\overline{Y}$ (b) WX (c) $XY\overline{Z}$ (d) $\overline{Y}$

38. For a four-variable map in W, X, Y, and Z draw the subcubes for:
   (a) $WX\overline{Y}\overline{Z}$ (b) $W\overline{Z}$ (c) $\overline{W}\overline{Z}$ (d) Y

39. Draw maps of the expressions in Question 40, then draw the subcubes for the shortened terms you found.

40. Apply the rule $AY + A\overline{Y} = A$ where possible to the following expressions:
   (a) $XY + X\overline{Y}$ (b) $\overline{A}BC + \overline{A}\overline{B}C$
   (c) $A\overline{B}C + ABC$ (d) $ABC + A\overline{B}C + A\overline{B}\overline{C} + AB\overline{C}$
   (e) $ABC + \overline{A}\overline{B}C + A\overline{B}C$ (f) $ABC + \overline{A}BC + \overline{A}\overline{B}C$

Note: There is a technique for writing minterms which is widely used. It consists in writing the letter m (to represent *minterm*) along with the value of the binary number given by the row of the table and combinations in which the minterm lies. For instance, in the variable X, Y, Z we have the following unfinished table of combinations:

INPUT			OUTPUT	PRODUCT TERMS	DESIGNATION AS m_i
X	Y	Z			
0	0	0		$\overline{X}\overline{Y}\overline{Z}$	m_0
0	0	1		$\overline{X}\overline{Y}Z$	m_1
0	1	0		$\overline{X}Y\overline{Z}$	m_2
0	1	1		$\overline{X}YZ$	m_3
1	0	0		$X\overline{Y}\overline{Z}$	m_4
1	0	1		$X\overline{Y}Z$	m_5
1	1	0		$XY\overline{Z}$	m_6
1	1	1		XYZ	m_7

For this table $m_0 = \overline{X}\overline{Y}\overline{Z}$, $m_1 = \overline{X}\overline{Y}Z$, $m_2 = \overline{X}Y\overline{Z}$, $m_3 = \overline{X}YZ$, and so to $m_7 = XYZ$. Now, we can substitute m_is for actual terms and shorten the writing of expressions. For instance, $m_1 + m_2 + m_4$ means $\overline{X}\overline{Y}Z + \overline{X}Y\overline{Z} + X\overline{Y}\overline{Z}$. Similarly, $m_0 + m_3 + m_5 + m_7$ means $\overline{X}\overline{Y}\overline{Z} + \overline{X}YZ + X\overline{Y}Z + XYZ$.

This can be extended to four or more variables. An expression in W, X, Y, Z can be written as $m_0 + m_{13} + m_{15} = \overline{W}\overline{X}\overline{Y}\overline{Z} + WX\overline{Y}Z + WXYZ$. Or $m_2 + m_5 + m_9 = \overline{W}\overline{X}Y\overline{Z} + \overline{W}X\overline{Y}Z + W\overline{X}\overline{Y}Z$. As can be seen, to change a minterm to its m_i, simply make uncomplemented variables 1s and complemented variables 0s. Thus $\overline{W}XY\overline{Z}$ would be 0110, or 6 decimal, $\overline{W}\overline{X}Y\overline{Z}$ would be 0010, or 2 decimal. These two terms would then be written m_6 and m_2. (Notice that we must know how many variables a minterm is in.)

41. Draw the Karnaugh maps in X, Y, Z for:

(a) $m_0 + m_1 + m_5 + m_7$ (b) $m_1 + m_3 + m_5 + m_4$

(c) $m_1 + m_2 + m_3 + m_5$ (d) $m_0 + m_5 + m_7$

42. Draw the subcubes for a three-variable map in X, Y, Z for:

(a) $m_1 + m_3 + m_5 + m_0$ (b) $m_5 + m_7$ (c) $m_0 + m_2$

43. Find the maximal subcubes for the maps drawn for Question 42.

44. Find minimal expressions for the maps drawn in Question 42.

45. Using maps, simplify the following expressions in four variables W, X, Y, and Z.

(a) $m_2 + m_3 + m_5 + m_6 + m_7 + m_9 + m_{11} + m_{13}$

(b) $m_0 + m_2 + m_4 + m_8 + m_9 + m_{10} + m_{11} + m_{12} + m_{13}$

46. Using maps, simplify the following expressions in four variables W, X, Y, and Z.

(a) $m_1 + m_3 + m_5 + m_7 + m_{12} + m_{13} + m_8 + m_9$

(b) $m_0 + m_5 + m_7 + m_8 + m_{11} + m_{13} + m_{15}$

47. Using maps, derive minimal product-of-sums expressions for the functions given in Question 46.

48. Using maps, derive minimal product-of-sums expressions for the functions given in Question 42.

49. Using maps, simplify the following expressions, using sum-of-products form.

$$
\text{(a) } \overline{A}\overline{B}C + A\overline{B}\overline{C} + \overbrace{ABC + \overline{A}BC + \overline{A}B\overline{C}}^{\text{don't-cares}}
$$

$$
\text{(b) } ABC + \overline{A}\overline{B}\overline{C} + \overbrace{A\overline{B}\overline{C} + A\overline{B}C}^{\text{don't-cares}}
$$

$$
\text{(c) } ABCD + \overline{A}B\overline{C}D + \overline{A}BCD + \overbrace{A\overline{B}\overline{C}D + \overline{A}\overline{B}CD + AB\overline{C}D}^{\text{don't-cares}}
$$

50. Using maps, derive minimal product-of-sums expressions for the functions given in Question 46.

51. Using maps, simplify the following expressions, using sum-of-products form.

$$
\text{(a) } ABC + \overline{A}\overline{B}C + \overbrace{\overline{A}BC + A\overline{B}C}^{\text{don't-cares}} + AB\overline{C}
$$

$$
\text{(b) } ABCD + \overline{A}B\overline{C}D + \overbrace{\overline{A}BCD + A\overline{B}CD}^{\text{don't-cares}} + \overline{A}\overline{B}CD
$$

$$
\text{(c) } A\overline{B}C\overline{D} + A\overline{B}CD + \overbrace{\overline{A}BCD + \overline{A}BC\overline{D}}^{\text{don't-cares}}
$$

Note: The following rules are useful in designing using NAND gates and NOR gates:

(1) To design a NAND-to-NAND gate network, use the sum-of-products form. For example, to design for $XY + \overline{X}\,\overline{Y}$:

(2) To design a NOR-to-NOR gate network, use the product-of-sums form. For example, to design for $(A+\overline{B})(B+\overline{C})$:

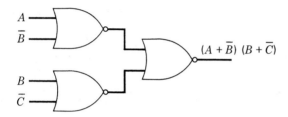

(3) To design a NAND-to-AND gate network, use the product-of-sums form but complement each input variable. For example, to design for $(A+B)(\overline{B}+C)$:

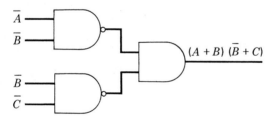

(4) To design a NOR-to-OR gate network, use the sum-of-products form but complement each input variable. For example, to design $A\overline{B} + \overline{A}BC$:

52. *(a)* Design an AND-to-OR gate combinational network for the Boolean algebra expression

$$ABCD + AB\overline{CD} + \overline{A}BCD + AB\overline{C}D + ABC\overline{D} + \overline{A}BCD$$

Use as few gates as you can.
(b) Design a NOR-to-NOR gate combinational network for the Boolean algebra function in part *(a)*, again using as few gates as you can.

53. The following is a NAND-to-NAND gate network. Draw a block diagram for a NOR-to-NOR gate network which realizes the same function, using as few gates as possible.

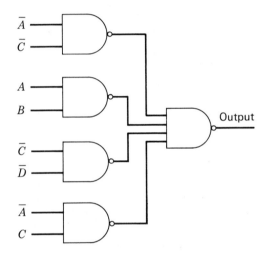

54. *(a)* Derive a Boolean algebra expression for the output *y* of the network shown below.
(b) Convert the expression for *y* derived in *(a)* to product-of-sums form.

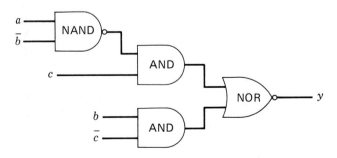

55. *(a)* Design an OR-to-AND gate combinatorial network for the Boolean algebra expression

$$ABCD + \overline{AB}\overline{CD} + \overline{A}B\overline{CD} + \overline{A}BCD + (\overline{AB}\overline{CD} + \overline{AB}CD)$$

The two terms in parentheses are don't-care terms.

(b) Using only NAND gates design a combinatorial network for the Boolean algebra function given in part *(a)*.

56. *(a)* Design an OR-to-AND gate combinatorial network for the Boolean algebra expression

$$ABCD + \overline{ABCD} + \overline{A}BC\overline{D} + \overline{AB}\overline{CD} + (\overline{AB}\overline{CD} + \overline{A}BCD)$$

The two terms in parentheses are don't-care terms.

(b) Using only NOR gates design a combinatorial network for the Boolean algebra function given in part *(a)*.

57. The following NAND-to-AND gate network is to be redesigned using a NOR-to-OR gate configuration. Make the change using as few gates as possible.

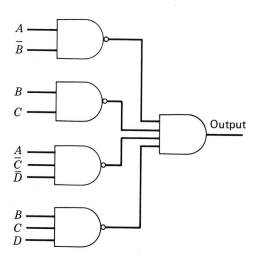

58. *(a)* Design an AND-to-OR gate combinational network for the Boolean algebra expression

$$ABCD + AB\overline{CD} + \overline{AB}C\overline{D} + AB\overline{CD} + ABC\overline{D} + \overline{ABCD}$$

Use as few gates as you can.

(b) Design a NOR-gate combinational network for the Boolean algebra function in part *(a)*, again using as few gates as you can.

59. Convert the following NOR-to-OR gate network into a NAND-to-AND gate network. Use as few gates as possible.

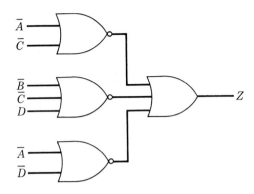

60. (a) Design an AND-to-OR gate combinational network for the Boolean algebra expression

$$ABCD + AB\overline{C}D + \overline{A}BCD + AB\overline{C}\overline{D} + AB\overline{C}\overline{D} + \overline{A}BCD$$

Use as few gates as you can.

(b) Design a NOR-to-NOR gate combinational network for the Boolean algebra function in part (a) again using as few gates as you can.

61. A combinational network has three control inputs c_1, c_2, and c_3; three data inputs a_1, a_2, and a_3; and a single output z. ($\overline{a}_1$, $\overline{a}_2$, $\overline{a}_3$, $\overline{c}_1$, $\overline{c}_2$, and $\overline{c}_3$ are also available as inputs.) Each input is a binary valued signal. Only one of the control inputs can be a 1 at any given time and all three can be 0s simultaneously. When c_1 is a 1, the value of z is to be the value of a_1; when c_2 is a 1 the value of z is to be the value of a_2; and when c_3 is a 1 the value of the output is to be the value of a_3. If c_1, c_2, and c_3 are 0s the output z is to have value 0. Design this network using only NOR gates. Make the network have two levels and use as few gates as possible.

62. The following NAND-to-AND gate network is to be redesigned using a NOR-to-OR gate configuration. Make the change using as few gates as possible.

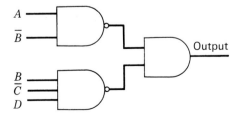

63. Convert the following NOR-to-OR gate network into a NAND-to-AND gate network. Use as few gates as possible in your network.

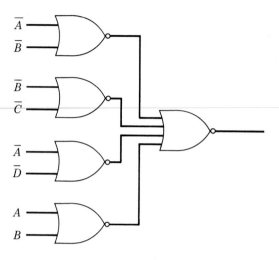

64. Will the minimal expression for the following function require fewer NAND gates or NOR gates? (d means don't-care.) Assume complements are available. How many gates for each? Give your minimal expressions.

X_1	X_2	X_3	X_4	OUTPUT
0	0	0	0	0
0	0	0	1	1
0	0	1	0	1
0	0	1	1	0
0	1	0	0	0
0	1	0	1	0
0	1	1	0	1
0	1	1	1	d
1	0	0	0	d
1	0	0	1	1
1	0	1	0	0
1	0	1	1	0
1	1	0	0	d
1	1	0	1	0
1	1	1	0	d
1	1	1	1	0

65. The following NAND-to-AND gate network must be converted to a NOR-to-OR gate network. Make the conversion using as few gates as possible in your final design.

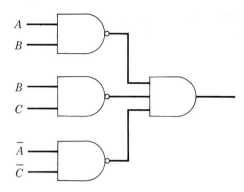

66. Will the minimal expression for the following function require fewer NAND gates or NOR gates? (d means don't-care.) Assume complements are available. How many gates for each? Give your minimal expressions.

X_1	X_2	X_3	X_4	OUTPUT
0	0	0	0	0
0	0	0	1	1
0	0	1	0	1
0	0	1	1	0
0	1	0	0	0
0	1	0	1	0
0	1	1	0	1
0	1	1	1	d
1	0	0	0	d
1	0	0	1	1
1	0	1	0	1
1	0	1	1	0
1	1	0	0	d
1	1	0	1	0
1	1	1	0	1
1	1	1	1	0

67. Simplify

(a) $(\overline{W} + \overline{X} + Y + Z)(\overline{W} + X + \overline{Y} + Z)(\overline{W} + X + Y + Z)$
don't-cares
$$\overline{(W + X + \overline{Y} + Z)(W + \overline{X} + Y + Z)(\overline{W} + \overline{X} + Y + \overline{Z})(W + X + Y + Z)}$$
don't-cares

(b) $\overline{\overline{a}\,\overline{b}\,\overline{c}\,\overline{d}} + \overline{a}\overline{b}\overline{c}d + \overline{a}bc\overline{d} + \overline{\overline{a}\overline{b}\overline{c}}d + \overline{a}bcd + \overline{a}bc\overline{d} + \overline{a}\overline{b}c\overline{d} + a\overline{b}c\overline{d}$

(c) For parts (a) and (b) design block diagrams for the logical circuitry of the simplified expressions using either NAND gates only or NOR gates only. Assume complements of the inputs are available. The same type gates do not have to be used for both (a) and (b).

68. Write a Boolean algebra expression in sum-of-products form for a gating network with three inputs A, B, and C (and their complements $\overline{A}$, $\overline{B}$, and $\overline{C}$) which is to have a 1 output only when two or three of the inputs has a 1 value.

69. Draw a block diagram for a gate network, using only NOR gates, with three inputs A, B, and C (and their complements) which have a 1 output only when two or three of the inputs has a 1 value as in Question 1.

70. Will the minimal expression for the following function require fewer NAND gates or NOR gates? (d means don't-care.) Assume complements are available. How many gates for each? Give your minimal expressions.

X_1	X_2	X_3	X_4	OUTPUT
0	0	0	0	0
0	0	0	1	1
0	0	1	0	1
0	0	1	1	0
0	1	0	0	0
0	1	0	1	0
0	1	1	0	1
0	1	1	1	d
1	0	0	0	d
1	0	0	1	1
1	0	1	0	1
1	0	1	1	d
1	1	0	0	d
1	1	0	1	0
1	1	1	0	1
1	1	1	1	0

71. The following is a NAND-to-NAND gate network. Draw a block diagram for a NOR-to-NOR gate network which realizes the same function, using as few gates as possible.

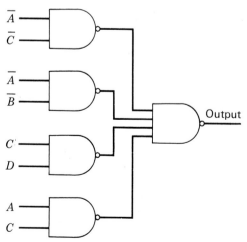

72. Convert the following NOR-to-OR gate network into a NAND-to-NAND gate network. Use as few gates as possible in your network.

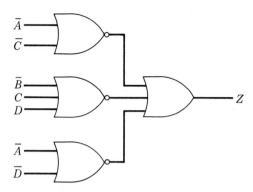

73. (*a*) Design an AND-to-OR gate combinational network for the Boolean algebra function

$$f = \overline{wxy}\overline{z} + \overline{wx}yz + w\overline{xyz} + w\overline{x}yz + \overline{w}xyz$$

Use as few gates as you can.

(*b*) Design a NOR gate combinational network for the Boolean algebra function in part (*a*), again using as few gates as you can.

4
LOGICAL DESIGN

The preceding chapter described gates and the analysis of gating networks using Boolean algebra. The basic devices used in the operational or calculating sections of digital computers consist of gates and devices called *flip-flops*. It is remarkable that even the largest of computers is primarily constructed of these devices. Accordingly, this chapter first describes flip-flops and their characteristics. From an intuitive viewpoint flip-flops provide memory and gates provide operations on, or functions of, the values stored in these memory devices.

Following the introduction to flip-flops, the use of flip-flops and gates to perform several of the most useful functions in computers is presented. The particular functions described include counting in binary and binary-coded-decimal, transferring values, and shifting or scaling values stored in flip-flops.

There are, incidentally, several other names which have been used instead of flip-flop. These include *latch, binary,* and *toggle,* but flip-flop has been the most frequently used. Also, there are several other types of memory devices in computers, and these will be studied in Chap. 7. For actual operations flip-flops remain dominant, however, because of their high speed, the ease with which they can be set or read, and the natural way gates and flip-flops can be interconnected.

This chapter also contains a section on clocks in digital computers. Computers do not run by taking steps at random times, but proceed from step to step at intervals precisely controlled by a clock which provides a carefully regulated time base for all operations. Some knowledge of the uses of clocks in computers is indispensable, and the subject is introduced here.

All the above material is presented without recourse to the study of electronic digital circuitry. In many cases, students have gained familiarity with digital circuits prior to studying this material; in other cases, where courses and users of the book are pressed for time, it is decided to progress without studying the actual circuit details of the gates and flip-flop circuits which are used. Accordingly, this book has been constructed so that it is possible to proceed while omitting the material on circuits, which is in Chap. 5. (Material can also be selected from Chap. 5 at the instructor's discretion.)

It is the fact that computers have come to be constructed of circuits which operate in a modular, or block, fashion that makes it possible to treat circuit material in this way. As integrated circuits have become increasingly complex, it has become necessary to examine them from a functional viewpoint rather than a component viewpoint, both in computer design and maintenance. We ask first, "What does the circuit do?", then, only later, "How does it work?"

4•1 THE FLIP-FLOP

The basic circuit for storing information in a digital machine is called a *flip-flop*. There are several fundamental types of flip-flops and many circuit designs; however, there are two characteristics shared by all flip-flops.

1. The flip-flop is a bistable device, i.e., a circuit with only two stable states, which we will designate the 0 state and the 1 state.

The flip-flop circuit can remember, or store, a binary bit of information because of its bistable characteristic. The flip-flop responds to inputs. If an input causes it to go to its 1 state, it will remain there and "remember" a 1 until some signal causes it to go to the 0 state. Similarly, once placed in the 0 state, it will remain there until told to go to the 1 state. This simple characteristic, the ability of the flip-flop to retain its state, is the basis for information storage in the operating or calculating sections of a digital computer.

2. The flip-flop has two output signals, one of which is the complement of the other.

Figure 4·1 shows the block diagram for a particular type of flip-flop, the *RS flip-flop*. There are two inputs, designated as S and R, and two outputs, marked with X and $\overline{X}$. To describe and analyze flip-flop operation, there are several conventions which are standard in the computer industry.

1. Each flip-flop is given a "name." Convenient names are generally letters such as X or Y or A or B, or letter-number combinations such as A_1 or B_2,

FIG. 4•1 *RS* flip-flop.

or sometimes, because of difficulty in subscripting on typewriters or printers, simply *A*1 or *B*2. The flip-flop in Fig. 4·1 is called *X*. It has two outputs, the *X* output and the $\overline{X}$ output.

The *X* and $\overline{X}$ output lines are always complements; i.e., if the *X* output line has a 1 signal, the $\overline{X}$ output line has a 0 signal; and if the *X* output line has a 0 signal, output line $\overline{X}$ has a 1 signal.

2. The state of the flip-flop is taken to be the state of the *X* output. Thus, if the output line *X* has a 1 signal on it, we say that "flip-flop *X* is in the 1 state." Similarly, if the *X* line contains a 0 signal, we say that "flip-flop *X* is in the 0 state."

These two sets of conventions are very important and convenient. Notice that when flip-flop *X* is in the 1 state, the output line $\overline{X}$ has a 0 on it, and when flip-flop *X* is in the 0 state, the output line $\overline{X}$ has a 1 on it.

There are two input lines to the *RS* flip-flop. These are used to control the state of the flip-flop. The rules are:

1. As long as both input lines *S* and *R* carry 0 signals, the flip-flop remains in the same state, i.e., does not change state.

2. A 1 signal on the *S* line (the SET line) and a 0 signal on the *R* line cause the flip-flop to "set" to the 1 state.

3. A 1 signal on the *R* line (the RESET line) and a 0 signal on the *S* line cause the flip-flop to "reset" to the 0 state.

4. Placing a 1 on the *S* and a 1 on the *R* lines at the same time is forbidden. If this occurs, the flip-flop can go to either state. (This is in effect an ambiguous input in that it is telling the flip-flop to both SET and RESET at the same time.)

An example of a possible sequence of input signals and the resulting state of the flip-flop is as follows:

S	*R*	*X*	*X* is the state of the flip-flop after inputs *S* and *R* are applied.
1	0	1	
0	0	1	Flip-flop remains in same state.
0	0	1	
0	1	0	Flip-flop is reset.
0	0	0	
0	0	0	
0	1	0	Flip-flop is told to reset but is already reset.
0	0	0	
1	0	1	Flip-flop is set.
0	0	1	

While the above conventions may seem formidable at first, they can be simply summarized by seeing that a 1 on the *S* line causes the flip-flop to SET (i.e., assume the 1 state) and a 1 on the *R* line causes the flip-flop to RESET (i.e., assume the 0 state). The flip-flop does nothing in the absence of 1 inputs and would be hopelessly confused by 1s on both *S* and *R* inputs.

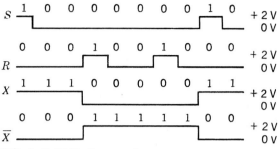

FIG. 4·2 *RS* flip-flop waveforms.

It is very convenient to be able to draw graphs of the inputs and outputs from computer circuits to show how they act as inputs vary. We shall assume the convention that a 1 signal is a positive signal and a 0 signal a ground, or 0 V, signal. This is conventional in most present-day circuits and is called *positive logic*. Figure 4·2 shows several signals as they progress in time, with the current binary values of each signal written above it. The signals in Fig. 4·2 are the sequence of signals given in the list above along with both the X and $\bar{X}$ output line signals from the flip-flop. We have arbitrarily chosen + 2 V for the 1 state of the signals and 0 V for the 0 state; however, these are very frequently used levels. Notice that the flip-flop changes only when the input levels command it to, and that it changes at once (actually, there would be a slight delay from when the flip-flop is told to change states and when it changes, since no physical device can respond instantly; so we assume the flip-flop's delay in responding is quite small, perhaps a small fraction of a microsecond).

4·2 THE TRANSFER

The *RS* flip-flop, although simple in operation, is adequate for all purposes and is a basic flip-flop circuit. Let us examine the operation of this flip-flop in a configuration called a *transfer circuit*. Figure 4·3 shows two sets of flip-flops named X_1, X_2, and X_3 and Y_1, Y_2, and Y_3. The function of this configuration is to transfer the states or *contents* of Y_1 into X_1, Y_2 into X_2, and Y_3 into X_3 upon the "TRANSFER," command, which consists of a 1 on the TRANSFER line.

Assume that Y_1, Y_2, and Y_3 have been set to some states which we want to remember or store in X_1, X_2, and X_3, while the Y flip-flops are used for further calculations. Placing a 1 on the TRANSFER line will cause this desired transfer of information. Understanding the transfer of the state of Y_1 into X_1 depends on seeing that if Y_1 is in the 0 state, the Y_1 output line has a 0 on it, and so the input line connected to the AND gate will be a 0 and the AND gate will place a 0 on the S input line of X_1, while the $\bar{Y}_1$ output from Y_1 will be a 1, causing, in the presence of a 1 on the TRANSFER line, a 1 on the R input of X_1. Similar reasoning will show that a 1 in Y_1 will cause a 1 to be placed in X_1 in the presence of a 1 on the TRANSFER line. As long as the TRANSFER line is a 0,

Transfer

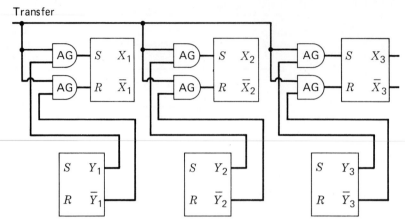

FIG. 4·3 Transfer circuit.

both inputs to the X flip-flops will be 0s and they will remain in the last state they assumed.

The above simple operation, the *transfer operation,* is quite important. Related sets of flip-flops in a computer are called *registers,* and we might call the three flip-flops Y_1, Y_2, and Y_3 simply *register Y*, and the three flip-flops X_1, X_2, and X_3 would be called *register X*. Then a 1 on the TRANSFER line would transfer the contents of register Y into register X. We shall return to this important concept.

4·3 THE CLOCK

A very important fact about digital computers (and flip-flops) as we now conceive of them is that they are almost invariably clocked. This means that there is some "master clock" somewhere sending out signals which are carefully regulated in time.

There are excellent reasons why machines are designed this way. The alternative way, with operations triggering other operations as they occur, is called *asynchronous operation* (the clocked way is called *synchronous operation*) and leads to considerable difficulty in design and maintenance. As a result, genuinely asynchronous operation is rarely used.

The clock is therefore the mover of the computer in that it carefully measures time and sends out regularly spaced clock signals which cause things to happen. We can then examine the operation of the flip-flops and gates before and after the clock "initiates an action." Initiating signals are often called, for historical reasons, *clock pulses.*†

---

† The term *clock pulse* has a historical origin. The early computers used short electrical pulses to initiate operations and these were naturally called *clock pulses*. Some circuits still use these narrow pulses but the majority of circuits now respond to edges of square waves as in Fig. 4 · 4.

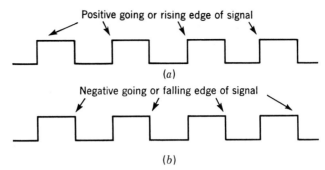

FIG. 4·4 Clock waveforms.

Figure 4·4 shows a clock. The clock waveform in Fig. 4·4(a) and (b) is called a *square wave*. The figure shows two important portions of a square wave, the *leading edge*, or *rising edge*, or sometimes *positive-going edge*, and the *falling edge*, or *negative-going edge.* These are particularly important since most flip-flops now in use respond to either (but not both) a falling edge or a rising edge. In effect, a system which responds to rising edges of the clock "rests" between such edges and changes state only when such positive-going edges occur. (The reason for the rest periods is to give the circuits time to assume their new states and to give all transients time to die down. The frequency at which such edges occur is generally determined by the speed with which the circuits can go to their new state; the delay times for the gates, since they must process the new signals; etc.)

Since clock signals are used to initiate flip-flop actions, a clock input is included on most flip-flops. This input is marked with a CL, as shown in Fig. 4·5. A clocked flip-flop can respond to either the positive-going edge of the clock signal or the negative-going edge.† If a given flip-flop responds to the positive-going edge of the signal, there is no "bubble" at the CL input on the block diagram, as in Fig. 4·5(a). If the flip-flop responds to a negative-going edge, or signal, a bubble is placed at the CL input, as in Fig. 4·5(b).

It is important to understand the above convention because clocked flip-flops actually respond to a *change* in clock input level, not to the level itself.

This is shown in Fig. 4·5(c) and (d). The flip-flop in Fig. 4·5(a) responds to positive-going clock edges (positive shifts), and a typical set of signals for the *clocked RS flip-flop* in Fig. 4·5(a) is shown in Fig. 4·5(c).

The flip-flop is operated according to these rules:

1. If the S and R inputs are 0s when the clock edge (pulse) occurs, the flip-flop does not change states but remains in its present state.
2. If the S input is a 1 and the R input is a 0 when the clock pulse (positive-going edge) occurs, the flip-flop goes to the 1 state.

---

† A flip-flop which responds to a rising or falling clock signal (as opposed to responding to a dc level) is called an *edge-triggering* or *master-slave* flip-flop for reasons which will be explained.

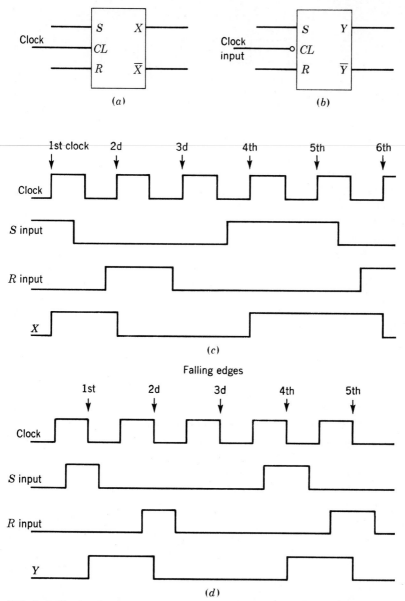

FIG. 4•5 Clocked flip-flops and waveforms. (a) Positive-edge-triggering flip-flop; (b) negative-edge-triggering flip-flop; (c) waveforms for positive-edge-triggering flip-flop in (a); (d) waveforms for flip-flop in (b).

3. If the S input is a 0 and the R input a 1 when the clock pulse occurs, the flip-flop is cleared to the 0 state.

4. Both the S and R inputs should not be 1s when a clock signal's positive-going edge occurs.

Of course, nothing happens to the flip-flop's state between occurrences of the initiating positive-going clock signal.†

Figure $4\cdot5(c)$ shows this with a square-wave clock signal. The flip-flop is set to a 1 by the first clock positive-going edge; a 0 at the occurrence of the second clock signal; no change occurs at the third positive-going clock edge; the flip-flop is set to 1 again on the fourth edge; and remains a 1 until the sixth clock edge occurs. Notice that the S and R inputs can be anything between the clock edges without affecting the operation of the flip-flop. (They can even both be 1s without effect, except when the positive-going edge occurs.)

Figure $4\cdot5(d)$ shows typical waveforms for the flip-flop in Fig. $4\cdot5(b)$. This flip-flop is *negative-edge triggering* because it responds to shifts in the clock level which are negative-going. The rules of operation are as before: 0s on S and R lead to no change; a 1 on S sets the flip-flop; and a 1 on R clears the flip-flop. The flip-flop responds to the S and R inputs only at the precise time the clock, or CL input, goes negative.

4•4 THE SHIFT REGISTER

Figure $4\cdot6$ shows a *shift register.* This circuit accepts information from some input source and then shifts this information along the chain of flip-flops, moving the information one flip-flop each time a positive-going clock signal occurs.

Figure $4\cdot6$ also shows a typical sequence of input signals and flip-flop signals in the shift register. The input value is taken by X_1 when the first positive-going clock signal arrives. Anything in this and the remaining flip-flops is shifted right at this time. We have assumed that all the flip-flops are initially in their 0 states. In the figure, the input waveform is at 1 when the first clock occurs; so X_1 goes to the 1 state.

When the second positive-going clock signal arrives, the input is at 0; so X_1 goes to the 0 state, but the 1 in X_1 is shifted into X_2. When the third clock edge appears, the input is a 1; so X_1 takes a 1, the 0 previously in X_1 is shifted into X_2, and the 1 in X_2 goes into X_3. This process continues. The values in X_3 are simply dropped off the end of the register.

Notice that each flip-flop takes the value in the flip-flop on its left when the shift register is stepped. The reasoning is as follows: If, for instance, X_1 is in the 1 state, its X output line is a 1 and thus the S input to X_2 will be a 1; and the $\overline{X}$ output of X_1 will be a 0, and so the R input of X_2 will be a 0. This causes X_2

---

† There is some delay from the time the positive-going edge of the clock signal tells a flip-flop to "go" until the flip-flop's outputs are able to change values. The clock signal itself will also require some small amount of time to rise, for physical reasons. For present systems the rise time on the clock signals, i.e., the time to rise 90 percent of total rise, ranges from about 1×10^{-9} to about 50×10^{-9} s. The delay from the clock-signal change until a flip-flop's output changes 90 percent, which is called the *delay time,* ranges from 10.5×10^{-9} to 50×10^{-9} s for most circuits.

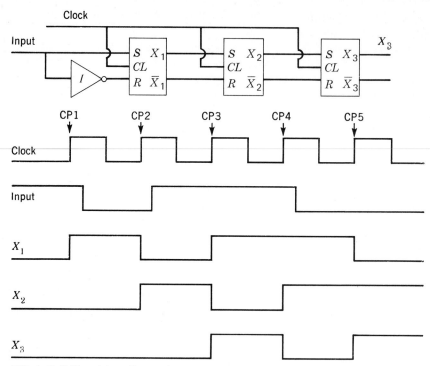

FIG. 4•6 Shift register with waveforms.

to take its 1 state when the clock pulse occurs. A 0 in X_1 will cause X_2 to go to 0 when the clock pulse occurs, and the reason for this should be analyzed.

There is one problem which could occur if certain design precautions were not taken with the flip-flops. If the flip-flop outputs changed too fast, a state could ripple, or race, down the chain. This is called the *race problem,* and is handled by designing the flip-flops so that they take the value at their inputs just as the clock positive-going edge occurs and not slightly after or during the clock's rise time. This leads to a certain complexity in flip-flop design, which we will not at this time consider. The designer and manufacturer of circuits provide us with this protection, and we shall accept it for the present, but an explanation in detail is in the final sections of this chapter and can be read now, if desired.

4•5 THE BINARY COUNTER

Inasmuch as the binary counter is one of the most useful of logical circuits, there are many kinds of binary counters. The fundamental purpose of the binary counter is to record the number of occurrences of some input. This is a basic function, that of counting, and is used over and over.

The first type of binary counter to be explained is shown in Fig. 4·7. This counter records the number of occurrences of a positive-going edge (or pulse) at the input.

It is desirable to start this counter with 0s in all three flip-flops; so one further line is added to each flip-flop, a DC RESET line. This line is normally at the 0 level; when it goes positive, or 1, it places a 0 in the flip-flop. This action does not depend on the clock; when a DC RESET line is at the 1 level, the flip-flop goes to 0 regardless of any other input and in the absence or presence of a clock pulse.

It is quite common for flip-flops to have a DC RESET line. Notice this input "overrides" all other inputs when it is a 1, forcing the flip-flop to the 0 state. A 0 on this line, however, does not affect flip-flop operation in any way.

Before counting begins, then, a 1 is placed temporarily on the RESET COUNTER line and the three flip-flops are cleared to 0. The RESET COUNTER line is then returned to 0.

When the first clock positive edge occurs, the flip-flop X_1 goes to its 1 state. This is because when the flip-flop X_1 is in the 0 state, the $\overline{X}_1$ output is high, or 1, placing a 1 on the S input (refer to Fig. $4 \cdot 7$), and the X_1 output is low, or 0, placing a 0 on the R input; so a 1 goes into flip-flop X_1.

Flip-flops X_2 and X_3 are not affected by this change, for although the $\overline{X}_1$ output is connected to the CL input of X_2, the signal has gone from 1 to 0. This is a negative shift, which does nothing to X_2.

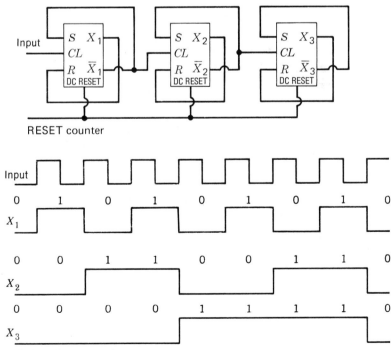

FIG. $4 \cdot 7$ Binary counter.

The counter now has $X_3 = 0$, $X_2 = 0$, $X_1 = 1$, or binary 001; so the first input clock edge has stepped the counter from 000 to 001.†

The occurrence of the second positive-going clock edge causes flip-flop X_1 to go from the 1 state to the 0 state. The reasoning is as follows: When X_1 is a 1, the X_1 output is a 1 and is connected to the R input, and the $\overline{X_1}$ output is a 0 and is connected to the S input. This tells the flip-flop to "go to 0," and when the second clock pulse occurs, it goes.

This is important. When a flip-flop is cross-coupled, i.e., when its uncomplemented output is connected to its R input and its complemented output to its S input, the occurrence of a clock edge will always cause it to "complement," or change values.

The change of value from 1 to 0 of flip-flop X_1 causes X_2 to change from a 0 to a 1. This is because $\overline{X_1}$'s output is connected to the CL input of X_2 and has gone from 0 to 1, a positive shift, and since X_2 is cross-coupled, it will complement (change values) and go from 0 to 1. This does not affect X_3, because the CL input of X_3 has gone from 1 to 0, a negative shift.

The counter has now progressed to $X_1 = 0$, $X_2 = 1$, and $X_3 = 0$; so the sequence of states has been 000, 001, 010.

Reasoning of this type will show that the progression of states by the counter will be as follows:

X_3	X_2	X_1
0	0	0
0	0	1
0	1	0
0	1	1
1	0	0
1	0	1
1	1	0
1	1	1
0	0	0
0	0	1
0	1	0

This is a list of binary numbers from 0 to 7, which repeats over and over. Thus, after five input pulses the counter contains 101, or binary 5; after seven pulses the counter contains 111, or binary 7. The maximum number of pulses this counter can handle, without ambiguity, is 7. After eight pulses the counter contains 0; after nine pulses, 1; etc. In the trade this is called a *modulo 8 counter,* or *three-stage counter.*

The counter can be extended by another flip-flop, X_4, which is cross-

---

† Notice that the binary numbers are written in the opposite direction from the block diagram layout, which has the least significant bit on the left. This makes for a neater block diagram and is frequently used. The standards, in fact, ask for left-to-right signal flow.

ENABLE

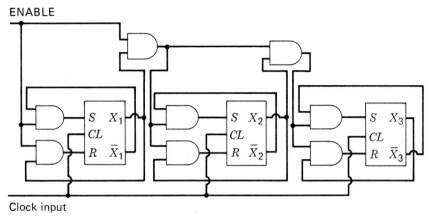

Clock input

FIG. 4·8 Gated-clocked binary counter.

coupled and which has its *CL* input connected to the output of flip-flop $\bar{X}_3$. This forms a *four-stage,* or *modulo 15,* counter, which can handle up to 15 counts. A fifth flip-flop would form a counter which would count to 31, a sixth to 63, etc.

We now consider a *gated-clocked binary counter.* This is an exceedingly popular counter in modern integrated circuit computers, and it demonstrates the fact that most operations are *enabled* by logic levels and activated by clock signals. The preceding counter is called a *ripple counter* because changes ripple down the flip-flop chain.

In Fig. 4·8 the ENABLE input to the first flip-flop in the chain X_1 goes to two AND gates, which also have the output of the flip-flop as inputs. Notice, if the ENABLE signal is a 0, the two AND gates will have 0 outputs and X_1 will remain in the same state regardless of how many clock pulses occur.

When the ENABLE signal is a 1, however, the outputs from flip-flop X_1 cause that flip-flop to always change values when a clock pulse occurs. Thus the counter records the number of clock pulses which occur while the ENABLE is on. Then the flip-flop X_2 will change only when X_1 is a 1, the ENABLE signal is a 1, and a positive-going clock signal occurs. Similarly, X_3 will change states only when X_1 and X_2 are 1s, the ENABLE is a 1, and a clock positive edge occurs.

The two AND gates combined with an *RS* flip-flop in Fig. 4·8 are so useful that most popular lines of flip-flops contain in a single integrated circuit container the flip-flop and its two AND gates, as shown in Fig. 4·9(*a*).

Figure 4·9(*b*) shows another very popular and useful flip-flop, which consists of the *RS* flip-flop and its two AND gates, but with the AND gates having the cross-coupling already permanently made inside the container. In this form the two lines taken outside are called *J* and *K,* and the flip-flop is called a *JK flip-flop.* This is most useful, because analysis indicates that the *J* and *K* inputs act just as *RS* inputs for two 0 inputs — in this case the flip-flop never changes states. However, with a 0 on *J* and a 1 on *K,* the flip-flop

Entire circuit is in
single container

(a)

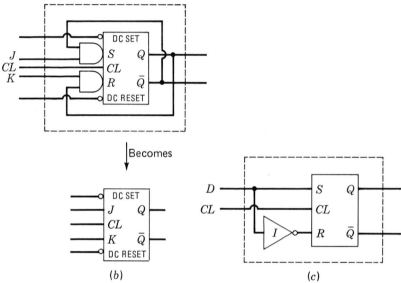

Becomes

(b)   (c)

FIG. 4·9 *JK* and *D* flip-flops. (*a*) *RS* flip-flop with AND gates; (*b*) how *JK* flip-flop
is made from *RS* flip-flops; (*c*) *D*-type flip-flop.

goes to the 0 state when a clock positive edge appears, and with a 1 on *J*
and a 0 on *K,* the flip-flop goes to 1 when a clock positive edge appears. The
significant fact is that when both *J* and *K* are 1s, the flip-flop always changes
states when a clock positive edge appears.

It is a general rule that bubbles, or small circles, at the DC SET and DC RE-
SET inputs mean that these inputs are activated by 0 levels. The absence of
these bubbles would mean that the inputs are activated by 1 levels and are
normally at 0.

The flip-flops in Fig. 4·9(*a*) and (*b*) both have DC RESET and DC SET inputs. The bubbles at the input on the block diagram indicate that these are
activated by 0 inputs and are normally held at a 1 level. When, for instance,
a 0 is placed on the DC SET input, the flip-flop goes to a 1 level regardless of
the clock or other inputs. DC SET and DC RESET should not be 0s at the same
time, because this is forbidden and leads to an undetermined next state.

It is a general rule that bubbles, or small circles, at the DC SET and DC RE-
SET inputs mean that these inputs are activated by 0 levels. The absence of
these bubbles would mean that the inputs are activated by 1 levels and are
normally at 0.

There is one other type of circuit, now in general use, the *D* flip-flop. This
flip-flop simply takes the value at its input when a clock pulse appears and re-

mains in its same state until the next clock pulse appears. As shown in Fig. 4·9(c), the D flip-flop can be made from a RS flip-flop and an inverter.

The D flip-flop is very useful because when clocked it takes the state on its input and holds it until clocked again. Only a single input line is needed for a transfer, whereas the RS or JK flip-flops require two input lines.

An example of the use of JK flip-flops is shown in Fig. 4·10(a) and (b). Figure 4·10(a) shows the simplicity of a gated binary counter with JK flip-flops. Figure 4·10(b) shows a block diagram for a *binary up-down counter*. When the UP ENABLE line is high or a 1, the counter will count up, that is, 0, 1, 2, 3, 4, ... When the DOWN ENABLE line is a 1, the counter will count down, that is, 6, 5, 4, ... In general, the counter will increase its value by 1 if the UP ENABLE line is a 1 and a clock pulse arrives, or will decrease its value by 1 if the DOWN ENABLE input is a 1 and a clock pulse occurs.

A RESET line is provided which is used to DC RESET the counter to 0. This is activated by a 1 on the RESET line.

FIG. 4•10 Binary counters with JK flip-flops. (a) Gated-ripple counter; (b) up-down counter.

4•6 BCD COUNTERS

The binary counters considered so far all count to their limit before resetting to all 0s. Often it is desired to have counters count in binary-coded-decimal (BCD) Figure 4·11(a) shows a typical BCD counter. Examination of this counter shows that it counts normally until it reaches 1001; that is, the sequence until that time is as follows:

X_4	X_3	X_2	X_1
0	0	0	0
0	0	0	1
0	0	1	0
0	0	1	1
0	1	0	0
0	1	0	1
0	1	1	0
0	1	1	1
1	0	0	0
1	0	0	1

When the next negative-going edge at the input occurs, however, the BCD counter returns to all 0s. At the same time (i.e., during the interval when the counter goes from 9 to 0) a negative-going signal edge occurs at the CARRY

FIG. 4•11 BCD counters. (a) Decade, or BCD, counter; (b) cascading BCD counter blocks.

output. This CARRY output can be connected to the INPUT of another BCD counter, which will then be stepped by 1 when the first BCD stage goes from 9 to 0. This is shown in Fig. $4 \cdot 11(b)$, where several four-flip-flop BCD stages are combined to make a large counter.

If we consider just two of the "BCD boxes," we find the sequence to be as follows:

8	4	2	1	8	4	2	1 value of bits
Y_4	Y_3	Y_2	Y_1	X_4	X_3	X_2	X_1
0	0	0	0	0	0	0	0
0	0	0	0	0	0	0	1
0	0	0	0	0	0	1	0
0	0	0	0	0	0	1	1
0	0	0	0	0	1	0	0
0	0	0	0	0	1	0	1
0	0	0	0	0	1	1	0
0	0	0	0	0	1	1	1
0	0	0	0	1	0	0	0
0	0	0	0	1	0	0	1
0	0	0	1	0	0	0	0
0	0	0	1	0	0	0	1
.	.	.	.	.	.	.	.
0	0	0	1	1	0	0	1
0	0	1	0	0	0	0	0
0	0	1	0	0	0	0	1
.	.	.	.	.	.	.	.

We have here counted to 21; this would continue until the counter reached 99, when the Y part would put out a signal which could be used to gate another stage to form a counter that could count to 999.

This sort of repetition of various "boxes," or "modules," such as a BCD counter, is facilitated by manufacturers placing an entire four-stage BCD counter in a single integrated circuit container, as is often the case.

One thing should be noted about the block diagram in Fig. $4 \cdot 11(b)$. The flip-flops trigger (i.e., are activated by) negative-going shifts in input levels at the input. This is indicated by the small circles of "bubbles" at the inputs. As a result, a flip-flop such as X_3 is activated when X_2 goes from a 1 to a 0, that is, when the 1 output makes a negative transition.

Also, note that unconnected inputs, such as the K inputs of all the flip-flops and the J inputs of X_1 and X_3, are assumed to be at 1 levels. This is due to the circuit construction.

4•7 INTEGRATED CIRCUITS

The flip-flops and gates used in modern computing machines—which range from calculators and microcomputers through the large high-speed computers—are constructed and packaged using what is called *integrated circuit technology*. When integrated circuits are used, one or more complete gates or flip-flops are packaged in a single integrated circuit (IC) container.

The IC containers provide input and output pins or connections which are then interconnected using plated strips on circuit boards, wires, or other means to form complete computing devices.

In earlier computers, flip-flop and gate circuits were constructed using discrete electrical components such as resistors, capacitors, transistors, and before that, vacuum tubes and relays. Individual components were interconnected to form flip-flops and gates which were then interconnected to form computers. With the present-day IC technology, flip-flops and gates are fabricated in containers and only the IC containers (or "cans") need be interconnected.

Two typical IC containers are shown in Fig. 4·12(a). One is called a *dual inline package* (in the trade it is called a "coffin" or a DIP), and this particular package has 14 pins which provide for external connections. For years this 14-pin package was a standard in the industry, and plastic and ceramic DIPs of this sort have been the largest-selling IC package for some years.

There has been a tendency as IC technology improved, however, to increase the number of pins per package. Packages with 16 and 20 pins are becoming popular, and up to 70 pins per package can now be found in some IC manufacturer's products.

Figure 4·12(b) through (e) shows how several gates and flip-flops are packaged in a single container. The inputs and outputs are numbered, and each number refers to an external pin on the IC container. A ground connection and a positive power voltage are both required for each container so that only 12 pins remain to be used for the actual inputs and outputs to gates and flip-flops. (For these circuits, each V_{CC} pin is connected to a 5.5 V power supply and GND to OV or system ground.)

The particular circuits in Fig. 4·12 are called transistor-transistor-logic (TTL) circuits and are widely used high-speed circuits (see Chap. 5). These particular configurations with identical pin connections are manufactured by just about every major IC manufacturer, and packages from one manufacturer can be fairly easily substituted for another manufacturer's packages (provided the speed requirements or loading capabilities are not violated). There are many other packages with, for instance, 3 three-input NAND gates, 2 *RS* flip-flops, exclusive OR gates, etc.

In order to illustrate the use of IC packages in logic design we now examine an implementation of Fig. 4·13, using the packages shown in Fig. 4·12. The logic circuit in Fig. 4·13 is called a *shift register with feedback,†*

---

† This particular type of shift register with feedback is so widely used that complete books have been written about it. It is sometimes called a *linear shift register,* a *random sequence generation,* or a *linear recurring sequence generator.* With similar feedback connections, a register with as many flip-flops as desired can be made, thus forming counters with sequences of $2^N - 1$ for any reasonable N (where N is the number of flip-flops).

Consider the set of consecutive states taken by X_4 in the shift register in Fig. 4·13 to be its output sequence. Each nonzero 4-tuple occurs once in any 15-bit segment of this sequence, each nonzero 3-tuple occurs twice, etc. Adding a 15-bit segment of this sequence to another 15-bit segment bit-by-bit mod 2 (exclusive OR) will give still another 15-bit segment. These sequences are used in instruments to form random number generators and to generate bandpass noise; in radar for interplanetary observations; in communications systems to generate noise and encode or encrypt; and for many other purposes. See Birkhoff and Bartee for more information and references.

FIG. 4·12 IC containers and flip-flop and gate circuits. (a) Dual inline and flat pack IC containers; (b) dual JK flip-flops with common clock and resets and separate sets; (c) dual JK flip-flop with separate resets and clocks; (d) dual four-input NAND gates; (e) quad two-input NAND gates.

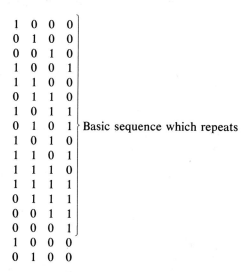

FIG. 4·13 Shift register with feedback.

for it consists of four flip-flops connected in a shift register configuration and "feedback" from these four flip-flops to the first flip-flop's inputs. This particular counter is started by setting a 1 in X_1 and 0s in X_2, X_3, and X_4. The sequence of states taken is then

$$
\left.
\begin{array}{cccc}
1 & 0 & 0 & 0 \\
0 & 1 & 0 & 0 \\
0 & 0 & 1 & 0 \\
1 & 0 & 0 & 1 \\
1 & 1 & 0 & 0 \\
0 & 1 & 1 & 0 \\
1 & 0 & 1 & 1 \\
0 & 1 & 0 & 1 \\
1 & 0 & 1 & 0 \\
1 & 1 & 0 & 1 \\
1 & 1 & 1 & 0 \\
1 & 1 & 1 & 1 \\
0 & 1 & 1 & 1 \\
0 & 0 & 1 & 1 \\
0 & 0 & 0 & 1
\end{array}
\right\} \text{Basic sequence which repeats}
$$

$$
\begin{array}{cccc}
1 & 0 & 0 & 0 \\
0 & 1 & 0 & 0
\end{array}
$$

Notice this sequence contains 15 of the 16 possible 4-bit numbers which might be taken by this circuit. (Only the all 0 combination is excluded.) This is a widely used sequence which occurs in many instruments and has many uses in radar systems, sonar systems, coding encryption boxes, etc.

Quite often the sequence of states taken by a logic circuit is written in a *counter table*. The counter table for the above sequence is

X_1	X_2	X_3	X_4
1	0	0	0
0	1	0	0
0	0	1	0
1	0	0	1
1	1	0	0
0	1	1	0
1	0	1	1
0	1	0	1
1	0	1	0
1	1	0	1
1	1	1	0
1	1	1	1
0	1	1	1
0	0	1	1
0	0	0	1

In the counter table the flip-flop's names are first listed, followed by the starting state. Then the successive states taken are listed in order, and the final line contains the state preceding the starting state.

There is a straightforward technique for designing a logic circuit to realize a counter table; this technique is developed in Sec. 4 · 12. For now we return to the implementation of the counter in Fig. 4 · 13.

In order to implement this counter, we require four flip-flops and a gate circuit which will yield the function $\overline{X_3}X_4 + X_3\overline{X_4}$. As shown, this can be made with a NAND-to-NAND gate network with 3 two-input NAND gates. An inverter is also required. (A NAND gate can be used for this by connecting both inputs together.)

One problem remains: We need to start the counter with X_1 in state 1 and the other three flip-flops in state 0. Since DC RESET inputs are connected together on the flip-flops [see Fig 4 · 12(b)], it is necessary to use a trick for flip-flop X_1. This simply involves renaming the J and K inputs and the two outputs so that J becomes K, K becomes J, and the two output names are reversed. The DC RESET input then becomes a DC SET input for the new (renamed) flip-flop.

Figure 4 · 14 shows the circuit as finally designed. Notice how X_1 differs in connections from X_2 and X_3.

The logic circuit in Fig. 4 · 14 could be implemented using a printed circuit board to make the connections between IC containers, or the connections could be made by individual wires using any one of a number of interconnection boards manufactured by various companies. Placing a 0 (ground) on the DC RESET input sets the flip-flops to the desired starting conditions, and the circuit will then step through the desired states.

There are nine major lines of integrated circuits now being produced in substantial quantities. Table 4 · 1 lists these lines and gives some of the characteristics of each line. The first six IC lines in the table are called *bipolar logic* because they utilize conventional transistors in the IC packages, and the final three of the lines use what are called field effect transistors (FETs)

FIG. 4·14 Design of shift register in Fig. 4·13 using TTL. Circled numbers are pin numbers on IC containers.

and are fabricated using a metallic oxide semiconductor (MOS) technology. The bipolar logic lines are widely used for constructing configurations on circuit boards which realize highspeed logic. Generally, there are not so many gates and flip-flops in a package using bipolar logic, but these lines are fast and can be interconnected more readily than the MOS lines. The reason for this is that the bipolar logic lines use more power (primarily more current) for each gate or flip-flop and can, as a result, produce more current drive and therefore drive long cables, long wires, and, in general, more other circuits.

Associated with each gate and flip-flop in a line of integrated circuits are data concerning the gate's or flip-flop's ability to drive other circuits and be driven by other circuits. Typically, the manufacturer gives data concerning the delays through the circuit, rise and fall times for output waveforms, the circuit's ability to drive other electrical loads, circuits, and long wires or cables. The manufacturer also generally provides information on how many other inputs to gates of a similar type a given gate can drive. In its simplest form, every input to every gate and flip-flop is the same, and the manufacturer simply stipulates how many inputs can be connected to a given output. Each input is then called a *standard load* and an output is said to be able to drive,

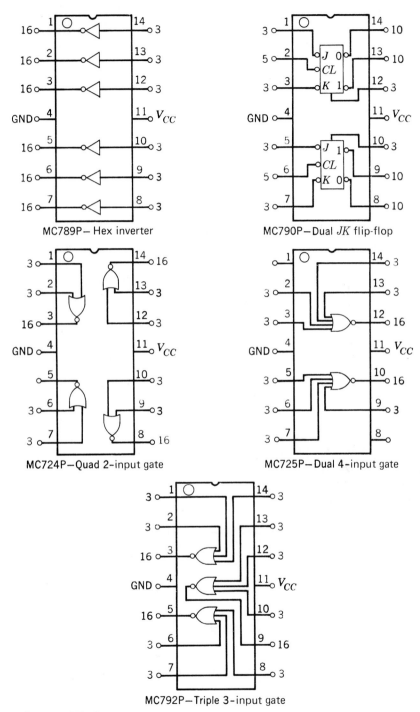

FIG. 4•15 RTL IC packages.

TABLE 4·1 INTEGRATED CIRCUIT LINES

NAME OF CIRCUIT LINE	ACRONYM	SPEED (DELAY PER GATE), ns	POWER PER GATE	GOOD FEATURES	PROBLEMS
Resistor-transistor logic	RTL	40	20 mW	Simple to manufacture and inexpensive. Easy to interconnect.	Sensitive to noise. Low fan-out ratios. Low packing density.
Diode-transistor logic	DTL	30	8 mW	Inexpensive, good noise rejection, easy to use and interconnect.	Relatively low speed. Low packing density.
High-level diode-transistor logic	HLDTL	40	15 mW	A line of DTL specially made for industrial applications because of high noise rejection. Easy to use and interconnect.	Low speed, relatively high power dissipation, low packing density.
Transistor-transistor Logic	TTL	7 (3 ns for Schottky clamped)	10 mW (20 mW for Schottky clamped)	Most popular line at present. Easy to interconnect; fast, wide selection of circuits available. MSI packages available, inexpensive.	Generates noise spikes, relatively high power dissipation, modest packing density.
Low-power transistor-transistor logic	LPTTL	30	1 mW	A low power per gate TTL developed for space and other portable applications, easy to use and interconnect.	Low speed.

Emitter-coupled logic	ECL	0.5	60 mW	Highest speed, generates little noise internally.	Difficult to interconnect. Low packing density. Difficult to cool.
p-channel metal oxide silicon	PMOS	50	0.1 mW	Low power, good packing density, easy to manufacture, inexpensive.	Slow and delicate, and has limited ability to drive lines and interface with other circuit lines.
n-channel metal oxide silicon	NMOS	20	0.1 mW	Faster than PMOS, relatively low power, good packing density, inexpensive and relatively easy to manufacture.	Has limited ability to drive lines and to interface with other circuits.
Complementary metal oxide silicon	CMOS	10	10 nW	Very low standby power required. Modest speed and packing density, reasonably priced.	Difficult to manufacture. Power consumption increases when switched at high speeds.

Note: In this table, **W** is for watts; n is for nano $= 10^{-9}$; m is for milli $= 10^{-3}$; and s is for seconds.

for instance, eight standard loads. For some circuit lines, different gates and flip-flop inputs present different loads, and so an input to a particular kind of gate might have a number such as 2 or 3 associated with it and an output drive number such as 12. Then, the designer must see that the sum of the input loads does not exceed the output drive number for a given output. As an example, Fig. 4·15 shows several RTL IC packages. Notice the numbers on the input and output pins. These give the input load for inputs and the output drive capability for outputs. The total of the input loads connected to an output must not exceed the output drive capability for that output.

The following chapter and the questions in this chapter develop this subject in more detail.

4•8 MEDIUM- AND LARGE-SCALE INTEGRATION

As has been explained, most circuits are now fabricated using the general technology of integrated circuitry. In this case the transistors, diodes, resistors, and any other components are fabricated together, using solid-state physics techniques, in a single container. In the most common technology, called *monolithic integrated circuitry,* a single semiconductor wafer is processed by photomasking, etching, diffusions, and other steps, thus producing a complete array of diodes, transistors, and resistors already interconnected to form one or more logic gates of flip-flops.

Two terms find wide use in discussing IC circuitry. When more than one or two flip-flops or a few gates are packaged in a single container, the process is called *medium-scale integration* (MSI). Notice that medium-scale integration still refers to integrated circuits, except that even more circuits are housed in a single container. There are no fixed specific rules, but generally, if more than 10 but less than 100 gates or flip-flops are in a single package, the manufacturer will refer to it as MSI.

When over 100 gates or flip-flops are manufactured in a single small container, the process is called *large-scale integration* (LSI). Some ideas of the complexity of arrays of this sort will be found in later chapters where memories and arithmetic-logic units consisting of thousands of flip-flops and gates in a single package will be studied.

Despite the various levels of integration, the circuits are surprisingly similar in principle, except that LSI tends to use a technology based on MOS, while MSI and "conventional" integrated circuits use "conventional" *npn* and sometimes *pnp* transistors fabricated on silicon chips. There are good reasons for this. MOS circuits require very small areas on a chip and use very little power, which is quite important considering the volume/complexity factor. On the other hand, as had been mentioned, conventional bipolar circuits are faster and more readily interconnected. As a result, the MOS technology is more often used for larger arrays which can be treated only as complete single units rather than on a circuit-by-circuit basis.

Figure 4·16(a) shows a typical MSI package containing a complete

BCD counter. This counter steps from 0 to 9 and then resets to 0 when X_1 (which is pin 5) is connected to clock 2 (which is pin 6). The counter is stepped each time an input clock waveform connected to clock 1 (pin 8) goes negative (on negative edges). The counter can be reset to the all 0s by connecting a 0 to the reset line (pin 13). Data from four input wires connected to Y_1, Y_2, Y_3, and Y_4 will be loaded into flip-flops X_1, X_2, X_3, and X_4, respectively, if the LOAD input is pulled down to a 0. (It is normally a 1.)

An example of gate networks in MSI packages is shown in Fig. $4 \cdot 16(b)$, which shows a *seven-segment decoder.* When decimal numbers are to be read from a digital calculator, instrument, microcomputer, etc., display devices using light-emitting diodes (LEDs) or liquid crystals are often used. Each digit of the display is formed from seven segments each consisting of one light-emitting diode or crystal which can be turned on or off. A typical arrangement is shown in Fig. $4 \cdot 16$ (c) which assigns the letters *a* through *g* to the segments. To make the digit 5, for example, segments *a, f, g, c,* and *d* are turned on. The set of digits as formed by these segments is shown in Fig. $4 \cdot 16$ (d).

The seven-segment decoder in Fig. $4 \cdot 16(b)$ can be connected to the outputs of the four flip-flops in the BCD counter in $4 \cdot 16(a)$ by connecting the X_1, X_2, X_3, and X_4 outputs from Fig. $4 \cdot 16(a)$ to the X_1, X_2, X_3, and X_4 inputs of Fig. $4 \cdot 16(b)$. If the seven outputs *a* through *f* of Fig. $4 \cdot 16(b)$ are then connected to a decimal digital display device, a counter with a decimal digit display, such as those in the familiar calculator, will be formed.

The BCD counter in Fig. $4 \cdot 16(a)$ can be extended to several digits by connecting the X_4 output from one digit to the clock 1 input of the next-highest-order digit in the counter.

The seven-segment decoder in Fig. $4 \cdot 16(b)$ has the ability to blank leading zeroes in a multidigit display, which is commonly done on calculators. Consider that a multistage BCD counter has been connected to several seven-segment decoders with one decoder per BCD counter stage. If the ripple blanking output (RBO) of each seven-segment decoder is connected to the ripple blanking input (RBI) of the seven-segment decoder of the next-higher-order digit in the counter and the ripple blanking input of the most significant digit's seven-segment decoder is connected to a 0 input, a blanking circuit will be formed. Then, for instance, in a four-stage counter the number 0014 will have the leading two 0s turned off or "blanked"; the number 0005 will be displayed as simply 5, with the 0 displays not turned on, etc. In effect, the circuit tests for a 0 value at its input and if the value is 0 and all the digits to its left are 0, then it turns off all seven segments and generates a blanking signal for the next rightmost digits light driver. The light test (LT) input can be used to test all seven segments simultaneously. Notice that making the light test input a 0 will cause all seven segments to go on.

In the MSI products of some manufacturers both a four-stage BCD counter and a seven-segment decoder are placed in the same package complete with a blanking input and output for each digit. This gives some feeling for the more complex MSI packages.

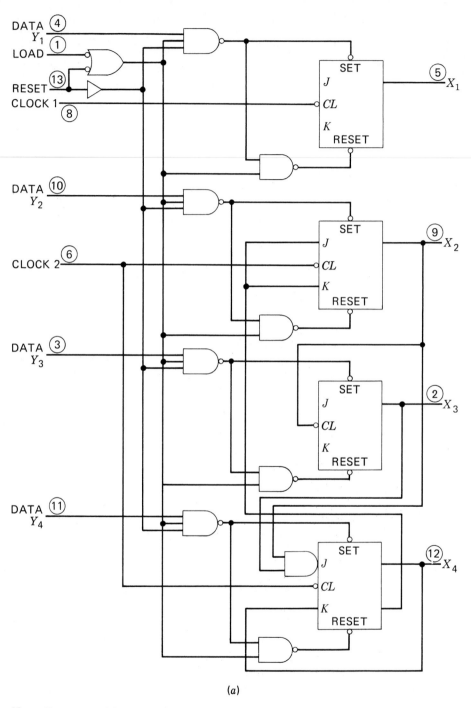

(a)

Note: Unconnected inputs are 1.

FIG. 4·16 (a) BCD counter in IC package; (b) logic diagram for seven-segment decoder; (c) designation for the seven segments; (d) numbers formed by seven segments; (e) general arrangement for connecting seven-segment decoder. (Courtesy Fairchild Semiconductor)

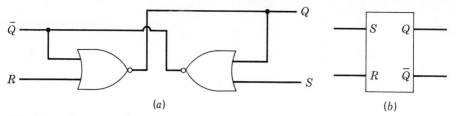

FIG. 4 • 17 RS flip-flop formed by cross-coupling NOR gates. (a) Cross-coupled NOR gates; (b) RS flip-flop corresponding to (a).

4 • 9 GATED FLIP-FLOP DESIGNS

It is important to note that flip-flops can be made from gates and, in fact, that this is a common practice. Figure 4 · 17 shows two NOR gates cross-coupled to form an RS flip-flop. The cross-coupled NOR gates in Fig. 4 · 17(a) have two inputs, S and R, and two outputs, Q and $\overline{Q}$. This configuration realizes the RS flip-flop in Fig. 4 · 17(b).

The operation of the NOR gates is as follows: Consider both S and R to be 0s. If Q is a 1, then the rightmost NOR gate has a 1 and a 0 input and its output will be a 0. This places a 0 on the $\overline{Q}$ output and two 0s at the point to the left-most NOR gate which will have a 1 output and the configuration will be stable. Similar reasoning will show that the configuration will be stable with a 1 on $\overline{Q}$ and a 0 on Q.

The S and R inputs work as follows: If a 1 is placed on the R input and a 0 on the S input, this will force the leftmost NOR gate to a 0 output and this will cause the rightmost NOR gate to have two 0s as inputs and a 1 output. The flip-flop has now been cleared with a 0 on the Q output and a 1 on the $\overline{Q}$ output. Similar reasoning will show that a 1 on the S input and a 0 on the R input will force the NOR gate to flip-flop to the 1 state with Q a 1 and $\overline{Q}$ a 0.

4 • 10 THE GATED FLIP-FLOP

Just as Fig. 4 · 17 showed that two NOR gates can be used to form an RS flip-flop, Fig. 4 · 18 shows that two NAND gates can be used to form an RS flip-flop. In this case, the inputs operate as follows. When both S and R are 1s, the flip-flop will remain in its present state, i.e., will not change states. If however, the R input goes to a 0, the NAND gate connected to R will have a 1 output regardless of the other feedback input to the NAND gate, and this will force the flip-flop to the 0 state (provided the S input is kept high or a 1).

Similar reasoning shows that making the S input a 0 will cause the NAND gate at the S input to have a 0 output, forcing the flip-flop to the 1 state (again provided the R input is kept high or 1).

If both inputs R and S are made 0s, the next state will depend on which input is returned to 1 first, and if both are returned to 1 simultaneously, the

FIG. 4 • 18 Two NAND gates used to form *RS* flip-flop.

resulting state of the flip-flop will be indeterminate. As a result, this is a "for-bidden," or "restricted," input combination.

The block diagram in Fig. 4 · 18 shows the flip-flop to be a conventional *RS* flip-flop, except that the two inputs are inverted. This is shown by the two "bubbles" at the *R* and *S* inputs. The circuit is therefore activated by *0*s, and inputs are normally at 1.

A limited form of clocked flip-flop can be formed by using four NAND gates, as shown in Fig. 4 · 19. The circuit has a *R* and a *S* input and also a clock input *CL*. This flip-flop is activated by a positive level on the clock input, and not on a positive transition. Thus, the flip-flop "takes" its input levels during the positive portion of clock signals, not changes in clock levels. To see how the circuit works, if the clock signal is at the 0 level, both NAND gates *A* and *B* will have 1 outputs, and so the NAND gate inputs to *C* and *D* will be 1 and, as before, the flip-flop will remain in its present state with either *C* or *D* on. (Both cannot be on because of the cross-coupling.)

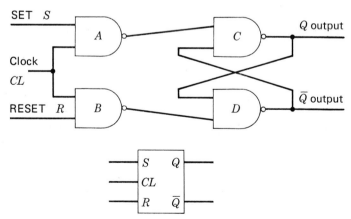

FIG. 4 • 19 Limited form of clocked flip-flop formed by using four NAND gates.

If the clock signal goes to the 1 level and both inputs R and S are at the 0 level, the NAND gate outputs of A and B will still be 1s and the flip-flop will remain in the same state.

If the R input is a 1 and the S input a 0, when the clock input goes positive (a 1), the NAND gate connected to R will have a 0 output and the NAND gate connected to S a 1 output, forcing the flip-flop consisting of C and D to the 0 state.

Similarly, a 1 at the S input and a 0 at the R input will cause the S input gate A to have a 0 output and the R input gate B a 1 output, forcing the flip-flop to the 1 state.

If both S and R are 1s and a clock pulse (1 level) occurs, the next state of the circuit is indeterminate.

A major problem with this circuit is that the R and S inputs should remain unchanged during the time the clock is a 1. This considerably limits the use of the circuit leading to more complicated circuits to give the designer more flexibility.

It is better for the flip-flop to take the state indicated by the R and S inputs at precisely the time the leading, or positive-going, edge of the clock occurs, and for the flip-flop's next state to be unaffected by changes occurring at the inputs after this time. As a result, most flip-flops in the bipolar lines are edge triggering, not level activated. We will study flip-flops of this sort in the next section.

When gated flip-flops of the kind shown in Fig. 4 · 19 are used, it is a common practice to have several different clock signals, each consisting of positive pulses but with the positive sections occurring at different times. A clock system of this type is called a *multiphase clock*.

4 • 11 THE MASTER-SLAVE FLIP-FLOP

In a computer, the flip-flops are connected, either directly or through gates, to other flip-flops, and when clock edges occur, the resulting changes in a given flip-flop's output may lead to a change in the input to another flip-flop. This race problem is generally alleviated by using flip-flops which take the input information applied at the time of the clock's change in value or at the time just before the clock's change in value. Naturally, these flip-flops are more complicated logically, but the elimination of worry about the effects of interaction between circuits had led to widespread use of such flip-flops.

To effect this "safety factor" in flip-flop operation, discrete component circuits use capacitors to store input signals and thus to "smooth out" and delay changes in input values.

Integrated circuits use pure logic to effect the same thing. The most used flip-flop design for IC flip-flops is that shown in Fig. 4 · 20. Figure 4 · 20 shows a JK flip-flop which actually consists of two flip-flops plus some gating. The two flip-flops are called "master" and "slave." In Fig. 4 · 20(a) the master

FIG. 4·20 (a) Gate arrangement for master-slave flip-flop; (b) *RS* flip-flop equivalent of (a); (c) master-slave flip-flop state table and symbol.

flip-flop is the leftmost NAND gates, and the slave flip-flop the rightmost NAND gates.

The flip-flop's output changes on the negative-going edge of the clock pulse. The basic timing is shown in Fig. 4·20(a). First, on the positive-going edge and during the positive section of the clock pulse, the master flip-flop is loaded by the two leftmost NAND gates. Then, during the negative-going edge of the clock signal, the two rightmost NAND gates load the contents of the master flip-flop into the slave flip-flop just after the two input NAND gates are disabled. This means that the master flip-flop will not change in value while the clock is low (0); so the slave remains attached to a stable flip-flop, with a value taken during the positive section of the clock pulse.

A more detailed account of the action of the flip-flop is as follows: If the clock signal is low, the two input NAND gates both have 1 outputs; so the master flip-flop does not change states since it is a NAND gate flip-flop and can be set or cleared only by 0 inputs.

At the same time, as long as the clock signal is low (a 0), the inverter causes the inputs to the E and F NAND gates to force the value of the master flip-flop into the slave flip-flop. The situation is stable. The master cannot change, and the output flip-flop is "slaved" to the master.

When the clock starts positive, however, the circuit thresholds are arranged so that first the E and F NAND gates are disabled, and the NAND gates A and B to the master flip-flop are then enabled. That is, the natural slope of the input signal plus delays and circuit values ensure that the two NAND gates E and F both have 1s at their output before any change in the master flip-flop can affect the slave flip-flop.

When the input signal is a 1, then, the master flip-flop will accept information from the J and K inputs, and the slave flip-flop is now isolated from the master and will not change states regardless of changes in the master.

The operation of the master flip-flop is according to the following rules when the clock level is a 1:

1. If both J and K are at 0 levels, the two input NAND gates will have 1 outputs and the master flip-flop will not change values.
2. If the J input is a 1 and the K input a 0, the master flip-flop will go to its 1 state, with the upper master NAND gate having a 1 output.
3. If the J input is a 0 and the K input a 1, the master flip-flop will go to its 0 state, with the upper NAND gate having a 0 output.
4. If both J and K are 1s, the master flip-flop will take the value of the complement of the slave flip-flop (i.e., a 0 if the slave is a 1 or a 1 if the slave is a 0).

When the clock signal goes negative to its 0 level, first the input NAND gates to the master flip-flop are disabled, i.e., each output goes to a 1, then the E and F NAND gates are enabled (by the inverted clock signal). This causes the state of the master flip-flop to be transferred into the slave flip-flop.

The effects of all this are shown in the next state table in Fig. 4·17(d), which indicate that the flip-flop is a *JK* flip-flop activated by a negative-going clock signal.

* 4 • 12 COUNTER DESIGN

The design of a counter to sequence through a given set of states is straight-forward, using the technique to be shown.

First, a counter table is made up listing the states to be taken. Let us assume we wish a counter to sequence as follows:

$$
\begin{array}{ccc}
\text{starting state} \rightarrow 0 & 0 & 0 \\
1 & 1 & 1 \\
1 & 0 & 1 \\
1 & 1 & 0 \\
0 & 0 & 1 \\
0 & 1 & 0 \\
0 & 0 & 0 \\
1 & 1 & 1 \\
1 & 0 & 1
\end{array}
\left.\begin{array}{l} \\ \\ \\ \\ \\ \\ \end{array}\right\} \text{this repeats}
$$

This will require three flip-flops. We first use *RS* flip-flops and name the three flip-flops C_1, C_2, and C_3. Now, each flip-flop has two inputs, an *R* input and an *S* input. We therefore give the *R* input to C_1 the name $C_1{}^R$, the *S* input to C_1 the name $C_1{}^S$, the *R* input to C_2 the name $C_2{}^R$, and so on through $C_3{}^S$.

The problem is now to derive Boolean algebra expressions for each of the six inputs to the flip-flops. To do this, we place the state table in a *counter design table* listing the three flip-flops and their states and also listing the six inputs to the flip-flops. This is shown in Fig. 4 · 21 (a).

The values for $C_1{}^S$, $C_1{}^R$, $C_2{}^S$, $C_2{}^R$, $C_3{}^S$, $C_3{}^R$ are then filled in using the following rule:

Design rule

Consider a row in the table and a specific flip-flop:

1. If the flip-flop's state is a 0 in the row and a 0 in the next row, place a 0 in the *S* input column and a d in the *R* input column for the flip-flop inputs.
2. If the flip-flop is a 1 in the row and a 1 in the next row, place a 0 in the *R* input column and a d in the *S* input column.
3. If the flip-flop is a 0 in the row and changes to a 1 in the next row, place a 1 in the *S* column and a 0 in the *R* column.
4. If the flip-flop is a 1 in the row and changes to a 0 in the next row, place a 1 in the *R* column and a 0 in the *S* column.

As an example, consider flip-flop C_1 in Fig. 4 · 21 (a). The flip-flop has value 0 in the first row and changes to a 1 in the second row. We therefore

_____

* This section can be omitted in a first reading.

place a 1 in $C_1{}^S$ in row 1 and a 0 in $C_1{}^R$ in row 1. In row 2, C_1 has value 1 and remains a 1 in row 3. We therefore fill a d in $C_1{}^S$ and a 0 in $C_1{}^R$.

A check of Fig. 4·21(a) will show how this rule works.

The design of the counter now progresses by forming a Boolean algebra expression from this table for $C_1{}^S$, $C_1{}^R$, $C_2{}^S$, $C_2{}^R$, $C_3{}^S$, $C_3{}^R$ and then minimizing each expression. This is shown in Fig. 4·21(b). Notice that any unused counter states can be included as d's in the map as they are don't-cares because the counter never uses them.

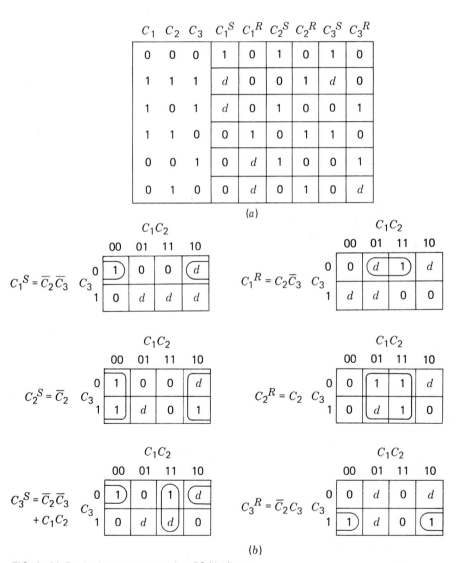

C_1	C_2	C_3	$C_1{}^S$	$C_1{}^R$	$C_2{}^S$	$C_2{}^R$	$C_3{}^S$	$C_3{}^R$
0	0	0	1	0	1	0	1	0
1	1	1	d	0	0	1	d	0
1	0	1	d	0	1	0	0	1
1	1	0	0	1	0	1	1	0
0	0	1	0	d	1	0	0	1
0	1	0	0	d	0	1	0	d

(a)

FIG. 4·21 Designing a counter using *RS* flip-flops.

CLOCK
FIG. 4 • 22 Counter with *RS* flip-flops.

The final step is to draw the block diagram for the counter using the minimal expressions. The final design for this counter is shown in Fig. 4 · 22.

When *JK* flip-flops are used, the technique is much the same except the inputs are $C_1{}^J$, $C_1{}^K$, $C_2{}^J$, $C_2{}^K$, $C_3{}^J$, $C_3{}^K$. The design rule is then

Design rule

For a given flip-flop in a selected row, the *J* and *K* inputs to the flip-flop are filled in as follows:

1. If the flip-flop is a 0 in the row and remains a 0 in the next row, place a 0 in the *J* input column and a d in the *K* input column.
2. If the flip-flop is a 1 in the row and remains a 1 in the next row, place a 0 in the *K* input column and a d in the *J* input column.
3. If the flip-flop is a 0 in the row and changes to a 1 in the next row, place a 1 in the *J* input column and a d in the *K* input column.
4. If the flip-flop is a 1 in the row and changes to a 0 in the next row, place a d in the *J* input column and a 1 in the *K* input column.

The design procedure again procedes by filling in the design table, forming the Boolean algebra expressions and minimizing them, and finally drawing the block diagram for the counter. Any unused combinations can again be

C_1	C_2	C_3	C_1^J	C_1^K	C_2^J	C_2^K	C_3^J	C_3^K
0	0	0	1	d	1	d	1	d
1	1	1	d	0	d	1	d	0
1	0	1	d	0	1	d	d	1
1	1	0	d	1	d	1	1	d
0	0	1	0	d	1	d	d	1
0	1	0	0	d	d	1	0	d

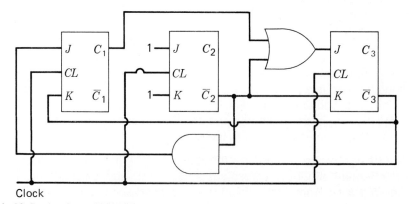

FIG. 4·23 Design for a *JK* flip-flop counter.

given d values in the map to aid in minimizing. A complete design for the counter previously designed is shown in Fig. 4·23. Notice this $\overline{JK}$ flip-flop requires fewer gates than the RS design and this will generally be the case, although sometimes the diagram will be the same.

QUESTIONS

1. Draw a set of waveforms for S and R and X and $\overline{X}$ (as in Fig. 4·2) so that the flip-flop in Fig. 4·1 will have the output signals 0011010 on the 1 output line.

2. If the $\overline{X}$ output of flip-flop X is connected to an inverter, the inverter's output will always be the same as the X output of the flip-flop. True or false. Why?

3. Draw a set of waveforms for S and R (as in Fig. 4·2) so that the flip-flop in Fig. 4·1 will have the output signals 101110001 on the output line.

4. If the AND gate connected to the R input of X_1 in Fig. 4·3 fails so that its output is always 0, we would expect, after a few transfers, that X_1 would always be in the _____ state. Why?

5. Draw a set of waveforms as in Fig. 4·5(d) for the flip-flop in Fig. 4·5(b) so that the flip-flop will have the output signals 0010110 on its output line.

6. Draw a set of waveforms as in Fig. 4·5(c) for the flip-flop in Fig. 4·5(a) so that the flip-flop will have the output signals 10111001 on its 1 output line.

7. Draw an input waveform as in Fig. 4·6 so that X_3 will have the output signal 000011010 if X_1, X_2, and X_3 are started in the 0 state.

8. In Fig. 4·6, if flip-flop X_2 "sticks" (that is, fails) in its 1 state, X_3 will have a 1 output after (a) clock pulse 1, (b) clock pulse 2, (c) clock pulse 3, and for each clock pulse thereafter.

9. The binary counter in Fig. 4·7 uses flip-flops which act on positive transitions. Draw a block diagram of a binary counter with "bubbles" on the CL inputs (that is, with flip-flops which act on *negative*-going clock, or CL, inputs).

10. If the X_3 line (the output of X_3) is connected to the INPUT line in Fig. 4·6, a *ring counter* is formed. If this circuit is started with $X_1 = 0$, $X_2 = 1$, and $X_3 = 1$, draw the waveform at X_1, X_2, and X_3 for six clock pulses.

11. Redraw Fig. 4·7 as it is but place bubbles on each CL input to X_1, X_2, and X_3 [that is, make the same drawing but use the flip-flop in Fig. 4·5(b) instead of that in 4·5(a)]. Redraw the waveforms in Fig. 4·7 for this circuit.

12. Does the counter in Question 11 count up or down?

13. Make a single change in Fig. 4·7 by connecting the output of flip-flop X_2 to the CL input of X_3 instead of the $\overline{X}_2$ output of X_2. Now redraw the waveforms in Fig. 4·7 for this changed configuration.

14. After answering Question 13, using the flip-flop in Fig. 4·5(a), design a counter which counts as follows:

X_3	X_2	X_1
0	0	0
0	1	1
0	1	0
1	0	1
1	0	0
1	1	1
1	1	0
0	0	1
0	0	0
0	1	1
0	1	0
1	0	1
.	.	.

15. After answering Question 13, using only the flip-flop in Fig. 4·5(a), design a counter which counts as follows:

X_3	X_2	X_1
0	0	0
1	1	1
1	1	0
1	0	1
1	0	0
0	1	1
0	1	0
0	0	1
0	0	0
1	1	1

This counter counts *down*. Figure 4·7 counts *up*.

16. Draw a clock waveform and waveforms for the output of the AND gate connected to the S input of X_1, the R input of X_2, and the 1 output of X_1, X_2, and X_3 for Fig. 4·8.

17. In Fig. 4·10(a), when the ENABLE line is a 1, the counter counts at the occurrence of a negative-going clock edge. Draw the output waveforms for FF0, FF1, and FF2 for these waveforms. Start the flip-flops at 0.

18. For Fig. 4·10(*b*) draw up enable, down enable, and clock waveforms so that the counter starts at 000 and counts as follows:

X_3	X_2	X_1
0	0	0
0	0	1
0	1	0
0	1	1
1	0	0
0	1	1
0	1	0
0	1	1

19. Suppose the AND gate in Fig. 4·11(*a*) fails so that its output is always a 1. Write the sequence or show the waveform through which this counter will go in response to clock signals.

20. Suppose the AND gate's output in Fig. 4·11(*a*) is connected to the *K* input of X_4 instead of the *J* input. How will the computer count?

21. For Fig. 4·11(*b*), the carry-out from block 1 to block 2 goes from 1 to 0 every _____ clock pulses. The carry-out from block 3 to block 4 goes from 1 to 0 every _____ clock pulses.

22. (*a*) If we replace block 2 in Fig. 4·11(*b*) with the four-stage ripple counter in Fig. 4·10(*a*), using the 1 output of FF3 in that counter as the carry-out line, the carry-out line from block 2 will go from 1 to 0 after how many clock pulses?

(*b*) For the configuration in Question 22(*a*), after how many clock pulses will the carry-out from block 2 go from 0 to 1?

23. Using the circuits in Fig. 4·12, design a gated-clocked binary counter.

24. Using the circuits in Fig. 4·12, design a BCD counter.

25. Using the circuits in Fig. 4·12, design a gating network with inputs *A*, *B*, and *C* which will have output 1 when $\overline{A}B\overline{C}$ or $A\overline{B}\overline{C}$ are 1s.

26. Design a BCD counter using the flip-flops in Fig. 4·12.

27. The inputs to the NOR gates in Fig. 4·15 have 0s on them when not connected. Does connecting only two inputs of a four-input NOR gate give a gate which acts as a two-input gate? Explain your answer. *Note:* Inputs to TTL gates, such as in Fig. 4·12, which are left unconnected, automatically act as if they have 1s on them.

28. Does a three-input NAND gate, as in Fig. 4·12, act as a two-input gate would if only two inputs were used? Explain your answer.

29. Design the counter in Fig. 4·13 using the blocks in Fig. 4·15.

30. Give the states of the flip-flops in the following circuit after each of the first five clock signals (pulses) are applied. The circuit is started in the state $A_1 = 0$, $A_2 = 0$, $A_3 = 1$.

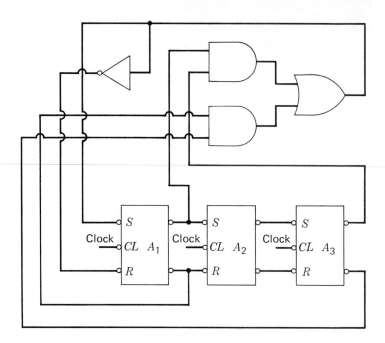

31. Redesign the following circuit using only *RS* flip-flops and NOR gates.

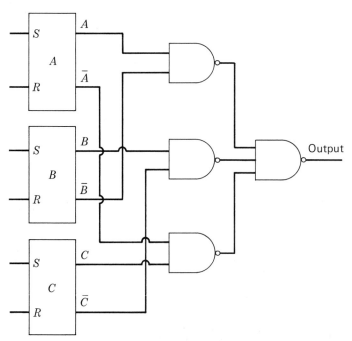

32. The gate block in the following circuit is an "equal to" combinational network realizing the Boolean function $\overline{X}_3\overline{X}_2 + X_3X_2$. If this set of three flip-flops is started in $X_1 = 1$, $X_2 = 0$, and $X_3 = 0$, what will the sequence of internal states be? As a start, the first three states can be listed as follows

X_1	X_2	X_3	
1	0	0	
1	1	0	after first clock pulse
0	1	1	after second clock pulse
.	.	.	(you are to continue this list)

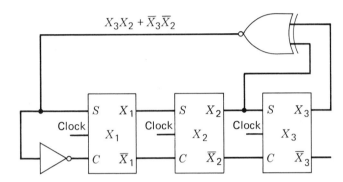

$$X_3X_2 + \overline{X}_3\overline{X}_2$$

33. The following circuit is started in $C_2 = 1$ and $C_2 = 0$. The circuit divides the number of positive-going input edges (positive pulses) by what number? (That is, every _____ input pulses the output will return to 0). Justify your answer.

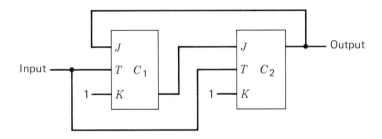

34. In Fig. 4·20, if the feedback connection from the C NAND gate output to the input of the D NAND gate is broken (open), in what state will we probably find the flip-flop?

35. In Fig. 4·20, why are E and F enabled at a lower level than A and B?

36. In Fig. 4·20, write 0s and 1s for all gate inputs and outputs when the CL input is 1, J is a 1, K is a 1, and the flip-flop is in the 1 state.

37. Using your result from Question 36, explain how the flip-flop in Fig. 4·19 complements when J and K are 1s and a negative edge appears.

38. The following sequence is to be realized by a counter consisting of three RS flip-flops. Use AND and OR gates in your design.

	A_1	A_2	A_3
	0	0	0	← starting state
	0	1	0
Sequence repeats after this segment	0	1	1
	0	0	1
	1	0	0
	1	1	0
	0	0	0
	.	.	.

39. Design a counter using only *JK* flip-flops, AND gates, and OR gates which counts in the following sequence.

0	0	0
0	1	0
0	1	1
1	0	0
0	0	0
0	1	0
0	1	1
1	0	0
0	0	0

this repeats

40. Design a counter using three *JK* flip-flops X_1, X_2, and X_3, and whatever gates you would like, which counts as follows

X_1	X_2	X_3	
0	0	0	starting state
0	1	1	after first clock pulse
0	1	0	after second clock pulse
1	1	1	after third clock pulse
1	0	1	after fourth clock pulse
0	0	0	after fifth clock pulse
0	1	1	
0	1	0	

41. The following sequence is to be realized by a counter consisting of three *JK* flip-flops. Use AND and OR gates in your design.

	A_1	A_2	A_3	
	0	0	0	starting state
	0	1	1	
Sequence repeats after this segment	0	1	0	
	0	0	1	
	1	0	1	
	1	1	0	
	0	0	0	
	.	.	.	

42. Design a counter using three *JK* flip-flops X_1, X_2, and X_3 and whatever gates you would like, which counts as follows

X_1	X_2	X_3	
0	0	0	starting state
0	1	1	after first clock pulse
0	1	0	after second clock pulse
1	1	1	after third clock pulse
1	0	1	after fourth clock pulse
0	0	0	after fifth clock pulse
0	1	1	
0	1	0	

43. The NAND gate flip-flop in Fig. 4·18 will have what outputs on the 0 and 1 lines if both the SET and RESET are made 0s?

44. If the *S* and *R* inputs to Fig. 4·18 are both made 0s and the *S* is made a 1 followed by *R*, what will be the resulting state of the flip-flop?

5
DIGITAL
CIRCUITS

Electronics circuitry and electronic devices have undergone vast improvements since the digital computer was first introduced. The large arrays of vacuum tubes with their glass shells and heated filaments have been squeezed into small plastic integrated circuit (IC) containers by industrious solid-state physicists and electronic circuit designers. Even the past 10 years has brought a significant change, and smaller, faster, less expensive devices and circuits are continually being introduced. Basic changes are not quite so rapid, however, and most of the improvements are now due to refinements of existing technology rather than radical new ideas. It should be noted, though, that the digital integrated electronics circuit industry is the largest segment of the electronics industry, and descriptions of new designs and improvements on old designs continue to fill the pages of the computer journals.

The study of the actual circuits used in electronic computers — from microcomputers to the largest systems — centers around IC technology. Further, the integrated circuits now in general use are generally variations of several basic circuit designs. In fact, it is safe to say that over 95 percent of all computers now contain circuits using the basic circuits in Table 4 · 1.

The intent of this chapter is first to explain some of the circuit principles which relate to all digital circuits and then to examine, one at a time, the major circuit technologies. Basic facts about the general properties of each circuit technology are given, and some of the advantages and disadvantages of each type of circuit are pointed out. No attempt is made to be comprehensive; only representative circuits have been selected and explained.

It is possible to omit this chapter on a first reading without loss of continuity, and it is also possible to sample selected sections and examine some, but not all, of the circuit lines. However, the author feels that an overview of this subject matter is well worth the effort involved, and having spent many hours designing circuits, has strong personal feelings concerning the value of this material. He also realizes, however, that this subject is often taught in other courses and that time limitations may not permit inclusion of the material.

5•1 COMPUTER CIRCUITS

Although a modern electronic computer is composed of a large number of electronic components, an entire machine will usually contain only a few types of basic circuits. The current theory of computer construction dictates the use of a few basic "blocks" which are used over and over. Construction of this sort greatly simplifies the design of the machines, increases reliability — since only a few well-tested circuits are used — and makes maintenance of machines easier and faster. The circuits used in these blocks are simple in principle. They are simpler, for instance, than most of the circuits used in modern radio and television sets. There are several types of circuits: circuits which perform logical operations on input signals; storage elements, such as flip-flops, which store bits of information; and accessory circuits, such as co-axial line drivers, neon-light indicator circuits, etc.

The circuits which will be described have been classified according to the functions they perform. For instance, following the description of diode and transistor characteristics, the first type of circuit to be described is the diode AND gate. This is followed by a diode-and-transistor AND gate. Then, finally, an all-transistor AND gate is described. The intent here is, therefore, to describe the function each circuit performs and how one circuit differs from another and, at the same time, to explain the manner in which the circuits function.

No attempt has been made to describe every circuit configuration now in use; only representative circuits of each type are included in the discussion.

5•2 CHARACTERISTICS OF DIODES AND TRANSISTORS USED IN SWITCHING CIRCUITS

Before analyzing logical circuits, we shall briefly describe the general characteristics of junction transistors and diodes when used as switching devices. This does not imply that the characteristics of these devices in switching circuits are radically different from those used in audio or other circuitry; however, most general introductions to transistors treat them as linear amplifying devices. When transistors are used in switching circuits, they are generally operated at or near the extremes of their operating points. That is, they are quite often operated either in a "cutoff" or a "saturated" condition. Therefore some of the characteristics which are most important to the computer circuit are of less importance in other fields.

Also, no attempt will be made to explain the physics of junction semiconductor devices. Semiconductor physics and detailed analysis of the operating characteristics of junction devices are so interwoven with the manufacturing techniques, the geometry of the junctions, and many other considerations that the subject has grown into a highly specialized (and very fascinating) field, which is treated in detail in other books. For our purposes, and for the purposes of most users of circuit devices, the operational characteristics of these devices is what is important, and we shall limit discussion to these operational characteristics.

The characteristics of semiconductor diodes will first be briefly noted. A semiconductor diode is made of two pieces of semiconductor material† of different types joined together. One type of semiconductor material is called *p-type* material, and the other *n-type* material [refer to Fig. 5·1(a)].‡ When two differing types of semiconductor material are joined together, a *semiconductor junction* is formed, and a single junction is also called a *diode*. In Fig. 5·1(a) the *p*-type material is referred to as the *anode* of the diode and the *n*-type material is called the *cathode* of the diode. Figure 5·1(a) also shows the schematic symbol for the diode.

A study of semiconductor, or solid-state, devices would explain the physical internal workings of the diode. However, our sole interest here is to view the diode as a component in electronic switching circuits; so we will examine the diode from the viewpoint of its electrical characteristics only. When we apply an electric voltage, possibly through a resistor as in Fig. 5·1(b), so that the anode of the diode is positive with respect to the cathode, the diode is said to be *forward biased*. A diode which is forward biased will conduct current rather freely. (*Conventional current* will be used in our discussion; conventional current flows from positive to negative.)

Figure 5·1(c) shows a typical characteristic curve for a semiconductor germanium diode and silicon diode. Most of the diodes in computer use are silicon diodes. Notice that, when forward biased, the silicon diode drops on the order of 0.7 V.§ Notice that the forward-biased region on the graph lies to the right of the ordinate of the graph.

When the cathode of a diode is positive with respect to the anode, the diode is said to be *reversed biased,* and it will present a very high resistance to current flow [refer to Fig. 5·1(b) and (c)]. This ranges from tens to hundreds of megohms.¶

A diode may therefore be thought of as a kind of electronic switch which is

---

† A semiconductor has a conductivity roughly halfway between those of metals, which are "good" conductors, and insulators, which conduct poorly.

‡ *n*-type material has an excess of negative current carriers (electrons), while *p*-type material has an excess of positive current carriers (holes). Thus current flows readily when the *p*-type material is positive and the *n*-type material negative. Alternatively, very little current flows when the *p*-type material is negative and the *n*-type material is positive.

§ Provided 1 mA or more of current flows (1 mA = 1 milliampere, or 1×10^{-3} A).

¶ The part of the curve for silicon diodes which is below the 0 current level is somewhat distorted since a diode actually passes less than a few hundred nanoamperes when reverse biased (1 N = 10^{-9} A).

FIG. 5•1 Diode symbol and characteristics.

closed (freely passes current) when forward biased and open (passes almost no current) when reverse biased.

The most commonly used transistors in computer circuits are *junction transistors,* constructed of either a piece of *n* material between two pieces of *p* material or a piece of *p* material between two pieces of *n* material. The first of these is called a *pnp* transistor, and the second an *npn* transistor. Figure 5·2(*a*) and (*b*) shows this. The pieces of *n* and *p* material are named; for the *pnp* transistor the "middle" piece is *n*-type and is called the *base,* while the two *p*-type pieces are called the *collector* and *emitter* and further identified with the schematic symbols shown in Fig. 5·2(*a*). For the *npn* transistor, the *p*-type material is the base, and the two pieces of *n*-type material the emitter and collector.

A transistor's operating characteristics are generally studied by connect-

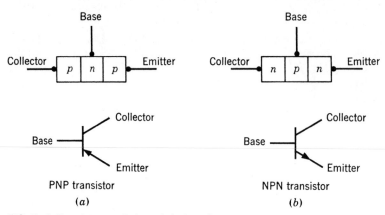

FIG. 5 • 2 Transistor symbols and designations.

ing the transistor in a circuit, varying the input currents and voltages, and plot-
ting the resulting output currents and voltages.

Figure $5 \cdot 3$ shows an *npn* transistor in a circuit with the emitter grounded.
The currents and voltages in the circuit are identified as follows: The current
into the base of the transistor is called I_b; the current *into* the collector is
called I_c; the current *into* the emitter is called I_e; the voltage of the collector
is called V_{ce} (this is the voltage between the collector and the emitter); the
voltage at the base is called V_{be} (the voltage between base and emitter).

In this configuration, the transistor can be operated in three modes: (1)
active region, (2) *saturated,* and (3) *cutoff.*

First let us define these terms, and then examine the transistor's characteristics in each region of operation.

1. *Active*   The *npn* transistor in Fig. $5 \cdot 3(a)$ is in the *active region* when
   current flows into the base, that is, when I_b is positive and when V_{ce} is
   more positive than V_{be} (the collector is more positive than the base).
2. *Saturated*   The *npn* transistor in Fig. $5 \cdot 3(a)$ is in the *saturated region*
   when positive current flows into the base (I_b is positive) and when V_{ce} is
   equal to or less than V_{be} (the collector is less positive than the base).
3. *Cutoff*   The *npn* transistor is said to be *cut off* when either no current flows
   into the base or when current flows out of the base (when I_b is either 0 or
   negative).

Active   When transistors are used in television or radio circuits, they are
most often operated in the active region, because a small change in base
current then causes a large change in collector current, thus making it possible to amplify the input. To examine this, a set of curves is presented in
Fig. $5 \cdot 3(b)$ for a widely used transistor, the 2N706.

To see an example of the current gain, notice that if, in Fig. $5 \cdot 3(b)$, the
voltage V_{ce} is held at 8 V and I_b, the base current, is at 0.45 mA, then I_c, the
collector current, will be about 15 mA. If I_b is changed to 0.85 mA, a change of

0.4 mA, I_c changes to 30 mA, a change of 10 mA. Thus the collector current has changed more than the base current by a factor of 30.

In the active region, the base-emitter junction is forward biased and the base-collector junction is reverse biased. This means that current flows easily from base to emitter but that base-to-collector current is small. As current is increased through the base-emitter junction, however, this stimulates current flow through the base from the collector to the emitter. The fact that a small

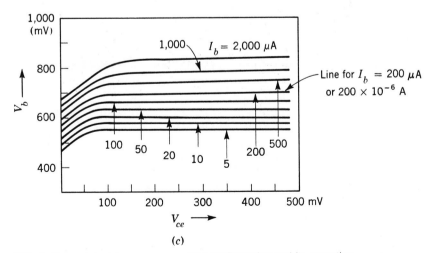

FIG. 5•3 *npn*-transistor common-emitter configuration and its operation.

change in base current causes a large change in current from the collector to the emitter is the "secret" of the transistor's usefulness as an amplifier. The base of a transistor is made very thin, which encourages the flow of current through the base (from collector to emitter), once the base area begins to "break down" (that is, to permit current flow) due to the current from base to emitter. Notice that this base-emitter current also controls the collector-emitter current.

Saturated When the input current I_b is positive but V_{ce} is less than V_{be}, then the base-collector and the base-emitter junctions will both be forward biased and the transistor will "look like" two forward-biased diodes. Current will flow freely in both the base and the base-collector junctions.†

Cutoff When no current or negative current flows into the base (that is, V_{be} is negative), the transistor is cut off and virtually no current flows in the collector ($I_c = 0$). This can be seen in Fig. 5·3(b), for with 0.25 mA into the base, less than 3 mA will flow in the collector, and for I_b equal to 0, virtually no current flows in the collector ($I_c = 0$).‡ If V_{be} is negative (the base is negative with respect to the emitter), both junctions of the transistor will be reverse biased and virtually no current will flow in the circuit (I_c and I_b will be 0).

Let us now examine the operation of the circuit in Fig. 5·4(a). A load resistor of 500 Ω has been added to the collector circuit, and an input resistor of 2,000 Ω to the base circuit. The plot of an input-output signal for this circuit is shown in Fig. 5·4(b).

In Fig. 5·4(b) the input starts at 0 V, so that no base current flows in the transistor and it is cut off. As a result, the output is at +5 V, since no current flows in the collector and no voltage is dropped across $R2$.

As the input starts positive, current begins to flow into the base and the transistor passes into the active region. This causes current to flow in the collector circuit, and this current flows through resistor $R2$, and so the output begins to fall. At some point the output will fall below the voltage at the base, which will be held at about 0.8 V—the base-emitter junction is well forward biased by the current through the resistor $R1$—and the transistor will be saturated.

When the voltage at the input goes back to 0 V, the process is reversed; the transistor passes from saturation through the active region and is again cut off.

Notice that the output from the transistor is an "inverted" near-replica of the input; so the circuit is generally called an *inverter*.

Note: One general comment should be made. An npn transistor is, strictly

---

† Some curves for a saturated transistor are shown in Fig. 5·3(c). Notice that the collector voltages are less than the base voltages. Also notice that the base voltages are very "flat" for wide ranges of collector voltage. For instance, with a base current I_b of 1,000 μA (microampere) (1 μA = 10^{-6} A), the base voltage will be about 0.75 V when the collector is from 0.1 to 0.5 V.

‡ The slight "turnup" in the ends of the curves in Fig. 5·3(b) is due to junction breakdown at higher voltages. The transistor is to be operated with collector voltage of less than +10 V.

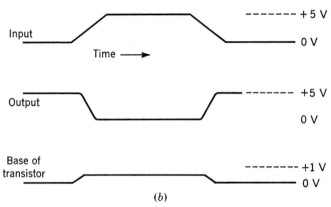

FIG. 5·4 The transistor inverter. (a) Inverter circuit; (b) waveforms for inverter circuit.

speaking, "cut off" when the base current is 0 or negative, which means, for our circuits, when the base voltage V_{be} is 0 or negative. In general practice, a transistor is said to be cut off when "negligible" current flows. This is, of course, not precise, nor can it be made so. What is meant is that so little current flows into the base that virtually no current flows in the collector circuit.

The operation of a *pnp* transistor is essentially the same as that of the *npn* transistor, except that all the polarities discussed are reversed. For instance, the *pnp* transistor is cut off when I_b is positive or into the base. The voltage V_{ce} is made negative for *pnp* transistors in the common-base circuit.

For completeness, a *pnp* transistor and its characteristics are shown in Table 5·1. The currents I_e and I_c are as before, but since the base and not the emitter is grounded, the voltages are measured from emitter to base (and not from base to emitter) and from collector to base (and not emitter to collector), and so are called V_{eb} and V_{cb}. Table 5·1 also shows several curves for values of emitter currents. Some characteristics of the active, cutoff, and saturated regions are also noted.

TABLE 5·1 *pnp* TRANSISTOR CHARACTERISTICS FOR A COMMON-BASE CIRCUIT

Collector breakdown voltage

DEFINITIONS

1 *Cutoff* The *pnp* transistor is defined as being "cut off" when the input current flowing from the emitter (I_e) of the transistor is 0, or when current flows from the emitter, and when the collector potential is negative with respect to the base. The cutoff region in the figure above lies to the right of the curve plotted for an emitter current equal to 0. This is designated as Region I on the figure, and extends vertically up to the x axis of the graph. The important thing to note is that the emitter-base junction is reverse biased. For the *pnp* transistor this means that the base is positive with respect to the emitter. (For the *npn* transistor, the base was negative.)

2 *Active* In this region the *pnp* transistor has a normal, or forward, emitter-to-base bias (the emitter is positive with respect to the base), and the collector is negative with respect to the base. The active region is designated as Region II in the figure. This is the normal operating region for the transistor, and most transistor amplifiers operate in this region.

3 *Saturation* When the collector is positive with respect to the base, the transistor is said to be *saturated*. This is Region III in the above figure.

CHARACTERISTICS OF THE THREE MODES OF OPERATION

The transistor exhibits different input and output characteristics in each of the three regions. Referring again to the figure, the three regions of operation have the following characteristics:

1 When the *pnp* transistor is cut off, the emitter and collector are both negative with respect to the base. As a result, both the emitter and collector appear as large resistances, and little current flows from either the collector or emitter. Some reverse current will flow, however, because of leakage current across

the surface and reverse current through the junction.* The magnitude of this current varies with the voltage across the junction and the temperature of the transistor, but generally lies somewhere between 1 to 100 nA for silicon transistors.

2 In the active region, the transistor exhibits all the characteristics common to signal amplifier circuits. The transistor possesses a power gain from input to output in this region, and the current which flows in the collector circuit is a function of the current into the emitter. The current gain from the emitter to the collector is designated as α, the ratio of small change in the emitter current to the resulting change in the collector current $\Delta I_c / \Delta I_e$, with the collector voltage held constant. This value generally lies between 0.9 and 0.99 for junction transistors. For a particular transistor, the value of α varies somewhat throughout the active region.†

If the positive collector voltage is increased beyond a certain point, known as the *breakdown voltage*, the collector current will increase rapidly with virtually no change in collector voltage. This may be caused either by avalanche of the minority carriers or by another phenomenon, known as *punchthrough*, which occurs when the collector space charge region extends to the emitter. Care is generally taken to see that transistors are not operated with voltages which will cause breakdown.

3 When the *pnp* transistor is saturated, both the emitter and collector are positive (forward biased) with respect to the base, and both the emitter-base and collector-base junctions present small resistance to current flow.

---

* The leakage current is often designated as "cutoff current" and identified as I_{co}.
† Notice that $1/1 - \alpha$ gives the current gain from base to collector.

5·3 THE EMITTER FOLLOWER

There are three transistor configurations which produce a power gain from input to output. The common-base and common-emitter configurations are shown in Fig. 5·3 and Table 5·1; the third configuration is the *common collector* shown in Fig. 5·5. In actual practice, the common collector is connected and used as in Fig. 5·5(a) and (b), which shows a single resistor at the emitter, an input to the base, and an output from the emitter. In this form the circuit is called an *emitter follower*, for as long as the input level does not exceed $+V$ or $-V$, the output at the emitter will be an exact replica of the input. That is, the emitter *follows* the base, except for a slight shift in level. (For the *npn* circuit the shift is *down* about 0.5 V, and for the *pnp up* about 0.5 V.) Because of its ability to simply follow the input signal level, the emitter follower is generally used to provide current gain. The emitter follower is operated in the active region. The characteristics of the emitter follower are:

1. The voltage gain of the circuit is approximately unity. A change of 3 V in the input voltage will cause a change of approximately 3 V at the output.
2. The dc output level from the emitter follower is approximately equal to the dc input level. If the input to the base of an emitter follower is a dc level of +3 V and the transistor is operating in the active region, the output level at the emitter will also be at approximately +3 V dc. For the circuit in Fig. 5·5(a), the output level at the emitter will be slightly negative with

FIG. 5•5 The emitter follower. (a) *npn* emitter follower; (b) *pnp* emitter follower; (c) common-collector configuration.

respect to the base because of the base-emitter junction drop, and the output dc level will effectively "follow" the input level.

3. The current gain of the emitter follower is greater than unity. For most transistors, the current gain through the emitter follower will be greater than 25. Since the voltage gain of the circuit is approximately unity and the current gain is greater than unity, the emitter follower has power gain.

4. The output of the emitter follower is *in phase,* or follows the input. This applies to both input and output currents and input and output voltages.

5. The emitter follower has a high input resistance and a low output resistance. (The input resistance is usually at least of an order of magnitude greater than the load resistance at the emitter.)

5•4 THE AND GATE

Since the information processed by a digital computer is represented by sets of electric signals which may be considered to represent binary values, a given signal may be thought of as representing either a 0 or a 1. Assume that a positive dc voltage represents a 1, and a negative voltage a 0. In this case, the function of an AND gate with two inputs is to produce a positive output signal (a 1) only when both of the inputs are positive (1s). If the AND gate has three inputs, the output will be positive only when all three of the inputs are positive (in all other cases the output level will be negative, representing a 0).

In most systems, 0s and 1s are represented by a positive dc signal (representing a 1) or a 0 V dc signal (representing a 0). The function of the AND gate circuit is then to produce a positive dc signal at its output only when a positive dc signal is applied to all the inputs to the circuit simultaneously. If the inputs to the circuit are labeled X, Y, and Z, the circuit will produce a positive dc signal only when a positive dc signal is simultaneously applied to X AND Y AND Z.

5•5 THE DIODE AND CIRCUIT

Figure 5·6 illustrates a two-input diode AND gate. In the circuit illustrated, a 0 V dc level represents a binary 0 and a +3 V signal a binary 1. If both inputs are at 0 V, both of the diodes will be forward biased and the output will be

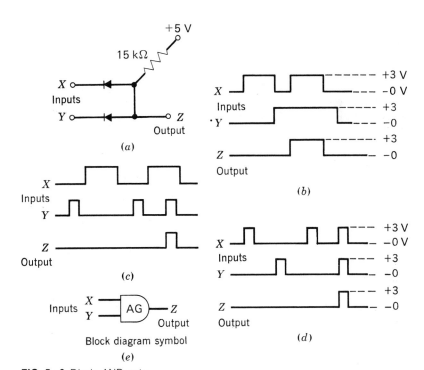

FIG. 5•6 Diode AND gate.

held at 0 V by the diodes. The total voltage drop across the resistor will be 5 V.†

If the X input line goes to 3 V and the Y input remains at 0 V, the diode connected to the Y input will still be forward biased, and the output will remain at 0 volts dc. (Notice that in this case the X-input diode will be reverse biased and 3 V will be dropped across the diode.) If the input at Y goes to +3 V and X remains at 0 V, the output will be at 0 V dc.

When the inputs at X and Y both go to the +3 V level, the output level will then rise to +3 V and the output will represent a 1.

The responses of the diode AND gate to several types of inputs are illlustrated in Fig. 5·6. The circuit in Fig. 5·6 could have more than two inputs. In this case, a diode would be required for each input, and each additional diode would be connected just as the two diodes are connected in the figure. If four diodes are connected as shown in Fig. 5·6, the output will rise to the +3 V signal level only when the input signals to all four diodes are positive. There is a practical limit to the number of diodes which can be connected in this manner, however, due to the fact that the diodes do not actually have an infinite back resistance or zero forward resistance. With a large number of inputs, the finite forward and back resistances of the diodes will cause varying output levels, depending on the state of the inputs.

5•6 THE OR GATE

The OR gate has the property that a signal representing a 1 will appear at the output if any one of the inputs represents a 1. Figure 5·7 illustrates a diode OR gate circuit. There are two inputs to the circuit (X and Y) and one output. The input signals to the circuit consist of 0 V signals representing 0s, and +3 V signals representing 1s. If both of the inputs to the circuit are at 0 V dc, both diodes will be forward biased and the output of the circuit will be at 0 V dc, representing a 0. If either of the inputs to the circuit rises to +3 V dc, the diode at this input will be forward biased and the output will rise to +3 V, representing a 1. The diode at the input remaining at 0 V will then be reverse biased by the +3 V signal at the output. This circuit has the property that the output level will be at the level of the most positive input.

If both of the inputs to the circuit rise to +3 V, the output will again be at +3 V. (This circuit is sometimes referred to as an *inclusive* OR circuit, because the output is a 1 when both inputs are 1s.)

More inputs may be added to the circuit illustrated in Fig. 5·7. A diode is then required for each input. If any one or any combination of the inputs rises to the +3 V level, the output will be at +3 V.

As in the case of the diode AND gate, it is not practical to have too many

---

† We have assumed, for simplicity of explanation, that no voltage is dropped across a forward-biased diode. In fact, for silicon diodes, the output would be at approximately +0.7 V and the drop across the resistor about 4.3 V.

Block diagram symbol for OR gate

FIG. 5•7 Diode OR gate.

inputs to the circuit because the forward and back resistances of the diodes are finite, and different combinations of input signals will then cause different signal levels at the outputs.

The logical block diagram symbol used for the OR gate is also illustrated in Fig. 5·7.

If the convention that a positive signal represents a 1 and a negative signal a 0 is reversed, the circuit of Fig. 5·7 will then perform the AND function. Also notice that if the AND gate which is illustrated in Fig. 5·6 has negative inputs representing 1s and positive input signals representing 0s, the circuit will then perform the OR function. To avoid confusion, the circuit in Fig. 5·7 is sometimes referred to as a *positive* OR gate or as a *negative* AND gate. The circuit in Fig. 5·6 would then be referred to as a *positive* AND gate or a *negative* OR gate. Unless otherwise noted, we will consider relatively positive signals to represent 1s and relatively negative signals to represent 0s. The term AND gate will then refer to a positive AND gate, such as the one in Fig. 5·6, and an OR gate will mean a positive OR gate, such as that in Fig. 5·7.

5•7 THE INVERTER CIRCUIT

The circuit shown in Fig. 5·8 is from an early and once very popular line of integrated circuits called RTL (resistor-transistor logic) circuits. These circuits are manufactured by almost every major IC manufacturer and have the

FIG. 5·8 RTL inverter.

advantage of being simple and quite inexpensive. Binary 0s are represented by 0 V signals and binary 1s by signals ranging from about +0.8 to +3.5 V. (The reason for the variation in 1 signals will be explained.) The logic for entire computers can be constructed from this simple circuit; so it is perhaps the most basic transistor circuit.

The input X in Fig. 5·8 can be a binary 0 which is 0 V, in which case, since the base will be at the same potential as the emitter, the transistor will be cut off, and no current will flow in the collector circuit; so the output will rise to a binary 1 or +3.5 V level.

If the input is at +3 V, a binary 1, the transistor will be turned on and in saturation and the collector will then be at 0 V, plus the emitter-collector drop, representing a binary 0.

This circuit can be used to illustrate an important point. If a single inverter output is connected to a single inverter as in Fig. 5·9(a), or to two inverters as in Fig. 5·9(b), or to three inverters as in Fig. 5·9(c), differing output voltages occur for the 1 level at the output of the first inverter.

If the input to the first inverter is a 0, the transistor will be off, and for the single-inverter load in Fig. 5·9(a), the resistor at the output of the first stage and input to the second stage form a voltage divider in series with the base-emitter junction of the transistor of the second stage. Assuming this drop is 0.5 V, the 640 Ω and 450 Ω resistors will drop 3 V and the point Z will be at +1.7 V.

With two inverters connected to the output of the first inverter, as in Fig. 5·9(b), point Z will be at +1.3 V, while with three inverters at the output, as in Fig. 5·9(c), point Z will be at +1.1 V.

Since all three of these voltages, 1.7, 1.3, and 1.1 V, represent 1s, and since even more circuits might be added, it is necessary to (1) limit the number of circuits connected to an output and (2) let 0s and 1s be represented by voltages lying in intervals.

As an example of (1) above, Fig. 4·15 shows several IC packages from the Motorola line. Included is a six-inverter package with six inverters in a single IC container of the sort shown in Figs. 5·8 and 5·9. The inner numbers on the MC 789P show the pin numbers; so the topmost inverter has pin 14 as an input and pin 1 as an output. The other numbers are for *loading*, or *fan-in, fan-out* purposes. For the topmost inverter we see that the input at pin 14 has a

FIG. 5·9 Inverters connected together. (*a*) Two inverters in series; (*b*) two inverters to a single output; (*c*) three inverters to a single output.

load factor of 3 and the output at pin 1 can drive 16 loads. Therefore we could connect five inverter inputs to a single inverter output (since $5 \times 3 = 15$, which is less than 16), but not six inverters, because that would overload a single output. Similarly, the pin 2 input of the dual *JK* flip-flop package is a *CL* input to a *JK* flip-flop with a load of five; so only three of the *CL* inputs could be connected to an inverter output. Similarly, three inverters could be connected to pin 14 of the dual *JK* flip-flop package, since this would give a load factor of 9, which is less than the load of 10 the 0 output of the flip-flop can support.

Regarding voltage levels, the circuits are designed so that levels of less than +0.5 V represent binary 0s, while signals of greater than 0.8 V represent 1s. There is, therefore, a 0.3 V indeterminate interval† which gives some protection against noise and some immunity against variations in circuits. (Proper design can further provide protection against noise. RTL is generally conceded to be more sensitive to noise than some other systems, however.) V_{cc}, the power supply level, is to be 3.5 V dc ± 10 percent. Each of the circuits in Fig. 4·15 can be obtained in the IC packages described in Chap. 4, as can the RTL made by any of the major manufacturers.

5•8 NOR GATES

By combining two of the circuits in Fig. 5·8 it is possible to make a *two-input NOR gate*. Figure 5·10 shows this: the two collectors are tied together and share a single load resistor.

X	Y	Output
0	0	1
0	1	0
1	0	0
1	1	0

FIG. 5•10 Two-input NOR gates.

---

† This is sometimes called the "region of ambiguity."

If either or both of the inputs X and Y to the circuit in Fig. 5·10 are high (or 1s), the transistor connected to that input will be turned on and saturated. This means that the collector will be at essentially ground, or 0, potential and the output will be a 0. For instance, if the input at X is at $+2$ V, $T1$ will be turned on and saturated and the output will be at 0 volts. If the input Y happens to be at 0 volts, it will not affect the output, and the collector-base junction of $T2$ will be at about the same potential.

The same applies if both inputs are at a 1 or high input level: both $T1$ and $T2$ will be saturated and the output a 0.

If both inputs X and Y happen to be 0s, then both $T1$ and $T2$ will be off and the output will be at $+3.5$ V.

A truth table for the circuit is shown in Fig. 5·10. This indicates that the presence of a 1 at either or both inputs leads to a 0 output; so the circuit is a two-input NOR gate. This is one of the circuits in Fig. 4·15.

Figure 5·11 shows that the circuit can be extended. Connecting the collectors of three inverters together forms a three-input NOR gate; four transis-

MC792P—TRIPLE 3-INPUT GATE

$R1 = 450\ \Omega$

$R2 = 640\ \Omega$

FIG. 5·11 Three- and four-input NOR gates. (Courtesy Motorola Corp.)

tors can form a four-input NOR gate; etc. Both of these circuits are RTL circuits and correspond to the block diagram in Fig. 4 · 15.

5 • 9 THE TRANSISTOR FLIP-FLOP

The basic characteristic of the flip-flop circuit is that it is bistable. This ability to be stable in only one of two possible states or conditions at a given time is almost always based on some variation of the basic two-transistor circuit shown in Fig. 5 · 12. The two-transistor circuits are arranged so that one of the transistors is always on and the other is always off.

Assume transistor $T2$ is off. Then the 640 Ω resistor $R4$ at its collector "pulls up" on the base of transistor $T1$ through resistor $R2$. This turns transistor $T1$ on and saturates it. The output at the collector of $T1$ is then at essentially ground, which applies about 0 V to the base of $T2$ through $R3$, keeping it off. At this time the Q output is at about $+1.7$ V, depending on the base-to-emitter drop of $T1$, and the $\overline{Q}$ output is at perhaps $+0.3$ V. This is then the 1 state for the flip-flop.

If $T1$ is off, then $R1$ and $R2$ turn $T2$ on and the collector of $T2$ then is near ground, keeping $T1$ off. The Q output is then at about ground (perhaps $+0.3$ V), and the $\overline{Q}$ output will be at about $+1.7$ V, and so the flip-flop is in the 0 state.

An examination will show that the circuit will not be stable in any condition but the 1 or 0 state outlined above.

This flip-flop has outputs but no inputs. Figure 5 · 13 shows an RS flip-flop with a SET and RESET input. The SET and RESET inputs are normally at 0. When a positive voltage is applied to the RESET input, transistor $T4$ goes on, and the collector of $T4$ goes to about ground; this turns $T1$ off, and the output of $T1$ rises, turning $T2$ on. If the positive voltage is now removed from the RESET input, the flip-flop will be in the 0 state, with $T1$ off and the $\overline{Q}$ output high and with $T2$ on and the Q output low.

A positive voltage applied to the SET input will turn $T3$ on, grounding the

FIG. 5 • 12 Two-transistor flip-flop.

FIG. 5 • 13 SET-RESET flip-flop.

base of *T2* and turning *T2* off. This will turn *T1* on and, removing the positive input voltage from the SET input, will leave the flip-flop with 1 state, with the *Q* output high and the *Q̄* output low.

Figure 5 · 13 also shows that this circuit consists of two NOR gates cross-coupled, which is how the basic *RS* flip-flop is made in RTL logic.

5 • 10 RESISTOR-TRANSISTOR LOGIC

We have already seen several examples of a class of logic circuits called RTL circuits. These circuits are distinguished by their use of only transistors and resistors as circuit elements and by the presence of a resistor at the input to each base. The circuits are also characterized by the use of the NOR gate as the standard gate. The circuits are generally medium-speed and medium-power, although low-power circuits are available, and a complete line of these circuits is available from just about every major manufacturer.

These circuits are widely used and are manufactured to standards throughout the industry, so that the circuit packages used are interchangeable in that one manufacturer's circuit can be replaced by another's. (An examination of the schematics of two circuits will generally show that both circuits are identical with regard to component values and configuration as well as external pin numbers.)

For the gates shown in Figs. 5 · 10 and 5 · 11, the delay through a single unloaded gate is on the order of 12 ns. The gates have an input load factor of 3 and an output capability of 16; so five inputs could be connected to a single output.

Figure 5 · 14 shows the schematic for a standard clocked *JK* flip-flop. This flip-flop has inverted inputs and outputs (notice the bubbles on the block diagram) because it is constructed of NOR gates which lead to inverted logic.

CLOCKED OPERATION

J	K	Q Output
0	0	Changes
0	1	Goes to 0
1	0	Gate 1
1	1	No change

$R1 = 450\ \Omega$
$R2 = 640\ \Omega$
$R3 = 510\ \Omega$
$R4 = 225\ \Omega$
$R5 = 300\ \Omega$

FIG. 5·14 RTL flip-flop.

Figure 5·14 shows a table of the clocked input operation values. This shows that if both inputs J and K are 1s when the negative-going edge of the clock pulse arrives, the flip-flop will remain in the same state. If, however, both inputs are 0s when the negative edge arrives, the flip-flop will change states. If the pin 3 input is a 1 and the pin 1 input is a 0 when the clock arrives, the flip-flop goes to the 0 state (since inputs are inverted), with pin 13 high (since the 1 output is inverted) and pin 14 low (since the 0 output is inverted). Similarly, if pin 3 is a 1 and pin 1 a 0 when the clock goes negative, afterward pin 13 will be low (a 0) and pin 14 high (a 1). This inverted input, inverted output requires some thinking in use, but it is common to all lines of RTL logic.

Pin 12 is used to clear the flip-flop to its 0 state, and a plus or 1 signal is used to activate the input. During normal clocked operation this input is at ground, or 0, potential.

5•11 DIODE-TRANSISTOR LOGIC

Diode-transistor logic (DTL) is again one of the most frequently used circuit lines. The circuits are characterized by diode gates followed by transistor inverters, which leads to a NAND gate as the basic gate. DTL has more resistance to noise than RTL, and the logic is more "natural" but the circuits are more complicated. DTL was the largest selling line for some years and is still widely used, particularly in industrial applications where protection against noise is an important factor in evaluating logic circuit performance. DTL has reasonably good performance in this area, and there is a circuit line called HLDTL (or high-level DTL) where the power supply voltage is +25 V instead of the +5 V used in basic DTL. This line of circuits has excellent noise protection and is widely used in industrial applications where, for instance, machinery causes electrical noise and there are large power-line transients.

The basic DTL gate is shown in Fig. 5·15(a). This particular circuit is standard with virtually all manufacturers. The circuit basically consists of a diode AND gate followed by a transistor inverter. There is also an additional transistor (an emitter follower) between the diode AND gate and the transistor inverter's input. This means that there is more gain through the input circuit, and therefore less input drive required. The extra transistor T1 also means a higher input level is required to turn T2 on since there are now three junctions (a diode and the base-emitter junctions of T1 and T2) between the output of the AND gate and ground, and so a higher voltage is required to start significant current flowing. This increases the protection against noise.

To analyze the operation of the circuit in Fig. 5·15(a), if any one of the three inputs is at ground potential, the base of T1 will be only slightly positive (the amount of the drop across a diode), and the three junctions in series, the base emitter of T1, the diode D1, and the base-emitter junction of T2, will not conduct, particularly since R3 is also holding the base to ground. As a result, the output will tend to rise to the output voltage of +5 V.

If all inputs are at a high or 1 level (3 V or more) the output from the diode AND gate will be high and the emitter of T1 will be at about the input level (notice that the base-emitter junction of T1 drops a voltage about equal to the rise across the diodes), so that T2 is turned on hard and saturates. This gives a low or 0 output. The circuit therefore operates as a NAND gate.

A block diagram and schematic for the standard RS flip-flop in DTL is shown in Fig. 5·15(b). The standard flip-flop has 2 two-input AND gates which come connected to the S and R inputs. In DTL, unused inputs are 1s; so simply using one R and one S input will give a conventional RS flip-flop. A table of next-state values for this flip-flop is shown in the figure. The flip-flop is initiated by negative-going edges on the clock. DC RESET and DC SET lines are included, and these are normally at a high, or 1, level (unconnected, they will be 1s) and are activated by "grounding," or making the input a 0.

There is one frequently used trick with this flip-flop. Connecting the Q output to an R input and the $\overline{Q}$ output to an S input gives a JK flip-flop (which complements with two 1 inputs).

The circuit in Fig. 5·15(b) can be further analyzed using the logic diagram

FIG. 5·15 (a) Basic DTL gate; (b) block diagram and schematic for standard RS flip-flop in DTL; (c) logic diagram.

in Fig. 5·15(c), which shows the circuit reduced to its block form. This shows the flip-flop to be a master-slave flip-flop, as previously described.

5•12 TRANSISTOR-TRANSISTOR LOGIC

The line of circuits called transistor-transistor logic (TTL) is now the most widely used circuit line because of the high speed of TTL circuits. These circuits are characterized by a multiple emitter transistor at the inputs. Otherwise, the circuits are very similar to DTL, with a standard NAND gate, except the output stage frequently contains two transistors.

The characteristic which distinguishes TTL circuits from other circuit lines is a multiple emitter transistor at the input circuit. The schematic diagram for this kind of transistor is shown as $T1$ in Fig. 5·16(a). The multiple emitter transistor simply has a larger than normal collector area and several base-emitter junctions. The two-emitter transistor in Fig. 5·16(a) functions like the two-transistor circuit because the two-emitter transistor is effectively two transistors with a common collector and base. Figure 5·16(b) and (c) shows the TTL input circuit in separate transistor and multiple-emtter transistor form. The transistors $T1A$, $T1B$, and $T1C$ are combined to form a single

FIG. 5•16 TTL gate circuit. (a) Schematic symbol and equivalent circuit; (b) discrete version of TTL gate; (c) multiple emitter TTL gate.

multiple-emitter transistor $T1$ in (c). This circuit operates as follows. If one of three inputs X, Y, and Z is at 0 V, current will flow through $R1$ and the base-emitter junction of $T1$ to the input. This will hold the base of $T1$ at about 0.5 V. The base collector of $T1$ and the base emitter of $T2$ form two junctions in series with resistor $R3$ to ground, and so the base of $T2$ will not be positive more than 0.2 V which is insufficient to turn $T2$ on; and little (leakage only) current will flow in the collector circuit of $T1$, and $T2$ will be off. As a result, no current will flow through the resistors $R2$ and $R3$ and the emitter of $T2$ will be at ground and the collector at +5 V.

If all three inputs are at a level of +3.5 V (the 1 level), then current will flow through $R1$ and the base-collector junction of $T1$ (which is forward biased) into the base of $T2$ turning it on. Current will flow through $R1$ and $R2$ until the transistor $T2$ is saturated with its emitter and collector both at about 2.5 V. At this time, notice that the three emitter-base junctions of the multiple emitter transistor will be reverse biased.

The two outputs from the collector and emitter of $T2$ operate like scissors which close when $T2$ is on and open when $T2$ is off. That is, the emitter and collector of $T2$ will be at about the same voltage (closed) when $T2$ is on, and the emitter will be at ground and the collector at +5 when $T2$ if off (open scissors).

Notice that $T2$ is on when the three inputs are high (1s) *and* $T2$ is off when any one of the three inputs are low (a 0), so the circuit operation is basically that of a NAND gate.

A complete TTL NAND gate is shown in Fig. 5·17. This is a "second generation" TTL circuit and is typical of the circuits offered by the major TTL manufacturers in their medium-speed lines.

Let us examine the operation of the circuit in Fig. 5·17 by assuming that input Y is at +3.5 V and X is at 0 V and therefore $T1$ has its base-emitter junction connected to Y reversed biased and the full current from $R1$ flows through the base-emitter junction connected to X. At this time, (1) $T2$ will be off; (2) $T4$ will be off because with no current through $R4$ its base will be at essentially ground; (3) $T3$ and $T5$ will be turned on by current flowing through $R2$. The transistors $T5$ and $T3$ are connected in what is called a *Darlington configuration* which gives large current gain. As a result, little current will be required through $R2$ to turn $T3$ on, and the output will be at +5 V minus the base-emitter drops for $T5$ and $T3$ and therefore at about +4 V.

Let us consider that the input voltage at X is slowly raised positive. As a result, the collector of $T1$ goes positive and $T2$ begins to conduct. As the emitter of $T2$ becomes more and more positive, $T4$ begins to conduct and as the collector of $T2$ becomes more and more negative, the $T5$ to $T3$ combination begins to turn off. Finally, (1) $T2$ will saturate; (2) $T4$ will be saturated; and therefore about +0.5 V or less.

The circuit in Fig. 5·17 will have about 7 ns turn-on delays and 11 ns turn-off delays and a power dissipation of about 10 mW.

The reason for the high speeds lie in the all-transistor construction of TTL and in the fact that the final stage drives current in both directions. The standard transistor inverter (see Figs. 5·8 or 5·15 for examples in RTL and

DTL) has an output which is "driven down" by the turning on of the output transistor. When the transistor is turned off, however, the rising edge is formed by the resistor at the circuit's output supplying current to all the stray capacity in this circuit and any circuits connected to the output. Therefore, the rise time is exponential. With TTL's two-transistor output (the circuit is called a *totem pole*), the rising edge is "driven up" by the upper transistor turning on and the lower transistor turning off. This gives a sharp edge, and the falling edge is similarly sharp.

In many aerospace, military, and industrial applications it is desirable to have a much lower power dissipation. If the resistor values in the basic circuit design shown in Fig. 5·17 are raised, the circuit will consume far lower power, and circuit manufacturers offer low-power TTL circuits. Typical resistor values are: $R1 = 40$ K, $R2 = 20$ K, $R3 = 500$ Ω, $R4 = 12$ K, and $R5 = 5$ K. Naturally there will be a decrease in speed, but low-power gates are still capable of 33 ns delays at only 1 mW power dissipation.

There is a famous problem with TTL circuits which can be illustrated using Fig. 5·17. When TTL circuits are switched, they generate large "spikes" on their outputs, and interconnections must be carefully watched to prevent ringing or even circuit damage. Generally, capacitors are even placed across the +5 volt-to-ground power supply on each circuit container to prevent spikes in the power supply voltage.

The problem develops because it is possible for both $T3$ and $T4$ to be on simultaneously when the circuit is switching. For instance, if the output is switching from a 0 to a 1 level, then $T4$ must go off and $T3$ must go on. But if

FIG. 5 • 17 Classic TTL NAND gate.

*T*3 goes on before *T*4 is completely off, then both transistors will be on simultaneously, almost shorting the +5 to ground.

The TTL current spike problem has plagued the TTL family and is clearly in evidence in the circuit of Fig. 5·17. While *T*3 and *T*4 can both be on during turn-on and turn-off, the turn-off case is usually worse since the storage time of *T*4 causes both transistors to be on for a greater time. Turn-on current spiking may be lowered by increasing the ratio of *R*2 to *R*4. In this way the collector of *T*2 reaches a lower voltage before *T*4 begins to conduct. There is a trade-off involved, however, since increasing *R*2 decreases the on drive for *T*4, decreasing its turn-on time. The increased value of *R*2 also results in decreased noise immunity. So far, no "perfect" answer to current spiking has been found.

Although the standard TTL circuits are fast, there is always a desire to speed up circuit lines. In order to increase still further the speeds of TTL logic, a basic problem must be dealt with. When a transistor is saturated and must be turned off, before the transistor begins to go off there is a delay (caused by the minority carriers) called the *storage time delay*. This is shown in Fig. 5·18(*a*) where a transistor inverter is turned off from saturation. While this delay is on the order of nanoseconds, it is still significant since several of the TTL circuit transistors become saturated at various times.†

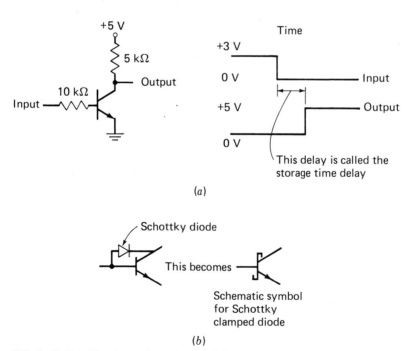

(*a*)

(*b*)

FIG. 5•18 Schottky clamped transistor. (*a*) Storage delay; (*b*) Schottky diode and transistor.

---

† Gold doping is often used to reduce minority carrier storage times in switching transistors.

In order to alleviate this problem the newest TTL circuits use a diode clamp between base and collector. This is shown in Fig. 5·18(*b*). The diode used is not a conventional diode, however, but is a special diode (called a Schottky diode) formed by the junction of a metal and a semiconductor.

The Schottky diode is faster than conventional diodes because electrons which have crossed the junction and entered the metal when current is flowing are not distinguishable from the conduction electrons of the metal. Since these electrons are majority carriers, there is no delay associated with minority carrier recombination as in semiconductor diodes. As a result, reverse recovery times for Schottky diodes are generally in the low picosecond range. Further, because of the choice of materials (aluminum or platinum silicides), the forward drop of the Schottky diode is less than a conventional diode.

The transistor with a Schottky diode connected from base to collector will switch faster because the transistor is not allowed to saturate. The minority carrier storage time normally associated with the transistor's operation when coming out of saturation is avoided and the circuit can operate faster.

When a transistor is fabricated with a Schottky diode connected from base to collector, the combination is given a special schematic diagram symbol as shown in Fig. 5·18(*b*).

The use of Schottky clamped transistors has resulted in a series of high-speed TTL circuits with delays on the order of 2 ns (rise and fall times are on the order of 3 ns). Figure 5·19(*b*) shows a typical circuit. Notice that the transistors which normally become saturated at some time are now Schottky clamped transistors and so storage delays are reduced. The operation of this circuit is essentially the same as that of Fig. 5·17 except the transistors do not saturate.

The diodes connected to ground at the inputs dampen negative spikes and negative-going signals which may occur during ringing. These circuits must be carefully inter-connected, however, and wire or printed circuit connections

TABLE 5·2 TTL CHARACTERISTICS

	VERY HIGH SPEED 74 S (SCHOTTKY CLAMPED)	HIGH SPEED	MEDIUM SPEED 74	LOW SPEED 74 L
High-level input (minimum)	2 V	1.8 V	2 V	2 V
Low-level input (maximum)	.8 V	.9 V	.8 V	.7 V
High-level output (minimum)	2.7 V	2.5 V	2.4 V	2.4 V
Low-level output (maximum)	.5 V	.4 V	.4 V	.3 V
High-level noise margin (minimum)	700 mV	700 mV	400 mV	400 mV
Low-level noise margin (minimum)	300 mV	500 mV	400 mV	400 mV
Maximum input load current	−2 mA	−2 mA	−1.6 mA	−1.8 mA
Average power per gate	20 mW	22 mW	10 mW	1 mW
Typical delay high to low	3 ns	6 ns	8 ns	31 ns
low to high	3 ns	6 ns	12 ns	35 ns
Supply voltage	5 V	5 V	5 V	5 V

FIG. 5·19 (a) Schottky MSI circuit; (b) Schottky clamped TTL
logic gate.

of more than 8 in. in length should be treated with respect and terminated
according to the rules given by the circuits manufacturers.

Table 5·2 gives some of the characteristics for several TTL lines. Notice
that speed is associated with power consumption.

TTL circuits are also available in MSI. The MSI seven-segment decoder
and BCD counters in Chap. 4 were TTL. A simplified TTL gate is used internally for such MSI circuits, and this gate is shown in Fig. 5·19(a).

A TTL flip-flop is shown in Fig. 5·20, the Fairchild 9022. This operates like any *JK* flip-flop, except that it provides AND gates at the *J* and *K* inputs and a *JK* or "gate" input, which can be used to inhibit the flip-flop's operation. Notice that the clock input presents no bubble; so positive clock transitions activate the flip-flop (that is, 0 to 1 shifts). The block diagram in Fig. 5·20 shows the flip-flop to be a master-slave flip-flop. DC RESET and DC SET inputs are activated by grounding the respective input line. This gives some

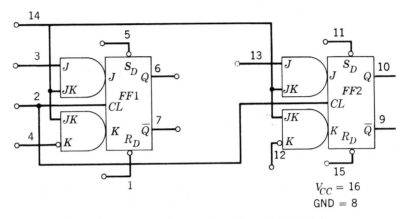

$V_{CC} = 16$
GND = 8

The numbers from 1 to 14 are pin numbers on the container.

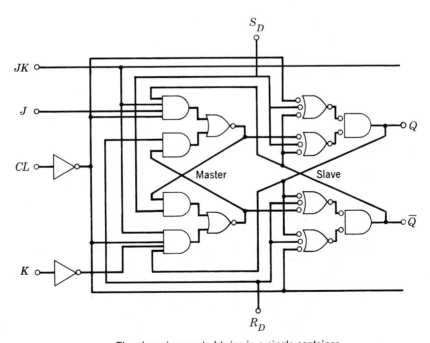

The above is repeated twice in a single container.

FIG. 5·20 TTL flip-flop. (Courtesy Fairchild Corp.)

idea of the complexity of circuits in TTL logic packages. Two of these flip-flops are packaged in one 14-pin container as shown in Fig. 4 · 12.

5 • 13 EMITTER-COUPLED LOGIC

Emitter-coupled logic (ECL) has several other common names, *current-mode logic* (CML), *current-steering logic,* and *nonsaturating logic.* The latter term is the key to this type of circuit: when transistors are operated in a saturated condition, they turn off slowly due to the delay caused by a charge stored in the collector and base region.† This delay in "turn-off time" can be eliminated by operating transistors only in either the active or off regions. As will be seen, in these circuits current is "steered" rather than having voltages or levels passed around.

The ECL logic line is the fastest currently available. Manufacturers of ECL have a number of basic circuits each with different features and drawbacks. ECL has not proved as popular as TTL, primarily because it is more expensive, harder to cool, and more difficult to interconnect, and is considered to have less noise immunity (this is debatable). Also, ECL may be faster than is necessary in many applications. On the other hand, a number of the "superfast" computers use ECL as do a number of the highest-speed special-purpose computers.

The basic ECL configuration can be best described by examining a particular inverter. Figure 5 · 21 shows an ECL inverter with an input X. The logic levels in this system are as follows: binary 0 is represented by -1.55 V, and binary 1 by -0.75 V. Notice that this is "positive logic," since, although both levels are negative, the more positive level, -0.75, is the binary 1. Also, notice the small signal difference between 0 and 1.

The circuit's operation is based on a *differential amplifier* consisting of $T4$ and $T3$. When the input to $T3$ is at -1.55 V, $T3$ will be off and current will flow through $R3$ and $R2$. Calculation will indicate a drop of about 0.8 V across $R2$; so, figuring a base-emitter drop of 0.75 V for $T1$, the X output will be at -1.55 V.

Since $T2$ is cut off by the -1.55 V input, very little current will flow through $R1$, and the output $\overline{X}$ will be at the base-emitter drop voltage across $T2$; so the output will be at -0.75 V.

An examination will show that if the input is at -0.75 V, transistor $T3$ will be on, $T4$ will be off, the X output will be at -0.75 V, and the $\overline{X}$ output at -1.55 V. (The key to analyzing this circuit is to notice that in a "differential amplifier" circuit such as $T3$ to $T4$ form, the current through the resistor $R3$ shared by the two emitters will be almost constant.) Notice that the transistors are never saturated. They are either in their active region or off.

A three-input gate is shown in Fig. 5 · 22. This is a combined NOR and OR

---

† This was called the storage delay in the preceding section.

FIG. 5 • 21 ECL-gate basic circuit. (Courtesy Motorola Corp.; Motorola has the trade name MECL for Motorola ECL.)

TRUTH TABLE

Inputs			Outputs	
8	7	6	5	4
0	0	0	1	0
0	0	1	0	1
0	1	0	0	1
0	1	1	0	1
1	0	0	0	1
1	0	1	0	1
1	1	0	0	1
1	1	1	0	1

FIG. 5 • 22 ECL three-input gate.

gate, as shown by the block diagram, depending on which output connection is used.

As time has passed several generations of ECL circuits have evolved. In general, the circuits have become faster and require more power with each generation. More facilities and more complicated logic per chip are also available in the new lines, including MSI chips. Notice that the circuits in Fig. 5·21 require three voltages: ground, −1.175 V, and −5.2 V. Later circuits provide a circuit on each chip to generate the intermediate (in this case −1.175 V) voltage, so that only a single power supply is required.

Figure 5·23 shows the four generations Motorola has gone through with their ECL logic which is called Motorola ECL or MECL, and also Fairchild's 10,000 series. Table 5·3 outlines some of the characteristics of these circuits, and the speed versus power and general noise characteristics can be deduced from the table. From Fig. 5·23 it is evident which variations were employed as technology advanced. For instance, notice that the circuit to produce the third −1.175 V bias voltage for the MECL I Line is not included on the chip, whereas all subsequent lines have this as an internal feature.

Second, corresponding resistor values differ among MECL lines. This is necessary to achieve the varying speed and power improvements. Of course, speed is not determined by resistor values alone; transistor geometries, while not shown on a schematic, are a major factor. The transistor geometries in conjunction with the resistor values provide the speed and power characteristics of the different families.

Notice also that Fairchild 10,000 and MECL III gates are supplied with base pull-down resistors (50,000 Ω) to each of the input transistors while the other two families are not. These resistors provide a path for base leakage current to unused input bases, causing them to be well turned off.

A final significant difference between the families is in the output circuits. MECL I circuits normally are supplied with output pull-down resistors on the chip. MECL II circuits can be obtained with or without output resistors. MECL III and Fairchild 10,000 circuits normally have open outputs.

The use of on-chip output resistors has both advantages and limitations. An advantage is that fewer external components are required. However, with

TABLE 5·3 GENERAL CHARACTERISTICS OF ECL CIRCUITS

Feature	MECL I	MECL II	FAIRCHILD		MECL III
			10k Series	100k Series	
Gate propagation delay	8 ns	4 ns	2 ns	0.75 ns	1 ns
Gate edge speed	8.5 ns	4 ns	3.5 ns	1.5 ns	1 ns
Flip-flop toggle speed (minimum)	30 MHz	70 MHz	125 MHz	500 MHz	500 MHz
Gate power	31 mW	22 mW	25 mW	65 mW	60 mW
Input pulldown resistors	No	No	50 kΩ	50 kΩ	2 kΩ, 50 kΩ

FIG. 5 • 23 Several generations of ECL circuits.

open outputs the designer can choose both the value and location of terminating resistance to meet system requirements. Finally, the use of external resistors reduces on-chip heating and power dissipation, allowing more complex LSI and increasing chip life and reliability.

An *RS* flip-flop in this system is shown in Fig. 5·24. DC SET and RESET

FIG. 5·24 ECL *RS* flip-flop.

inputs are included. This flip-flop can be used in counters at rates up to 30 million counts per second. More complicated flip-flops operate at even higher rates.

5·14 METAL-OXIDE SEMICONDUCTOR CIRCUITS

The circuits so far described are all termed *bipolar* circuits and use "conventional" transistors. For large-scale integration (LSI), quite often another type of transistor, called a *field effect transistor* (FET), is used. While the characteristics of these FETs have not proved desirable for some applications (because of their slowness, delicacy, and lack of drive characteristics), the ease of manufacture, small size, and small power dissipation have offset the negative factors and have led to FETs constructed of MOS (metal-oxide semiconductor) as the primary technology for use in large arrays. FETs constructed of MOS are called MOSFETs.

The manufacture of MOS circuits using FETs involves different techniques at different companies. Most MOSFET circuits now manufactured use a structure called *insulated gate p-channel enhancement mode field effect transistors,* or *insulated gate n-channel enhancement mode field effect transistors.* We shall deal with these structures primarily.

Figure 5·25(a) shows a cross section of an FET of *p*-channel type. As shown in Fig. 5·25(b), a substrate of *n*-type (silicon) material is first formed, and two separate low-resistivity *p*-type regions are diffused into this substrate. Then the surface of this structure is covered with an insulating oxide layer. Holes are cut into the oxide, and two metal contacts are made to the two pieces of *p* material, and a thin piece of metal called the gate (*G*) is placed over what is called the *channel.*

With no voltages applied, the above structure (refer to Fig. 5 · 25) forms two diodes back to back, and if we attempt to force current from source to drain, the alternate *pn* junction followed by an *np* junction will not permit current flow (in either direction).

The gate is used to cause and control current flow in the following manner. Consider the source to be grounded and the drain connected to a negative voltage through a resistor. Figure 5 · 26 shows this [the schematic symbol for the FET is shown in Fig. 5 · 25(*d*)]. The metal area of the gate, along with the insulating oxide layer and semiconductor channel, form a capacitor, with the metal gate the top plate and the *n*-material substrate the lower plate. Making the gate potential negative causes a corresponding positive charge in the *n*-type semiconductor substrate along the channel, as shown in Fig. 5 · 25(*c*). Given sufficient negative potential on the gate, the positive charge induced in the channel finally causes this section of material to become *p*-type, and current begins to flow from source to drain — thus the term *current enhancement mode.*

The more negative the gate becomes, the more "*p*-type" the semiconductor channel becomes, and the more current flows. As a result, this type of MOS is also called PMOS.

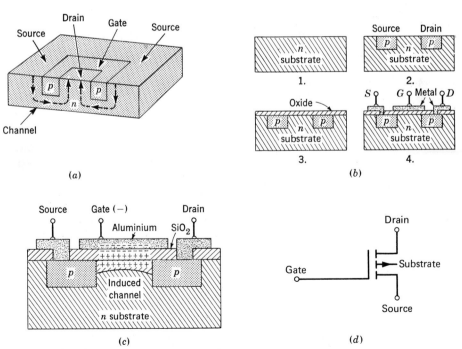

FIG. 5 ● 25 MOSFET structure. (*a*) General configuration; (*b*) fabrication steps; (*c*) cross section with gate-biased negative; (*d*) schematic symbol. (Courtesy Motorola Corp.)

FIG. 5•26 Alternate schematic symbols for MOSFET resistive element.

As a switching circuit, an FET can be used to form an inverter. With a 0, or ground, input the output of the circuit shown in Fig. 5·26 will have a −10 V output, and with a −7 V or more negative input, the output will go to about 0 V.

Two things should be noted about this circuit. First, the voltages used are larger than for the circuits in preceding sections. Second, the FET circuit has a high input impedance (perhaps 10^{12} Ω) because the gate input is a capacitor, in effect.

One other fact should be noted. Instead of forming actual resistors for these circuits, another FET is used, thus simplifying manufacture. This is shown in Fig. 5·26. The FET resistor's gate areas are controlled so that the FET represents a high resistance (perhaps 10 to 100 kΩ) when the gate is at the drain potential. Some manufacturers show this FET using the regular symbol, and some show the resistor-plus-bar symbol, also seen in the figure.

When a p-type substrate with n doping for the source and drain are used, as in Fig. 5·27, then the n-channel transistor is formed as shown in the figure. The schematic diagram symbol for the n-channel transistor and an inverter circuit are shown in Fig. 5·27(a) and (b). Notice the circuit uses a positive

(a)   (b)

FIG. 5•27 (a) n-channel MOSFET transistor (NMOS); (b) n-channel inverter.

voltage and behaves similar to an *npn* transistor inverter circuit. This type of MOS is called NMOS.

A NOR gate can be formed in NMOS as shown in Fig. $5 \cdot 28(a)$. The logic levels for this circuit are $+2$ to 0 V for a binary 0 and $> +8$V for a binary 1. (This is positive logic.) If any of the inputs A, B, or C is a 1, the corresponding FET will conduct, causing the output to go to about $+2$ V or less. If all inputs are at $+2$ V or less, the FETs will all be off and the output will be at $+8$ V (or more).

Several different gates and flip-flops using NMOS are shown in Fig. $5 \cdot 28$. (PMOS is the same except for negative V_{CC} voltages and negative logic.) The high resistances used in these circuits mean low power dissipation. This, combined with the small areas needed to fabricate an FET, makes it possible to fabricate large numbers of circuits on a single small chip. Commonly, one or two 1024-bit shift registers are included in a single container with 14 leads. Gating arrays with thousands of gates and flip-flops are also manu-

(a)

(b)

(c)

FIG. 5 • 28 FET logic circuit. (a) Three-input OR gate; (b) three-input NAND gate; (c) *RS* flip-flop.

factured in standard containers, and these are often used in IC memories, which will be studied in Chap. 7, and in microprocessor chips, as described in Chap. 10.

5•15 CMOS LOGIC CIRCUITS

A series of circuits using MOSFET transistors called complementary MOS (CMOS) was originally developed for the aerospace and oceanographic industries. These circuits have very low power consumption and considerable resistance to noise. These circuits are, however, slow relative to the high-speed logic lines, but large numbers of circuits can be placed on a single chip, the power supply voltage can vary over a large range, and the circuits are relatively economical to manufacturer. The newest CMOS circuits have become relatively fast and are widely used for everything from electronic watches and calculators to microprocessors.

The CMOS circuits are fabricated as shown in Fig. 5·29(a), which shows that both n-channel and p-channel transistors can be fabricated on the same substrate.

The simplest form of CMOS integrated circuit consists of one n-channel and one p-channel MOS transistor, with both gate contacts tied together to form the input and both drain contacts tied together to form the output. This circuit is the basic CMOS inverter [Fig. 5·29(b)]. When the voltage at the input is near ground level, the gate-to-source voltage of the p-channel transistor approaches the value ot the supply voltage, +V, and the p channel is turned on. A low-resistance path is created between the supply voltage and output, while a high-resistance path is between the output and ground, due to the n-channel transistor being off. The output voltage will approach that of the supply voltage V+. When the input voltage is near V+, the p channel turns off and the n channel turns on, causing the output voltage to approach ground.

Notice that in either state, the circuit's power consumption is extremely low because one transistor is always off and because n- and p-channel transistors

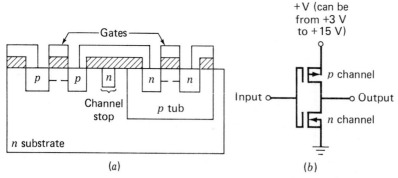

FIG. 5•29 CMOS inverter. (a) CMOS elements; (b) circuit that is the basic CMOS inverter.

exhibit very high resistance when off permitting very low leakage current to flow through the transistor which is in the off condition.

When conventional metal- and silicon-gate technologies are used, protective channel stops are provided to minimize leakage current between separate transistors as shown in Fig. 5·29(a). All p-channel devices must be surrounded by a continuous n-channel stop, which can also act as a conducting path for the external power supply to appropriate locations. Similarly, p-channel stops surround all n-channel devices and provide a conducting path between those n-channel devices which are electrically connected to the lowest potential and the external ground contact.

A two-input NOR gate can be constructed as shown in Fig. 5·30. Each additional input requires an additional p- and n-channel pair of MOS transistors.

(a)

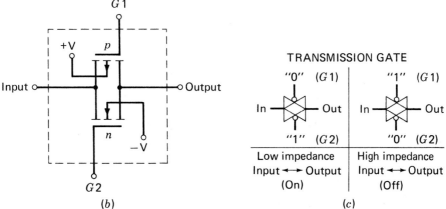

(b)   (c)

FIG. 5·30 CMOS NOR gate and transmission gate. (a) NOR gate in which an additional transistor pair is required for each gate leg added; (b) transmission gate schematic; (c) schematic symbol.

A unique feature of CMOS circuits is the *transmission gate* shown in Fig. 5·30(*b*). This circuit presents a low resistance (impedance) from input to output when the gate is on and a very high resistance (impedance) when the gate is off. The gate is enabled when the gate input G1 is near ground and when G2 is near the V+ level. When G1 is near V+ and G2 is near ground, the gate is off and has a resistance from input to output which is generally greater than 10^9 Ω. Figure 5·28(*b*) also shows the logic diagram symbol for the transmission gate.

Transmission gates are widely used in CMOS designs. Often a three-state circuit is used and this will be described in later chapters. Figure 5·31 shows this circuit and its three states.

Figure 5·32 shows a *D*-type flip-flop in CMOS technology which uses transmission gates to simplify the design. Notice the simplicity of this configuration versus the TTL and DTL circuits shown earlier.

Table 5·4 gives some details of CMOS operation versus other circuit lines. Notice the low power consumption (nanowatts when not being switched), competitive speeds, and noise protection.

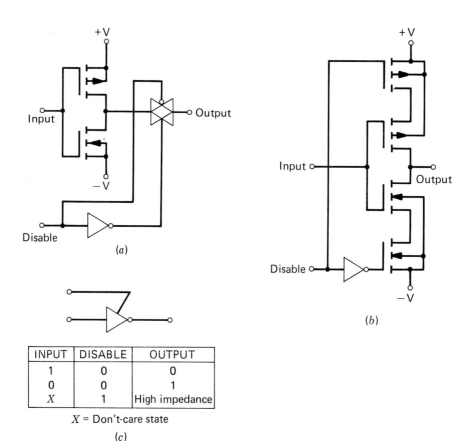

INPUT	DISABLE	OUTPUT
1	0	0
0	0	1
X	1	High impedance

X = Don't-care state

(*c*)

FIG. 5•31 Three-state CMOS circuit.

TABLE 5·4 CIRCUIT LINE CHARACTERISTICS

	STANDARD TTL 74	LOW-POWER TTL	DTL	SCHOTTKY CLAMPED TTL	CMOS 5 V SUPPLY	CMOS 10 V SUPPLY	ECL
Quiescent power	10 mW	1 mW	8.5 mW	20 mW	10 nW	10 nW	60 mW
Propagation delay	7 ns	30 ns	30 ns	3 ns	15 ns	10 ns	0.5 ns
Flip-flop toggle frequency	35 MHz	3 MHz	5 MHz	80 MHz	5 MHz	10 MHz	500 MHz
Noise immunity	1 V	1 V	1 V	0.8 V	2 V	4 V	0.5 V
Fan out	10	10	8	10	50	50	5

FIG. 5 • 32 D-type flip-flop in CMOS.

QUESTIONS

1. For a current of $+2$ mA the forward-biased silicon diode in Fig. 5·1(c) has a voltage drop of about _____ V. A germanium diode would have a drop of _____ V.

2. Consider the circuit

If we make IN a voltage of $+10$ V, the OUT point will be at about _____

volts, and about _____ amperes will flow through the resistor. (Answer for both germanium and silicon diodes.)

3. For what current does the silicon diode graphed in Fig. 5·1(c) have a voltage drop of +0.5 V?

4. If, for Question 2, IN were −10 V, give the corresponding OUT voltage and resistor currents.

5. If V_{ce} is held at +8 V and I_b is changed from 0.85 to 1 mA, what is the resultant change in I_c for the 2N706 in Fig. 5·3?

6. What is the current gain through the transistor for Question 5 (the ratio of the change in I_b to I_c)?

7. For the saturated transistor graphed in Fig. 5·3(c), what is the base voltage, which is also the base-emitter drop, when $I_b = 1,000\ \mu A$ and V_{ce} is 300 mV?

8. For Question 7, what is the difference between the base voltage and the collector voltage at that time?

9. For the emitter follower in Fig. 5·5(a), if the +V is 0 V and −V is −5 V, the resistor is 1,000 Ω, and the transistor base-emitter voltage drop is 0.75 V, a −2 volt input will result in an output of _____ volts. Is the transistor in the active region? Why?

10. For the emitter follower in Fig. 5·5(a), if −V is ground, +V is +5 V, the resistor is 2 kΩ, and the base-emitter drop of the transistor is 0.5 V, for a +1 V input give the output voltage and current through the resistor. Is the transistor in the active region? Why?

11. If the X input in Fig. 5·6 is at +3.5 V and the Y input at +3 V, what will the output voltage level at Z be? Assume a silicon diode with a forward drop of 0.6 V.

12. If the X input to the circuit in Fig. 5·6 is at +0.5 V and the Y input at 0.25 V, for a silicon diode with a forward drop of 0.6 V what will be the output voltage at Z?

13. Draw the schematic for a diode AND gate with four inputs.

14. If the X input to the OR gate in Fig. 5·7 is at +2 V and the Y input is at 0.5 V, what will the output voltage be? Assume a silicon diode with a forward drop of 0.6 V.

15. For the circuit described in the preceding question, what will be the output level if X is at 0.1 V and Y at 0.7 V?

16. Draw the schematic for a four-input diode OR gate.

17. Draw the schematic for a diode AND-to-OR gate network which realizes the Boolean algebra function $AB + CD$.

18. Analyze the output levels for the circuit you designed in the preceding question for input levels of +3 V for a logical 1 and +0.5 V for a logical 0.

19. Draw the block diagram and schematic for a single RTL inverter, as in Fig. 5·8, but with its output connected to four other inverters.

20. For the drawing you made in Question 19, calculate the output voltage for the first inverter when it has a 1 output.

21. Draw a block diagram for the following circuit. The inputs are A, B, and C and each carries a signal of 0 or +2 V, representing 0 or 1 respectively. What will the output levels be if the *output* is not connected to anything?

+3.6 V

640 Ω   640 Ω   640 Ω

Output

A   450 Ω   450 Ω   450 Ω   450 Ω   450 Ω   450 Ω   B

22. Assume the inputs *A* and *B* are both at ground potential (0 V) and that transistor *T2* is off. If the input *B* is raised to +2 V and then lowered back to 0 V, describe the operation of the circuit.

+3.6 V

640 Ω   640 Ω

Output

A   450 Ω T_3 450 Ω T_1 450 Ω T_2 B   450 Ω T_4

23. Discuss the noise protection of RTL circuits versus DTL circuits.
24. For the TTL circuit in Fig. 5·15(c), if all inputs are at +3 V, what will be the approximate voltages at the emitter and collector of *T2*?
25. Which transistors in the circuit in Fig. 5·17 are saturated when both inputs are low?
26. Which transistors in the circuit in Fig. 5·17 are saturated when both inputs are high?
27. Using the information gained in the preceding two questions, discuss how the use of Schottky clamped transistors might speed up the circuit in Fig. 5·17.
28. Compare the virtues and problems of the TTL circuits in Table 5·2.
29. Comment on the simplicity and low power consumption of the circuit in Fig. 5·19(a).
30. Does connecting the output of a DTL gate as in Fig. 5·15(a) to several DTL gate inputs tend to cause lower output levels when the output is a 1? Compare this with the RTL gate.
31. If we connect three inputs from DTL gates as in Fig. 5·15(a) to the output of a single gate, what will be the collector current of *T2* when turned on? Assume that *T1* has so much gain, its base draws 0 current.

32. Explain the action of the two output transistors in the TTL gate in Fig. 5·17.

33. Write the values at the output of each gate in Fig. 5·15(c) for inputs of $S_1 = 1$, $S_2 = 1$, $R_1 = 0$, and $R_2 = 1$. Assume that $CL = 1$ and the flip-flop is in the 1 state.

34. Redo the above, but with $S_1 = 0$. To what state will the flip-flop go when CL goes to 0? Explain.

35. If $T4$ shorts in Fig. 5·21 so that the emitter and collector are both permanently connected to the base, what will be the output at $\overline{X}$? Explain.

36. Given a single *npn* transistor, how would you connect it to make the three-input MECL gate in Fig. 5·22 a four-input gate?

37. $T4$ in Fig. 5·28(a) and (b) acts as a resistor. Analyze the operation of both of these gates if $A = 0$, $B = 1$, and $C = 1$. Make V_{cc} equal to 30 V, 25 V a 1, and 0 V a 0.

38. Draw block diagrams for the flip-flop in Fig. 5·28(c).

39. In Fig. 5·28(c) does the 0 output go positive or to 0 if $R = 10$ V and $S = 0$ V? Explain.

40. In Fig. 5·12, if the 640 Ω resistor from $T1$ to +3.5 V is open (or disconnected), the flip-flop will always be in the _____ state. Explain your answer.

41. If the RESET and SET inputs to the NOR gate flip-flop in Fig. 5·13 are both connected to +3.5 V, the 0 and 1 outputs will be at what levels?

42. Assume the inputs x and y to the following circuit are at ground potential and transistor T_1 is off. Explain the operation of the circuit if the input x is made positive 5 V and then returned to ground.

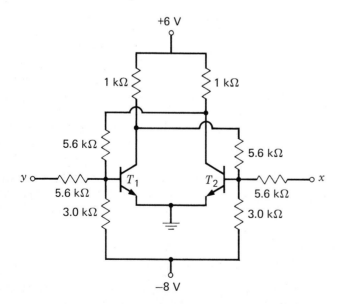

43. Write a Boolean algebra expression relating the inputs A, B, and C and their complements to the output Z for the following circuit.

44. The inputs to the following circuit are *A*, *B*, *C*, *D*, and *E*, each of which is

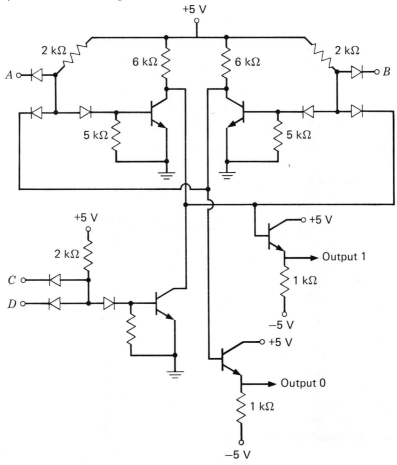

a signal of 0 or +3 V, representing 0 and 1 respectively. Draw a block
diagram for this circuit using AND, OR, NAND, NOR, or whatever gates
you would like.

45. The following DTL circuit has inputs A, B, C, and D and a single output Z.
Draw a block diagram of this circuit using AND, OR, NAND, NOR gates,
inverters, or flip-flops.

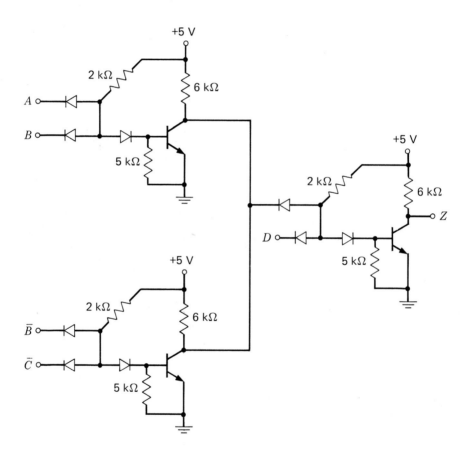

46. Draw a block diagram for the following circuit using any gates or flip-flops
you choose. The inputs A, B, and C are signal levels of either 0 or +3 V
representing 0 and 1, respectively.

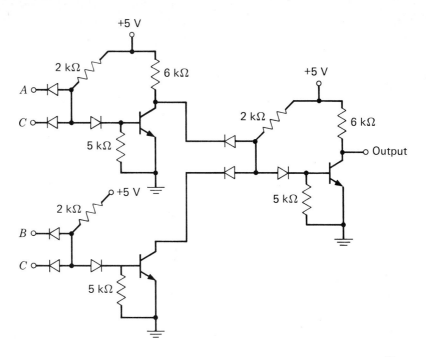

47. Draw a block diagram for the following circuit using any gates or flip-flops you choose. The inputs *A*, *B*, and *C* are signal levels of either 0 or +3 V, representing 0 and 1, respectively.

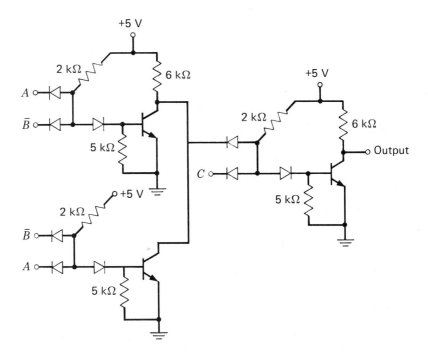

48. Write a Boolean algebra expression for the function realized by the following circuit. The inputs are *W*, *X*, *Y*, and *Z* and the output is to be expressed in these variables. Inputs are 0 or +3 V, representing binary 0 and 1 respectively.

49. The ability of a given TTL circuit to drive other circuits is often given in terms of what is called a *unit load*. For Fairchild's 7400 series TTL a unit load is 40 μA (to ground) when the level is in the high state and is the ability to accept 1.6 mA in the low state. Then, an input to a NAND gate in the 7400 series requires one unit load to be driven low or high. A NAND gate's output in the 7400 series can drive 20 unit loads when high and 10 unit loads when low. If a TTL NAND gate was connected to five inputs to other NAND gates and the output was high, how many amperes might the output supply to ground?

50. Using the data in the preceding question, how many gate inputs can be safely connected to a given gate output? (This is called the *fan-out* for the gate.)

51. Compare the *fan-out* ratios for the 7400 TTL gates with the RTL gates in Fig. 4·15.

52. Why is the unit load greater for the low level than the high level? Examine the basic TTL circuit to get your answer.

53. Explain why TTL outputs go from low to high faster than DTL when a long wire or other capacitive load must be driven.

54. What are some advantages of MOS over conventional bipolar circuits?

55. Why do CMOS gates require so little power when they are not changing states?

56. Draw a graph comparing speed and power consumption for Motorola's 10,000 and MECL III ECL circuits. Does this graph indicate any relationship?

57. Explain the operation of the circuit in Fig. 5·28(a). Explain the operation of the circuit in Fig. 5·28(b).

58. Draw block diagram symbols for the circuit in Fig. 5·28(c).

59. Compare NMOS and PMOS circuits with regard to speed.

60. Explain the operation of the circuit in Fig. 5·30(a).

61. Explain the operation of the circuit in Fig. 5·30(b).

62. Why is the circuit in Fig. 5·31 called a three-state circuit? What is the third state?

63. For the *data* input a 1 explain the operation of the circuit in Fig. 5·32 during a clock pulse. Assume the flip-flop starts in the 0 state.

64. For the *data* input a 0 and the flip-flop in the 1 state, show what happens to the flip-flop in Fig. 5·32 when a clock pulse is applied.

65. Compare CMOS with low-power TTL circuits. What might some disadvantages of CMOS be?

66. Discuss the problems and virtues of three of the circuit lines in Table 5·4.

67. *(a)* Draw a block diagram which shows the logical operation of the following circuit. You can use AND gates, NAND gates, OR gates, NOR gates, etc., in your diagram.
(b) Explain some advantages and disadvantages of the circuit.

68. Calculate the power dissipated in resistor $R2$ when the ECL circuit in Fig. 5·21 is in both of its output states.

69. Compare the MECL III and Fairchild 10,000 ECL series of circuits with regard to the power dissipation. Are these circuits very similar?

6
THE ARITHMETIC-LOGIC UNIT

The arithmetic-logic unit (ALU) is the section of the computer which performs arithmetic and logical operations on the data processed by the computer. This section of the machine can be relatively small, consisting of perhaps one or more large-scale integration (LSI) chips, or, for large "number crunchers" (scientific-oriented computers), it can consist of a considerable array of high-speed logic components. Despite the variations in size and complexity, the small machines generally perform their arithmetic and logic operations using the same principles as the large machines. What changes is the speed of the logic gates and flip-flops used; also, special techniques are used for speeding up operations and performing several operations in parallel.

Although many functions can be performed by the ALUs of present-day machines, the basic arithmetic operations—addition, subtraction, multiplication, and division—continue to be "bread-and-butter" operations. Even the literature gives evidence of the fundamental nature of these operations, for when a new machine is described, the times required for addition and multiplication are always included as significant features. Accordingly, this chapter first describes the means by which a computer adds, subtracts, multiplies, and divides. Other basic operations, such as shifting, logical multiplication, and logical addition, are then described.

It should be remembered that the control unit directs the operation of the ALU. What the ALU does is to add, subtract, shift, etc., when it is provided with the correct sequence of input signals. It is up to the control element to provide these signals, as it is the function of the memory units to provide the arithmetic element with the information which is to be used. It will therefore be assumed that the control and memory sections of the machine are capable of delivering the correct control signals, and that the data on which the operations are to be performed are available. The function of the ALU is therefore to add, subtract, or perform whatever operation the control element directs.

6•1 CONSTRUCTION OF THE ALU

The information handled in a computer is generally divided into "words" each consisting of a fixed number of bits.† For instance, the words handled by a given binary machine may be 32 bits in length. In this case, the ALU would have to be capable of adding, subtracting, etc., words of 32 bits in length. The operands used are then supplied from computer storage, and the control element directs the operations which are performed. If addition is to be performed, the addend and augend will be supplied to the ALU which must add the numbers and then, at least temporarily, store the result (sum).

To introduce several concepts, let us consider the construction of a typical computer ALU. The storage devices will consist of a set of flip-flop *registers,* each of which consists of one or more flip-flops. The *length* of each register is defined as the maximum amount of information the register can store. In a binary register, the register length is equal to the maximum number of binary digits which can be stored; and in a binary-coded-decimal (BCD) register, the register length will be the number of decimal digits the register can store.

For convenience, the various registers of the ALU are generally given names such as X register, B register, MQ register, etc., and the flip-flops are then given the same names, so that the X register would contain flip-flops X_1, X_2, X_3, etc.

Some computers have a register called an *accumulator* which is the principal register for arithmetic and logical operations. This register stores the result of each arithmetic or logical operation, and gating circuitry is attached to this register so that the necessary operations can be performed on its contents and any other registers involved.

An accumulator is therefore a basic storage register of the arithmetic element. If the machine is instructed to *load* the accumulator, the control element will first clear the accumulator of whatever may have been stored in it and then put the operand selected in storage into the accumulator register. If the computer is instructed to *add,* the number stored in the accumulator will represent the augend. The addend will then be located in memory, and the computer's circuitry will add this number (the addend) to the number previously stored in the accumulator (the augend) and store the sum in the accumulator. Notice that the original augend will no longer be stored in the accumulator after the addition. Furthermore, the sum may then either remain in the accumulator or be transferred to memory, depending on the type of computer. This chapter will deal only with the processes of adding, subtract-

---

† Some computers also provide the ability to handle variable length operands.

ing, etc., and not the process of locating the number to be added in memory or the transferring of numbers to memory. These operations will be covered in following chapters.

Some computers, instead of having a single accumulator, will have two or more accumulators and these are called, for instance, accumulator *A* and accumulator *B* (as in the Hewlett-Packard computers) or ACC1, ACC2, etc., (as in the Data General Corporation computers). When the number of registers provided to hold operands becomes larger than four, however, the registers are often called *general registers,* and individual registers are given names, such as general register 4, general register 8, etc.

6•2 INTEGER REPRESENTATION

The numbers used in digital machines must be represented using such storage devices as flip-flops. The most direct number representation system for binary-valued storage devices is an *integer representation system.* Figure $6 \cdot 1(a)$ shows a register of four flip-flops, X_1, X_2, X_3, and X_4, used to store numbers. Simply writing the values or states of the flip-flops gives the number in integer form, so that $X_1 = 1, X_2 = 1, X_3 = 0, X_4 = 0$ gives 1100, or decimal 12, while $X_1 = 0, X_2 = 1, X_3 = 0, X_4 = 1$ gives 0101, or decimal 5.

It is generally necessary to represent both positive and negative numbers; so an additional bit is required called the *sign bit.* This is generally placed to the left of the magnitude bits. In Fig. $6 \cdot 1(b)$ we choose X_0 as the sign bit, and X_1, X_2, X_3, and X_4 will give the magnitude. A 0 in X_0 means that the number is positive, and a 1 in X_0 means that the number is negative (this is the usual

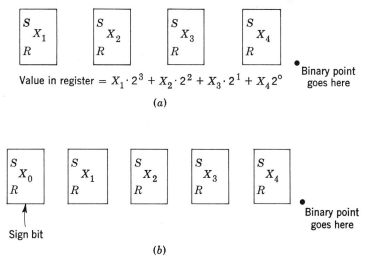

FIG. 6•1 Representation systems. (*a*) Integer representation; (*b*) sign-plus-magnitude system.

convention); so $X_0 = 0$, $X_1 = 1$, $X_2 = 1$, $X_3 = 0$, and $X_4 = 1$ gives positive 1101, or +13 in decimal, and $X_0 = 1$, $X_1 = 1$, $X_2 = 1$, $X_3 = 0$, and $X_4 = 1$ gives negative 1101, or −13 in decimal.

This system is called the *signed integer binary system,* or *signed magnitude binary integer system.*

If a register contains eight flip-flops, a signed binary number in the system would have 7 magnitude, or integer, bits and a single sign bit; so 00001111 would be +15 and 10001111 would be −15, since the leading 0 and 1 give the + and − only.

The magnitudes of numbers which can be stored in the two representative systems in Fig. 6·1 are as follows:

1. For binary integer representation, an *n*-flip-flop register can store from (decimal) 0 to $2^n - 1$. Thus, for a 6-bit register, we can store from 000000 to 111111, where 111111 is 63, which is $2^6 - 1$, or 64 − 1.
2. The signed binary integer representation system has a range of from $-(2^{n-1} - 1)$ to $+2^{n-1} - 1$ for a binary storage device. For instance, a 7-flip-flop register can store from −111111 to +111111, which is −63 to +63 $[-(2^6 - 1)$ to $+(2^6 - 1)]$.

In the following sections we shall learn how to perform various arithmetic and logical operations on registers.

6•3 THE BINARY HALF ADDER

A basic module used in binary arithmetic elements is the *half adder.* The function of the half adder is to add two binary digits, producing a sum and a carry according to the binary addition rules shown in Table 6·1. Figure 6·2 shows a design for a half adder. There are two inputs to the half adder, designated as X and Y in Fig. 6·2, and two outputs, designated as S and C. The half adder performs the binary addition operation for two binary inputs shown in Table 6·1. This is *arithmetic addition,* not logical or Boolean algebra addition.

As shown in Fig. 6·2, there are two inputs to the half adder and two outputs. If either of the inputs is a 1, but not both, the output on the S line will be a 1. If both of the inputs are 1s, the output on the C (for carry) line will be a 1; for

TABLE 6•1

INPUTS	SUM BIT	
0 + 0	0	
0 + 1	1	
1 + 0	1	
1 + 1	0	with a carry of 1

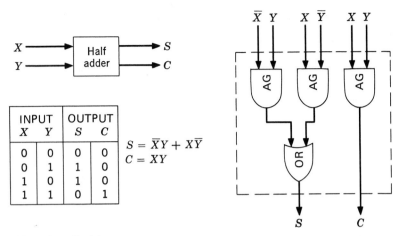

FIG. 6•2 Half adder.

all other states there will be a 0 output on the CARRY line. These relationships may be written in Boolean form as follows:

$$S = X\bar{Y} + \bar{X}Y$$
$$C = XY$$

A *quarter adder* consists of the two inputs to the half adder and the S output only. The logical expression for this circuit is therefore $S = X\bar{Y} + \bar{X}Y$. This is also the *exclusive OR* relationship for Boolean algebra (refer to Chap. 3).

6•4 THE FULL ADDER

When more than two binary digits are to be added, several half adders will not be adequate, for the half adder has no input to handle carries from other digits.

Consider the addition of the following two binary numbers:

```
    1 0 1 1              1 0 1 1
+   1 1 1 0          +   1 1 1 0
  1 1 0 0 1 = sum        0 1 0 1 = partial sum
                       1   1     = carry bits
                       1 1 0 0 1 = complete sum
```

As shown, the carries generated in each column must be considered during the addition process; therefore adder circuitry capable of adding the contents of two registers together must include provision for handling carries as well as addend and augend bits. There must therefore be three inputs to each stage of a multidigit adder — except the stage for the least significant bits —

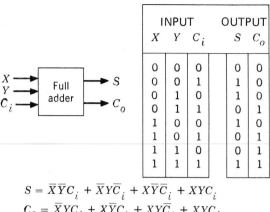

INPUT			OUTPUT	
X	Y	C_i	S	C_o
0	0	0	0	0
0	0	1	1	0
0	1	0	1	0
0	1	1	0	1
1	0	0	1	0
1	0	1	0	1
1	1	0	0	1
1	1	1	1	1

$$S = \overline{X}\overline{Y}C_i + \overline{X}Y\overline{C}_i + X\overline{Y}\overline{C}_i + XYC_i$$
$$C_o = \overline{X}YC_i + X\overline{Y}C_i + XY\overline{C}_i + XYC_i$$
or
$$C_o = XC_i + XY + YC_i$$

FIG. 6·3 Full adder.

one for each input from the numbers being added and one for any carry which might have been generated or propagated by the previous stage.

The block diagram symbol for a *full binary adder,* which will handle these carries, is illustrated in Fig. 6·3, as is the complete table of input-output relationships for the full adder. There are three inputs to the full adder: the X and Y inputs from the respective digits of the registers to be added, and the C_i input, which is for any carry generated by the previous stage. The two outputs are S, which is the output value for that stage of the addition, and C_o, which produces the carry to be added into the next stage.† The Boolean expressions for the input-output relationships for each of the two outputs are also presented in Fig. 6·3, as is the expression for the C_o output in simplified form.

A full adder may be constructed of two half adders, as illustrated in Fig. 6·4. Constructing a full adder from two half adders may not necessarily be the most economical technique, however, and generally full adders are designed directly from the input-output relations illustrated in Fig. 6·3.

6•5 A PARALLEL BINARY ADDER

A 4-bit parallel binary adder is illustrated in Fig. 6·5. The purpose of this adder is to add together two 4-bit binary integers. The addend inputs are named X_1 through X_4, and the augend bits are represented by Y_1 through Y_4.‡

---

† C_i is for *carry-in* and C_o for *carry-out.*

‡ These inputs would normally be from flip-flop registers X and Y and the adder would add the number in X to the number in Y giving the sum, or S_1 through S_4.

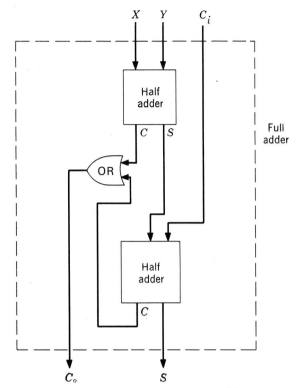

FIG. 6•4 Half adder and full adder relationship.

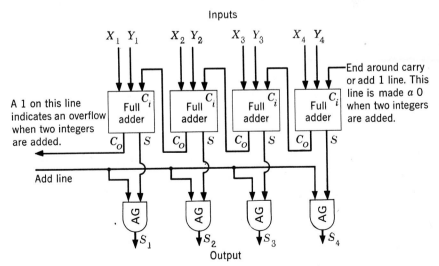

FIG. 6•5 Parallel adder.

The adder shown does not possess the ability to handle sign bits for the binary words to be added, but only adds together the magnitudes of the numbers stored. The additional circuitry needed to handle sign bits is dependent on whether negative numbers are represented in true magnitude or in the 1s or 2s complement systems, and this problem will be described later.

Consider the addition of the following two 4-bit binary numbers:

$$\begin{array}{ll} 0\ 1\ 1\ 1 & \text{where } X_1 = 0,\ X_2 = 1,\ X_3 = 1,\ \text{and } X_4 = 1 \\ \underline{0\ 0\ 1\ 1} & \text{where } Y_1 = 0,\ Y_2 = 0,\ Y_3 = 1,\ \text{and } Y_4 = 1 \\ \text{Sum} = 1\ 0\ 1\ 0 \end{array}$$

The sum should therefore be $S_1 = 1$, $S_2 = 0$, $S_3 = 1$, and $S_4 = 0$.

The operation of the adder may be checked as follows: Since X_4 and Y_4 are the least significant digits, they cannot receive a carry from a previous stage. In the problem above, X_4 and Y_4 are both 1s, their sum is therefore 0, and a carry is generated and added into the full adder for bits X_3 and Y_3. Bits X_3 and Y_3 are also both 1s, as is the carry input to this stage; therefore the sum output line S_3 carries a 1 and the CARRY line to the next stage also carries a 1. Since X_2 is a 1, Y_2 a zero, and the CARRY input is 1, the sum output line S_2 will carry a 0 and the carry to the next stage will be a 1. Both inputs X_1 and Y_1 are equal to 0, and the CARRY input line to this adder stage is equal to 1; therefore the sum output line S_1 will represent a 1 and the CARRY output line, designated as "overflow" in Fig. 6·5, will have a zero output.

The same basic configuration illustrated in Fig. 6·5 may be extended to any number of bits. A 7-bit adder may be constructed using 7 full adders, and a 20-bit adder using 20 full adders.

It should be noted that the OVERFLOW line could be used to enable the 4-bit adder in Fig. 6·5 to have a 5-bit output. This is not generally done, however, because the addend and augend both come from storage, and so their length is the length of the basic computer word, and a longer word cannot be readily stored by the machine. It was explained earlier that a machine with a word length of n bits [consisting of a sign bit and $(n-1)$ bits to designate the magnitude] could express binary numbers from $(-2^{n-1}+1)$ to $(2^{n-1}-1)$. A number within these limits is called *representable*. Since the simple 4-bit adder in Fig. 6·5 has no sign bit, it can only represent binary integers from 0 to 15. If 1100 and 1100 are added in the adder illustrated in Fig. 6·5, there will be a 1 output on the OVERFLOW line because the sum of these two numbers is 11000. This number is 24 decimal and cannot be represented in this system. Such a number is referred to as *nonrepresentable* for this particular very small register, and when two integers are added such that their sum is nonrepresentable (i.e., contains too many bits), then we say the sum *overflows*, or an *overflow* occurs. A 1 on the CARRY line for the full adder connected to the most significant digits indicates this. The overflow generated in this case is often connected to circuitry which alerts the computer, generating an indication that an overflow operation has occurred. It is one of the functions of the computer to detect such overflows and to deal with them.

The AND gates connected to the S output lines from the four adders are used to gate the sum into the correct register.

6•6 POSITIVE AND NEGATIVE NUMBERS

When writing numbers in the decimal system, the common practice is to write the number as a magnitude preceded by a plus or minus sign, which indicates whether the number is positive or negative. Hence $+125$ is positive and -125 is negative 125. The same practice is generally used with binary numbers: $+111$ is positive 7, and -110 is negative 6. To handle both positive and negative numbers, the computer must have some means of distinguishing a positive from a negative number, and as was previously explained, the computer word usually contains a sign bit, generally adjacent to the most significant bit in the computer word. In the systems to be described, a 1 in the sign bit will indicate a negative number and a 0 in the sign bit a positive number.

We have examined the representation of numbers in Sec. 6•1 using a signed integer magnitude representation system. There are two other representation systems, however, which are more often used—the 1s and 2s complement systems. (The 2s complement system is the most frequently used system at present.) The advantage of these systems is that both positive and negative numbers can be added or subtracted using only an adder of the type already explained.

Here are the three basic systems.

1. Negative numbers may be stored in their *true magnitude form*. The binary number -0011 will therefore be stored as 1.0011, where the 1 indicates that the number stored is negative and the 0011 indicates the magnitude of the number.†

2. The *1s complement* of the magnitude may be used to represent a negative number. The binary number -0111 will therefore be represented as 1.1000, where the 1 indicates that the number is negative and 1000 is the 1s complement of the magnitude. (The 1s complement is formed by simply complementing each bit of the positive magnitude.)

3. The *2s complement* may be used to represent a negative binary number. For instance, -0111 would be stored as 1.1001, where the 1 in the sign bit indicates that the number is negative and the 1001 is the 2s complement of the magnitude of the number. (The 2s complement is formed by 1s complementing the magnitude part 0111, giving 1000, and then adding 1 to the least significant digit, giving 1001.)

---

† Again we note that a binary point is used to separate the sign bit from the magnitude bits. Thus 0.011 is $+3$. Other symbols have been used, but this is conventional and we will use it.

6•7 ADDITION IN THE 1S COMPLEMENT SYSTEM

The 1s complement system for representing negative numbers is often used in parallel binary machines. The main reason for this is the ease with which the 1s complement of a binary number may be formed, since only complementing each bit of a binary number stored in a flip-flop register is required. Before discussing the implementations of an adder for the 1s complement system, the four possible basic situations which may arise in adding combinations of positive and negative numbers in the 1s complement system will be noted:

1. When a positive number is added to another positive number, the addition of all bits, including the sign bit, is straightforward. Since both sign bits will be 0s, no sum or carry will be generated in the sign-bit adder and the output will remain 0. Here is an example of the addition of two 4-bit positive numbers:†

NORMAL NOTATION	COMPUTER WORD
+0 0 1 1	0 . 0 0 1 1
+0 1 0 0	0 . 0 1 0 0
+0 1 1 1	0 . 0 1 1 1

2. When a positive and a negative number are added together, the sum may be either positive or negative. If the positive number has a greater magnitude, the sum will be positive; and if the negative number is greater in magnitude, the sum will be negative. In the 1s complement system, the answer will be correct as is if the sum of the two numbers is negative in value. In this case no overflow will be generated when the numbers are added. For instance:

+0 0 1 1	0 . 0 0 1 1
−1 1 0 0	1 . 0 0 1 1
−1 0 0 1	1 . 0 1 1 0

In this case the output of the adder will be 10110, the last 4 bits of which are the 1s complement of 1001, the correct magnitude of the sum. The 1 in the sign bit is also correct, indicating a negative number.

3. If the positive number is larger than the negative number, the sum before the end-around carry is added will be incorrect. The addition of the end-around carry will correct this sum. There will be a 0 in the sign bit indicating that the sum is positive.

---

† In this and in all discussion that follows, we assume that the result (sum) does not exceed the capacity of the number of digits being used. This will be discussed later.

$$
\begin{array}{llll}
+1001= & 0.1001 & +0011= & 0.0011 \\
-0100= & 1.1011 & -0010= & 1.1101 \\
\hline
+0101 & 0.0100 & +0001 & 0.0000 \\
& \quad\quad\rightarrow 1 & & \quad\quad\rightarrow 1 \\
\hline
& 0.0101 & & 0.0001
\end{array}
$$

Notice what happens when two numbers of equal magnitude but opposite sign are added:

$$
\begin{array}{llll}
+1011=0.1011 & & +0000=0.0000 \\
-1011=1.0100 & & -0000=1.1111 \\
\hline
0000 \quad 1.1111 & & 0000 \quad 1.1111
\end{array}
$$

The result in these cases will be a negative zero (1.1111), which is correct.

4. When two negative numbers are added together, an end-around carry will always be generated, as will a carry from the adder for the first bits of the magnitudes of the numbers. This will place a 1 in the sign bit.

$$
\begin{array}{llll}
-0011= & 1.1100 & -0100= & 1.1011 \\
-1011= & 1.0100 & -0111= & 1.1000 \\
\hline
-1110 & 1.0000 & -1011 & 1.0011 \\
& \quad\quad\rightarrow 1 & & \quad\quad\rightarrow 1 \\
\hline
& 1.0001 & & 1.0100
\end{array}
$$

The output of the adder will be in 1s complement form in each case, with a 1 in the sign-bit position.

From the above we see that in order to implement an adder which will handle 4-bit magnitude signed 1s complement numbers, we can simply add another full adder to the configuration in Fig. 6·5. The sign inputs will be labeled X_0 and Y_0, and the C_o output from the adder connected to X_1 and Y_1 will be connected to the C_i input of the new full adder for X_0 and Y_0. The C_o output from the adder for X_0 and Y_0 will be connected to the C_i input for the adder for X_4 and Y_4. The S_0 output from the new adder will give the sign digit for the sum. (Overflow will not be detected in this adder, additional gates are required.)

6·8 ADDITION IN THE 2S COMPLEMENT SYSTEM

When negative numbers are represented in the 2s complement system, the operation of addition is very similar to that in the 1s complement system. In parallel machines, the 2s complement of a number stored in a register may be formed by first complementing the register and then adding 1 to the least significant bit of the register. This process requires two steps and is therefore more time consuming† than the 1s complement system; however, the 2s complement system has the advantage of not requiring an end-around carry during addition.

The four situations which may occur in adding two numbers when the 2s complement system is used are as follows:

1. When both numbers are positive, the situation is completely identical with that in case 1 in the 1s complement system which has been discussed.

2. When one number is positive and the other negative, and the larger number is the positive number, a carry will be generated through the sign bit. This carry may be discarded, since the outputs of the adder are correct, as shown below.

$$
\begin{array}{ll}
+0111 = 0.0111 & +1000 = 0.1000 \\
-0011 = +1.1101 & -0111 = +1.1001 \\
\hline
+0100 \quad \llcorner 0.0100 & +0001 \quad \llcorner 0.0001 \\
\qquad \ \ \hookrightarrow\text{carry is discarded} & \qquad \ \ \hookrightarrow\text{carry is discarded}
\end{array}
$$

3. When a positive and negative number are added and the negative number is the larger, no carry will result in the sign bit and the answer will again be correct at it stands.

$$
\begin{array}{ll}
+0011 = 0.0011 & +0100 = 0.0100 \\
-0100 = 1.1100 & -1000 = 1.1000 \\
\hline
-0001 \quad 1.1111 & -0100 \quad 1.1100
\end{array}
$$

Note: A 1 must be added to the least significant bit of a 2s complement negative number when converting it to a magnitude. For example:

$$
\begin{array}{rl}
1.0011 = & 1100 \ \text{form 1s complement} \\
& \underline{0001} \ \text{add 1} \\
& -1101
\end{array}
$$

When both numbers are the same magnitude, the result is as follows:

$$
\begin{array}{l}
+0011 = 0.0011 \\
-0011 = 1.1101 \\
\hline
0000 \quad 0.0000
\end{array}
$$

When a positive and negative number of the same magnitude are added, the result will be a positive zero.

4. When two negative numbers are added together, a carry will be generated

---

† Generally, this 1 is "sneaked in" during calculation, as will be shown.

in the sign bit and also in the bit to the right of the sign bit. This will cause a 1 to be placed in the sign bit, which is correct, and the carry from the sign bit may be discarded.

$$
\begin{array}{rcl}
-0011= & 1.1101 \\
-0100= & 1.1100 \\
\hline
-0111 & 1.1001 \\
\end{array}
\qquad
\begin{array}{rcl}
-0011= & 1.1101 \\
-1011= & 1.0101 \\
\hline
1110 & 1.0010 \\
\end{array}
$$

└──→ carry is discarded

For parallel machines, addition of positive and negative numbers is quite simple, since any overflow from the sign bit is simply discarded. Thus, for the parallel adder in Fig. 6·5, we simply add another full adder, with X_0 and Y_0 as inputs and with the carry line C_0 from the full adder, which adds X_1 and Y_1, connected to the carry input C_i to the full adder for X_0 and Y_0. A 0 is placed on the C_i input to the adder connected to X_4 and Y_4.

This simplicity in adding and subtracting has made the 2s complement system the most popular for parallel machines. In fact, when signed-magnitude systems are used, the numbers generally are converted to 2s complement before addition of negative numbers or subtraction is performed; then the numbers are changed back to signed magnitude.

6·9 ADDITION AND SUBTRACTION IN A PARALLEL ARITHMETIC ELEMENT

We now examine the design of a gating network which will either add or subtract two numbers. The network is to have an ADD input line and a SUBTRACT input line as well as the lines that carry the representation of the numbers to be added or subtracted. When the ADD line is a 1, the sum of the numbers is to be on the output lines and when the SUBTRACT line is a 1, the difference is to be on the output lines. If both ADD and SUBTRACT are 0s, the output is to be 0.

First we note that if the machine is capable of adding both positive and negative numbers, subtraction may be performed by complementing the subtrahend and then adding. For instance, $8 - 4$ yields the same result as $8 + (-4)$, and $6 - (-2)$ yields the same result as $6 + 2$. Subtraction therefore may be performed by an arithmetic element capable of adding, by forming the complement of the subtrahend and then adding. For instance, in the 1s complement system, four cases may arise:

TWO POSITIVE NUMBERS

$$
\begin{array}{r}
0.0011 \\
-0.0001 \\
\hline
\end{array}
\qquad
\begin{array}{l}
\text{Complementing the subtrahend} \\
\text{and adding}
\end{array}
\qquad
\begin{array}{r}
0.0011 \\
1.1110 \\
\hline
0.0001 \\
\end{array}
$$

└──→ carry 1
$$
\begin{array}{r}
\hline
0.0010 \\
\end{array}
$$

TWO NEGATIVE NUMBERS

```
     1.1101                                        1.1101
    -1.1011       Complementing                    0.0100
                                              ┌────0.0001
                                              └──→ carry 1
                                                   0.0010
```

POSITIVE MINUEND   NEGATIVE MINUEND
NEGATIVE SUBTRAHEND   POSITIVE SUBTRAHEND

```
   0.0010 _ 0.0010                  1.0101 _ 1.0101
  -1.1101 = 0.0010                 -0.0010 = 1.1101
           0.0100                        ┌────1.0010
                                         └──→ carry 1
                                              1.0011
```

The same basic rules apply to subtraction in the 2s complement system except that any carry generated in the sign-bit adders is simply dropped. In this case, the 2s complement of the subtrahend is formed, and the complemented number is then added to the minuend with no end-around carry.

We now examine the implementation of a combined adder and subtracter network. The primary problem is to form the complement of the number to be subtracted. This complementation of the subtrahend may be performed in several ways. For the 1s complement system, if the storage register is composed of flip-flops, the 1s complement can be formed by simply connecting the complement of each input to the adder. The 1 which must be added to the least significant position to form a 2s complement may be added when the two numbers are added by connecting a 1 at the CARRY input of the adder for the least significant bits.

A complete logical circuit capable of adding or subtracting two signed 2s complement numbers is shown in Fig. 6·6. One number is represented by X_0, X_1, X_2, X_3, and X_4, and the other number by Y_0, Y_1, Y_2, Y_3, Y_4. There are two control signals, ADD and SUBTRACT. If neither control signal is a 1 (i.e., both are 0s), then the outputs from the five full adders, which are S_0, S_1, S_2, S_3, S_4, will all be 0s. If the ADD control line is made a 1, the sum of the number X and the number Y will appear as S_0, S_1, S_2, S_3, and S_4. If the SUBTRACT line is made a 1, the difference between X and Y (that is, $X - Y$) will appear on S_0, S_1, S_2, S_3, and S_4.

Notice that the AND-to-OR gate network connected to each Y input selects either Y or $\overline{Y}$, so that, for instance, an ADD causes Y_1 to enter the appropriate full adder, while a SUBTRACT causes $\overline{Y}_1$ to enter the full adder.

To either ADD or SUBTRACT, each X input is connected to the appropriate full adder. When a subtraction is called for, the complement of each Y flip-flop is gated into the full adder, and a 1 is added by connecting the SUBTRACT signal to the C_i input of the full adder for the lowest-order bits X_4 and Y_4. Since the SUBTRACT line will be a 0 when we ADD, a 0 carry will be on this line when addition is performed.

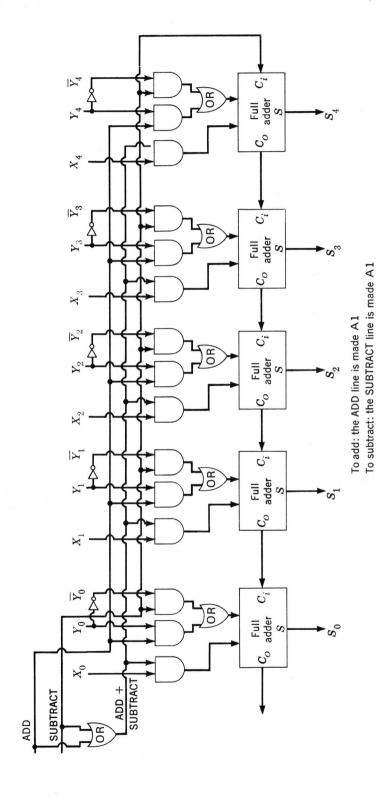

To add: the ADD line is made A1
To subtract: the SUBTRACT line is made A1
Numbers are to be in 2s complement form

FIG. 6 • 6 Parallel addition and subtraction.

233

The simplicity of the operation of Fig. $6 \cdot 6$ makes 2s complement addition and subtraction very attractive for computer use, and it is the most frequently used system.†

The configuration in Fig. $6 \cdot 6$ is the most frequently used for addition and subtraction because it provides a simple direct means for either adding or subtracting positive or negative numbers. Quite often the $S_0, S_1, \ldots, S_4$ lines are gated back into the X flip-flops, so that the sum or difference of the numbers X and Y replaces the original value of X.

An important consideration is overflow. In digital computers an *overflow* is said to occur when the performance of an operation results in a quantity beyond the capacity of the register (or storage register) which is to receive the result. Since the registers in Fig. $6 \cdot 6$ have a sign bit plus 4 magnitude bits, they can store from $+15$ to -16 in 2s complement form. Therefore, if the result of an addition or subtraction were greater than $+15$ or less than -16, we would say that an overflow had occurred. Suppose we add $+8$ to $+12$; the result should be $+20$, and this cannot be represented (fairly) in 2s complement on the lines S_0, S_1, S_2, S_3, and S_4. The same thing happens if we add -13 and -7 or if we subtract -8 from $+12$. In each case logical circuitry is used to detect the overflow condition and signal the computer control element. Various options are then available, and what is done can depend on the type of instruction being executed. (Deliberate overflows are sometimes used in double-precision routines. Multiplication and division use the results as are.) We shall defer this to Chap. 9, except that one of the questions at the end of the chapter asks for a circuit to test for overflow.

The parallel adder-subtractor configuration in Fig. $6 \cdot 6$ is quite important, and it is instructive to try adding and subtracting several numbers in 2s complement form using pencil and paper and this logic circuit.

6•10 THE FULL ADDER

The full adder is a basic component of an arithmetic element. Figure $6 \cdot 3$ illustrates the block-diagram symbol for the full adder, along with a table of combinations for the input-output values and the expressions describing the sum and carry lines. Succeeding figures and text described the operation of the full adder. Notice that a parallel addition system requires one full adder for each bit in the basic word.

There are of course many gate configurations for full binary adders. Examples of an IBM adder and an MSI package containing two full adders follow.

1. *Full binary adder*   Figure $6 \cdot 7$ illustrates the full binary-adder configura-

---

† A 1s complement parallel adder-subtracter can be made by connecting the carry-out line for the X_0, Y_0 adder to the carry-in line for the X_4, Y_4 adder (disconnecting the subtract line to this full adder, of course).

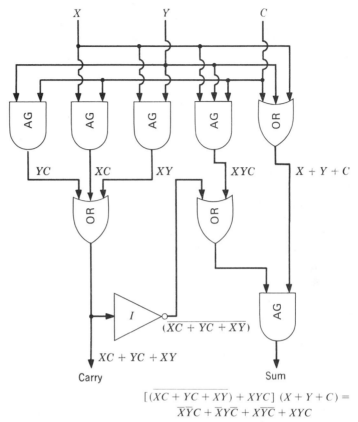

X Y C

AG AG AG AG OR

YC XC XY XYC $X + Y + C$

OR OR

I $\overline{(XC + YC + XY)}$

$XC + YC + XY$

AG

Carry   Sum

$$[\,\overline{(XC + YC + XY)} + XYC\,](X + Y + C) =$$
$$\overline{X}\overline{Y}C + \overline{X}Y\overline{C} + X\overline{Y}\overline{C} + XYC$$

FIG. 6•7 Full adder used in IBM machines.

tion used in several IBM general-purpose digital computers. There are three inputs to the circuit: the X input is from one of the storage devices in the accumulator, the Y input is from the corresponding storage device in the register to be added to the accumulator register, and the third input is the CARRY input from the adder for the next least significant bit. The two outputs are the SUM output and the CARRY output. The SUM output will containe the sum value for this particular digit of the output. The CARRY output will be connected to the CARRY input of the next most significant bit's adder (refer to Fig. 6·5).

The outputs from the three AND gates connected directly to the X, Y, and C inputs are logically added together by the OR gate circuit directly beneath. If either the X and Y, X and C, or Y and C input lines contain a 1, there should be a CARRY output. The output of this circuit, written in logical equation form, is shown on the figure. This may be compared with the expression derived in Fig. 6·3.

The derivation of the SUM output is not so straightforward. The CARRY output expression $XY + XC + YC$ is first inverted (complemented), yielding $(\overline{XY + XC + YC})$. The logical product of X, Y, and C is formed by an AND gate and is logically added to this, forming $(\overline{XY + XC + YC}) + XYC$. The logical sum of X, Y, and C is then multiplied, forming the expression

$$[(\overline{XY + XC + YC}) + XYC](X + Y + C)$$

When multiplied out and simplified, this expression will be $X\overline{Y}\overline{C} + \overline{X}Y\overline{C} + \overline{X}\overline{Y}C + XYC$, the expression derived in Fig. 6·3. Tracing through the logical operation of the circuit for various values will indicate that the SUM output will be 1 when only one of the input values is equal to 1, or when all three input values are equal to 1. For all other combinations of inputs the output value will be a 0.

2. *Two full adders in an integrated circuit (IC) container* Figure 6·8 shows two full adders. This package was developed for integrated circuits using transistor-transistor logic (TTL). The entire circuitry is packaged in one IC container. The maximum delay from an input change to an output change for an S output is on the order of 8 nanoseconds (ns).† The maximum delay from input to the $C2$ output is about 6 ns.

   The amount of delay associated with each carry is an important figure

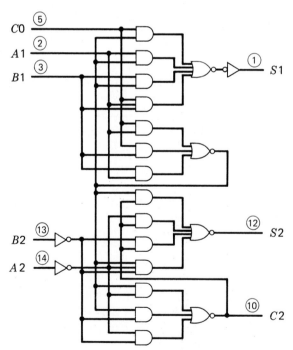

FIG. 6•8 Two full adders in an IC container. (Courtesy Texas Instruments)

---

† 1 ns = 10^{-9} s.

in evaluating a full adder for a parallel system, because the amount of time required to add two numbers is determined by the maximum time it takes for a carry to propagate through the adders. For instance, if we add 01111 to 10001 in the 2s complement system, the carry generated by the 1s in the least significant digit of each number must propagate through four carry stages and a sum stage before we can safely gate the sum into the accumulator. A study of the addition of these two numbers using the configuration in Fig. 6·5 will make this clear. This problem is called the *carry-ripple problem.*

There are a number of techniques which are used in high-speed machines to alleviate this problem. The most used is a bridging or carry-look-ahead circuit which calculates the carry-out of a number of stages simultaneously and then delivers this carry to the succeeding stages. (This is covered in the questions.)

6•11 THE BINARY-CODED-DECIMAL (BCD) ADDER

Arithmetic units which perform operations on numbers stored in BCD form must have the ability to add 4-bit representations of decimal digits. To do this a BCD adder is used. A block diagram symbol for a adder is shown in Fig. 6·9. The adder has an augend digit input consisting of four lines, an addend digit input of four lines, a carry-in and a carry-out, and a sum digit with four output lines. The augend digit, addend digit, and sum digit are each represented in 8, 4, 2, 1 BCD code.

The purpose of the BCD adder in Fig. 6·9 is to add the augend and addend digits and the carry-in and produce a sum digit and carry-out. This adder could be designed using the techniques in Chap. 3 and the rules for decimal addition. It is also possible to make a BCD adder using full adders and AND or OR gates. An adder made in this way is shown in Fig. 6·10.

FIG. 6•9 Serial-parallel addition.

FIG. 6 • 10 BCD adder.

There are eight inputs to the BCD adder, four X_i, or augend, inputs and four Y_i, or addend, digits. Each of these inputs will represent a 0 or a 1 during a given addition. If 3(0011) is to be added to 2(0010), then $X_8 = 0$, $X_4 = 0$, $X_2 = 1$, and $X_1 = 1$; $Y_8 = 0$, $Y_4 = 0$, $Y_2 = 1$, and $Y_1 = 0$.

The basic adder in Fig. 6·10 consists of the four full binary adders at the top of the figure and performs base 16 addition when the intent is to perform base 10 addition. Some provision must therefore be made to (1) generate carries and (2) correct sums greater than 9. For instance, if $3_{10}(0011)$ is added to $8_{10}(1000)$, the result should be $1_{10}(0001)$ with a carry generated.

The actual circuitry which determines when a carry is to be transmitted to the next most significant digits to be added consists of the full binary adder to which sum (S) outputs from the adders for the 8, 4, 2 inputs are connected and of the OR gate to which the carry (C) from the eight-position bits is connected. An examination of the addition process indicates that a carry should be generated when the 8 AND 4, or 8 AND 2, or 8 AND 4 AND 2 sum outputs from the base 16 adder represent 1s, or when the CARRY output from the eight-position adder contains a 1 (this occurs when 8s or 9s are added together).

Whenever the sum of two digits exceeds 9, the CARRY TO NEXT HIGHER ORDER ADDER line contains a 1 for the adder in Fig. 6 · 10.

A further difficulty arises when a carry is generated. If 7_{10} (0111) is added to 6_{10} (0110), a carry will be generated, but the output from the base 16 adder will be 1101. This (1101) does not represent any decimal digit in the 8, 4, 2, 1 system and must be corrected. The method used to correct this is to add 6_{10} (0110) to the sum from the base 16 adders whenever a carry is generated. This addition is performed by adding 1s to the weight 4 and weight 2 position output lines from the base 16 adder when a carry is generated. The two half adders and the full adder at the bottom of the diagram perform this function. Essentially then, the adder performs base 16 addition and corrects the sum, if it is greater than 9, by adding 6. Several examples of this are shown below.

$$
\begin{array}{ll}
8 + 7 = 15 & \qquad 1000 + 0111 = \\
\end{array}
\qquad
\begin{array}{r}
(8)(4)(2)(1) \\
1 \quad 1 \quad 1 \quad 1 \\
+0 \quad 1 \quad 1 \quad 0 \\
\hline
1 \quad 0 \quad 1 \quad 0 \quad 1 = 5 \\
\end{array}
$$
     with a carry generated

$$
9 + 5 = 14
\qquad
\begin{array}{r}
(8)(4)(2)(1) \\
1 \quad 0 \quad 0 \quad 1 \\
0 \quad 1 \quad 0 \quad 1 \\
\hline
1 \quad 1 \quad 1 \quad 0 \\
+0 \quad 1 \quad 1 \quad 0 \\
\hline
1 \quad 0 \quad 1 \quad 0 \quad 0 \text{ or } 4 \\
\end{array}
$$
     with a carry generated

Figure 6 · 11 shows a complete BCD adder in an IC package.† The inputs are digit A and digit B, and the output is S. A carry-in and carry-out are included. The circuit line used is CMOS.

6 • 12 POSITIVE AND NEGATIVE BCD NUMBERS

The techniques for handling BCD numbers greatly resemble those for handling binary numbers. A sign bit is used to indicate whether the number is positive or negative, and there are three methods of representing negative

---

† The IC packages in Figs. 6 · 11, 6 · 13, 6 · 14, and 6 · 15 are typical BCD MSI packages. The notation $A1$, $A2$, $A3$, $A4$ (instead of X_1, X_2, X_4, X_8) is often used for the 4 bits of a BCD digit and the weights 1, 2, 4, 8 are understood. Thus a BCD digit in $B1$, $B2$, $B3$, $B4$ would have weight 1 or $B1$, weight 2 or $B2$, weight 4 or $B3$, and weight 8 or $B4$.

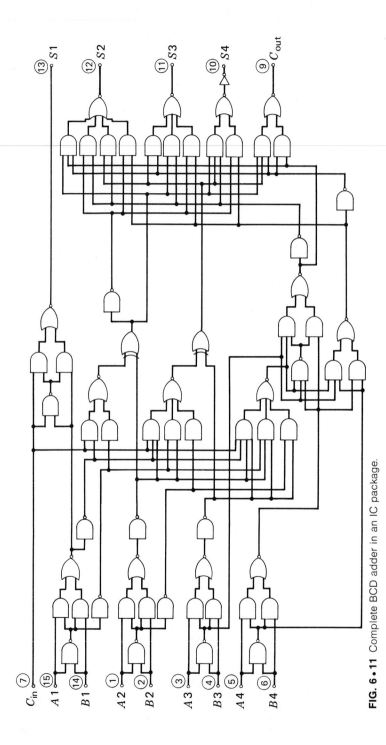

FIG. 6•11 Complete BCD adder in an IC package.

numbers which must be considered. The first and most obvious method is, of course, to represent a negative number in true magnitude form with a sign bit, so that −645 is represented as 1.645. The other two possibilities are to represent negative numbers in a 9s or a 10s complement form, which forms resemble the binary 1s and 2s complement forms.

6 • 13 ADDITION AND SUBTRACTION IN THE 9S COMPLEMENT SYSTEM

When decimal numbers are represented in a binary code in which the 9s complement is formed when the number is complemented, the situation is roughly the same as when the 1s complement is used to represent a binary number. Four cases may arise: two positive numbers may be added; a positive and negative number may be added, yielding a positive result; a positive and a negative number may be added, yielding a negative result; and two negative numbers may be added. Since there is no problem when two positive numbers are added, the three latter situations will be illustrated.

Negative and positive number — positive sum:

$$
\begin{array}{r}
+692 = 0.692 \\
-342 = 1.657 \\
\hline
+350 \quad 0.349 \\
\longrightarrow 1 \\
\hline
0.350
\end{array}
$$

Positive and negative number — negative sum:

$$
\begin{array}{r}
-631 = 1.368 \\
+342 = 0.342 \\
\hline
-289 \quad 1.710 = -289
\end{array}
$$

Two negative numbers:

$$
\begin{array}{r}
-248 = 1.751 \\
-329 = 1.670 \\
\hline
-577 \quad 1.421 \\
\longrightarrow 1 \\
\hline
1.422 = -577
\end{array}
$$

The rules for handling negative numbers in the 10s complement system are the same as those for the binary 2s complement system in that no carry must be ended-around. A parallel BCD adder may therefore be constructed using only the full BCD adder as the basic component, and all combinations of positive and negative numbers may thus be handled.

There is an additional complexity in BCD addition, however, because the

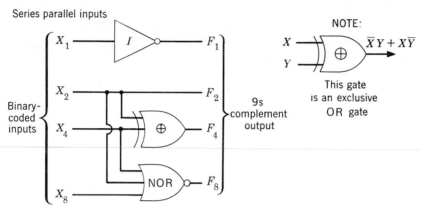

FIG. 6·12 Logical circuit for forming 9s complement of 8421 BCD digits.

9s complement of a BCD digit cannot be formed by simply complementing each bit in the represention. As a result, a gating block called a *complementer* must be used.

To illustrate the type of circuit which may be used to form complements of the code groups for BCD numbers, a block diagram of a logical circuit which will form the 9s complement of a code group representing a decimal number in 8421 BCD form is shown in Fig. 6·12. There are four inputs to the circuit, X_1, X_2, X_4, and X_8. Each of these inputs carries a different weight: X_1 has weight 1, X_2 has weight 2, X_4 has weight 4, and X_8 has weight 8. If the inputs represent a decimal digit of the number to be complemented, the outputs will represent the 9s complement of the input digit. For instance, if the input is 0010 (decimal 2), the output will be 0111 (decimal 7), the 9s complement of the input.

Figure 6·13 shows a complete 9s complementer in an IC package. The circuits used are CMOS, and so transmission gates† appear in the block diagram as well as conventional gates. (This does not bother the circuit's user because the user is primarily interested in the circuit's function.) When the COMP input is a 1, the outputs F1–F4 represent the complement of the digit on A1–A4. While if COMP is a 0, the A1–A4 inputs are simply placed on F1–F4 without change.

By connecting the IC packages in Figs. 6·11 and 6·13 together, a BCD adder-subtracter can be formed as shown in Fig. 6·14. This shows that a two-digit adder-subtracter IC package would be required for more digits. In order to add the digits in the inputs the ADD-SUBTRACT input is made a 1; to subtract this signal is made a 0. (Making the ZERO input a 1 will cause the

---

† Transmission gates can be explained in terms of conventional gates. Figure 5·30 explains transmission gates.

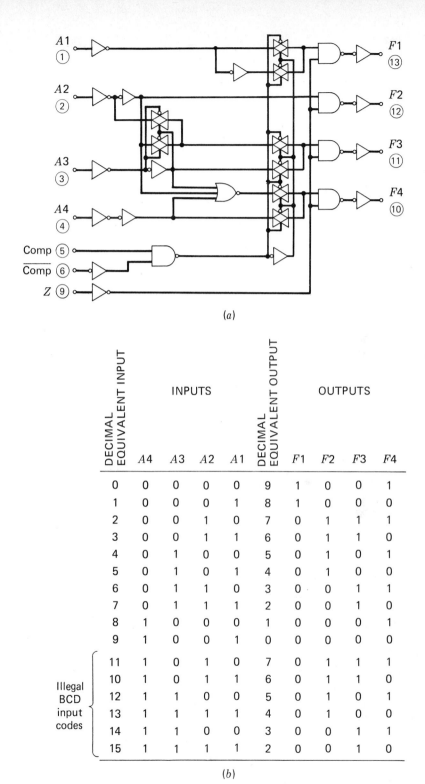

FIG. 6 • 13 9s complements in IC package. (*a*) Logic diagram; (*b*) truth table.

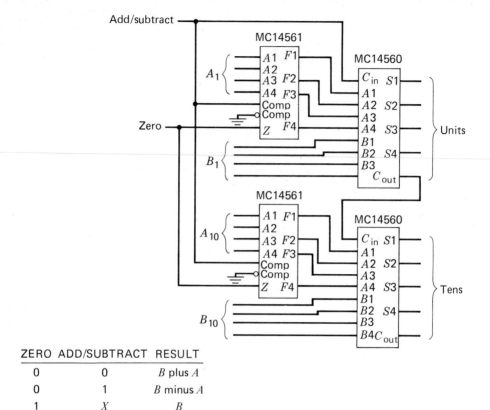

ZERO	ADD/SUBTRACT	RESULT
0	0	B plus A
0	1	B minus A
1	X	B

X = don't care

FIG. 6•14 Parallel add-subtract circuit (10s complement).

value of B to pass through unchanged.) BCD numbers may also be represented in parallel form, as we have shown, but a mode of operation called *series-parallel* is often used. If a decimal number is written in binary-coded form, the resulting number consists of a set of code groups, each of which represents a single decimal digit. For instance, decimal 463 in a BCD 8421 code is 0100 0110 0011. Each group of 4 bits represents one decimal digit. It is convenient to handle each code group which represents a decimal digit as a unit, that is, in parallel. At the same time, as the word lengths for decimal computers are apt to be rather long, it is desirable to economize in the amount of equipment used.

The *series-parallel* system provides a compromise in which each code group is handled in parallel but the decimal digits are handled sequentially. This requires four lines for each 8421 BCD character, each input line of which carries a different weight. The block diagram for an adder operating in this system is shown in Fig. 6·15. There are two sets of inputs to the adder; one consists of the four input lines which carry the coded digit for the addend, and the other four input lines carry a coded augend digit. The sets of inputs

FIG. 6 • 15 Series-parallel BCD adder-subtracter using shift register.

arrive sequentially from the *A* and *B* registers, each of which consists of four shift registers; the least significant addend and augend binary-coded decimal digits arrive first, followed by the more significant decimal digits.

If the 8421 code is used, let 324 represent the augend and 238 the addend. The ADD signal will be a 0. The adder will first receive 0100 on the augend lines, and at the same time it will receive 1000 on the addend lines. After the first clock pulse, these inputs will be replaced by 0010 on the augend lines and 0011 on the addend lines. Before the first clock signal, the sum lines should contain 0010, and before the second, 0110. A carry will be generated during the addition of the first two digits; this will be delayed and added in using the *D* flip-flop. The process will continue until each of the three digits have been added. To subtract *B* from *A*, we have only to make the ADD-SUBTRACT input a 1 and then apply the clocks.

6 • 14 THE SHIFT OPERATION

A SHIFT operation is an operation which moves the digits stored in a register to new positions in the register. There are two distinct SHIFT operations, a SHIFT-LEFT operation and a SHIFT-RIGHT operation. A SHIFT-LEFT operation moves each bit of information stored in a register to the left by some specified number of digits. Consider the following 6 binary digits, 000110, which we will assume to be stored in a parallel binary register. If the contents of the register are shifted left 1, after the shift the register will contain 001100. If a shift right of 1 is performed on the word 000110, after the shift the register will

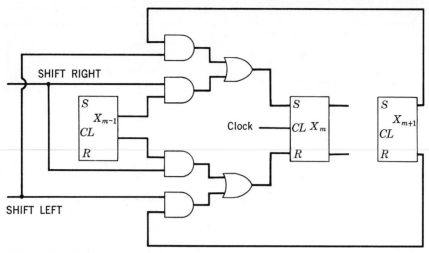

FIG. 6•16 Shift-left and shift-right stage of register.

contain 000011. The shifting process in a decimal register is similar: if the register contains 0.01234, after a right shift of 1 the register will contain 0.00123, or after a left shift of 1 the register will contain 0.12340. The SHIFT operation is used in the MULTIPLY and the DIVIDE instructions of most machines and also is provided as an instruction which may be used by programmers. For instance, a machine may have instructions SHR and SHL, where the letters represent in mnemonic form the order for SHIFT-RIGHT and SHIFT-LEFT instructions.

A block diagram of logical circuitry for a single stage (flip-flop) in a register which can be shifted either left or right is shown in Fig. 6·16. As can be seen, the bit to the left is shifted into X as if SHIFT RIGHT is a 1 and the bit to the right is shifted into X when SHIFT LEFT is a 1.

Figure 6·17 shows an MIS package which contains four flip-flops and gating circuitry so that the register can be shifted right or left, and also so that the four flip-flops can be parallel loaded from four input lines W, X, Y, and Z. The circuits are TTL circuits and are clocked in parallel. By combining modules such as this one, a register of a chosen length can be formed which can be shifted left or right or parallel loaded.

6•15 BASIC OPERATIONS

The arithmetic-logic unit of a digital computer consists of a number of registers in which information can be stored and a set of logical circuits which make it possible to perform certain operations on the information stored in the registers and to perform certain operations between registers.

As we have seen, the data stored in a given flip-flop register may be operated on in the following ways:

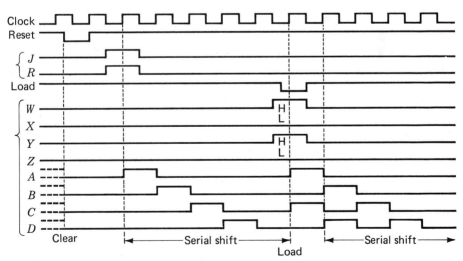

FIG. 6·17 Shift register (model SN 74195) with a parallel load ability. (Courtesy Texas Instruments.)

1. The register may be reset to all 0s.
2. The contents of a register may be complemented to either 1s or 2s complement form for binary, or for decimal to 9s or 10s complement form.
3. The contents of a register may be shifted right or left.
4. The contents of a register can be incremented or decremented.

Several operations between registers have also been described. These include:

1. Transferring the contents of one register to another register
2. Adding to or subtracting from the contents of one register the contents of another register

Most arithmetic operations which an arithmetic-logic unit performs consist of these or sequenced sets of these two types of operations. Complicated instructions, such as multiplication and division, can require a large number of these operations, but these instructions may be performed using only sequences of the simple operations already described.

One other important point needs to be made. Certain operations which occur within instructions are *conditional.* That is, a given operation may or may not take place, depending on the value of certain bits of the numbers stored. For instance, it may be desirable to multiply using only positive numbers. In this case, the sign bits of the two numbers to be multiplied together will be examined by control circuitry, and if either is a 1, the corresponding number will be complemented before the multiplication begins. This operation, complementing of the register, is a conditional one.

Many different sequences of operations can yield the same result. For instance, two numbers could be multiplied together by simply adding the multiplicand to itself the number of times indicated by the multiplier. If this were done with pencil and paper, 369 × 12 would be performed by adding 369 to itself 12 times. This would be a laborious process compared with the easier algorithm which we have developed for multiplying, but we would get the same result. The same principle applies to machine multiplication. Two numbers could be multiplied together by transferring one of the numbers into a counter which counted downward each time an addition was performed, and then adding the other number to itself until the counter reached zero. This technique has been used, but much faster techniques are also used and will be explained.

Many algorithms have been used to multiply and divide numbers in digital machines. Division, especially, is a complicated process, and in decimal machines in particular, many different techniques are used. The particular technique used by a machine is generally based on the cost of the machine and the premium on speed for the machine. As in almost all operations, speed is expensive, and a faster division process generally means a more expensive machine.

To explain the operations of binary multiplication and division, we will use a block diagram of a generalized binary machine. Figure 6 · 18 illustrates, in block diagram form, the registers of an ALU. The machine has three basic

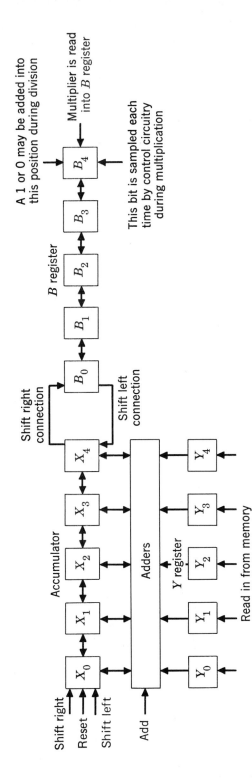

FIG. 6·18 Generalized parallel arithmetic element.

registers, an accumulator, *Y* register, and *B* register. The operations which can be performed have been described:

1. The accumulator can be cleared.
2. The contents of the accumulator can be shifted right or left. Further, the accumulator and *B* register may be formed into one long shift register. If we then shift this register right two digits, the two least significant digits of the accumulator will be shifted into the first two places of the *B* register. Several left shifts will shift the most significant digits of the *B* register into the accumulator. Since there are 5 bits in the basic machine word, there are five binary storage devices in each register. A right shift of five places will transfer the contents of the accumulator into the *B* register, and a left shift of five places will shift the contents of the *B* register into the accumulator.
3. The contents of the *Y* register can be either added to or subtracted from the accumulator. The sum or difference will then be stored in the accumulator register.
4. Words from memory may be read into the *Y* register. To read a word into the accumulator, it is necessary first to clear the accumulator, then to read the word from memory into the *Y* register, and then add the *Y* register to the accumulator.

An arithmetic element which can perform these operations on its registers can be sequenced to perform all arithmetic operations. It is, in fact, possible to construct a machine using fewer operations than these, but most general-purpose computers will usually have an arithmetic element with at least these capabilities.

6 • 16 BINARY MULTIPLICATION

The process of multiplying binary numbers together may be best examined by writing out the multiplication of two binary numbers:

$$
\begin{array}{r}
1\,0\,0\,1 = \text{multiplicand} \\
1\,1\,0\,1 = \text{multiplier} \\
\hline
1\,0\,0\,1 \\
0\,0\,0\,0 \\
1\,0\,0\,1 \\
1\,0\,0\,1 \\
\hline
1\,1\,1\,0\,1\,0\,1 = \text{product}
\end{array}
$$

partial products

The important thing to notice in this process is that there are really only two rules for multiplying a single binary *number* by a binary *digit;* (1) If the multiplier digit is a 1, the multiplicand is simply copied, and (2) if the multiplier digit is a 0, the product is 0. The above example illustrates these rules as follows: The first digit to the right of the multiplier is a 1; therefore the multiplicand is copied as the first partial product. The next digit of the multiplier to the left is a 0; therefore the partial product is a 0. Notice that each time a partial product is formed, it is shifted one place to the left of the previous partial product. Even if the partial product is a 0, the next partial product is shifted one place to the left of the previous partial product. This process is continued until all the multiplier digits have been used, and then the partial products are summed.

The three operations which the computer must be able to perform to multiply in this manner are therefore (1) the ability to sense whether a multiplier bit is either a 1 or a 0, (2) the ability to shift partial products, and (3) the ability to add the partial products.

It is not necessary to wait until all the partial products have been formed before summing them. They may be summed two at a time. For instance, starting with the first two partial products in the above example,

$$
\begin{array}{r}
1\,0\,0\,1 \\
0\,0\,0\,0 \\
\hline
0\,1\,0\,0\,1
\end{array}
$$

The next partial product may then be added to this sum, displacing it one position to the left:

$$
\begin{array}{r}
0\,1\,0\,0\,1 \\
1\,0\,0\,1 \\
\hline
1\,0\,1\,1\,0\,1
\end{array}
$$

and finally,

$$
\begin{array}{r}
1\,0\,1\,1\,0\,1 \\
1\,0\,0\,1 \\
\hline
1\,1\,1\,0\,1\,0\,1
\end{array}
$$

A multiplier can be constructed in just this fashion. By sampling each bit of the multiplier in turn, adding the multiplicand into some register, and then shifting the multiplicand left each time a new multiplier bit was sampled, a product would be formed of the sum of the partial products. In fact, the process of multiplying in most binary machines is performed in a manner very similar to this.

To examine the typical technique for multiplying, the generalized arithmetic elements in Fig. 6·18 will be used. Referring to Fig. 6·18, let the multiplier be stored in the B register, and the multiplicand in the Y register; the accumulator contains all 0s. Let us also assume that both multiplier and multiplicand are positive; if either is negative, it must be converted to positive form before the multiplication begins. Assume n bits in each operand.

A multiplication requires n basic steps. Each step is initiated by the control circuitry examining the rightmost bit in the B register. The basic step is then performed as follows. If the rightmost bit in the B register is a 0, the combined accumulator and B register is shifted right one place; if the rightmost bit in the B register is a 1, the number in the Y register is added to the contents of the accumulator, and the combined accumulator and B register is then shifted right one place. The new rightmost bit of the B register is then again examined, and the next of the n steps is initiated.

Let us consider the same multiplication which was used in the previous example, that is, 1101×1001, where 1101 is the multiplier. In this case, the accumulator contains 0.0000, the B register 0.1101, and the Y register 0.1001.

Since the rightmost bit of the B register contains a 1 (the least significant bit of the multiplier), during the first step the contents of the Y register are added to the accumulator, and the combined accumulator and B register are then shifted to the right. The second least significant bit of the multiplier will now occupy the rightmost bit of the B register and will control the next operation.

The Y register will still contain the multiplicand 0.1001, the contents of the accumulator will be 0.0100, and the contents of the B register will be 1.0110. The rightmost bit of the B register is a 0, and since it controls the next operation, a SHIFT-RIGHT signal will be initiated and the accumulator and B register will be shifted right, giving 0.0010 in the accumulator and 0.1011 in the B register. A 1 will now be in the rightmost bit of the B register.

The Y register will therefore again be added to the accumulator, and the combined accumulator–B register will again be shifted right. The least significant bit of the B register will be another 1; so the Y register will again be added to the accumulator and the accumulator shifted right.

After the above shift right, the combined accumulator and B register will contain 0.011101010. A final right shift gives 0.001110101, the correct product for our integer number system. The most significant digits will be stored in the accumulator, and the least significant digits in the B register.

The reason for the combined accumulator and B register can now be seen. The product of two 5-bit signed numbers can contain up to nine significant digits (including the sign bit), and so two 5-bit registers, not one, are required to hold the product. The final result is treated like a 10-bit number extending through the two registers with the leftmost bit in the left register, the sign bit and rightmost bit in the right register, and the least significant binary digit in the product. Thus, our result in the two combined registers was 0.001110101, which is $+117$ in decimal.

The control circuitry is designed to perform the examination of the multiplier bits, then either shift or add and shift the correct number of times, and then stop. In this case, the length of the multiplier, or Y register, was 4 bits plus a sign bit; so four such steps are performed. The general practice is to examine each bit of the machine word except the sign bit, in turn. For instance, if the basic machine word is 25 bits, that is, 24 bits in which the magnitude of a number is stored plus a sign bit, each time a multiplication is performed the machine will examine 24 bits, each in turn, performing the ADD-AND-SHIFT or just the SHIFT operation 24 times. As many be seen, this makes the multiplication operation longer than such operations as add or subtract. Some parallel machines double their normal rate of operation during multiplication: if the machine performs such operations as addition, complement, transfers, etc., at a rate of 4 MHz per sec for ordinary instructions, the rate will be increased to 8 MHz for the add-and-shift combinations performed while multiplying. Some machines are able to shift right while adding; that is, the sum of the accumulator and Y register appears shifted one place to the right each time, and the SHIFT-RIGHT operation after each addition may be omitted.

The sign bits of the multiplier and multiplicand may be handled in a number of ways. For instance the sign of the product can be determined by means of control circuitry before the multiplication procedure is initiated. This sign bit is stored during the multiplication process, after which it is placed into the sign bit of the accumulator, and the accumulator is then complemented, if necessary. Therefore the sign bits of the multiplier and multiplicand are first examined; if they are both 0s, the sign of the product should be 0; if both are 1s, the sign of the product should be 0; and if either but not both are 1s, the sign of the product should be 1. This information, retained in a flip-flop while the multiplication is taking place, may be transferred into the sign bit afterward. If the machine handles numbers in the 1s or 2s complement system, both multiplier and multiplicand may be handled as positive magnitudes during the multiplication, and if the sign of either number is negative, the number is complemented to a positive magnitude before the multiplication begins. Sometimes the multiplication is performed on complemented numbers using more complicated algorithms. These are described in the references.

6 • 17 DECIMAL MULTIPLICATION

Decimal multiplication is a more involved process than binary multiplication. Whereas the product of a binary digit and a binary number is either the number or 0, the product of a decimal digit and decimal number involves the use of a multiplication table plus carrying and adding. For instance,

$$7 \times 24 = (7 \times 4) + (7 \times 20) = 28 + 140 = 168$$

Even the multiplying of two decimal digits may involve two output digits, for instance, 7×8 equals 56. In the following discussion we call the two digits which may result when a decimal digit is multiplied times a decimal digit the *left-hand* and *right-hand digits*. Thus, for 3×6, we have 1 for the left-hand digit and 8 for the right-hand digit. For 2×3, we have 0 for the left-hand digit and 6 for the right-hand digit.

Except for simply adding the multiplicand to itself, the number of times indicated by the multiplier, a simple but time-consuming process, the simplest method for decimal multiplication involves loading the rightmost digit of the multiplier into a counter which counts downward and then adding the multiplicand to itself and simultaneously indexing the counter until the counter reaches 0. The partial product thus formed may be shifted right one decimal digit, the next multiplier digit loaded into the counter, and the process repeated until all the multiplier digits have been used. This is a relatively slow but straightforward technique.

The process may be speeded up by forming products using the multiplicand and the rightmost digit of the multiplier as in the previous scheme, but by actually forming the left-hand and right-hand partial products obtained when multiplying a digit by a number and then summing them. For instance, 6×7164 would yield 2664 for the right-hand product digits and 4032 for the left-hand product digits. The sum would then be

$$
\begin{array}{r}
2\,6\,6\,4 \\
+\,4\,0\,3\,2 \\
\hline
4\,2\,9\,8\,4
\end{array}
$$

Decimal-machine multiplication is in general a complicated process if speed is desired, and there are almost as many techniques for multiplying BCD numbers as there are types of machines.† IC packages are produced containing a gate network which has two BCD characters as inputs which produce the two-digit output required. The questions and references explore this in more detail.

*6•18 DIVISION

The operation of division is the most difficult and time consuming which the ALU of most general-purpose machines performs. Although division may appear no more difficult than multiplication, there are several problems in connection with the division process which introduce time-consuming extra steps.

Division, using pencil and paper, is a trial-and-error process. For instance, if we are to divide 77 into 4610, we first notice that 77 will not "go" into 46; so we attempt to divide 77 into 461. We may guess that it will go six times, however:

$$
\begin{array}{r}
6 \\
77\,\overline{)\,4\,6\,1\,0} \\
4\,6\,2 \\
\hline
-\,1
\end{array}
$$

---

† Several machines use table-look-up techniques for forming products, where the product of each pair of digits is stored in the memory.

* This section can be omitted in a first reading.

Therefore we have guessed too high and must reduce the first digit of the quotient, which we will develop, to 5.

The same problem confronts the computer when it attempts to divide in this manner. It must "try" a subtraction each step of the process and then see if the remainder is negative. Consider the division of 1111 by 11.

$$
\begin{array}{r}
1\ 0\ 1 \\
1\ 1\ )\overline{1\ 1\ 1\ 1} \\
\underline{1\ 1} \\
0\ 0\ 1\ 1 \\
\underline{1\ 1} \\
0\ 0
\end{array}
$$

It is easy to determine visually at any step of the process whether the quotient is to be a 1 or a 0, but the computer cannot determine this without making a trial subtraction each time. After a trial quotient has been tried and the divisor subtracted, if the result is negative, either the current dividend must be "restored" or some other technique for dividing used.

There are several points to be noted concerning binary fixed-point integer-value division. The division is generally performed with two signed binary integers of the same fixed length. The result, or quotient, is stored as a number, with as many digits as the divisor or dividend, and the remainder is also stored as a number of the same length.†

Using the registers shown in Fig. 6·18, we will show how to divide a number stored in the accumulator by a number in the Y register. The quotient is then stored in the B register, and the remainder in the accumulator. This is the most common division format.

Assume the B and Y registers in Fig. 6·18 to be 5 bits in length (4 bits + sign bit) and the accumulator also 5 bits in length. Before starting the procedure, the dividend is read into the accumulator, and the divisor into the Y register. After the division, the quotient will be stored in the B register and the remainder will be in the accumulator. Both divisor and dividend are to be positive.

There are two general techniques for division for binary machines: the *restoring* and *nonrestoring* techniques. Our example will use the restoring technique.

The *basic step* in the restoring technique consists of a trial division which is made by attempting to subtract the Y register from the accumulator.

1. If the result is negative, the divisor will not "go"; a 0 is therefore placed in the right-most bit of the B register, and the dividend (accumulator) is

---

† If we divide one integer into another, the quotient and remainder will both be integers. The rule is as follows: if a is the dividend, y the divisor, b the quotient, and r the remainder, then $a = y \times b + r$.

TABLE 6·2

B REGISTER	ACCUMULATOR	Y REGISTER	REMARKS
0.0000	0.0110	0.0011	We divide 6 by 3.
0.0000	0.0110	0.0110	Y register is shifted left once, aligning 1s in accumulator Y registers; the basic step must be performed two times.
0.0000	0.0000	0.0110	The Y register has been subtracted from the accumulator. The result is 0, so the B register and accumulator are shifted left and a 1 placed in the rightmost bit of the B register.
0.0001	0.0000	0.0110	
0.0001	1.1010	0.0110	The Y register is subtracted from the accumulator.
0.0010	0.0000	0.0110	The Y register is added to the accumulator, and the B register and accumulator are shifted left 1. A 0 is placed in the B register's last bit.
0.0010	0.0000	0.0110	The accumulator must now be shifted right two times but it is 0 so no change results.

restored by adding the divisor to the result of the subtraction. The combined *B* register and accumulator will then be shifted left.

2. If the result of a trial division is positive or zero, there is no need to restore the partial dividend in the accumulator for the trial division has succeeded. A 1 is placed in the rightmost bit of the *B* register, and the accumulator and *B* register are both shifted left.

The computer determines whether or not the result of a trial division is positive or negative by examining the sign bit of the accumulator after each subtraction.

In order to demonstrate the entire procedure, it is first necessary to explain how to initiate the division and how to start and stop performing the basic steps.

1. As described above, if the divisor is larger than the dividend, then the quotient should be 0 and the remainder is the value of the dividend. (For instance, if we attempt to divide 7 by 17, the quotient is 0 and the remainder is 7.) To test this, the dividend in *Y* can be subtracted from the accumulator and if the result is negative, all that remains is to restore the accumulator by adding the *Y* register to the accumulator. The *B* register now has value 0 which is right for the quotient, and the accumulator has the original value which is the remainder.

2. After the above test is made, it is necessary to align the leftmost 1 bit in the divisor with the leftmost 1 bit in the dividend by shifting the divisor left, and to record the number of shifts required to make this alignment. If

TABLE 6·3

B REGISTER	ACCUMULATOR	Y REGISTER	REMARKS
0.0000	0.1101	0.0011	We divide 13 by 3.
0.0000	0.1101	0.0110	Shift Y register left.
0.0000	0.1101	0.1100	Shift Y register left. Leftmost 1 bits in accumulator and Y register are aligned. Basic step will be performed three times.
0.0000	0.0001	0.1100	Y register has been subtracted from accumulator. Result is positive.
0.0001	0.0010	0.1100	B register–accumulator shifted left and 1 placed in B register.
0.0001	1.0110	0.1100	Y register is subtracted from accumulator. Result is negative.
0.0010	0.0100	0.1100	Y register is added to accumulator. Both are then shifted left and a 0 placed in the B register.
0.0010	1.1000	0.1100	Y register is subtracted from accumulator. Result is negative.
0.0100	0.1000	0.1100	Y register is added to accumulator. Accumulator and B register are shifted left. A 0 is placed in the B register's bit.
0.0100	0.0001	0.1100	The accumulator has been shifted right 3. The quotient is 4 and the remainder is 1.

the number of shifts is M, then the basic step must be performed $M + 1$ times.†

3. Now, the basic step is performed the necessary $M + 1$ times.

4. Finally, to adjust the remainder, the accumulator must be shifted right $M + 1$ times after the last basic step is performed. Examples are shown in Tables 6·2 and 6·3. Step 1 above, testing for a zero quotient, is not shown in the two examples.

Figure 6·19 shows a flowchart of the algorithm. Flowcharts are often used to represent algorithms. A more detailed flow chart would separate some of the steps, such as "shift the accumulator right $M + 1$ times," into single shifts performed in a loop which is controlled by a counter. Often, when algorithms are reasonably complicated, as this algorithm is, it is convenient to draw a flowchart of the algorithm before attempting to implement the control circuitry.

---

† This can be accomplished by making Y a shift register and providing a counter to count the shifts until the first 1 bit of Y is aligned with the 1 bit of the accumulator. Both the accumulator and Y could be shifted left until there is a 1 bit in their first position, but the remainder will then have to be adjusted by moving it right in the accumulator.

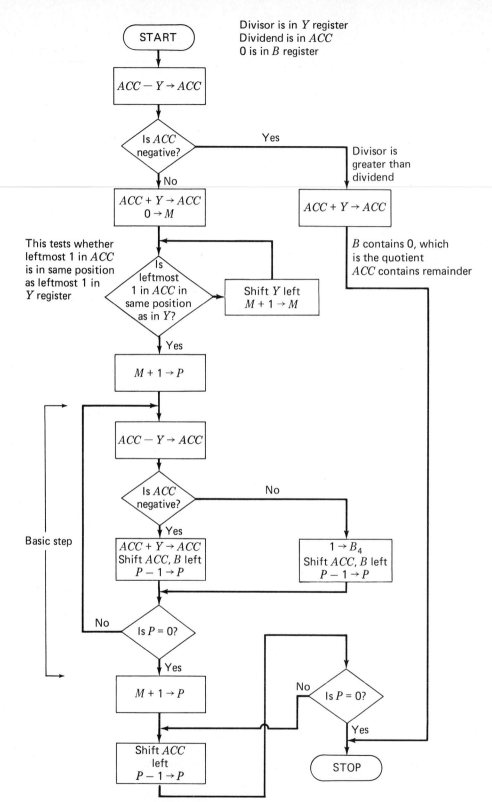

FIG. 6·19 Flowchart of division algorithm.

There are several techniques for nonrestoring division, but one widely used algorithm uses a procedure in which the divisor is alternately subtracted and added.

The principle involved here may be explained as follows: Let X equal the number stored in the accumulator and Y equal the divisor. If the divisor is subtracted, the result is $X - Y$. If this result is stored in the accumulator and then shifted left 1 bit, the result will be $2(X - Y)$. If $X - Y$ was negative, the divisor is now added to the accumulator, resulting in $2(X - Y) + Y$, or $2X - Y$, which will be correct for this step. The quotient is formed in the same way as in restoring division. If the result of a trial division is positive, a 1 is placed in the rightmost bit of the quotient, and if the result of a trial division is negative, the quotient is left unchanged. After each trial, both the accumulator (the partial dividend) and the quotient are shifted left.

The basic steps required for each trial division are therefore as follows:

1. For the first step the Y register is subtracted from the accumulator.
2. If the result is positive or zero, a 1 is placed in the least significant bit of the B register, and the accumulator and B register are shifted left. The next step will be another subtraction.
3. If the result of step 1 is negative, a 0 is placed in the least significant bit of the B register, and the accumulator and B register are shifted left. For the next step the Y register is added instead of subtracted. If the result is positive, a 1 is placed in the least significant bit of the B register, and the accumulator and B register are shifted left. The next step is to subtract the Y register from the accumulator. If the result is negative, a 0 is placed in the least significant bit of the B register, and the accumulator and B register are shifted left. The Y register is again added and shifted left until a positive result is yielded, in which case the procedure reverts to the subtract step 1.

Although it is more complicated, fewer steps are required to perform a division by this technique, since the dividend need not be restored at each step. For this reason, the procedure has often been used.

In some machines the sign bit of the result of the trial division (subtraction) may be examined by control circuitry without performing the actual subtraction. Then, if the sign bit is a 1, no subtraction is performed; otherwise, the subtraction is performed. In this case it is, of course, not necessary to restore; the result of the trial division which fails is not placed in the accumulator.

During division, the sign bits are handled in much the same way as during multiplication. The first step is to convert both the divisor and dividend to positive magnitude form; the value of the sign bit for the quotient must be stored while the division is taking place. The rule is that if the signs of the dividend and divisor are both either 0s or 1s, the quotient will be positive. If either but not both of their signs is a 1, the quotient will be negative. The relationship of the sign bit of the quotient to the sign bit of the divisor and dividend is therefore the quarter adder, or exclusive OR, relationship, that is, $S = X\overline{Y} + \overline{X}Y$. The value for the correct sign of the quotient may be read into a flip-flop while the division is taking place, and this value may then be placed in the sign bit of the register containing the quotient after the division of magnitudes has been completed.

6•19 LOGICAL OPERATIONS

In addition to the arithmetic operations, many logical operations are performed by ALUs. Three logical operations will be described here: logical multiplication, logical addition, and *sum modulo 2* addition (the exclusive OR operation). Each of these will be operations between registers, where the operation specified will be performed on each of the corresponding digits in the two registers. The result will be stored in one of the registers.

The first operation, logical multiplication, is often referred to as an *extract, masking,* or AND operation. The rules for logical multiplication have been defined in the chapter on logical algebra. The rules are $0 \cdot 0 = 0$; $0 \cdot 1 = 0$; $1 \cdot 0 = 0$; and $1 \cdot 1 = 1$. Suppose the contents of the accumulator register are "logically multiplied" by another register. Let each register be five binary digits in length. If the accumulator contains 01101 and the other register 00111, the contents of the accumulator after the operation will be 00101.

The masking, or extracting, operation is useful in "packaging" computer words. To save space in memory and keep associated data together, several pieces of information may be stored in the same word. For instance, a word may contain an item number, wholesale price, and retail price, packaged as follows:

To extract the retail price, the programmer will simply logically multiply the word above by a word containing 0s in the sign digit through digit 15, and with 1s in positions 16 through 24. After the operation, only the retail price will remain in the word.

The logical addition operation, or the sum modulo 2 operation, is also provided in most computers. The rules for these operations are:

LOGICAL ADDITION	MODULO 2 ADDITION
$0 + 0 = 0$	$0 \oplus 0 = 0$
$0 + 1 = 1$	$0 \oplus 1 = 1$
$1 + 0 = 1$	$1 \oplus 0 = 1$
$1 + 1 = 1$	$1 \oplus 1 = 0$

Figure 6•20 shows how a single accumulator flip-flop and *B* flip-flop can

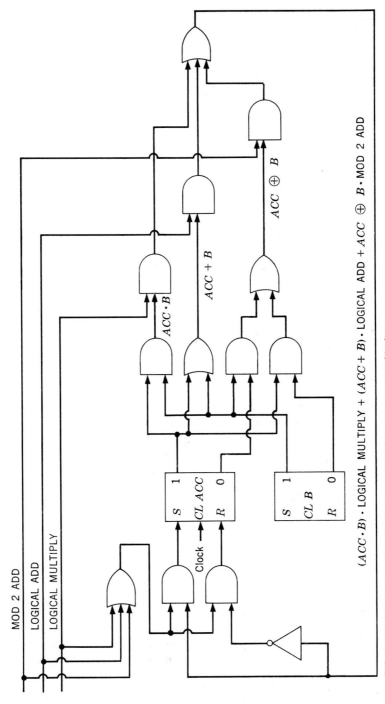

MOD 2 ADD

LOGICAL ADD

LOGICAL MULTIPLY

$ACC \cdot B$

$ACC + B$

$ACC \oplus B$

S 1

$CL\ ACC$

R 0

S 1

$CL\ B$

R 0

Clock

$(ACC \cdot B) \cdot$ LOGICAL MULTIPLY $+ (ACC + B) \cdot$ LOGICAL ADD $+ ACC \oplus B \cdot$ MOD 2 ADD

FIG. 6·20 Circuit for gating logical operations into accumulator flip-flop.

be gated together so that all three of these logical operations can be performed. The circuit in Fig. 6·20 would be repeated for each stage of the accumulator register.

There are three control signals, LOGICAL MULTIPLY, LOGICAL ADD, and MOD 2 ADD. If one of these is up, or 1, when a clock pulse arrives, this operation is performed and the result placed in the ACC (accumulator) flip-flop. If none of the control signals is a 1, nothing happens and the ACC remains as it is.

The actual values desired are found by three sets of gates; that is, ACC · B and ACC + B and ACC ⊕ B are all formed first. Each of these is then AND-gated with the appropriate control signal. Finally, the three control signals are ORed together, and this signal is used to gate the appropriate value into the ACC flip-flop when one of the control signals is a 1.

Figure 6·20 shows how a choice of several different function values can be gated into a single flip-flop using control signals. We could include an ADD signal and a SHIFT RIGHT and SHIFT LEFT by simply adding more gates. More about this will be found in Chap. 9.

*6 • 20 FLOATING-POINT NUMBER SYSTEMS

The preceding sections describe number representation systems where positive and negative integers are stored in binary words. In the representation system used, the binary point is "fixed" in that it lies at the end of each word, and so each value represented is an integer. When computers calculate with binary numbers in this format, the operations are called *fixed-point arithmetic.*

In science, it is often necessary to calculate with very large or very small numbers. Scientists have therefore adopted a convenient notation in which a *mantissa* plus an *exponent* are used to represent a number. For instance, 4,900,000 may be written as 0.49×10^7, where 0.49 is the mantissa and 7 is the value of the exponent, or 0.00023 may be written as 0.23×10^{-3}. The notation is based on the relation $y = a \times r^p$, where y is the number to be represented, a is the mantissa, r is the base of the number system ($r = 10$ for decimal, and $r = 2$ for binary), and p is the power to which the base is raised.

It is possible to calculate with this representation system. To multiply $a \times 10^n$ times $b \times 10^m$, we form $(a \times b) \times 10^{m + n}$. To divide $a \times 10^m$ by $b \times 10^n$, we form $a/b \times 10^{m-n}$. To add $a \times 10^m$ to $b \times 10^n$, we must first make m equal to n. If $m = n$, then $a \times 10^m + b \times 10^n = (a + b) \times 10^m$. The process of making m equal to n is called *scaling* the numbers.

Considerable "bookkeeping" can be involved in scaling the numbers, and there can be difficulty in maintaining precision during computations when the numbers vary over a very wide range of magnitudes. For computer usage, these problems are alleviated by means of two techniques whereby the com-

---

* This section can be omitted during a first reading.

puter (not the programmer) keeps track of the radix (decimal) point, automatically scaling the numbers. In the first, programmed *floating-point routines* automatically scale the numbers used during the computations while maintaining the precision of the results and keeping track of the scale factors. These routines are used with small computers having only fixed-point operations. A second technique lies in building what are called "floating-point operations" into the computer's hardware. The logical circuitry of the computer is then used to perform the scaling automatically and to keep track of the exponents when calculations are performed. To effect this, a number representation system called the floating-point system is used.

A floating-point number in a computer uses the exponential notation system described above, and during calculations the computer keeps track of the exponent as well as the mantissa. A computer number word in a floating-point system may be divided into three pieces: the first is the sign bit, indicating whether the number is negative or positive; the second part contains the exponent for the number to be represented; and the third part, the mantissa.

As an example, let us consider a 12-bit word length computer with a floating-point word. Figure 6·21 shows this. It is common practice to call the exponent part of the word the *characteristic* and the mantissa section the *integer part;* we shall adhere to this practice.

The integer part of the floating-point word shown represents its value in signed-magnitude form (rather than 2s complement, although this has been used). The characteristic is also in signed-magnitude form. The value of the number expressed is $I \times 2^c$, where I is the value of the integer part and C is the value of the characteristic.

Figure 6·22 shows several values of floating-point numbers in both binary form and after being converted to decimal. Since the characteristic has 5 bits and is in signed-magnitude form, the C in $I \times 2^c$ can have values from -15 to $+15$. The value of I is a sign-plus-magnitude binary integer of 7 bits, and so I can have values from -63 to $+63$. The largest number represented by this system would have a maximum I and would be 63×2^{15}. The least number would be -63×2^{15}.

This example shows the use of a floating-point number representation system to store "real" numbers of considerable range in a binary word.

One other widely followed practice is to express the mantissa of the word as a fraction instead of as an integer. This is in accord with common scientific usage since we commonly say that 0.93×10^4 is in "normal" form for exponential notation (and not 93×10^2). In this usage, a mantissa in decimal normally has a value from 0.1 to 0.999 . . .. Similarly, a binary mantissa in nor-

FIG. **6·21** 12-bit floating-point word.

$\overbrace{\hspace{1.5cm}}^{C} \quad \overbrace{\hspace{2cm}}^{I}$

| 0 | 0 | 1 | 1 | 1 | 0 | 0 | 0 | 1 | 0 | 1 | 1 | Value is $2^7 \times 11 = 1408$

$\quad C = +7 \qquad\quad I = +11$

| 0 | 0 | 0 | 1 | 1 | 1 | 0 | 0 | 0 | 1 | 1 | 1 | Value is $2^3 \times (-7) = -56$

$\quad C = +3 \qquad\quad I = -7$

| 1 | 0 | 1 | 0 | 1 | 0 | 0 | 0 | 0 | 1 | 0 | 1 | Value is $2^{-5} \times 5 = \dfrac{5}{32}$

$\quad C = -5 \qquad\quad I = +5$

| 1 | 0 | 1 | 1 | 0 | 1 | 0 | 0 | 1 | 0 | 0 | 1 | Value is $2^{-6} \times -9 = -\dfrac{9}{64}$

$\quad C = -6 \qquad\quad I = -9$

FIG. 6•22 Values of floating-point numbers in 12-bit all-integer systems.

mal form would have a value from 0.5 (decimal) to less than 1. Most computers maintain their mantissa sections in normal form, continually adjusting words so a significant (1) bit is always in the leftmost mantissa position (next to the sign bit).

When the mantissa is in fraction form, this section is called the *fraction*. For our 12-bit example we can express floating-point numbers with characteristic and fraction by simply supposing the binary point to be to the left of the magnitude (and not to the right as in integer representation). In this system a number to be represented has value $F \times 2^c$, where F is the binary fraction and C is the characteristic.

For the 12-bit word considered before, fractions would have values from $1 - 2^{-6}$, which is 0.111111, to $-(1 - 2^{-6})$, which is 1.111111; thus numbers from $(1 - 2^{-6}) \times 2^{15}$ to $-(1 - 2^{-6}) \times 2^{15}$ can be represented, or about +32,000 to −32,000. The smallest value the fraction part would have is now the fraction 0.1000000, which is 2^{-1} times the smallest characteristic, which is 2^{-15}, so the smallest positive number representable is $2^{-1} \times 2^{-15}$ or 2^{-16}. Most computers use this factional system for the mantissa, although computers of Burroughs Corporation and the National Cash Register Company use the integer system previously described.

The Univac 1108 represents single-precision floating-point numbers in this format

	1	2		9	10		36	Bit number

S	C	F

↑ Sign bit   ↑ Characteristic 8 bits   ↑ Fraction part 27 bits

For positive numbers, the characteristic C is treated as a binary integer, the sign bit is a 0, and the fraction part is a binary fraction with value $0.5 \le F < 1$. The value of the number represented is $2^{C-128} \times F$. This is called an *offset system* because the value of the characteristic is simply the integer value in that portion of the word minus an offset which in this case is 128. The exponent can therefore range from -128 to $+127$, since the integer in the characteristic section is 8 bits in length.

As an example, the binary word

$$0.10000001 \qquad 1100......0$$
$$\text{Characteristic} \qquad\quad \text{Fraction}$$

has value $2^{129-128} \times \frac{3}{4} = 2 \times \frac{3}{4} = 1.5$. The representation for a negative number can be derived by forming the representation for the positive number with the same magnitude and then forming the 1s complement of this representation (considering all 36 bits as a single binary number.)

In computers using 16-bit words (including some made by DEC, Hewlett-Packard, Data General, and IBM), floating-point words are represented by *two* adjacent words and thus have 32 bits per word. The actual format for floating-point words for several of these computers is shown in Fig. 6·23. In these computers the fraction part F consists of 24 bits representing a 23-bit fraction and a sign bit. The exponent or characteristic consists of 8 bits. (In Hewlett-Packard computers the fraction part and the characteristic part are represented in 2s complement form, as programmed for Fortran.) Each of these computers can represent magnitudes of up to 2^{127} (or about 10^{38}) and fractions of about as small as 2^{-138} (about 10^{-38}).

Another example of a computer with internal circuitry which performs floating-point operations and uses a single computer word representation of floating-point numbers is the IBM 360/370 series.

IBM calls the exponent part the *characteristic* and the mantissa part the *fraction.* In the 360/370 series floating-point data words can be either 32 or 64 bits in length. The basic formats are as follows:

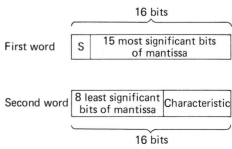

FIG. 6 • 23 Floating-point representation using two words.

Short or single-word floating-point number:

S CHARACTERISTIC FRACTION

0	1 ⟶ 7	8 → 31

Long or double-word floating-point number:

S CHARACTERISTIC FRACTION

0	1 ⟶ 7	8 → 63

In both cases the sign bit *S* is in the leftmost position and gives the sign of the number. The characteristic part of the word then comprises bits 1–7 and is simply a binary integer, which we shall call *C*, ranging from 0 to 127. The actual value of the scale factor is formed by subtracting 64 from this integer *C* and raising 16 to this power. Thus the value 64 in bits 1 to 7 gives a scale factor of $16^{C-64} = 16^{64-64} = 16^0$; a 93 (decimal) in bits 1 to 7 gives a scale factor of $16^{C-64} = 16^{93-64}$ which is 16^{29}; and a 24 in bits 1 to 7 gives a 16^{-40}.

The magnitude of the actual number represented in a given floating-point word is equal to this scale factor times the fraction contained in bits 8 to 31 for the short number, or 8 to 63 for a long number. The radix point is assumed to be to the left of bit 8 in either case; so if bits 8 to 31 contain 1000 . . . 00, the fraction has value $\frac{1}{2}$ (decimal); that is, the fraction is .1000 . . . 000 in binary. Similarly, if bits 8 to 31 contain 11000 . . . 000, the fraction value is $\frac{3}{4}$ decimal, or .11000 . . . 000 binary.

The actual number represented then has magnitude equal to the value of the fraction times the value determined by the characteristic. Consider a short number:

	SIGN	CHARACTERISTIC	FRACTION
Floating-point no.:	0	1 0 0 0 0 0 1	1 1 1 0 0 . . . 0
Bit position:	0	1 2 3 4 5 6 7	8 9 10 11 12 . . . 31

The sign bit is a 0, and so the number represented is positive. The characteristic has binary value 1000001, which is 65 decimal, and so the scale factor is 16^1. The fraction part has value .111 binary, or $\frac{7}{8}$ decimal, and so the number represented is $\frac{7}{8} \times 16$, or 14 decimal.

Again, consider the following number:

	SIGN	CHARACTERISTIC	FRACTION
Floating-point no.:	1	1 0 0 0 0 0 1	1 1 1 0 0 . . . 0
Bit position:	0	1 2 3 4 5 6 7	8 9 10 11 12 . . . 31

This has value -14 since every bit is the same as before except the sign bit. (The number representation system is signed magnitude.)

As further examples:

SIGN	CHARACTERISTIC	FRACTION	
0	1 0 0 0 0 1 1	1 1 0 . . . 0	$16^3 \times \frac{3}{4} = 3072$
0	0 1 1 1 1 1 1	1 1 0 . . . 0	$16^{-1} \times \frac{3}{4} = \frac{3}{64}$

6 • 21 PERFORMING ARITHMETIC OPERATIONS WITH FLOATING-POINT NUMBERS

A computer obviously requires additional circuitry to handle floating-point numbers automatically. Some machines come equipped with floating-point instructions. (For computers such as DEC PDP-11/45 and others, floating-point circuitry can be purchased and added to enable them to perform floating-point operations.)

To handle the floating-point numbers, the machine must be capable of extensive shifting and comparing operations. The rules for multiplying and dividing are

$$(a \times r^p) \times (b \times r^q) = ab \times r^{p+q}$$
$$(a \times r^p) \div (b \times r^q) = \frac{a}{b} \times r^{p-q}$$

The computer must be able to add or subtract the exponent sections of the floating-point numbers, and also perform the multiplication or division operations on the mantissa sections of the numbers. In addition, precision is generally maintained by shifting the numbers stored until significant digits are in the leftmost sections of the word. With each shift, the exponent must be changed. If the machine is shifting the mantissa section left, for each left shift the exponent must be decreased.

For instance, in a BCD computer, consider the word

0	10	0064
Sign	Exponent	Mantissa

To attain precision, the computer shifts the mantissa section left until the 6 is in the most significant position. Since two shifts are required, the exponent must be decreased by 2, and the resulting word is 0.08 6400. If all numbers to be used are scaled in this manner, the maximum precision may be maintained throughout the calculations.

For addition and subtraction, the exponent values must agree. For instance, to add 0.24×10^5 to 0.25×10^6, we must scale the numbers so that the exponents agree. Thus

$$(0.024 \times 10^6) + (0.25 \times 10^6) = 0.274 \times 10^6$$

The machine must also follow this procedure. The numbers are scaled as was described, so that the most significant digit of the computer mantissa section of each word contains the most significant digit of the number stored. Then the larger of the two exponents for the operands is selected, and the other number's mantissa is shifted and its exponent adjusted until the exponents for both numbers agree. The numbers may then be added or subtracted according to these rules:

$$(a \times r^p) + (b \times r^p) = (a + b) \times r^p$$
$$(a \times r^p) - (b \times r^p) = (a - b) \times r^p$$

QUESTIONS

1. Draw a block diagram of circuitry for two registers X and Y of three flip-flops each, so that Y can be transferred into X or the 1s complement of Y can be transferred into X.

2. Two parallel binary registers, designated as register X and register Y, both consist of three flip-flops. Draw a block diagram of the registers and the necessary logical circuitry so that (a) register X can be cleared, or 1s complemented, and (b) the contents of register Y can be transferred into register X.

3. If a binary computer handles numbers in the sign-plus-magnitude integer system, and numbers are 5 bits (sign plus 4 bits) each, how would the following decimal numbers be represented? For example, $+5 = 0.0101$.
   (a) $+6$ (b) $+10$ (c) -12 (d) -16

4. If a binary computer represents numbers in a sign-plus magnitude with 5 bits per number, now would the following decimal numbers be represented:
   (a) $+7$ (b) $+10$ (c) -6
   (d) -8 (e) -17 (f) -14

5. If a binary machine handles negative numbers in the true magnitude form, how would -4 be stored in a register with a sign bit and 4 bits representing magnitude? If the same machine stored numbers in the 1s complement system, how would -4 be stored?

6. If we use the $\oplus$ symbol to mean exclusive OR and define it as $X \oplus Y = \overline{X}Y + X\overline{Y}$, then the output S from a full adder can be written as $S = X \oplus Y \oplus C_i$. Show why this is the case.

7. The inputs to the full adder in Fig. 6·3 are as follows: $X = 1$, $Y = 1$, and $C = 1$. What will the output on the S and C lines represent?

8. If a register contains five flip-flops as in Fig. 6·1(b) and the register contains $X_0 = 1$, $X_2 = 1$, $X_3 = 0$, $X_4 = 1$, $X_5 = 1$, give the decimal value of the number in the register if the 1s complement number system is used? What is the value if 2s complement is used?

9. If we load the binary number 1.0011 into the flip-flops in Fig. 6·1(*b*), that is, if $X_0 = 1$, $X_1 = 0$, $X_2 = 0$, $X_3 = 1$, and $X_4 = 1$, what will the value of the register be in the 1s complement number system? Give the answer in decimal. What will the value of this number be if the 2s complement number system is used?

10. If register X contains 0.0110 and register Y contains 1.1011, what do the two numbers represent in decimal if 1s complement is used? If 2s complement is used? Add the two numbers in 1s complement, then in 2s complement, and give the results in decimal.

11. Register X contains 0.1100, and register Y contains 0.1101 (where the 0s preceding the binary point designate that the number stored is positive). If the two registers are added together, what will the result be?

12. If 1s complement is used, for which of the following expressions will an overflow or end-around carry be generated? Why? Assume 5-bit registers, including a sign bit.

(*a*) $+5 + (-6)$ (*b*) $+5 + (-3)$
(*c*) $+12 + (-12)$ (*d*) $+12 + 2$

13. Add a stage to the LOAD and SHIFT register in Fig. 6·17. Copy only D in your drawing, omitting A, B, and C.

14. A binary register consists of five binary storage devices; one stores the sign bit, and the other four store the magnitude bits. If the number stored is 0.0100 and this number is then shifted right one binary place, what will be the result? Assume a 0 goes into the sign bit.

15. Design a half adder using only NOR gates.

16. Design a half adder using only NAND gates.

17. A binary half subtracter has two inputs x and y and two outputs which are the "difference" value $x - y$ and a "borrow" output which is 1 if the value of $x - y$ is negative ($x - y$ then is given the value 1). Draw a block diagram for a half subtracter using NAND gates and assuming x, $\bar{x}$, y, and $\bar{y}$ are all available as inputs.

18. Design a half subtracter using only NOR gates.

19. If a borrow input is added to the half subtracter in Questions 17 and 18, a full subtracter is formed. Design a full subtracter using only NAND gates.

20. Design a full subtracter using only NOR gates.

21. Design a full adder using only NAND gates.

22. Can an overflow occur during multiplication in a binary machine with numbers stored in fixed-point sign-plus magnitude? Assume a double-length product.

23. Explain how the 2s complement of the subtrahend is formed when we subtract using the configuration in Fig. 6·6. How is the 1 added in to form this complement?

24. Show how the configuration in Fig. 6·6 adds and subtracts by adding and subtracting +6 and +3 in binary showing what each output will be.

25. Add and subtract +6 and −4 using the configuration in Fig. 6·6, showing what each output will be and checking correctness of the sum and difference.

26. Add a control line NAND and circuitry to Fig. 6·20 so that the NAND of ACC and B can be transferred into ACC.

27. If a register containing 0.110011 is logically added to a register containing 0.101010, what will the result be? What will be the result if the registers are logically multiplied? If the registers are exclusive ORed together?

28. Find a sequence of logical operations which will cause the ACC to have value 0 regardless of how ACC and B start in Fig. 6·20.

29. Referring to Fig. 6·20, show that a logical multiply followed by a logical addition will transfer the contents of B into ACC.

30. Add a control line NOR and circuitry to Fig. 6·20 so that the NOR of ACC and B can be transferred into ACC.

31. Demonstrate by means of a table of combinations that two half adders plus an OR gate do make a full adder as shown in Fig. 6·4.

32. Add gates and a flip-flop X_{m+2} so that we can shift left and right into X_{m+1} in Fig. 6·16.

33. Add gates to the following drawing so that if the control input signal C is made a 1, the value $\overline{XY}$ will appear on the output line. If A is a 1 then $X+Y$ appears on the output; if B is a 1 then $X \times Y$ appears on the output; if A, B, and C are 0s, then the output is to be a 0; and only one of A, B, or C can be a 1 at a given time.

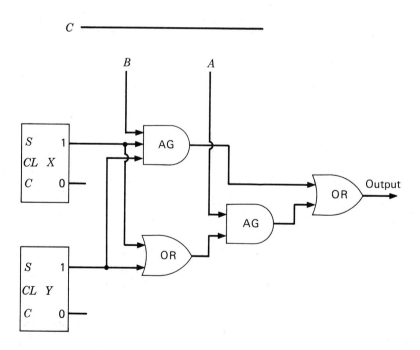

34. In what case will subtracting a negative number from 0 cause an overflow in the 2s complement system?

35. If numbers are represented in a 2s complement, 6-bit magnitude plus 1 sign bit integer system and we ignore overflow (that is, any result will be stored, even if it requires more magnitude bits), then the largest positive integer which can result from the addition of two numbers is _____ and the largest positive integer which can result from the subtraction of one number from another is _____? The least negative numbers which can result from an addition and subtraction are _____ and _____. As a result, any sum or difference can be stored in _____ bits.

36. Write down all 4-bit 2s complement numbers (i.e., sign-plus 3-bit numbers) and their decimal values. Show that there is one more negative number than positive number. Consider 0 to be neither negative nor positive.

37. When addition is performed in a binary machine using the 2s complement number system to represent negative numbers, an overflow may occur in a register only when two positive or two negative numbers are added. Show that the addition of a positive number and a negative number cannot result in an overflow condition.

38. Show that there are as many negative as positive numbers in a 1s complement system.

39. The Boolean algebra expressions on the output lines from the gates in Fig. $6 \cdot 8$ are not filled in. Develop the Boolean algebra expressions for the S_1, S_2, and C_2 outputs from the network.

40. Which of the following number systems has two 0s:
(a) Sign-plus magnitude *(b)* 1s complement *(c)* 2s complement

41. When the 2s complement number system is used and addition is performed, let us designate the carry-out of the full adder connected into the full adder for the sign digits as C_1 (refer to Fig. $6 \cdot 6$). The rule for overflow is that two numbers cause an overflow when they are added if both numbers are positive and C_1 equals a 1, or if both numbers are negative and C_1 does not equal a 1. Therefore, by examining the sign digits of the two numbers being added and the carry-out of the full adder which adds the two most significant digits of the magnitude of the numbers being added, we can form a logic network the output of which will be a 1 when an overflow condition arises and 0 if the addition is legitimate. Let X_0 store the sign digit of the addend, Y_0 store the sign digit of the augend, and C_1 again be the carry-out of the full adders connected to the X_1 and Y_1 flip-flops as in Fig. $6 \cdot 6$. Show that the logic equation for an overflow condition is $X_0 Y_0 \overline{C_1} + \overline{X_0} \overline{Y_0} C_1 = $ overflow.

42. Modify Fig. $6 \cdot 16$ so that the complement of X_{m+1} can be shifted into X_m, that is, so that SHIFT LEFT causes $\overline{X}_{m+1}$ to go into X_m.

43. Show that when we add 7 to 9 in the BCD system using the series-parallel BCD adder in Fig. $6 \cdot 10$, the answer will be correct. Do this by tracing the outputs of the circuit, filling in the binary value for each X and Y shown in the figure, and also by showing the values of Z_8, Z_4, Z_2, and Z_1.

44. Show how the BCD adder in Fig. $6 \cdot 11$ adds $+6$ to $+5$ by calculating each output from the gates and then the final outputs.

45. Check how the gates in Fig. 6·12 form a 9s complement by trying 6 and 2 in BCD at the inputs.

46. Explain the operation of Fig. 6·15 by explaining how 324 can be added or subtracted to/from 523 in this configuration.

47. What is the function of the *D* flip-flop in Fig. 6·15?

48. Explain how to load the input values on *W*, *X*, *Y*, and *Z* into the flip-flops in Fig. 6·17.

49. Explain how to cause the flip-flops in Fig. 6·17 to shift right three times. Suppose we (1) make the *reset* input a 0, then a 1, (2) hold *J* and *K* at 1 and shift at 1, and then (3) apply three clock pulses to the *clock* line. Draw the output waveforms for *A*, *B*, *C*, and *D* for this sequence of inputs.

50. What is the result if we multiply 0.1101 times 0.0011 in our generalized machine in Fig. 6·18? Give the values in each *X* and *B* flip-flop.

51. What is the binary number which represents −1 in the 2s complement fractional number system if we represent the number using a sign digit plus four magnitude digits?

52. Using the 8421 BCD system with a single digit for the sign digit, write the following numbers using a sign-plus-magnitude number system.
(a) +0015   *(b)* +0191
(c) −2246   *(d)* −0264

53. Using the 8421 BCD system, write in binary form the following decimal numbers. Use a single digit for the sign digit, and express the numbers as magnitude plus sign.
(a) +0042   *(b)* −0122   *(c)* +1034   *(d)* −1097

54. Using the 8421 code as in Question 52, give the same numbers but use 9s complement for the negative numbers.

55. Express each of the numbers in Question 53 using the 9s complement and the 8421 BCD system. For example, −1024 = 1.1000 1001 0111 0101.

56. Write the binary form of the numbers in Question 52 using 8421, but use 10s complements for negative numbers.

57. Write the decimal numbers in Question 53 using the 10s complement number system and again the 8421 BCD system to represent these numbers. For example, −1420 = 1.1000 0101 1000 0000.

58. If we add two 20-digit binary numbers using the full adders shown in Fig. 6·8 and if 3 ns is required for a signal to pass through a gate, what is the maximum time it will require a CARRY signal to propagate from the lowest-order bits to the highest-order bits, assuming a full adder which is parallel as in Fig. 6·6? The carry circuit in Fig. 6·8 could be replaced by a "carry bridge" with expression $C2 = C0 \cdot A1 \cdot B2 + C0 \cdot A1 \cdot B2 + C0 \cdot A2 \cdot B1 + C0 \cdot B1 \cdot B2 + A1 \cdot B1 \cdot A2 + A1 \cdot B1 \cdot B2 + A2 \cdot B2$. Show how this would work and how a carry bridge for 3 bits might work.

59. Explain how you would add gates and inputs to Fig. 6·17 so the flip-flop register could be shifted left as well as right.

60. If we multiply 6 × 11 in the registers in Fig. 6·18, show the placement of binary digits at the start and end of the multiplication.

61. Show how 7×9 and 5×6 would be multiplied in the registers in Fig. 6 · 18.

62. Draw a flowchart (as in Fig. 6 · 19) for the binary miltiplication procedure described.

63. If we divide 23 by 5 in the registers in Fig. 6 · 18, show the beginning positioning of the numbers (in binary) and the result at the end. (Show where the quotient and remainder are placed.)

64. Show how to divide 14 by 3 using the registers in Fig. 6 · 18 and showing how the quotient and remainder are placed after the division.

65. Go through the division of 14 by 5 using the technique shown in the text.

66. Using the algorithm shown in Fig. 6 · 19, show how to divide 11 by 3.

67. Show how to represent $+7$ in the 12-bit floating-point word in Fig. 6 · 21.

68. Show how to represent -12 in the 12-bit floating-point word in Fig. 6 · 21.

69. (a) Give the IBM 360/370 floating-point representation for 52.5 and -52.5.

  (b) Give the Univac 1108 floating-point representation for $+24.0$ and -24.0.

  (c) Compare the ranges, accuracy, and other system design considerations for the above two computer floating-point number systems.

70. Show two decimal numbers which when converted into the IBM 360/370 floating-point number system will have .0001 in bits 9, 10, 11, and 12.

71. Can you give any reasons that might be behind the systems architects at IBM's decision to use hexadecimal as the base for the 360/370 series floating-point number system instead of conventional base 2? That is, in System 360/370 a floating-point full word of 32 bits has as characteristic a 7-bit integer with value C and as fraction a binary signed-magnitude-fraction 25-bit number with value F. The value of the number represented is then $(16^{C-64})F$. Why 16^{C-64} rather than 2^{C-64}? Give system design considerations.

72. Give the value of a positive nonzero *integer* less than 16^{62} which cannot be represented in the IBM 360/370 floating-point number system (using a single 32-bit word.) Do not be afraid to use an expression such as $2^{16} + 3$ for your answer but do give the reason you think your answer is correct.

73. A binary computer with a basic 16-bit code uses an integer 2s complement number system. The arithmetic element contains an accumulator and *MQ* register, each containing 16 flip-flops (or bits). When a multiply is performed, the 16-bit word taken from the memory is multiplied times the 16-bit word in the accumulator and the product is stored in the combined ACC-*MQ* with the least significant bit in the rightmost bit of the *MQ*. The sign bit of the MQ is set the same as the sign of the ACC and not used to store a magnitude bit. In what bit of the ACC does the most significant bit of a product appear for numbers of maximum magnitude?

THE MEMORY ELEMENT

The memory of a computer is not actually concentrated in one place; storage devices are scattered throughout the machine. For instance, the *operation registers* are flip-flop registers which are used in the arithmetic and control units of the computer. The actual calculations on data take place in these registers. For instance, additions, multiplications, shifts, etc., are all performed in these registers of the machine. The actual processing of information is performed in and at the direction of these registers.

Looking outward, the next category of storage device which is encountered is called the *high-speed memory, inner memory,* or *main memory.* This section of the computer's memory consists of a set of storage registers, each of which is identified with an address which enables the control unit either to write into or read from a particular register.

It is desirable that the operating speed of this section of the computer's memory be as fast as possible, for most of the transfers of data to and from the information processing section of the machine will be via the main memory. For this reason, storage devices with very fast access times are generally chosen for the main memory; unfortunately, the presently available devices which are fast enough to perform this function satisfactorily do not possess the storage capacity which is sometimes required. As a result, additional memory, which is called the *auxiliary memory* or *secondary memory,* is added to most large computers. This section of the computer's memory is characterized by low cost per digit stored, but it generally has an operating speed far slower than that of either the operation registers or the main memory. This section of the memory is sometimes designated the *backup store,* for its function is to handle quantities of data in excess of those which may be stored in the inner memory.

The final and outermost storage devices are those which are used to introduce information into the computer from the "outside world" and to store
results from the computer to the computer user. The storage media in this
case generally consist of such input media as punched cards or perforated
paper tape, and the outputs from the machine generally consist of printed
characters. Again, the cost per bit is low, but the operating speeds of the tape
and card readers, printers, etc., are liable to be on the order of 1,000 times
slower than the speeds of the operation registers. These devices will be described in Chap. 8 under input-output devices. This chapter will be limited to
the *internal storage* of the machine, which is defined as those storage devices
which form an integral part of the machine and are directly controlled by the
machine.

Each of the divisions of memory has certain characteristics. For instance,
the premium on speed is very high for the operation registers. These registers
must generally perform operations at several times the speed of the main
memory. The main memory also requires high operating speeds, but because
it is desirable to store larger quantities of data (perhaps 10^4 to 10^8 bits) in
this section of the memory, a compromise between cost and speed must
generally be made. The same sort of compromise must often be made in the
case of the auxiliary memory. In a large machine the auxiliary memory may
have to store from 10^8 to 10^{12} binary digits, and in these instances, it might
prove too expensive to use devices such as those used in the main memory.

An important point to notice when considering operating speed is that,
before a word can be read, it is necessary to locate it. The time required to
locate and read a word from memory is called the *access time*. The procedures for locating information may be divided into two classes, random
access and sequential access. A *random-access* storage device is one in
which any location in the device may be selected at random, access to the
information stored is direct, and approximately equal access time is required
for each location. A flip-flop register is an example of a random-access
storage device, as is the magnetic core memory system, which will be described below. A sequential-access device is one in which the arrival at the
location desired may be preceded by sequencing through other locations, so
that access time varies according to location.† For instance, if we try to read
a word stored on a reel of magnetic tape and the piece of tape on which the
word is stored is near the center of the reel, it will be necessary to sequence
through all the intervening tape before the word can be read.

Another way to subdivide storage devices is according to whether they are
static or dynamic storage devices. A *static* storage device is one in which the
information does not change positions; flip-flop registers, magnetic core

---

† Sequential-access devices are further separated into *direct-access storage devices* (DASD) and
serial-access devices. Direct-access storage devices have addresses, but the access time to reach the data
at a given address may vary. For instance, the time to locate data on a movable head disk (to be explained)
depends on the head position and disk position when the address is given. Serial-access devices are truly
serial in their access properties; magnetic tape is the classic example.

registers, and even punched cards or tape are examples of static storage devices. *Dynamic* storage devices, on the other hand, are devices in which the information stored is continually changing position. Circulating registers utilizing delay lines are examples of dynamic storage devices.

This chapter will concentrate on the four most frequently used devices for storing digital information in the internal memory sections of computers. These are (1) magnetic core memories, which are random-access devices used principally in the inner memory because of their high operating speeds and moderate cost per bit; (2) IC memories, which are high speed and of moderate cost; (3) magnetic drum and disk memories, which are direct-access storage devices generally used for auxiliary storage; and (4) magnetic tape memories, which are used exclusively as an auxiliary, or backup, storage but which are capable of storing large quantities of information at low cost. Following the sections on drum, disk, and magnetic tape devices, the techniques used to record digital information on a magnetic surface will be described.

7•1 RANDOM-ACCESS MEMORIES

The main memory of a computer is organized in a way which is particularly desirable. Figure 7·1 shows that a high-speed main memory in a computer is organized into words of fixed lengths. As the figure indicates, a given memory is divided into N words, where N generally is some power of 2, and each word is assigned an *address* or *location* in the memory. Each word has the same number of bits, called the *word length,* and if we read, for instance, the word at location 72, we shall receive a word from the memory with this number of bits.

The addresses or address numbers in the memory run consecutively, start-

FIG. 7•1 Words in high-speed memory.

ing with the address 0 and running up to the largest address. Thus, at address 0 we find a word, at address 1 a second word, at address 2 a third word, and so on up to the final word at the largest address.

The computer can read a word from or write a word into each location in the memory. For a memory with an 8-bit word, if we write the word 01001011 into memory address 17 and later read from this same address, we shall read the word 01001011. If we again read from this address at a later time (and have not written another word in), the word 01001011 will again be read. This means the memory is *nondestructive read* in that reading does not destroy or change a stored word.

It is important to understand the difference between the *contents* of a memory address and the address itself. A memory is like a large cabinet containing as many drawers as there are addresses in memory. In each drawer is a word, and the address of each word is written on the outside of the drawer. If we write or store a word at address 17, it is like placing the word in the drawer labeled 17. Later, reading from address 17 is like looking in that drawer to see its contents. We do not remove the word at an address when we read, but change the contents at an address only when we store or write a new word.

From an exterior viewpoint, a high-speed main memory looks very much like a "black box" with a number of locations or addresses into which data can be stored or from which data can be read. Each address or location contains a fixed number of binary bits, the number being called the *word length* for the memory. A memory with 4096 locations each with a different address and with each location storing 16 bits is called a "16-bit 4096-word memory," or, in the vernacular of the computer trade, a "4K 16-bit memory." (Since memories generally come with a number of words equal to 2^n for some n, if a memory has $2^{14} = 16,384$ words, computer literature and jargon would refer to it as a "16K memory" because it is always understood that the full 2^n words actually occur in the memory. Thus, a 2^{15}-word 16-bit memory is called a "32K 16-bit memory.")

Memories can be "read from" (that is, data can be taken out) or "written into" (that is, data can be entered into the memory). Memories which can be both read from and written into are called *read-write memories.* Some memories have programs or data permanently stored and are called *read-only memories.*

A block diagram of a read-write memory is shown in Fig. 7·2. The computer places the address of the location into which the data is to be read into the *memory address register.* This register consists of n binary devices (generally *flip-flops*), where 2^n is the number of words which can be stored in the memory. The data to be written into the memory are placed in the *memory buffer register,* which has as many binary storage devices as there are bits in each memory word. The memory is told to write by means of a 1 signal on the WRITE line. The memory will then store the contents of the memory buffer register in the location specified by the memory address register.

Words are read by placing the address of the location to be read from into

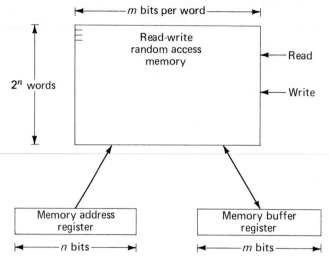

FIG. 7·2 Read-write random-access memory.

the memory address register. A 1 signal is then placed on the READ line, and the contents of that location are placed by the memory in the memory buffer register.

As can be seen, the computer communicates with the memory by means of the memory address register, the memory buffer register, and the READ and WRITE inputs. Memories are generally packaged in separate modules or packages. It is possible to buy a memory module of a specified size from a number of different manufacturers and, for instance, an 8K 16-bit memory module can be purchased on a circuit board ready for use. Similarly, if a computer is purchased with a certain amount of main memory, more memory can generally later be added by purchasing additional modules and "plugging them in."

If it is possible to read from or write into any location "at once," that is, if there is no more delay in reaching one location as opposed to another location, the memory is called a *random-access memory*. Modern computers almost invariably use random-access read-write memories for their high-speed main memory and then use backup or slower-speed memories to hold auxiliary data.

The two principal types of high-speed random-access memories are the magnetic core memory and the IC. These are described in the immediately following sections.

7·2 MAGNETIC CORE STORAGE

The basic storage device in a magnetic core memory consists of a small toroidal (ring-shaped) piece of magnetic material called a magnetic core.

| Current is applied | Core is magnetized with flux through core in counterclockwise direction | Current is reversed; the core reverses its magnetic state | Current is removed; core remains magnetized with flux in clockwise direction |

FIG. 7·3 The magnetic core.

The magnetic core is generally a solid piece of ferromagnetic ceramic material.

Figure 7·3 illustrates a magnetic core, many times actual size. Each magnetic core in the memory is capable of storing 1 bit of digital information. An input winding (wire) is shown threaded through this core; if current is passed through this winding, magnetic flux will be produced, with a direction dependent on the direction of the current through the winding. The core is ring-shaped and formed of material with a high permeability, so that it will present a low-reluctance path for the magnetic flux. Depending on the direction of the current through the input winding, the core will become magnetized in either a clockwise or counterclockwise direction.† The retentivity of the material used in the core is such that when the magnetizing force is removed, the core remains magnetized, retaining a large part of its flux.

The characteristics of a given type of magnetic core are generally studied by means of a graph, with the magnetizing force H produced by the winding current plotted along the abscissa, and the resulting flux density B through the core along the ordinate (Fig. 7·4). If a cyclical current which is alternately positive and negative is applied to the input winding in Fig. 7·3, for each value of the input current there will be a magnetizing force H applied to the core. If the flux density B in the core is then plotted against this magnetizing force, the resulting curve is called a *hysteresis loop*. In Fig. 7·4, the force H applied is sufficient to saturate the core material at both the positive and negative extremities of the input current. The maximum flux density through the core when the core is saturated with a positive value of H is designated $+B_m$, and the corresponding negative value of H is denoted $-B_m$.

Notice that for each value of magnetizing force there are two values of flux density. One occurs when the magnetizing force is increasing, and the other when the magnetizing force is decreasing. If the magnetizing force is varied from $-H_m$ to $+H_m$, the flux density will move along the lower part of the curve, and if the magnetizing force is moved from $+H_m$ to $-H_m$, the flux density will

---

† There is a nice rule for determining the direction of the flux around a conductor. Grasp the wire with the right hand with the thumb in the direction of current flow. The fingers then point in the direction of the flux around the conductor. This is called the "right-hand rule."

FIG. 7·4 Hysteresis loop for a magnetic material.

move along the upper part of the curve, again following the arrows, to point $-B_m$.

If a current sufficient to cause the core to be saturated is applied at the input winding and then removed, the flux density through the core will revert to either point $+B_r$ or to point $-B_r$ depending on the polarity of the current. These two operating points are called the *remanent* points, and when the flux through the core is at either of these points, the core resembles a small permanent magnet. If a core is at the $+B_r$ point of the graph and a current of sufficient amplitude to cause a force of $-H_m$ is applied, the flux produced will be in opposition to the remanent flux in the core, $+B_r$, and the flux through the core will be reversed, moving the operating point to $-B_m$. After the current has been removed, the majority of the flux will remain, and the flux density in the core will be at the $-B_r$ point of the curve. The fact that the core can be in either one of two unique states of magnetization makes it possible to consider one state as representing a 0 ($-B_r$ in the figure) and the other state as a 1 ($+B_r$ in the figure).

Another winding, called a *sense winding* [Fig. 7·5(b)], is used to determine whether a core contains a 0 or a 1. To sense the state of the core, a current sufficient to produce a magnetizing force $-H_m$ is applied to the input winding. If the core was at $+B_r$, the operating point will be moved downward along the arrows in Fig. 7·4 to the $-B_m$ point. If the core was at the $-B_r$ point, the operating point will be moved horizontally to $-B_m$. The amount of change in flux in the core will be quite different for each of these cases. If the core was initially in the 1 state (at point $+B_r$ on the hysteresis curve), the direction of magnetization of the core will be changed and the flux through the core will change from $+B_r$ to $-B_m$. The magnitude of this change in the magnetization of the core is indicated as $+B_r$ to $-B_m$ on the figure. If, however, the core was originally in the 0 state at $-B_r$ on the curve, the change in magnetization will be small, only from $-B_r$ to $-B_m$, and the magnitude of this change in flux is indicated as $-B_r$ to $-B_m$ on the figure. A change in the flux density through the core will induce a voltage in the sense winding which is proportional to the rate of change of flux. If the core was originally in the 0 state, the change and rate of change in flux will be small, and therefore the voltage induced in the sense winding will be small. If the core was originally in the 1 state, the amount of change and rate of change in flux will be large, and consequently the voltage induced in the sense winding will be large. A small output from the sense winding will therefore indicate that the core originally contained a 0, and a large output will indicate that the core originally contained a 1.

The difficulty in the use of this technique for sensing the state of a core is that the core is always reset to the 0 state. This readout technique is therefore "destructive" in that the core no longer contains the information which was previously stored in it. It is generally desirable to retain information in storage after it has been read. Since reading from a core is destructive, it is necessary to write the original state of the core back into it. By detecting and amplifying the output of the sense winding when the core's state is sensed, it is possible to use the signal to set a flip-flop or other temporary, erasable storage device. The contents of the flip-flop may then be written back into the core via the input winding, returning the core to its original state.

7·3 STORAGE OF INFORMATION IN MAGNETIC CORES IN A TWO-DIMENSIONAL ARRAY

The preceding discussion showed how a single bit of information may be stored in and read from a single core. In digital computer systems, however, it is necessary to store many bits of information; some of the larger computers have core memories with over 10 million cores. To utilize these cores, the computer must be able to write information into any given core and also to read from any given core. Techniques for writing or reading information into or from a selected core or group of cores in a memory are known as *selection techniques*. The selection technique which will be described is called the *coincident-current technique*, and it is the most commonly used one in large computer systems.

Figure 7·5(a) plots the values of flux density for a magnetic core versus current I through the input winding of a core. If the current reaches a value of $+I_m$, which is sufficient to saturate the core, and is then removed, the core will be placed in the $+B_r$, or 1, state. If the operating point on the curve is at $+B_r$ with no input current through the winding, and a negative pulse of current with amplitude $-I_m$ is applied, the core will be switched to the 0 state. The important thing to notice in Fig. 7·5 is that, if the core is in the 1 state and a current of only $-I_m/2$ is applied and then removed, the state of the core will not be changed. Instead, the operating point will move from $+B_r$ to $+B_d$ and, when the current is removed, will move back to approximately $+B_r$. The same prin-

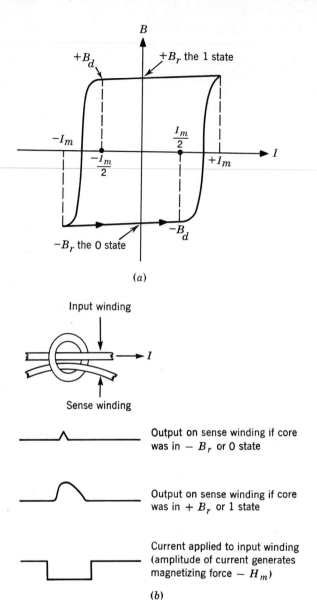

FIG. 7·5 (a) Current versus flux density hysteresis loop for a magnetic core; (b) sense winding.

ciple applies if the core is in the 0 state at point $-B_r$ on the curve. A current of $+I_m$ will switch the core to the 1 state, but a current of $+I_m/2$ will only move the operating point to $-B_d$, and when the current is removed, the core will return to point $-B_r$.

Figure 7·6(a) shows 16 cores arranged in a square array. Each core has two input windings, one from a set of X input lines and one from a set of Y

(a)

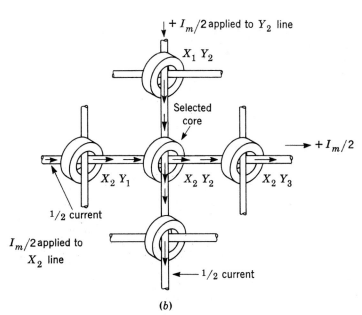

(b)

FIG. 7•6 Two-dimensional core plane. (a) Wiring; (b) selection of X_2Y_2.

input lines. Assume that all the cores are in the 0 state and a 1 is to be written into core X_2Y_2. If a current with an amplitude of $+I_m$ is applied on the X_2 line, core X_2Y_2 will be switched to the 1 state; however, all the cores connected to the X_2 input line will also be switched to the 1 state. The same holds true if a current of $+I_m$ is applied to input line Y_2, in which case all the cores connected to this Y input line would be switched to the 1 state.

If, however, currents of $+I_m/2$ are applied to both the X_2 line and the Y_2 line at the same time, only core X_2Y_2 will receive a total current of $+I_m$ (Fig. $7 \cdot 6(b)$). Each of the other cores along the Y_2 input line will receive a current of $+I_m/2$, as will each of the cores along the X_2 input line. Since these cores will have started at point $-B_r$ on the graph and will receive a current of $+I_m/2$, their operating point will be moved as far as $-B_d$ on the curve; however, the operating point will not be moved as far as the steep incline which leads to the $+B_r$ section of the graph. When the current is removed, these cores, with the exception of X_2Y_2, will return to the $-B_r$ point and will be in the 0 state. Therefore only core X_2Y_2 will receive a total current of $+I_m$ and will be switched into the 1 state.

By this technique, any given core can be selected from the array. For instance, core X_1Y_3 can be selected by applying currents of $+I_m/2$ to the X_1 and the Y_3 input lines at the same time. This is known as the coincident-current selection technique. The core which receives a full $+I_m$ current is known as a *fully selected* core, and all the cores which receive a current of $+I_m/2$ are known as *half-selected* cores. For instance, if a current of $+I_m/2$ is connected to input lines X_1 and Y_3, core X_1Y_3 will be fully selected, and cores X_1Y_1, X_1Y_2, X_2Y_3, and X_3Y_3 will be half selected.

Notice that regardless of the previous state of each of the cores in the array, a current of $+I_m/2$ applied to one X and one Y input line will result in sufficient current to switch only one core of the array. If cores in the 0 state are half selected, they will remain in the 0 state; and if cores in the 1 state are half selected, they will remain in the 1 state.

The state of any given core can be sensed using the same technique. If currents of $-I_m/2$ are applied to input lines X_2 and Y_2, a full $-I_m$ current will be applied to core X_2Y_2, causing it to change states if it contained a 1 and remain in the same state if it contained a 0. The fully selected core will be the only core which can change states, and therefore the only core which is capable of causing an appreciable output on a sense winding. A sense winding would be threaded through all the cores; if a certain core is selected, the output at the sense winding will represent the state of that core only.

It may be seen that there are two separate operations involved: first, the writing of information into a core, and second, the reading of information which has been stored in a core. A 0 or a 1 may be written into any core in the array by applying a current of either $-I_m/2$ or $+I_m/2$ to the correct pair of input lines, and the state of any core may be sensed by applying a current of $-I_m/2$ to the correct pair of input lines and sensing the magnitude of the output voltage on the sense winding.

7•4 ASSEMBLY OF CORE PLANES INTO A CORE MEMORY

Figure 7 · 7 illustrates a small *core-memory plane*. Any core in this plane may be selected, and a 0 or 1 written into the core, or the state of any core may be sensed, by applying the correct currents to one of the X input lines and one of the Y input lines simultaneously. A complete core memory consists of a number of such planes, stacked in a rectangular array. The X windings of each plane are connected in series, so that current applied to the X_1 winding of the first plane must travel through the X_1 winding of the second plane, and so on, until it passes through the X_1 winding for the last plane in the array. If the plane illustrated in Fig. 7 · 7 were connected in an array, the X_1 winding at the top left of the drawing would be connected to one end of the X_1 winding from the preceding core plane, and the X_1 winding at the bottom left would be connected to the X_1 connection of the following core plane. If 10 core planes of the size in Fig. 7 · 7 were stacked in this manner, a pulse on the X_1 input line would have to travel through 80 cores. The Y windings are connected in the same manner. Each plane has its own sense winding, however, and the sense windings for the planes are not connected together in any way; instead, a *sense amplifier* is connected to the sense-winding output from each plane.

Let us call a $+I_m/2$ current pulse a WRITE 1 pulse, for such a current applied to an X or Y winding tends to write a 1 into the cores along the winding. It may be seen that simultaneously applying a WRITE 1 pulse on a selected Y line and a selected X line will write a 1 into a single core in the same relative position in each of the planes. For instance, if the X_3 and Y_4 input lines are pulsed with a current of $+I_m/2$, the X_3Y_4 core in each plane will receive a $+I_m$ current. If a $-I_m/2$ pulse is then applied to the same X and Y selection lines, an output will be sensed on the sense winding† of each plane.

In general, there will be as many core planes in the array as bits in the word length of the memory in which the array is used. If the word length is 15 bits, there will be 15 planes in the array; if the word length is 35 bits, 35 planes. There will be a sense winding for each plane, so that the output from each core which is selected will be sensed.

One problem still remains: a WRITE 1 $(+I_m/2)$ pulse on a pair of X and Y input lines will write a 1 into the core in the same relative position of each plane, and therefore into every position of the word, and it may be necessary to write 0s into some cores and 1s into others. A fourth winding through each core is therefore added. This winding is called the *inhibit winding,* and it is used to inhibit the writing of a 1 into a given selected core in a plane. A single inhibit winding is threaded through each core in a plane in a direction so that a current of $-I_m/2$ on the winding will oppose the WRITE 1 cur-

---

† The sense windings are threaded through the cores diagonal to the other windings to reduce the coupling between drive and sense windings (Fig. 7 · 7) and to cancel the output signals from half-selected cores caused during a READ pulse.

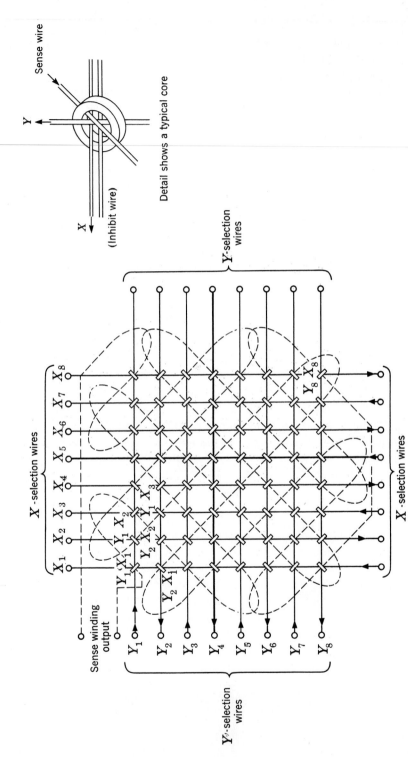

Sense wire

Y

X

(Inhibit wire)

Detail shows a typical core

Y-selection wires

X-selection wires

X-selection wires

X_1 X_2 X_3 X_4 X_5 X_6 X_7 X_8

$Y_1 X_1$ $Y_1 X_2$ $Y_1 X_3$

$Y_2 X_1$ $Y_2 X_2$ $Y_2 X_3$

$Y_2 X_1$

$Y_8 X_8$

Sense winding output

Y_1
Y_2
Y_3
Y_4
Y_5
Y_6
Y_7
Y_8

Y-selection wires

FIG. 7 • 7 Core-memory plane.

rent. There are therefore as many inhibit windings as core planes. There is also a single driver for each inhibit winding, which can be gated on or off, depending on whether a 1 or a 0 is to be written into the selected core of the plane. The amplitude of the current through the inhibit winding is the same as the $-I_m/2$ current used in the X and Y selection lines. The inhibit winding is threaded through the cores so that the magnetizing force from the current through the inhibit winding always opposes the magnetizing force of the WRITE 1 currents.

Since the WRITE 1 pulse from the X and Y drivers is of $+I_m/2$ amplitude and the pulse from the INHIBIT driver is of $-I_m/2$ amplitude, if a WRITE 1 pulse is applied from a given pair of X and Y drivers at the same time as an INHIBIT pulse is applied, the total current through the selected core will be $(+I_m/2) + (+I_m/2) + (-I_m/2) = +I_m/2$, which is not sufficient to switch the core to a 1. A 1 or 0 may therefore be written into the selected core of a given plane by first clearing the cores with a $-I_m/2$ pulse on the correct pair of X and Y select lines, and then turning the INHIBIT driver on for each plane where a 0 is desired and off for each plane where a 1 is desired, while applying a WRITE 1 pulse to the X and Y select lines.

7·5 TIMING SEQUENCE

The same timing sequence is generally used whether the computer is to write information into the core memory or to read information from the core memory. The total time taken by the entire timing sequence is called a *memory cycle,* and is one of the principal speed-determining factors for a machine. Each memory cycle consists of two periods, the first of which is called the read time, and the second of which is called the write time. Figure 7·8 shows a complete memory cycle. The operation of writing a word into the memory will

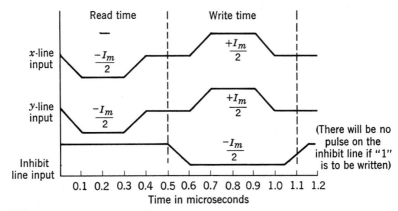

FIG. 7·8 Timing sequence for core memory.

be examined first, then the READ operation. Assume that there are five core planes in the total array and that each core plane contains 64 cores, as in Fig. 7·7.

1. *Writing into a core memory*   Assume that the binary number 10100 is to be written into core location X_3Y_4 of the memory. Zeros are therefore to be written into the selected cores of planes 2, 4, and 5, so that the INHIBIT drivers for each of these planes are enabled; that is, when the write time begins (Fig. 7·8), the drivers connected to the INHIBIT windings of planes 2, 4, and 5 will drive current through the INHIBIT windings of these core planes.

First the correct drivers are selected; since core X_3Y_4 in each plane is to be written into, the drivers connected to the X_3 line are enabled, as are the drivers connected to the Y_4 line of the array. When the *read time* pulses are applied, 0s are written into the X_3Y_4 core in each of the five planes; after 0.4 μs, each of the selected cores will contain a 0. At 0.5 μs after the sequence is initiated, the INHIBIT drivers connected to planes 2, 4, and 5 are turned on; in addition, the write time begins. A 1 will then be written into the selected core in planes 1 and 3, and the subtraction of the INHIBIT current from the coincident current through the selected cores in planes 2, 4, and 5 will result in the selected cores in these planes remaining in the 0 state. After the sequence of pulses, the selected cores in planes 1 and 3 will contain 1s, the selected cores in planes 2, 4, and 5 will contain 0s, and the computer word 10100 will have been stored in the memory in location X_3Y_4.

2. *Reading from a core memory*   Assume that at a later time the location X_3Y_4, which was written into in the WRITE operation above, is to be read from. The timing sequence illustrated in Fig. 7·8 still applies, although there are several differences in operation. First, the READ currents are applied to the selected cores (from 0 time to 0.5 μs in Fig. 7·8). If a large signal is received at the sense amplifier connected to a given plane during this period, the selected core in that plane contained a 1; if a small signal is received, the selected core in the plane contained a 0. The sense windings connected to planes 1 and 3 will therefore produce signals indicating 1s, and the sense windings connected to planes 2, 4, and 5 will produce small signals, indicating 0s. The word stored was therefore 10100. This word must now be written back into the memory array. The output of each sense winding is amplified and used to set a storage device to the 0 or 1 state during the read time, and the contents of each of these storage devices are then used to control the INHIBIT winding drivers during the write time. Only the INHIBIT drivers connected to planes 2, 4, and 5 will therefore be enabled by signals from the respective storage devices and conduct during the write time, and the selected cores in these planes will remain in the 0 state. After the write time, the selected cores will again contain 10100, just as before the READ operation.

7 • 6 CHARACTERISTICS OF CORE-MEMORY ARRAY

Each core of a core memory of the type described is threaded by four windings, as in Fig. 7 · 7.† Since the cores are generally quite small, perhaps 12/1,000 to 50/1,000 in. or mil,‡ outer diameter, the total size of the arrays can be made quite small. Each plane of one of the memories used in the TX-2 computer at Lincoln Laboratory is a 64 × 64 core plane and therefore contains 4096 cores; there are 37 planes in the array, and therefore a total of 151,552 cores in the complete array. This array is about the size of a 5-in. cube. There are 64 X-selection winding inputs to the array and 64 Y-selection inputs, 37 sense windings, and 37 inhibit windings.

Some general characteristics of coincident-current core memories are evident from this: the number of planes used equals the number of bits in the memory word; the number of X input lines times the number of Y input lines equals the number of words which can be stored in the array.

Not all core memories consist of individual cores assembled and individually threaded. Some memories utilize apertured ferrite plates consisting of a ferrite plate with a number of holes through which the X and Y selection lines, sense windings, and inhibit windings may be threaded. The plate is constructed so that each of the areas around the apertures acts as a single core; the plate has similar characteristics to a plane of cores.

7 • 7 MEMORY ADDRESS AND MEMORY BUFFER REGISTERS

The computer communicates with the core memory through two registers: (1) the *memory address register,* which contains the address of the word which is to be read from or written into, and (2) the *memory buffer register,* which contains the word which was read from the memory (after a READ cycle) or the word which is to be written into memory. To locate a word in memory, the address of the word is first loaded into the memory address register. If the memory is to be read from, the states of the cores at the address specified will be sensed and written into the memory buffer register. The computer can then read the word which was looked up from the memory buffer register. If a word is to be written into the memory, the address to be written into is loaded into the memory address register, and the word to be written into the memory is loaded in the memory buffer register. After the memory cycle, the word will be stored in the memory at the address specified.

---

† The windings shown in Fig. 7 · 7 are in a commonly used form. It has the advantages of minimum coupling from drive to sense windings, optimum cancellation of half-select noises, and uniform distribution of driving circuits and terminals about the memory plane.

‡ Core dimensions are generally given in mils thus: a 50-mil outer-diameter, 30-mil inner-diameter core, or, in computerese, a 50-mil OD, 30-mil ID core.

7•8 DRIVING THE X- AND Y-SELECTION LINES

Let us examine the sequencing of currents through a core memory using a simple idealized model. Flip-flops are generally used as the storage devices for both the memory address register and memory buffer register. Figure 7·9 illustrates, in block diagram form, the operation of a selection system for a core memory, with each plane the size of the plane illustrated in Fig. 7·7. Since there are eight X-selection lines and eight Y-selection lines, three flip-flops will be required to select an X line and three more to select a Y line. There are therefore six flip-flops in the memory address register, so that any one of the 64 (2^6) locations in each plane may be selected. The flip-flops in the register illustrated have been designated X_1, X_2, X_3 and Y_1, Y_2, Y_3, to indicate that the first three are used to select the X winding and the second three to select the Y winding.

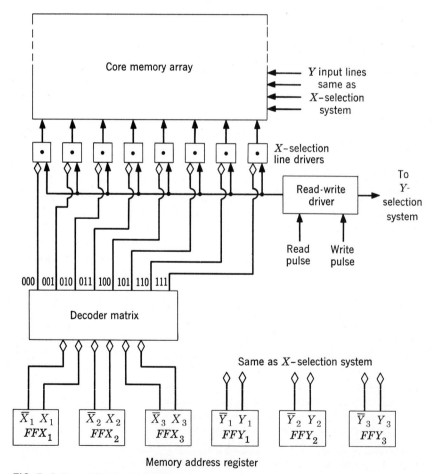

FIG. 7•9 X- and Y-selection system.

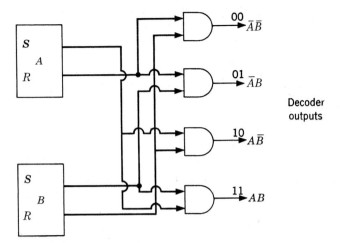

FIG. 7 • 10 Four-output decoder.

1. *Decoder matrix*   The outputs of the X_1, X_2, and X_3 flip-flops in Fig. 7 · 9 are connected to a *decoder*. This is a frequently used configuration having several input and output lines and the characteristic that for each combination of input values, only one output line will represent a 1. Figure 7 · 10 illustrates a decoder constructed of AND gates. There are four input lines to the decoder: two from a flip-flop designated A and two from a flip-flop designated B. The two flip-flops may be in any one of four possible states. For instance, flip-flop A may contain a 0 and B a 1, in which case the $\bar{A}$ input will be "high" and the B input will be "high." In this case the $\bar{A}B$ output line will be high (representing a 1) and the other three output lines will be "low," or 0.

   This type of decoder is often referred to as a *many-to-one decoder* because the inputs select one of the output lines. If we have inputs from three flip-flops, as in Fig. 7 · 9, and designate the flip-flops as FFX_1, FFX_2, FFX_3, the states of the flip-flops may be written as a binary number such as 011, meaning FFX_1 contains a 0, FFX_2 a 1, and FFX_3 a 1. We may then designate each output line with a binary number (Fig. 7 · 10), and the output line which will be high will correspond to the input number represented by the state of the input flip-flops.

   Since there are three X flip-flops in Fig. 7 · 9, the flip-flops may take any one of eight states, representing from 000 to 111. For each input state, only one of the outputs from the decoder will be high, and therefore only one of the X-selection line drivers (Fig. 7 · 9) will be enabled.

   If the decoder is large, it may be more economical to use other configurations than that shown, but the function of these decoders is the same: one output line is selected for each input state.

2. *X-selection line drivers*   There are eight X-selection line drivers in Fig. 7 · 9, each of which has two inputs, one from the decoder and one from the

READ-WRITE driver. The output currents from the READ-WRITE driver may be either negative or positive; the X-selection line drivers are therefore capable of passing current in either direction. The X-selection line drivers also function as AND gates, for they will pass current only when the input signal from the decoder matrix represents a 1. Only one of the X-selection line drivers will be enabled by the decoder at any given time. For instance, if the X flip-flops in the memory address register contain 000, only the left-most driver in the illustration will be enabled. All the X-selection line drivers will receive a READ and then a WRITE current pulse (of opposite polarity) from the READ-WRITE driver. Since only one X-selection line driver is enabled by a 1 signal from the decoder, only one of the X windings in the array will receive the drive currents. The same holds true for the Y-selection line system, which is identical with the X system. Since only one X line and only one Y line are pulsed during each memory cycle, only one core in each plane will receive a full-select READ and WRITE pulse.

3. *READ-WRITE driver* The READ-WRITE driver receives two clock pulses each memory cycle. The first is the READ pulse, which causes the READ-WRITE driver to deliver a positive HALF-SELECT pulse of current to both the X- and Y-selection line drivers. The second input pulse to the READ-WRITE driver is the WRITE pulse, which initiates a negative pulse of current to the X- and Y-selection line drivers. The current supplied by the READ-WRITE drivers is generally on the order of 0.1 to 1 A.

The operation of the memory address register and its associated circuitry cause a single core in each plane of the memory to receive a full-read and then a full-write current pulse. The memory address register is generally loaded directly from the instruction which is being interpreted by the machine. That is, the address section of the word is read directly into the memory address register. (This will be described in Chap. 9.)

7•9 MEMORY BUFFER REGISTER AND ASSOCIATED CIRCUITRY

The memory buffer register consists of a flip-flop register which contains one flip-flop for each plane in the array. The number of planes in the array, and hence the length of the memory buffer register, is equal to the number of bits in the basic computer word. The arithmetic element and control element of the machine generally communicate directly with the memory buffer, either loading the word to be written in storage into it or reading from it.

Figure 7·11 illustrates two flip-flops of a memory buffer register along with their associated circuitry. Each bit in the memory buffer register has identical circuitry. Two distinct sequences may occur: the first involves the reading of a word from memory and the second the writing of a word into the memory.

1. *Reading from memory* The location of the word to be read from the memory is first loaded into the memory address register (Fig. 7·9). The memory buffer register is then cleared. During the read time (Fig. 7·8) the

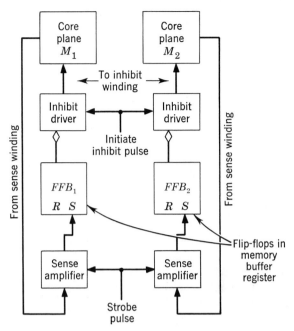

FIG. 7·11 Operation of memory buffer register.

selected core in each plane receives a full current pulse and is set to 0. If the selected core in a given plane contains a 1, a signal is received on the sense winding. This is amplified by the sense amplifier and then used to set a 1 into the memory buffer flip-flop used to control the INHIBIT driver for the core plane. If the selected core in the plane contains a 0, the signal received by the sense amplifier will be small, and no pulse will appear at the output of the sense amplifier, and the flip-flop will remain in the 0 state.

The sense amplifier is "strobed" (Fig. 7·11) with a narrow pulse, because, despite the fact that a core containing a 0 will produce a small signal when "sensed," many of the cores in each plane will receive half-select pulses, and each will generate a small amount of noise on the sense winding. If this noise is additive, it may approach the level of the signal from a core whose polarity is reversed. It has been found that the noise generated by the half-selected cores dies out shortly after the half-select pulses are started; therefore the sense amplifier is strobed during the latter part of the read time, when the output from a selected core reversing states is highest in proportion to the noise from half-selected cores. Only the output signal during the strobe pulse is gated into the SET line of the flip-flop.

During write time (Fig. 7·8), each of the selected cores receives a full-select current from the X- and Y-selection system. As a result of the reading operation, all these cores have previously been set in the 0 state; however, the memory buffer flip-flops now contain 1s for each plane in which a 1 was stored in the full-selected core. The outputs from these flip-flops are used to enable the INHIBIT drivers for each plane in which a 0 is to remain. All other full-selected cores will be set to the 1 state. The 0 output from each flip-flop is therefore used to enable the INHIBIT driver for the plane associated with the flip-flop. After the write time, the selected core in each plane will be in its original state.

2. *Writing into core memory*   The X- and Y-selection system goes through the same timing sequence when a word is to be written into memory as when a word is read from memory. The operation of the memory buffer register differs, however. The word to be written into the selected location is loaded into the memory buffer register, and the address in memory to be written into is loaded into the memory address register. During the read time the sense amplifier is not strobed; so the memory buffer register is not disturbed.

After the read time, all the selected cores will have been set to 0. During the write time, the same cores all receive full-current WRITE pulses from the X- and Y-selection system; however, the planes in which 0s are to remain have their inhibit drivers enabled by the memory buffer flip-flops (Figs. $7 \cdot 9$ and $7 \cdot 11$), and the half-current pulses from these drivers cancel the selection current, leaving the full-selected cores in the 0 state. All other full-selected cores are set to 1.

After the write time, the word in the memory buffer register will have been written into the cores.

7•10 CHARACTERISTICS OF CORE MEMORY

The small memory described is typical of the random-access memories now used, except for its size. Memories are now in use which contain over 10 million cores. Although the fundamentals of such memories are the same, the circuitry will of necessity differ in details.

The memory-cycle times vary with different machines, but most commercial machines have memory-cycle times in the 0.275- to 2-μs region. *Reading access time* is defined as the duration of the delay before a word may be used during the reading process. This is less than the memory-cycle time, because the read time occurs first, and the word may be used as soon as the sense amplifier is strobed and the word loaded into the memory buffer register. The access time for some high-speed memories is less than 0.1 μs.

Table $7 \cdot 1$ shows the characteristics of some cores manufactured by Electronic Memories, Inc. As an example, the core with a 30-mil outer diameter, manufacturer type 31-103, has a 580-mA FULL-READ or FULL-WRITE current, and therefore a 290-mA half-select current. READ and WRITE pulses are to be 0.5 μs, with 0.05-μs rise and fall times. This leads to a core output on the sense line of 61 mV when the core's flux is switched from 1 to 0, versus an output of 8 mV for a 0 ($-B_r$ to $-B_m$ in Fig. $7 \cdot 4$). The sense-line output

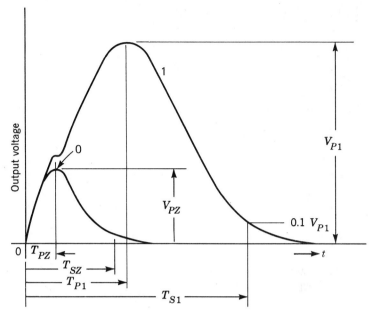

FIG. 7 • 12 Core sense-line signals.

signal peaks 0.23 μs after the READ pulse is applied. These figures are typical for fast, small cores. Figure 7 · 12 shows how these parameters are defined, along with typical READ 1 and READ 0 signals.

7 • 11 DECODERS

An important part of the system which selected the cores to be read from and written into in a coincidence-current memory is the decoder matrix shown in Fig. 7 · 10. This particular circuit is called a *many-to-one decoder,* a *decoder matrix,* or simply a *decoder,* and has the characteristic that for each of the possible 2^n binary input numbers which can be taken by the n input cells, the matrix will have a unique one of its 2^n output lines selected.

Figure 7 · 13 shows a decoder which is completely parallel in construction and is designed to decode three binary cells, or flip-flops. In this case, there are six input lines to the network (X_1, $\overline{X}_1$, X_2, $\overline{X}_2$, X_3, and $\overline{X}_3$). There are then $2^3 =$ 8 output lines, and for each of the eight states which the three flip-flops may take, a unique output line will be selected. This type of decoder is often constructed using diodes in the AND gates. The rule is: The number of diodes used in each AND gate is equal to the number of inputs to each AND gate. For Fig. 7 · 13, this is equal to the number of flip-flops which are being decoded. Further, the number of AND gates is equal to the number of output lines, which is equal to 2^n (n is the number of flip-flops being decoded). The total number

TABLE 7·1 SUMMARY OF TYPICAL CORE CHARACTERISTICS*

DESCRIPTION	MILS	TYPE	SIZE OD/ID/ht, mils	PULSE DRIVE CHARACTERISTICS			OUTPUT SIGNALS (TYPICAL OPERATING CONDITIONS AT 25°C)			
				AMPLITUDE, ma	DURATION, μsec	RISE AND FALL TIME, μsec	AMPLITUDE 1, mv	AMPLITUDE 0, mv	PEAK TIME, μsec	SWITCH TIME, μsec
Coincident current	20	22-100	22/14/05	700/350	0.4	0.05	55	5	0.13	0.22
	30	31-103	31/20/07	580/290	0.5	0.1	61	8	0.23	0.37
		31-108	31/20/07	720/360	0.5	0.1	62	5	0.21	0.39
	50	52-106	50/30/15	500/250	2.0	0.2	90	9	0.43	0.75
		51-110	50/30/15	500/250	2.0	0.2	68	8	0.52	1.02
		51-119	50/30/15	400/200	2.0	0.5	90	5	0.75	1.25
	80	81-104	80/50/25	410/203	6.0	0.5	60	6	1.4	2.6
Coincident-current lithium for wide temperature range applications	20	24-100	22/14/05	780/390	0.4	0.05	40	4	0.145	0.270
	30	34-102	31/20/10	760/380	0.5	0.1	63	4	0.26	0.49
Coincident current for 2½D applications	20	22-101	22/14/04	850/425	0.4	0.05	60	5	0.12	0.20
	30	31-115	30/21/07	750/375	0.5	0.1	52	4	0.21	0.37

*Courtesy of Electronic Memories, Inc.

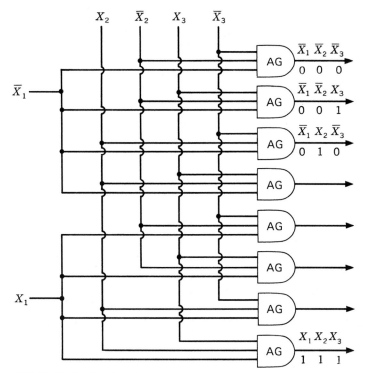

FIG. 7 • 13 Parallel decoder.

of diodes is therefore equal to $n \times 2^n$, and for the binary decoding matrix in Fig. 7 · 13, 24 diodes are required to construct the network. As may be seen, the number of diodes required goes up sharply with the number of inputs to the network. For instance, to decode an eight-flip-flop register, we would require $8 \times 2^8 = 2048$ diodes if the decoder were constructed in this manner.

As a result, there are several other types of structures which are often used in building decoder networks. One such structure, called a *tree-type decoding network,* is shown in Fig. 7 · 14. The particular tree network shown in Fig. 7 · 14 decodes four flip-flops, and therefore has $2^4 = 16$ output lines, a unique one of which is selected for each state of the flip-flops. An examination will show that 56 diodes are required to build this particular network, while $2^4 \times 4 = 64$ diodes would be required to build the parallel decoder type shown in Fig. 7 · 13.

Still another type of decoder network is shown in Fig. 7 · 15, and this network is called a *balanced multiplicative decoder network.* Notice that this particular network requires only 48 diodes. It can be shown that the type of decoder network shown in Fig. 7 · 15 requires the minimum number of diodes for a complete decoder network, and the difference in the number of diodes, or decoding elements, to construct a network such as shown in Fig. 7 · 15,

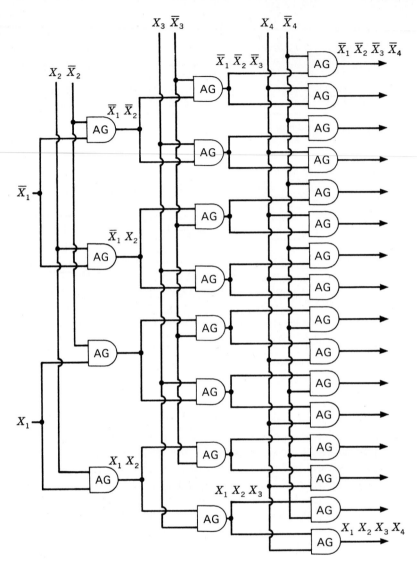

FIG. 7•14 Tree decoder.

compared with that in Figs. $7 \cdot 14$ and $7 \cdot 13$, becomes more significant as the number of flip-flops to be decoded increases. The type of network shown in Fig. $7 \cdot 11$, however, has the advantage of being the fastest of the three types of networks. This is counter-balanced by the fact that it is the most costly.

Having studied the three types of decoding matrices which are now used in digital machines, we will simply draw the decoder networks as a box with n inputs and 2^n outputs, with the understanding that one of the three types of circuits shown in Figs. $7 \cdot 13$ to $7 \cdot 15$ will be used in the box.

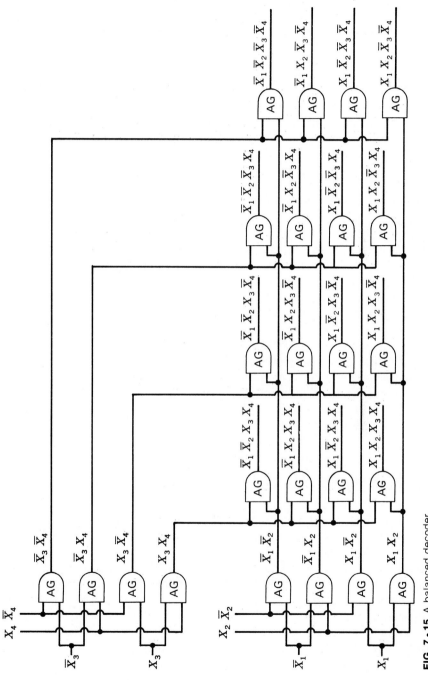

FIG. 7·15 A balanced decoder.

7 • 12 CORE-MEMORY ORGANIZATION AND WIRING SCHEMES

The core-memory organization which has been described is the classic *coincident-current four-wire random-access core memory*. Several variations on this basic scheme will be outlined in this section.

First, notice that the sense-line and the inhibit-line windings can be combined into a single winding. The sense amplifier is used only during the read section of the memory timing cycle, while the inhibit driver is on only during the write portion of the memory timing cycle. By simply connecting the sense amplifier to the inhibit winding and removing the sense winding, an array with only three wires per core can be formed. To visualize this, picture Fig. 7 · 7 with the sense winding removed. The sense amplifier is then connected to the inhibit winding, and this winding is called the *digit winding*, or *bit winding*. The sense amplifier must, of course, be capable of withstanding the large input from the inhibit driver. A three-wire coincident-current memory of this type is shown in Fig. 7 · 16, which is a 16-word 4-bit memory.

Aside from simplifying memory construction, reducing the number of windings through the cores has the desirable effect of making it possible to reduce the size of the cores. Smaller cores can be switched faster than larger cores, and the limiting factor on core size is often the number of wires through the cores; so the fastest memories are made with fewer wires. The price that is paid is in additional circuit complexity.

There is another selection scheme which is often used in core memories. This is called *linear selection*. The basic selection of a core from each plane for coincident-current memories is shown in Fig. 7 · 17(a), which is a three-wire coincident-current memory. Figure 7 · 15(b) shows the basic linear-selection technique, in which each word has a separate *word,* or *drive,* line and there are thus as many *word lines* as words in the memory. The sense and inhibit lines are combined in Fig. 7 · 17(b), in what is generally called a *digit line,* and there are as many digit lines as bits (binary digits) in the word. Notice that there are only two wires per core in Fig. 7 · 17(b), so the cores can be quite small. The READ and WRITE currents are both full currents; so the selected word line sends first a $-I_m$ READ, then a $+I_m$ WRITE current through the single selected line. The sense amplifiers than determine whether the bit previously stored along the digit line was a 0 or a 1 during the read time. During the write time, the inhibit driver for each digit line is turned on (to write a 0), and the current from this driver is $-I_m/2$, or not turned on (to write a 1). Since the current is a half current, it does not affect other cores along the digit line, but when on, it cancels half of the normal $+I_m$ current through the word line, so that the core at the intersection of the digit line and selected word line receives only $+I_m/2$ current and remains in the 0 state.

Since there are as many word lines as words in a linear-select memory, the decoder switch must be much larger. On the other hand, the READ and WRITE currents can be made large and turned on and off "hard," since only the selected cores receive any current. Linear-select memories are generally fast, but they cost more to construct because of the decoder and for various

Sense amplifiers and inhibit drivers

Memory buffer register flip-flops

Sense

Inhibit when appropriate

$\frac{1}{2}I$

$\frac{1}{2}I$

Y decoders and drivers

X decoders and drivers

Memory address register flip-flops

FIG. 7 • 16 Three-wire coincident-current memory.

Sense and inhibit lines (sometimes called digit lines)

(a)

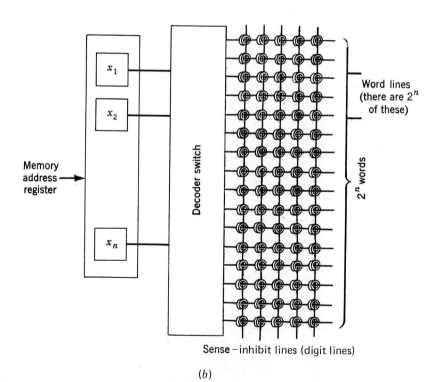

(b)

FIG. 7·17 Memory selection system techniques. (a) Coincident-current or three-dimensional selection system; (b) word-organized or linear-select memory which is two-dimensional.

FIG. 7·18 Linear-select memory.

Inhibit drivers and sense amplifiers

Flip-flops in memory buffer register

Memory register

Sense

Inhibit

I_S

Selected address

Decoder and word line drive circuit

0
1
0
1
0
1
0
1

Memory address register flip-flops

"small" reasons. (For instance, the smaller cores give smaller outputs, so that the sense amplifiers must be carefully set up.)

A 16 word 4-bit linear-select memory is shown in Fig. 7·18.

There is another core-memory arrangement called a $2\frac{1}{2}$D memory. One variation of the $2\frac{1}{2}$D memory is used for large inexpensive memories, and another for small fast memories. We shall not study this type of memory in detail except to note that the basic principle consists in making a stack, which is basically a coincident-current selection stack, but where the X windings are continuous from plane to plane; however, each plane has a separate Y winding. During the READ cycle, current is then gated through the selected X winding, which goes through all planes, and also through all Y windings; so each selected Y driver is turned on. During the WRITE cycle only those Y drivers for planes in which a 1 is to be written are turned on, while the X drivers are used in the customary way. CDC has a core memory with 12-mil cores which has a 275-ns memory cycle and a $2\frac{1}{2}$D organization.

The $2\frac{1}{2}$D memory can be three wires with a separate sense winding, or there are some two-wire memories where the output of the selected core is sensed on the Y-drive line by a circuit technique. (This is used in a very large IBM memory.) The $2\frac{1}{2}$D memory is a strategy which uses the coincident-current selection technique of half currents, but uses a dividend Y winding to facilitate writing, using more complicated gating of the Y windings rather than inhibit windings.

7•13 RANDOM-ACCESS SEMICONDUCTOR MEMORIES

The ability to fabricate large arrays of electronic components using straight-forward processing techniques and to make these arrays in small containers at reasonable prices has made it possible to manufacture electronic circuit, or *semiconductor,* memories which are competitive with core, memories. The first of these memories were small flip-flop memories called "scratch-pad memories," which were high-speed (faster than core) and were used for small buffer or operational memories.

The small flip-flop scratch-pad memories range from sixteen to several hundred words in size and can be read from or written into, in from several to tens of nano-seconds. A single flip-flop is used for each bit of storage, and gates are used to select words and to read into and from the flip-flops.

As the fabrication costs became less and larger arrays became feasible, semiconductor memories became much larger. Although there are a number of different schemes and devices available, there are three main categories of IC memories at this time.

1. *Bipolar memories*   These are essentially flip-flop memories with the flip-flops fabricated using standard *p-n* junction transistors. These memories are fast but tend to be expensive.
2. *Static MOS memories*   These are fabricated using MOS field effect devices to make flip-flop circuits. These memories are lower in speed than

TABLE 7·2 SEMICONDUCTOR MEMORY CHARACTERISTICS

| CHARACTERISTIC | MOS p-CHANNEL | MOS n-CHANNEL | | BIPOLAR |
		HIGH SPEED	HIGH DENSITY	
Number of bits per chip	4096	4096	16,384	2048
Access time, ns	300–400	50	150	20
Power dissipation, mW/bit	0.2	0.1	0.02	0.25
Average large-quantity cost, cents per bit	0.15	0.5	0.1	0.6

the bipolar memories but cost less, consume less power, and have high packing densities.

3. *Dynamic MOS memories*   These are fabricated using MOS devices but instead of using a flip-flop for the basic memory cell, a charge is deposited on a capacitor (or capacitors) fabricated on the IC chip, and the presence or absence of this charge determines the state of the cell. The MOS devices are used to sense and to deposit the charge on the capacitors used. Since the charge used will slowly dissipate in time, it is necessary to periodically refresh this charge, and the memories are therefore called *dynamic memories* (MOS or bipolar flip-flop memories are called *static memories*). These memories tend to be slower than the other types, but they are also less expensive, consume less power, and have a high packing density.

All three of the above types of memories have an advantage over core memories — the reading of data is nondestructive. Table 7·2 gives some key memory characteristics.

The selection techniques, sensing techniques, and other basic ideas used in core memories also apply to semiconductor memories. Since the storage devices are fabricated on a chip, the sense amplifiers, decoders, etc., can be placed on the same chip and quite often individual chips contain essentially complete small memories. The following sections cover some of the important features and details of semiconductor memories.

7•14 BIPOLAR IC MEMORIES

Bipolar memories are fabricated using high-density versions of the bipolar transistor flip-flop. One problem in increasing the density is isolating individual transistors from one another, but manufacturers have developed processes for reducing the space needed for transistor isolation. An advantage of bipolar devices is the simplicity of the interface circuitry required because of compatibility with bipolar logic. Another is the speed attainable.

Bipolar memories are manufactured using processes similar to those described in Chap. 5, and the primary circuit types are TTL and ECL emitter-coupled logic. (Gold doping to reduce transistor recovery time, as well as

X_i	Y_j	W_0	W_1	S_0	S_1	
0	X	0	0	0	0	
0	X	1	0	0	1	
0	X	0	1	1	0	
X	0	0	0	0	0	
X	0	1	0	0	1	
X	0	0	1	1	0	
1	1	1	0	0	1	Write 0
1	1	0	0	1	0	Sense 0
1	1	0	1	1	1	Write 1
1	1	0	0	0	1	Sense 1

Positive Logic
0 – Low level
1 – High level
X – Don't care

(from 15 other cells)

R_6 910
R_5 220 R_7 220   Y selection
Q_3 Q_4

X selection

Sense and write (digit) lines go to all 16 flip-flops.

Basic memory cell
(flip–flop)

(a)

$Y_1\ Y_2\ Y_3\ Y_4$ $Y_5\ Y_6\ Y_7\ Y_8$ $S_0\ S_1\ W_0\ W_1$
(Bit 1)
(Bit 2)
(Bit 3)
(Bit 4)
(Bit 5)
(Bit 6)
(Bit 7)
(Bit 8)
$S_0\ S_1\ W_0\ W_1$

(b)

FIG. 7·19 High-speed coincident-current semiconductor memory. (a) Basic memory model (courtesy of RCA); (b) modules assembled into a memory of 8 bits and 64 words.

Schottky diode clamping to prevent transistor saturation are used with TTL configurations to increase speed. ECL memories are suitable only where cost is secondary to very high speed.)

A basic memory cell for bipolar technology is shown in Fig. $7 \cdot 19(a)$. This flip-flop is fabricated of two multiple emitter transistors. The Q_3 and Q_4 transistors form the flip-flop, and either Q_3 will be on and Q_4 off, or Q_3 will be off and Q_4 on so the circuit is bistable.

These flip-flops are assembled in an array to form a memory. Figure $7 \cdot 19(a)$ also shows a two-dimensional array of these flip-flops and how they are placed in an IC container. Each square in the block diagram of the IC package showing the connections and general layout represents a single flip-flop in the 16-flip-flop array.

A flip-flop in the array is selected by means of the X and Y selection lines. The two SENSE lines S_0 and S_1 are shared by all the flip-flops and are returned to ground through a low resistance and the outputs are connected to sense amplifiers.

The operation of the memory is as follows. The four X-selection lines X_1, X_2, X_3, and X_4 and the four Y-selection lines Y_1, Y_2, Y_3, and Y_4 are normally low, or a 0. Making a single X line and a single Y line a 1 selects the cell at the intersection of the two lines. To write a 1 into a selected cell, the cell is selected by raising an X and Y input at the same time. W_0 is then made a 0 and W_1 a 1. To write a 0, the cell is selected, W_0 is made a 1, and W_1 is made a 0.

To read from the memory, both W_0 and W_1 are held at 0 and a cell is selected by raising an X and Y line. Then either the S_1 or S_0 line will have a current output; for instance, if the selected cell contains a 0, then S_0 will supply current. (Thus S_0 and S_1 are SENSE lines.) Reading is nondestructive because the value read need not be written back into the cell.

As manufactured by RCA, TI, and Fairchild, each IC container is a standard 14-pin container, as shown, containing 16 bits, including drive circuits and sense amplifiers. Figure $7 \cdot 19(b)$ shows 32 of these packages interconnected to form a 64-word 8-bit memory.

The preceding memory is very fast, with read and write times of a few nanoseconds. Quite often, more bits are packaged in a single IC container, and often the decoders to drive the X and Y lines are included in the package.

An example of a linear-select IC memory is shown in Fig. $7 \cdot 20$. Each cell or bit is as in Fig. $7 \cdot 20(a)$, which shows that to read from a cell the ADDRESS line is made a 1. To write into a cell, the ADDRESS line and the WRITE ENABLE lines are made a 1, and the DATA line then given the value to be written. Figure $7 \cdot 20(b)$ shows a block diagram for a 16-word 4-bit memory which is linear select, in that, to read or write, a single ADDRESS line of the 16 is made high and then, when reading, the values on S_1, S_2, S_3, and S_4 are sensed. To write, a single ADDRESS line is made a 1, the values to be written are placed on I_1, I_2, I_3, and I_4, and then the WRITE ENABLE line is made a 1.

Figure $7 \cdot 21$ shows a block diagram of a single package containing all the decoders and buffers for a 256-bit random-access memory. The dimensions are also shown. In actual practice, memories contain as many as 4,000 bits on a single semiconductor chip, including all decoders, buffers, and drivers.

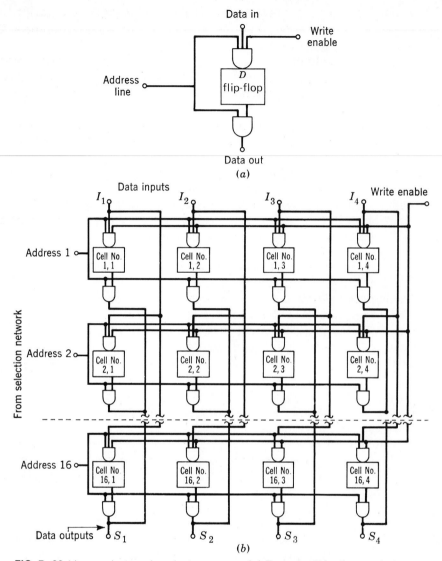

FIG. 7·20 Linear-select semiconductor memory. (*a*) Typical cell for linear-select memory in (*b*); (*b*) selection and read-write details.

7·15 STATIC MOS MEMORIES

It was realized very early in semiconductor memory development that MOS devices offer simplicity of manufacture and economy of layout. (MOS is made with only one diffusion and perhaps two-thirds the number of masks as bipolar devices.) MOS cells take up only one-half to one-fourth the area of bipolar cells, and hence they offer a considerable cost advantage. Figure 7·22 illustrates an MOS flip-flop analogous to the bipolar device of Fig. 7·19(*a*).

FIG. 7·21 Single-chip 256-bit memory. (Courtesy of INTEL Corp.)

This flip-flop is for a linear-select memory, however, and selection of a cell is by simply raising the word line. Transistors Q3 and Q4 act as resistors, replacing the relatively large-area resistors used in the collector circuits of bipolar units. Q5 and Q6 serve as gates, connecting to the digit lines. The state of the storage cell can be read by raising the word line which will turn

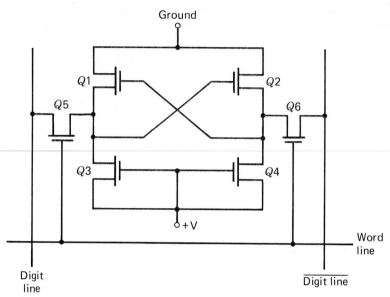

FIG. 7•22 Static MOS bit storage cell for linear-select memory.

on either Q5 or Q6 depending on the state of the flip-flop. The WRITE operation is carried out by raising the word line, and then setting the desired value
in by placing a high and low voltage on the correct digit lines.

The predominant type of MOS device in early memories was the p-channel
enhancement mode (PMOS) unit, in which holes are the vehicle of current
flow. Although easy to produce, inexpensive, and reliable, PMOS is relatively
slow and limited in LSI packing density. n-channel devices have now become the most popular, offering important performance advantages, such as
low operating voltage and higher speed, over their p-channel counterparts.
Because electron mobility is greater than hole mobility, n-channel transistors
are two to three times faster than p-channel transistors, which is equivalent to
saying that n-channel devices have greater gain than p-channel devices of
the same size. For equal speeds, n-channel units are smaller, permitting
greater packing density; and higher substrate doping levels may be employed, increasing density even further.

If we compare bipolar and MOS technologies, bipolar offers a speed advantage, although, until recently, limitations imposed by the need for isolation
between transistors have limited packing density and hence per-chip storage
capacity. Bipolar components can provide access times of under 10 ns, in
contrast with 300 or more ns for PMOS and 30 for NMOS. MOS devices
have relatively high internal capacitance and impedance, leading to longer
time constants and access times. Our schematic symbols will not show the
channel connections on the FETs as is conventional for memory devices. All
devices will be NMOS.

The operation of a typical 4096-bit static memory chip is detailed in Figs.

FIG. 7·23 MOS static memory cell. (Figures 7·23–7·26 courtesy of Electronic Memories and Magnetics Corp.)

7·23 to 7·26. The 4096 bits of memory are organized in an array of 64 rows by 64 columns. The memory cells are accessed by simultaneously decoding the X address A_0 through A_5 for the rows and the Y-address A_6 through A_{11} for the columns. (Each column contains a presense amplifier, the outputs of which are ORed and connected to the output stage.) Each bit or memory cell is a standard flip-flop as shown in Fig. 7·23, consisting of $R1$, $R2$ (which are actually MOS devices), Q2, Q4, Q1, and Q3. The load resistors $R1$ and $R2$ are typically 60 MΩ and connect to the power supply. Q1 and Q3 are used to connect the cell to the digit lines whenever the X select line is high. To read from this cell the X line is raised; then the cell will pull one of the digit lines low from its normally high state. The presense circuit selected by the Y column decoder will detect the differential voltage on the digit line selected and amplify it. To write into the cell, an X line is selected and then a digit line is selected and forced low by the circuit and the selected cell assumes the state forced by the selected digit line.

The CHIP SELECT (CS) input controls the operation of the memory. When CHIP SELECT is low, the input address buffers, decoders, sensing circuits, and output stages are held in the off state and power is supplied only to the memory elements. When the CHIP SELECT goes high, the memory is enabled. The CHIP SELECT pulse clocks the TTL logic level addresses, READ-WRITE, and DATA input into D flip-flops and enables the output stage. When a cell is read from one of the two outputs will source current (DO for data originally input as a 1, $\overline{\text{DO}}$ for data originally input as a 0). The DO and $\overline{\text{DO}}$ outputs are returned to ground through an impedance; as a result, the voltage at the output sourcing current will approach a value between 0.35 and 2 V (typically 1 V) above ground. The voltage at the other output will be below 100 mV. (A differential amplifier is used to detect the polarity of the signal.) A differential output of 25 mV (V_{out}) or more is considered a valid 1 output.

FIG. 7 • 24 Block diagram of MOS static memory.

Top view

Pin assignment

FIG. 7 • 25 MOS static memory
pin assignment.

As shown in Fig. 7·25, this memory chip is packaged in a 22-pin dual in-line package. By assembling a number of these chips, a large, moderately fast memory can be constructed. Memory cycle times for this chip are on the order of 100 ns. Figure 7·26 shows the timing for the memory cycles.

Notice the basic memory cell in this memory is a linear-select device. A two-dimensional selection is obtained by breaking the memory into rows and columns and using many (64) sense amplifiers and inhibit (digit) drivers on these columns. When a READ or WRITE operation is performed, the appropriate digit driver or "presense" amplifier is selected by the Y decoder. Thus, a row of memory cells is enabled by the X winding, but only the cell at the intersection of the enabled X winding and the selected sense amplifier or digit line driver will be actually used. This scheme requires more digit drivers and

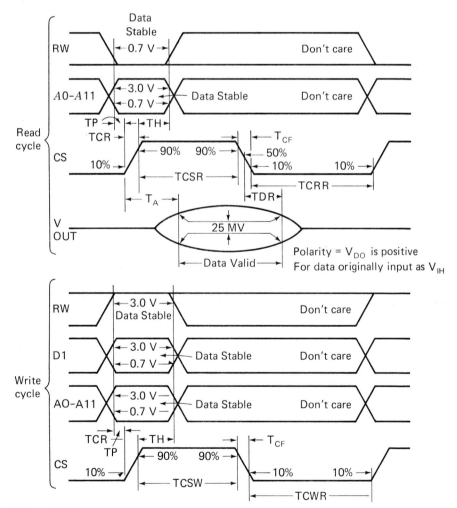

FIG. 7•26 Timing diagrams.

"presense" amplifiers but simplifies construction of the individual flip-flop memory cells. (Two more MOS transistors per cell are required to make a conventional two-dimensional selection as in the bipolar cell previously shown.) In general, two-dimensional selection of semiconductor cells requires more circuitry (generally two transistors per cell) but simplifies the decoders used. One-dimensional (linear) selection makes for larger decoders but simpler individual cells. As a result, compromise strategies such as that shown in Figs. 7 · 23 and 7 · 24 are often used.

As can be seen, the same selection systems and basic operational features of core memories carry over to semiconductor memories. Semiconductor memories are nondestructive read, however, and can be directly written into.

7 • 16 DYNAMIC MEMORIES

MOS cells are often used as the basis for a dynamic memory system. In a given memory cell, a 1 is written in by placing a charge on a capacitor; not charging or discharging the capacitor stores a 0. Reading then entails sensing the presence or absence of a charge on the capacitor. However, because there is always some leakage of the charge to ground, periodic refreshing is necessary.

Figure 7 · 27 depicts the simplest type of data storage cell, using a single MOS switching transistor and a storage capacitor (also an MOS device). During the WRITE cycle, a charge may or may not be stored on the capacitor. During the READ cycle, the capacitor charge determines the voltage on the DATA line. Although the single-transistor memory cell requires sophisticated sense and write circuits, its small size suits it to high-density storage such as in memories with 16,000 cells per IC chip.

A three-transistor cell used in several dynamic MOS memories is shown in Fig. 7 · 28. The gate capacitance of Q1 is used to store the charge, eliminating the need for an additional capacitor, so this cell can be made extremely small, permitting high bit packing density. To read from the cell, the WRITE DATA line is raised to the 1 level. The READ SELECT line is than raised so that Q2 can conduct. If the voltage on the Q1 gate exceeds the transistor threshold,

FIG. 7 • 27 Single-transistor memory cell.

FIG. 7 • 28 Three-transistor memory cell for dynamic memory.

Q1 conducts, so that the READ DATA line discharges to a 0 V potential. If the charge on the Q1 gate is insufficient to turn on Q1, the line remains pre-charged at the negative potential. The potential of the READ DATA line is sensed using an amplifier integral with the chip. A refresh amplifier (similar to a sense amplifier) must then sense the information on the line and rewrite it into the WRITE DATA line, refreshing the stored information. During a WRITE cycle, information on the WRITE DATA line is stored in the cell.

The dynamic memory cell in Fig. 7 · 29 has two transistors connected to form a flip-flop, with two additional transistors required for gating. The data

FIG. 7 • 29 Dynamic MOS memory cell with four MOS transistors.

bit and its complement are stored on the gate capacitances of the flip-flop transistors.

The primary advantages of dynamic MOS memories lie in the simplicity of the individual cells. There is a secondary advantage in the fact that power need not be applied to the cells when they are not being read from or written into. This makes for higher packing densities per chip. The obvious disadvantage lies in the need to refresh these cells every few milliseconds. (Generally, less than every 2 ms is required.) External circuitry to read and then rewrite may be required or the memories may include special circuits to refresh when commanded. As a result, extra refresh memory cycles are required, but these occupy only a small percentage of the overall operating time.†

The selection systems and SENSE and WRITE operations for dynamic memories are similar to those for static memories except that more complicated timing is required. Dynamic memories are generally slower than static memories but also tend to cost less per bit.

7•17 READ-ONLY MEMORIES

Many digital systems use a type of storage device called a *read-only memory* (ROM). These memory devices have the unique characteristic that they can be read from, but that the computer cannot write information into them. The information stored in these memories is therefore introduced into the memory in some manner such that the information is semipermanent or permanent. Sometimes the information stored in a ROM is placed in the memory at the time of construction, and sometimes devices are used where the information can be manually changed. In this section we shall study several types of ROMs, bearing in mind that a number of different types are now being constructed. Those types of memory which we shall study, however, are characteristic of this particular class of memory devices, and most devices are variations on the principles which will be presented.

Basically, a ROM is a device with several input and output lines such that, for each input combination, there is a unique output combination. Thus a ROM physically realizes a truth table, or table of combinations. A typical (small) table might be that in Table 7·3.

This list of input-output values is actually a list of binary-to-Gray code values (the Gray code will be discussed in the next chapter). It is important to see that the list can be looked at in two ways, however: first, as a table for a gating network with four inputs and four outputs, and, second, as a list of addresses from 0 to 15, as given by the X values, and the contents of each address, as given by the values of the Z's.

---

† There are even some interesting internal refresh mechanisms called *charge pumps* which require application of a sine wave on one of the inputs and make refreshing transparent (invisible) to the user. Other refresh strategies rewrite entire columns using a single refresh pulse.

TABLE 7·3 BINARY-TO-GRAY CODE VALUES

INPUT				OUTPUT			
X_1	X_2	X_3	X_4	Z_1	Z_2	Z_3	Z_4
0	0	0	0	0	0	0	0
0	0	0	1	0	0	0	1
0	0	1	0	0	0	1	1
0	0	1	1	0	0	1	0
0	1	0	0	0	1	1	0
0	1	0	1	0	1	1	1
0	1	1	0	0	1	0	1
0	1	1	1	0	1	0	0
1	0	0	0	1	1	0	0
1	0	0	1	1	1	0	1
1	0	1	0	1	1	1	1
1	0	1	1	1	1	1	0
1	1	0	0	1	0	1	0
1	1	0	1	1	0	1	1
1	1	1	0	1	0	0	1
1	1	1	1	1	0	0	0

Thus we might construct a gating network as in Fig. 7·30 which would give the correct Z output for each X input. (The boxes with ⊕ inside are mod 2 adders.)

The table could also be realized by a 16-word 4-bit-per-word core memory into which we had read 0000 at the address 0; 0001 at the address 1; 0011 in the next address; and so on until 1000 in the last address. If we did not ever thereafter write into this memory, it would be a ROM memory and would serve the same purpose as the gating network in Fig. 7·30.

Figure 7·31(a) shows a scheme for implementing the table using a de-coder network with four inputs X_1, X_2, X_3, and X_4 and a number of diodes. With a given input combination (or address), a single output line from the decoder will be high. Let us assume the input value is $X_1 = 0$, $X_2 = 1$, $X_3 = 1$, $X_4 = 1$. This corresponds to 0111 on the decoder output in Fig. 7·31(a). Diodes are connected at the junction of this line and the output lines which are 1s, and no diodes are placed where 0s are to appear. Thus, for the input 0111, we have a single diode connected to output line Z_2, since the desired output is to be

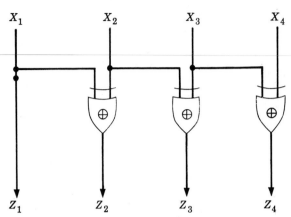

FIG. 7·30 Combinational network for binary-to-Gray code.

0100. Similarly, for the input 0110, we connect diodes to Z_2 and Z_4, since the output is to be 0101. The operation of the network is as follows: Only one decoder line output will be high at a time. Current flows from this line to only those output lines to which a diode is connected. Thus, for the input 0101, current flows into lines Z_2, Z_3, and Z_4 but not Z_1; so Z_2, Z_3, Z_4 will be 1s and Z_1 a 0.

The entire scheme outlined above realizes the ROM with electronic gates (the diodes form OR gates). By using LSI techniques, arrays of this sort can be inexpensively fabricated in small containers at low prices. 512-word 8-bit memories are of about average size for the LSI ROMs; these memories effectively store 4096 bits in all.

The diodes in Fig. 7·31(a) are often transistors, and the manufacturing processes are of various types. Figure 7·31(b) shows typical memory cells for semiconductor ROMs using MOS and bipolar transistors. These cells are from a one-dimensional selection system; notice the word-selection lines and the bit line. Both one- and two-dimensional selection is used in ROMs. MOS ROMS generally have 50- to 200-ns access times; bipolar memories range from 5- to 100-ns access time.

When a ROM is constructed so the user can electrically (or using other techniques) write in the contents of the memory, the memory is called a *programmable ROM* or PROM.† Often, a scheme is used where a memory

---

† These memories are also called *field programmable* ROMs.

(a)

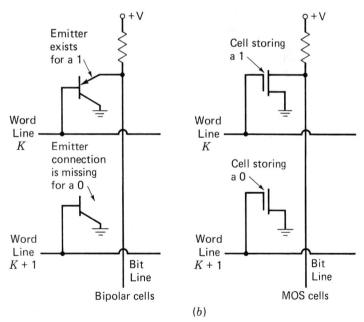

(b)

FIG. 7 • 31 (a) Diode ROM; (b) ROM cells using MOS and bipolar transistors.

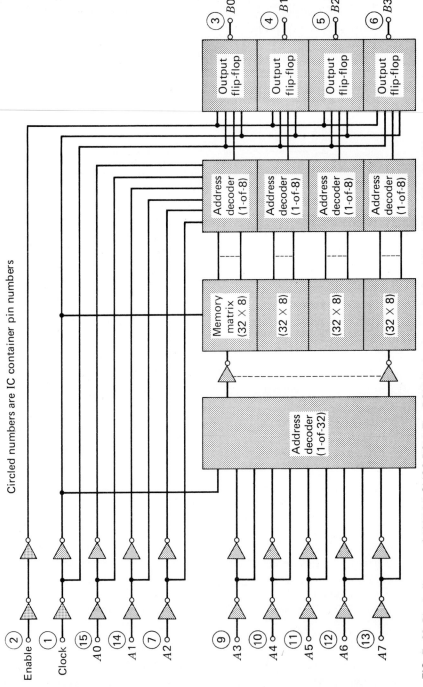

Circled numbers are IC container pin numbers

FIG. 7·32 Block diagram of 1024-bit CMOS ROM. The ROM device is organized as 256 × 4 bits. (Courtesy Motorola Corp.)

chip is delivered with 1s in every position but 0s can be introduced at given positions by placing an address on the input lines and then raising each output line which is to be a 0 to a specified voltage, thus destroying a connection to the selected cell. (Sometimes the memories contain all 0s, and 1s are written in by the user.) Devices are also manufactured which program PROMs by reading paper tapes, magnetic tapes, punched cards, etc., and placing their contents into the PROM.

Custom ROM manufacturers provide forms whereby a user can fill 1s and 0s on a form which is provided and the manufacturer will produce a custom-made mask and will then produce LSI chips which will realize the memory contents specified by the user. A single chip may cost more for such a memory, but large production runs generally cost less per chip.

Figure 7·32 shows a block diagram of a 1024-bit MOS memory which is organized as a 256 word 4-bit-per-word memory. The user places the address on the eight input lines A_0 through A_7, and then raises the ENABLE line. Lowering the clock line will cause the output flip-flops to be loaded and the desired word will appear on lines B_0, B_1, B_2, and B_3. This is a custom-made memory where the desired memory contents are supplied to the manufacturer by the user on a form. The manufacturer then makes a mask to create the desired bit patterns on an IC chip and manufactures ROMs with this pattern to order. Delay time for the memory is on the order of 100 ns.

When a ROM is manufactured so that the memories' contents can be set as desired by the user and the memory can later have the contents erased and new values placed in the memory, the ROM is said to be *erasable* and *reprogrammable*. For example, some memory chips are made with a transparent lid. Exposing the chip (through the lid) to ultraviolet light† will erase the pattern on the chip, and a new pattern can be written in electrically. This can be repeated as often as desired.

7·18 MAGNETIC DRUM STORAGE

The storage devices which have been described utilize the principle of setting a device that is essentially bistable into one of its two states. Access to the devices was essentially random—once addressed, a core is immediately available and a flip-flop continuously produces an indication of its state. The limitations on this type of storage are based on the complexity, and therefore the cost and reliability, of storing a large number of bits. While core memories have been constructed which can store tens of millions of bits, some large machines require the storage of as many as 10^{13} bits. This would require 1 million core memories. The high speed of core-memory storage is therefore paid for in the complexity and cost of the storage.

---

† Standard ultraviolet lamps can be used to erase the memory. About 20- to 30-min exposure is required.

READ-WRITE heads

Tracks

(a)

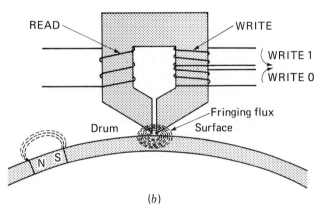

(b)

FIG. 7 • 33 Magnetic drum memory. (a) Magnetic drum tracks; (b) READ-WRITE head.

Magnetic drums were among the first devices to provide a relatively inexpensive means of storing information and have reasonably short access times. A magnetic drum consists basically of a rotating cylinder coated with a thin layer of magnetic material which possesses a hysteresis loop similar to that of the material used in magnetic cores (Fig. 7 · 4). A number of recording heads [Fig. 7 · 33(a)] are mounted along the surface of the drum. These are used to write and read information from the surface of the drum by magnetizing small areas, or sensing the magnetization of the areas on which information has been recorded. While Fig. 7 · 33(a) shows only a few heads, some magnetic drums have several hundred recording heads scattered about their periphery.

As the drum rotates, a small area continually passes under each of the heads. This area is known as a *track* [Fig. 7 · 33(a)]. Each track is subdivided into cells, each of which can store 1 binary bit.

Generally, one of the tracks is used to provide the timing for the drum. A series of timing signals is permanently recorded around this timing track, and each signal defines a *time unit* for the drum system. The timing track is then used to determine the location of each set of storage cells around the tracks. For instance, if the timing track is 60 in. in length and timing pulses are recorded at a density of 100 per inch, there will be 6,000 locations for bits (cells) around each of the tracks. If the drum has 30 tracks plus the timing track, the drum will have the capacity to store a total of 180,000 bits.

Information is written onto the drum by passing current through a winding on the WRITE heads. This current causes flux to be created through the core material of the head. Figure 7·33(*b*) illustrates a head for writing or reading information from a drum. Some drum systems use separate heads for reading and writing, and others use combined READ-WRITE heads. The head in Fig. 7·33(*b*) consists of a ring formed of high-permeability material around which wire is wound. When information is to be written on the surface of the drum, pulses of current are driven through the WRITE 0 or WRITE 1 winding. The direction of flux through the head, and in turn the polarization of the magnetic field recorded on the surface of the drum, depends upon whether WRITE 1 or WRITE 0 is on.

The gap in the core presents a relatively high-reluctance path to the flux generated by the current through the coil. Since the magnetic material on the surface of the drum is passing near the gap, most of the flux passes through this material. This causes a small area of the drum surface to be magnetized, and since the material used to coat the surface of the drum has a relatively high retentivity, the magnetic field remains after the area has passed from under the head, or the current through the coil is discontinued. It should be noted that the head does not actually touch the surface of the drum. Instead, to prevent wear, the heads are located very close to the drum surface but not touching it. The drum must therefore be of very constant diameter in order to keep the heads at a constant distance. If the head moves farther from the surface of the drum, the signals recorded will become weaker. In practice, the heads are able to move slightly into or away from the surface and are pushed toward the surface by a spring loading mechanism. A cushion of air between the head and the rotating surface then maintains the required relatively constant distance from the magnetic surface.

The signals recorded on the surface of the drum are read in a similar manner. When the areas which have been magnetized pass under the head, some of the magnetic flux is coupled into the head, and changes in this flux induce signals in the winding. These signals are then amplified and interpreted. A description of the recording techniques used will be found in the final section of this chapter.

The sizes and storage capacities of magnetic drums vary greatly. Small drums with capacities of less than 25,000 bits have been constructed. Drums of this size generally have from 15 to 25 tracks and from 15 to 50 heads. To decrease access time, heads are sometimes located in sets around the periphery of the drum, so that a drum with 15 tracks may have 30 heads divided

TABLE 7·4 MAGNETIC DRUM CHARACTERISTICS

CHARACTERISTICS	FH 432 UNIVAC 1108	2301 IBM 360	2303 IBM 360	1964 ICL 1900 SERIES	FASTRAND II UNIVAC 1108
Tracks per drum	144	220	800	512	6,144
Characters per track	12,288	20,483	4,892	4,048	10,752
Characters per unit	1,572,864	4,096,600	3,910,000	2,072,576	132,120,756
Transfer rate, kilobits	1,440	1,200	312	100	153
Head arrangement (fixed or movable)	Fixed	Fixed	Fixed	Fixed	Movable
Heads per drum	128	200	800	512	32 × 192 positions
Drum diameter, in.	10.5	10.7		18.5	32.8
Drum speed, rpm	7,100	3,490	3,428	1,500	870
Packing density, bits/in.	627	1,250	1,105	1,000	1,000
Average access time, ms	4.25	8.6	8.75	20.5	93
Approximate cost per 6-bit character stored, cents	8	5	4	3	0.2

into two sets of 15 heads, each set located 180° from the other. For very fast access time, there may be even more than two sets of heads.†

Much larger drums can store up to 10^9 bits and may have from 500 to 1,000 tracks. The larger drums are generally rotated much more slowly than small drums, and speeds vary from 120 rpm (for laboratory models) up to 75,000 rpm. The access times obviously decrease as the drum speeds increase; however, there is another important factor: the packing density along a track. Most present-day drums have a packing density of from 600 to 1,000 bits/in., although by maintaining the heads very close to the drum surface and rotating the drum slowly, packing densities in excess of 1000 bits/in. may be achieved. One drum system, the IBM 2303, has 800 tracks and 4892 bytes per track (and so about a 3.9 million-bytes capacity), and the drum makes a complete rotation in 17.5 ms. Table 7·4 gives some characteristics of present-day drum systems.

7•19 PARALLEL AND SERIAL OPERATION OF A MAGNETIC DRUM

It is possible to operate a drum in either a serial or parallel mode. For parallel operation, all the bits of a word may be written simultaneously, and read in the same manner. If the basic computer word contains 40 bits, the drum might read from 41 tracks (one for timing) simultaneously, thus reading an entire computer word in one bit time. When the drum is read from and written into in parallel, a separate READ and WRITE amplifier is required for each track that is used simultaneously, so that to read a 40-bit word in a bit time, 40 READ amplifiers are required. The correct set of heads is then selected, and the drum system locates the selected set of cells.

Notice that words in a parallel system may be located by means of a timing track. If each track contains 8192 bits, a 13-bit counter may be set to zero at the same position each time the drum revolves, and stepped by one each time a timing pulse appears. In this way, the location 1096 will be the 1096th slot around the track from the 0 location. If the address of the word to be read is loaded into a register, the signals from the drum can be gated into the computer when the counter agrees with the register's contents. In this way words may be located on the drum.

A magnetic drum may also be operated in a serial mode. In this case only one track will be read from or written into at a given time. Since there are a number of tracks for each drum, the correct track as well as the location of the desired bits around the track must be selected.

Each track is therefore assigned a number. In addition, each track is divided into *sectors,* each sector containing one or more full computer words.

---

† The actual access time can be reduced by clever coding of the computer program. If the computer writes into or reads words near the reading or writing heads when an instruction is initiated, the access time may be minimized.

To specify the address of a word on a magnetic drum operated serially, both the track number and sector number must first be given. If only one word is in a sector this will suffice; if more than one word is in each sector, this word must be specified also. Consider a drum with 32 tracks plus a timing track and 32 words (sectors) around each track. The address of a word on the drum in a binary machine will consist of 10 bits, 5 bits to specify the track and 5 bits the sector. When written, the address will contain 10 bits. The first 5 bits may be used to designate the track number, and the second 5 bits the sector number.

Address register

| 1 | 0 | 0 | 1 | 1 | 1 | 0 | 1 | 1 | 1 |

Track
number

Sector
number

The five flip-flops containing the track number may be connected to a *decoder,* which will then select the correct READ-WRITE head.

Several techniques involving the timing tracks may be used to locate the selected sector. One technique involves the use of several timing tracks instead of one. Figure 7·34 shows a technique utilizing three timing tracks. One of the tracks contains a set of signals indicating the location of each bit around the tracks. The second track contains a set of pulses with a pulse at the beginning of each word time. (The word-time signals illustrated are 12 bits apart; so the basic word would be 11 or 12 bits in length.) In addition, the *sector number* of the *next* word around the drum is recorded around a third timing track. The computer reads sector numbers from this track, and when the number read agrees with the sector number in the address, the computer can then read the selected word from the next sector, beginning with the next word-time pulse.

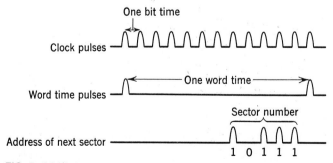

FIG. 7•34 Timing signals for a magnetic drum.

7•20 MAGNETIC DISK MEMORIES

Another type of memory, called a *magnetic disk memory,* greatly resembles the magnetic drum memory in operation. The magnetic disk memory provides very large storage capabilities with moderate operating speeds. There are quite a large number of different types of magnetic disk memories now on the market. Although differing in specific details, all of them are based on the same principles of operation.

In appearance, a magnetic disk memory resembles the coin-operated automatic record player, or "juke box." A number of rotating disks coated with a magnetic material are stacked with space between each disk (refer to Fig. 7•35). Information is recorded on the surface of the rotating disks by magnetic heads which are positioned against the disks. (Information is recorded in bands rather than on a spiral.) Each band of information around a given disk is called a "track." On one side of a typical disk there may be from one hundred to several thousand of these data tracks. Bits are recorded along a track at a density of from perhaps 500 to 7000 bits/in. In some systems, the outer tracks contain more bits than the inner tracks, because the circumference of an outer track is greater than that of an inner track, but many disks have the same number of bits around each track. The speed at which the disks rotate varies, of course, with the manufacturer, but typical speeds are on the order of 3,000 rpm.

Since each disk contains a number of tracks of information and there may be several disks in a given memory, several techniques have evolved for placing the magnetic READ and WRITE head in the correct position on a selected track. Since the same head is generally used for reading and for writing, the problem becomes that of placing this head accurately and quickly on the track which has been selected.

There are two basic types of disk systems. The first type of system has its heads fixed in position on each track. These are called *fixed-head systems.* The second kind of system has one or more pairs of READ-WRITE heads for each pair of adjacent disk surfaces (because information is generally written on both the top and bottom of each disk). These READ-WRITE heads are mounted on arms which can be moved in and out. These are called *movable-head systems.*†

The positioning of the heads by means of the mechanical movement of arms is a difficult and tricky business, particularly since the tracks are often recorded less than hundredths of an inch apart on the disk. It should be apparent that disk-file memories with many heads can locate and record or read from a selected track faster than ones with only a few heads, since the

---

† A few systems have been made with only one pair of READ-WRITE heads for the entire memory. In these systems, the two recording heads are positioned on an arm which is first moved between the correct pair of disks, and then selects the correct surface of the adjacent surfaces (again because information is written on both the top and bottom of each disk). The READ-WRITE head is finally placed upon the correct selected track of the disk.

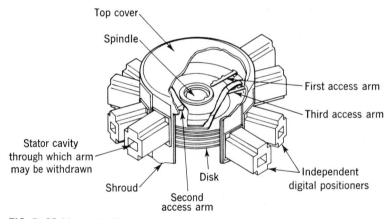

Top cover

Spindle

First access arm

Third access arm

Stator cavity through which arm may be withdrawn

Shroud

Disk

Second access arm

Independent digital positioners

FIG. 7 • 35 Magnetic disk memory system.

amount of mechanical movement before the track is reached will be less for the multihead system.

The total time it takes to begin reading selected data or to begin writing one selected track in a particular place is called the *access time.*

The time it takes to position a head on the selected track is called the *seek time,* and it is generally somewhere between an average of several milliseconds to fractions of a second. The other delay in locating selected data is the *latency,* or *rotational, delay,* which is the time required for the desired data to reach the magnetic head once the head is positioned. Thus, the total access time for a disk is the seek time plus the latency.

For a rotational speed of 2,400 rpm, for example, latency is a maximum of

25 ms and averages 12.5 ms. Latency represents a lower limit to access time in systems using fixed heads. As a result, for minimum access time, fixed heads are used. Typically, heads are arranged in groups of eight or nine, perhaps including a spare, and are carefully aligned in fixed positions with respect to the disk. Although head spacing in each group is typically 8 to 16/in., track densities of 30 to 60/in. can be achieved by interlacing groups.

Although they are faster, fixed-head systems provide less storage capacity than moving-head systems having comparable disk recording areas because the moving-head systems have more tracks per inch. Further, the large number of heads required can increase cost for a given capacity; however, where only modest storage capacity is required, a fixed-head system may be the most economical, because no head positioning mechanism is required.

An important advantage of moving magnetic heads concerns their alignment with very closely spaced data tracks. Although track spacing is limited by "crosstalk" between adjacent tracks and mechanical tolerances, spacing of 10 mils between adjacent tracks is common. Further, track widths of approximately 3.5 to 5 mils are consistent with head positioning accuracies of 0.5 to 1.5 mils.

The READ and WRITE heads used on magnetic disk memories are almost invariably of a type called *flying heads*. A simplified diagram of a flying head is shown in Fig. 7 · 36. When a disk rotates at a high speed, a thin but resilient boundary layer of air rotates with the disk. The head is so shaped that it rides on this layer of rotating air, which causes the disk to maintain separation from the head, thus preventing wear on the surface of the disk. In effect, the layer of air rotating with the disk acts like a spring with a stiffness exceeding several thousand pounds per inch, thus forcing the head away from the surface of the disk. To force the head into the correct proximity with the disk, a number of mechanisms have been used. Often compressed air is simply blown into a

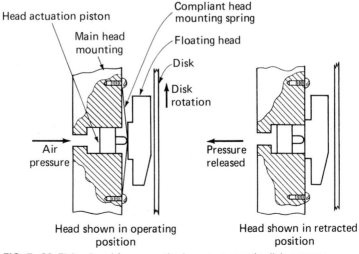

FIG. 7 • 36 Flying head for magnetic drum or magnetic disk memory.

(a)

(b)

FIG. 7·37 (a) IBM 2314 magnetic disk memory; (b) disk pack for IBM 2314 (only five disks are shown).

mechanism which forces the head toward the surface of the disk, using a pistonlike arrangement, as shown in Fig. 7·36.

There are many sizes and speeds for disk memories. Some disks are quite large, running up to 4 ft in diameter. Others are smaller, rotate faster, are changeable, etc. Because of the large market for these memories and the seemingly infinite variety of configurations in which they can be manufactured, the system user is afforded considerable freedom in selection.

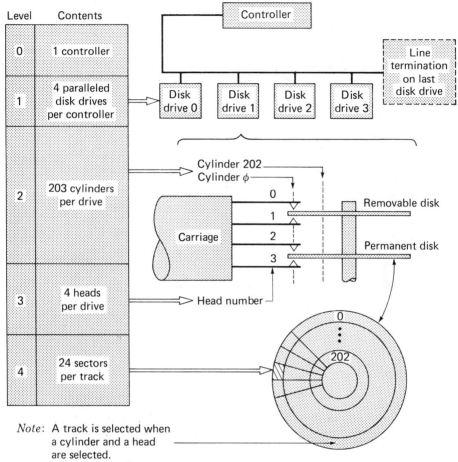

FIG. 7•38 Storage system containing up to four disk drives, each with two disks recorded on both sides. (Courtesy Hewlett-Packard Co.)

Disk memories which have changeable disk packs (or *modules*†) are very popular. Each disk pack contains a set of disks which rotate together. The IBM 2314 shown in Fig. 7•37(*a*) uses a changeable disk pack, for instance, which contains 20 recording disk surfaces consisting of 10 disks. [Refer to Fig. 7•37(*b*).] In this particular configuration, the top of the top disk and the bottom of the bottom disk are not used. Eighteen READ-WRITE heads are used, two for each surface on which information is recorded. The disks revolve at a speed of 2,400 rpm. The heads are mounted in a comblike positioning mechanism as shown. Each disk surface is divided into 200 concentric magnetic tracks per inch and each track contains about 4400 bits/in.

Figure 7•38 shows characteristics of a lower-priced disk system manufactured by Hewlett-Packard.

---

† A *module* is a disk pack which has the READ-WRITE heads and positioning arms all packaged together with the disks. These modules are costly, but enable a higher performance system.

TABLE 7·5 DISK DRIVE/DISK PACK TECHNOLOGY

DISK DRIVE TECHNOLOGY	IBM 2314	CDC 215	UNIVAC 8440	IBM 3330	IBM 3330-11	IBM 3340
Pack design	IBM 2316	IBM 2316	2316*	IBM 3336	IBM 3336-11	IBM 3348
Number of surfaces	20	20	20	19	19	24
Storage capacity megabytes	29	54	108	100	200	35 to 70
Tracks per inch	200	200	200	192	384	300
Transitions per inch	4,400	4,400	4,400	4,040	4,040	5,072
Data rate (million bits/s)	2.5	2.5	5.0	6.5	6.5	7.1
Average access time (ms)	60	30	30	30	30	25
Rpm	2,400	2,400	2,400	3,600	3,600	3,000
Detent	Mech.†	Optical	Optical	Servo	Servo	Servo
Actuator	Hydr.†	Voice coil	Voice coil	Voice coil	Voice coil	Voice coil
Disk coating, minimum (μin.)	90	90	50	50	40	40
Head fly height, minimum (μin.)	80	80	70	50	30	30

* Special pack made with 2316-pack hardware and 3336 disks.

† Non-IBM hybrids exist with voice coil and optical mask.

Table 7·5 lists the characteristics of several of the larger disk systems and Table 7·6 some characteristics for a smaller, less expensive system.

Because of the relative inexpensiveness per bit of information stored in disk memories and because of the relatively low access times and the high transfer rates attainable when reading or writing data from or into a disk file, magnetic disk memories have become one of the most important storage devices in modern digital computers.

7•21 FLEXIBLE DISK STORAGE SYSTEMS — THE FLOPPY DISK

An innovation in disk storage, originally developed at IBM, uses a flexible, "floppy" disk with a plastic base, in place of the more conventional rigid, metal-based disk. This storage medium is approximately the size and shape of a 45-rpm record and can be "plugged in" about as easily as a tape cartridge. Each floppy disk costs only a few dollars.

The floppy disks are changeable and each disk comes in an envelope as shown in Fig. 7·39. The disks are mounted on the disk drive with the envelope in place, and information is written and read through an aperture in the en-

TABLE 7·6 SPECIFICATIONS FOR HP 2888A DISK DRIVE

CHARACTERISTIC	SPECIFICATION
Data access time	
Minimum	7 ms
Average	29 ms
Maximum	55 ms
Rotational delay (latency)	
Average ($\frac{1}{2}$ revolution)	12.5 ms
Maximum (1 revolution)	25 ms
Total average response time	
Position and rotation	41.5 ms
Maximum response	80 ms
Operational characteristics	
Start up	20 s
Stop time	25 s maximum
Disk rotation speed	2,400 rpm
Number of heads	20
Number of cylinders	40 (20 tracks per cylinder)
Storage capacity	47,104,000 bytes
Data transfer rate	320,000 bytes/s; 236,000 bytes/s burst rate (average)
Actuator	Electromagnetic actuator with closed-loop optical servo positioning
Disk pack—HP 30333A	
Surfaces	20
Tracks/surface	400, plus 6 spare

velope. (Some systems require removing the envelope.) Several manufacturers now provide complete systems for well under $1000 for use with these disks. Convenience in use and low prices have broadened the use of floppy disk memories in many applications.

On most floppy disk drives, the READ-WRITE head assembly is in actual physical contact with the recording material. (For increased life, head contact is generally maintained only when reading or writing.) The flexible disk is enclosed in an 8-in. square jacket, and the disk has a diameter of 7.88 in. The recording surface is a 100-μin.-thick layer of magnetic oxide on a 0.003-in.-thick polyester substrate. The jacket gives handling protection, and, in addition, it has a special liner that provides a wiping action to remove wear products and other dirt which would be abrasive to the media and head if left on the surface.

In the IBM version there is a single 0.100-in.-diameter index hole 1.5 in. from the center of the disk to indicate the start of a track. A written track is 0.012-in. wide, and standard track spacing is 48/in. The number of tracks is 77. The capacity of a surface using a standard code and a bit density of

8 in.
(20 cm)

8 in.
(20 cm)

Index hole

The outer circle shows a hole in the jacket;
the inner circle shows the index hole in the
disk. When these two holes are aligned as
the disk revolves during data processing
operations, a beam of light shining on one
side of the diskette is sensed from the other
side and used for timing functions.

Drive access opening in jacket

Drive spindle hole in disk

After the diskette has been placed in the
machine and the disk drive spindle has been
inserted into the drive spindle hole in the
disk, the drive mechanism clamps onto a
portion of the disk exposed by the drive
access opening in the jacket.

Pressure pad slot
(A similar opening on the other side of the
diskette is called the head slot.)

The head slot exposes the recording surface
of the disk as the disk turns in its jacket in
the machine. The data recording and sensing
unit of the disk drive, which is called a *read-
write head* and is similar to the record/play-
back head in a tape recorder, moves to specified positions along the length of the slot.
Moving to a specified position is called
accessing a track. (Data are recorded only
on the side of the diskette that contains the
head slot.)

FIG. 7·39 Floppy disk with envelope.

TABLE 7·7 CHARACTERISTICS FOR
AN IBM COMPATIBLE FLEXIBLE DISK DRIVE

CHARACTERISTIC	SPECIFICATION
Capacity*	400,000 bytes
Rotational speed	360 rpm
Transfer rate	250,000 bits/s
Track-to-track access time	16–20 ms
Average access time	176 ms
Bit density	
Inner track	3268 bits/in.
Outer track	1836 bits/in.
Track density	48 tracks/in.
Number of tracks	77

* This is a maximum; using IBM's formatted recording
system, only 250,000 bytes of data are recorded per disk.

TABLE 7·8 FLEXIBLE DISK DRIVE SPECIFICATIONS
(Courtesy Pertec Corporation)

CHARACTERISTIC	SPECIFICATION
Media	IBM diskette or equivalent
Tracks per inch	48
Number of tracks	77
Track width	0.012 in.
Recording parameters	
Transfer rate	250 kbits/s
Bit density	6631 bits/rad
Max. bits per disk (unformatted)	3.2 million
Max. bits per track (unformatted)	41,665
Format*	
Sectors per track	26
Index tracks	1
Data tracks	73
Spare tracks	2
Reserved tracks	1
Bytes per sector	128
Performance	
Disk speed	360 rpm ± 1.5%
Start/stop time	3 s maximum
Seek time	10 ms track-to-track
Head settling time	10 ms (last track addressed)
Head loading time	20 ms maximum
Error rate (maximum)	1 per 10^9 recoverable, 1 per 10^{12} nonrecoverable
Head life	10,000 h in normal use
Media life	3500 h
Dimensions	3.45 in. high, 8.58 in. wide, 13.28 in. deep
Weight	5.5 kg maximum

  * Compatible with disks recorded on IBM 3540 or 3740 systems. Easily interfaced with non-IBM compatible systems.

3268 bits/in. on the innermost track is about 400,000 bytes of 8 bits each. Table 7·7 shows some characteristics of this kind of flexible disk system.†

    Several companies offer floppy disk systems using adaptations of the flying-head concept. An example system is made by Pertec, and their specifications are shown in Table 7·8. Most floppy disks use an address system (like disks) where the disk drive, track, and sector are given; however, some systems write "headers" on each block of recorded data on a track and the header information is specified for each access.

---

  †IBM uses only about 250,000 bytes for data; the remaining bits are used for formatting, error correction, and timing signals.

7•22 MAGNETIC TAPE

At present, the most popular medium for storing very large quantities of information is magnetic tape. Although, because of its long access time, magnetic tape is not a desirable medium for the main high-speed storage of a computer, modern mass-production techniques have made the cost of tape very low, so that vast quantities of information may be stored inexpensively. Furthermore, since it is possible to erase and rewrite information on tape, the same tape may be used again and again. Another advantage of magnetic tape is that the information stored does not "fade away," and therefore data or programs stored one month may be used again the next.

Another advantage of using magnetic tape for storing large quantities of data derives from the fact that the reels of tape on a tape mechanism may be changed. In this way the same magnetic tape handling mechanism and its associated circuitry may be used with many different reels of tape, each reel containing different data.

There are four basic parts of a digital magnetic tape system:

1. *Magnetic tape*   This is generally a flexible plastic tape with a thin coating of some ferromagnetic material along the surface.
2. *The tape transport*   This consists of a mechanism designed to move the tape past the recording heads at the command of the computer. Included are the heads themselves and the storage facilities for the tape being used, such as the reels on which the tape is wound.
3. *The reading and writing system*   This part of the system includes the reading and writing amplifiers and the "translators" which convert the signals from the tape to digital signals which may be used in the central computing system.
4. *The switching and buffering equipment*   This section consists of the equipment necessary to select the correct tape mechanism if there are several, to store information from the tape and also information to be read onto the tape (provide buffering), and to provide such facilities as manually directed rewinding of the tape.

The tape transports used in digital systems have two unique characteristics: (1) the ability to start and stop very quickly, and (2) a high tape speed. The ability to start and stop the tape very quickly is important for two reasons. First, since the writing or reading process cannot begin until the tape is moving at a sufficient speed, a delay is introduced until the tape gains speed, slowing down operation. Second, information is generally recorded on magnetic tape in "blocks" or "records." Since the tape may be stopped between blocks of information, the tape which passes under the heads during the stopping and starting processes is wasted. This is called the *interblock* or *interrecord* gap. Fast starting and stopping conserves tape.

Figure 7·40(a) shows a typical tape system. To accelerate and decelerate the tape very quickly, an effort is made to isolate the tape reels, which have a high inertia, from the mechanism which moves the tape past the recording

FIG. 7•40 (a) IBM 3420 tape system; (b) magnetic tape mechanism using tension arms; (c) magnetic tape mechanism using vacuum columns.

TABLE 7·9 TYPICAL TENSION ARM TAPE DRIVE CHARACTERISTICS

REEL SIZE, IN.	BITS PER IN.	DATA RATE, KILOBITS	START-STOP TIMES, ms	CAPACITY, MILLIONS OF BYTES	COST OF A TYPICAL REEL OF TAPE
7	1600	40	15	11.5	$ 7.50
8.5	1600	60	10	23	$ 8.50
10.5	1600	72 kbits/s at 45 in./s; 120 kbits/s at 75 in./s	8.33 (5 ms at 75 in./s)	46	$11.00

heads. Figure 7·40(b) shows a high-speed start-stop tape mechanism which uses a set of tension arms around which the tape is laced. The upper and lower tension arms in Fig. 7·40(b) are movable, and when the tape is suddenly driven past the heads by the capstan, the mechanism provides a buffering supply of tape. A servomechanism is used to drive the upper and lower reels, maintaining enough tape between the capstan and tape reels to keep the supply of tape around the tension arms constant. Table 7·9 shows some characteristics of this kind of system.

Another arrangement for isolating the high-inertia tape reels from the basic tape drive is shown in Fig. 7·40(c). This system isolates the tape from the capstan drive by means of two columns of tape held in place by a vacuum. A servosystem then maintains the correct length of tape between reel and capstan drive. Both this and the previous system use continuously rotating capstans to actually drive the tape, and "pressure rolls" to press the tape against the capstan when the transport is activated. Brakes are also provided for fast stopping. Table 7·10 shows some typical figures on this kind of system.

Using systems of this sort, the start and stop times can be less than 5 ms. These are the times required to accelerate a tape to a speed suitable for reading or writing and the time required to fully stop a moving tape. The speeds at which the tapes are moved past the heads vary greatly, most tape transports having speeds in the range from 12.5 to 250 in./s. A very fast (900 in./s)

TABLE 7·10 TYPICAL VACUUM COLUMN TAPE DRIVE CHARACTERISTICS FOR 10.5-IN. TAPE REEL SYSTEMS

SPEED, IN./S	BITS/IN.	MAXIMUM DATA RATE, KILOBYTES/s	START AND STOP TIMES, ms	CAPACITY, MILLIONS OF BYTES
50	1600	80	7.5	46
75	1600	120	5	46
125	1600	200	3	46
125	6250	780	1.2	180

Two-gap read-write head   Gap read-write head

FIG. 7 • 41 One- and two-gap tape heads.

mechanism has been constructed at Lincoln Laboratory in which the tape is driven directly by the reels of the tape transport. A tape system of this sort is designed to transfer only large quantities of data to and from the machine's main fast-access storage in a single operation. The slower tape speeds, combined with fast starting and stopping, are probably more adaptable to systems in which smaller amounts of data must be transferred. Some systems have changeable cartridges with a reel of tape in each cartridge. The manufacturers of these systems feel that this protects the tape and facilitates changing the reels. These will be discussed in a following section.

Most tape systems have two-gap READ-WRITE heads. The two gaps (refer to Fig. 7 · 41) are useful because, during writing, the READ gap is positioned after the WRITE gap and is used to check what has been written by reading and comparing.

Tapes vary from $\frac{1}{4}$ to 3 in. in width; however, most tape is $\frac{1}{2}$-in.-wide 1.5-mil-thick mylar tape. A 10.5-in. reel typically has 2,400 ft of tape. Generally about nine channels or tracks are used for $\frac{1}{2}$ in. of width. The surface of the tape is usually in contact with the READ-WRITE head. Output signals from the READ heads are generally in the 0.1- to 0.5-V range. The recording density varies; however, 200, 556, 800, 1600 and 6250 bits/in. per channel are fairly standard.

Data are recorded on magnetic tape using some coding system. Generally, one character is stored per row (refer to Fig. 7 · 42) along the tape. The tape in Fig. 7 · 42 has seven tracks, or channels, one of which is a parity bit, which is added to make the number of 1s in every row odd (this will be studied in the next chapter, as will the codes used for magnetic tape). Data are recorded on magnetic tape in blocks, with gaps between the blocks and usually with unique start and stop characters to signal the beginning and the end of a block.

A small piece of metallic reflective material is fastened to the tape at the beginning and end of the reel, and photoelectric cells are used to sense these markers and prevent overrunning of the tape [refer to Fig. 7 · 43(a)].

The codes used to record on tape vary, but two commonly used IBM codes are shown in Fig. 7 · 43(b) and (c). IBM standard tape is $\frac{1}{2}$ in. wide and 1.5

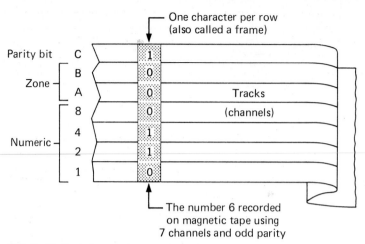

FIG. 7•42 Basic layout of magnetic tape.

milli-in. thick, with either seven or nine tracks. The seven-track code is shown in Fig. 7·43(b), where the 0s are simply blank and 1s are indicated by a vertical line. Figure 7·43(c) shows the nine-track code. Recording densities are 200, 556, 800, 1600, or 6250 bits (or rows) per inch (which means 200, 556, 800, 1600, or 6250 characters (or bytes) per inch, since a character is recorded in each row).

Some further characteristics of tape systems are shown in Table 7·11, and Table 7·12 gives the characteristics for an inexpensive Hewlett-Packard system.

7•23 TAPE CASSETTES AND CARTRIDGES

The changeable tape cassette used in the familiar home recorder is an attractive means for recording digital data. The cassettes are small, changeable, and inexpensive. Unfortunately, the quality of tape and the tape moving mechanism in the conventional "home" tape cassette are not of sufficient quality for computer usage. As a result, a number of high-quality digital cassettes with prices in the dollar ($2 to $15 in general) region have been developed. These are of a small size—on the order of the familiar cassette—and have a similar appearance.

There are also larger *tape cartridges* which contain long strips of magnetic tape and which resemble large cassettes. These cartridges provide a more convenient way to package tape, and greatly simplify the mounting of tape reels (which can be a problem with conventional reels of tape where the tape must be manually positioned on the mechanism). The tape cartridges also provide protection against dirt and contamination, since the tape is sealed in the cartridge.

(a)

(b)

† The P bit position produces odd parity.

(c)

FIG. 7 • 43 Magnetic tape coding. (a) Beginning and end of tape marking;
(b) magnetic recording of seven-track BCD code on tape; (c) nine-track
(EBCDIC) and seven-track tape data format comparison.

TABLE 7·11 CHARACTERISTICS OF MAGNETIC TAPE UNITS

CHARACTERISTIC	IBM 2401			IBM 2420	BGH 424	BGH 9392	UNIVAC VIII C	UNIVAC 16
	MODEL 4	MODEL 5	MODEL 6	MODEL 7				
Bytes/s	60,000	120,000	180,000	15,000	66,400	72,000	96,000	192,000
Density, bytes/in.	1,600	1,600	1,000	1,600	800	800	800	1,600
Tape speed, in./s	37.5	75.0	112.5	200	83	90	125	125
Nominal interrecord gap, in.	0.6	0.6	0.6	0.6	0.75	0.75	0.75	0.75
Nominal IRG time, ms	16.0	8.0	5.3	5	25	25	12	12
Rewind time, min	3.0	1.4	1.0	1.0	1.5	1.6	3	2

TABLE 7·12 HEWLETT-PACKARD 7090E TAPE SYSTEMS

CHARACTERISTIC	SPECIFICATION
Number of tracks	9
Read-write speed	
2100-based systems	25, 37.5, 45 in./s
3000 system	45 in./s
Density	1600 characters/in.
	(8 bits/character)
Data transfer rate	72,000 characters/s max
Reel diameter	$10\frac{1}{2}$ in. maximum
Tape (computer grade)	
Width	0.5 in.
Thickness	1.5 mils
Rewind speed	160 in./s
Start-stop times	8.33 ms (READ-AFTER-WRITE) at 45 in./s
End of tape and beginning of tape reflective strip detection	IBM compatible

FIG. 7·44 Magnetic tape cassette.

Figure 7·44 shows a typical cassette. A number of different digital cassettes are now in production and each has different characteristics.† As an example, Data General Corporation offers a cassette with an average tape speed of 31 in./s, a 200-ft. 0.15-in. magnetic tape per cassette, storage per tape of 800,000 bits, and transfer (reading) rate of 12,800 bits/s. The cassette can rewind in 85 s. A 22-in. reflective leader and trailer are used to mark the beginning and end of the tape (a photodiode senses this strip).

---

† Standards organizations have attempted to develop standards for cassettes. The "Phillips" cassette is such a standard.

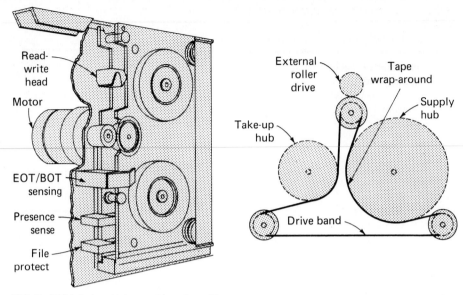

FIG. 7·45 Digital cartridge and interface. (Courtesy 3M Co.)

Cartridges are a high-performance magnetic tape storage medium. There are several cartridge designs available. These vary, not only in performance capabilities, but also in the division of hardware between cartridge and transport.† The 3M cartridge and drive shown in Fig. 7·45 is representative. The

TABLE 7·13 SPECIFICATIONS OF 3M CARTRIDGE AND DCD-3 CARTRIDGE DRIVE

CHARACTERISTIC	SPECIFICATION
Operating speeds	
Read-write	30 in./s forward and reverse
Fast forward, rewind, gap search	90 in./s forward and reverse
Packing density	1600 bits/in.
Transfer rate	48 kilobits/s maximum
Inter-record gap	1.33 in. typical; 1.2 in. minimum per proposed ANSI standard
Maximum recommended start-stop rate	Three operations per second without forced air cooling
Total speed variation	±4% max
Tape head	1-, 2-, or 4-channel READ-WHILE-WRITE heads available
Interface logic	TTL compatible
Power	5 V dc ±5%, ±18 V dc ±5%

† For instance, the heads may or may not be included in each cartridge.

TABLE 7·14 STORAGE MEDIA COMPARISON*

SYSTEM CHARACTERISTIC	PHILLIPS TYPE CASSETTE	3M-TYPE CARTRIDGES	FLOPPY DISKS
Cost per bit, cents	10^{-4}	0.5×10^{-4}	2.5×10^{-4}
Capacity	3×10^6 bits maximum	2×10^7 bits on four tracks	0.3×10^6 bits typical
Access times	Tens of seconds average	20 s average	Hundreds of milliseconds, but depends on rotational speed
Data transfer rates	25×10^3 bits/s	50×10^3 bits/s	Hundreds of kilobits per second

* Typical figures are given.

cartridge contains 300 ft of $\frac{1}{4}$-in. tape capable of recording up to four tracks at 1600 bits/in. for a maximum storage capacity of more than 2×10^7 bits. The 3M transport operates at 30 in./s when reading or writing, and at 90 in./s in search mode. A novel elastic band drive moves the tape and also supplies tape tension. Tape drive, hub, and guide components are referenced to the base of the cartridge and require no external guidance.

Table 7·13 gives some specifications of the 3M cartridge and the 3M cartridge drive. Table 7·14 compares some of the memory devices which have been described giving some idea of the potential of these devices. Notice these are estimates of potentiality, and most present-day devices fall short of these limits. Table 7·15 gives some data on low-cost devices suitable for mini- computers and microcomputers as opposed to more expensive devices. These are again representative figures.

TABLE 7·15 SOME LOW-COST STORAGE SYSTEM CHARACTERISTICS

SYSTEM CHARACTERISTIC	CAPACITY	COST, CENTS
Floppy disk	250 kilobits	4×10^{-3}
High-performance cassette	2 million bits	5×10^{-4}
Phillips cassette	3 million bits (maximum)	1×10^{-4}
Low-performance cassette	100 kilobits	20×10^{-4}
3M cartridge	20 million bits	0.5×10^{-4}
7-in. tape reels	30 million bits	0.5×10^{-4}

*7 • 24 DIGITAL RECORDING TECHNIQUES

Although the characteristics and construction of such storage devices as magnetic drums, tape recorders, and magnetic disk storage devices may vary greatly, the fundamental storage process in each consist of storing a binary 0 or 1 on a small area of magnetic material. Storage in each case is dynamic, for the medium on which the information is recorded is moved past the reading or writing device.

Although the process of recording a 0 or 1 on a surface may appear straightforward, considerable research has gone into both the development of the recorded patterns used to represent 0s and 1s and the means for determining the value recorded. There are two necessities here: (1) the packing density should be made as great as is possible; that is, each cell or bit should occupy as little space as is possible, thus economizing, for instance, on the amount of tape used to store a given amount of information; and (2) the reading and writing procedure should be made as reliable as is possible. These two interests are conflicting because, when the recorded bits are packed more and more closely together, the distortion of the playback signal is greatly increased.

In writing information on a magnetic surface, the digital information is supplied to the recording circuitry, which then codes this information into a pattern which is recorded by the writing head. The techniques used to write information on a magnetic medium can be divided into several categories, the *return-to-zero* (RZ) technique, the *return-to-bias* (RB) technique, and the *non–return-to-zero* (NRZ) technique. The methods for reading information written using these techniques also vary. The basic techniques will be described below, along with the recorded waveshapes and the waveshapes later read by the READ heads and translated by the reading system.

*7 • 25 RETURN-TO-ZERO AND RETURN-TO-BIAS RECORDING TECHNIQUES

Figure 7 · 46 illustrates the return-to-zero recording technique. In Fig. 7 · 46(a) there is no current through the winding of the WRITE head, except when a 1 or a 0 is to be recorded. If a 1 is to be recorded, a pulse of positive polarity is applied to the winding on the WRITE head, and if a 0 is to be written, a negative pulse is applied to the winding. In either case the current through the WRITE-head winding is returned to zero after the pulse, and remains there until the next bit is recorded. The second set of waveforms on this drawing illustrates the remanent flux pattern on the magnetic surface after the writing head has passed. There is some distortion in this pattern due to the fringing of flux around the head.

---

* The sections on recording techniques can be omitted without loss of continuity.

If this pattern of magnetization is passed under a READ head, some of the magnetic flux will be coupled into the core of the head. The flux takes the lower reluctance path through the core material of the head instead of bridging the gap in the head (Fig. 7·33), and when the amount of flux through the core material changes, a voltage will be induced in the coil wound around the core. Thus a change in the amplitude of the recorded magnetic field will

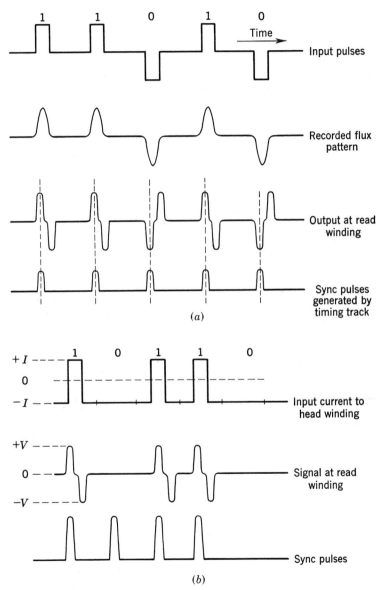

FIG. 7•46 Recording techniques. (a) Return-to-zero (RZ) recording; (b) return-to-bias (RB) technique.

result in a voltage being induced in the coil on the READ head. The waveforms in Fig. 7·46(a) and (b) illustrate typical output signals on the READ-head windings for each of the techniques. Notice that the waveform at the READ head is not a reproduction of the input current during the WRITE process, nor of the pattern actually magnetized on the magnetic material.

The problem is, therefore, to distinguish a 1 or a 0 output at the sense winding. Several techniques have been used for this. One consists in first amplifying the output waveform from the output waveform from the READ winding in a linear amplifier. The output of this amplifier is then strobed in the same manner that the output from the sense winding of a core plane is strobed. For drum systems the correct timing for the strobe, which must be very accurate, may be determined by the timing signals recorded on the timing track. If the output from the READ amplifier is connected to an AND gate and the strobe pulse is also connected as an input to the same AND gate, the output will be a positive pulse when the recorded signal represents a 1.

It is important that the timing pulse be very sharp and occur at the right time relative to the reading and writing of the bits.

A fundamental characteristic of return-to-zero recording [(Fig. 7·46(a)] is that, for a 1, the output signal during the first half of each bit time will be positive with regard to the second half; and that for a 0, the first half of the output signal during each bit time will be positive in regard to the second half signal. This is sometimes exploited in translating the signal read back.

In the return-to-zero system in Fig. 7·46(a), the magnetic field returns to zero flux when a 1 or 0 pulse is not present. This makes it impossible to write over information which has previously been written, unless the position of each cell is very accurately located. If a 0 pulse is written directly over a previously recorded 1, the flux generated will reverse the polarity of the recorded field only if the writing head is in exactly the right position when the 0 is recorded. The timing of the writing of information is therefore very critical for this system, and it is rarely used except with magnetic drums, where the timing may be accurately established by timing tracks. An alternative technique involves erasing all flux before writing new information, but this involves an additional erase head and is seldom used.

The second method for recording information is the return-to-bias system, illustrated in Fig. 7·46(b). In this case the current through the winding maintains the head saturated in the negative direction unless a 1 is to be written. When a 1 is written, a pulse of current in the opposite direction is applied to the winding at the center of the bit time. The outputs at the sense winding are also illustrated in the figure. In this case there will be an output at the sense winding only when a 1 is written. This output may be amplified and strobed just as in the previous case. The timing here is not so critical when information is being "written over," because the negative flux from the head will magnetize the surface in the correct direction regardless of what was previously recorded. The current through the winding in this case, and in all those which follow, is assumed to be sufficient to saturate the material on which the signals are being recorded. A primary problem here concerns sequences of 0s. For magnetic tape, either a clock track must be used or the code used must be such that at least one 1 occurs in each line of the tape. Notice that this is because only 1s generate magnetic flux changes, and therefore output signals at the read head.

*7 • 26 NON–RETURN-TO-ZERO RECORDING TECHNIQUES

Figure 7 · 47 illustrates three recording techniques, each of which is classified as a non–return-to-zero system. In the first, the current through the winding is negative through the entire bit time when a 0 is recorded, and is positive through the entire bit time when a 1 is recorded. The current through

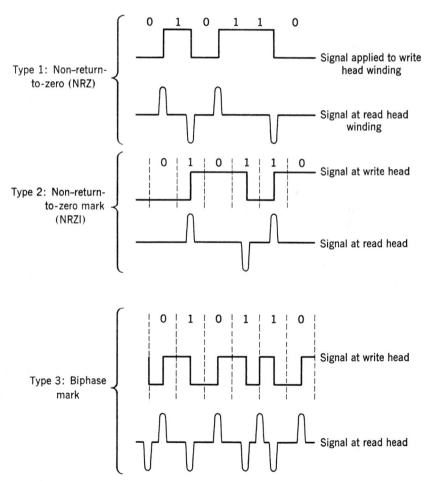

FIG. 7 • 47 Three types of non–return-to-zero recording.

the winding will therefore remain constant when a sequence of 0s or 1s is being written, and will change only when a 0 is followed by a 1 or when a 1 followed by a 0 is written. In this case a signal will be induced in the sense winding only when the information recorded changes from a 1 to a 0, or vice versa.

The second technique illustrated is sometimes referred to as a "modified non–return-to-zero," or "non–return-to-zero mark" (NRZI), technique. In this system, the polarity of the current through the WRITE winding is reversed each time a 1 is recorded and remains constant when a 0 is recorded. If a series of 1s is recorded, the polarity of the recorded flux will therefore change for each 1. If a series of 0s is recorded, no changes will occur. Notice that the polarity has no meaning in this system; only changes in polarity. Therefore a signal will be read back only when a 1 has been recorded. This system is often used for tape recording, when, in order to generate a clock or strobe, a 1 must be recorded somewhere in each cell along the tape width. That is, if 10 tracks are recorded along the tape, one of these must be a timing track which records a sequence of 1s, each of which defines a different set of cells to be read, or the information must be coded so that a 1 occurs in each set of 10 cells which are read. Alphanumeric coded information† is often recorded on tape, and the code may be arranged so that a 1 occurs in each code group.

The third non–return-to-zero technique in Fig. 7·47 is sometimes called a *phase-encoded,* biphase-mark, Harvard, Manchester, or split-frequency system. In this case a 0 is recorded as a $\frac{1}{2}$-bit-time negative pulse followed by $\frac{1}{2}$-bit-time positive pulse, and a 1 is recorded as a $\frac{1}{2}$-bit-time positive pulse followed by a $\frac{1}{2}$-bit-time negative pulse. This technique is often used in high-speed systems.

The reading of information which has been recorded consists of two steps. First, the output from the READ head is amplified, and then the amplified signals are translated by logical circuitry. Figure 7·48 shows a translation technique for the first non–return-to-zero system illustrated in Fig. 7·47. The output signals may be either from the output flip-flop or serial pulses. The sync pulses occur each time a cell passes under the READ heads in the system.

The flip-flop (Fig. 7·48) responds to positive pulses only. Positive-pulse signals at the recording head will therefore "set" the flip-flop to 1. The inverter at the C input will cause negative pulses to be made positive. These positive pulses then will clear the flip-flop. The output of the flip-flop may be used directly by the computer, or pulse outputs can be generated by connecting an AND gate to the 1 output, delaying the sync pulses, and connecting them to the AND gate. Also, a serial representation of the number stored along the surface may be formed.

---

† Alphanumeric codes will be described in Chap. 8.

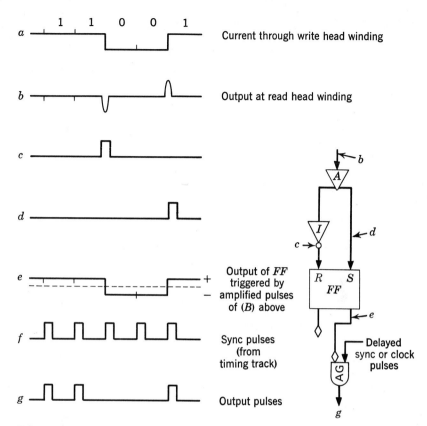

FIG. 7 • 48 Non–return-to-zero recording.

QUESTIONS

1. How many magnetic cores are required in a core-memory array for a computer with a word length of 35 binary bits and 4096 different addresses in core memory? How many storage devices (flip-flops) will be required for the memory address register?

2. Several microcomputers come with a basic 4096-word 8-bit memory. Assuming a plane for each bit, how many flip-flops in:
   (a) The memory address register?
   (b) The memory buffer register?

3. If we construct a 4096-word 36-bit-per-word coincident-current magnetic-core memory, how many cores will be in the memory? How many sense amplifiers will be required? How many INHIBIT-line drivers? How many word-line drivers? How many X-selection drivers and how many Y-selection drivers? How many planes in the core memory and how many cores per plane?

4. A 4096-word 8-bit memory with eight planes is to be operated in linear-select mode. How many word lines? If the memory was coincident-current, how many drive lines in the X axis and how many in the Y axis?

5. The INHIBIT drivers are not used when a word is read from a core memory using a coincident-current selection system. True or false? Why?

6. For the 30-mil coincident-current cores in Table $7 \cdot 1$, type 3-103, the drive current of 290 mA on each winding causes a 1 output of about 61 mV and a 0 output of 8 mV. Discuss the setting of a threshold level in the sense amplifier so that 1s and 0s will be correctly identified. How long after the READ drive pulses are applied would you measure or strobe the sense line?

7. If we use the coincident-current memory system described, and if the current driver which drives the $-i_m/2$ current through the selection line X_2 in Fig. $7 \cdot 6$ is broken so that no current is ever driven through this line, we will never be able to read from or write satisfactorily into three cores, one of which is core X_2Y_1. What are the designations of the other two cores into which we will never be able to read or write correctly?

8. In a linear-select memory, the driver can be set to "overdrive" cores by applying more current than is necessary to saturate the core. This will make it necessary also to increase the amount of inhibit current that is applied. Why?

9. If the INHIBIT driver which is connected to the core plane storing the first binary digit of each computer word fails, what will be the value of the binary digit written into the selected core in this plane during each memory cycle?

10. Draw the input signal, recorded flux pattern, and output at the READ head for return-to-zero and for return-to-bias recording if the bits 1001 are recorded.

11. Draw the waveforms for recording the binary sequence 101, showing the signal applied to the WRITE-head winding and the signal at the READ-head winding for the type 1, type 2, and type 3 non–return-to-zero recording techniques.

12. A block diagram of an INTEL MOS LS1 memory chip is shown in Fig. $7 \cdot 21$. The A_1 through A_8 lines are for the 256 addresses. R/W tells whether to read or write (a 0 on this line is READ, a 1 is WRITE). The "chip select" disables the memory for a 1 input and enables the memory with a 0 input. Discuss the construction of a 256-word 8-bit memory using these packages. How many packages are required? Each flip-flop in the address register (external) would have its 1 output connected to how many chips?

13. Draw the schematic for a many-to-one decoder matrix with inputs from four flip-flops and 16 output lines. Use the same basic configuration as is illustrated in Fig. $7 \cdot 10$.

14. The INTEL package in Question 12 is representative of several integrated circuit manufacturers' products. Show how the *chip select* can be used to add words to a memory.

15. How is it possible to combine the sense and INHIBIT lines in a core memory to form a single digit or bit line? Why is this desirable?

16. Answer the following questions on expansion of a coincident-current magnetic core memory.

(a) Increasing the number of bits per word in a 4096-word 18-bit memory from 15 to 20 bits increases the number of core planes from _____ to _____.

(b) Increasing the number of words in a 4096-word 18-bit memory from 4096 to 8192 increases the number of X and Y drive windings from _____ to _____.

(c) Increasing the number of words in a 4096-word 15-bit memory to 8192 and the number of bits to 24 increases the number of INHIBIT windings from _____ to _____.

17. (a) Explain why the slower, less expensive core memories tend to use a coincident-current selection and the faster, more expensive core memories use linear selection.

(b) How does the number of dimensions in a core memory's selection scheme affect the minimal size of the cores which can be used?

(c) Do IC memories tend to be destructive or nondestructive read memories? Why?

18. (a) Discuss the effects on memory cycle time of destructive versus nondestructive read devices.

(b) Why do the sense amplifiers have to be protected against the inhibit drive current in a three-wire coincident-current-core memory but not in a four-wire coincident-current-core memory?

19. Discuss the concept of dimensionality in memory-selection techniques and its effects on memory speed, cost, and complexity. (As examples, you might contrast 2-dimensional and 3-dimensional selection schemes in IC memories or compare linear-select and coincident-current selection in core memories.)

20. What is the purpose of the INHIBIT line in a core memory?

21. Give an advantage of core memory over semiconductor memory.

22. What are the primary advantages of bipolar memory over MOS memory?

23. Explain the operation of the digit line in a linear-select core memory.

24. Explain the difference in a dynamic and static MOS memory.

25. Contrast the parallel tree and balanced decoder net-words for a 32-output decoder. Figure the number of diodes used for each and the delay incurred because of the number of gates a signal must pass through for each assuming diode AND gates are used.

26. If there is a power failure, most core memories have cutoff circuits so the computer is stopped after writing its registers into core memory and the core memory is then stopped before the power drops so low that errors occur. The contents of the core memory are not then lost and the machine can be restarted. Is this possible with IC memories?

27. Batteries are often used as backup power for IC memories to "smooth out" power failures. Discuss this, giving reasons for doing this.

28. In larger machines, when the ac power drops below a certain level, the contents of the control unit and arithmetic-logic unit are dumped on tape or disks so the computer can be restarted with no loss of data. If IC memories are used, their contents must also be dumped. Explain why.

29. Explain the operation of the memory cell in Fig. $7 \cdot 19$.

30. Explain the operation of the memory cell in Fig. $7 \cdot 22$.

31. When linear selection is used for IC memories, individual cells tend to be simpler than if for two-dimensional cell select systems, but the decoders tend to be more complicated. Explain why.

32. Explain why NMOS is replacing PMOS for IC memory use.

33. The memory in Figs. $7 \cdot 23$ and $7 \cdot 24$ has linear-select memory cells; it then breaks the memory into another dimension, using several bit or digit lines and their associated circuitry. This simplifies individual memory cell complexity while increasing sense and WRITE circuitry. Explain why this might be cost effective for a memory of this type.

34. Dynamic memories that require external refreshing introduce extra complexity into computer operation. Can you give reasons why?

35. Explain the advantages and disadvantages of dynamic IC memories.

36. A magnetic drum has a circumference of 50 in. and a packing density of 1000 bits/in. If the drum has 40 tracks, how many bits can be stored on the surface of the drum?

37. In designing a 256-word 8-bit memory, pin 1 is connected to pin 1 for each container of the Intel chip in Question 12. This applies to all A inputs and to CHIP SELECT bits and to READ-WRITE, but not to DATA OUT or DATA IN. Why?

38. A magnetic drum has 128 tracks (exclusive of timing tracks) and 1920 cells or binary bits recorded around each track. If the drum is used in a serial computer with a word length of 29 binary bits, and 1 "spacer bit" is left between words when recording, how many bits will be required to address a word on the drum? How many binary bits will be required to address a track? How many binary bits will be required to address a sector?

39. Show how to expand the 256-word 1-bit memory in Question 12 to a 1024-word 1-bit memory using the CHIP SELECT and a two-input–four-output decoder.

40. For the IBM 3330 disk memory described, how many binary digits can be recorded on one surface of a given disk?

41. If a magnetic drum rotates at 25,000 rpm, what is the maximum access time required to read a word in a parallel system, assuming that there is no delay in decoding the address? What is the average random-access time?

42. Which of the IBM tape units described will transfer data fastest, and how fast can characters and bits be read or written?

43. Assuming that a disk in the IBM 2314 system rotates at a speed of 2,400 rpm as stated and that we read from eight tracks simultaneously, how many bits per second can be read from one of these disks?

44. Make up a formula for how many bits a second can be read for a disk memory which revolves at a rate of r revolutions per second and has b bits per track. What will the average access time be?

45. A magnetic tape system has seven tracks for each $\frac{1}{2}$-in. width of tape. The packing density per track is 250 bits/in., and the tape is moved at a speed of 75 in./s. If the tape width is 1 in., how many bits may be read per second?

46. Explain seek time and latency for disk memories.

47. Fixed-head disk memories reduce total access time by avoiding either seek time or latency. Which is avoided and why?

48. What is the danger to disk packs when flying heads are used?

49. Contrast three of the disk packs described in Table $7 \cdot 5$, giving your ideas on their desirability. Do you think price might be an important factor in evaluating these systems?

50. Explain the figures given for delays in the HP 2888A disk system described in Table $7 \cdot 6$.

51. Contrast the floppy disk figures for the Pertec system with the HP 2888A disk pack system.

52. Is price a factor in evaluating the systems in Question 51?

53. Compare the Hewlett-Packard 7090E tape system with one of the IBM tape systems.

54. Tape cassettes and tape cartridges have advantages and disadvantages compared to conventional tape systems. Can you give several of each?

55. The table comparing storage media brings out some of the contrasts in price and performance for memory systems. Tell what devices would you choose for the following kinds of computers and why.
  (a) Microcomputers
  (b) Minicomputers
  (c) Large computer systems

56. Draw a diode ROM, as in Fig. $7 \cdot 31$, but which converts from BCD 8421 to the 2421 code.

57. If we read from eight heads or write from eight heads simultaneously on the magnetic disk memory described which is manufactured by the Data Products Corporation, how many bits per second can we transfer in that system?

58. Draw a diode ROM as in Fig. $7 \cdot 31$ which translates from BCD to excess 3 code.

59. For the coincident-current memory, the word-line drivers are turned on twice, and for the thin-film memory the word-line drivers are turned on only once. Discuss the reason for this. Do thin-film word-line drivers need to drive current in two directions? Do the bit-line drivers?

60. Design four locations in a diode ROM for a microprogrammed computer by adding diodes to the following drawing. The control signal C_1 is to be a 1 in locations 01110 and 01111 and is otherwise a 0; the control signal C_2 is to be a 1 in locations 01101 and 10000 and is 0 otherwise; the control signal C_3 is to be a 1 in 01101, 01110, and 01111 and is 0 otherwise. A given decoder output line is high when selected.

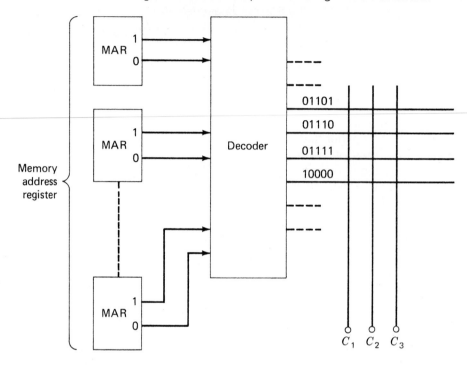

61. Here are some data on the PDP-11 disk pack.

Number of cylinders, 203
Tracks per cylinder, 2
Bytes per track, 6144
Disk rotation time, 40 ms
Seek time S to move N cylinders
For $N = 0$ to 8, $S = 6 + 2N$
For $N = 9$ to $N = 24$, $S = 16 + 3N/4$
For N greater than 24, $S = 26 + N/3$

Discuss the total search time for finding a specific piece of data considering the heads to be positioned in the center cylinder when the search order is given. A cylinder is the set of all tracks which can be read from or written on for a given position of the head-positioning mechanism.

8
INPUT-OUTPUT DEVICES

The input-output devices provide the means of communication between the computer and the outer world. To solve problems or process data, the data and instructions must be inserted into the machine, and the machine must deliver the results of its calculations. It has been difficult to produce input and output devices that can keep up with the computer speeds, and there is a constant demand for faster and faster printers, card readers, etc.

In its simplest form, the sequence of events in the processing of information for business or the solving of scientific problems is as follows: First a program is written describing the sequence of calculations which the machine is to perform; the data, such as the cost of a ton of steel in Pittsburgh or the distance of Mars from Venus at some particular time, are then collected and also readied for insertion into the machine. The machine then reads the program plus the data and stores this information. Having stored the necessary program and data, the machine is started at the first instruction in the program. After completing the series of caluclations which it must perform, the machine prints out the results. The program contains orders which direct the machine to print the final results for the user of the machine. Partial results are sometimes also printed, often for purposes of program checking.

It is first necessary to insert the program and the data into the machine via the input devices. The input devices to an ordinary calculator consist of the keys of the calculator. Numerical data are introduced into the machine via these push buttons; when some sort of operation button is pushed, the machine performs the necessary operations.

As can be seen, in order to use a computer it is desirable to have some means for recording both instructions and data in a way which may be read by the computer at high speeds and then performed at computer speeds. A medium proposed by Babbage and still used today is the punched card. A rectangular card is perforated by a number of holes, and the position of each hole determines its meaning. The programs and data are punched into cards. The cards are then placed in a card reader connected to the machine, and the command to read is given. The card reader senses the holes in the cards and transmits this information to the computer, which then stores it. In this manner, either program or data can be read into the machine.

When the program has been read and the necessary operations have been completed, it is necessary for the computer to print out the data so that they may be used. A great variety of output devices are now available. Business applications generally require that the results be printed in tabular form, or perhaps on a series of checks as in a payroll accounting operation. Scientific results are more likely to consist of numerical data which must be clearly printed with little chance of error (and such accuracy is also of prime importance in computers used to calculate payroll checks) or graphs showing the results of the calculations. For each of these applications, one type of output device may be more desirable than another. However, the great majority of applications require that the outputs from the machine be printed on a piece of paper. The principal output devices are therefore printers, ranging from electromechanical typewriters which print one letter or digit at a time, to high-speed printers capable of printing hundreds of characters at a time. Several of these, as well as several more specialized output devices, will be described.

8•1 DIFFERENCES IN BUSINESS AND SCIENTIFIC USES

There are distinct differences in the ratio of data to program length in business and scientific problems. The business problems generally have shorter programs which process large amounts of data. For instance, programs which calculate payrolls or programs which maintain an inventory control are liable to be relatively short in length by comparison with the volume of data they must process. On the other hand, scientific problems are more liable to have long, complicated programs performing many calculations but using relatively little input data.

Computers used for business problems must be able not only to handle large amounts of input data but also to deliver much information, generally in the form of printouts, to the user. A machine which calculates the payroll for a large company must print thousands of checks. The same fact applies to machines doing calculations for banks or other large businesses where large numbers of business statements must be printed. For this reason, there is a particularly great premium on speed and economy in the input-output devices for business machines.

8·2 PERFORATED TAPE

Perforated (punched) tape was one of the first popular mediums for storing the programs and data to be read into a digital machine. When the first large computers were designed, telegraph systems had been using perforated paper tapes for some time, and as a result, devices for punching and reading paper tapes had already been fairly well developed. The tape used is of many types and sizes. A medium-thickness paper tape has been used a great deal, and oiled tapes and plastic tapes are also used. The widths of the tapes used have varied from $\frac{1}{2}$ to 3 in. Information is punched into the tape a line at a time. Figure 8·1 illustrates a section of a perforated tape. Multiple channels are used (just as on magnetic tape, a channel runs lengthwise along the tape), and a single character or code is punched as a pattern of bits in each lateral line.

The preparation of these paper input tapes is sometimes referred to as *keyboarding,* and a typical paper-tape-punching machine is shown in Fig. 1·7. In this step the operator of a tape-punching machine is presented with a copy of a program or input data. The operator then punches, by means

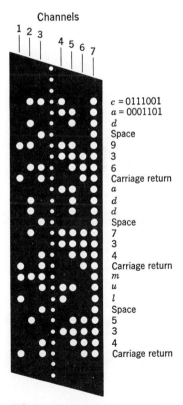

Channels

$c = 0111001$
$a = 0001101$
d
Space
9
3
6
Carriage return
a
d
d
Space
7
3
4
Carriage return
m
u
l
Space
5
3
4
Carriage return

FIG. 8·1 Punched paper tape.

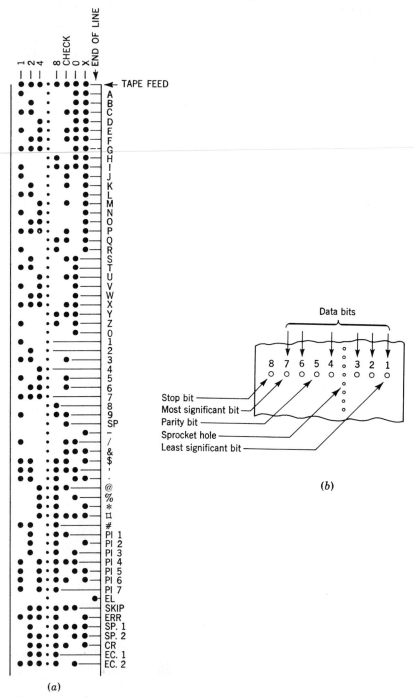

FIG. 8•2 (a) Punched tape with eight-channel code; (b) format for eight-channel tape.

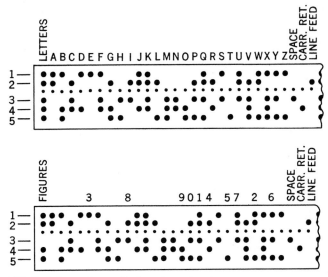

FIG. 8•3 Paper tape with five-channel code.

of the tape-punching machine (tape punch), a number of holes into the tape. The holes represent, in coded form, the input information to the machine. The tape-punching device used may be one of a number of types; however, the more popular devices resemble a typewriter, and the keyboards of these tape punches contain conventional symbols, similar to those on an ordinary typewriter. The keyboards of many tape-punch machines are identical with the keyboards of manual typewriters used in businesses, and sometimes electric typewriters are converted to tape-punching machines by attaching a punching device which is actuated by the typewriter mechanism.

When a key on the tape-punch keyboard is depressed, the binary-coded symbol for the character selected is punched into the tape, and the tape then advances to the next line. In most cases, the tape-punch device also prints on a separate piece of paper, in the same manner as a typewriter, the character which was punched, as well as printing the characters along the rows of the tape. There is then a typewritten copy of the program which may be .checked for errors in addition to the paper type punched with the coded symbols. This printed copy of the program is referred to as the "hard copy." Many of the tape-punch machines are able to read a perforated tape and to type printed copy from this tape. A punched section of tape may be placed in the tape reader attached to the tape-punch machine, and a typed copy of the information which was punched in the tape may be made.

Figures 8·2 and 8·3 show two codes which have been frequently used for paper tape systems. Figure 8·2 shows an eight-channel code wherein there are eight channels running lengthwise along the tape. A hole in a given one of these channels represents a 1, and the absence of a hole a 0. The 1, 2, 4, and 8 channels are used to represent the digits for 0 to 9; thus

0s or no holes in positions *EL*, *X*, and 0 indicate that the encoded character is a digit with the value given by the sum of the positions 8, 4, 2, 1, in which there are holes. The check position is used for an *odd-parity check*. Its value is determined so that the number of 1s or holes in each character is odd. The 0 and *X* positions are used in conjunction with the 8, 4, 2, 1 positions to encode alphabetic and special characters.

The code has two special features. A punch in the end-of-line position indicates the end of a record on the tape. When there are punches in all seven of the positions, this indicates a blank character called TAPE FEED, and the tape reader skips over such positions. This is useful for correcting mistakes in keyboarding or in editing tapes, because an erroneous character can be eliminated by simply punching in the nonpunched positions.

The five-channel code shown in Fig. 8·3, called the Baudot code, was very popular in communications systems. Since five positions are insufficient to encode the requisite number of characters, a special trick is used utilizing two special characters to change the meaning of those characters which follow. Thus a LETTERS character followed by a line with punches in the 1 position indicates an *E*, while a FIGURES character followed by a punch in the 1 position indicates a 3. Whenever a LETTERS character occurs, all following characters are in the LETTERS code until a FIGURES character occurs, and similarly, a FIGURES character means that all following characters are in that mode until a LETTERS character occurs.

8•3 TAPE READERS

The function of the paper tape reader is to sense the coded information punched in the tape and deliver this information to the computer. Most of the tape readers used in teletype and office equipment are electromechanical devices. In many of these devices mechanical "sensing pins" are used to determine the symbol punched into each line of the tape. In a system of this type, there will be a sensing pin for each information channel, plus a means of moving the tape and positioning it for reading. The tape is not moved continuously, but only a single line at a time, stopped while the coding is sensed, and then moved to the next line. The motion of the sensing pins operates a switch, the contacts of which are opened or closed, depending on whether or not there is a hole in the tape. Another type of reader uses a "star wheel" to sense the absence or presence of holes in the tape, as shown in Fig. 8·4. A complete reader mechanism is shown in Fig. 8·5, indicating the relative complexity of these devices.

When the input is to a digital machine, the motion of the tape through the reader will generally be controlled by the computer. Each time the tape is to be advanced and a new character read, the computer will supply the reader with a pulse which will cause it to advance the tape to the next character. To read characters as fast as possible, a line will generally be read

FIG. 8•4 Star-wheel mechanism for reading perforated tape.

at the same time as the advancing pulse is transmitted. Since there will be a delay due to inertia before the tape is actually moved, the reading of the state of the sensing relays will occur during this delay period. In this case, when a STOP character is sensed, the reader will proceed to the next character before actually stopping.

To speed up the reading process, many tape readers use photoelectric cells or photodiodes to read the characters punched into the tape. In this case, a light-sensitive cell is placed under each channel of the tape, including the "tape feed hole, or "sprocket channel." A light source is placed above the tape, so that the light-sensitive element beneath the hole in the tape will be energized and will produce a signal indicating the presence of the hole. The signals from the light-sensitive elements are then amplified and supplied to the computer as input information.

The tape feed hole will be used in this case to determine when the outputs of the light-sensitive elements are to be sensed. The tape in a reader of this type is generally friction-driven and moved continuously until a STOP character is sensed. Extremely fast starting and braking of the tape are very desirable features, and most readers are capable of stopping the tape on any given character.

The operation speeds attainable with various tape readers are generally expressed as the number of characters per second which can be read. Mechanical sensing readers have been designed to operate at speeds as high as 250 characters per second, although speeds of from 10 to 60 characters per second are more common. Present-day photoelectric readers operate at speeds of up to 1,000 characters per second.

FIG. 8·5 Mechanism of electromechanical tape reader.

8•4 PUNCHED CARDS

The most widely used input medium is the punched card. While there are a number of sizes of punched cards, the most frequently used card at present is a 12-row 80-column card $3\frac{1}{4}$ in. wide and $7\frac{3}{4}$ in. long (see Fig. 8·6). The thickness of the cards used varies, although at one time most of the cards were 0.0067 in. thick. There is now a tendency to make the card somewhat thinner.

Just as with tape, there are numerous ways in which punched cards may be coded. The most frequently used code is the Hollerith code, an alpha-numeric code in which a single character is punched in each column of the card. The basic code is illustrated in Fig. 8·6. As an example, the symbol A is coded by means of a punch in the top and 1 rows of the card, and the symbol 8 by a punch in the 8 row of the card. There are other types of cards with different hole positions on the cards, just as there are many ways of preparing the cards to be read into the computer. The most common tech-nique is very similar to that for preparing punched tape, in that a card punch machine with a keyboard like that of a typewriter is used, as was shown in Fig. 1·8. The card punch usually also makes a hard copy of the program as it is punched into the cards. Generally, the card punch also prints the char-acters punched into a card on the face of the card itself. In this way, a card may be identified without examining the punches. Each character is usually printed at the top of the card directly above the column in which the character is punched.

The card punch machine contains a hopper in which the blank cards are stacked. The operator of the card punch then causes a card to enter the punching area, and the program's list of instructions or the data to be processed are then punched into the card. The card punch punches the card laterally, a column at a time, starting at the left. If a key of the card punch

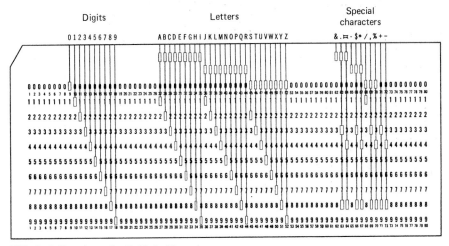

FIG. 8•6 Punch card with Hollerith code.

is depressed, the code for the character is punched into a column of the card, and the card is then moved so that the next column on the right is under the punch.

Generally, when a program is punched into cards, only one instruction and its associated address or addresses are punched into each card. Then, if an error is made in programming, the erroneous instruction may be changed by throwing the incorrect card away and replacing it with a correct card.

Figure 8·7 shows a card punch with a small integrated circuit (IC) memory capable of holding all the data which can be punched into two 80-column records and six program cards. The keypunch operator keyboards the data into the small memory and can backspace and change characters until the data keyboarded are correct. After all the data are in the small memory, an "enter data" key is depressed, and the card is then punched from the characters in the memory. Facilities for controlling the format of the card are included by means of IC logic.

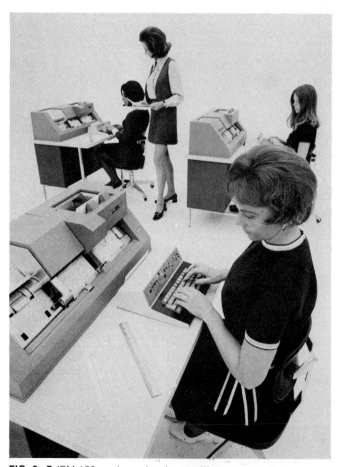

FIG. 8·7 IBM 129 card punches in operation.

The preparation of cards containing data for business systems is a highly developed area. Large businesses such as insurance companies, credit agencies, and banks must gather and process almost incredible amounts of data. Most of this data processing is now done by electronic computers, but even prior to the advent of the digital computer, punched cards were extensively used, and a considerable technology for handling punched cards was developed.

In any case, the data — information, checking account, income tax rates, or whatever — must first be entered into a punched card by a keypunch operator. To give some idea of the magnitude of this operation, there are over 500,000 keypunching consoles (as shown in Figs. 1·8 and 8·7) at this time.

The preparation of punched cards and some of the operations which can be performed on cards are facilitated by the several special devices, as shown in Fig. 8·8. For example, a *verifier* is used to check the keypunching of cards. After a card has been punched, since the alphanumeric characters are printed above the keypunches, some checking can be done by comparing the cards with the input data. A common procedure, however, is to place the deck of cards punched by an operator in the hopper of a verifier and to have a second operator keyboard the same data. The verifier does not punch new cards, but compares what the second operator punches with the deck prepared by the first operator and, if a discrepancy occurs, notifies the second operator so that the card can be compared against the data.

Other machines shown in Fig. 8·8 are the *sorter,* which is used to sort cards into different sequences according to certain keys in the data, and *collator,* which compares or merges several decks into a single deck according to some instructions wired into the machine.

There are several other card processing machines, such as summary punches, which combine data from a number of cards into a few cards, and reproducers, which duplicate decks. The operations performed by these machines, however, can be performed by electronic machines, which, in most cases, cost less to operate, and perform the necessary operations faster and more efficiently.

The card punch remains the most frequently used device for entering data into a computer, and the relatively inexpensive card ($\frac{1}{10}$ cent per card, perhaps) is still in widespread use.

8•5 CARD READERS

Most card readers are electromechanical devices which read the information punched into a card, converting the presence or absence of a hole into an electric signal representing a binary 0 or 1. The punched cards are placed into a hopper, and when the command to read is given, a lever pushes a card from the bottom of the stack. Generally, the card is then moved lengthwise over a row of 80 "read brushes." These brushes read the information punched along the bottom row of the card. If a hole is punched in a par-

(a)

(b)

(c)

FIG. 8•8 Punched-card-processing machines. (a) Verifier; (b) sorter; (c) collator.

ticular row, a brush makes electrical contact through the hole in the card, providing a signal which may be used by the computer. The next row up is then read, and this process continues until all rows have been read, after which the next card is moved into position on the brushes.

Faster card readers are constructed using photoelectric cells under the 12 punch positions along a column and an illuminating source above the card. As each column on the card is passed over the 12 photoelectric cells, whether or not a given position is punched is determined by the presence or absence of light on the corresponding cell. Card readers operate at speeds of from 12 to 1,000 cards per minute.

Notice that when cards are read a row at a time, programs must "decipher" the characters punched in the card. Often "binary" decks are used, particularly for programs where the computer words are distributed along rows rather than in columns and data may be loaded directly as the rows are read.

8•6 ALPHANUMERIC CODES

Data and programs are almost invariably entered in alphanumeric form, and the internal operation of computers, particularly those which involve business records, make extensive use of alphanumeric codes. Because of the diversity of applications and the many viewpoints on codes and code construction, many different alphanumeric codes have been suggested and used. Computers such as IBM's 1401, 1410, and others, as well as Honeywell's 200 series, have (basically) 6-bit characters with corresponding codes. We have already examined several codes for magnetic tape and 5- and 8-bit codes for paper tape, as well as the 12-bit Hollerith code. Each of these has been widely used. The 6-bit, so-called *BCD code*, used in the IBM 1401, 1410, 7010, 7040, and 7044 and the Honeywell 200 series, as well as many other machines, is shown in Fig. 8·9. This code uses the conventional 8, 4, 2, 1 positions for decimal digits, except that 0 is represented by a 1 in the 8 and 2 positions. The "report" and "program" are for two different types of systems. Thus, for some systems, a 1 in the 8, 2, 1 position yields a # and in other systems a =.

There has been an attempt to standardize on an alphanumeric code which will be agreeable to both manufacturers and users, and the American National Standards Institute has published an American Standard Code for Information Interchange (abbreviated the ASCII code). This code is now widely used in the newer machines, and a number of the major manufacturers are now using the code in order that their equipment may be compatible with that of other manufacturers. This code is shown in Fig. 8·10. Notice that the decimal digits are represented by the normal 8, 4, 2, 1 code preceded by the three binary digits 011, so that decimal 1 becomes 0110001, decimal 2 is 0110010, decimal 7 is 0110111, etc. To expand on the code, the letter A is 1000001, B is 1000010, etc. There are various codes such as "end of message," "who are you," "skip," "carriage return," etc., which are very

CHARACTER Report	Program	C	B	A	8	4	2	1
b		C						
.			B	A	8		2	1
□	)	C	B	A	8	4		
[			B	A	8	4		1
<			B	A	8	4	2	
‡		C	B	A	8	4	2	1
&	+	C	B	A				
$		C	B		8		2	1
*			B		8	4		
]		C	B		8	4		1
;		C	B		8	4	2	
Δ			B		8	4	2	1
—			B					
/		C		A				1
'		C		A	8		2	1
%	(			A	8	4		
⌒		C		A	8	4		1
\		C		A	8	4	2	
₊₊				A	8	4	2	1
b				A				
#	=				8		2	1
@		C			8	4		
:					8	4		1
>					8	4	2	
√		C			8	4	2	1
?		C	B	A	8		2	
A			B	A				1
B			B	A			2	
C		C	B	A			2	1
D			B	A		4		
E		C	B	A		4		1
F		C	B	A		4	2	
G			B	A		4	2	1
H			B	A	8			
I		C	B	A	8			1
!			B		8		2	
J		C	B					1
K		C	B				2	
L			B				2	1
M		C	B			4		
N			B			4		1
O			B			4	2	
P		C	B			4	2	1
Q		C	B		8			
R			B		8			1
‡				A	8		2	
S		C		A			2	
T				A			2	1
U		C		A		4		
V				A		4		1
W				A		4	2	
X		C		A		4	2	1
Y		C		A	8			
Z				A	8			1
Ø		C			8		2	
1								1
2							2	
3		C					2	1
4						4		
5		C				4		1
6		C				4	2	
7						4	2	1
8					8			
9		C			8			1

Low→ ... COLLATING SEQUENCE ... High→

Symbol	Name
‡	Group Mark
‡	Record Mark
₊₊	Segment Mark
⌒	Word Separator
@	At Sign
#	Number Sign
&	Ampersand
+	Plus
*	Asterisk
%	Percent
/	Slash
\	Backslash
□	Lozenge
b	Blank
ƀ	Substitute Blank
(	Left Parenthesis
)	Right Parenthesis
[	Left Bracket
]	Right Bracket
√	Tape Mark
<	Less than
>	Greater than
=	Equal to
;	Semicolon
:	Colon
.	Period or Point
'	Prime or Apostrophe
—	Minus or Hyphen (Dash)
Δ	Delta

FIG. 8•9 BCD code.

	000	001	010	011	100	101	110	111
0000	NULL	DC_0 ①	ƀ	0	@	P		
0001	SOM	DC_1	!	1	A	Q		
0010	EOA	DC_2	''	2	B	R		
0011	EOM	DC_3	#	3	C	S		
0100	EOT	DC_4 (Stop)	$	4	D	T		
0101	WRU	ERR	%	5	E	U		
0110	RU	SYNC	&	6	F	V		
0111	BELL	LEM	'	7	G	W		
1000	FE_0	S_0	(	8	H	X	Unassigned	
1001	HT / SK	S_1	)	9	I	Y		
1010	LF	S_2	*	:	J	Z		
1011	V_{TAB}	S_3	+	;	K	[		
1100	FF	S_4	(Comma) ,	<	L	＼		ACK
1101	CR	S_5	–	=	M	]		②
1110	SO	S_6	·	>	N	↑		ESC
1111	SI	S_7	/	?	O	←		DEL

Example: | 100 | 0001 | = A

b_7 ---------------- b_1

The abbreviations used in the figure mean:			
NULL	Null Idle	CR	Carrige return
SOM	Start of message	SO	Shift out
EOA	End of address	SI	Shift in
EOM	End of message	DC_0	Device control ① Reserved for data Link escape
EOT	End of transmission	DC_1-DC_3	Device control
WRU	"Who are you ?"	ERR	Error
RU	"Are you . . . ?"	SYNC	Synchronous idle
BELL	Audible signal	LEM	Logical end of media
FE	Format effector	SO_0-SO_7	Separator (information)
HT	Horizontal tabulation		Word separator (blank, normally non-printing)
SK	Skip (punched card)	ACK	Acknowledge
LF	Line feed	②	Unassigned control
V/TAB	Vertical tabulation	ESC	Escape
FF	Form feed	DEL	Delete Idle

FIG. 8 • 10 American Standard Code for Information Interchange.

useful in communications systems and in editing data processes in computers. As a result, this is probably the most frequently used code for inter-computer communications systems.

Finally, most IBM computers, and a number of other computer systems, use the extended BCD interchange code (called EBCDIC) shown in Fig. 8·11.

FIG. 8 • 11 Extended BCD interchange code (EBCDIC).

8•7 DATA PREPARATION

One form of buffering consists in first recording the program to be read in on magnetic tape and then reading from the tape into the machine. A number of devices are available which will read punched tape or cards and transfer the information punched into them onto magnetic tape. This process takes place outside the central computer. Since the magnetic tape may be read much faster than punched cards or paper tape, the time required to read in information will be reduced.

The process of converting from punched cards to magnetic tape has been bypassed by a number of input devices. Several companies now offer a line of keyboard-to-magnetic-tape devices. Figure 8•12 shows a console of this type. In its simplest form, when the operator depresses a key, the character selected appears on a display and is also entered on the tape. When the magnetic tape has been filled or all records have been transcribed, the tape can be read by the computer to be used.

More advanced systems permit the keyboard operator to type a number of characters; these characters are displayed on a console where they may be read and checked and also are stored in a small memory. The characters can be edited (changed), and when the operator is satisfied that the data

FIG. 8•12 Keyboard-to-magnetic-tape console. (Courtesy Honeywell Corp.)

are correct, a "record" button is depressed, the data are entered on magnetic tape, and new data may be keyboarded.

Even more complex systems use a number of keyboards, all connected to a small memory and processor equipped with a magnetic tape recorder. This permits extensive editing; checking by the small processor-computer comparing inputs; error detection, particularly format checking of many types; and many sorting and collating operations. The magnetic tape prepared by a system of this sort has had many "preprocessing" operations already performed, and the data have been subjected to considerable checking and preprocessing. For companies with extensive data processing requirements, such systems are gaining popularity.

The preparation of tapes, including cassettes and cartridges, has proved very popular, offering some economy, because tape is cheaper than cards for bulk storage and more convenient for system operation. However, the absence of cards containing printing which can be stored, examined, and manually handled has met with some resistance.

Some idea of the importance of input-data preparation can be seen from the fact that 30 to 50 percent of installation cost is often for data preparation. This is especially true, of course, for the larger business systems, but even strictly scientific installations of modest size find that as much as 20 percent of their systems cost can go into preparation of data for computer input. As a further example, in 1968 the Internal Revenue Service alone used about 400 million punched cards.

Numerous special devices and media are used to reduce the cost to business for data entry. For example, agencies such as American Express use a combination of punched cards with printed characters for their billing. The customer returns the card with his check, and the card is then directly given to the computer.

Some companies use identification cards with special coding for their employees. In these systems, the employee inserts his or her card in a special reader which reads the identification and also enters the time from a clock. These data are recorded on tape or a disk, and later the computer reads all the check-in and check-out data recorded during the day. Still other systems use a time clock to simply punch check-in and check-out time in a card which has the employee's identification already punched into it. These cards are then collected at the end of each week. Each of these schemes reduces the expense of operators punching the data. Gas pumps which read customers' credit cards and record the amounts of sales, cash registers which carry sales data to a central tape file in a large department store, and many similar techniques are all being used to alleviate the problems and expense of preparing data for computer entry.

8 • 8 CHARACTER RECOGNITION

Techniques for data entry extend in many directions. The reading of handwritten or typewritten characters from conventional paper appears to offer an

FIG. 8 • 13 A magnetic reader character set.

ideal input system for many applications. The systems currently in use are primarily as follows.

1. *Magnetic ink character reading* (MICR) The recording of characters using an ink with special magnetic properties and with characters having special forms was originally used in quantity by banks. The American Banking Association settled on a type font, and several of their characters are shown in Fig. 8 · 13. A *magnetic character reader* "reads" these characters by examining their shapes using a 7 × 10 matrix and determines, from the response of the segments of the matrix to the magnetic ink, which of the characters has passed under the reader's head. This information is thus transmitted to the system. The determination of the character which is read is greatly facilitated by the careful design of the characters and the use of the magnetic ink.

2. *Optical character reading* This area takes one of two forms. In the first, a special type font (or fonts) is used to print on conventional paper using conventional ink. The printed characters are examined by passing them under a strong light and a lens system which differentiates light (no ink) from inked areas and a logical system which attempts to determine which of the possible characters in the system is being examined. The systems in actual use depend heavily on the fact that only a limited number of characters in a particular font are used, but such systems are still quite useful. The standard type font agreed on by the ANSI optical character committee is shown in Fig. 8 · 14.

The ideal system would, of course, be able to adapt to many different type fonts. Some systems, particularly one developed by the Post Office, even reads handwritten characters. The limited success of these systems is due to the many shapes that a given character can have; consider the ways you can write an *a* and the similarity between a handwritten *a* and an *o* or a *b* and an *f*. These problems are increased by the optical reader's difficulty with the porosity of paper, ink smearing at the edges of lines, etc. Much work

FIG. 8·14 Type font for optical character recognition.

continues in this area, and much more is needed, but the advantages of such systems continue to cause this work to be sponsored and performed.

8·9 OUTPUT EQUIPMENT

Although many types of output equipment are now in use in the computer industry, the most popular form of output from a computer is undoubtedly the printed word. Other types of display devices in common use include neon lights and oscilloscopes, and some computers are even equipped with loudspeakers. (Programs which will play music through the loudspeakers are common, and attempts are often made to compose music using a computer.)

Lights are generally used to indicate the states of the storage devices of the principal registers of the machine (the accumulator, selected in-out registers, etc.). These lights are sometimes used as output devices for simple programs where the answers may then be read visually; however, such lights are generally used as troubleshooting aids, often to troubleshoot the operation of the machine. Figure 8·15 shows the lights on the console of the IBM 370 Model 155. Each light is connected to a flip-flop output (via a light driver). The outputs of most of the important flip-flops are monitored using the lights. Various sets of flip-flops can be selected using the rotary switches at the bottom of the panel, and the toggle switches and push buttons can be used to enter data into flip-flop registers and to sequence operations of the computer (as well as to start and stop the computer). The lights are sometimes used to troubleshoot programs for small machines. If, for instance, a program works itself into an endless loop, the machine can be stopped and the location† of the

---

† The program counter contains the address of the instruction being performed. Details of this section of the control element will be presented in the next chapter.

FIG. 8 • 15 Console of a large computer system, the IBM 370-155. (Courtesy of IBM Corp.)

faulty instruction sequence in the program can be read from the lights on the console of the machine.

8 • 10 PRINTERS

Generally, the most convenient and useful method by which the computer can deliver information is by means of printed characters. For the sake of convenience, the printer should have the ability to print alphabetical characters, decimal digits, and also common punctuation marks. It would be possible to print all the information processed by the computer in pure binary form or some form of coded binary, but not many banks would appreciate receiving a check for $1010.011, and most scientists and engineers, despite their admitted abilities in this direction, would prefer to have a printout which reads 130 rather than 10000010.

It is obvious that the printer must therefore operate from binary-coded characters rather than directly from binary. The process here is the inverse of the encoding procedure in which a key corresponding to an alphanumeric character is depressed, causing a coded binary character to be punched into a tape or card. In this case, coded groups of binary bits are delivered to the printer, which decodes them and then prints the correct characters. The basic binary-code groups may contain 5 through 9 bits, depending on the coding for alphanumeric characters which the printer provides.

The information delivered to a printer operated online will be in the form of electronic signals directly from the machine. If the printer is operated offline, the reading and decoding of data stored on punched tape, punched cards, or magnetic tape may be a part of the printing operation. Since the electronic circuitry of a computer is able to operate at speeds much higher than those of mechanical printing devices, it is desirable that a printer operated online be capable of printing at a very high speed. Even if the printer is operated offline, speed is highly desirable, since the volume of material to be printed may be quite large.

Most of the original printers were converted electric typewriters, and this type of printer is still popular. If the code used contains 8 bits per character and the printer is operated online, the computer will deliver 8 bits to the printer, which will decode them and energize a solenoid which will actuate the correct key of the typewriter. The codes used generally include coded characters such as those discussed earlier, including codes for spacing between words, carriage return, and other operations necessary to typing. The speed of such typewriter type printers is relatively low, perhaps from 10 to 30 characters per second.

Other types of character-at-a-time printers utilize slightly different principles. One type has a number of "pallets," each of which has a raised character on the surface nearest the roller or contact drum, mounted in a movable type basket. The type basket is positioned electromechanically by a decoder, and the back of the pallet is then struck by a hammer which forces the pallet against the page. An inked ribbon is positioned between the pallet and the page (like a typewriter ribbon); the character on the pallet is thereby printed on the page, the roller is then moved to the left, and another character is printed. Sometimes the pallets are contained in a rectangular "type box" which is also positioned by the action of the decoding mechanism, and the correct pallet is then struck by a hammer. Both the typewriter mechanisms and type-bar and type-box mechanisms are capable of printing up to perhaps 40 characters per second.

In order to further increase printer speed without significantly adding to cost, several manufacturers make *dot matrix printers* in which a set of pins in a 9×7 solenoid-actuated array are used to print characters. A character is printed by selecting the proper pins in the 9×7 matrix and the selected pins are then driven against the paper by small hammers. Speeds of up to 330 characters per second are attainable with these printers.

If a number of type bars are located in a row along the drum, and positioning mechanisms and hammers are provided for each bar, a *line-at-a-time printer* may be constructed. In this case, it is generally desirable for the printer to be provided with some sort of accumulator that can store all the bits which will determine the characters in a complete line. If each character contains 6 bits, and 50 characters are printed across the page, storage for 300 binary bits will be necessary. Each 6-bit coded character must be decoded and the respective type bar positioned before the hammers can cause a line to be printed. This type of printer can print up to four lines per second, a speed much higher than that of the character-at-a-time printer.

Even faster printers are constructed in which the raised characters are distributed around a "print wheel" which revolves constantly. In this case, the print wheel does not contain moving parts like the pallets just described, but consists of a motor-driven drum with a number of bands equal to the number of characters printed per line. A set of all the characters which are used is distributed around each band. The print wheel is revolved continuously. When the selected character is in position, the print hammer strikes the ribbon against the paper, and thus against the raised character on the print wheel located behind the paper. A printer of this type requires a decoder and a memory for each character position along the line, and also a character-timing encoder for each position, which determines when the selected character is in position. Printers of this type can print up to 1,250 lines per minute with 160 characters per line.

Two types of these printers are shown in Figs. 8 · 16 and 8 · 17. Figure 8 · 16 shows the IBM 1403 printer, in which the paper is moved vertically in front of a *chain* of raised characters of type. This chain is continually moving in the horizontal direction so that each of the 48 different characters continually pass by each of the 100 printers' positions in each line. (Other numbers of characters per line are available.) When a character to be printed passes the position where it is to be printed, the armature hammer magnet is energized, striking a hammer and forcing the paper against the type at that position. An inked ribbon is placed between paper and type so that the character is impressed on the paper in ink.

Figure 8 · 17 shows the major mechanical components of the Dian series N printer, which has a type roll or wheel with 17 circular tracks of printed characters, and is therefore a 17-character-per-line printer. This type roll is continually revolving, and when a selected character passes by the position it is to be printed in, the print actuator pushes the chosen ballistic hammer against the paper, forcing the paper against the selected character on the type roll. The type roll is continually inked by an ink roll, and no ribbon is used. In this system, a code disk and shaft encoder are used to tell which character is currently in a position to be printed. Shaft encoders will be discussed in a section which follows. Figure 8 · 17 shows that the paper is moved horizontally after each line is printed.

Refer to Figure 1 · 12, which shows a printer for the ledger cards used in accounting systems. This printer is typical of those used in many business-oriented systems. The ledger cards are dropped in the feed slot in the center

(a)

(b)

FIG. 8 • 16 (a) High-speed line printer; (b) type chain for the printer.

FIG. 8 • 17 Line-at-a-time drum printer.

just above the keyboard. The printer is often used in conjunction with a disk file, automatically posting data from the files in the ledger cards.

The natural limitations of speed in electromechanical devices have led to the development of printers called *nonimpact printers.* These printers are primarily in the following categories:

1. *Electromagnetic*   Using magnetic recording techniques, a magnetic image of what is to be printed can be written on a drum surface. This surface is then passed through magnetic power which adheres to the charged areas. The powder is then pressed onto the paper. Speeds of up to 250 characters per second are obtained in such systems.
2. *Electrostatic*   For electrostatic printers the paper is coated with a non-conducting dialectric material which holds charges when voltages are applied using writing "nibs" (heads). These heads write "dots" on the paper as it passes. Later, the paper passes through a toner containing material with colored particles carrying an opposite charge to that written by the nibs and, as a result, particles adhere to the magnetized areas forming printed characters.
3. *Thermal printers*   An electric pulse can be converted to heat on selected sections of a printing head or on wires or nibs. When this heat is applied to heat sensitive paper, a character is printed.
4. *Ink jets*   Some printers direct a high velocity stream of ink toward the paper. This stream is deflected, generally by passing the stream through an electrostatic field such as that used to deflect beams in oscilloscopes.

In some systems the ink stream is broken into droplets by an ultrasonic transducer.

The wide variety of printers available and the continuing development of new ideas makes the printer field a fascinating area. The cost-performance tradeoffs often make selection of a satisfactory printer difficult.

8 • 11 CATHODE-RAY-TUBE OUTPUT DEVICES

Cathode-ray tubes are often used as auxiliary output devices. The tubes were first used to display curves, the coordinates of which were calculated by programs. More recently, the cathode-ray tube has been used a great deal to display characters as well, especially in real-time online systems. The cathode-ray tube is a very fast output device, but does not deliver permanent copy. Therefore such tubes are sometimes used in conjunction with a camera, so that the display on the tube face can be photographed and thereby recorded permanently.

The cathode-ray tubes used in computer displays are the same type as those used in oscilloscopes and television sets, and entire television sets are sometimes used. For these display systems, the displayed points are made by positioning and turning on an electron beam in the tube, just as in television sets or oscilloscopes. The displays are sometimes called *oscilloscope,* or "scope," displays. Figure 8 · 18 shows a cathode-ray-tube display with a keyboard.

Several systems have been used to encode data for transmission to oscilloscope displays. The simplest system consists in simply sending, in binary, the *x, y* coordinates of each point to be displayed. The scope electronics then, using D-to-A converters, convert the binary numbers to voltages, which are used to position the beam.

The above system is simple, but inefficient, in that many points must be transmitted, which takes considerable computer time. Also, if the console or display is at a remote location and telephone lines are used, as is often the case, the transmission of the points can be expensive. (In most of these oscilloscope displays the points must be illuminated at least 30, and generally more, times each second. There are, however, *storage scopes,* which hold displayed points and do not require "refreshing." These must be erased, however, before rewriting, and are relatively expensive at present.)

Because of the problem of repeatedly sending data points to the display device, generally the display-device electronics include a small memory which stores the data from the computer and then generates the display from the last data transmitted, changing or updating the display only when the computer so directs.

Some more complicated but also more efficient techniques for data transmission to scope displays are frequently used. If only alphanumeric data are to be displayed, the ASCII code is generally used for the transmission of each character to be displayed. The oscilloscope electronics then converts

FIG. 8 • 18 Cathode-ray-tube display. (Courtesy of Computek, Inc.)

from each 8-bit coded ASCII character to the sequence of points required to display the character.† Lines for graphical displays such as that shown in Fig. 8 · 18 are often drawn using a technique by which the computer sends the difference in coordinates between the electronic beam's present location and the line segment to be drawn.

---

† Scopes are quite often scanned a line at a time, as in television sets, and so some conversion electronics is required.

One-shot extrusion method
of forming characters

Matrix – Shapes electron beam into
a character by extrusion process

Convergence coil – Directs shaped
beam to reference plates

Metal shield

Viewing screen

Electron gun –
Shoots unshaped
electron beam

Selection plates – Direct
unshaped electron beam
to illuminate a preselected
aperture in the matrix

Reference plates – Align shaped
beam on axis of tube

Displayed character

Focus coil – Focuses shaped-beam
character on screen

Helical accelerator –
Gives shaped-beam
character "speed"
for increased brightness

Deflection yoke – Bends beam to position shaped-
beam character on viewing screen

FIG. 8 • 19 Charactron shaped-beam display tube. (Courtesy of Stromberg-
Carlson Division, General Dynamics Corp.)

An example of a special tube developed for data display is the Charactron
tube. A cutaway view of a Charactron tube is shown in Fig. 8 · 19. This tube is
capable of displaying data at the rate of over 100,000 words per minute. The
character-forming part of the Charactron tube illustrated contains a small
matrix through which 64 characters have been cut. The electron beam passes
through the selection plates which direct it through the selected character
in the matrix. The beam is thus formed in the shape of the selected character.
The focus coil controls the size of the character formed, and the deflection
yoke then positions the shaped beam on the tube face.

8 • 12 OTHER OUTPUT DEVICES

Two other output devices are high-speed card- or tape-punching machines.
The information from the computer is punched into either paper cards or

tapes, so that the output medium resembles the input medium. If the output is to be used, the punched cards or tapes must then be interpreted and printed; the perforated tapes and cards may therefore be thought of as an intermediate step.

Magnetic tape is also used as an intermediate storage medium for offline output equipment operation. Since magnetic tape may be recorded much faster than either cards or tape may be punched, the computer's output operation is speeded up. In this case, a magnetic tape reader and translator is required to sense and interpret the binary-coded information recorded, and finally a printer is needed to print the information.

One advantage of these devices lies in the speed-to-cost ratio attainable. A high-speed magnetic tape recorder will be much faster than a high-speed printer, and the final printing may then take place on a slower printer, which interprets the recorded tape and prints the final result. This is another case of offline operation, in which the final operation is performed at the speed of a faster output device and the computer is therefore not slowed down as much as it would be if a low-speed printer were used. Even the magnetic tape recorder devices, however, are inherently much slower than the computer.

8•13 ERROR-DETECTING AND ERROR-CORRECTING CODES

The process of transferring information into the machine and from the machine is especially liable to error. Although card and tape readers are constructed with the highest possible regard for correct operation, and the occurrence of errors is relatively infrequent, errors still do occur, and it is desirable to detect them whenever possible. To facilitate the detection or correction of errors, two classes of codes have been invented, (1) error-detecting codes and (2) error-correcting codes. The first type of code enables the equipment to detect the errors which occur in the coded groups of bits, and the second type of code corrects the errors automatically.

Both error-detecting and error-correcting codes require that redundant information be sent along with the actual information being processed. The most commonly used type of error-detecting code is undoubtedly the parity-check code. Parity-check codes are commonly used for card and tape readers and for the storage of information on magnetic tape.

Parity checking

The parity check is based on the use of an additional bit, known as a "parity bit," or parity-check bit, in each code group. The parity bit associated with each code group in an *even-parity-bit* checking system has such a value that the total number of 1s in each code group plus the parity bit is always even. (An *odd-parity-bit* checking code has a parity bit such that the sum of the 1s in the code group plus the parity bit is always an odd number.) The ex-

TABLE 8·1

DECIMAL	BCD	EVEN PARITY BIT
0	0000	0
1	0001	1
2	0010	1
3	0011	0
4	0100	1
5	0101	0
6	0110	0
7	0111	1
8	1000	1
9	1001	0

ample shown in Table 8·1, which uses an 8, 4, 2, 1 code, has an even parity bit which makes the sum of the 1s in each code group an even number.

If a single error occurs in transmitting a code group—for instance, if 0010, 1 is erroneously changed to 0011, 1—the fact that there is an odd number of 1s in the code group plus the parity bit will indicate that an error has occurred. If the values of the parity bits had been selected so that the total sum of the 1s in each code group plus the parity bit were odd instead of even, each parity bit would be the complement of the parity bit shown above and the code would be an odd-parity-bit checking code.

The technique of parity checking is doubtless the most popular method of detecting errors in stored code groups, especially for storage devices such as magnetic tape, paper tape, and even for core-and-drum systems.

If the parity-bit system is used, an additional bit must be sent with each code group. For instance, if the 5-bit Baudot code group is used, each line of a punched tape will have an additional hole position which will contain a 1 or 0. When the tape is read by the tape reader, each code group will be examined, together with the parity bit; and in an odd-parity-bit system, an alarm will be generated if the number of 1s in a group is even.

This type of checking will detect all odd numbers of errors. Suppose that an even-parity check is used as in Table 8·1 and the code group to be sent is 0010; the parity bit in this case will be a 1. If the code group is erroneously read as 0110, the number of 1s in the code group plus the parity bit will be odd, and the error will be detected. If, however, a double error is made and 0010 is changed to 0111, the error will not be detected since the number of 1s will again be even. A parity-bit check will only detect odd numbers of errors.

(The rule above will also apply when the parity bit is in error. For instance, consider an even-parity-bit checking system where 0010 is to be sent and the parity bit is 1. If the parity bit is changed to 0, the number of 1s in the code group plus the parity bit will be odd, and the error will be detected.)

The parity check may also be used to check entire words. In this case, the procedure is the same as it is with the shorter code groups; the parity bit is arranged to make the total number of 1s in each word plus the parity bit even or odd, depending on the system used.

There are many types of error-correcting codes, and some very clever and sophisticated coding schemes are used in both communications and computer systems. For instance, magnetic tape is a memory device which is especially prone to errors. Most of these errors are due to either imperfections in the tape or foreign matter which gets between reading heads and the tape, causing the tape to be physically pushed away from the reading head and the recorded signal to be incorrectly interpreted. Such errors are said to be caused by "dropout." These errors tend to lie in a single track, and there are several clever codes which have been used to detect and correct such errors.†

8 • 14 TERMINALS

When a keyboard is combined with an oscilloscope display or a printing mechanism and suitable electronics is provided so that characters struck on the keyboard can be entered into a computer and the computer can also have the ability to print on the oscilloscope or printing mechanism, the keyboard-printer or keyboard-oscilloscope is called a *terminal.*

Terminals are widely used to input programs and data to computers. The teletype shown in Fig. 1 · 7 was an early terminal which continues to be widely used as a computer terminal. Teletypes provide a means for entering alphanumeric characters into a computer. They enable the computer to print responses to a user, and a tape punch and tape reader are generally included so that programs or data can be permanently recorded on paper tape, and so that such programs or data can be read into the computer when desired.

Figure 8 · 18 shows a terminal consisting of an oscilloscope and a keyboard. Characters struck on the keyboard will appear on the oscilloscope face, and output signals are also provided which are suitable for computer usage. A computer can also print on the oscilloscope, providing for two-way communications. The primary disadvantage is that no "hard copy" or record of what is typed by the terminal operator or printed by the computer remains when the terminal is turned off. Some means of recording selected data are now being introduced in the more expensive systems and these include cameras to photograph the scope face, small printers, and tape cassettes to record data.

Terminals range from minimal systems containing almost no memory to "smart" terminals where a small microcomputer or minicomputer is included.

---

† A study of error-correcting and error-detecting codes in some depth may be found in W. W. Peterson, *Error Correcting Codes,* and in G. Birkhoff and T.C. Bartee, *Modern Applied Algebra.*

Smart terminals provide many facilities for the user, sometimes including text editing, input formatting, and checking for typing errors made by operators.

Oscilloscope-keyboard combinations almost always contain a small memory in which the present contents of the screen are stored so that the screen can be refreshed by the terminal electronics instead of requiring the computer to continually rewrite data on the screen. In this case, a small memory and some electronics is required, and microprocessors are often used to control the terminal's operation. By enlarging the memory capabilities and program in the microprocessor, a smart terminal can be formed without too much additional cost.

Terminals generally generate output data in serial form and accept input data in serial form. The formats, coding, and electrical properties of the signals generated vary from terminal to terminal, but there are now strong movements to standardize the interface designs.

Teletypes and most of the terminals in present-day use generate an 11-bit output in serial form whenever a key on the keyboard is depressed. This same stream is generally used to activate the printer mechanism; however, on teletypes and many other devices it is possible to disengage the keyboard from the printing mechanism. In this case, when a key is struck, the code for the character is read by the computer which must then write this character back into the terminal's printer. This is called "echoing" the character.

Figure $8 \cdot 20$ shows how the present standard character transmission operates. The output line from the keyboard is normally in the high† state, but when a key is depressed a *start bit* at a low level is generated. This start bit is followed by the proper 8-bit ASCII-coded character, and then two *stop bits* at the high level are inserted before another character can be started (that is, before another start bit can be generated). The start bit, each stop bit, and the bits in the ASCII-coded character are each of the same time duration. For most current systems this is $\frac{1}{110}$ s for each, and, since 11 such time periods or *bit times* are required, a single character requires $\frac{11}{110}$ or $\frac{1}{10}$ s.

There are several other speeds which are currently used, including 300, 600, and 1200 bits/s. In each case, the same character construction with start and stop bits is used, and so character rates of $\frac{11}{300}$, $\frac{11}{600}$, and $\frac{11}{1200}$ s are attainable.

The character transmission system described here is called *asynchronous transmission,* for the character and start bits can occur at any time. *Synchronous transmission* systems have the bits clocked into fixed time periods, and characters are also placed in fixed positions in the bit stream. These systems require both bit timing and character timing to be established between the transmitting device and receiver and are therefore more complicated. Character transmission can be at higher rates, however. (Since start and stop bits are not required, the character beginnings and ends are established by

---

† Communications people call this a *mark* value and the other level a *space.*

Note: To make an 8-bit character from a
7-bit ASCII code, an odd parity
bit is placed in the 8th position

FIG. 8 • 20 Sending a character using the standard code.

the system.) As a result, high-speed data communication is generally in
synchronous form.

The output levels and interface requirements for the coded characters are
examined in the questions and several standards are noted.

When terminals are operated at some distance from a computer, the telephone system is often used to provide the necessary communications link. If
a terminal is to be operated into the telephone system, special devices are
needed to translate the logic levels produced by the terminal into signals
acceptable for telephone-line transmission.

Figure 8 · 21 shows a terminal with an *acoustic coupler*. The handset from
the telephone is placed in this acoustic coupler. When a key is depressed,
the bits comprising the character are converted into audio tones using a
small speaker in the coupler. Generally one frequency is used for a 0 and
another for a 1. These signals enter the transmitter part of the handset and
are transmitted into the telephone line. At the computer end these frequencies
are received by a microphone connected to a handset and then converted
back to 1s and 0s in electrical form, so that the electrical logic levels output
at the receiver are replicas of the signals originally generated at the terminal.

The computer "talks" back to the terminal using an acoustic coupler at its

Telephone
receiver

When telephone receiver is placed in
acoustic coupler, terminal can
communicate (both ways) with a computer

Oscilloscope
display

Keyboard

FIG. 8 • 21 Oscilloscope display and terminal.

end of the telephone line, and the acoustic coupler at the terminal converts
the computer's signals back to logic levels which are used to drive the
display.

When output signals in logic level form are converted directly into electrical signals suitable for telephone transmission using electronic circuitry
(instead of acoustic coupling), the converting device is called a *modem*. A
modem can generally convert logic levels into electrical signals for the telephone system and can convert received signals from the telephone line back
into logic levels. This means, of course, that the connections to the telephone
line are made electrically and directly into the telephone line, and a headset
is not used. It also means that the electrical signals must comply with telephone system regulations; and the design of modems which will (1) send
bits through telephone lines at high speeds, (2) make few errors in transmission, and (3) comply with telephone company regulations is a highly developed and interesting scientific area.

Like acoustic couplers, modems generally use a (different) frequency for
a 1 and a 0. As an example, the Bell 103 modem sends data through telephone lines at either 110 or 300 bits/s. The modem at one end of a telephone
line uses 1,070 Hz (for 1s) and 1,270 Hz (for 0s) to send, while the modem
at the other end uses 2,025 Hz (for 1s) and 2,225 Hz (for 0s). The reason for
the two sets of frequencies is that transmission can be in either direction and

while one modem is transmitting a character, the other will still be sending its high (mark) frequency. (A single telephone line handles communications in both directions. Both ends can "talk" at the same time. You can, for instance, interrupt someone who is talking.)

8 • 15 INPUT-OUTPUT DEVICES FOR SYSTEMS WITH ANALOG COMPONENTS

Not all the inputs to digital machines consist of alphanumeric data which may be directly punched into cards or tape. Computers used in data-reduction systems or in real-time control systems often have inputs which are expressed as the physical position of some device, or as electric signals which are analog in nature. An example of a physical position which might be used as an input to a digital computer is a real-time control system in which a computer is used automatically to point a telescope. If, by some system of gears, the position of the telescope along an axis is related to the position of a shaft, the position of this shaft must be read into the computer. This will involve the translation of the shaft position into a binary-coded number which may be read by the machine.

Changing a physical displacement or an analog electrical signal to a digital representation is called *analog-to-digital* (A-to-D) *conversion*. Two major types of A-to-D converters are: (1) those which convert mechanical displacements into a digital representation and (2) those which convert an electric analog signal into digital-coded signals.

Suppose an analog device has as its output a voltage which is to be used by a digital machine. Let us assume that the voltage varies within the limit 0 to 63 V dc. We can then represent the voltage values with a set of 6-bit numbers ranging from 000000 to 111111 and, for each value the input voltage may assume, assign a corresponding value of the 6-bit number. If the input voltage is 20 V, the corresponding digital value will be 010100. If, however, the input signal is at 20.249 V dc, the 6-bit binary number will not completely describe the input voltage, but will only approximate the input value. The process of approximating the input value is called *quantizing*. The number of bits in the binary number which represents the analog signal is the *precision* of the coder, and the amount of error which exists between the digital output values and the input analog values is a measure of the *accuracy* of the coder.

Not only are the inputs to the computer sometimes in analog form, but it is often desirable for the outputs of the computer to be expressed in analog form. An example of this lies in the use of a cathode-ray tube as an output device. If the output from the computer is to be displayed as a position on an oscilloscope tube, then the binary-coded output signals from the computer must be converted to voltages or currents, which may be used to position the electron beam, and which are proportional to the magnitude of the output binary number represented by the computer's output signals. This involves digital-to-analog conversion, and a device which performs this conversion is called a D-to-A *converter*. When digital computers are used in control systems, it is generally necessary to convert the digital outputs from the machine to analog-type signals, which are then used to control the physical system.

8•16 ANALOG-TO-DIGITAL CONVERTERS—SHAFT ENCODERS

The first type of coder which will be briefly described below converts a shaft position to a binary-coded digital number. A number of different types of devices will perform this conversion; the type described is representative of the devices now in use, and it should be realized that more complicated coders may yield additional accuracy. Also, it is generally possible to convert a physical position into an electric analog-type signal and then convert this signal to a digital system. For instance, a shaft may be mechanically coupled to a potentiometer with a dc voltage across the ends of the resistance. If the output signal is then taken from the potentiometer tap, the dc output signal will be related to the shaft position. In general, though, more direct and accurate coders can be constructed by eliminating the intermediate step of converting a physical position to an analog electric signal.

Figure 8·22(a) illustrates a coded-segment disk which is coupled to the shaft. A set of brushes is then attached so that a single brush is positioned in the center of each concentric band of the disk. Each band is constructed of several segments made of either conducting material (the darkened areas) or some insulating material (the unshaded areas). A signal is connected to the conductor, and if a given brush makes contact with a segment of conducting material, a 1 signal will result, but if the brush is over the insulating material, the output from the brush will be a 0. The four output lines of the coder shown will represent a 4-bit binary number. There are 16 distinct in-

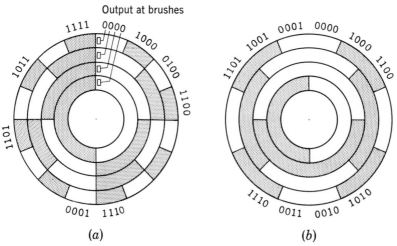

FIG. 8•22 Shaft-position encoder disks. (*a*) Binary-coded disks; (*b*) unit distance code disk.

tervals around the coder disk, each corresponding to a different shaft-position interval and each causing the coder to have a different binary number output.

A photoelectric coder may be constructed using a coder disk with bands divided into transparent segments (the shaded areas) and opaque segments (the unshaded areas). A light source is put on one side of the disk, and a set of four photoelectric cells on the other side, arranged so that one cell is behind each band of the coder disk. If a transparent segment is between the light source and a light-sensitive cell, a 1 output will result; and if an opaque area is in front of the photoelectric cell, there will be a 0 output. By increasing the number of bands around the disk, more precision may be added to the coder. The photoelectric type of coder has greater resolution than the brush type, and even greater resolution may be obtained by using gears and several disks. The state of the art is about 18 bits or 2^{18} positions per shaft revolution but most commercial coders have 14 bits or fewer.

There is one basic difficulty with the coder illustrated: if the disk is in a position where the output number is changing from 011 to 100, or in any position where several bits are changing value, the output signal may become ambiguous. Since the brushes are of finite width, they will overlap the change in segments; and no matter how carefully it is made, the coder will have erroneous outputs in several positions. If this occurs when 011 is changing to 100, several errors are possible; the value may be read as 111 or 000, either of which is a value with considerable errors. To circumvent this difficulty, a number of schemes have been used, generally involving two sets of brushes, with one set displaced slightly from the other. By logically choosing from the outputs available, the "ambiguity" may be eliminated at a slight cost in accuracy.

TABLE 8·2

DECIMAL	GRAY CODE $a_3 a_2 a_1 a_0$
0	0000
1	0001
2	0011
3	0010
4	0110
5	0111
6	0101
7	0100
8	1100
9	1101
10	1111
11	1110
12	1010
13	1011
14	1001
15	1000

Another scheme for avoiding ambiguity involves the use of a "Gray," or "unit-distance," code to form the coder disk [Fig. 8·22(b)]. In this code, 2 bits never change value in successive coded binary numbers. Using a Gray-coded disk, a 6 may be read for a 7 or a 4 for a 5, but larger errors will not be made. Table 8·2 shows a listing of a 4-bit Gray code.

If the inputs to the machine are from a coder using a Gray code, the code groups must be converted to conventional binary or BCD before use. This conversion may be simply performed, either sequentially or combinatorially. The questions treat the Gray code and conversion in more detail.

8•17 DIGITAL-TO-ANALOG CONVERTERS

The problem of converting a digital output to an analog voltage can be re-solved by several techniques, the most straightforward of which involves the use of a resistor network. A basic type of resistor-network D-to-A converter is illustrated in Fig. 8·23, which shows a resistor net with four inputs. Each input is converted to a switch which connects a resistor to either 0 V or V_+. When a switch is in the position converting to V_+, the binary bit represents a 1, and when the switch connects to 0 V, the input bit is a binary 0. The output at E_0 will then be a dc potential in the range 0 to V_+ and will be proportional to the value of the binary number represented by the inputs.

For instance, if the input number is 0111, the output voltage at E_0 will be $\frac{7}{15}V_+$; if the input is 1111, the output E_0 will be V_+; and if the input is 0001, the output E_0 will be at $\frac{1}{15}V_+$ V dc. To achieve accuracy, the resistors should all be of the precision type. Also, the input voltages representing the binary values must be accurately established, and since the load on the inputs will vary with the value of the input numbers, the input should be capable of de-livering the necessary current without a shift in the voltage level. More pre-cision can be added by increasing the number of inputs and adding a resistor for each input.

FIG. 8•23 D-to-A resistor network.

FIG. 8 • 24 R/2R resistor D-to-A converter.

Figure 8 · 24 shows another type of resistor network which can be used for D-to-A conversion. The advantage of this network is that only two different values of resistors are used. The inputs are shown as switches, but semi-conductor switches or *level-setting amplifiers* are often used. The disadvantage of this converter is that two resistors are required per input.

There are many other types of D-to-A converters, and the design and construction of these devices represents a growing area in the computing field. Many decoders are very specialized, especially those used in control systems. For instance, automatic milling machines are often controlled by a digital computer which must have its digital outputs converted into the mechanical motion of the milling machinery. The use of digital computers in large industries, such as the petroleum industry, paper manufacturing, and camera manufacturing, also involves the utilization of many different types of A-to-D and D-to-A converters.

8 • 18 ELECTRONIC HIGH-SPEED ANALOG-TO-DIGITAL CONVERTERS

There are several techniques used for converting an electric analog signal to digital form. What is basically needed is a device which converts a dc signal to a binary number proportional to the dc level of the signal. Suppose we have a dc voltage with an amplitude which is in the interval 0 to +15 V. If we wish to convert this to a four-digit binary number, we will want the number 0000 for 0 to 0.5 V, 0001 for 0.5 to 1.5 V, 0010 for 1.5 to 2.5 V, 1111 for 14.5 V or greater, etc. (Notice that the binary number corresponds to the center of the interval.)

A simple A-to-D converter can be made using a resistor network such as that in Fig. 8·23, a START-STOP flip-flop, a four-flip-flop binary counter, four level converters, and a high-gain dc amplifier.

The basic configuration is shown in Fig. 8·25. The flip-flops X_1, X_2, X_3, and X_4 are arranged in a binary counter which counts 0000, 0001, 0010, ..., 1111. Each flip-flop drives a level converter such that, when the flip-flop's output is a 1, the output of the level converter is −16 V dc; and when the flip-flop's output is a 0, the level-converter output is 0 V dc.

The high-gain dc amplifier is designed so that when the input to the amplifier is positive, the output of the amplifier represents a 0; but when the input is negative, the output goes to a 1, thus setting the START-STOP flip-flop (and stopping the counter).

Now let us assume that a START signal is given, clearing the flip-flop counter to 0000. All the outputs from the level converters will be at 0 V (unless the input analog signal is less than +0.5 V dc, the 160-kΩ resistor to −16 V will cause the input to the amplifier to be negative†), the amplifier's output will be a 0, and the clock pulse will pass the first AND gate.

If the input signal is 0 to 0.5 V, the amplifier will have a level output of a 1 and will set the start-stop flip-flop to a 1 so that no clock pulses will pass.

If the input signal is greater than +0.5 V, the counter will count, thereby causing the negative current into the junction of the 10-, 20-, 40-, and 80-kΩ resistors to increase until the input to the amplifier goes negative, thus stopping the counter.

If, for instance, the analog signal input is at +9 V dc, the input to the amplifier will be positive until the counter goes from 1000 to 1001; and when the counter is a 1001, the clock pulses will be stopped, giving the right value for the signal.

There are several other techniques which are used for A-to-D conversion. The most used is the *successive approximation method* because of its combination of high resolution and high speed. The successive approximation converter operates with a fixed conversion time per bit, independent of the value of the analog input. The method can be explained using Fig. 8·24 since it is a variation on this technique.

Consider that we have control of the individual flip-flops in Fig. 8·25 instead of their being in a counter. At the start of the conversion, the D-to-A converter's most significant bit is set to the 1 state and the converter's output, which is now one-half the full-scale analog input range, is compared with the input. If it is smaller than the input, the most significant bit is left on and the next bit is tried. If the most significant bit output from the level converter to the most significant bit is larger than the input, the most significant bit is turned off when the next least significant bit is turned on.

This process of comparison is continued on each bit in turn down to and in-

---

† The 160-kΩ and −16-V combination contributes as much current to the junction of resistors at the amplifiers' input as a +0.5-V signal at the input for the analog signal.

FIG. 8·25 A-to-D converter.

cluding the least significant bit, after which the output register contains the complete output digital number.

Speeds as high as 100 ns/bit can be achieved by this method. Successive approximation converters can also be quite accurate, but the accuracy depends on the stability of the reference, the level converters, the D-to-A resistor network, and the comparator.

The fastest converters are parallel-type converters. These converters can be made to have rates of up to 25 million conversions for 4 bits. Sometimes these converters are called *simultaneous* or *flash converters*.

The parallel method of making an n-bit converter employs an input quantizer comprised of $2^n - 1$ comparators biased 1 least significant bit apart by resistors connected to a reference voltage; refer to Fig. 8·26, which shows a 2-bit A-to-D converter that therefore has $2^2 - 1$, or 3, comparators. Each comparator looks at the signal input and compares it with its particular reference voltage. If the signal input is less the comparator turns on; if the signal input is greater the comparator turns off. As a result, for a given signal input voltage to the comparators, all comparators with inputs from the resistor network which are below the signal input level turn on while all comparators above it are off. Therefore, the quantization process is accomplished in the switching time of a single comparator. The comparator outputs, however, are not in binary code and must, therefore, go through a logic network to be converted to binary, as shown in the figure.

The parallel method has the advantage of the fastest speed but is limited to a relatively few bits, usually 4, due to the large number of comparators required. In order to convert a large number of bits it is necessary to employ

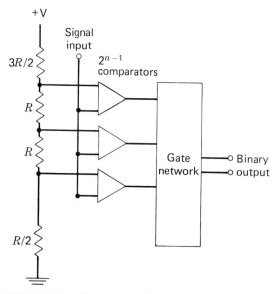

FIG. 8 • 26 Parallel-type A-to-D converter.

TABLE 8 • 3 A-TO-D AND D-TO-A CONVERSION TERMINOLOGY

Resolution The smallest analog change that can be distinguished by an A-to-D converter or produced by a D-to-A converter. Resolution is the analog voltage value of the least significant bit, which is *full-scale voltage* $\div$ 2^n for an *n*-bit binary converter. Resolution is often specified in percentage of full scale.

Linearity The maximum deviation from a straight line drawn between the minimum and maximum input levels of the converter. Linearity may be expressed as a percentage of full scale or as a fraction of the least significant bit's voltage size. (The linearity of a good converter is $\pm\frac{1}{2}$ least significant bit.)

Quantizing error The basic uncertainty associated with digitizing an analog signal, due to the finite resolution of an A-to-D converter. An ideal converter has a maximum quantizing error of $\pm\frac{1}{2}$ least significant bit.

a mixed strategy whereby a parallel conversion stage is followed by a fast D-to-A converter, the output of which is subtracted from the input voltage; the difference is then amplified and converted using another parallel stage. This results in a speed compromise but higher resolution.

A-to-D converters are commonly made to give either 7 to 20 binary digits or 3 to 7 decimal digits for outputs. The fastest converter now on the market makes 250 million conversions per second; more modestly priced converters operate at much lower frequencies. Slow A-to-D converters primarily intended for manual use or slow-speed recording are called *digital voltmeters*. These almost invariably operate using BCD. Display devices then convert the BCD to a decimal number which is displayed and can be read by an operator or printed.

Table 8 · 3 lists some of the terms which are used in describing A-to-D and D-to-A converters.

QUESTIONS

1. Using the code in Fig. 8 · 2, an operator keyboards the following:

ADD 641

CAD 932

SUB 841

How many lines will be punched in the paper tape? How many holes will be punched in the tape?

2. The code in Fig. 8 · 2(a) has at least one punch or hole for each character. This makes it possible for the reader to detect when to read. Explain the TAPE FEED character.

3. Write out in binary form the first line of the program in Question 1 using the code in Fig. 8 · 3.

4. The code in Fig. 8·2 is a parity-checking code. Is the parity check odd or even?

5. If the short program in Question 1 is punched into cards according to the code in Fig. 8·6 using normal procedures, how many holes will be punched into the cards used? If a mistake is made during keyboarding, will it be easier to correct if cards or tape are used? Explain why.

6. The TAPE FEED character can be used to take out any character in the code in Fig. 8·2 except one. Which character and why? *Hint:* Remember the parity checks.

7. Generally, programs are punched into cards with an instruction word per card. The first line of the program in Question 1 would go on one card. How many holes will be punched in the first card for the code in Fig. 8·6?

8. In EBCDIC, when the first four bits are 1s, the remaining four bits represent a digit. Is the code for these bits BCD or straight binary? Give a reason for your answer.

9. List the binary-code groups for each decimal digit in the excess 3 BCD-code in Chap. 3, and assign a parity bit for an even-parity-bit checking system to each code group. List the values of the parity bits for the same excess 3 code for an odd-parity-bit checking system.

10. Discuss any problems you can foresee in attempting to read characters optically which would not occur for magnetic characters. Do these reasons somewhat explain why banks adopted magnetic readers before optical readers?

11. Each of the following rows of digits consists of a code group in the ASCII code. A single parity check has been added as the rightmost bit in each row, and a single row of parity checks has been added at the end, as explained in Question 15. In addition, errors have been added so that the data are not correct at present. Correct these groups of data, and then convert each seven-digit character to the alphanumeric character it represents. The parity checks are odd parity checks:

(a)	(b)
0 0 1 0 0 0 1 1	0 1 1 0 0 1 0 0
0 1 1 0 1 0 0 0	0 1 0 0 0 1 1 0
0 1 1 0 0 0 0 1	0 1 0 1 0 1 0 1
0 0 1 0 0 0 1 1	0 0 1 0 0 0 1 1
0 0 1 1 0 0 1 0	0 0 0 1 0 0 0 0
0 0 0 1 0 0 0 0	0 0 1 0 0 0 1 0
0 1 0 0 1 1 0 1	0 0 1 0 0 0 1 1
0 1 1 1 1 1 0 1	0 1 0 0 0 1 1 0
0 1 1 0 0 0 1 1	0 1 0 1 0 1 1 1
0 1 1 0 1 0 0 0	1 0 1 0 0 0 1 1 parity-check row
0 0 1 0 0 0 1 1	
1 1 0 0 1 0 0 0 parity-check row	

12. Using the error-detecting and error-correcting scheme in Question 11, a

message has been sent. It arrives as below. Determine if errors have occured, and correct any you find in the following message:

$$1\ 0\ 1\ 0\ 0\ 1\ 0\ 0$$
$$1\ 0\ 0\ 0\ 0\ 0\ 1\ 0$$
$$1\ 0\ 0\ 0\ 1\ 1\ 0\ 1$$
$$1\ 0\ 0\ 1\ 0\ 0\ 0\ 1$$
$$1\ 0\ 1\ 0\ 1\ 0\ 0\ 0$$
$$0\ 1\ 1\ 1\ 1\ 1\ 1\ 1$$

13. How many bands must a coder disk similar to that in Fig. 8·22 have for an A-to-D converter which has a precision of 10 binary digits? List the successive code groups for a 5-bit unit-distance code which counts from 0 to 31_{10}.

14. A 2, 4, 2, 1 code for encoding the 10 decimal digits into 4 binary digits can be made so that no more than two positions change each time a single digit is increased by one. Write this code down.

15. More powerful parity-check systems can be formed by adding columns with the number of 1s in each column written at the end as a binary number. For instance, if we wish to encode

$$1\ 0\ 1\ 1$$
$$1\ 1\ 0\ 1$$
$$1\ 1\ 0\ 0$$
$$1\ 1\ 1\ 0$$

we add

```
0⎫
0⎪
1⎬ parity checks
0⎭
0 1 0 0 1⎫
0 1 1 1 0⎬ no. of 1s in each column
1 0 0 0 0⎭
↑      ↑——indicates two 1s
⎣indicates four 1s
```

Adding this to the data forms this encoded block of data:

$$1\ 0\ 1\ 1\ 0$$
$$1\ 1\ 0\ 1\ 0$$
$$1\ 1\ 0\ 0\ 1$$
$$1\ 1\ 1\ 0\ 0$$
```
0 1 0 0 1⎫
0 1 1 1 0⎬ check digits
1 0 0 0 0⎭
```

Now if one or more errors occur in the same column, they can be corrected by simply noting that the column does not agree with the number of 1s recorded at the end, and that there are parity checks in the rows of the block of data containing errors. By simply changing these errors, we will convert the message back to its original form. Here are two other blocks of data which include errors. Correct the errors in these blocks of data and write the alphanumeric code for each set of seven digits in a row to the right of the rows. The code is that in Fig. 8·10; so the parity checks are as indicated in the figure, and not in the rightmost column.

(a) 0 0 1 0 0 0 1 1
    0 1 1 0 1 0 1 0
    0 1 1 0 0 0 1 1
    0 0 1 0 0 0 0 1
    0 0 1 1 0 0 1 0
    0 0 0 1 0 0 0 0
    0 1 1 1 0 1 1 0
    0 1 1 1 1 0 0 1
    0 1 0 0 0 1 0 1
    0 1 1 1 0 1 0 1
    0 0 0 1 0 1 0 0 ⎫
    0 1 0 0 1 1 0 1 ⎬ check digits
    0 1 0 1 0 0 1 1 ⎭
    0 0 1 0 0 0 0 0

(b) 0 1 1 0 0 0 1 0
    0 1 0 0 0 0 0 1
    0 1 0 0 0 1 0 0
    0 0 0 1 0 0 0 0
    0 0 1 0 0 0 1 1
    0 1 1 0 0 0 0 1
    0 1 0 1 0 1 1 1
    0 1 1 1 0 1 0 1
    0 0 1 1 0 0 1 0
    0 0 0 1 0 0 0 0
    0 0 1 1 0 1 0 1 ⎫
    0 1 1 0 0 1 0 0 ⎬ check digits
    0 1 1 1 0 0 1 1 ⎭
    0 0 0 0 0 0 0 0

16. Explain why the Gray code cannot be used if we are to use a D-to-A resistor network as in Fig. 8·23. Explain why the 2, 4, 2, 1 code in Question 14 could be used.

17. If the signals of each of the four inputs to the D-to-A converter resistor network in Fig. 8·23 are from the 1 outputs of flip-flops which have +8- and 0-V logic levels (+8 V represents a 1), what will be the potential at E_0 if the flip-flops represent the binary number 0101? 1010? 1111?

18. Put errors into the message in Question 12 which the coding will neither correct nor detect.

19. Show an error pattern the code in Question 15 will not correct but will detect and one which it will neither correct nor detect.

20. If the ASCII code in Fig. 8·10 is transmitted serially in binary, draw the waveform for the character 8, assuming a 1 is +4 V and a 0 is −4 V.

21. Characters are generally read from punched paper tape a line at a time. When the code in Fig. 8·2(a) is used, the computer will be supplied with information bits each time a line is read. If the computer used is a serial computer, the bits will arrive in parallel and must be changed to serial form. By loading a seven-place shift register in parallel and then shifting the register at the machine's pulse-repetition frequency, the bits representing the character can be converted to serial form. Draw a block diagram of a seven-flip-flop shift register, along with the input lines nec-

essary to load the register. (Assume that there are seven input lines —
one to each flip-flop — from the tape reader and that a given input line
will contain a pulse if a hole is in the respective position of the tape.)

22. Explain why, in large computer systems, output data to be printed are
almost always recorded on magnetic tape for offline printing and not
printed at once.

23. Which of the sets or errors in Question 11 would have been detected if
the error-catching system in Question 15 had been used? Which of these
sets of errors in Question 15 could have been corrected by the error-
detecting and error-correcting scheme in the Question 11, and which
would only have been detected?

24. Is it possible to invent a 7-binary-bit code which includes an odd-parity-
check bit and which contains 70 characters? Give a reason for your
answer.

25. For the A-to-D converter in Fig. 8·25, if the 40-kΩ resistor were made
50-kΩ by error, which of the following voltages would be incorrectly
converted:
(a) +10 V   (b) +3 V
(c) +2 V   (d) +18 V
(e) +8 V   (f) +13 V

26. Design a 6-bit A-to-D converter using the same scheme shown in Fig.
8·25.

27. The code in Question 15 is not generally able to correct double errors
in a row or errors in the checking numbers at the end, but will almost
always detect each of these. Explain this statement.

28. Discuss the relationships between accuracy, precision, and speed in
an A-to-D converter.

29. Show how a teletype would read out the character C when this key was
depressed. Draw the output waveform.

30. What is the ASCII code for "who are you" which is also WRU in Fig.
8·10?

31. What is the EBCDIC code for D in Fig. 8·11?

32. Notice that the characters in the magnetic reader character set in Fig.
8·13 are "blocked," not curved. Why might this be a good idea?

33. Notice the difference in a 0, a Q and an O in Fig. 8·14. Find other
letters which have similar printed shapes that have been altered to make
them more machine readable.

34. What is the difference between an acoustic coupler and a modem?

35. Can you think of any reasons why it might be a good idea for a computer to echo a character struck on a keyboard it is to read from instead
of having the character printed immediately?

36. Why are start bits and at least one stop bit necessary for the teletype
code transmission explained for terminals?

37. Explain the difference between synchronous and asynchronous transmission of digital data.

38. Explain how the Bell 103 modem described would send the ASCII char-

acter D on a line in a chosen direction. How would it send in the other direction? Use the teletype scheme to encode using start and stop bits.

39. Use 1- and 2-kΩ resistors and draw the schematic diagram for a D-to-A converter as in Fig. 8·24.

40. For the schematic you drew in the preceding question, use +7 and 0 V as the two levels and figure the output for two nonzero digital input values.

41. Repeat the preceding question but use 5- and 10-kΩ resistors.

42. Design a D-to-A converter which converts using the successive approximation technique. Use a modified version of Fig. 8·25.

43. Show how long it would take a D-to-A converter using the successive approximation technique to convert 6 bits. Assume it takes 10 ms for the D-to-A converter-resistor network to stabilize its output. Explain by showing how conversions are made for three specific input voltages.

44. Again assuming it takes 10 ms for the D-to-A converter network to stabilize, show how a 6-bit converter uses the successive approximation technique for three voltages +9, +1, and +7 V, assuming a 0- to 10-V range for inputs (0 and +10 V as voltage levels for the level converter outputs).

45. Show how the converter in Fig. 8·25 converts the three voltages in the preceding question and compare the conversion times.

46. Using the information in the preceding three questions, can you compare the average time for conversion for an A-to-D converter as in Fig. 8·25 with a successive approximation converter? Assume 6 bits.

47. Show how a flash converter works for a 3-bit system using 10-kΩ resistors. Assume voltages in an interval from 0 to 6 V, so $000_2 = 0$ V, $001_2 = 2$ V, $100_2 = 4$ V, $110_2 = 6$ V, etc. Draw the gates from the comparator outputs to the binary numbers.

48. Explain how the converter in the preceding question converts +0.5, +3.2, and +5.4 V.

49. Discuss resolution, linearity, and quantizing error. Can the quantizing error be less than resolution? Why or why not?

9
THE
CONTROL
UNIT

This chapter describes the control section of digital computers. Preceding chapters have described techniques whereby arithmetic and logical operations may be performed and information read into and from various memory devices. To utilize the speeds and information handling capabilities of the techniques and devices which have been illustrated, it is necessary to sequence automatically the various operations which occur at speeds compatible with those of the rest of the machine. The control element must therefore be constructed of high-speed circuitry. The basic elements used in the control element of a digital computer are those described in Chaps. 4, 5, and 7, and most of the concepts underlying the functioning of the control element are those presented in Chaps. 3 to 6.

Present-day digital computers are generally divided into two classes: the special-purpose and the general-purpose computer. A *special-purpose computer* is one in which the sequence of operations is predetermined by the actual construction of the control circuitry. A special-purpose machine therefore has a fixed sequence of operations which cannot be changed. A *general-purpose* machine, on the other hand, is one in which the sequence of instructions (program) which the machine performs is read into the machine via the input devices, and may be changed by simply reading in a new program. This type of machine is also referred to as a *stored-program* computer.

This division of digital computers into two categories is not as clear-cut as it may at first appear. Many computers, such as those used in aircraft and missile control systems or as a part of industrial process control systems, are special-purpose because the sequence of the operations performed is wired directly into the control circuitry. Other computers, such as the large computers used at computing centers for business and science, are clearly general-purpose, since the programs for these machines are always read in and are changed quite frequently. On the other hand, a class of computers exists in which the program sequence is determined by a read-only memory (ROM), the contents of which may be changed, thus changing the sequence of operations. For instance, microprocessors are frequently used with a program in a semiconductor ROM. The ROM can be replaced, thus changing the program; and some ROMs are reprogrammable in that their contents can be changed whenever desired. The techniques employed here are relatively inefficient, but viewed externally, the computers appear to operate in the area defined as general purpose, and manufacturers of microprocessors point out that quite often these computers are programmed to operate as general-purpose computers. The classification at this point is purely arbitrary, and the differences between the two types of computers are relative since both are performing similar functions.

It should be noted that most of the computers classed as special-purpose are capable of altering their sequence of operations, depending on the input data. That is, they have *conditional branches* which depend on the numerical results, but the sequence of operations is altered in that the computer skips to another position in the program. The basic sequence of operations in each section of the program does not change; only the path the computer takes through the program is altered.

The *control unit* may be defined as "those parts of a digital computer which effect the carrying out of instructions in proper sequence, the interpretation of each instruction, and the application of the proper commands to the arithmetic element and other circuits in accordance with this interpretation."†

The function of the control circuitry in a general-purpose computer is therefore to interpret the instruction words and then sequence the necessary signals to those sections of the machine which will cause the machine to perform the instruction. Previous chapters have shown how the application of the correct sequence of control signals to the logical circuitry in the arithmetic element enables the computer to perform arithmetic operations, and how binary words may be stored and later read from several types of memory devices. For the machine to function, the operation of the sections of the machine must be directed, and the control circuitry performs that function.

9•1 CONSTRUCTION OF INSTRUCTION WORD

We have defined a computer word as an ordered set of characters handled as a group. Also, the computer word is considered to be a basic unit of in-

---

† Institute of Electronic and Electrical Engineers, *IEEE Standards on Electronic Computers*, Definition of Terms.

formation in a machine.† Basically, all words consist of a set of binary digits, and the meaning of the digits depends upon several different factors. For instance, the bits 01000100 could represent the decimal number 68 in a pure binary computer, and the decimal number 44 in a BCD computer which uses an 8421 code. Thus the meaning of a set of digits is sometimes determined by its usage. In addition, other interpretations are possible, for instruction words are stored just as are data words, and the digits could represent an instruction to the computer. Since memory locations can store either instruction words or data words, the programmers and system operators must see that the instruction words are used to determine the sequence of operations which the computer performs, and that reasonable meanings are assigned to the data words.

If we assume each memory location can contain a single instruction word, a computer will start with the word stored in some specified address, interpret the contents of this location as an instruction, and then continue taking instruction words from the memory locations in order, unless a HALT or BRANCH instruction is encountered. The data to be used in the calculations will be stored in another part of the memory. Since the computer can store either instructions or data in the same storage registers, considerable flexibility of operation results. For instance, if the computer memory element can store only 8000 words, one program might contain 5000 instructions, leaving 3000 locations for the storage of data, while another program might use only 1000 instruction words, leaving 7000 locations for data. The computer user is therefore free to allocate the memory as necessary, and problems with many instructions and few numbers, or with much data and few instructions, can be handled by the same computer.

It should be noted that computers which have both a high-speed inner memory and a lower-speed auxiliary memory will use the high-speed inner memory for the instruction words and for intermediate results, and the lower-speed storage devices for any data which cannot be accommodated in the high-speed memory. For instance, if a computer has a high-speed magnetic core memory plus a number of magnetic tape devices, the program instructions may be stored in the magnetic core storage, and the data to be used in the tape storage. Then, as portions of the data are read into the core memory and calculations are performed, more data are read from tape to core and more calculations are performed, until all the data have been processed. The machine takes its instruction words only from the inner memory; if instructions are stored on tape, they must be transferred into the inner memory before they are performed by the computer.

An instruction word in a digital machine generally consists of several sections. The number of divisions in the word depends on the type of computer. Because of its wide usage and simplicity, we will describe what are

---

† Some of the new computers will handle words of different lengths, in which case the "basic word" is generally considered to be the word normally handled as a unit. Some computers have completely variable word lengths.

Raytheon
7180

FIG. 9·1 Instruction-word format for Raytheon 7180.

called *single-address instruction words* in this and the following sections, leaving more complicated formats to later sections. The single-address instruction word is widely used in microcomputers and minicomputers, as well as in many of the larger computers, and serves as a good basis for introducing control unit operations. Basically, each single-address instruction word contains two sections: the *operation code* (OP code), which defines the instruction to be performed, such as addition, subtraction, etc.; and the *address part,* which contains the location of the number to be added or subtracted or otherwise used (the operand).

If 5 binary digits of the word are used to specify which instruction is to be performed, there must be some coding system to indicate each of the various instructions. Since 5 bits have been allocated to designate which instruction is to be performed, 2^5, or 32, different instructions could be used, and a different binary number would be associated with each. Each type of instruction will then have a specific OP code consisting of the set of binary digits which the machine is to interpret.

The Raytheon 7180 is an example of a single-address binary machine having 32 basic instructions and an OP code of 5 binary digits packaged in a 21-binary-digit word. Fifteen binary digits are used for the address of the operand in the memory, and a single digit is used to indicate whether or not an index register is to be used. (This subject will be discussed later.) The basic format of the instruction word for this computer is such that the operation code occupies digits 1 through 5; digit 6 is used to indicate whether or not the particular instruction is indexed; and digits 7 through 21 are used to designate the address in memory of the word to be used. (See Fig. 9·1.)

Six typical instructions in this machine are shown in Table 9·1, and the effect of each instruction in the machine is shown in the same table. If, for instance, the machine reads a binary instruction word from the memory for which the five OP-code digits are 00100, the machine will multiply the number which is in the accumulator of the machine when the instruction word is read by the number located at the address given by binary digits 6 through 20 in the instruction word.

The DDP-24 is manufactured by Minneapolis-Honeywell and is a medium-sized single-address computer. The complete set of instructions for the DDP-24 is shown in Table 9·2. In this table, A refers to the accumulator, B to the register used to store the least significant digits of products, etc., and EA is the address portion of a computer instruction word. Octal OP codes, as well as the mnemonic codes, are given. To explain a typical instruction, the addition instruction has an octal OP code of 10; so the binary code is 001000. The mnemonic code is ADD, and the notation (A) + (EA)

TABLE 9·1 INSTRUCTIONS AND OPERATION CODE FOR RAYTHEON 7180 COMPUTER

OP CODE (MNEMONIC CODE)	OP CODE IN BINARY	MEANING OF INSTRUCTION
ADD	00010	Adds the number at the address in memory given by the address part of the instruction word to the number in the accumulator and stores that number in the accumulator.
MUL	00100	Multiplies number at the address in memory given by address part of the instruction word by the number in the accumulator, and stores the most significant digits and sign in the accumulator and the least significant digits in an MQ register.
DVD	00101	The combined number formed by the accumulator and MQ register is divided by the number at the address given in the address part of the instruction word. The quotient replaces the number originally in the MQ, and the remainder replaces the number originally in the accumulator.
STO	11000	The contents of the accumulator are stored in the location given by the address part of the instruction word.
AND	01111	Each bit in the accumulator is AND-ed with the corresponding bit of the word located at the address in memory given by the address part of the instruction word. The resulting bits replace the original contents of the accumulator.
CLA	00001	Loads the number at the address in memory given by the address part of the instruction word into the accumulator.

$\rightarrow$ (A) says that the sum of the accumulator plus the word in memory at the address given by EA (which is the location given by the address part of the instruction word) is placed in the accumulator.†

---

† The parentheses are used to indicate "the contents of," therefore, the notation (A) means "the contents of the accumulator" and the notation (A) → (B) means "the contents of register *A* are transferred into register *B*." [This is often written (A) → B, but Honeywell uses (A) → (B).]

TABLE 9·2 OPERATION CODES FOR DDP-24 COMPUTER

	OP CODE MNEMONIC	OCTAL	FUNCTION	X	I	O'F
LOAD & STORE	CRA	60	$0 \to (A)$			
	IAB	57	$(A) \quad (B)$			
	LDA	24	$(EA) \to (A)$	X	X	
	LDB	23	$(EA) \to (B)$	X	X	
	STA	05	$(A) \to (EA)$	X	X	
	STB	03	$(B) \to (EA)$	X	X	
	STC	04	$(A)_{1-9} \to (EA)_{1-9}$	X	X	
	STD	06	$(A)_{10-24} \to (EA)_{10-24}$	X	X	
	TAB	55	$(A) \to (B)$			
ARITHMETIC	ADD	10	$(A) + (EA) \to (A)$	X	X	X
	ADM	20	$(A) + |(EA)| \to (A)$	X	X	X
	BCD*	36	(EA) BCD $\to (A)$ Binary	X	X	
	BIN*	37	(EA) Binary $\to (A)$ BCD	X	X	(X)
	DIV	35	$(A, B)/(EA) \to$ (quotient to B, remainder to A)	X	X	(X)
	MPY	34	$(B) \times (EA) \to (A, B)$			X
	RND	62	$(A) + 1 \to (A)$, if $(B)_2 = 1$			
	SBM	21	$(A) - |(EA)| \to (A)$	X	X	X
	SUB	11	$(A) - (EA) \to (A)$	X	X	X
LOGICAL	ANA	15	$(A) \cap (EA) \to (A)$	X	X	
	ERA	17	$(A) \oplus (EA) \to (A)$	X	X	
	ORA	16	$(A) \cup (EA) \to (A)$	X	X	
SHIFT	ALS**	41	Shift $(A)_{2-24}$ left, positions specified by $(EA)_{19-24}$	X	X	
	ARS**	40	Shift $(A)_{2-24}$ right, positions specified by $(EA)_{19-24}$	X	X	
	LGL**	47	Shift $(A)_{1-24}$ left, positions specified by $(EA)_{19-24}$	X	X	
	LLR**	43	Rotate $(A, B)_{1-24}$ left, positions specified by $(EA)_{19-24}$	X	X	
	LLS**	45	Shift $(A, B)_{2-24}$ left, positions specified by $(EA)_{19-24}$	X	X	
	LRR**	42	Rotate $(A, B)_{1-24}$ right, positions specified by $(EA)_{19-24}$	X	X	
	LRS**	44	Shift $(A, B)_{2-24}$ right, positions specified by $(EA)_{19-24}$	X	X	
	NRM	46	Shift $(A, B)_{2-24}$ left until $(A)_2 = 1$, See Manual			
	SCL**	65	Shift $(A, B)_{2-24}$ left and decrement index register, positions specified by $(EA)_{19-24}$	X	X	
	SCR**	64	Shift $(A, B)_{2-24}$ right and increment index register, positions specified by $(EA)_{19-24}$	X	X	

X = indexable
I = indirectly addressable
O'F = overflow possible
(X) = improper divide possible   *Optional.
$\cap$ = symbol for AND   **If indirect address not specified (I = O),
$\cup$ = symbol for OR   address portion of instruction is effective operand.

| | OP CODE | | FUNCTION | X I O'F |
	MNEMONIC	OCTAL		
JUMP	JMP	74	Jump to EA	X X
	JOF	73	Jump to EA, if overflow indicator set	X X
	JPL	70	Jump to EA, if sign $(A) = 0$	X X
	JRT	25	Jump to location specified by $(EA)_{11-24}$, restore interrupt	X X
	JST	27	Jump to EA + 1 and store location in (EA)	X X
	JZE	71	Jump to EA, if $(A) = 0$	X X
	SKG	12	Skip next instruction, if $(A) > (EA)$	X X
	SKQ	13	Skip next instruction, if $(A) \geq (EA)$	X X
INDEX	ADX**	54	$(X) + (EA)_{11-24} \rightarrow (X)$	X X
	IRX	67	$(EA)_{11-24} + 1 \rightarrow (EA)_{11-24}$ and (X)	X X
	JIX	72	Jump to EA, if $(X) \neq 0$	X X
	JXI	75	$(X) + 1 \rightarrow (X)$, Jump to EA, if resultant $(X) = 0$	X X
	LDX**	56	$(EA)_{11-24} \rightarrow (X)$	X X
	STX	66	$(X) \rightarrow (EA)_{11-24}$	X X
	TAX	63	$(A)_{11-24} \rightarrow (X)_{11-24}$	
INPUT/OUTPUT	DMB	32	Dump memory starting at EA	X X
	FMB	31	Load memory starting at EA	X X
	INA**	52	Input $\rightarrow (A)$, according to mask in (EA)	X X
	INM	07	Input $\rightarrow (EA)$	X X
	ITC**	51	Inhibit or enable interrupt, according to mask in (EA)	
	OCP**	53	Select I/O, according to mask in (EA)	X X
	OTA**	50	$(A) \rightarrow$ Output, according to mask in (EA)	X X
	OTM	22	$(EA) \rightarrow$ Output	X X
	SKS**	61	Skip next instruction, if sense line not set sense line specified by $(EA)_{11-24}$	X X
CONTROL	HLT	00	Stop computer operation until start button pressed	
	NOP	77	Perform no operation	
	XEC	02	Execute instruction at EA	X X

Word formats

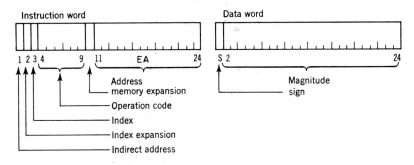

411

As a further example, JMP with a binary OP code of 111100 causes the machine to take the next instruction word from the address given by the address portion of the JMP instruction word. Notice that the multiplication instruction multiplies a word in memory by the B register, not the accumulator, which was a characteristic of many earlier IBM machines.

Subscripts such as in $A_{2\text{-}24}$ are very useful notational devices. They indicate the bits of the register involved, so that, for instance, STD in Table 9·2 causes only the bits in the tenth to the twenty-fourth positions in the accumulator to be stored at the location given by the address (EA) in the instruction word, and these go into the tenth through the twenty-fourth positions in that word of the memory.

9•2 INSTRUCTION-CYCLE AND EXECUTION-CYCLE ORGANIZATION OF CONTROL REGISTERS

A digital computer proceeds through the execution of a program with a basic rhythm or pattern in its sequence of operation which is produced by the necessity of drawing both instructions and operands from the same memory. Let us examine the single-address type of computer, bearing in mind that the two-address, as well as three- and four-address machines, operate in essentially the same manner and require essentially the same control registers, although the pattern of the execution of an instruction differs according to the number of operands in the particular machine and the format of the instruction word.

The basic pattern or sequence of operations for most instructions in a digital machine of the single-address type consists of an alternation of a time period called the *instruction cycle,* followed by a period of time called the *execution cycle.* During the instruction cycle, an instruction word is obtained from the memory and interpreted, and the memory is given the address of the operand to be used. During the execution cycle, the memory obtains the operand to be used (for instance, the multiplier if the instruction is a multiplication, or the augend if the instruction is an addition), and the operation called out by the instruction word is then performed upon this operand.

Almost all machines now being made use either a core memory or an IC memory for the storing of both instruction words and operands or data. There will be no harm in assuming that we have a core memory since most types of memory operate with essentially the same characteristics when viewed externally.

The cycle time for a core memory is fixed, and once we tell the memory that we wish to read from it or write into it, a certain period of time will elapse before we can instruct the memory that we are again ready to read or write. If we are reading from the memory, the selected word will be delivered a short time after the memory has been given the address of the word to be read and instructed to read. During the remaining portion of the memory cycle, the memory will rewrite this word into the location from which it was read.

If the memory is to be written into, the word to be written as well as the address at which we wish to write it must be given the memory. A WRITE signal must also be given, telling it to write this word at the location or address which we have given. As discussed in Chap. 7, the address at which we write into or read from in the memory is given by means of a memory address register, and the word to be written into the memory is delivered to a register called the memory buffer register; when we read from the memory, the word is also delivered to a memory buffer register.

During the instruction cycle, the instruction word is transferred by the memory into the memory buffer register. To obtain this word, we must tell the memory to read and give the memory the address to read from. During the instruction cycle the instruction word which was read into the memory buffer register is interpreted, and the address of the operand to be used is delivered to the memory address register. For many instructions this will be a part of the instruction word, the address part of which was read from the memory during the instruction cycle. During the execution time or execution cycle, an operand is obtained from the memory or written into the memory, depending upon the instruction word which was interpreted during the previous instruction time period.

If the instruction being interpreted is an ADD instruction, the location of the augend is given in the address part of the instruction word, and this address must be given the memory address register. The memory then obtains the desired word from the memory and puts it into the memory buffer register. The computer must add this word to the word already in the accumulator. Afterward, the computer must give the memory the address of the next instruction word to be used and command the memory to read this word.

Notice that the machine alternates between instruction cycles and execution cycles. Also notice that during an execution cycle, we must store somewhere in our control circuitry the OP code of the instruction word which was read from the memory, the address of the operand to be used (which was a part of the instruction word read from the memory), and also the address of the next instruction word to be read from the memory and used.

As a result, there are several registers which are basic to almost every digital computer. These are shown in Fig. 9·2 and are described as follows:

1. *The instruction counter*   This is a counter of the same length as the address section of the instruction word. The counter can be either reset or incremented. A typical logic diagram for the instruction counter could consist of the counter shown in Fig. 4·10(a), having a RESET line and an increment or enable line. This counter keeps track of the instructions to be used in the program, so that normally, during each instruction time, the counter will be incremented by 1, which will give the location of the next instruction word to be used in the program. If, however, the instruction is a BRANCH or JUMP instruction, we may wish to place the *B* register's con-

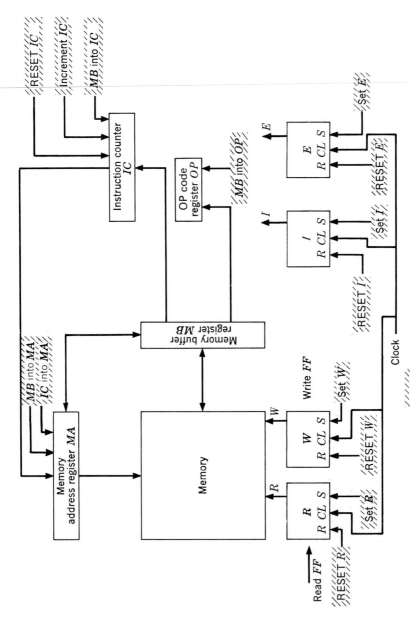

Note: Control signals are shaded thus Set E

FIG. 9 • 2 Control registers.

tents into this counter, and the MB INTO IC line does this. The counter can be reset to 0 when a program is started.†

It must also be possible to transfer the contents of this counter into the memory address register, which is used to locate a word in memory. Normally, the instruction counter will be increased by 1 during the performance of each instruction, and the contents of the counter will be transferred into the memory address register at the beginning of each instruction time.

2. *The OP-code register*   When an instruction word is read from the memory, the OP-code section of this word must be stored in order to determine what instruction is to be performed. If the computer has an OP code with a length of 5 binary digits, the operation register will be 5 binary digits in length and will contain the OP-code part of the instruction word which is read from the memory. We must therefore be able to transfer a section of the memory buffer register into the OP-code register during the instruction time period.

3. *The memory address register*   This register contains the location of the word in memory to be read or the location to be written into.

4. *R flip-flop*   When this flip-flop is turned on, it tells the memory to read a word. (The flip-flop can be turned off shortly thereafter, for it need not be on during the entire memory cycle.)

5. *W flip-flop*   Turning this flip-flop on tells the memory to write the word located in the memory buffer register at the location given by the memory address register.

6. *I flip-flop*   When this flip-flop is on, the computer is in an instruction cycle.

7. *E flip-flop*   When this flip-flop is on, the machine is in an execution cycle.

9•3 SEQUENCE OF OPERATION OF CONTROL REGISTERS

Let us further consider the construction of the control circuitry of a digital computer, again using the block diagram of the control registers, memory, memory address register, and memory buffer register shown in Fig. 9•2.

The control signals necessary to the operation of this small single-address machine are also shown on the diagram and are as follows: There is a RESET IC line which will clear the instruction counter to 0. (This is often connected to a push button which clears the counter when the program is to be started.) There is an MB INTO IC control signal which causes the contents of the memory buffer register to be transferred into the instruction counter, and there is an INCREMENT IC control signal which causes the instruction coun-

---

† Most machines make it possible to load a selected address into the operation counter and thereby start the machine at that selected address.

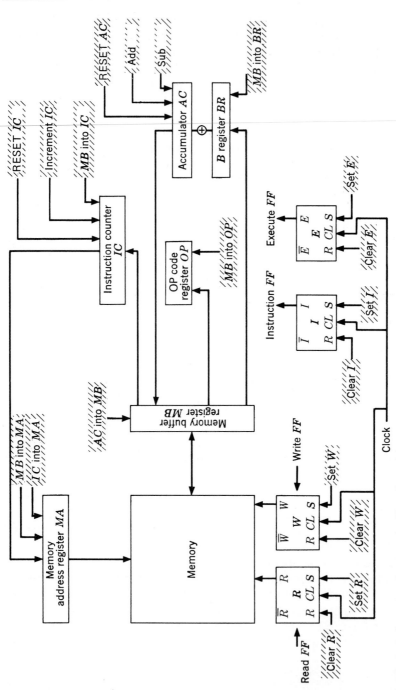

FIG. 9 • 3 Control registers and arithmetic registers.

ter to be incremented by 1. Another control signal is the MB INTO OP, which transfers the first five digits of the memory buffer register that contains the operation code of an instruction word into the five flip-flops in the operation register. The memory address register has two control signals. The IC INTO MA control signal causes the contents of the instruction counter to be transferred into the memory address register, and the MB INTO MA control signal causes the last 16 digits of the memory buffer register (which constitute the address part of an instruction word) to be transferred into the memory address register.

During each instruction cycle of the machine we must first turn the READ flip-flop on, and at the same time (or earlier) transfer the contents of the instruction counter into the memory address register. The memory will now read an instruction word into the memory buffer register, after which time we can enable the MB INTO OP line, transferring the OP-code section of the instruction word into the OP-code register. The next actions which the machine will take will now be dependent upon the contents of the OP-code register.

9•4 CONTROLLING ARITHMETIC OPERATIONS

Consider the problem of directing the arithmetic element as it performs an instruction word. Let us add an accumulator and a B register to the registers in Fig. 9·2, thus forming the block diagram shown in Fig. 9·3. Five more control signals are required to perform such instructions as add, subtract, clear and add, and store:

1. RESET ACC   This signal sets all the flip-flops in the accumulator to 0.
2. ADD   This signal causes the B register to be added to the accumulator and the sum transferred into the accumulator.
3. SUBTRACT   This signal causes the B register to be subtracted from the accumulator and the difference placed in the accumulator.
4. MB INTO BR   This signal transfers the memory buffer register into the B register.
5. AC INTO MB   This causes the contents of the accumulator to be transferred into the memory buffer register.

Figure 9·4 shows a single accumulator flip-flop and a single B-register flip-flop, along with the control signals and gates required for these operations. The accumulator and B register are basically composed of as many of these blocks as there are bits in the basic computer word. (The carry into the least significant bit is connected to the SUBTRACT signal when 2s complement addition is used, or to the carry-out of the sign digit when the 1s complement system is used.)

One further thing is needed. We must distribute our control signals in an orderly manner; some sort of a time base which will indicate where we are in

FIG. 9·4 Accumulator flip-flop and *B*-register flip-flop with control signals.

FIG. 9 • 5 Timing signal distributor.

the sequence of operations to be performed is required. To do this, each memory cycle is broken into four equal time periods, the first of which we call T_0, the second T_1, the third T_2, and the fourth T_3. If we are in the first of these time periods, we need a signal which will tell us it is now time T_0; then, during the second period, we need a signal which will tell us it is time T_1, etc.

Figure 9 · 5 shows a way of generating such timing signals. There is a clock signal input, and the clock is assumed to be running so that during a memory cycle we obtain four clock pulses. If it requires 2 μs to read into or write from the memory, a clock pulse should be generated every $\frac{1}{2}$ μs. Therefore the clock will run at a rate of 2 MHz.

The circuit has four output lines designated T_0, T_1, T_2, and T_3. When the machine is in time period T_0, the output line T_0 will carry a 1 signal and T_1, T_2, and T_3 will be 0s; at time T_1 only, line T_1 will have a 1 signal on it, etc.

Let us now write, in a short table, the squence of operations which must occur during each of the ADD, SUBTRACT, CLEAR AND ADD, and STORE instructions. Notice that when the instruction-cycle flip-flop I is on, the operations during times T_0 and T_1 are always the same. In Table 9 · 3 the control signal to be turned on or made a 1 is listed to the left, and what the signal does is listed to the right.

From this table of operations, it is possible to design the control section of this small machine. The inputs are the operation code stored in the OP-code register, the timing-signal distributor, and the I and E flip-flops.

TABLE 9·3 SEQUENCING OF CONTROL SIGNALS

ADD	LIST OF CONTROL SIGNALS TO BE TURNED ON	COMMENTS
I and T_0	SET R	Tells memory to read instruction word.
I and T_1	MB INTO OP, RESET R	Transfers OP-code part of instruction word into OP-code register; turns READ flip-flop off.
I and T_2	INCREMENT IC	Adds one to the instruction counter, preparing for the next instruction.
I and T_3	MB INTO MA, RESET I, SET E	Transfers the address part of the instruction word (which is in the memory buffer register) into the memory address register. Puts the computer in the execution cycle.
E and T_0	SET R	Turns the READ flip-flop on, telling the memory to read a word.
E and T_1	MB INTO BR, RESET R	Transfers the contents of the memory buffer register into the B register. Since the memory buffer register now contains what was read from the memory, the subtrahend is transferred into the B register; also turns READ flip-flop off.
E and T_2	ADD	The contents of the B register are subtracted from the accumulator and the difference placed in the accumulator.
E and T_3	IC INTO MA, SET I, RESET E	The contents of the instruction counter are transferred into the memory address register giving the location of the next instruction word to the memory. The instruction-cycle flip-flop is turned on and the execution-cycle flip-flop turned off.

CLEAR AND ADD	LIST OF CONTROL SIGNALS TO BE TURNED ON	COMMENTS
I and T_0	SET R	Tells memory to read instruction word.
I and T_1	MB INTO OP, RESET R	Transfers OP-code part of instruction word into OP-code register; turns READ flip-flop off.
I and T_2	INCREMENT IC	Add one to the instruction counter, preparing for the next instruction.
I and T_3	MB INTO MA, RESET I, SET E	Transfers the address part of the instruction word (which is in the memory buffer register) into the memory address register.
E and T_0	SET R	Turns the READ flip-flop on telling the memory to read a word.

420

CLEAR AND ADD	LIST OF CONTROL SIGNALS TO BE TURNED ON	COMMENTS
E and T_1	MB INTO BR, RESET AC, RESET R	Transfers the memory buffer register into the B register and also clears the accumulator so if the B register is now added to the accumulator, the accumulator will contain the word read from memory.
E and T_2	ADD	The contents of the accumulator are added to the B register and the sum placed in the accumulator.
E and T_3	IC INTO MA, SET I, RESET E	The contents of the instruction counter are transferred into the memory address register, giving the location of the next instruction word to the memory. The instruction-cycle flip-flop is turned on and the execution-cycle flip-flop turned off.

SUBTRACT	LIST OF CONTROL SIGNALS TO BE TURNED ON	COMMENTS
I and T_0	SET R	Tells memory to read instruction word.
I and T_1	MB INTO OP, RESET R	Transfers OP-code part of instruction word into OP-code register; turns READ flip-flop off.
I and T_2	INCREMENT IC	Adds one to the instruction counter, preparing for the next instruction.
I and T_3	MB INTO MA, RESET I, SET E	Transfers the address part of the instruction word (which is in the memory buffer register) into the memory address register. Puts the computer in the execution cycle.
E and T_0	SET R	Turns the READ flip-flop on, telling the memory to read a word.
E and T_1	MB INTO BR, RESET R	Transfers the contents of the memory buffer register into the B register. Since the memory buffer register now contains what was read from the memory, the subtrahend is transferred into the B register; also turns READ flip-flop off.
E and T_2	SUB	The contents of the B register are subtracted from the accumulator and the difference placed in the accumulator.
E and T_3	IC INTO MA, SET I, RESET E	The contents of the instruction counter are transferred into the memory address register giving the location of the next instruction word to the memory. The instruction-cycle flip-flop is turned on and the execution-cycle flip-flop turned off.

Table 9.3 (*Continued*)

STORE	LIST OF CONTROL SIGNALS TO BE TURNED ON	COMMENTS
I and T_0	SET R	Tells memory to read instruction word.
I and T_1	MB INTO OP, RESET R	Transfers OP-code part of instruction word into OP-code register; turns READ flip-flop off.
I and T_2	INCREMENT IC	Add one to the instruction counter, preparing for the next instruction.
I and T_3	MB INTO MA, RESET I, SET E	Transfers the address part of the instruction word (which is in the memory buffer register) into the memory address register.
E and T_0	SET W, AC INTO MB	Transfers word to be read into memory from accumulator into the memory buffer register.
E and T_1	RESET W	Turns WRITE flip-flop off.
E and T_2		Contents of memory buffer register written into memory.
E and T_3	IC INTO MA, SET I, RESET E	The contents of the instruction counter are transferred into the memory address register, giving the location of the next instruction word to the memory. The instruction-cycle flip-flop is turned on and the execution-cycle flip-flop turned off.

Notice, for instance, that when it is time T_0 and we are in an instruction cycle, we always turn the READ flip-flop on, telling the memory to read the instruction word located at the address in the memory address register. Then we assume that the memory places this word in the memory buffer register before time T_1; so at time T_1 we transfer the OP-code part of the instruction word into the OP-code register. These two facts tell us that we should logically AND the output line T_0 from the timing-signal distributor with the 1 output of the I flip-flop, and connect the $T_0 \cdot I$ signal to the SET input of the READ flip-flop; and then we should connect a $T_1 \cdot I$ signal to the control line which transfers the first 5 bits of the memory buffer register into the OP register. This is shown in Fig. 9·6.

What happens next is always dependent on the OP-code register; so we now connect a decoder or selector matrix with $2^5 = 32$ outputs to that register (assuming we will use all the combinations by adding more instructions). We then have a set of signal lines, so that line 00000 = ADD will carry a 1 signal when we are adding (since the operation code for ADD is 00000); 00001 = SUB will carry a 1 if, and only if, we are subtracting, since the OP code for subtract is 00001; 00010 = CLA will be a 1 only when we clear and add, etc. We combine these lines and the timing-signal distributor lines and the I and E flip-flop lines to give us all the control signals needed to run the

FIG. 9 · 6 Control circuitry for four-instruction computer.

machine. Figure 9·6 shows the complete control circuitry required. A comparison of this figure with the timing and control-signal chart will show how the control circuitry words and signals are manufactured when they are needed.

More instructions can be added by adding to the timing and control-signal chart and also by adding the required gates to the control circuitry. Analyzing the machine in this way, we can readily see how the control circuitry directs the operations performed in the machine, alternating the acquiring of instructions from the memory and the performance of the instructions.

9•5 TYPICAL SEQUENCE OF OPERATIONS

It will be instructive to analyze the control circuitry in Fig. 9·6 during both an ADD instruction and a STORE instruction. Each instruction will be started with the I (instruction cycle) flip-flop on, and with the timing-signal distributor having an output on line T_0 so that the AND gate at the upper right of the figure will be turned on by I and T_0, thus setting the READ flip-flop to the 1 state and initiating a READ from the memory. At this time, the memory address register is assumed to have the address of the instruction which will be read into the memory buffer register.

By time T_1, the word read from the memory will have been read into the memory buffer register, so that when we have the control state I and T_1, the contents of the memory buffer register which constitute the OP-code section of the instruction will be transferred into the OP-code register, and the computer will be in a position to decode the OP code and determine what instruction is to be performed.

At time I and T_2 the instruction counter is incremented by 1, so that the instruction counter now contains the address of the next instruction to be read from the memory. The AND gate connected to the I and T_2 input signals is used in turn on the INCREMENT IC control signal, and its output is designated with the name of the control signal.

Similarly, at time I and T_3, the memory buffer register is transferred into the memory address register by the MB INTO MA signal, thus transferring the address part of the instruction word into the memory address register. The next word read from the memory or written into the memory will then be at the address designated by the address part of the instruction word which was just read from the memory.

At the same time, the instruction-cycle flip-flop is cleared by the RESET I signal and the execution flip-flop is set on by the SET E signal, thus changing the state of the machine from an instruction cycle to an execution cycle.

At time E and T_0, then, during an ADD instruction, we set the R flip-flop on, thus telling the memory to read the word at the address currently in the memory address register. In this case, this address will be the address part of the instruction word which is being executed. Then, at time E and T_1, we transfer the contents of the memory buffer register into the B register. The memory buffer register at that time contains the word which has been read from the memory, so that we now have the word which has been addressed by the instruction word in the B register for the addition. At the same time, we reset the READ flip-flop.

Notice that the RESET R and RESET W lines are used to reset both the READ and the WRITE flip-flop simultaneously. There is no harm in resetting both flip-flops, since only one will be on at any given time.

If the instruction is an ADD instruction at time E and T_2, we shall add the contents of the B register to the contents of the accumulator. The B register contains the word which has been read from the memory and the accumulator has not been changed, so their sum will be transferred into the accumulator. Thus, the sum of the word read from the memory and the previous contents of the accumulator will be placed in the accumulator. Then, at time E and T_3, we transfer the instruction counter into the memory address register (thus giving the address of the next instruction to be performed to the memory), at the same time clearing the EXECUTE flip-flop, setting the instruction cycle flip-flop on, and changing the machine from an execution cycle to an instruction cycle.

Since the I flip-flop is on and it is time T_0, the SET R control line will now go high, thus telling the memory to read a word. The next instruction word will be read from the memory and can then be interpreted.

Let us also examine the operation of the STORE instruction which was just described. When the instruction flip-flop is on and we are in an instruction cycle when time T_0 arrives, the R flip-flop will be set on, telling the memory to read just as for an addition, subtraction, or clear and add; and the same thing will happen during time I and T_1. Since the memory-buffer-register flip-flops now contain the OP-code of the instruction at time I and T_1, it will be transferred into the OP-code register.

At time I and T_2, we will increment the instruction counter so that the address of the next instruction in memory now lies in the instruction counter; and at time I and T_3, we will reset the instruction flip-flop and turn on the execution-cycle flip-flop, thus putting the machine in an execution cycle.

At time E and T_1, however, if the instruction is a STORE instruction, we will set the WRITE flip-flop on instead of the READ flip-flop, thus initiating a WRITE into the memory. We will also transfer the contents of the accumulator into the memory buffer register, so that the word written into the memory will be the current contents of the accumulator register, and so that after the WRITE cycle has been terminated, the accumulator will have been written into the memory at the address which was given by the instruction word.

At time E and T_1, we reset the WRITE flip-flop, since we have already told the memory to write; nothing need be done at E and T_2, for we are now writing the word into the memory. At time E and T_3 the instruction counter is transferred into the memory address register by the IC INTO MA control signal, thus giving the address of the next instruction to the memory. The instruction-cycle flip-flop is turned on, and the execution-cycle flip-flop turned off, thus turning the machine to the instruction-cycle state. The machine will now execute an instruction cycle by reading the next instruction word from the memory, interpreting it, and continuing onward in the program.

FIG. 9•7 General configuration of control circuitry.

The preceding example demonstrates how it is possible to design a machine which will execute a given sequence of operations and thereby cause the machine to perform each instruction word which is read from the memory. Although only four instructions were demonstrated in this particular example, more instructions can be added in exactly the same manner by simply writing down what must be done when an instruction word is read from the memory, listing the operations which must be performed, and providing gates which will generate the control signals necessary to the performance of each instruction. Subsequent sections will discuss shifting instructions, branching instructions, floating-point instructions, and indexing instructions. All these may be incorporated into the machine shown by simply adding gates to the control circuitry and providing for the additional gates necessary for the transfers and operations between the registers of the machine.

The general form of the control-signal generating scheme is shown in Fig. 9·7. It shows a timing-pulse distributor with eight different time divisions, in which case each time period would be one-eighth of the memory-cycle time.

9•6 BRANCH, SKIP, OR JUMP INSTRUCTIONS

The BRANCH, JUMP, or SKIP instruction varies from the normal instruction in several ways.† For single-address machines, only one word, the instruction

---

†A survey indicates that some manufacturers call these instructions BRANCH instructions, others call them TRANSFER instructions, while still others call them SKIP or JUMP instructions. All are the same thing.

word, must be located in memory. Also, the contents of the instruction counter may be modified instead of being simply increased by 1. There are two types of BRANCH instructions, conditional and unconditional. For the unconditional BRANCH instruction, the contents of the address portion of the memory buffer register are always transferred into the instruction counter. The next instruction performed will then be the instruction at the location indicated by the address section of the instruction word. In most single-address machines, however, the conditional BRANCH instruction will cause the machine to branch only if the number stored in the accumulator register of the arithmetic element is negative. If the number in the accumulator is positive, the contents of the instruction counter will simply be increased by 1, and the next instruction will be taken in the normal order.

During a conditional BRANCH instruction, the sign bit of the accumulator of the arithmetic element must be examined by control circuitry. If the sign bit is a 1, the number stored is negative, and so the number in the address part of the instruction word is transferred into the instruction counter. If the sign bit is a 0, a 1 is added to the instruction counter and the computer proceeds.

To demonstrate how a typical BRANCH-ON-MINUS instruction (BRM) operates in a single-address computer, we will modify the control circuitry shown in Fig. 9·6 so that the small machine will also include a BRM instruction. Let us give the operation code 00100 to BRM, so that the line beneath the 00011 = STO line will be high from the decoder attached to the OP-code register in Fig. 9·6 when a BRM instruction is in the register.

The first two time periods of the instruction cycle are the same for all instructions. First the memory is told to read, and then the instruction word is read from memory into the memory buffer register. The OP-code part is then transferred into the OP-code register, so that, after time T_1 and the beginning of time T_2, the line 00100 = BRM will be high and all the other output lines from the decoder will be low. Now, let us make a small table for a BRM instruction showing what must be done in order to carry out this instruction. Table 9·4 shows the steps which must be taken.

If at time T_2 during the instruction cycle, a BRM instruction OP code is in the OP-code register, one of two things must happen. Either we wish to increment the instruction counter and give this number as the address of the next instruction to be taken from the memory, or we wish to transfer the contents of the address portion of the instruction word into the instruction counter. Which of the two choices we take depends upon the sign bit of the accumulator, called AC_0. If the accumulator contains a negative number, it will have a 1 in AC_0, and if it contains a positive number, it will have a 0 in flip-flop 0. Therefore, if I AND T_2 AND AC_0, we want to increment the instruction counter; and if I AND T_2 AND AC_0 happens to be the case, we wish to transfer the memory buffer register into the instruction counter. This is shown in the table. During time T_3 of this instruction cycle, we want to transfer the instruction counter into the memory address register. We do not need to put the machine in an execution cycle, but can simply continue on to another instruction cycle, taking the word at the address which has been transferred into the memory address register as the next instruction. Therefore we do not clear the instruction-cycle

TABLE 9·4

BRANCH ON MINUS	LIST OF CONTROL SIGNALS TO BE TURNED ON	COMMENTS
I and T_0	SET R	Tells memory to read instruction word.
I and T_1	MB INTO OP, RESET R	Transfers OP-code part of instruction word into OP-code register; turns READ flip-flop off.
I and T_2 and $\overline{AC_0}$	INCREMENT IC	If the sign digit of the accumulator AC_0 is a 0, we want to increment the instruction counter and use its contents as the address of the next instruction.
I and T_2 and AC_0	MB INTO IC	If the sign digit of the accumulator is a 1, the accumulator is negative, and we want to use the address in the instruction word as the address of the next instruction word.
I and T_3	IC INTO MA	This transfers the instruction counter into the memory address register. Notice the E flip-flop is not turned on as we are ready to read another instruction word; an execute cycle is not needed.

FIG. 9•8 Modification of control circuitry for BRANCH instruction.

flip-flop or put a 1 in the execution-cycle flip-flop, but simply transfer the instruction counter into the memory address register.

The control circuitry which will implement these operations is shown in Fig. 9·8. The meaning of this is that the two particular AND gates in Fig. 9·6 which are connected to the I, T_2 and I, T_3 inputs will be replaced with the two circuits shown in Fig. 9·8. Notice that this logical circuitry, plus the circuitry in Fig. 9·6, is all that is needed to generate the control signals required for the BRM instruction.

Notice also that a $\overline{\text{BRM}}$ signal (the complement of BRM) is used rather than ORing together the instructions which are not BRM instructions. This saves control circuitry in that $\overline{\text{BRM}}$ can be made as shown in the figure by simply connecting the BRM signal to an inverter and designating this as $\overline{\text{BRM}}$.

Notice that the BRM instruction requires only one access to memory, and therefore only one instruction cycle for its execution.

9•7 SHIFT INSTRUCTIONS

The instructions we have examined to date have been instructions which were always performed within a basic fixed number of memory cycles; that is, the ADD, SUBTRACT, CLEAR AND ADD, and STORE instructions were performed within exactly two memory cycles and the TRANSFER or BRANCH instructions required only one memory cycle. There are several classes or types of instructions which may require several memory cycles, because the instruction cannot be performed within, say, two memory cycles. Typical of these instructions are multiplication and division, which generally require more time than the two memory cycles normally require. Similarly, an instruction such as SHIFT RIGHT or SHIFT LEFT could conceivably be performed in a single-memory cycle, since the operand is in the accumulator when the instruction word is obtained. However, if the instruction calls for a large number of shifts, it may require more than a memory cycle to complete the number of operations required. In this case, we could not initiate another memory cycle until we had finished shifting the requisite number of times. Similarly, for multiplication and division, we could not initiate another memory cycle until we had finished our multiplication and division process.

To implement these types of instructions, we will therefore turn over our control of the machine to a simple control element which is dominated by a counter. This counter will sequence and count the number of steps which must be performed until the instruction has been completed, and will then put the machine in an instruction cycle and tell the memory to read the next instruction word.

The SHIFT-RIGHT instruction consists of two parts, an OP code and an address part. The OP code of 00101 tells the machine to shift the word in the accumulator right the number of times given in the address part, so that if we write 00101 for the OP code in an instruction word and then write 8 in binary form in the address part, the machine has been instructed to shift the binary number in the accumulator right 8 binary digits.

Assuming that we have an accumulator with gates so that we can shift the accumulator digits right as was explained in Chap. 6, all we need is to apply eight consecutive SHIFT-RIGHT control signals to the accumulator and we will have shifted the number right 8 places. Since there are only four pulses per memory cycle, we will not want to use the memory until we have completed our shifting. If, for instance, the instruction said shift right 1, we could finish in one pulse time and start the next instruction cycle immediately after; but if the instruction word said shift right 4, 5, or 15 or more times, we would have to wait until we had completed shifting before we could initiate another instruction cycle and fetch the next instruction word from the memory.

To do this, we first prepare the machine for the shifting operation by incrementing the instruction counter so that the next word obtained from the instruction counter will contain the address of the next instruction word; and in order to count the number of shifts that we perform, we add another register, called the step-counter register, which is a counter that counts downward from a given number to 0. We then transfer the memory-buffer-register address part into the step counter, so that the step counter contains the number of shifts to be performed. Then each time we shift, we decrement the counter by 1, so that when the counter reaches 0, we will have performed the requisite number of shifts.

Figure 9·9 shows two stages of a decrementing counter and also the gates necessary to transfer the memory-buffer-register contents into the step counter, which is designated SC. The two rightmost, or least significant, digits of the counter are shown (SC_{n-1} and SC_n), as are also the two rightmost digits of the memory buffer register (MB_{n-1} and MB_n).

The actual number of stages in the step counter will be determined by the maximum number of shifts which the machine must ever make and, since we will also use the same counter for multiplication and division, by the maximum number of steps which will ever be required to multiply or divide. For a machine containing 21 binary digits in the basic computer word, the counter might well contain five flip-flops. For a machine with a basic computer word of perhaps 35 or 36 binary digits, the step counter might well contain six or even seven flip-flops.

Consider a sequence of operations for a SHIFT instruction. Times I AND T_0 and I AND T_1 are as usual. At I AND T_2 we increment the instruction counter and transfer count to the step counter. At I AND T_3, we set a flip-flop called SR on which tells the machine to start shifting (SR stands for *shift right*). At the same time we clear the I flip-flop, so that the machine is in neither an instruction nor execution cycle, although it is actually executing an instruction. Thus we do not initiate subsequent memory cycles, and the machine effectively freezes in the shifting state until the step counter has counted to 0, indicating that the requisite number of shifts have been performed. (Actually, notice that the step counter counts only to binary 1 rather than to 0 before the order to stop counting is given, for counting when the counter is at 0 would introduce an extra shift.) If we turn the counter SR flip-flop off when the output of the counter is at 00 . . . 001 signal, and if we at the same

FIG. 9 • 9 Two stages of decrementing counter and transfer network.

TABLE 9·5

SHIFT RIGHT	CONTROL SIGNAL TURNED ON	COMMENTS
I and T_0	SET R	Tells memory to read.
I and T_1	MB INTO OP, RESET R	OP code of instruction word is transferred into OP-code register. READ flip-flop is turned off.
I and T_2	INCREMENT IC, MB INTO SC	The instruction counter is prepared to obtain the next instruction word. The address part of the instruction word is transferred into the step counter.
I and T_3	RESET I, SET SR	The instruction cycle flip-flop is turned off. The shift-right flip-flop is turned on.

time turn the I or instruction cycle on, the machine will proceed to the next instruction cycle, fetching the next instruction word from the memory and performing it. Table 9·5 shows this.

When the SR flip-flop is on, it will be necessary to stop the timing-signal distributor; so we arrange to disable this circuit using the SR flip-flop's output for this purpose.

Implementation of the above procedure is straightforward. A three-input AND gate with inputs I, T_3, and $00101 = $ SHR (the output from the decoder in Fig. 9·6) can be used to turn a SR flip-flop on and the stop output from the step counter to turn it off, also turning I on. The input to the clock can be turned off when SR is on.

9 • 8 MICROPROGRAMMING

In the preceding sections, the control signals which sequence the operations which are performed to execute computer instructions were generated using gates. There is another method, called *microprogramming*, which is used to generate the control signals in an orderly fashion. This method generally involves use of a ROM to effectively store the control signals in a manner which will be described.

When a computer is microprogrammed, the individual operations between and on registers are called *microoperations*. For instance, transferring the program counter's contents into the memory address register is a microoperation. Similarly, incrementing the program counter is a microoperation, as is transferring the accumulator's contents into the memory buffer register. In each of these cases a microoperation is initiated by raising a single control signal. Thus, sequencing microoperations involves sequencing the appropriate control signals.

Figuring out a sequence of microoperations to do something is called *microprogramming.* The microprogrammer generally writes the list of operations or *microprogram* using a special language, and quite often a computer program is used to translate this microprogram into a listing which describes the appropriate contents for a ROM which will be used to store the microprogram. The statements the microprogrammer writes are therefore in a microprogramming language. This language can be very primitive or can be very complex. (Variations of the PL/1 compiler language are used in some systems.) Also, ROM manufacturers often provide a service where a punched paper tape with the desired contents of the ROM punched into the tape can be automatically placed in the ROM.

In order to explain microprogramming, we will use the computer layout and instructions in the previous sections and redo the design using a ROM to store the control signals. Therefore, the registers and control signals in Fig. 9·3 will be used in the design. First we note that the basic list of microoperations needed are shown in Table 9·6. Each microoperation is described using a symbolic notation (in effect, a microprogramming language), and

TABLE 9•6 MICROOPERATIONS

MICROOPERATION	CONTROL-SIGNAL NAME	BIT IN READ-ONLY CONTROL MEMORY
$0 \rightarrow IC$	RESET IC	C7
$IC + 1 \rightarrow IC$	INCREMENT IC	C8
$MB \rightarrow IC$	MB INTO IC	C9
$0 \rightarrow AC$	RESET AC	C10
$AC + BR \rightarrow AC$	ADD	C11
$AC - BR \rightarrow AC$	SUBTRACT	C12
$1 \rightarrow E$	SET E	C13
$0 \rightarrow E$	RESET E	C14
$1 \rightarrow I$	SET I	C15
$0 \rightarrow I$	RESET I	C16
$1 \rightarrow W$	SET W	C17
$0 \rightarrow W$	RESET W	C18
$1 \rightarrow R$	SET R	C19
$0 \rightarrow R$	RESET R	C20
$0 \rightarrow AC$	CLEAR AC	C21
$MB_{5-21} \rightarrow MA$	MB INTO MA	C22
$IC \rightarrow MA$	IC INTO MA	C23
$AC \rightarrow MB$	AC INTO MB	C24
$MB_{0-4} \rightarrow OP$	MB INTO OP	C25
$MB \rightarrow BR$	MB INTO BR	C26
$IAR + 1 \rightarrow IAR$	INCREMENT IAR	C27
$C_{0-6} \rightarrow IAR$	C INTO IAR	C28
$OP + IAR + 1 \rightarrow IAR$	ADD OP TO IAR	C29
$0 \rightarrow IAR$	RESET IAR	C30

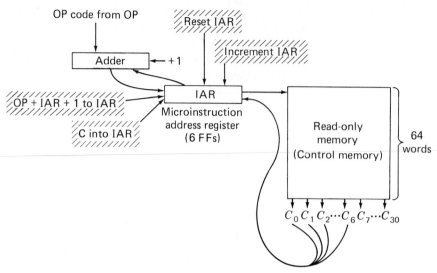

FIG. 9 • 10 Block diagram for control system.

the corresponding control signal which will cause this operation to occur is also shown.

For instance, the microoperation MB → BR, which means "transfer the contents of the memory buffer register (MB) into the *B* register (BR), is caused to occur by raising the control signal MB INTO BR. Notice the considerable similarity between the description in the microprogramming language and the control signal's name. This is a convenient practice although the control signals could be named X_1, A_1, or anything desired, of course.

Figure 9·10 shows a block diagram for the control system as it will be implemented. There is a ROM with 64 locations and 30 bits per address and an address register for this memory called IAR (for microinstruction address register). Each output bit from the ROM is a control signal which will generate a microoperation, and these control signals are named C_0 to C_{30}. Seven of these outputs are special as they are *next addresses* which can be loaded into the IAR and which will be used to sequence the IAR in several cases. (This ROM is often called a *control memory*.)

The operations which can be performed on this control unit are that a 1 can be added to the IAR (in microprogramming language IAR + 1 → IAR, the control signal is called INCREMENT IAR) and the output bits from the control memory labeled C_0 through C_6 can be transferred into the IAR. It is also possible to add the value in OP (see Fig. 9·3) plus 1 to the current contents of the IAR.

Now, the basic scheme is this; The control signals to generate a given computer instruction, say ADD, are stored in a section of the control memory. The IAR sequences through this section and at each location the outputs from the control memory will comprise the control signals. These ROM outputs then replace the control signals generated by the gates in Fig. 9·6.

The first problem is that the IAR must be set to the correct address at the beginning of the section in control memory which contains the bits storing the control signals for the instruction to be executed. To do this, we must examine the OP-code register's contents after we have read the instruction word from memory and then moved the OP-code section in the memory buffer register into the OP-code register. The complete microprogram for the control memory is shown in Table 9·7. Notice that the first microoperations performed are:

LOCATION IN CONTROL MEMORY	MICROPROGRAM
0	$1 \rightarrow R$ $IAR + 1 \rightarrow IAR$
1	$MB_{0-4} \rightarrow OP$ $IAR + 1 \rightarrow IAR$
2	$OP + IAR + 1 \rightarrow IAR$
3	$C_{0-6} \rightarrow IAR$
4	$C_{0-6} \rightarrow IAR$
5	$C_{0-6} \rightarrow IAR$
6	$C_{0-6} \rightarrow IAR$

The operation here is as follows: first the memory is told to read (the prior instruction has loaded the memory address register with the location of the instruction word). The instruction word is then in the memory buffer register when the next microoperation is performed and this microinstruction loads the OP-code register with the first 5 bits in the memory buffer register. Next, this value is added to the IAR register plus 1. Now, if the instruction is an ADD instruction with OP code 00000, then 1 will be added to the current IAR's contents (which will give 3 in decimal). Thus, the next word in the control memory to be accessed would be at location 3, and in location 3 the value for C in the first 7 bits is 20. When C is loaded into the IAR, the next microinstruction word addressed will be that at address 20 in the ROM which contains the first microinstruction in the ADD section. If the instruction in OP was a subtract, the OP code will be 00001 and so the next location in the control memory to be used will be at location 4 decimal, which will cause a transfer to location 30 which contains the microinstructions for the SUBTRACT instruction.

Therefore, an ADD instruction will cause a jump to location 20 (decimal) in the control memory and a SUBTRACT will cause a branch to location 25. In each case these locations begin the section of memory containing the microinstructions which will cause the instruction to be executed.

At the end of each microprogram section which causes an instruction to be executed, the IAR is set to 0 which is the starting point for the operations which lead to reading in the next instruction and branching to the correct section in the control memory to cause the instruction to be executed.

TABLE 9·7 MICROPROGRAM FOR FOUR-INSTRUCTION COMPUTER

LOCATION IN CONTROL MEMORY	MICROPROGRAM	COMMENTS
0	$1 \rightarrow$ R, IAR $+ 1 \rightarrow$ IAR	Tell memory to read, increment IAR.
1	$MB_{0-4} \rightarrow$ OP, IAR $+ 1 \rightarrow$ IAR	Place OP code in instruction in OP.
2	OP $+$ IAR $+ 1 \rightarrow$ IAR	Add OP code to 3, this gives next address in IAR to be used.
3	$C_{0-6} \rightarrow$ IAR C_{0-6} has value 20 decimal	Instruction was ADD go to location 20 in ROM.
4	$C_{0-6} \rightarrow$ IAR C_{0-6} has value 25 decimal	Instruction was SUBTRACT go to location 25 in ROM.
5	$C_{0-6} \rightarrow$ IAR C_{0-6} has value 30 decimal	Instruction was CLA go to location 30 in ROM.
6	$C_{0-6} \rightarrow$ IAR C_{0-6} has value 35 decimal	Instruction was STO go to location 35 in ROM.
7		
8		
9	Left blank to add more instructions	
10		
11		
12		
13		
14		
15		
16		
17		
18		
19		
20	$0 \rightarrow$ I, $1 \rightarrow$ E, $MB_{5-21} \rightarrow$ MA	Begin ADD instruction microoperations; place address of augend in memory address register.

Line	Microoperation	Description
21	$1 \rightarrow R, IC + 1 \rightarrow IC$	Read augend from memory, increment instruction counter.
22	$MB \rightarrow BR, 0 \rightarrow R$	Place augend in B register.
23	$AC + BR \rightarrow AC$	Add and place sum in accumulator.
24	$IC \rightarrow MA, 1 \rightarrow I, 0 \rightarrow E, 0 \rightarrow IAR$	Set up for next instruction by placing instruction counter in memory address register and going to location 0 in control memory.
25	$MB_{5-21} \rightarrow MA, 0 \rightarrow I, 1 \rightarrow E$	Begin subtract instruction microoperations.
26	$1 \rightarrow R, IC + 1 \rightarrow IC$	
27	$MB \rightarrow BR, 0 \rightarrow R$	Place subtrahend in B register.
28	$AC - BR \rightarrow AC$	Subtract and place difference in accumulator.
29	$IC \rightarrow MA, 1 \rightarrow I, 0 \rightarrow E, 0 \rightarrow IAR$	Place address of next instruction word in memory address register and go to 0 in control memory.
30	$MB_{5-21} \rightarrow MA, 0 \rightarrow I, 1 \rightarrow E$	Begin CLA instruction operations.
31	$1 \rightarrow R$	Reset accumulator.
32	$MB \rightarrow BR, 0 \rightarrow AC, 0 \rightarrow R$	Add B register to accumulator.
33	$AC + BR \rightarrow AC$	End CLA instruction; place address of next instruction in memory address register and go to 0 in control memory.
34	$IC \rightarrow MA, 1 \rightarrow I, 0 \rightarrow E, 0 \rightarrow IAR$	Begin STO instruction.
35	$0 \rightarrow I, 1 \rightarrow E, MB_{5-21} \rightarrow MA$	Place accumulator's contents in memory buffer register so it can be stored, tell memory to write.
36	$1 \rightarrow W, AC \rightarrow MB$	
37	$0 \rightarrow W$	Set up for next instruction.
38	$IC + 1 \rightarrow IC$	End of instruction, place address of next instruction in memory address register and go to 0 in control memory.
39	$IC \rightarrow MA, 1 \rightarrow I, 0 \rightarrow E, 0 \rightarrow IAR$	

9·10 VARIATIONS IN MICROPROGRAMMING CONFIGURATIONS

Figure 9·11 shows the microprogram in Table 9·7 stored in a memory. The implementation here has the control memory in Fig. 9·10 with its contents as in Fig. 9·11. This basic configuration is used in most modern microprogrammed computers. There are many variations on this idea, however, and there are many microprogramming languages. The references contain further descriptions and information in this area.

The microprogramming configuration shown in Fig. 9·11 has an output bit from the memory for each control signal. This is called *horizontal microprogramming*. For larger computers there may be many control signals and so there would be many bits in the control memory. (In general, the number of control signals will vary from about 60 for small computers to about 3,000 for the largest machines.) Since this would involve too large a control memory, the control signals are examined and an attempt is made to reduce the number of outputs from the memory. After this is done the resulting configuration is said to use *vertical microprogramming*.

As an example of how the number of outputs might be reduced, consider that in some cases when one control signal is raised, another is always raised and so these two signals could be combined into a single signal.

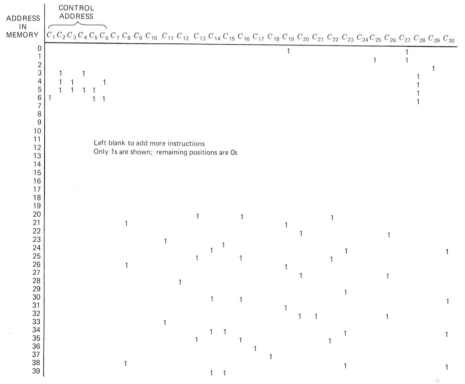

FIG. 9•11 Microprogram in memory. Control address C_0 has 0s in all positions.

In some cases different control signals are never turned on at the same time. If N such signals can be found, then only M control lines, where $2^M \geq N$, will be required and a decoder can be used to provide the necessary control signals. For instance, the ADD, SUB, RESET AC, and MB INTO BR signals are never turned on at the same time, and so two control output lines with a four-output decoder could be used to generate these signals.

When vertical microprogramming is used the system becomes less flexible since, if a microprogram is to be changed or enlarged, fewer options in control signal generation will be available. As a result most commercial machines are arranged so they are somewhere between horizontal and vertical in their construction. (Many schemes have been used and several are described in the questions.)

Microprogramming is widely used in the new computer lines. Since the instruction repertoire for the computer is effectively stored in the ROM, the instructions provided can be changed or added to by changing or adding to the ROM.

Further, microprogramming is useful in *simulating* one computer on another. What this means is that we have a computer which has a basic set of registers and operations between registers and we have the ability to microprogram this computer. Further, we have a second computer with a certain set of instructions and a set of programs written to run on this second computer. We now wish to make the first computer run these programs and deliver the same results as the second computer would have delivered. This is called *simulation,* and the first computer is said to *simulate* the second computer. To do this, we microprogram the simulator computer so that a given instruction has the same effect as the same instruction in the second machine.†

As can be seen, a computer which is microprogrammed can be made to simulate another computer. Clearly some computers have architectures which are much better suited for simulation than others. A computer which is very well adapted for simulation is, for instance, the Burroughs 1700, which has great flexibility in its operations between registers and a considerable set of microoperations available.

The microprograms provided by a manufacturer (or anyone else) to be used on his microprogrammed computer are generally called *firmware*. The instructions which a microprogrammed computer provides can be very complex and can be carefully designed to satisfy the programmer's needs. The primary objections to microprogramming are (1) speed, because the logic gates used in a "conventional" computer will be faster than the ROM in most cases and so the conventional machine may run faster; and (2) the gates can be minimized in number since the instructions are to be fixed and so the total amount of equipment can often be made smaller. (This is not always the case; however, ROMs are quite compact and inexpensive so that the advantage of gates decreases as time passes.) As a result, most large,

---

†This is often called *emulation* when microprogramming is used. It is necessary to rename registers and arrange for other changes to really effect this, but the principle is essentially given here.

fast "super" computers tend to use logic gates for control while the medium and smaller computers now tend to be microprogrammed.

QUESTIONS

1. A single-address, one-instruction-per-word computer has a word length of 22 binary digits. The computer can perform 32 different instructions, and it has three index registers. The inner memory is a 16,000-word magnetic core memory. Draw a diagram of the computer word, allocating space for each part of the basic instruction word (OP-code part, address part, index-register part). Do not use the sign digit (leftmost digit) of the word.

2. The octal code 15 (for ANA) causes the contents of the accumulator to be ANDed, with the contents (word) at the address given in the instruction word in the DDP-24 in Table 9·2. Make bits 1 through 3 each a 0, and also make bit 4 a 0; then write, in binary, the instruction word which will AND the accumulator with the contents of address 16 in the memory.

3. If the basic computer word in a machine has 24 binary digits and we have 55 different instructions, make up an instruction-word format for a single-address machine. How many different memory locations can be directly addressed by the address portion of this computer instruction word? Make up the computer instruction word for a double-address computer with 24 binary digits in the computer word and 55 instructions. How many different locations can now be addressed directly by a single instruction word?

4. If the accumulator of the DDP-24 computer contains all 1s (has a 1 in each bit) and address 30 in the memory contains all 0s, an STC 30_{10} instruction, in which 30 refers to (decimal) location 30, will result in what in location 30 in the memory?

5. Write a simple program, using the operation codes for the Raytheon 7180 computer given in Table 9·1, which will evaluate the polynomial $ax^2 + bx + c$, given that $a, b, c,$ and x are in memory addresses 29, 28, 27, and 26, respectively. Store the result in 30.

6. Would you expect the instruction counter of a single-address computer to have as many bits as the address portion of the computer word? Why?

7. The instruction code for the DDP-24 is listed in Table 9·2, along with a diagram of the basic instruction word. Write in binary form the instruction word which will cause the contents of the B register to be multiplied by the word stored at location 24 of the computer's inner memory.

8. Design a single stage of an accumulator and B register which will add and shift left in one operation (step) or will simply shift left in one step. Use SHIFT LEFT and ADD AND SHIFT LEFT as control signals, a full adder, AND and OR gates, and RS flip-flops.

9. Make out a timing table and modify the control circuitry in Fig. 9·6, including the modification in Fig. 9·8, so that the machine has an unconditional BRANCH instruction BRA, as well as a conditional BRANCH instruction BRM, generating the necessary control signals.

10. Explain the RND instruction in Table 9·2.

11. Write a program for the DDP-24, using the OP codes in Table 9·2, which will evaluate the expression $(x + y^2)/z$, assuming that x, y, and z are at addresses 301, 302, and 303 in the memory. Assume no scaling is necessary and store the result at address 304 in the memory.

12. Explain the STD instruction in Table 9·2. This is called an address-modifying instruction. Why?

13. Explain the SBM instruction in Table 9·2.

14. The microprogramming language outlined in this chapter is generally called a *register-transfer language*. Discuss how you would expand or perhaps improve this language. Do you think that microprogramming in a higher-level language, such as PL/1 or one of its variations, would yield an efficient microprogram in the control memory? Discuss this.

15. Show how to modify Fig. 9·8 so that the BRM instruction becomes a BRP instruction, meaning that the computer jumps or branches when the ACC is positive instead of negative.

16. Show how to generate timing signals (such as, T_0, T_1, T_2, and T_3 in Fig. 9·5) using a shift register with the rightmost stages' outputs connected to the leftmost stages' inputs. This is called a *ring counter*. In what states would you DC set the flip-flops to start?

17. Why is the instruction counter always placed in the memory address register at time T_3 during the execution part of an instruction in Table 9·3?

18. Explain why some instructions require both execution and instruction cycles and some require only instruction cycles. Give examples of both kinds of instruction.

19. Why can the SET W and AC INTO MB control signals be combined in Fig. 9·6?

20. Why can the IC INTO MA, SET I, and CLEAR E control signals be combined in Fig. 9·6?

21. Show how to add a push button connected to a RESET and START wire which will (using DC SETs and DC RESETs on the flip-flops) cause the computer in Fig. 9·6 to start executing a program beginning at location 0 in the memory when depressed.

22. Add a BRANCH ON ZERO instruction similar to that in Table 9·4 and Fig. 9·8, except that the computer branches when accumulator value is all zeros.

23. Add a SHIFT-LEFT instruction to the example computer control using a technique as in Table 9·5 and Figs. 9·8 and 9·9.

24. When microprogramming is used to generate control signals and a ROM is used, how can the instruction repertoire of the computer be changed?

25. In Fig. 9·10 the control signals could be loaded into D flip-flops and the flip-flops' outputs used as the actual control signals. Give advantages and disadvantages of this.

26. Explain the difference between a microoperation and the control signal which implements it.

27. In order to implement BRANCH or JUMP ON ACCUMULATOR NEGATIVE instructions, another control signal C_{30} can be added which, when it is a 1, causes a test of the sign bit of the accumulator and a jump in the control memory to a section of microoperations which cause the desired change in the computer sequence of operations. Design this instruction.

28. In writing microprograms, it is convenient to have an IF microoperation. For instance, to write a microprogram to implement a branch instruction, we might like an IF($AC_0 = 1$) THEN $C_{0-6} \rightarrow$ IAR ELSE IAR + 1 $\rightarrow$ IAR microoperation. This says if AC_0 is a 1, then place the current value of C_0 to C_6 in IAR, which means the next microinstruction will be from the address given in C_0–C_6. If AC_0 is a 0, the next microinstruction will be from the next location in the control store. Write a microprogram for the branch-register-memory instruction using this microoperation.

29. Write a microprogram for a BRP (branch or positive) instruction using the information in the preceding question.

30. Show how to implement the instruction in the preceding question.

31. Write a microprogram for a SHIFT-RIGHT instruction using the IF type of statement just described. (You will also need a counter.)

32. Show how to implement the microprogram in the preceding question.

33. Write a microprogram to implement a multiplication instruction.

34. Show how to implement the multiplication instruction in the preceding question.

35. Write a microprogram to implement a DIVIDE instruction.

36. Show how to implement your DIVIDE instruction from the preceding question.

37. Reduce the number of control signals used in Fig. 9·11.

38. Explain what features you might like in a computer which is to be micro-programmed to simulate several other computers.

39. Discuss some of the advantages and disadvantages of microprogramming as you see them.

19
COMPUTER ORGANIZATION

Computers are now available in a tremendous range of sizes, costs, and capabilities. The smallest computers are called microcomputers, the next largest are minicomputers, followed by small, medium-sized, and finally the large, super or "maxi" computers. The price range is from a few dollars (for a chip set for a microcomputer) to several million dollars. Speeds are from tens of microseconds per instruction (or operation) to tens of instructions per microsecond.

The microcomputer is the newest addition in the computer hierarchy, and a given microcomputer generally consists of several integrated circuit (IC) chips including a central processing unit (CPU) chip (or chips) called a *microprocessor* chip (or chips), several memory chips, and one or more input-output interface chips. These sets of chips can be quite inexpensive (a few dollars in large quantities) or fairly expensive (several hundred dollars for high-speed chip sets). The familiar hand calculators are often assembled from IC chips including one of the lower-priced microprocessor chips. Fully assembled microcomputers can cost as little as several hundred dollars.

Microprocessor chips are widely used in what is called original equipment manufacturer (OEM) devices or systems; and traffic lights, printers, communications controllers, automatically controlled instrument complexes, cash registers, and automatic checkout facilities in grocery and department stores, etc., all make wide usage of microprocessors.

Similarly, minicomputers, which generally have prices from one thousand to tens of thousands of dollars (including memory and input-output) are widely used in control systems and OEM systems as well as in scientific applications and business data processing for small businesses, schools, laboratories, etc. The minicomputer preceded the microcomputer in time, and the minicomputer continues to be widely used since computers in this price range provide many users with enough additional capabilities to warrant the extra cost.

The small and medium-scale computer market finds applications in businesses and laboratories of all kinds as well as hospitals, warehouses, small banks, etc. The largest computers are to be found in large corporations such as insurance companies, large banks, large scientific laboratories, large universities, etc. These "super" computers range from scientific-application-orientied "number crunchers" to large complexes of input-output devices and memories used in busines where emphasis is on maintaining large files of data, producing management reports, billing, automatic ordering, inventory control, etc.

The characteristics of these categories of computers differ considerably from category to category and also from design to design. Computers for business data processing have different systems features than those for scientific work. There is also considerable variation in opinion as to how computers for the same application area should be configured, which leads to differing computer designs.

The subject of *computer architecture* ranges through almost every aspect of computer organization. Included are the length of the instruction words, whether the length is variable or there are several different lengths, and how many addresses in memory are referenced by an instruction word. Other architectural considerations concern the number of bits in each memory word, whether instructions and data words are of the same size as the memory words, whether numbers are handled in 1s or 2s complement form or in BCD or some combination of these. What are the instructions provided, how are the memories organized, and how are input-output devices interfaced? As can be seen, computer architecture is a large and rich subject which deals with most aspects of computer design and organization and interacts with every aspect of the computer.

This chapter will first describe some of the instruction word formats now in use. Then some typical computer architectures will be described. Actual details of real computers will be used to illustrate the principles covered, and, while no computer will be described in detail, enough information should be given so that the architecture and operation of most computers can be readily understood. The intent is therefore to concentrate on the principles involved, using actual computers to illustrate these principles.

10•1 INSTRUCTION WORD FORMATS—NUMBER OF ADDRESSES

A given computer has one or more basic formats for its instruction words. We have emphasized the single-address instruction word which is very popular for microcomputers and was once the predominant type of instruction word (including use with most large computers). There are now several other formats in use, however, and these are described below.

Two-address instructions

The number of divisions in the basic computer instruction word is determined primarily by the number of addresses which are referred to. Many computers have two-address instruction words. A two-address computer will generally have a basic instruction word with three sections (Fig. 10 · 1), the first consisting of the OP-code section and the second and third sections each containing the address of a location in memory.

Different machines use these addresses differently. Generally, both addresses in a two-address machine may specify operands, and the result is stored at the first of the addresses. The Minneapolis-Honeywell 200 and IBM 1400 and 360/370 series have two-address instructions which provide examples in which each address refers to an operand in memory.

In many computers, instead of a single accumulator there are two or more registers which are either called *multiple accumulators* or *general-purpose registers*. An instruction word will then have the first address section [the "address of operand (A)" section in Fig. 10 · 1] tell which general register contains one of the operands. The second address section of the instruction word will then give the address in memory of the second operand. If only 2 accumulators or general registers are provided, only 1 bit is needed for the first address section; if 16 general registers are used, then 4 bits will be

Operation code	Address of operand

Single address instruction

Operation code	Address of operand (A)	Address of operand (B)

Two address instruction

Operation code	Address of operand (A)	Address of operand (B)	Address for result (C)

Three address instruction

Operation code	Address of operand (A)	Address of operand (B)	Address for result (C)	Address of next instruction (D)

Four address instruction

FIG. 10 • 1 Formats for instructions.

needed for the first address. Results are generally stored in the general register (accumulator) specified by the first address.

In some computers instruction words are provided in which each of the two addresses refer to general registers; and so, for instance, in a computer with 16 general registers an instruction word would consist of the OP code plus two 4-bit address sections.

Two-address instruction words in which one or both addresses refer to general registers are shorter than two-address instruction words where both addresses refer to the memory, and this format is popular in minicomputers.

Three-address instructions

The three-address instruction generally uses two addresses to indicate the operands to be used and the third address to indicate the location in which the result is to be stored (Fig. 10·1). The operation code section of the word indicates the operation to be performed—for instance, ADD, SUBTRACT, MULTIPLY, etc. The first two of the three addresses are used to indicate the locations of the operands to be used. For instance, if the instruction is an ADD instruction, the contents of location A will be added to the contents of location B. The last address indicates the location in which the result is to be stored, as in the instruction "add A to B and store the result in C." The machine will take its instructions from the memory in order, unless instructed to branch or jump. The instruction word, and therefore the basic computer word for a three-address system, must be of moderate length. The three-address machines are not terribly popular at this time, except in the Soviet Union, although at one time they were more popular than two-address machines. Typical three-address machines were the National Bureau of Standards' Dy-Seac, the Datamatic Corporation's Datamatic 1000 and Datamatic 800, and the Radio Corporation of America's Bizmac.

Four-address instructions

If the basic instruction word contains four addresses (Fig. 10·1), three are generally used as in the three-address machine, and the fourth is used to indicate the location of the next instruction. If we designate the four addresses as A, B, C, and D, a MULTIPLY instruction will cause the contents of address A to be multiplied by the contents of B and stored in C. The next instruction will then be taken from memory address D. Typical four-address machines were the National Bureau of Standards' Swac and the Raytheon Manufacturing Company's Raydac. There are few, if any, four-address machines at present.

Zero-address instructions — stacks

There is a type of instruction word which does not specify any location in memory for an operand but which relies on what is called a *stack* to provide operands.

Basically, a stack is a set of consecutive locations in a memory into which operands (data items) can be placed. The name "stack" is derived from the fact that the memory is organized like a stack of plates in a cafeteria. (Each operand can be thought of as a plate.) The first operand placed on the stack is said to be at the bottom of the stack. Placing an operand on the stack is called *pushing,* and removing an operand is called *popping* the operand. The operand most recently placed on the stack is said to be on the *top* of the stack. Only this top operand is immediately available.

If we push operands *A, B,* and *C* onto an empty stack and then pop an operand, *C* will be removed. If we push *A, B,* and *C* in order and then pop three operands, first *C* will be popped, then *B* and finally *A.* (This last-in first-out principle leads to stacks sometimes being called LIFO lists.)

Figure 10·2 shows the operation of a stack. Stacks are generally maintained as a set of words in a memory. Each word therefore has a fixed length (number of bits) and an address. The *stack pointer* is a register which contains the address of the top operand in the stack. The stack pointer is incremented or decremented when an operand is pushed or popped.

If an ADD instruction is given a computer using a stack architecture, the top two operands in the stack will be removed and added and the sum then placed on the top of the stack. Similarly, a MULTIPLY instruction would cause the top two operands to be multiplied together and the product placed on the stack.

Since only the OP-code section of an arithmetic instruction need be given to specify an arithmetic operation, these instruction words can be very short. It will still be necessary, however, to move operands from memory onto the stack and from the stack back into the memory, and the instruction words for this will be longer since memory addresses must be specified. (These instruction words will be like single-address instruction words except the op-

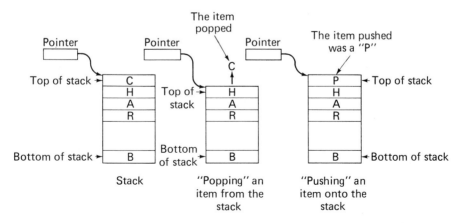

Note: In this case each item in the stack is a single character. The stack items could be numbers, words, records, etc. The pointer contains the address of the "top of the stack."

FIG. 10·2 Stack operations.

erands are moved to and from the stack instead of to and from the accumulator.)

The advocates of stacked computer architecture have some convincing arguments, but problems do exist. Stacked computers include the Burroughs 5500 and 1700 and the Hewlett-Packard 3000. Stacks are widely used in other sections of computers, as will be shown.

10 • 2 REPRESENTATION OF INSTRUCTIONS AND DATA

Important features of a computer's architecture concern the number of bits in instruction words, the size of memory words, and the way data are represented in the computer. In most early computers and in many present-day computers, the high-speed memory contains the same number of bits at each address (in each location) as the instruction words. Similarly, numbers are represented again using the same number of bits. This makes for straightforward implementation. An example of a computer with this structure can be found in the PDP-8, which has a 12-bits-per-word core memory, and 12-bit instruction words with a 3-bit OP code, and numbers are represented using a 12-bit signed 2s complement number system. Many large computers were and are made with this structure; the IBM 700, 704, 709, 7094, and the Minneapolis-Honeywell 6000 and 60 series of computers, all have 36-bit memory words and 36-bit instruction words, and binary numbers are represented using 2s complement signed 36-bit numbers (floating-point numbers are basically 36 bits, also). Most of the large scientific number-crunching machines also use this structure, and CDC produces a number of 64-bits-per-word large computers with this basic structure as well as some smaller 24-bits-per-word computers.

There is a desire to be efficient with the length of instruction words. Also, business data processing involves much manipulation using character strings (names, addresses, text, etc.). The desire to create computer architectures which conserve on instruction word length and also permit storing of strings of characters of arbitrary length efficiently has led to a number of computer architectures with (1) only 8 bits at each address in memory, so a single alphanumeric character can be stored at each address, (2) instruction words with variable lengths (each word length is generally some multiple of 8 bits).

The IBM 1400 and 1600 series of computers, as well as the Honeywell 200 series, all had 8 (or 9) bits per word in the high-speed memory and instruction word OP codes were one alphanumeric character (8 bits) plus whatever bits were needed to provide the two memory addresses required for each instruction. This kind of computer is described in Sec. 10 · 11.

The IBM 360/370 series has 8 bits per word in the memory and a number of different instruction word lengths ranging from 16 to 48 bits.

In many of the newer, larger computers, numbers can be represented in BCD as well as binary and floating point, and calculations can be performed in each of these number representation systems.

Microcomputers tend to have data words and memory words of 4, 8, or 16 bits. Instruction words are generally variable in length, but the lengths are almost always multiples of the number of bits in the memory.

10•3 ADDRESSING TECHNIQUES

When an address in memory is given in an instruction word, the most obvious technique is simply to give the address in memory in binary form. This is called *direct addressing,* and the instruction words in the examples in Chap. 9 all used direct addressing.

While direct addressing provides the most straightforward (and fastest) way to give a memory address, many other techniques are also used. These techniques are generally motivated by one of the following considerations.

1. *Desire to shorten address section* For instance, if we have a minicomputer with 16-bit words and a 32K memory, 15 bits will be required for a direct address leaving only 1 bit for the OP code—an intolerable situation.
2. *Programmer convenience* There are several addressing techniques (such as index registers, which will be covered) which provide a convenience to the programmer in writing programs.
3. *System operation facilities*   In most large computer systems the computer will have several different programs in its memory at a given time and will alternate the running of these programs. In order to efficiently load and remove these programs from memory in differing locations, addressing techniques are provided which make the programs *relocatable,* meaning the same program can be run in many different sections of memory.

The following sections describe several of the techniques in common use which are variations on the direct addressing method.

10•4 INDEX REGISTERS

There is a variation on conventional direct memory addressing which facilitates programming, particularly the programming of sequences of instructions that are to be repeated many times on sets of data distributed throughout the machine. This technique is called *indexing.*

Indexing was first used in a computer developed at the University of Manchester. A register named the *B-box* was added to the control section. The contents of the B-box could be added to the contents of the memory address register when desired. When the B-box was used, the address of the operand located in memory would be at the address written by the programmer plus the contents of the B-box. The Manchester computer had only one B-box, but the idea proved so valuable that many modern computers have several. The American term for B-box is *index register,* and this term will be used.

Use of index registers eases writing programs that process data in tables,

such as those described in Chap. 1, greatly reducing the number of instructions required in an iterative program. The index registers permit the automatic
modification of the addresses referred to without altering the instructions
stored in memory.

When index registers are included in a machine, an additional division is
generally made in the computer instruction word. This section of the instruction word tells the computer if an index register is to be used, and if so,
which index register to use. The basic instruction word is therefore broken,
for a single-address computer, into three parts instead of two. A typical division is shown in Fig. 10·3.

Two additional instructions are also added; one is used to "load" the
index register, and the other modifies the number stored in the specified
index register or causes the computer to branch.

If an index register is not to be used, the programmer places 0s in the
index-register-designation section of the word. If there are three index registers, there will be two binary digits in the index-register section of the
word, and the index register desired can be selected by placing the correct
digits in the index-register-designation section.

To describe the operation of the index registers, two new instructions will
be introduced. We will designate one of these by the mnemonic code SIR
(set index registers), and this instruction will cause the address section of
the instruction word to be transferred into the index register designated by
the index-register-designation bits in the word. For instance, 01 SIR 300 will
load the number 300 into index register 01. Since the address register normally contains the address section of the computer word, all that is required
is that the contents of the address register be transferred into the index
register designated.

We will designate the second instruction with the mnemonic code BRI
(branch on index). This instruction will cause the contents of the index register designated to be decreased by one if the number stored in the index
register is positive. At the same time, the computer will branch to the address
in the address section of the instruction word, taking its next instruction from
that address. If the index register designated contains a 0, the computer will
not branch but will instead perform the next instruction in normal order.

The index registers may be used during any normal instruction by simply
placing the digits indicating the index register to be used in the index-
register-designation section of the computer word. For instance, if index

FIG. 10·3 Index-register instruction word.

TABLE 10 • 1

ADDRESS IN MEMORY	INDEX-REG. DESIGNATION	OPERATION CODE	ADDRESS SECTION	COMMENTS
	INSTRUCTION WORD			
0	01	SIR	99	The number 99 into index register 01.
1	01	CAD	201	Picks up number to be added.
2	00	ADD	301	Adds to total thus far.
3	00	STO	301	Stores the current sum.
4	01	BRI	1	Subtracts 1 from index register 01 and then branches to first instruction until index register 01 contains 0, then proceeds to next instruction.
5	00	HLT	0	
201 to 300	Contain numbers to be added.			
301	Location at which sum is stored.			

register 01 contains 300, and we write a clear and add instruction (CAD) as follows:

01 CAD 200

the computer will add the contents of index register 01 to the contents of the address register, and the address used will be the total of these two. Since index register 01 contains 300 and the address register will contain 200, the address from which the operand will be taken will be address 500 in memory.

An example of the use of an index register may be found in the short program shown in Table 10 · 1, which will add together all the numbers stored in memory addresses 201 to 300 and store the sum in address 301.

The program repeats the instructions at addresses 1 through 4 until index register 01 is finally at 0; then the computer does not branch and is halted by the next instruction.

10 • 5 PAGING AND INDIRECT ADDRESSING

The low prices and ready accessibility of integrated circuits and inexpensive memories has led to the marketing of small general-purpose digital computers called *microcomputers* and *minicomputers*.

Since the manufacturer is pressed to keep costs down, several ingenious strategies are used in these machines. First, the basic memory word lengths are generally short, with lengths of from 8 to 16 bits. If instruction words are the same length as the memory words, this limits the length of the OP-code section, and therefore the number of different instructions which can be used. Also, the short word length means short memory address sections in instruction words; so special techniques must be used to address the entire memory.

The microcomputer and minicomputer designer alleviates his first problem, a small instruction repertoire, by mixing ingenious and tricky instructions in with the conventional instructions. For instance, the basic minimal PDP-8, a popular minicomputer manufactured by the Digital Equipment Corporation, has a 12-bit instruction word with a 3-bit OP code. The machine has a single conventional arithmetic instruction, 2s complement addition. Subtraction must then be programmed and consists of forming the 2s complement of the subtrahend and then adding. (This is facilitated by an instruction which forms the 2s complement of a number in the accumulator.) Multiplication and division must also be programmed. A single logical instruction, AND, is used in conjunction with a complement instruction (where each bit in the accumulator is complemented) and the ADD instruction to form exclusive OR's, inclusive OR's, and all other logic operations. An "increment and skip if zero" instruction which will add one to a selected memory location and then "skip if a 0" is used to form index registers in memory locations. Several circular shift or rotate accumulator instructions round out the basic repertoire, along with the required input-output instructions. This set of cleverly designed instructions is not only adequate for all purposes, but is highly efficient in performing most operations. The instruction word for this machine will be discussed in a subsequent section.

The above computer, although well designed and quite popular, is neither unique nor particularly novel.† Most small computers combine relatively small instruction sets with ingenious organizations to form efficient computers despite small size. The prices paid for small numbers of instructions in a machine are, primarily, increased operating time for programs and increased ingenuity required for the systems programmers who write the assemblers and compilers. (The actual user is generally not too much affected by the latter.)

Microcomputers and minicomputers often alleviate the problem of addressing a large memory with a short word by using a technique which actually arose in a large computer called Atlas. This technique is called *paging.* When paging is used, the memory is divided into *pages,* each of a fixed length.

Example For the PDP-8 mentioned above, the basic core memory of 4096 words of 12 bits each is divided into 32 pages of 128 words each. Thus page 0 contains

---

† However, it was highly original and well-developed, and it set a standard for all minicomputers which followed.

FIG. 10•4 Layout of 31-page memory with 4096 words of 12 bits.

the memory locations from 0 to 127 (decimal), page 1 refers to the memory locations from 128 to 255,..., and, finally, page 31 refers to the locations from 3968 to 4095, as shown in Fig. 10·4. Then 5 bits are required to reference a page, and 7 bits to reference a location within a page.

The addressing of data in a computer with paging varies from computer to computer. Generally, the address given in the instruction word can refer either to the page in which the instruction word lies or possibly to some other particular page, previously specified.

Example For the PDP-8 the fourth bit in a 12-bit instruction word is called the *page bit*. This bit tells whether the 7-bit address in the instruction word refers to the page in which the instruction lies, in which case the bit is a 1, or to the first page in the memory, in which case the bit is a 0. For instance, if the fourth bit is a 1 and the address given is 23 and the instruction word is on page 20, then the actual location referenced is the 23d location on page 20 or the 2583d word in memory.† If the fourth bit is a 0, the address 20 simply refers to location 20 in the memory.

The above example of paging enables the use of addresses containing fewer digits than would normally be required to address memory. Generally, this is adequate, since a program is most likely to either address nearby

---

† The twentieth page begins with location $20 \times 128 = 2560$ and the location referenced would therefore be $2560 + 23 = 2583$.

locations or some data in a particular area. When addresses outside of these areas are required, either a technique called *indirect addressing* or special longer instruction words are used.

Often paging is relative to the instruction word, in which case the address part tells how many addresses ahead of (or behind) the instruction word the operand word lies. Thus, if the instruction word is at address 960, the address part has value 140, and relative paging was used, the address referenced would be address 1100. The Data General Computers, DECs PDP-11, the Lockheed Sue, and many other computers use relative address paging. The actual address is formed by simply adding the contents of the instruction counter to the address section of the instruction word.

Another widely used variation in the conventional addressing technique is called *indirect addressing*. When used, indirect addressing causes the instruction word to give the address, not of the operand to be used, but of the address of the operand. As an example, if we write ADD 302 and the instruction is a conventional *direct*-addressing addition instruction, the word at location 302 will be added to the word currently in the accumulator.

If the addition instruction is indirect addressed and we write IAD 302 (IAD for *indirect add*), then the number stored at address 302 will give the actual address of the operand to be used. As an example, when the instruction word at address 5 in the memory in the following program is performed, it will cause the number 164 to be added to the current contents of the accumulator.

MEMORY ADDRESS	CONTENTS
5	IAD 302
. . .	. . .
302	495
. . .	. . .
495	164

As an example, consider that both index registers and indirect addressing are used in many of the newer computers. For example, the Varian Data Model 6201 is a small general-purpose computer with a 16-bit basic word length which uses 2s complements for negative numbers. The basic instruction word is as follows:

15	14	13	12	11	10	9	8	7	6	5	4	3	2	1	0
		O			m						M				
	OP Code				Address mode						Address				

The OP-code section tells what instruction is to be performed; the M bits give a basic 9-bit memory address, while the three m bits tell the *mode* of addressing.

Four basic registers can be used in the various addressing modes. These are the instruction counter, IC (which Varian calls the P register, or program counter), the B register, which is the "lower half" of the accumulator, as in Fig. 9·3, and an X register, which is an index register.

The m bits then tell the mode of addressing as follows:

$m = 000$ The address of the operand is given directly by the 9-bit binary number M.

$m = 100$ The address of the operand is found by adding the value of M to the current value in the instruction counter.

$m = 101$ The address of the operand is found by adding the value of M to X, the value of the index register.

$m = 110$ The address of the operand is formed by adding the value of M to B, the value in the B register.

$m = 111$ Addressing is indirect. The address of the operand is stored at the location given by M.

There is one variation on the indirect-addressing scheme used by Varian, Data General, and several others. For indirect addressing, the address at location M above is a 15-bit address plus a sign bit which tells if the address is the operand's address or the address of yet another indirect address. That is, if the instruction word says ADD and bits 9 to 11 are 111 and the address M is 320 (decimal), then if the memory address 320 contains a 0 in the sign bit, the remaining bits contain the address of the number to be added to the present value of the accumulator. If, however, the sign bit at memory address 320 is a 1, this says "use the remaining bits as the address of the next place to look for an address." Suppose these bits give the number 325; the contents of this memory location are treated similarly. If the sign bit at 325 is a 0, the remaining bits give the address of the operand to be added to the accumulator; if the sign bit is a 1, the address formed from the remaining bits gives the address of the next place to look for the operand's address.

This indirect-addressing scheme permits indefinite *chaining* of indirect addresses, and is surprisingly useful in programs. Notice that when indirect addressing is used an entire word can be used as an address; this is very useful in a paged computer since the entire word will be larger than the address part of a word and most if not all of the memory will be addressable.

10•6 INTERCONNECTING SYSTEM COMPONENTS

The components of a computer system, that is, the memories, input-output devices, etc., must be interconnected to form a computer system. The way these components are put together and how they communicate with each other profoundly affect the system's performance characteristics.

The arithmetic-logic unit and control unit are generally placed physically together and called the central processing unit (CPU). The CPU is then "in charge" of the system's operation, directing the operation of the other parts of the system.

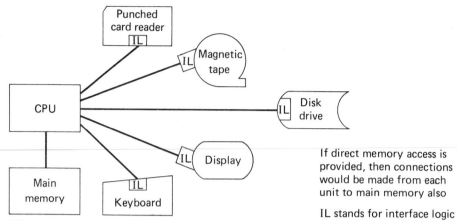

FIG. 10•5 Individual connections between computer system units.

In the earlier computers and in some present-day smaller computers, the CPU is connected directly to each input-output device and memory unit using a separate cable for each connection. This is shown in Fig. 10·5. Then, if a card is to be read from a card reader, the CPU must accept the information and if it is to be stored in memory, the CPU must store it. The CPU is therefore central and involved directly in each transaction.

The above system has the disadvantages of many different cables (or buses) and considerable interface logic (at each end of each cable).

In order to make interconnection of the system components less expensive and to standardize on the interface logic used, a very popular technique now involves interconnecting all components using a single *bus*. This bus consists of a number of wires or connections and in the bus are provisions for addressing the components and transferring data from or to each component.

Figure 10·6 shows the DEC PDP-11 bus which DEC calls a UNIBUS. Notice the same wires are used to transfer data from the CPU to the memory as from the CPU to a tape punch or other input-output device.

In the simplest systems, the CPU is the director of all traffic on the bus, and if a transfer of data must be made from, for instance, a disk pack to the core memory, the CPU, under program control, will read each piece of data into its CPU general registers and then store each piece of data in the core memory.

There is a problem here in the computer's ability to know when a peripheral device† has performed a given operation. Suppose we wish to find some data on a magnetic tape and are unwilling to wait for the tape to be searched, desiring to perform other calculations while waiting. If the computer must

---

† *Peripheral devices* are the input-output devices, disk packs, tape drives, and other devices not including the main (core or IC) memory.

continually look to see if the tape drive now has the right data, time is lost and programming complexity increased. In order to alleviate this, the computer bus is generally provided with control lines which are called *interrupt lines*, and a peripheral device can raise one of these lines when it has completed an action and is ready for attention.

The computer must then be provided with some kind of interrupt facility so that it can "service" the interrupt without losing its place in the program being executed. This problem becomes serious in systems where a number of input-output devices (such as A-to-D converters) must be serviced frequently, and computers are designed to service these interrupts as efficiently as possible.

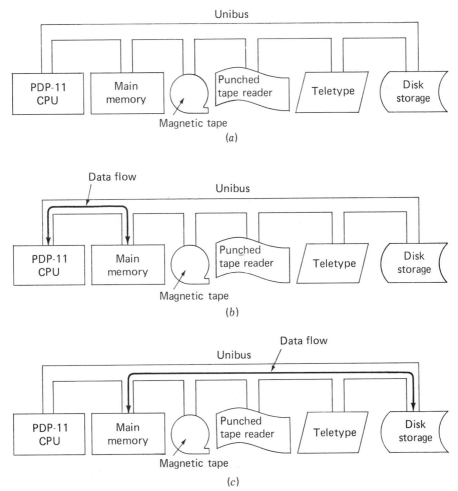

FIG. 10•6 Bus for PDP-11. (*a*) CPU, memory, and other devices are connected by a single bus; (*b*) CPU controls transfers of data in normal use; (*c*) when system has direct memory access (DMA) feature, peripherals can send data directly to the memory on the bus. (Courtesy Digital Equipment Corp.)

Even with a good interrupt facility, the computer is still involved in every data transfer, and this can be very time consuming. It is possible to add what is called a direct memory *access* (DMA) feature to most systems where a disk pack or tape reader transfers data directly into core memory without passing the data through the CPU. This is done by "stealing" memory cycles (called *cycle stealing*). The CPU is simply held in its present state for a memory cycle while a piece of data is transferred from the disk pack directly into the core memory. The CPU does not see this transfer when it occurs, but simply continues executing its program which is slowed down a little because of the cycle "stealing" but not nearly so much as if the CPU had to make each transfer itself. The CPU must, of course, originate these DMA transfers by telling both the disk pack and core memory where the data are to be read from and into which locations in memory the data are to be read. (Transfers can generally be made in either direction when the DMA feature is added to a system, that is, for example, tape-to-core or core-to-tape.)

Because of the economy of operation, a single bus is now the most used way to interconnect components of a microcomputer or minicomputer system.

Large systems have quite different problems from very small systems, and so different interconnection configurations are used. Since large systems contain many components, they are quite expensive and it is important to utilize the CPU and other components to the maximum, and so the cost of more expensive interconnection configurations is warranted.

As a result, in order to keep large processor configurations such as that shown in Fig. 10·7 working at their maximum speed, the systems are operated in what is called a *multiprocessing mode.* What this means is that

FIG. 10•7 Parts of a large general-purpose computer.

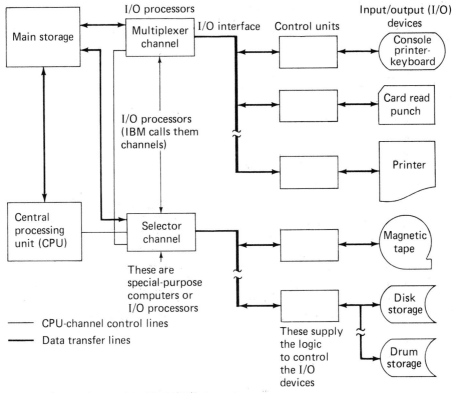

FIG. 10 • 8 Organization of IBM 360/370 computer series.

several programs are kept in memory at the same time. A given program is then executed until it demands an input-output device or perhaps a disk drive. Since these devices are slow compared to the CPU, the device is started in its function but the CPU then begins executing another different program until this program asks for input-output. When this happens, the CPU begins executing a third program and this process continues.

When a program completes execution, another program is read in. As can be seen, the CPU must keep track of where it is in each program and must control all the data transfers between system components but would be hopelessly held up if it had to participate in each transfer.

One way to configure a large system of this sort is shown in Fig. 10·8 which shows the IBM 360/370 configuration. This particular figure shows a single 370 CPU and two input-output processors; one of which IBM calls a multiplexer channel and the other a selector channel.† Some systems have

---

† A multiplexer channel has logic particularly suited to relatively slow devices with random characteristics. Selector channels are for fast bursts of data generated by disk packs and tape drives, for instance.

more input-output processors, and some even have more than one CPU, in which case the system is called a *multiprocessor.*

The system operates as follows: All transfers to and from *peripheral devices,* such as card readers, printers, tape drives, etc., are initiated by the CPU telling an input-output processor what is to be done. The actual transfers are then made by the special-purpose processors, which work independently of the CPU. To initiate a data transfer, the CPU tells the input-output processor where in memory to put (or find) the data, which input-output device to use, and (if necessary) where in that device the data are located. The actual transferring of data is guided by a *channel program* executed by the input-output processor which has been written in advance, and the CPU also sees that the correct channel program is used.

Once an input-output data transfer has been initiated by the CPU, the CPU can go about executing other programs, and when the input-output processor completes its work, the CPU is notified so it can return and continue where it was in the program which called for the input-output transfer.

Another large computer configuration is that in Fig. 10·9 which shows the organization of the CDC Cyber 70 computer. In this case, the input-output operations are all handled by small "computers" called *peripheral processing units* (PPUs). The PPUs have their own memories and programs and work independently of the Cyber 70 CPU. The way the Cyber 70 commands input-output operations is to "plant" messages in a specified area in

FIG. 10·9 Cyber 70 computer organization.

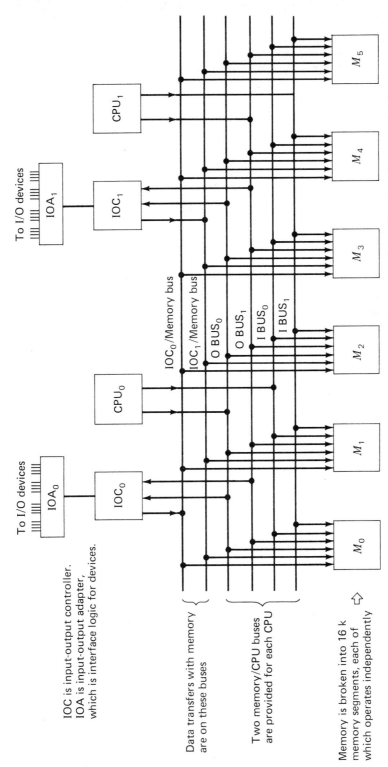

To I/O devices

To I/O devices

IOA₀

IOA₁

IOC is input-output controller.
IOA is input-output adapter,
which is interface logic for devices.

IOC₀

CPU₀

IOC₁

CPU₁

IOC₀/Memory bus

IOC₁/Memory bus

O BUS₀

O BUS₁

I BUS₀

I BUS₁

M_0

M_1

M_2

M_3

M_4

M_5

Data transfers with memory
are on these buses

Two memory/CPU buses
are provided for each CPU

Memory is broken into 16 k
memory segments, each of
which operates independently

Note: Data on bus lines is bidirectional; arrows indicate direction of request signal

FIG. 10·10 Univac AN/UYK-7 multiprocessor.

its memory telling what it would like. The PPUs then search this memory looking for orders and when they find one, they execute the necessary operations and plant a message telling the CPU that its orders have been fulfilled and the necessary operations performed.

The reason that complex structures such as the IBM 360/370 and Cyber 70 make good sense is that a number of peripheral or input-output devices can be operating simultaneously at the relatively low speeds they can maintain, while the CPU races from job to job. In this way the overall throughput for the computer system can be increased because of the parallel operation of all parts of the system.

The idea of providing several CPUs which execute programs in parallel is an attractive one for large systems. As was just mentioned, such systems are called *multiprocessor systems,* and these systems again have high throughput and make good usage of both large memories and the many input-output devices often found in very large systems. Fig. 10·10 shows such a system.

There are several problems having to do with multiprocessor systems which lead to other strategies. The best known such strategy is to build a single "super" CPU with the fastest possible circuitry and then try to force instructions through this CPU at a high rate. When the CPU contains a set of logic circuits which simultaneously operate on several instructions in order, performing operations on different steps of each instruction's execution at the same time using a unit as shown in Fig. 10·11, then the computer is called a *pipeline* computer. The CDC Star, Amdahl computers, and the University of Manchester's MU5 are examples of this kind of architecture.

In some computer systems the CPU simply has a number of different units, each of which can perform a different category of instruction (a multiplier, a divider, a floating-point unit, for example; refer to Fig. 10·12). An instruction's OP code is then decoded and the instruction sent to the appropriate unit for execution. Then, several instructions can be executed in parallel by these different units. CDC produces several computers (including the Cyber 70) which operate in this way. These computers and the pipeline computers all have to have enough logic circuitry to consider interaction between

FIG. 10·11 Pipeline CPU and memory.

FIG. 10•12 CPU with multiple units.

instructions (because an instruction which precedes another instruction can alter the second instruction's operand, for example) and see that the calculations are correctly performed. This makes for large, expensive CPUs, but because these systems are very large and already expensive the price can be paid.

10•7 INTERFACING—BUSES

When input-output devices, memory devices, and the arithmetic-logic unit and control unit are all combined to form a computer system, all of these must be connected together. When one device or unit is connected to another, an interface is required which includes the necessary logic.

   The primary disadvantages of using a large number of individual cables to interconnect parts of a system are cost and complexity. The necessary interface logic must be repeated for each connection along with cable-driving circuits and receiving circuits.

   A widely used technique to interface modules efficiently and with small

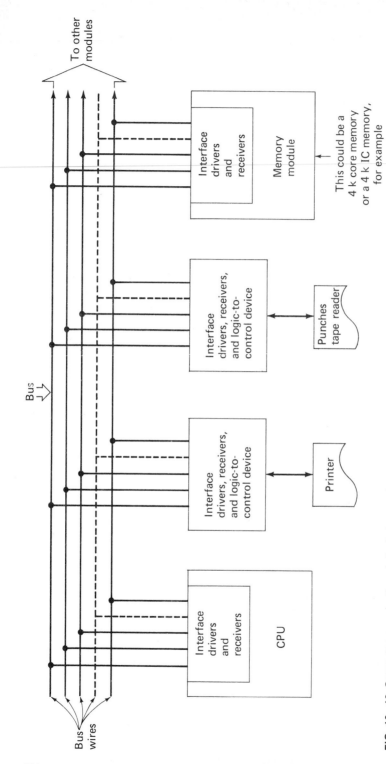

FIG. 10·13 Computer organization of single-bus system.

464

cost uses a single bus† to interconnect all the units. This is shown in Fig. 10 · 13 where the several lines or conductors which form the bus pass through and connect to a number of units or modules. In general, each module can read from the bus or write into the bus. The bus interface is generally standardized, since the same bus connects all units. Since each unit connects only once to the bus, the amount of interface circuitry and logic required tends to be lower than for separate connections between units. As a result, buses are widely used in microcomputers and minicomputers and even in large computer systems for modules where the data flow is not excessive.

Since the modules which are bused together must share the same data lines, it is necessary that each module be able to both write onto and read from a given wire. There are three general techniques for doing this and these are shown in Fig. 10 · 14. (Some of the electrical considerations are treated in the questions.)

In Fig. 10 · 14(a), the wire connection to be shared is normally in the high state. A given module can write on this wire by forcing the wire to the 0 or ground level. A typical writing circuit or driver is shown in the inset of the figure. Each module also has a receiver, which is a simple inverter. (Often the high state on the bus wire is made a logical 0 and the low state a 1.)

In Fig. 10 · 14(b), the bus connection is normally at ground level. The module's writing circuit or driver writes high levels (for logic 1s) on this line, leaving the line low when 0s are to be written. The receiver can consist of either a noninverting amplifier or two inverters in series.

Some logic lines provide what are called *three-state line drivers*. These circuits have a *disable* input as well as a logic level input, as shown in Fig. 10 · 14(c). When the disable is low (a 0), the circuit drives the bus wire to the level at the logic input. Thus, if the disable input is a 0 and the logic input a 0, the bus wire will be driven to 0. If the disable is a 0 and the logic input a 1, the bus wire will be driven high. If the disable input is a 1, however, the circuit presents a very high impedance to the bus wire, which permits another three-state line driver to drive the bus line to whatever lever is selected. Receivers are again conventional logic circuits or inverters. Manufacturers of TTL, ECL, CMOS, and other circuit lines generally include three-state line drivers in their IC package lines.

Since several units are sharing the same bus lines, the interface procedures for bused modules must be carefully worked out so that, for instance, two modules do not attempt to write data on the bus at the same time and so that, for instance, the module for which the data are intended knows it is the selected module, etc.

Various standards organizations (such as the American National Standards Institute) have undertaken to develop interfaces and procedures or, as they are frequently called, *protocols* for digital systems. A widely used

---

† A bus is a set of parallel lines or connections. Most buses use wires for the connections although some research has been done with light beams and other media.

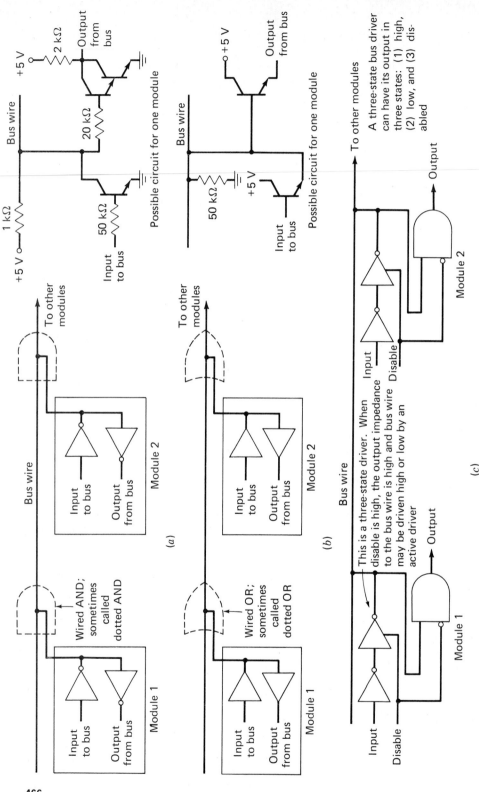

FIG. 10·14 Sharing a bus wire. (a) Bus connections using wired AND; (b) bus connections using wired OR; (c) three-state bus driver.

protocol which has been developed for interfacing instruments will be briefly outlined, as it is representative of the interfaces worked out for buses.

Figure 10·15 shows the basic interface and bus lines which can be used to interconnect a number of modules. Each bus line performs at least one interface function, depending on the interface capabilities.

At a given time, any particular module connected to the bus may be idle, monitoring the activity on the bus, or functioning as (1) a talker, (2) a listener, or (3) a controller. As a talker, a module sends data over the bus to a listener (or listeners). As a listener, a module receives such data. As a controller, it directs the flow of data on the bus, mainly by designating which modules are to send data and which are to receive data.

Notice that the bus consists of 16 signal lines, grouped functionally into three component buses. The *data bus* (eight lines) is used to transfer data in parallel, from talkers to listeners; it also transfers certain commands from the controller to subordinate modules. The *transfer bus* (three lines) is used for the handshaking process, by which a talker or controller can synchronize its readiness to receive data. The *general interface management bus* (five lines), as its name suggests, is principally used by the controller.

Each system must have one module to designate listeners and talkers and this module is called a *controller*. The controller uses a group of commands, referred to as *interface messages,* to direct the other modules on the bus in carrying out their functions of talking and listening.

Normally the controller would be the CPU of the computer, and this unit would generate the command signals on the bus to the other modules which would then respond. Because this interface is designed to handle a large number of different types of modules, the specification is reasonably complicated and general. The basic procedure for generating a transfer of data on this bus is as follows, however. First, the controller designates a listener by placing the listener's address (each listener is given a 5-bit address) on the data bus and raising the appropriate control lines. A talker is then designated by placing the talker's address on the data lines and raising the appropriate control lines. Finally, the talker and listener are told to proceed and the talker places data, 8 bits at a time, in parallel on the data lines.

In the transfer of data from talker to listener, certain basic problems arise in the operation of every bus.† These problems are solved by means of a handshaking procedure whereby talker and listener interact using the control lines. It is convenient to describe this procedure using a *flowchart* as shown in Fig. 10·16. This diagram shows that three control lines, called DAV, NRFD, and NDAC, are used to control each data byte transfer. The talkers and receivers each raise and lower the control signals, as shown by

---

† These problems concern: (1) How does the listener know when data are on the bus? (2) How does the talker know when the listener has received the data? The bus described here is an *asynchronous bus.* Microprocessors and minicomputers often use synchronous buses where one wire in the bus contains a clock and the clock signal is used to time data transfers. In these systems, the talker must place the data on the data wires and the listener must be ready to receive data when the clock edge arrives. A synchronous system is faster and simpler but less flexible.

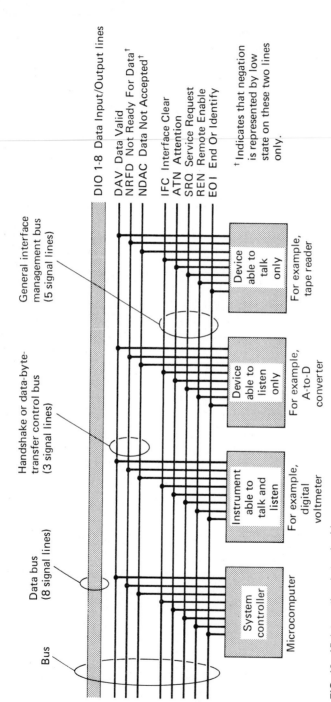

Bus

Data bus
(8 signal lines)

Handshake or data-byte-
transfer control bus
(3 signal lines)

General interface
management bus
(5 signal lines)

DIO 1-8 Data Input/Output lines

DAV   Data Valid
NRFD Not Ready For Data[†]
NDAC Data Not Accepted[†]

IFC Interface Clear
ATN Attention
SRQ Service Request
REN Remote Enable
EOI End Or Identify

[†] Indicates that negation
is represented by low
state on these two lines
only.

System
controller

Microcomputer

Instrument
able to
talk and
listen

For example,
digital
voltmeter

Device
able to
listen
only

For example,
A-to-D
converter

Device
able to
talk
only

For example,
tape reader

FIG. 10 · 15 International standard bus.

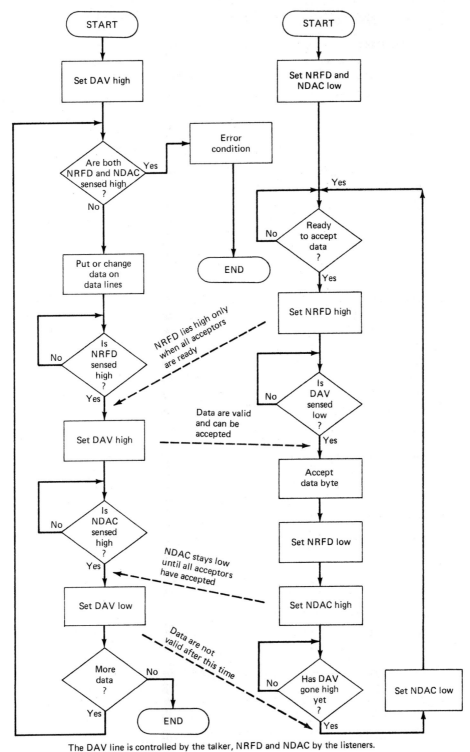

The DAV line is controlled by the talker, NRFD and NDAC by the listeners.

FIG. 10·16 Flowchart for handshaking on a bus. (Courtesy Hewlett-Packard Corp.)

the flowchart, and the talker places data on the data bus at the appropriate time.

The necessary control circuitry to implement this handshaking and the other required functions must be provided by each module's interface circuitry. It is possible to design a line of input-output equipment including instruments, tape punches, etc., and to interface each of these to the same bus using the interface specification, and IC manufacturers often provide single chips made to provide the necessary logic for an interface.

Even connector types and electrical loading and driving rules are called out so that circuit designers can proceed with the necessary details. Minicomputer and microcomputer manufacturers also provide bus specifications for the buses they use so that peripheral manufacturers can comply with their interface specifications, and so that purchasers of these computers can design their own equipment when necessary. Large computer manufacturers provide similar specifications for their buses and other interfaces.

The bus shown is adequate for most instrument computer purposes. A higher-speed bus could be designed by adding more control lines and address lines in parallel with the data lines, and many computers have buses with 50 or more lines. The following section will show a higher-speed bus with parallel address and data lines which is used in a microcomputer.

10 • 8 MICROPROCESSORS AND MICROCOMPUTERS

Microprocessor or microcomputer systems are based around a set of IC chips. These chips are interconnected and communicate with each other using a bus. The interface circuitry for the bus is generally included in the individual chips.

Figure 10 · 17 shows the layout for a small microcomputer system using four modules. The address bus, data bus, and control bus are the three sections of the bus. The microprocessor or CPU controls the bus and contains the arithmetic-logic unit and control unit.† The memory modules can be of any desired size and will consist of however many chips are required. The interfaces to external devices are provided by interface chips called *peripheral interface adapters*. In the figure, connection to a teletype unit is shown, but interface chips are available to connect to tape punches, acoustic couplers, modems, A-to-D and D-to-A converters, printers, etc.

The basic layout shown here applies to most microprocessors. (In fact, the same layout is used for most minicomputers except the bus now becomes a set of wires in a physical frame, and the modules are generally complete circuit boards which are interconnected by this bus and each of which contains a number of chips.‡) The amount of memory per chip, interface chips

---

† The number of the CPU chip is generally used as the number of the microprocessor developed using the chips in the series. For instance, 6800 is the CPU number but the RAMs, ROMs, etc., have other numbers; however, the series of chips is called the 6800 series.

‡ Buses are given various names by minicomputer manufacturers, for instance, unibus, omnibus, callabus, etc.

FIG. 10 • 17 Microcomputer system with four modules.

available, and instruction repertoire of the CPU or microprocessor chip vary from manufacturer to manufacturer, of course.

The number of lines in the data bus is an important consideration. For early microprocessors (and for calculators) this tends to be four lines so that one 4-bit byte can be transferred or operated on. Later microprocessors tend to have 8 or 16 data lines so that words of modest size can be moved. Notice that the instruction words are also transmitted over these data lines since they are stored in the ROM and RAM. This means in many cases that several transfers are required to move one instruction word from memory. In effect, the CPU assembles the instruction word in its registers until it has enough bits to execute the instruction. Generally, the first transfer from memory will contain the OP-code section of the instruction word, and this will tell the CPU how many additional transfers are needed to provide the address information.

Since the CPU controls all transfers on the bus, this means the CPU must direct the transfers of instruction word segments and operands from the memory, and logic circuitry for this purpose is provided on the CPU chip.

The address section of the bus is used to read addresses into the RAMs, ROMs, and interface chips. The address section must contain enough wires to provide a complete address in one transfer, and 16 wires are commonly

A15 A14 A13 A12 A11 A10 A9 A8
25 24 23 22 20 19 18 17

A7 A6 A5 A4 A3 A2 A1 A0
16 15 14 13 12 11 10 9

Output buffers

Output buffers

Program counter H
Stack pointer H
Index register H
Instruction register (OP code)

Program counter L
Stack pointer L
Index register L
Accumulator A
Accumulator B
Condition code register
ALU

Instruction decode and control

Data buffer

All registers are 8 bits. H means high-order bits and L means low-order bits.

Clock φ1 (3)
Clock φ2 (37)
Reset (40)
Nonmaskable Interrupt (6)
Halt (2)
Interrupt Request (4)
Three-state Control (39)
Data Bus Enable (36)
Bus Available (7)
Valid Memory Address (5)
Read/Write (34)

26 27 28 29 30 31 32 33
D7 D6 D5 D4 D3 D2 D1 D0

Note: Circled numbers are pin numbers on IC container.

FIG. 10•18 Block diagram of CPU chip for 6800 microprocessor. (Courtesy Motorola Corp.)

used; otherwise, several address transfers would have to be made for each data bus transfer.

The input-output devices are generally given addresses just like memory addresses in these systems. In order to read a character from a tape reader (or keyboard), the CPU simply places the address assigned the tape reader on the address wires and calls for a READ. The tape reader must then place the character read on the data wires. Similarly, to print a character on a printer, the CPU places the printer's assigned address on the address bus wires and then places the character on the data wires. This writes the character into the printer which then prints it. Naturally, some status information must also be transferred (does the reader have a character ready, for instance) and this information is also transferred over the data wires.†

As an example of a microcomputer we will describe the 6800 microprocessor-microcomputer system first developed by Motorola. (Chips for this system are also available from a number of other manufacturers.) The basic CPU is on a single 40-pin IC chip, as shown in Fig. 10·18. The 6800

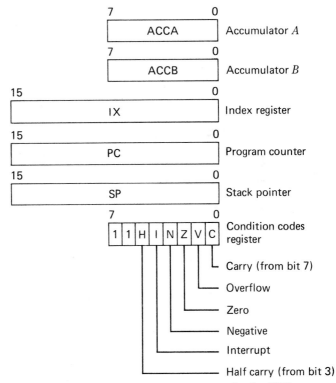

FIG. 10 • 19 Basic registers used in programming the 6800 microprocessor.

---

†An input device will have an address for its status register as well as an address for its data, and similarly an output device will have a data and status address.

has an 8-bit data bus and a 16-bit address bus; refer to Fig. 10 · 18. From a programming viewpoint, the CPU chip contains six basic registers which are shown in Fig. 10 · 19.

1. *Accumulator A*   This is an 8-bit accumulator.
2. *Accumulator B*   This is an 8-bit accumulator.
3. *Index register*   There is a single 16-bit index register.
4. *Stack pointer*   This is a 16-bit register which points to a stack in memory.
5. *Program counter*   This is the instruction counter or program counter and contains 16 bits.
6. *Status register*   This is a 6-bit register containing six flip-flops H, I, N, Z, V, and C. The results of arithmetic and other operations are stored in these bits, as will be described.

The instruction repertoire for this CPU chip includes over 100 different instructions. The operation code is 8 bits, the size of a word in memory. There are seven different addressing modes, which are described in Table 10 · 2. A partial list of the instructions for this microprocessor chip are shown in Tables 10 · 3 to 10 · 5.

The way that conditional branch instructions operate deserves mention. When an arithmetic or Boolean operation is performed, the status bits are set according to the result of this operation. Tables 10 · 6 and 10 · 7 show the status bits and detail their function. The branch instructions use the values of these bits to determine whether a branch is to be made or not.

For instance, if an arithmetic addition is performed, let us say accumulator A is added to accumulator B, then if the sum is negative the N bit will be set to a 1. We also assume no overflow so V will be set to a 0. Now, if a "branch if LT 0" (BLT) instruction follows, the computer will branch to the address given in the address part of the instruction. If the result of the addition had been 0 or positive, no branch would have occurred and the next instruction in sequence would be taken.

The use of status bits which record the result of arithmetic and logic operations, and branch instructions which use these values in the bits to determine whether to branch or not, is widely used in present-day computers.

The *interrupt mask bit* (I) in the status register is set on when external input-output devices are allowed to interrupt the computer. When an interrupt occurs, the computer jumps to an interrupt servicing routine (program) which is stored in the memory. To simplify and shorten the interrupt servicing program, this microprocessor automatically transfers the values in all the CPU registers into a stack in memory and places the address of these stored register contents in the stack pointer. The interrupt servicing program can then simply service the printer, reader, or whatever generated the interrupt and can later replace the contents of the CPU registers to their status when interrupted and restart the program where it was interrupted.

Maintaining these stored registers in a stack also enables the interrupt servicing program to be interrupted since the contents of the registers are again placed in the stack. In this way, several interrupts can follow one an-

TABLE 10·2 ADDRESSING MODES FOR MICROPROCESSOR

MODE	OPERATION
Accumulator (ACCX) addressing	In accumulator only addressing, either accumulator *A* or accumulator *B* is specified. These are 1-byte instructions.
Immediate addressing	In immediate addressing, the operand is contained in the second byte of the instruction except LDS and LDX which have the operand in the second and third bytes of the instruction. The 6800 addresses this location when it fetches the immediate instruction for execution. These are 2- or 3-byte instructions.
Direct addressing	In direct addressing, the address of the operand is contained in the second byte of the instruction. Direct addressing allows the user to directly address the lowest 256 bytes in the machine, i.e., locations 0 through 255. Enhanced execution times are achieved by storing data in these locations. In most configurations, it would be a random-access memory. These are 2-byte instructions.
Extended addressing	In extended addressing, the address contained in the second byte of the instruction is used as the higher 8 bits of the address of the operand. The third byte of the instruction is used as the lower 8 bits of the address for the operand. This is an absolute address in memory. These are 3-byte instructions.
Indexed addressing	In indexed addressing, the address contained in the second byte of the instruction is added to the index register's lowest 8 bits. Any carry generated is then added to the higher-order 8 bits of the index register. This result is then used to address memory. The modified address is held in a temporary address register so there is no change to the index register. These are 2-byte instructions.
Implied addressing	In the implied addressing mode the OP code gives the address (i.e., stack pointer, index register, etc.). These are 1-byte instructions.
Relative addressing	In relative addressing, the address contained in the second byte of the instruction is added to the program counter's lowest 8 bits plus 2. The carry or borrow is then added to the high 8 bits. This allows the user to address data within a range of −125 to +129 bytes of the present instruction. These are 2-byte instructions.

other, and the program can still service each interrupt in turn and then return to the original program which was operating when the first interrupt occurred.

Details of the operating features of this CPU can be found in the manufacturers' manuals listed in the bibliography.

TABLE 10·3 ACCUMULATOR AND MEMORY INSTRUCTIONS (Courtesy Motorola Corp.)

OPERATIONS	MNEMONIC	IMMED OP	DIRECT OP	INDEX OP	EXTND OP	IMPLIED OP	BOOLEAN ARITHMETIC OPERATION (All register labels refer to contents)
Add	ADDA	8B	9B	AB	BB		$A + M \rightarrow A$
	ADDB	CB	DB	EB	FB		$B + M \rightarrow B$
Add accumulators	ABA					1B	$A + B \rightarrow A$
Add with carry	ADCA	89	99	A9	B9		$A + M + C \rightarrow A$
	ADCB	C9	D9	E9	F9		$B + M + C \rightarrow B$
And	ANDA	84	94	A4	B4		$A \cdot M \rightarrow A$
	ANDB	C4	D4	E4	F4		$B \cdot M \rightarrow B$
Bit test	BITA	85	95	A5	B5		$A \cdot M$
	BITB	C5	D5	E5	F5		$B \cdot M$
Clear	CLR			6F	7F		$00 \rightarrow M$
	CLRA					4F	$00 \rightarrow A$
	CLRB					5F	$00 \rightarrow B$
Compare	CMPA	81	91	A1	B1		$A - M$
	CMPB	C1	D1	E1	F1		$B - M$
Compare accumulators	CBA					11	$A - B$
Complement 1s	COM			63	73		$M \rightarrow M$
	COMA					43	$A \rightarrow A$
	COMB					53	$B \rightarrow B$
Complement 2s (negate)	NEG			60	70		$00 - M \rightarrow M$
	NEGA					40	$00 - A \rightarrow A$
	NEGB					50	$00 - B \rightarrow B$
Decimal adjust, A	DAA					19	Converts binary addition of BCD characters into BCD format

Operation	Mnemonic	IMMED	DIRECT	INDEX	EXTND	INHER	Boolean/Arithmetic Operation
Decrement	DEC			6A	7A		$M - 1 \to M$
	DECA					4A	$A - 1 \to A$
	DECB					5A	$B - 1 \to B$
Exclusive OR	EORA	88	98	A8	B8		$A \oplus M \to A$
	EORB	C8	D8	E8	F8		$B \oplus M \to B$
Increment	INC			6C	7C		$M + 1 \to M$
	INCA					4C	$A + 1 \to A$
	INCB					5C	$B + 1 \to B$
Load accumulator	LDAA	86	96	A6	B6		$M \to A$
	LDAB	C6	D6	E6	F6		$M \to B$
Inclusive OR	ORAA	8A	9A	AA	BA		$A + M \to A$
	ORAB	CA	DA	EA	FA		$B + M \to B$
Push data	PSHA					36	$A \to M_{SP}, SP - 1 \to SP$
	PSHB					37	$B \to M_{SP}, SP - 1 \to SP$
Pull data	PULA					32	$SP + 1 \to SP, M_{SP} \to A$
	PULB					33	$SP + 1 \to SP, M_{SP} \to B$
Rotate left	ROL			69	79		$\left.\begin{array}{l} M \\ A \\ B \end{array}\right\}$
	ROLA					49	
	ROLB					59	
Rotate right	ROR			66	76		$\left.\begin{array}{l} M \\ A \\ B \end{array}\right\}$
	RORA					46	
	RORB					56	
Shift left, arithmetic	ASL			68	78		$\left.\begin{array}{l} M \\ A \\ B \end{array}\right\}$
	ASLA					48	
	ASLB					58	
Shift right, arithmetic	ASR			67	77		$\left.\begin{array}{l} M \\ A \\ B \end{array}\right\}$
	ASRA					47	
	ASRB					57	
Shift right, logic	LSR			64	74		$\left.\begin{array}{l} M \\ A \\ B \end{array}\right\}$
	LSRA					44	
	LSRB					54	

TABLE 10·3 ACCUMULATOR AND MEMORY INSTRUCTIONS (CONTINUED)

		ADDRESSING MODES					BOOLEAN ARITHMETIC OPERATION (All register labels refer to contents)
		IMMED	DIRECT	INDEX	EXTND	IMPLIED	
OPERATIONS	MNEMONIC	OP	OP	OP	OP	OP	
Store accumulator	STAA		97	A7	B7		$A \rightarrow M$
	STAB		D7	E7	F7		$B \rightarrow M$
Subtract	SUBA	80	90	A0	B0		$A - M \rightarrow A$
	SUBB	C0	D0	E0	F0		$B - M \rightarrow B$
Subtract accumulator	SBA					10	$A - B \rightarrow A$
Subtract with carry	SBCA	82	92	A2	B2		$A - M - C \rightarrow A$
	SBCB	C2	D2	E2	F2		$B - M - C \rightarrow B$
Transfer accumulators	TAB					16	$A \rightarrow B$
	TBA					17	$B \rightarrow A$
Test, zero or minus	TST			6D	7D		$M - 00$
	TSTA					4D	$A - 00$
	TSTB					5D	$B - 00$

OP Operation code (hexadecimal)
+   Arithmetic plus
−   Arithmetic minus
.   Boolean AND
M_{SP} Contents of memory location pointed to by stack pointer
+   Boolean inclusive OR

⊕   Boolean exclusive OR
$\bar{M}$ Complement of M
→   Transfer into
0   Bit = zero
00   Byte = zero

Note: Accumulator addressing mode instructions are included in the column for *implied* addressing.

TABLE 10·4 INDEX REGISTER AND STACK MANIPULATION INSTRUCTIONS

POINTER OPERATIONS	MNEMONIC	IMMED OP	DIRECT OP	INDEX OP	EXTND OP	IMPLIED OP	BOOLEAN ARITHMETIC OPERATION
Compare index register	CPX	8C	9C	AC	BC		$X_H - M$, $X_L - (M+1)$
Decrement index register	DEX					09	$X - 1 \rightarrow X$
Decrement stack pointer	DES					34	$SP - 1 \rightarrow SP$
Increment index register	INX					08	$X + 1 \rightarrow X$
Increment stack pointer	INS					31	$SP + 1 \rightarrow SP$
Load index register	LDX	CE	DE	EE	FE		$M \rightarrow X_H$, $(M+1) \rightarrow X_L$
Load stack pointer	LDS	8E	9E	AE	BE		$M \rightarrow SP_H$, $(M+1) \rightarrow SP_L$
Store index register	STX		DF	EF	FF		$X_H \rightarrow M$, $X_L \rightarrow (M+1)$
Store stack pointer	STS		9F	AF	BF		$SP_H \rightarrow M$, $SP_L \rightarrow (M+1)$
Index register → stack pointer	TXS					35	$X - 1 \rightarrow SP$
Stack pointer → index register	TSX					30	$SP + 1 \rightarrow X$

TABLE 10·5 JUMP AND BRANCH INSTRUCTIONS

OPERATIONS	MNEMONIC	RELATIVE OP	INDEX OP	EXTND OP	IMPLIED OP	BRANCH TEST
Branch always	BRA	20				None
Branch if carry clear	BCC	24				$C = 0$
Branch if carry set	BCS	25				$C = 1$
Branch if $= 0$	BEQ	27				$Z = 1$
Branch if ≥ 0	BGE	2C				$N \oplus V = 0$
Branch if > 0	BGT	2E				$Z + (N \oplus V) = 0$
Branch if higher	BHI	22				$C + Z = 0$
Branch if ≤ 0	BLE	2F				$Z + (N \oplus V) = 1$
Branch if lower or same	BLS	23				$C + Z = 1$
Branch if < 0	BLT	2D				$N \oplus V = 1$
Branch if minus	BMI	2B				$N = 1$
Branch if not equal 0	BNE	26				$Z = 0$
Branch if overflow clear	BVC	28				$V = 0$
Branch if overflow set	BVS	29				$V = 1$
Branch if plus	BPL	2A				$N = 0$
Branch to subroutine	BSR	8D				
Jump	JMP		6E	7E		
Jump to subroutine	JSR		AD	BD		
No operation	NOP				02	Advances prog. cntr. only
Return from interrupt	RTI				3B	
Return from subroutine	RTS				39	
Software interrupt	SWI				3F	
Wait for interrupt	WAI				3E	

TABLE 10·6 CONDITION CODE REGISTER BITS

Condition code register The condition code register indicates the results of an arithmetic-logic-unit operation: negative (N), zero (Z), overflow (V), carry from bit 7 (C), and half carry from bit 3 (H). These bits of the condition code register are used as testable conditions for the conditional branch instructions. Bit 4 is the interrupt mask bit (1). The unused bits of the condition code register (b_6 and b_7) are 1s.

When a set of chips of this kind are used with a fixed program, for instance, in an industrial controller, the program is generally developed using systems software provided by the chips' manufacturer and the software vendors. It is a common practice to write the program for the microprocessor and assemble this program using another larger computer. The program is also generally tested using this larger computer which runs the program on a simulator. The larger computer then produces a punched tape which is used to set up the ROM in which the program will be stored.

Considerable effort is made by the manufacturers of the microprocessor chips to facilitate programming the microprocessor and to facilitate preparing the ROMs and loading the RAMs, when required. Sometimes, higher-level languages are provided which enabled programs to be written in Fortran, PL/1, or other compiler languages which are then translated into the program for the microcomputer.

10•9 SINGLE-ADDRESS COMPUTER ORGANIZATION

A straightforward example of a single-address computer is the DEC PDP-8 minicomputer. This was the first major entry in the minicomputer race and continues to be an important computer (in terms of sales) for DEC. This computer will be used to point out some basic principles in computer architecture.

TABLE 10·7 CONDITION CODE REGISTER MANIPULATION INSTRUCTIONS

OPERATIONS	MNEMONIC	OP	BOOLEAN OPERATION
Clear carry	CLC	0C	$0 \rightarrow C$
Clear interrupt mask	CLI	0E	$0 \rightarrow 1$
Clear overflow	CLV	0A	$0 \rightarrow V$
Set carry	SEC	0D	$1 \rightarrow C$
Set interrupt mask	SEI	0F	$1 \rightarrow I$
Set overflow	SEV	0B	$1 \rightarrow V$
Accumalator $A \rightarrow$ CCR	TAP	06	$A \rightarrow$ CCR
$CCR \rightarrow$ accumulator A	TPA	07	$CCR \rightarrow A$

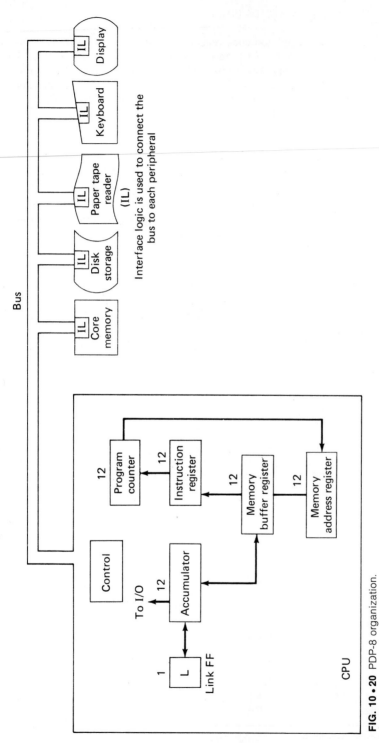

FIG. 10·20 PDP-8 organization.

The PDP-8 has a 12-bit instruction word as shown in Fig. 10·20. The memory is also organized in 12-bit words and a basic memory block consists of $2^{12} = 4096$ words. Since the instruction word is very short, the designers have allowed only 3 bits for the OP-code part, and so, as shown in Fig. 10·21, there are only eight basic classes of instruction words.

Several of the basic instructions are very straightforward. For instance, the TAD instruction (for 2s complement ADD) simply performs a 2s comple-

FIG. 10·21 Instruction repertoire for PDP-8. (Courtesy Digital Equipment Corp.)

Main program

This instruction calls subprogram

The subprogram returns control to the instruction following

Subprogram

Last instruction in subprogram returns control to calling program

(a)

Subprogram

(b)

Location in memory

354
355
211

When JMS is executed, the program counter +1 is stored at the address in the JMS instruction. The program then jumps to the next address in memory.

JMP I 354

Subprogram

The subprogram is exited by an indirect address jump instruction which returns control to the instruction following the JMS.

Location in memory

210   JMS 354
211

Main program

(c)

FIG. 10·22 (a) Calling a subprogram; (b) same subprogram may be called several times; (c) how the PDP-8 handles subprogram calls and returns.

ment addition of the operand addressed in memory to the operand currently in the 12-bit single accumulator and places the sum in this accumulator. There is an extra flip-flop called the *link* or *L bit* which receives any overflow from this addition. The OP code for TAD is 000_2 or 0_8.

Similarly, the AND instruction simply performs a bit-by-bit AND on the operand addressed in memory and the contents of the accumulator, placing the result in the accumulator. The OP code for AND is 001_2 or 1_8.

The addressing techniques used by the 9 bits to form addresses have been described. The 3 bit in an instruction word is a 0 if the address is direct and a 1 if indirect (the address of the address). The 4 bit is a 0 if the remaining 7 bits (bits 5 to 11) give the actual address on page 0 of the memory and a 1 if the address is on the same page as the instruction word.

There is an ISZ (for increment and skip if zero) instruction which increments the word addresssed and returns it to memory. If this word becomes a 0, the next instruction following the ISZ instruction is not executed; instead, the computer next executes the word in memory following this word. This particular instruction is very useful in indexing through tables and is provided as a substitute for index registers.

The DCA instruction (for deposit and clear the accumulator) stores the accumulator in the memory at the address specified and also clears the accumulator to all 0s. The OP code for DCA is 011 or 3_8.

The JMS (for jump to subroutine) brings up an important feature in instruction repertoires for computers. It is good form in writing a computer program to break the program into as many subprograms (separable pieces of the program) as possible. These subprograms or subroutines are then jumped to whenever the function they perform is required. Refer to Fig. $10 \cdot 22(a)$.

The problem confronting the computer designer is that a given subprogram can be jumped to from several different locations in the program. This is shown in Fig. $10 \cdot 22(b)$. For instance, in most minicomputers and microcomputers no square root instruction is provided. If many square roots are called for in a program, the programmer writes a single square root subprogram (or subroutine) and whenever the program must find a square root a JUMP is made to this subprogram. After the square root has been formed the subprogram then causes a jump back to the instruction following the JMS subprogram instruction in the original program section. The subprogram is then said to be *called,* and it exits by returning to the *calling program.*

The problem is to arrange for a smooth jump to the called subprogram and to make it easy for the subprogram to return or jump back to the original program. To implement this it is necessary to "plant" the address of the instruction to be returned to when the subprogram is finished in some convenient place for the subprogram. Since the program counter (instruction counter) contains this address when the jump is made, most computers provide a JMS instruction which will store the program counter before the jump is made.

The JMS instruction in the PDP-8 operates as follows. The program counter is stored at the address given in the address portion of the JMS instruction. The computer then jumps to the next address in memory. That is, if we write

JMS 50_8 (where 50_8 is the 50th location in memory) and if our instruction word is at 201_8 in memory, when the JMS 50_8 instruction is executed, the value 202_8 will be stored at location 50_8 in the memory and the computer will actually jump to or execute the word at location 51_8 next.†

The planting of the program counter's contents at location 50_8 in the above example enables the writer of the subroutine to exit from the subprogram by placing a JUMP or JMP instruction at the end of the subprogram and using the address 50_8 in the address section, but making the address an indirect address. Therefore, the computer will actually jump to the address stored at location 50_8 which will be 202_8, and the next instruction executed will be that at location 202_8.

Notice that a subprogram set up in this way can be jumped to by a JMS and exited using a JMP indirect from any place in memory and the return will always be correct.

The above scheme is a good one and has been used (with variations) in several machines but it has the problem that if a subprogram calls another subprogram which then calls the first subprogram, the return address for the original return will be wiped out. While this may seem unlikely, programs can become very complicated and this must be guarded against.

If a subprogram can call itself or can call another program which then calls it without damage, then the subprogram is said to be *recursive.*

A scheme whereby jumps to subprograms can be made so that a subprogram can call itself will be given in a later description.

The PDP 8 is a bused computer, and input-output devices are connected to this bus. Input-output in the PDP-8 is provided by the IOT (for input-output transfer) instruction. The input-output devices are each assigned a number from 0 to $2^6 - 1$, and when an IOT instruction is given, the number in bits 3 to 8 of the IOT is placed on six wires in the bus which each input-output device inputs to see if it is being addressed. The remaining 3 bits are also transmitted on the bus and tell the input-output device what it is to do. (READ, WRITE, REWIND, etc.) The selected input-output device responds to the bus signals generated by the IOT instruction using logic circuits in its interface to interpret the instruction and to place data on the data section of the bus, read from it, etc.

The input-output devices are allowed to interrupt the processor and demand service during program operation using the computer's interrupt facility. There is an instruction, the ION (interrupt ON) instruction, which raises a bus wire called ION to the input-output devices telling them it is their right to raise the INTERRUPT line on the bus and demand service.

If an input-output device raises its interrupt line while the computer is operating a program, the address of the next instruction word which would normally be executed is placed in location 0 in the memory and the next instruction executed is at location 1 in the memory. (This is generally a jump to the subprogram which services input-output devices.)

---

† DEC uses octal numbers in PDP-8 programming almost exclusively.

Address in
memory

If interrupt signal is given by peripheral device when this instruction is being executed

The computer automatically places the address of the next instruction which would have been executed in location 0 in memory

The computer jumps to address 1 in the memory

After the interrupt has been serviced, a jump instruction with indirect address 0 will cause a jump back to the next instruction which would have been executed

FIG. 10 • 23 Interrupts in PDP-8.

Since the address of the next instruction word in the program which was interrupted is in location 0, the interrupt service program† can exit using that address to return to the original program. This is shown in Fig. 10·23.

Again, an interrupt of an interrupt will cause the original return address (at 0 in the memory) to be destroyed. The programmer must see this does not occur, and the right of devices to interrupt is revoked as soon as an interrupt occurs. (The bus line for ION is lowered.) The program must also issue another ION in order to restore the interrupt privilege to input-output devices.

The PDP-8 has a number of features which have helped to make it attractive but which are outside the context of this description. For instance, since there is only a single arithmetic instruction, the TAD, it is necessary to complement an operand and then add in order to subtract. To perform this complement and also to provide ROTATE or SHIFT instructions, some SKIP instructions, and some other logical operations, the OP code 111 is a "no address" instruction class where the remaining 9 bits tell which of a number of different possible operations can be made to occur. (Details can be found in the manufacturers' manuals listed in the references.)

---

† The program (or subprogram) which handles the peripheral that generates the interrupt is called an *interrupt service program.*

10 • 10 A SINGLE-ADDRESS MICROPROCESSOR

The Intel 8080 is an example of a microprocessor chip series with a basic 40-pin IC chip containing the 8080 CPU. Other chips available include RAMs, ROMs, interface chips, etc. The chips are interconnected using a bus which contains 8 data lines, 16 address lines, and 6 control lines.

The 8080 CPU is basically a single-accumulator organization, but a number of other registers are provided, as shown in Fig. 10 · 24 (see p. 496). The instruction word formats are shown in Fig. 10 · 25 (see p. 497). Since 8 bits are used for the OP code, a large instruction repertoire has been provided. Some of these instructions are shown in Tables 10 · 8 and 10 · 9.

At the beginning of each instruction cycle, the 8-bit OP code is read by the 8080 CPU, and this determines how many more fetches from memory the CPU must make to execute the instruction. Some instructions require only the 8-bit OP code while some require 8-bit and some 16-bit addresses or operands, and so the CPU must make the necessary accesses to perform the instruction.

The Intel 8080 has a good set of addressing modes (see Table 10 · 10 on p. 497). It also has conditional BRANCH or JUMP instructions which jump or do not jump depending on the values in what are called *condition flags*. These consist of five flip-flops (see Table 10 · 11 on p. 498) that are set to the 0 or 1 state by the results of arithmetic instructions. For instance, if an addition is performed and the result is 0, then the Z flag will be set to 1 and the S, P, and C flags to 0 (provided no carry was generated). A conditional JUMP instruction which tested the Z flag would then cause a jump, whereas a conditional JUMP instruction which tests the S, P, or C flags would not cause a jump.

This computer uses what is now becoming the most used technique for subroutine calls and for servicing interrupts.

For a subroutine jump a CALL instruction is used. The address of the subroutine is in the 16 bits (two memory addresses) following the CALL OP code. This instruction first increments the program counter to the address of the next instruction in sequence and then places (pushes) the contents of the program counter on a stack in the memory. The stack pointer (Fig. 10 · 24) is adjusted to point to this address on the stack. The jump to the subprogram is then made.

At the end of the subprogram, a RETURN instruction is placed. This instruction specifies no address but simply causes a return to the address currently on top of the stack and then "pops" this address.

An investigation of this scheme will show that if a subroutine calls another subroutine which calls another subroutine which then calls the first subroutine, the successive addresses needed are stacked one on the other, and the subprograms will finally work their way back to the original calling program without loss of any of the necessary address links.

Interrupts are handled in a similar way in this computer. The program

(*Text continues on page 498*)

TABLE 10·8 INSTRUCTION REPERTOIRE FOR 8080 CPU (NOTATION USED IN TABLE 10·9)

SYMBOL	MEANING
Accumulator	Register A
Addr	16-bit address quantity
Data	8-bit data quantity
Data 16	16-bit data quantity
Byte 2	The second byte of the instruction
Byte 3	The third byte of the instruction
Port	8-bit address of an input-output device
r,r1,r2	One of the registers A,B,C,D,E,H,L
DDD, SSS	The bit pattern designating one of the registers A,B,C,D,E,H,L (DDD = destination, SSS = source):

DDD or SSS	Register name
111	A
000	B
001	C
010	D
011	E
100	H
101	L

SYMBOL	MEANING
rh	The first (high-order) register of a designated register pair.
rl	The second (low-order) register of a designated register pair.
rp	One of the register pairs: B represents the B,C pair with B as the high-order register and C as the low-order register; D represents the D,E pair with D as the high-order register and E as the low-order register; H represents the H,L pair with H as the high-order register and L as the low-order register; SP represents the 16-bit stack pointer register.

SYMBOL	MEANING
RP	The bit pattern designating one of the register pairs B,D,H,SP:

RP	Register pair
00	B,C
01	D,E
10	H,L
11	SP

SYMBOL	MEANING
PC	16-bit program counter register (PCH and PCL are used to refer to the high-order and low-order 8 bits, respectively).
SP	Stack pointer
r_m	Bit m of the register r (bits are number 7 through 0 from left to right).
Z,S,CY,AC	The condition flags: zero, sign, parity, carry, and auxiliary carry, respectively.
( )	The contents of the memory location or registers enclosed in the parentheses.
←	"Is transferred to"
$\wedge$	Logical AND
$\forall$	Exclusive OR
$\vee$	Inclusive OR
+	Addition
−	2s complement subtraction
*	Multiplication
↔	"Is exchanged with"
¯	The 1s complement [e.g., $(\bar{A})$]
n	The restart number 0 through 7
NNN	The binary representation 000 through 111 for restart number 0 through 7, respectively.

TABLE 10·9 INSTRUCTION REPERTOIRE FOR 8080 CPU

MOV r1, r2 (move register)

(r1) ← (r2)

The content of register r2 is moved to register r1.

0	1	D	D	D	S	S	S

Addressing: register   Flags: none

MOV r, M (move from memory)

(r) ← ((H)(L))

The content of the memory location, whose address is in registers H and L, is moved to register r.

0	1	D	D	D	1	1	0

Addressing: register indirect   Flags: none

MOV M, r (move to memory)

((H)(L)) ← (r)

Addressing: register indirect   Flags: none

MOV M, r (move to memory)

((H)(L)) ← (r)

The content of register r is moved to the memory location whose address is in registers H and L.

0	1	1	1	0	S	S	S

Addressing: register indirect   Flags: none

ADD r (Add register)

(A) ← (A) + (r)

The content of register r is added to the content of the accumulator. The result is placed in the accumulator.

1	0	0	0	0	S	S	S

Addressing: register   Flags: Z,S,P,CY,AC

ADD M (add memory)

(A) ← (A) + ((H)(L))

The content of the memory location whose address is contained in the H and L registers is added to the content of the accumulator. The result is placed in the accumulator.

1	1	0	0	0	1	1	0

Addressing: register indirect   Flags: Z,S,P,CY,AC

ADI data (add immediate)

(A) ← (A) + (byte 2)

The content of the second byte of the instruction is added to the content of the accumulator. Result is placed in the accumulator.

1	1	0	0	0	1	1	0
data

Addressing: immediate

INR M (increment memory)

$((H)(L)) \leftarrow ((H)(L)) + 1$

The content of the memory location whose address is contained in the H and L registers is incremented by one. *Note:* All condition flags except CY are affected.

0	0	1	1	0	1	0	0

Addressing: register indirect   Flags: Z,S,P,AC

LDA addr (load accumulator direct)

$(A) \leftarrow ((\text{byte 3})(\text{byte 2}))$

The content of the memory location, whose address is specified in byte 2 and byte 3 of the instruction, is moved to register A.

0	0	1	1	1	0	1	0
low-order addr							
high-order addr							

Addressing: direct   Flags: none

STA addr (store accumulator direct)

$((\text{byte 3})(\text{byte 2})) \leftarrow (A)$

Content of the accumulator is moved to the memory location whose address is specified in byte 2 and 3 of the instruction.

0	0	1	1	0	0	1	0
low-order addr							
high-order addr							

Addressing: direct   Flags: none

SUB M (subtract memory)

$(A) \leftarrow (A) - ((H)(L))$

The content of the memory location whose address is contained in the H and L registers is subtracted from the content of the accumulator. The result is placed in the accumulator.

1	0	0	1	0	1	1	0

Addressing: register indirect   Flags: Z,S,P,CY,AC

SUI data (subtract immediate)

$(A) \leftarrow (A) - (\text{byte 2})$

The content of the second byte of the instruction is subtracted from the content of the accumulator. The result is placed in the accumulator.

1	1	0	1	0	1	1	0
data							

Addressing: immediate   Flags: Z,S,P,CY, AC

SBB r (subtract register with borrow)

$(A) \leftarrow (A) - (r) - (CY)$

The content of register r and the content of the CY flag are both subtracted from the accumulator. The result is placed in the accumulator.

1	0	0	1	1	S	S	S

Addressing: register   Flags: Z,S,P,CY,AC

491

TABLE 10·9 INSTRUCTION REPERTOIRE FOR 8080 CPU *(CONTINUED)*

DCR r (decrement register)

$(r) \leftarrow (r) - 1$

The content of register r is decremented by 1. *Note:* All condition flags except CY are affected.

0	0	D	D	D	1	0	1

Addressing: register

LDAX rp (load accumulator indirect)

$(A) \leftarrow ((rp))$

The content of the memory location, whose address is in the register pair rp, is moved to register A. *Note:* Only register pairs rp = B (registers B and C) or rp = D (registers D and E) may be specified.

0	0	R	P	1	0	1	0

Addressing: register indirect   Flags: none

STAX rp (store accumulator indirect)

$((rp)) \leftarrow (A)$

The content of register A is moved to the memory location whose address is in the register pair rp. *Note:* Only register pairs rp = B (register B and C) or rp = D (registers D and E) may be specified.

0	0	R	P	0	0	1	0

Addressing: register indirect   Flags: none

XCHG (exchange H and L with D and E)

$(H) \leftrightarrow (D)$
$(L) \leftrightarrow (E)$

The contents of registers H and L are exchanged with the contents of registers D and E.

1	1	1	0	1	0	1	1

Addressing: register   Flags: none

INR r (increment register)

$(r) \leftarrow (r) + 1$

The content of register r is incremented by 1. *Note:* All condition flags except CY are affected.

0	0	D	D	D	1	0	0

Addressing: register   Flags: Z,S,P,AC

MVI M, data (move to memory immediate)

$((H)(L)) \leftarrow$ (byte 2)

The content of byte 2 of the instruction is moved to the memory location whose address is in registers H and L.

0	0	1	1	0	1	1	0
Data						

Addressing: immediate register indirect
Flags: none

LXI rp, data 16   (load register pair immediate)

(rh) ← (byte 3)   (rl) ← (byte 2)

Byte 3 of the instruction is moved into the high-order register (rh) of the register pair rp. Byte 2 of the instruction is moved into the low-order register (rl) of the register pair rp.

0	0	R	P	0	0	0	1
Low-order data							
High-order data							

Addressing: immediate   Flags: none

BRANCH GROUP

This group of instructions alters normal sequential program flow. *Condition flags are not affected* by any instruction in this group.

The two types of branch instructions are unconditional and conditional. Unconditional transfers simply perform the specified operation on register PC (the program counter). Conditional transfers examine the status of one of the four processor flags to determine if the specified branch is to be executed. The conditions that may be specified are as follows:

Condition		CCC
NZ	– not zero (Z = 0)	000
Z	– zero (Z = 1)	001
NC	– no carry (CY = 0)	010
C	– carry (CY = 1)	011
PO	– parity odd (P = 0)	100
PE	– parity even (P = 1)	101
P	– plus (S = 0)	110
M	– minus (S = 1)	111

JMP addr   (jump)

(PC) ← (byte 3) (byte 2)

Control is transferred to the instruction whose address is specified in byte 3 and byte 2 of the current instruction.

1	1	0	0	0	0	1	1
Low-order addr							
High-order addr							

Addressing: immediate
Flags: none

Jcondition addr   (conditional jump)

If (CCC), (PC) ← (byte 3) (byte 2)

If the specified condition is true, control is transferred to the instruction whose address is specified in byte 3 and byte 2 of the current instruction: otherwise, control continues sequentially.

1	1	C	C	C	0	1	0
Low-order addr							
High-order addr							

Addressing: immediate
Flags: none

TABLE 10·9 INSTRUCTION REPERTOIRE FOR 8080 CPU (CONTINUED)

CALL addr (Call)

$((SP) - 1) \leftarrow (PCH)$ $(SP) \leftarrow (SP) - 2$
$((SP) - 2) \leftarrow (PCL)$ $(PC) \leftarrow$ (byte 3) (byte 2)

The high-order 8 bits of the next instruction address are moved to the memory location whose address is one less than the content of register SP. The low-order 8 bits of the next instruction address are moved to the memory location whose address is 2 less than the content of register SP. The content of register SP is decremented by 2. Control is transferred to the instruction whose address is specified in byte 3 and byte 2 of the current instruction.

1	1	0	0	1	1	0	1
Low-order addr							
High-order addr							

Addressing: immediate/register indirect
Flags: none

RET (return)

$(PCL) \leftarrow ((SP))$ $(PCH) \leftarrow ((SP) + 1)$
$(SP) \leftarrow (SP) + 2$

The content of the memory location whose address is specified in register SP is moved to the low-order 8 bits of register PC. The content of the memory location whose address is one more than the content of register SP is moved to the high-order 8 bits of register PC. The content of register SP is incremented by 2.

1	1	0	0	1	0	0	1

Addressing: register indirect
Flags: none

STACK, INPUT-OUTPUT, AND MACHINE CONTROL GROUP

This group of instructions performs input-output, manipulates the stack, and alters internal control flags.

Unless otherwise specified, *condition flags are not affected by any instructions in this group.*

PUSH rp (push)

$((SP) - 1) \leftarrow (rh)$
$((SP) - 2) \leftarrow (rl)$
$(SP) \leftarrow (SP) - 2$

The content of the high-order register of register pair rp is moved to the memory location whose address is 1 less than the content of register SP. The content of the low-order register of register pair rp is moved to the memory location whose address is 2 less than the content of register SP. The content of register SP is decremented by 2. *Note: Register pair rp = SP may not be specified.*

1	1	R	P	0	1	0	1

Addressing: register indirect
Flags: none

PUSH PSW (push processor status word)

$((SP) - 1) \leftarrow (A)$
$((SP) - 2)_0 \leftarrow (CY), ((SP) - 2)_1 \leftarrow 1$
$((SP) - 2)_2 \leftarrow (P), ((SP) - 2)_3 \leftarrow 0$
$((SP) - 2)_4 \leftarrow (AC), ((SP) - 2)_5 \leftarrow 0$
$((SP) - 2)_6 \leftarrow (Z), ((SP) - 2)_7 \leftarrow (S)$
$(SP) \leftarrow (SP) - 2$

The content of register A is moved to the memory location whose address is 1 less than register SP. The contents of the condition flags are assembled into a processor status word and the word is moved to the memory location whose address is 2 less than the content of register SP. The content of register SP is decremented by 2.

1	1	1	1	0	1	0	1

Addressing: register indirect
Flags: none

POP rp (pop)

$(rl) \leftarrow ((SP))$
$(rh) \leftarrow ((SP) + 1)$
$(SP) \leftarrow (SP) + 2$

The content of the memory location, whose address is specified by the content of register SP, is moved to the low-order register of register pair rp. The content of the memory location, whose address is 1 more than the content of register SP, is moved to the high-order register of register pair rp. The content of register

SP is incremented by 2. *Note: Register pair rp = SP may not be specified.*

1	1	R	P	0	0	0	1

Addressing: register indirect
Flags: none

POP PSW (pop processor status word)

$(CY) \leftarrow ((SP))_0$
$(P) \leftarrow ((SP))_2$
$(AC) \leftarrow ((SP))_4$
$(Z) \leftarrow ((SP))_6$
$(S) \leftarrow ((SP))_7$
$(A) \leftarrow ((SP) + 1)$
$(SP) \leftarrow (SP) + 2$

The content of the memory location whose address is specified by the content of register SP is used to restore the condition flags. The content of the memory location whose address is 1 more than the content of register SP is moved to register A. The content of register SP is incremented by 2.

1	1	1	1	0	0	0	1

Addressing: register indirect
Flags: Z,S,P,CY,AC

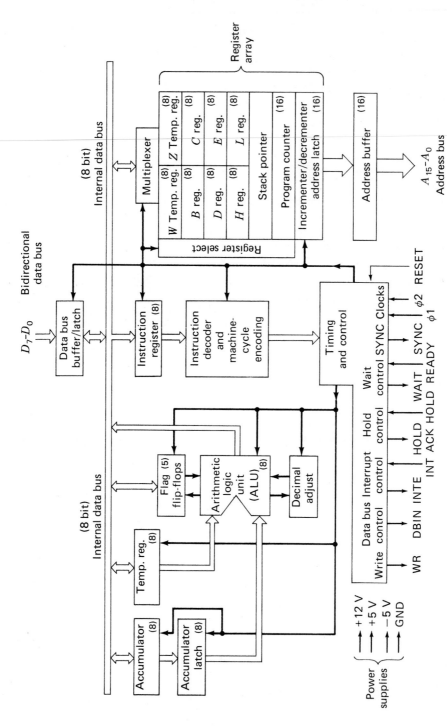

FIG. 10·24 8080 CPU functional block diagram. (Courtesy Intel Corp.)

TABLE 10•10 ADDRESSING MODES FOR THE 8080 CPU

ADDRESSING MODES

When multibyte numeric data are used, the data, like instructions, are stored in successive memory locations, with the least significant byte first, followed by increasingly significant bytes. The 8080 has four different modes for addressing data stored in memory or in registers:

Direct   Bytes 2 and 3 of the instruction contain the exact memory address of the data item (the low-order bits of the address are in byte 2, the high-order bits in byte 3).

Register   The instruction specifies the register or register pair in which the data are located.

Register indirect   The instruction specifies a register pair which contains the memory address where the data are located (the high-order bits of the address are in the first register of the pair, the low-order bits in the second).

Immediate   The instruction contains the data. This is either an 8-bit quantity or a 16-bit quantity (least significant byte first, most significant byte second).

Unless directed by an INTERRUPT or BRANCH instruction, the execution of instructions proceeds through consecutively increasing memory locations. A BRANCH instruction can specify the address of the next instruction to be executed in one of two ways:

Direct   The BRANCH instruction contains the address of the next instruction to be executed. (Except for the RST instruction, byte 2 contains the low-order address and byte 3 the high-order address.)

Register indirect   The BRANCH instruction indicates a register pair which contains the address of the next instruction to be executed. (The high-order bits of the address are in the first register of the pair, the low-order bits in the second.)

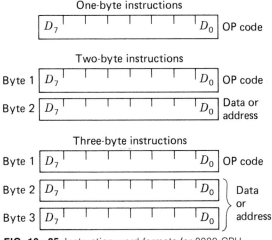

FIG. 10•25 Instruction-word formats for 8080 CPU.

TABLE 10•11 FLAGS USED IN 8080 CPU

Flag Word							
D_7	D_6	D_5	D_4	D_3	D_2	D_1	D_0
S	Z	0	AC	0	P	1	CY

CONDITION FLAGS

There are five condition flags associated with the execution of instructions on the 8080. They are zero, sign, parity, carry, and auxiliary carry, and are each represented by a 1-bit register in the CPU. A flag is "set" by forcing the bit to 1; "reset" by forcing the bit to 0.

Unless indicated otherwise, when an instruction affects a flag, it affects it in the following manner:

Zero If the result of an instruction has the value 0, this flag is set; otherwise it is reset.

Sign If the most significant bit of the result of the operation has the value 1, this flag is set; otherwise it is reset.

Parity If the modulo 2 sum of the bits of the result of the operation is 0, (i.e., if the result has even parity), this flag is set; otherwise it is reset (i.e., if the result has odd parity).

Carry If the instruction resulted in a carry (from addition), or a borrow (from subtraction or a comparison) out of the high-order bit, this flag is set; otherwise it is reset.

Auxiliary carry If the instruction caused a carry out of bit 3 and into bit 4 of the resulting value, the auxiliary carry is set; otherwise it is reset. This flag is affected by single precision additions, subtractions, increments, decrements, comparisons, and logical operations.

---

being executed is interrupted, and the address of the next instruction which was to be executed is placed on the top of the stack maintained by the stack pointer. Returns from the interrupt servicing subroutine can then use the RETURN instruction to return to the original program. This is shown in Fig. 10·26.

When this sort of stacking of subprogram and interrupt addresses is used, then it is possible to have subroutines interrupted, interrupts interrupted, and so on, and still return to each strip of instructions correctly as long as the stack does not overflow the area in memory allocated for it.

It is also necessary to save the registers in the CPU when interrupts occur if they are changed by the interrupt servicing subroutine. (The same applies for subroutine CALLs.) The interrupt program must take care of this saving and restoring of registers. Some idea of how this is done using a stack can be gathered by examining the PUSH and POP instructions, and the questions treat this in more detail.

Address in memory   For the 8080 CPU

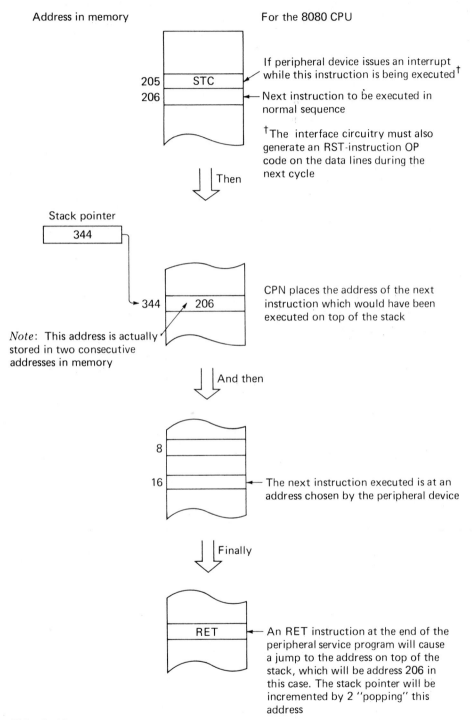

If peripheral device issues an interrupt while this instruction is being executed[†]

205 | STC

206 |

Next instruction to be executed in normal sequence

[†]The interface circuitry must also generate an RST-instruction OP code on the data lines during the next cycle

Then

Stack pointer

344

344 | 206

CPN places the address of the next instruction which would have been executed on top of the stack

Note: This address is actually stored in two consecutive addresses in memory

And then

8 |

16 |

The next instruction executed is at an address chosen by the peripheral device

Finally

RET

An RET instruction at the end of the peripheral service program will cause a jump to the address on top of the stack, which will be address 206 in this case. The stack pointer will be incremented by 2 "popping" this address

FIG. 10 • 26 Interrupt servicing using a stack.

10•11 TWO-ADDRESS COMPUTERS

The two-address computer has become increasingly popular. There are a number of "pure" two-address computers in existence and quite a few other computers with both multiple accumulators and instructions which are basically two-address instructions.

A great deal of the success of the two-address format can be traced to the great popularity of the IBM 1400 and 1600 series of computers. At one time there were more 1400 series computers in existence than all of the rest of the computers combined. This was some years ago and IBM has since discontinued this line of computer, replacing it with the 360/370 series. The 360/370 series can emulate or imitate the 1400 series, however, and many of the instructions in the 360/370 series are close copies of the 1400 instructions. Further, the Honeywell 200 series is a very popular line of computers which closely follows the instruction-word formats and operational features of the IBM 1400 series. We will use the Honeywell 200 series as an example for this kind of computer.

Several typical instruction-word formats are shown for the Minneapolis-Honeywell 200 series of computers in Fig. 10·27. All these computers basically operate in a system where the memory is *character addressable*, which is to say that a given address in the memory contains not a computer word or field, but a single alphanumeric character.

In the Honeywell series of machines, a single alphanumeric character is expressed as 9 binary digits, where 6 of the 9 are used for the actual alphanumeric digit. One digit is a parity check, and the eighth binary digit indicates whether or not a given digit is the last in a computer word or field and

FIG. 10•27 Typical instruction-word formats.

is called an "end-of-word" bit. This machine also has a ninth digit called an *item-mark digit* which indicates that a particular alphanumeric digit is the last alphanumeric character in an item generally containing several words.

The 200 series of machines is used a great deal in the processing of business-type data, where names, addresses, and other alphanumeric information need be stored, and there is a great advantage in being able to vary the length of a computer word in the system. The end-of-word digit is used to indicate the last digit in a given word, and the program instruction simply indicates the first digit in a word. Characters are then read from the memory, one alphanumeric character at a time. Operands are read starting with the highest numbered location in memory at which the operand is stored, and the memory address register is decremented as each alphanumeric character is read until an end-of-word bit is read from the memory. Instruction words are read consecutively from the memory, with the memory address register counting upward instead of downward. End-of-word marks or bits are used to indicate the last alphanumeric character in an instruction word or in an operand.

The operation codes in these machines consist of a single alphanumeric character. Since the words are of variable length, instruction words are also of variable length, although only five basic lengths of instruction words are used. The simplest of these is a single alphanumeric digit which indicates a single simple operation, such as "read a card into the memory." The next most complicated instruction word consists of an OP code, such as *B* for branch, and an address to which the machine is to branch. In this case, one alphanumeric digit gives the OP code and four alphanumeric digits give the address to which the machine is to branch.

The more usual two-address instruction contains an OP code of one digit and two 4-digit addresses, designated the *X* address and the *Y* address, making a total of nine alphanumeric characters in this type of instruction word. When these computers receive an OP code such as *A*, indicating addition, they add the number located at the address given in the *X* address part to the number located at the address given in the *Y* address part, and store this number at the location in memory given in the *Y* address part.

There are also instruction words with only an OP-code character and an OP-code modifier, and even longer instruction words which contain an OP code, an *I* address, a *Y* address, and a *D* character. The *D* character for this latter type of instruction is used to augment the number of instructions; that is, the *D* character is used to modify the meaning of the OP code given in the single alphanumeric character used as the basic OP-code character.

The internal operation is not too different from the single-address type of machine described in the section on control circuitry implementation. The primary differences arise from the BCD nature of the arithmetic and the fact that the memory is read from in a serial-parallel manner. However, the same basic registers are used in the control circuitry; that is, the OP-code register, the instruction counter, memory address register, and memory buffer registers are very much as previously described, as well as the READ and

Instruction word

OP code	X address	Y address
Ⓐ	1197	0009

Address in memory	1193	1194	1195	1196	1197	1198	1199
Data in each location	⑤	9	2	6	4	⑤	

Address in memory	4	5	6	7	8	9	10
Data in each location	6	②	4	2	5	7	⑨

FIG. 10·28 Execution of word on the Honeywell 200.

WRITE instructions to the memory and the fact that the machine alternates between instruction cycles and execution cycles. A primary difference is that the execution cycles are liable to require a good deal more time than instruction cycles, since two addresses in memory, and hence two operands, are used, and each may require several memory accesses. Also notice that two counters must be kept operating in order to handle the alternate addressing of the two operands in the memory.

As mentioned, each character in the Minneapolis-Honeywell system consists of 9 binary digits, of which 6 are used for the alphanumeric character. The three remaining bits consist of a parity digit, a word-mark digit, and an item-mark digit. To simplify programming, Honeywell draws a circle around those alphanumeric characters in which there is a word mark of 1 indicating the end of a word. Then instruction words address single characters in the memory, and the machine sequences through consecutive increasing addresses, pulling out character after character from the memory and incrementing the memory or instruction address register as each character is pulled out, until a character with a word mark of 1 is reached.

Figure $10 \cdot 28$ shows a typical instruction word with the operation code A, an X address 1197, and a Y address 9. This instruction word would occupy nine character positions or addresses in the memory and would be read serially from the memory. However, the X address would be stored in one register, the Y address in another register, and the OP code in the OP-code register.

The meaning of this instruction is as follows: Add the field or number which starts at address 1197 in the memory to the field or number lying at address 9 in the memory, and place the sum of these two numbers starting at address 9. This particular instruction operates on BCD characters, and possible contents for each of the character locations in the memory are also shown in the figure. The machine will continue adding characters while decreasing both of the instruction counters until it encounters a word mark in the Y-address series of characters, in which case it will terminate the addition. For instance, the character 2 at location 5 in the memory is circled, indicating that the word-mark bit is a 1 for that particular character.

The computer will first add the digit at location 9 to the digit at location 1197; so it adds 4 plus 7, places a 1 in location 9, and stores a carry digit to be added into the next pair of digits. The next digits are in locations 8 and 1196, which are 5 and 6, plus a carry of 1 from last time; so a 2 is placed in location 8 and a 1 is carried over to the addition of the next digits. These lie in 1195 and 7, respectively. The addition of these results in a 5 being placed in location 7. Then the character in 1194, which is a 9, is added to the number at location 6, giving a sum of 3 plus a carry, and finally we add 5 and 2 plus a carry, giving 8 to be put in location 5. After the addition, the data in locations 1193 and 1197 are as when the addition was initiated, whereas the number at locations 5 through 9 in the memory now contain 83521.

This computer can also add binary numbers, in which case six of the digits at each character location are considered to comprise six digits of a binary number and are added in 2s complement fashion.

FIG. 10 • 29 ADD instruction in Minneapolis-Honeywell 200.

Figure 10 · 29 shows another typical instruction word, which is a SUB-TRACT instruction, the OP code for this being an S; the X address given is 297, and the Y address 164. Nine locations in memory would be used for the instruction word shown, one location for each of the alphanumeric characters. The instruction would cause the subtraction of the numerical data in the X field from the numerical data in the Y field and the storing of this difference in the Y field. The subtraction terminates when a word mark is encountered; so it will terminate when the character at 293 is subtracted from the character at 160 in the memory.

The execution of this instruction word will cause 65143 to be subtracted from 83182 and the difference, 18039, to be placed in locations 160 through 164 in the memory, replacing the 83182 which was there at the beginning of the execution of the instruction.

Another instruction word, a "branch if character equal" instruction, is also shown in the figure. The OP code for this is B. The figure indicates an I address which is 93, a Y address which is 167, and a so-called D character A. Ten alphanumeric characters would be required to store this particular instruction word; hence it would occupy ten locations in the memory. This instruction causes the single character at the Y address to be compared with the D character, and if it has the same bit configuration as the D character, the program branches to the *I* address. Otherwise, the program continues sequentially. The *D* character can be any desired character combination of the six digits used for each BCD digit. (The presence or absence of a word mark is not considered.) For the particular instruction word given, if the character located at address 167 is an *A*, the program will take the next instruction word starting at location 93 in the memory. If the character is not an *A*, the next instruction word will be pulled from the memory at the address following this particular instruction word.

Another example of two-address computer lines are the Nova and Super Nova machines manufactured by the Data General Corporation. These computers are minicomputers and are the same in general organization, so we will describe the Nova. The basic word in this machine has 16 bits, as shown in Fig. 10·30. This computer is an example of a *multiple-accumulator* computer. The Nova has four accumulators, and a basic arithmetic or logical in-

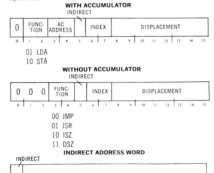

ARITHMETIC AND LOGICAL INSTRUCTIONS

The structure of an arithmetic or logical instruction word is shown below.

1	AC SOURCE ADDRESS	AC DEST. ADDRESS	FUNCTION	SHIFT	CARRY	NO LD.	SKIP
0	1 2	3 4	5 6 7	8 9	10 11	12	13 14 15

000	COM	01 L	01 Z	001	SKP
001	NEG	10 R	10 O	010	SZC
010	MOV	11 S	11 C	011	SNC
011	INC			100	SZR
100	ADC			101	SNR
101	SUB			110	SEZ
110	ADD			111	SBN
111	AND				

Each instruction in this class specifies one or two accumulators to supply operands to the function generator, which performs the function specified and produces a carry bit, whose value depends upon a base value specified by the instruction, the function performed, and the result obtained. The base value may be derived from the Carry flag, or the instruction may specify an independent value.

SOME TYPICAL INSTRUCTIONS

COM Complement. Place the (logical) complement of the word from ACS in ACD.

NEG Negate. Place the twos complement of the number from ACS into ACD. Complement Carry if ACS contains zero. (Forming the twos complement of zero generates a carry, because complementing zero produces a word containing all 1s, and adding 1 to that produces all zeros again, plus a carry.)

MOV Move. Place the contents of ACS in ACD.

INC Increment. Add 1 to the number from ACS and place it in ACD. If the result is 2^{16}, complement Carry.

ADC Add Complement. Add the (logical) complement of the number from ACS to the number from ACD and place the result in ACD. If the original ACD $\ge$ ACS, complement Carry.

SUB Subtract. Add the twos complement of the number from ACS to the number from ACD and place the result in ACD. If the original ACD $\ge$ ACS, complement Carry.

ADD Add. Add the number from ACS to the number from ACD and place the result in ACD. If the result is $\ge 2^{16}$, complement Carry.

AND And. Place the logical AND function of the word from ACS and the word from ACD in ACD.

MEMORY REFERENCE INSTRUCTIONS

There are two formats for memory reference instructions, depending on whether an accumulator is specified.

WITH ACCUMULATOR
INDIRECT

0	FUNC- TION	AC ADDRESS	INDEX	DISPLACEMENT
0	1 2	3 4	5 6 7	8 9 10 11 12 13 14 15

01 LDA
10 STA

WITHOUT ACCUMULATOR
INDIRECT

0	0	0	FUNC- TION	INDEX	DISPLACEMENT
0	1	2	3 4	5 6 7	8 9 10 11 12 13 14 15

00 JMP
01 JSR
10 ISZ
11 DSZ

INDIRECT ADDRESS WORD
INDIRECT

	ADDRESS
0 1 2 3 4 5 6 7	8 9 10 11 12 13 14 15

NOTES ON MEMORY ADDRESSING

Each instruction word contains information for determining the effective address, which is the actual address used to fetch or store the operand or alter program flow. The address information comprises an 8-bit displacement, a 2-bit index selection, and a single indirect bit. The displacement can directly address any location in four groups of 256 locations each. It can be an absolute address. That is, it may be used simply to address a location in page zero, the first 256 locations in memory. It can also be taken as a signed number used to compute an absolute address by adding it to a 15-bit base address supplied by an index register. The index bits can select AC2 or AC3 as the index register; either of these accumulators can thus be used as an ordinary index register to vary the address computed from a constant displacement, or as a base register for a set of different displacements. The program can also select the program counter as the index register, so any instruction can address 256 words in its own vicinity (relative addressing).

The computed absolute (15-bit) address can be the effective address. However, the instruction can use it as an indirect address. That is, it can specify a location to be used to retrieve another address. The word read from an indirectly addressed location contains an absolute address and an indirect bit; this address can be the effective address, or it can be another indirect address.

FIG. 10·30 Instruction-word formats for the Nova computer. (Courtesy Data General Corp.)

struction refers to two of these accumulators. All arithmetic or logical instructions perform only operations between accumulators. For example, an AND instruction would AND the contents of two accumulators specified by the instruction word—not an accumulator and a location in the main (core) memory.

Since 2 bits are required to address each of the four accumulators, only 4 bits are required for both of the addresses in a two-address instruction. As shown in the figure, bits 1 through 4 are used for addressing; bits 1 and 2 address the *source accumulator,* called ACS, and bits 3 and 4 address the *destination accumulator,* called ACD.

An addition instruction in the Nova causes the accumulator addressed by bits 1 and 2 (that is, ACS) to be added to the accumulator addressed by bits 3 and 4 (that is, ACD), and the result is placed in the ACD. Since arithmetic is only between accumulator registers, these must be loaded with data from the memory before the operations are performed, and *memory reference instructions* such as LOAD, which transfers the word addressed in memory into the specified accumulator, and STORE, which transfers the selected accumulator's contents into the addressed memory location, are used to move data into and from the accumulators.

In memory referencing instructions, memory locations are addressed by a *displacement,* which occupies bits 8 through 15, and an *index,* which refers to one of the accumulators, and the actual address used is the sum of the number in the selected accumulator and the displacement (refer to the figure). Indirect addressing is indicated by a 1 in bit 5 of a memory reference instruction, and a 1 in the sign bit of an indirectly addressed word indicates that it is another indirect address, as was explained previously (the machine permits indirect chaining of addresses).

The arithmetic instructions have options for additional operations after the basic arithmetic operation is performed. Thus a result may be shifted (notice the shift bits in Fig. 10 · 30) or not used [see the NO LD (for NO LOAD) bit], or the instruction can select from several options or skipping, whether or not an arithmetic result is positive, negative, zero, overflows, etc. This ability to combine several operations to be performed in order in a single instruction is used by several minicomputer manufacturers.

10 • 12 IBM 360/370 COMPUTER SERIES

We will now consider the IBM 360/370 series of computers. This line ranges from small to very large computers. The designs are arranged so that the computers are *upward compatible,* and what this means is that a program written for a small computer will run on any computer in the 360/370 series which is larger. (The general trick in determining "larger" is that the 40 is larger than the 30, the 50 is larger than the 40, etc., the 370/158 is larger than any of these and, in general, a larger model number means a larger computer.) To keep the computers upward compatible, the instruction repertoire of a small computer is made a subset of the instruction repertoire for a larger computer.

The various models are designed in different IBM labs and use differing circuit lines and memory technologies, and some are microprogrammed and some are not. Nevertheless, keeping the architectures consistent and standardizing the instruction repertoires enables this upward compatibility to work. Other manufacturers do the same thing, incidentally, and DEC's PDP-11 series, Honeywell's 6000 series, etc., are all lines of computers where the instruction repertoires and general capabilities of the larger computers are expanded versions of the instruction repertoires and capabilities of the small computers.

The IBM 360/370 series is also designed so that it can compete effectively in both the scientific computing market and the business data processing computer market. The scientific-application area calls for an instruction repertoire including both numeric instructions which operate (add, subtract, multiply, etc.) on both integer representation and floating-point numbers. These calculations must be performed on operands which are relatively long (in this case long is 32 and 64 bits per operand). The business applications, on the other hand, demand instructions which operate on character strings (as in the 1400 series) which consist of 8-bit alphanumeric characters and are of arbitrary length such as might be found in names, addresses, inventory descriptions, etc. It is also a good idea for business data processing computers to be able to calculate using BCD (since this reduces conversion time), and such numbers are also liable to be of different lengths and are generally stored in strings.

IBM's answer to these demands is to have a very large instruction repertoire which includes the necessary instructions to satisfy both application areas. Then Fortran compilers — which generally handle the numerical-type problem — generate the word-oriented binary arithmetic instructions, while Cobol compilers generate character string handling instructions.

Another important consideration in large systems is the use of a programmed *operating system* to control the operation of the computer. An operating system consists of a set of programs which are used to control the running of the *user* or *applications* programs. To use the system, the operating system programs are first read in and then these programs start and "operate" other programs by reading them into the memory, starting them, stopping programs which run too long or use too much memory, etc. These programs effectively aid the manual operators of the system in order to achieve maximum system throughput. The operating system sometimes types commands to operators on systems printers telling them to mount tapes or disk packs, to add paper to printers, etc.

In order to use large systems to their utmost potentiality, they are generally used in the *multiprogramming* mode where the operating system reads in one program and if it calls for some slow operation (an input-output operation, for instance), the operating system then reads in and starts another program. This continues, and programs are restarted where they were last interrupted by the operating system when input-output is available or when other programs end, etc.

In order to aid the writer of the operating system and to make computer operation more efficient, many computers now have architectures which permit the following:

1. A given program is *relocatable*. This means a program can be placed in different locations in memory at different times and it will still run. This permits the operating system to locate several different programs in different parts of the memory and to operate first on one, and then others, as convenient.
2. There must be some way for the operating system to set upper and lower bounds on the memory used by a given program. By allocating a specific area in memory to a program and not permitting the program to use other locations in memory, the program can be prevented from damaging the operating of other programs which are in memory at the same time. This also aids in what is called *security,* which refers to preventing programs from deliberately reading other programs or otherwise interfering with them. For instance, one user might try and read another user's files, steal that user's programs, send himself a check, etc.

In order to help achieve the above goals, the IBM 360/370 series (and most manufacturers' larger computers) have two classes of instructions: *supervisory mode instructions* and *user mode instructions*. The operating system programs use the *supervisory mode instructions,* and when they are being executed, a flip-flop is on in the CPU so the computer knows it is in this mode. When user or application mode programs are being executed, certain privileged instructions are not available to the program. Included in supervisory mode instructions but not application mode instructions are those which set the upper and lower bounds in memory where a program can operate and control input-output—in particular the reading of files—and a number of special instructions to handle emergencies, signal operators, etc.

Because of its size and complexity, we will only examine some of the more important aspects of the IBM 360/370 computer series. The manufacturer's manuals carry complete details.

In the 360/370 series, instruction words come in various sizes and lengths, and Fig. 10·31 shows three different types of instruction words and their lengths. Notice that the machine is basically a two-address machine. The computer has 16 accumulators, which are called *general registers,* and these are shown in Fig. 10·32. Each of these general registers consists of 32 bits, and each is addressable. There are also four *floating-point registers,* each consisting of 64 bits, and these are given the addresses 0, 2, 4, and 6, respectively. There are instructions so that one can load any of the general registers from the memory or can transfer the contents of any general regis-

Note: The 2s refer to operand numbers. In the one-word format, for example, $R1$ gives the register number of the first operand and $X2$, $B2$, and $D2$ the address of the second operand

Three IBM 360 word formats

FIG. 10·31 Typical instruction-word formats.

FIG. 10·32 General registers.

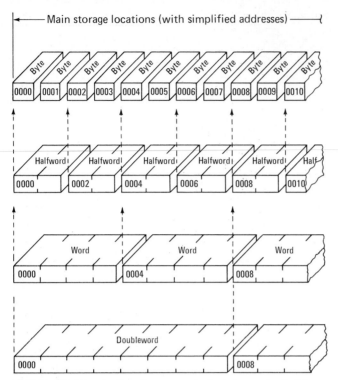

FIG. 10•33 Organization of memory—halfwords, words, double-words, and bytes.

ter into the memory, and the same may be said for each of the floating-point registers.

The memory is organized with 8 bits at each address, and so the memory is said to be *character* or *byte addressable.* The basic computer word consists of 32 bits, and so four consecutive memory locations are required to form a single word. There are also *half words* and *double words,* as shown in Fig. 10·33. There are instructions which operate on words, instructions which use half words, instructions which use double words, and instructions which operate on character strings.

In general, when we add one 32-bit word to another word, we can (1) add one of the general registers to another general register and store the sum in one of the general registers, or (2) add one of the general registers to a word located in the memory and store the sum in the general register.

Further, there are floating-point and fixed-point instructions, so that a floating-point word located in the memory can be multiplied by the contents of one of the floating-point registers and the product stored in one of the floating-point registers. As noted in Chap. 6, for floating-point words the word addressed in memory will consist of either 32 or 64 digits. These consist of a sign digit plus a 7-digit characteristic and a 24-digit fraction if a short floating-point instruction is used, or of a sign digit plus a 7-digit characteristic and a 56-digit floating-point fraction or mantissa when a long floating-point word is used.

The general registers not only contain operands, but are also used to store addresses, so that many instructions form an address by adding a number in a general register to another number to form the number of the location to be used in an operand.

Let us examine several typical words in this system to see how various instructions operate. The first instruction shown in Fig. 10·34 is an ADD instruction, the OP code for which is 1A (base 16) lying in bits 0 through 7. Two operands are then designated. These operands are located in general register 7 and general register 9, so that the number in general register 7 will be added to the number in general register 9 and the sum stored in general register 7. Notice that the two addresses given in this particular type of instruction actually indicate directly the locations of the two words to be added.

The second instruction shown, which is a STORE instruction, is more complicated. The operation code for store in this system is 50. This OP code is followed in the instruction word by four numbers in the system. The first number, which lies in bits 8 through 11, gives the number of one general register to be used; the contents of this register are to be stored in the memory. The second set of three numbers occupies bits 12 through 31 in the instruction word and gives the address in memory where this number is to be stored. However, this address is not given directly. The address is

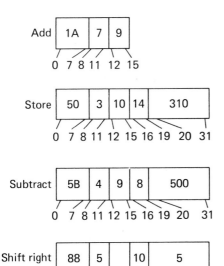

Add the contents of general register 7 to the contents of general register 9 and store the sum in general register 7

Store the contents of general register 3 at the main storage address given by the sum of 310 and the low-order 24 bits of general registers 14 and 10

Subtracts the word located at 500 plus the contents of the 24 least significant digits of general registers 8 and 9 from the word in register 4 and stores the difference in general register 4

Shifts the word in general register 5 to the right 5 times plus the number located in general register 10

Note: All characters are hexadecimal, for example, 1A is 0001 1010

FIG. 10 • 34 Typical instruction words.

instead formed by adding the number in general register 10 to the number in general register 14, taking the 24 least significant digits of this number, and adding these to the number stored in bits 20 through 31 in the instruction word, which in this case is 310. For instance, if general register 10 contained the number 400 and if general register 14 contained the number 200, we would add these two numbers, giving 600, and add that to 310, giving the number 910, so that the word in general register 3 would be stored in location 910 in the memory.

Subtract instructions operate somewhat similarly. The subtract instruction is indicated by the OP code 5B, and the particular type of instruction shown in the figure subtracts the number stored at an address which is determined by adding the numbers stored in general register 9 to the number stored in general register 8, and to this adding the number lying in bits 20 to 31 of the subtract instruction. When these three numbers are combined to form an address in the memory, the word located at that address is then subtracted from the word located in general register 4, and the difference is stored in general register 4.

For instance, if general register 4 contains 300, general register 9 contains 100, general register 8 contains 200, and in the memory the location 800 contains the word 1000, we will form the address number 800 by adding together the number 200 lying in general register 8 to the number 100 lying in general register 9, and then adding this to the 500 given in bits 20 through 31 in the instruction word, giving the number 800. We then look in the memory at location 800 and find the word 1000. If this number is subtracted from 300, which lies in general register 4, the difference -700 will be stored in general register 4 when the instruction is completed.

As one last example of the instruction code for this machine, let us examine a SHIFT-RIGHT instruction, the OP code for which is 88. In this case, the general register indicated by bits 8 through 11 in the instruction word is to be shifted right. The number of times the word is to be shifted is calculated by adding the number in bits 20 through 31 of the instruction word to the number in the register designated by bits 16 through 19 of the instruction word.

In the example shown, the general register 10 is called out by bits 16 through 19; so the number stored in general register 10 will be added to the 5 stored in bits 20 through 31, and the general register 5 will be shifted right, this many times. If, for instance, general register 10 contains the number 7, then we would add 7 to 5, saying that the word in general register 5 should be shifted right a total of 12 times.

There are several reasons for the complicated addressing technique used here. The use of two general-purpose registers to form each address is (1) to permit the operating system programs to relocate user programs in memory, (2) to permit the programmer to use one of the registers as an index register. Common practice in the 360/370 is for the second register in each address (the one specified in bits 12 to 15) to be used only by the operating system. This register is then called the *base register,* and if the base register is the same—say register 5—in each instruction word in a program, then the number in this register will be added to each address generated. By placing an appropriate number in this register, the operating system can cause a given program to be loaded at locations in memory of its choice and the program will operate there because each instruction word and data word address will be appropriately located. This then leaves the remaining register—that specified by bits 11 to 13—to be used by the programmer as an index register.

There is a set of instructions in this computer similar to those shown for the Minneapolis-Honeywell 200 series. This computer series is typical of the computers used in large systems in that it has a rich instruction repertoire and many features which the designers feel are useful to the computer's user. Some computer lines are much more scientific-application-oriented and some are almost exclusively business-oriented. A good blend is maintained by several computer firms, however.

QUESTIONS

1. A three-address computer has a word length of 11 decimal digits plus sign. The computer can perform 50 different instructions, and the inner memory has 1000 words. Draw a diagram of the basic computer instruction word, leaving the sign bit unusued.

2. A two-address computer has a single core memory with a 1-μs memory cycle time and a small high-speed memory with a 0.25-μs memory cycle time.

    An addition instruction word looks like

ADD	1st address	2d address

The first address refers to the small high-speed memory and the second address to the core memory. The sum is placed in the high-speed memory at the first address. How long will it take to perform an addition instruction? Why?

3. How many trips to memory must be made to perform an addition instruction in a three-address type of computer?

4. If we use 3 binary digits in the instruction word to indicate which index register is used, or if one is to be used, how many index registers can be used in the machine?

5. Using the index instructions in Sec. 10·4, write a program which adds 40 numbers located in the memory, starting at address 200 and storing the sum in register 300.

6. Modify the program in Sec. 10·4 so that the numbers located at memory addresses 353 through 546 are added together and stored at address 600.

7. Modify the program in Sec. 10·4 so that the numbers located at addresses 300 through 305 are multiplied together and the product stored at address 310.

8. The use of paging enables the relocation or moving around of programs in the memory without extensive modification of the addresses in the program. Explain why.

9. For the Varian computer in Sec. 10·5, the use of a 100 mode involves a form of paging called *relative addressing,* where the actual address is formed by adding the address at which the instruction lies to the number given in the address portion of the instruction word. If the instruction word is at location 293 in the memory, an ADD instruction is used with $m = 100$, and the address portion contains 63 (decimal), what address is actually used in the addition?

10. Compare the 4-accumulator organization in the Nova with the 16-accumulator organization in the IBM 360 series, noting any differences in the use of the two addresses in the instruction words.

11. Explain how paging and indirect addressing can be useful in relocating subprograms when a program is rewritten. What are some disadvantages of paging and indirect addressing?

12. Explain "handshaking" on a bus when data is transferred from a sender to a receiver. How can this be used to prevent errors due to signal skew caused by signals on different wires arriving at different times (skewed) because of the differences in line length and characteristics and differences in delays through IC line drivers, etc.

13. Describe some advantages and disadvantages of multiple-accumulator (general-purpose registers) versus single-accumulator computer architecture. Include effects on instruction-word length, convenience in programming, use of base or index registers, etc.

14. The following is a short program in assembly language for the PDP-8:

```
*700
            CLA    CLL
            TAD    DAT1
    GO,     ISZ    DAT2
            JMP    GO
            RAL
            JMP    GO
    DAT1,   0077
    DAT2,   0
    $
```

After this program has been assembled and loaded, it appears as follows in memory (all digits are octal), except that the contents of two addresses in memory need to filled in. Supply the contents of (octal) locations 700 and 701 in memory.

	ADDRESS NUMBER	CONTENTS
	0700	
	0701	
	0702	2307
	0703	5302
	0704	7004
	0705	5302
	0706	0077
	0707	0000

15. Evaluate the use of multiple general registers and an IBM 360 format in addressing versus the use of index registers in the DDP-24 for adding together numbers arranged in three tables.

16. Explain how paging as an addressing technique can be useful in re-locating programs, and then explain how small pages can sometimes force programmers to "think in segments." Are the above characteristics desirable or undesirable?

17. For the standard instrument interface draw the signals DAV, NRFD, NDAC for a data transfer from a talker to a listener. Assume there are no problems in transferring data and indicate who is raising and lowering each signal.

18. For the standard instrument interface indicate how the controller selects a "talker" and "listener."

19. How is "signal skew" handled on the standard instrument interface?

20. Details on Nova instructions are given in Fig. 10·30. Given the initial configuration

$$
\begin{array}{lllllll}
\text{AC1} & 0 & 100 & 011 & 010 & 001 & 000 \\
\text{AC2} & 0 & 000 & 000 & 000 & 000 & 001
\end{array}
$$

give the contents of the two registers (AC1, AC2) and carry bit after the following instructions are executed. Describe what happens, and where, during the execution of the first *two* instructions.

	ACS	ACD	FCTN	SH	C'Y		SKIP
1	01	10	000	00	01	0	000
1	10	01	110	01	00	1	010
1	10	10	011	00	11	0	000
1	10	01	110	10	00	0	011
1	01	01	011	00	11	0	000

21. Explain the addressing of pages in the PDP-8 series and the displace-ment-plus-index addressing technique used by DGC Nova computers. Give reasons why you think systems architects have elected to use these systems.

22. The following is a section of program and memory contents from an assembly listing for a PDP-8. The programmer who wrote this contends that after the instruction at location 255_8 is executed the location 256_8 in memory will contain the difference $A - B$ of the numbers A and B at locations 260_8 and 2053_8. Is the programmer correct? Give the reason for your answer, explaining the program operation.

```
                        *250
        0250   7300           CLA    CLL
        0251   1657           TAD    I       F
        0252   7040           CMA
        0253   1260           TAD    A
        0254   3256           DCA    C
        0255   7402           HLT
        0256   0004           C,     Y
        0257   2053           F,     2053
        0260   0005           A,     5
                        *2053
        2053   0006           B,     6
```

```
  └───┘└───┘ └──────────────────────────────┘
     ↖      ↖                    ↖
   Memory  Contents        Program written
   address    of            in assembly
          memory              language
```

23. Write the binary code sequence, in Nova machine code, for comparing two numbers, one in the second accumulator, and another in the word beginning at the address specified in the third accumulator. The program is to skip the next instruction word if the contents of the accumulator (second) are greater than those of the memory location.

24. Sketch, describe, and discuss the merits of one of the machine architectures which have been presented, or of any other machine with which you are familiar (or with which you would *like* to be familiar — including any of your own "ideal" designs, if you have any such notions).

25. A real-time system for manufacturing control is to be constructed using a computer. The system is to perform two functions
   (a) Automatically test cameras as they are manufactured. This involves, among other things, reading 1,000 values each second from several A-to-D converters and checking to see if the values are within prescribed limits.
   (b) The computer is to service four terminals which run inquiries against the data base maintained on the cameras and also the computer is to run some Fortran and Cobol programs.
   The designer decides to buy a computer with a single bus which is used

to interconnect all the A-to-D converters with the computer as well as the disk packs, terminals, core and IC memories, etc. Discuss the merits and disadvantages of this use of a single bus in such a system.

26. In the Minneapolis-Honeywell 200, how many binary digits are required to store the following decimal numbers when the alphanumeric format is used?

(a) 1924   (b) 22   (c) 87   (d) 10,924

27. The block diagram which follows is of the control and arithmetic registers of the Honeywell 200. The *I*-address register contains the address of the next instruction character to be used by the stored program. The number in this register is increased each time a character is read. The *A*- and the *B*-address registers contain the addresses of the two operands alphanumeric characters currently being used. These registers are decreased by 1 each time a character is used. The memory address register addresses the core memory; the *A* and *B* registers are 9-bit registers which hold the characters read from memory with *B*, always receiving what is read directly from the memory. The OP register also has 8 bits and is designed to hold the OP-code character from each instruction word. Discuss the sequencing of the operation of these registers during the SUBTRACT instruction described in Sec. 10·11.

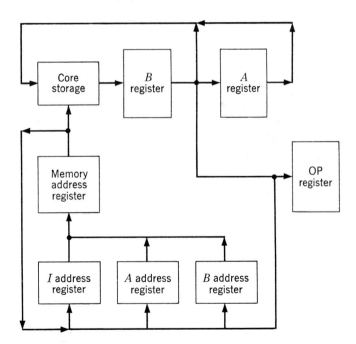

28. Using the same block diagram as for the preceding instruction, describe the sequencing of these registers in the Minneapolis-Honeywell 200 during the addition instruction in Sec. 10·11.

29. In the IBM 360, how many binary digits are required to store the following decimal numbers in BCD and in binary. (In BCD, sign requires 4 bits and BCD numbers are always organized into bytes.)
(a) 20   *(b)* 10,241   *(c)* 984   *(d)* 6

30. Describe the calculation of an effective address for the IBM 360, and outline logical hardware which will implement this calculation (control signals, data paths, registers, etc.).

31. Explain the addressing of pages in the PDP-8 series and the technique used by DGC Nova computers. Discuss the advantages and disadvantages of these techniques relative to each other.

32. Suppose we push *A*, *B*, *D*, and *F* on a stack, pop the stack twice, and then push *M* and then *N* onto the stack. If we then pop letters from the stack three times, what letters and in what order will be popped?

33. Explain how peripheral devices interrupt a computer with a single bus organization.

34. Explain the meaning of *direct memory access* (DMA) and why it is desirable in some cases.

35. Can you think of any problems that might arise in multiprocessor systems?

36. Contrast a pipeline computer organization with a multiple-unit organization. Where do problems arise when jump or branch instructions are executed in these computers?

37. Discuss assigning locations on the bus for a microcomputer with two 4K RAMs, one 4K ROM, and a teletype.

38. Explain extended addressing, implied addressing, and relative addressing in the 6800 microprocessor.

39. Explain how the "branch if zero" instruction works on the 6800 microprocessor.

40. Explain the difference in an ADD accumulator (ABA) and an ADD (ADDA or ADDB) instruction for the 6800 microprocessor.

41. Explain a ROTATE-RIGHT instruction on the 6800.

42. What are the differences between ROTATE and SHIFT instructions on the 6800? Why are both useful?

43. Explain the "branch to subroutine" instruction and the "return from subroutine" instructions for the 6800 microprocessor and explain how they would be used to enter and then exit from a subroutine.

44. Contrast the JMS instruction in the PDP-8 with the JSR instruction in the 6800.

45. Explain the register indirect and immediate addressing modes for the 8080 microprocessor.

46. Explain how two of the arithmetic-type instructions for the 8080 microprocessor affect the setting of the condition flags.

47. Explain how conditional JUMP instructions work in the 8080 microprocessor.

48. Explain the PUSH and POP instructions in the 8080.

49. Explain the CALL and RET instructions for the 8080 and compare these with the JSR and RTS instructions for the 6800.

50. Explain the STA and LDA instructions for the 8080 microprocessor.

51. Explain the ADI instruction for the 8080 and contrast it to the ADM instruction.

52. Compare the ADM instruction for the 8080 microprocessor with the ADDA and ADDB instructions for the 6800 microprocessor.

53. Contrast the PUSH and POP instructions for the 8080 with the DES and INS instructions for the 6800 microprocessor.

54. Compare the BRANCH instructions for the 6800 with those for the 8080 microprocessor.

BIBLIOGRAPHY

CHAPTER 1

Allan, R.: Microprocessors Galore, *IEEE Spectrum,* vol. 13, no. 1, January 1976.

Barron, D. W.: *Assemblers and Loaders,* MacDonald American Elsevier, New York, 1975.

Bartee, T. C.: *Introduction to Computer Science,* McGraw-Hill Book Company, New York, 1975.

Bell, G., and A. Newell: *Computer Structures: Readings and Examples,* McGraw-Hill Book Company, New York, 1971.

Chapin, N.: *360/370 Programming in Assembly Language,* McGraw-Hill Book Company, New York, 1973.

Cole, R. W.: *Introduction to Computing,* McGraw-Hill Book Company, New York, 1972.

Colin, A. J. T.: *Introduction to Operating Systems,* MacDonald American Elsevier, New York, 1972.

Donovan, J. J.: *Systems Programming,* McGraw-Hill Book Company, New York, 1972.

Estes, J. W., and B. R. Ellis: *Elements of Computer Science,* Canfield Press, 1972.

Gear, C. W.: *Computer Organization and Programming,* McGraw-Hill Book Company, New York, 1974.

Gschwind, H. W., and E. J. McCluskey: *Design of Digital Computers,* Springer-Verlag, New York, 1975.

Hellerman, H.: *Digital Computer System Principles,* McGraw-Hill Book Company, New York, 1973.

Maurer, W. D.: *Programming,* Holden-Day, Inc., Publisher, San Francisco, 1970.

Peatman, J. B.: *The Design of Digital Systems,* McGraw-Hill Book Company, New York, 1972.

Ralston, A.: *Introduction to Programming and Computer Science,* McGraw-Hill Book Company, New York, 1972.

Rice, J. K., and R. R. Rice: *Introduction to Computer Science,* Holt, Rinehart and Winston, Inc., New York, 1969.

Souček, B.: *Minicomputers in Data Processing and Simulation,* John Wiley & Sons, Inc., New York, 1972.

Stark, R. H., and D. W. Dearhold: *Computer Concepts and Assembler Programming: 360/370 Systems,* Academic Press, New York, 1975.

Stone, H. S.: *Introduction to Computer Science and Data Structures,* McGraw-Hill Book Company, New York, 1972.

Watson, R. W.: *Timesharing System Design Concepts,* McGraw-Hill Book Company, New York, 1970.

Weiss, E.: *The PL/1 Converter,* McGraw-Hill Book Company, New York, 1969.

CHAPTER 2

Booth, T. L., and Y. T. Chien: *Computing,* Hamilton, Santa Barbara, Calif., 1974.

Estes, J. W., and B. R. Ellis: *Elements of Computer Science,* Canfield Press, 1972.

Gschwind, H. W., and E. J. McCluskey: *Design of Digital Computers,* Springer-Verlag, New York, 1975.

Hellerman, H.: *Digital Computer System Principles,* McGraw-Hill Book Company, New York, 1973.

O'Mally, J.: *Introduction to the Digital Computer,* Holt, Rinehart and Winston, Inc., New York, 1971.

Scott, N. R.: *Electronic Computer Technology,* McGraw-Hill Book Company, New York, 1970.

CHAPTER 3

Bartee, T. C., I. L. Lebow, and I. S. Reed: *Theory and Design of Digital Machines,* McGraw-Hill Book Company, New York, 1962.

Birkhoff, G., and T. C. Bartee: *Modern Applied Algebra,* McGraw-Hill Book Company, New York, 1970.

Boole, G.: *An Investigation of the Laws of Thought,* Dover Publications, Inc., New York, 1966. First published 1854.

Brzozowski, J. A., and M. Yoeli: *Digital Networks,* Prentice-Hall, Inc., Englewood Cliffs, N.J., 1975.

Harrison, M. A.: *Introduction to Switching and Automata Theory,* McGraw-Hill Book Company, New York, 1965.

McCluskey, E. J., and T. C. Bartee: *A Survey of Switching Circuit Theory,* McGraw-Hill Book Company, New York, 1962.

McCluskey, E. J., Jr.: *Introduction to the Theory of Switching Circuits,* McGraw-Hill Book Company, New York, 1965.

Oberman, R. M. M.: *Discipline in Combinational and Sequential Circuit Designs,* McGraw-Hill Book Company, New York, 1970.

Wood, P. E.: *Switching Theory,* McGraw-Hill Book Company, New York, 1968.

CHAPTER 4

American Microsystems, Inc.: *Guide to Standard MOS Products,* Santa Clara, Calif., 1975.

Birkhoff, G., and T. C. Bartee: *Modern Applied Algebra,* McGraw-Hill Book Company, New York, 1970.

Brzozowski, J. A., and M. Yoeli: *Digital Networks,* Prentice-Hall, Inc., Englewood Cliffs, N.J., 1975.

Fairchild Semiconductor: *TTL Data Book,* Mountain View, Calif., 1976.

Gschwind, H. W., and E. J. McCluskey: *Design of Digital Computers,* Springer-Verlag, New York, 1975.

Hodges, D. A.: Trends in Computer Hardware Technology, *Computer Design,* vol. 15, no. 2, February 1976.

Intel Corporation: *Intel 8080 Microcomputer System User's Manual,* Santa Clara, Calif., 1975.

Motorola Corporation: *M6800 Microprocessor Applications Manual,* Phoenix, Ariz., 1975.

Rottner, J., J. Cornet, and M. E. Hoff: Bipolar LSI Computing Elements Usher in New Era of Digital Design, *Electronics,* September 1976.

Texas Instruments, Inc.: *The TTL Data Book,* Dallas, Tex., 1976.

CHAPTER 5

American Microsystems, Inc.: *Guide to Standard MOS Products,* Santa Clara, Calif., 1975.

Deem, W., K. Muchow, and A. Zeppa: *Digital Computers, Circuits and Concepts,* Reston Publishing Company, Inc., Reston, Va., 1974.

Fairchild Semiconductor: *TTL Data Book,* Mountain View, Calif., 1976.

Hodges, D. A., Trends in Computer Hardware Technology, *Computer Design,* vol. 15, no. 2, February 1976.

Intel Corporation: *Intel 8080 Microcomputer System User's Manual,* Santa Clara, Calif., 1975.

Malvino, A. P., and D. P. Leach: *Digital Principles and Applications,* McGraw-Hill Book Company, New York, 1974.

Motorola Corporation: *M6800 Microprocessor Applications Manual,* Phoenix, Ariz., 1975.

Motorola Semiconductor Products, Inc.: Semiconductor Data Library, Phoenix, Ariz., 1975.

Rottner, J., J. Cornet, and M. E. Hoff: Bipolar LSI Computing Elements Usher in New Era of Digital Design, *Electronics,* September 1976.

Texas Instruments, Inc.: *The TTL Data Book,* Dallas, Tex., 1976.

CHAPTER 6

Bartee, T. C., I. L. Lebow, and I. S. Reed: *Theory and Design of Digital Machines,* McGraw-Hill Book Company, New York, 1962.

Flores, I.: *The Logic of Computer Arithmetic,* Prentice-Hall, Inc., Englewood Cliffs, N.J., 1963.

Foster, C. C.: *Computer Architecture,* D. Van Nostrand Company, Inc., Princeton, N.J., 1971.

Freiman, C. V.: Statistical Analysis of Certain Binary Division Algorithms, *Proceedings of the IRE,* vol 49, no. 1, January 1961.

Gear, C. W.: *Computer Organization and Programming,* McGraw-Hill Book Company, New York, 1974.

MacSorley, O. L.: High Speed Arithmetic in Binary Computers, *Proceedings of the IRE,* vol. 49, no. 1, January 1961.

Rice, J. K., and R. R. Rice: *Introduction to Computer Science,* Holt, Rinehart and Winston, Inc., New York, 1969.

Stone, H. S.: *Introduction to Computer Science and Data Structures,* McGraw-Hill Book Company, New York, 1972.

CHAPTER 7

American Microsystems, Inc.: *Guide to Standard MOS Products,* Santa Clara, Calif., 1975.

Carothers, J. D.: A New High Density Recording System: The IBM 1311 Disc Storage Drive with Interchangeable Disc Packs, *Proceedings of the 1963 Fall Joint Computer Conference,* American Federation of Information Processing Societies.

Cole, R. W.: *Introduction to Computing,* McGraw-Hill Book Company, New York, 1972.

Davis, S.: Selection and Application of Semiconductor Memories, *Computer Design,* January 1976.

Deem, W., K. Muchow, and A. Zeppa: *Digital Computers Circuits and Concepts,* Reston Publishing Company, Inc., Reston, Va., 1974.

Intel Corporation: *Intel 8080 Microcomputer System User's Manual,* Santa Clara, Calif., 1975.

Motorola Corporation: *M6800 Microprocessor Applications Manual,* Phoenix, Ariz., 1975.

Motorola Semiconductor Products, Inc.: Semiconductor Data Library, Phoenix, Ariz., 1975.

Postoriza, J.: Tradeoffs among Binary Codes in Magnetic Tape Cassettes, *Computer Design,* vol. 15, no, 1, 1976.

Rottner, J., J. Cornet, and M. E. Hoff: Bipolar LSI Computing Elements Usher in New Era of Digital Design, *Electronics,* September 1976.

Smith, C. H., and L. D. Wittie: Memory Hardware for High Speed Job Selection, *IEEE Transactions on Computers,* vol. C-25, no. 2, February 1976.

Thomas, A. T.: Design Techniques for Microprocessor Memory Systems, *Computer Design,* August 1975.

Walther, T. R.: Dynamic N-MOS RAM with Simplified Refresh, *Computer Design,* February 1973.

CHAPTER 8

Anderson, T. O.: Code Conversion for Parallel A-D Converters, *Computer Design,* July 1973.

Booth, T. L., and Y. T. Chien: *Computing,* Hamilton, Santa Barbara, Calif., 1974.

Davis, S.: Printer Selection Factors, *Computer Design,* December 1972.

Deem, W., K. Muchow, and A. Zeppa: *Digital Computers Circuits and Concepts,* Reston Publishing Company, Inc., Reston, Va., 1974.

Foster, C. C.: *Computer Architecture,* D. Van Nostrand Company, Inc., Princeton, N.J., 1977.

Hodges, D. A.: Trends in Computer Hardware Technology, *Computer Design,* vol. 15, no. 2, February 1976.

O'Mally, J.: *Introduction to the Digital Computer,* Holt, Rinehart and Winston, New York, 1971.

Postoriza, J.: Tradeoffs among Binary Codes in Magnetic Tape Cassettes, *Computer Design,* vol. 15, no. 1, 1976.

Scott, N. R.: *Electronic Computer Technology,* McGraw-Hill Book Company, New York, 1970.

Talambiras, P. P.: Digital-to-Analog Converters: Some Problems in Producing High-fidelity Systems, *Computer Design,* vol. 15, no. 1, January 1975.

CHAPTER 9

Bartee, T. C.: *Introduction to Computer Science,* McGraw-Hill Book Company, New York, 1975.

Bell, G., and A. Newell: *Computer Structures: Readings and Examples,* McGraw-Hill Book Company, New York, 1971.

Booth, T. L., and Y. T. Chien: *Computing,* Hamilton, Santa Barbara, Calif., 1974.

Boulage, G., and J. Mermet (eds.): *Microprogramming,* Hermann & Cie, Paris, 1972.

Estes, J. W., and B. R. Ellis: *Elements of Computer Science,* Canfield Press, 1972.

Fagg, P., et al.: IBM System 360 Engineering, *Proceedings of the 1964 Fall Joint Computer Conference,* American Federation of Information Processing Societies.

Foster, C. C.: *Computer Architecture,* D. Van Nostrand Company, Inc., Princeton, N.J., 1971.

Hellerman, H.: *Digital Computer System Principles,* McGraw-Hill Book Company, New York, 1973.

Logan, J. D., and P. S. Kreager: Using a Microprocessor, *Computer Design,* September 1975.

Marchin, P.: Multi-level Nesting of Subroutines in a One-Level Microprocessor, *Computer Design,* vol. 15, no. 2, February 1976.

Peatman, J. B.: *The Design of Digital Systems,* McGraw-Hill Book Company, New York, 1972.

Ralston, A.: *Introduction to Programming and Computer Science,* McGraw-Hill Book Company, New York, 1972.

Souček, B.: *Minicomputers in Data Processing and Simulation,* John Wiley & Sons, Inc., New York, 1972.

Stone, H. S.: *Introduction to Computer Science and Data Structures,* McGraw-Hill Book Company, New York, 1972.

Waldecker, D. E.: Comparison of a Microprogrammed and a Non-microprogrammed Computer, *Computer Design,* June 1970.

CHAPTER 10

Allan, R.: Microprocessors Galore, *IEEE Spectrum,* vol. 13, no. 1, January 1976.

Anderson, H. A., M. Reiser, and G. L. Galati: Tuning a Virtual Storage System, *IBM Systems Journal,* vol. 14, no. 3, 1975.

Ashenhurst, R. L., and R. H. Vonderohe: A Hierarchical Network (of Minicomputers), *Datamation,* vol. 21, no. 2, February 1975.

Barron, D. W.: "Assemblers and Loaders," MacDonald American Elsevier, New York, 1975.

Bowra, J. W., and H. C. Torng: The Modeling and Design of Multiple Function Unit Processors, *IEEE Transactions on Computers,* vol. C-25, no. 3, March 1976.

Chapin, N.: *360/370 Programming in Assembly Language,* McGraw-Hill Book Company, New York, 1973.

Colin, A. J. T.: *Introduction to Operating Systems,* MacDonald American Elsevier, New York, 1972.

Cowry, F. F.: Advanced Architecture and Applications of Microcomputers, *Computer,* vol. 9, no. 1, January 1976.

Data General Corporation: *How to Use the Nova Computers,* Southboro, Mass., 1975.

Digital Equipment Corporation: *Introduction to Programming,* Maynard, Mass., 1972.

Digital Equipment Corporation: *PDP 11/45 Processor Handbook,* 1976.

Donovan, J. J.: *Systems Programming,* McGraw-Hill Book Company, New York, 1972.

Estes, J. W., and B. R. Ellis: *Elements of Computer Science,* Canfield Press, 1972.

Farber, D. J.: A Ring Network, *Datamation,* vol. 21, no. 2, February 1975.

Fleisher, H., and L. I. Maissel: An Introduction to Array Logic, *IBM Journal of Research and Development,* vol. 19, no. 2, March 1975.

Foster, C. C.: *Computer Architecture,* D. Van Nostrand Company, Inc., Princeton, N.J., 1971.

Gear, C. W.: *Computer Organization and Programming,* McGraw-Hill Book Company, New York, 1974.

Gschwind, H. W., and E. J. McCluskey: *Design of Digital Computers,* Springer-Verlag, New York, 1975.

Intel Corporation: *Intel 8080 Microcomputer System User's Manual,* Santa Clara, Calif., 1975.

Kinoshito, K., T. Sasao, and J. Matsuda: On Magnetic Bubble Logic Circuits, *IEEE Transactions on Computers,* vol. C-25, no. 3, March 1976.

Lowrie, D. H.: Access and Alignment of Data in an Array Processor, *IEEE Transactions on Computers,* vol. C-24, no. 12, December 1975.

Madnick, S., and J. Donovan: *Operating Systems,* McGraw-Hill Book Company, New York, 1973.

Motorola Corporation: *M6800 Microprocessor Applications Manual,* Phoenix, Ariz., 1975.

Salisbury, A. B., *Microprogrammable Computer Architecture,* MacDonald American Elsevier, New York, 1976.

Souček, B.: *Minicomputers in Data Processing and Simulation,* John Wiley & Sons, Inc., New York, 1972.

Stark, R. H., and D. W. Dearholt: *Computer Concepts and Assembler Programming: 360/370 Systems,* Academic Press, New York, 1975.

Thomas, A. T.: Design Techniques for Microprocessor Memory Systems, *Computer Design,* August 1975.

Ward, A. R.: LSI Microprocessors and Microcomputers: A Bibliography, *Computer,* vol. 9, no. 1, January 1976.

Weissberger, A. J.: Microprocessors Expand Industry Applications of Data Acquisitions, *Electronics,* September 1974.

ANSWERS TO SELECTED ODD-NUMBERED QUESTIONS

CHAPTER 1

5.

ADDRESS	OPERATION CODE	ADDRESS PART
1	CLA	40
2	ADD	41
3	ADD	42
4	STO	43
5	HLT	000

40 contains X
41 contains Y
42 contains Z
43 contains O

7.

ADDRESS	OPERATION	OPERAND
1	CLA	20
2	MUL	20
3	STO	40
4	CLA	21
5	MUL	21
6	ADD	40
7	STO	40
8	CLA	22
9	MUL	22
10	ADD	40
11	STO	40
12	HLT	
20	contains	X
21	contains	Y
22	contains	Z
40	contains	O

11.

ADDRESS	OPERATION	OPERAND
1	CLA	20
2	STO	21
3	CLA	21
4	MUL	20
5	STO	21
6	CLA	50
7	ADD	51
8	STO	50
9	BRM	3
10	CLA	21
11	ADD	20
12	STO	21
13	HLT	
20	contains	X
21	contains	0
50	contains	−5
51	contains	1

We will store our sum $X^5 + X$ in the address assigned by the assembler to the variable D.

ADDRESS	OPERATION	OPERAND
A	DEC	0
B	DEC	−5
C	DEC	1
D	DEC	0
	CLA	X
	STO	D
E	CLA	D
	MUL	X
	STO	D
	CLA	B
	ADD	C
	STO	B
	BRM	E
	CLA	D
	ADD	X
	STO	D
	HLT	

17.

If we assume the integers *are* in ascending or descending order only:

ADDRESS	OPERATION	OPERAND
1	CLA	30
2	SUB	31
3	BRM	5
4	HLT	
5	HLT	

The computer stops at address 4 if the numbers are in ascending order and at 5 if the numbers are in descending order.

We must check to see whether the numbers are in ascending or descending order.

ADDRESS	OPERATION	OPERAND
1	CLA	30
2	SUB	31
3	BRM	10
4	CLA	31
5	SUB	32
6	BRM	13
7	HLT	
10	CLA	31
11	SUB	32
12	BRM	15
13	HLT	
15	HLT	

This program stops at address 13 if the numbers are in neither ascending nor descending order; at address 7 if the numbers are ascending; and at address 15 if the numbers are descending.

21.

ADDRESS	OPERATION	OPERAND
1	CLA	26
2	SUB	25
3	BRM	300
4	BRA	400

23.

ADDRESS	OPERATION	OPERAND
P	CLA	A
	SUB	B
	BRM	M
	CLA	A
	SUB	C
	BRM	M
	CLA	A
	STO	X
	HLT	
M	CLA	B
	SUB	C
	BRM	N
	CLA	B
	STO	X
	HLT	
N	CLA	C
	STO	X
	HLT	

25. A = 10;
   B = 20;
   C = 5;
   D = (A * B) ** C;
   END;

27. 72

29. Z = 0
   A = 0
   LOOP. DO WHILE Z LE A
   X = −X
   Y = −Y
   Z = X − Y
   END LOOP
   PRINT (Z)
   END

31.

ADDRESS	OPERATION	OPERAND	ADDRESS	OPERATION	OPERAND
1	CLA	300	13	CLA	6
2	BRM	5	14	ADD	400
3	STO	300	15	STO	6
4	BRA	7	16	CLA	401
5	SUB	300	17	ADD	400
6	SUB	300	18	STO	401
7	CLA	3	19	BRM	1
8	ADD	400	20	HLT	
9	STO	3	300⎱ contains numbers		
10	CLA	5	329⎰		
11	ADD	400	400	contains	1
12	STO	5	401	contains	−30

33. *(a)* 45   *(b)* 2000   *(c)* 55   *(d)* 70

35. *(a)* A ** C / B ** D   *(b)* A ** 2 + B ** 2 + C * D   *(c)* A/B + (C/D) ** E
   (d) (A * B) ** C + (B * D)/E

CHAPTER 2

1. (a) 100111 (b) 111011 (c) 1000000000 (d) 0.011100
(e) 0.11001 (f) 0.110011 (g) 100,000,000.11
(h) 10,000,001.1001 (i) 1,000,000,000,000.11101

3. (a) 101011 (b) 1000000 (c) 100000000000 (d) 0.011
(e) 0.11011 (f) 0.0111 (g) 1000000000.1 (h) 10000011.1001
(i) 10000000000.0001

5. (a) 13 (b) 27 (c) 23 (d) 0.6875 (e) 0.203125 (f) 0.21288065
(g) 59.6875 (h) 91.203125 (i) 22.3408203125

7. (a) 11 (b) 36 (c) 19 (d) 0.8125 (e) 0.5625 (f) 0.3125
(g) 11.1875 (h) 9.5625 (i) 5.375

9. (a) $10100.11 = 20.75$ (b) $1001010 = 74$ (c) $1.1 = 1.5$
(d) $10101 = 21$

11. (a)
```
 1 1 0 1 . 1     1 3 . 5
 1 0 1 1 . 1     1 1 . 5
─────────────   ────────
1 1 0 0 1 . 0     2 5
```
(b)
```
 1 0 1 1 0 1     4 5
 1 1 0 1 1 0     5 4
──────────────   ────
1 1 0 0 0 1 1     9 9
```
(c)
```
0 . 0 0 1 1     0 . 1 8 7 5
0 . 1 1 1 0     0 . 8 7 5
───────────    ───────────
1 . 0 0 0 1     1 . 0 6 2 5
```
(d)
```
 1 1 0 0 . 0 1 1     1 2 . 3 7 5
 1 0 1 1 . 0 1 1     1 1 . 3 7 5
───────────────    ────────────
1 0 1 1 1 . 1 1 0     2 3 . 7 5 0
```

13. (a)
```
 1 0 0 0 0 0 0
- 1 0 0 0 0 0
───────────
   1 0 0 0 0 0
```
(b)
```
 1 1 1 1 1 1 1
-   1 1 1 1 1 1
───────────
 1 0 0 0 0 0 0
```
(c)
```
 1 0 1 1 1 0 1 . 1
- 1 0 1 0 1 0 . 1 1
─────────────────
 1 1 0 0 1 0 . 1 1
```
(d)
```
 1 0 1 0 1 0 0 . 0 1 0 0 1
- 1 1 0 0 0 0 . 0 1 0 1 0
───────────────────────
 1 0 0 0 1 1 . 1 1 1 1 1
```

15. (a)
```
   1 0 0 1 0 1
-  1 0 0 0 1 1
───────────
   0 0 0 0 1 0
```
(b)
```
 1 0 0 0 0 0 0 0
 0 1 0 0 0 0 0 0
───────────────
   1 0 0 0 0 0 0
```
(c)
```
 1 0 1 1 1 1 0 . 1
   1 0 1 0 1 1 . 1 1
─────────────────
 1 1 0 0 1 0 . 1 1
```
(d)
```
 1 1 1 1 1 1 1 1
   1 1 1 1 1 1 1
───────────────
 1 0 0 0 0 0 0 0
```

17. (a) 100100000 (b) 11111100 (c) 100 (d) 101
(e) 10100000001.101 (f) 10.1

19. (a)
```
       1 1 1 1
       1 1 0 1
     ─────────
       1 1 1 1
     1 1 1 1 0
   1 1 1 1
 ───────────
 1 1 0 0 0 0 1 1
```
(b)
```
       1 1 1 1
       1 0 1 0
     ─────────
       1 1 1 1 0
     1 1 1 1 0
   ───────────
 1 0 0 1 0 1 1 0
```
(c)
```
       1 0 1 1 0 0
         1 0 1 1
       ─────────
       1 0 1 1 0 0
     1 0 1 1 0 0
   1 0 1 1 0 0 0
 ─────────────
 1 1 1 1 0 0 1 0 0
```
(d)
```
       1 0 1 0 1 0
         1 1 0 0
       ─────────
     1 0 1 0 1 0 0 0
   1 0 1 0 1 0
 ─────────────
 1 1 1 1 1 1 0 0 0
```

(e)   1 1 1 . 1 1   (f)   1 0 1 1 0 . 1
               1 0 . 1   1 0 0 . 1 1
           _____   _____
               1 1 1 1 1   1 0 1 1 0 1
           1 1 1 1 1 0   1 0 1 1 0 1
           _____   _____
        1 0 0 1 1 . 0 1 1   1 0 1 1 0 1 0 0
                                            _____
                                        1 1 0 1 0 1 0 . 1 1 1

21.   9S COMPLEMENT   10S COMPLEMENT
(a)   4563   4564
(b)   8067   8068
(c)   54.84   54.85
(d)   81.706   81.707

23.   9S COMPLEMENT   10S COMPLEMENT
(a)   6345   6346
(b)   7877   7878
(c)   45.80   45.81
(d)   62.736   62.737

25.   1S COMPLEMENT   2S COMPLEMENT
(a)   0100   0101
(b)   00100   00101
(c)   0100.10   0100.11
(d)   00100.10   00100.11

27.   1S COMPLEMENT   2S COMPLEMENT
(a)   01000   01001
(b)   011011   011100
(c)   01000.01   01000.10
(d)   01100.00   01100.01

29.   9S COMPLEMENT   10S COMPLEMENT
(a)   9 4 8   9 4 8
            7 6 5   7 6 6
          _____   _____
        1   7 1 3   7 1 4
         └─────→ 1
          _____
            7 1 4

(b)   3 4 7   3 4 7
            7 3 6   7 3 7
          _____   _____
        1   0 8 3   0 8 4
         └─────→ 1
          _____
            0 8 4

(c)   3 4 9 . 5   3 4 9 . 5
          7 5 4 . 6   7 5 4 . 7
        _____   _____
      1   1 0 4 . 1   1 0 4 . 2
       └───────→ 1
        _____
          1 0 4 . 2

(d)   4 1 2 . 7   4 1 2 . 7
          5 9 0 . 7   5 9 0 . 8
        _____   _____
      1   0 0 3 . 4   3 . 5
       └───────→ 1
        _____
              3 . 5

31.

	9S COMPLEMENTS	10S COMPLEMENTS
(a)	1 0 2 4 9 0 8 6 0 1 1 0 → 1 1 1 1	1 0 2 4 9 0 8 7 0 1 1 1
(b)	2 4 9 8 6 2 1 1 1 → 1 1 1 2	2 4 9 8 6 3 1 1 2
(c)	2 4 . 1 8 6 . 5 1 0 . 6 → 1 1 0 . 7	2 4 . 1 8 6 . 6 1 0 . 7
(d)	2 3 9 . 3 8 8 0 . 5 1 1 9 . 8 → 1 1 1 9 . 9	2 3 9 . 3 8 8 0 . 6 1 1 9 . 9

33.

	1S COMPLEMENT	2S COMPLEMENT
(a)	1 0 1 1 1 0 1 0 1 0 1 0 1 → 1 0 1 1 0	1 0 1 1 1 0 1 1 0 1 1 0
(b)	1 1 0 1 1 0 0 1 1 0 1 0 0 0 0 1 → 1 1 0	1 1 0 1 1 0 0 1 1 1 0 0 0 1 0
(c)	1 0 1 1 1 . 1 0 1 1 0 0 . 0 1 0 0 0 1 1 . 1 → 1 1 0 0 . 0	1 0 1 1 1 . 1 0 1 1 0 0 . 1 1 0 0 . 0
(d)	1 1 0 1 1 . 0 0 0 1 1 0 0 . 0 0 1 0 0 1 1 1 . 0 0 → 1 1 1 1 . 0 1	1 1 0 1 1 . 0 0 0 1 1 0 0 . 0 1 1 1 1 . 0 1

35. $2^6 = 64$

37. 1,000 different numbers in each case (from 0 to 999, for instance)

39. 0, 1, 2, 3, 10, 11, 12, 13, 20, 21

41. 0, 1, 2, 3, 4, 5, 6, 7, 8, 9, A, 10, 11, 12, 13, 14, 15, 16, 17, 18, 19, 1A, 20, 21, 22

43. *(a)*

```
   .1 0 0 1
   .1 0 0 1
 ─ 0 0 1 0
 └──────→ 1
   .0 0 1 1
```

(b)

```
   .1 1 1 0
   .1 0 0 1
 ─ 0 1 1 1
 └──────→ 1
   .1 0 0 0
```

(c)

```
   0 1 1 1 1
   1 0 1 1 0
 ─ 0 0 1 0 1
 └───────→ 1
   .0 0 1 1 0
```

(d)

```
   1 1 0 1 1
   0 0 1 1 0
 ─ 0 0 0 0 1
 └───────→ 1
   0 0 0 1 0
```

(e)

```
     1 1 1 0 1 0 1
     0 1 0 1 1 0 1
 1   0 1 0 0 0 1 0
 └───────────→ 1
     0 1 0 0 0 1 1
```

47. *(a)*

```
 4 5 0 5 6
   1 5 3 6
     1 9 2
         7
 4 6 7 9 1
```

(b)

```
 2 4 5 7 6
   1 0 2 4
     1 6 0
       1 2
 2 5 7 7 2
```

(c)

```
 4 0 9 6 0
   1 0 2 4
     1 4 4
         2
 4 2 1 3 0
```

(d)

```
 8 5 1 9 6 8
     8 1 9 2
     1 7 9 2
         9 6
           3
 8 6 2 0 5 1
```

51. *(a)* 55   *(b)* 556   *(c)* 267   *(d)* 66.3   *(e)* 3.554

55. *(a)* 1644.   *(b)* 514   *(c)* 1041.3   *(d)* 1170.76051.   *(e)* 10515.5

59. *(a)* B7   *(b)* 9C   *(c)* 5F   *(d)* 0.7E   *(e)* B7A

63. *(a)*

```
      1
    1 5₈
  + 1 4₈
    3 1₈
```

(b)

```
      1
    2 4₈
  + 3 6₈
    6 2₈
```

(c)

```
      1
  1 2 6₈
  3 4 7₈
  4 7 5₈
```

(d)

```
      1
    6 7₈
    4 5₈
  1 3 4₈
```

(e)

```
      1
  1 3 6₈
  6 3 6₈
  7 7 4₈
```

CHAPTER 3

1. *(a)*

x	Y	$\bar{Y}$	XY	$X\bar{Y}$	$XY + X\bar{Y}$
0	0	1	0	0	0
0	1	0	0	0	0
1	0	1	0	1	1
1	1	0	1	0	1

(b)

X	Y	Z	$\bar{Y}$	$\bar{Z}$	$X\bar{Y}Z$	$\bar{Y}Z$	$X\bar{Y}Z + \bar{Y}Z$
0	0	0	1	1	0	1	1
0	0	1	1	0	0	0	0
0	1	0	0	1	0	0	0
0	1	1	0	0	0	0	0
1	0	0	1	1	0	1	1
1	0	1	1	0	1	0	1
1	1	0	0	1	0	0	0
1	1	1	0	0	0	0	0

3. (a)

X	Y	Z	XYZ	$X\bar{Y}\bar{Z}$	$XYZ + X\bar{Y}\bar{Z}$
0	0	0	0	0	0
0	0	1	0	0	0
0	1	0	0	0	0
0	1	1	0	0	0
1	0	0	0	1	1
1	0	1	0	0	0
1	1	0	0	0	0
1	1	1	1	0	1

(b)

A	B	C	ABC	$A\bar{B}\bar{C}$	$\bar{A}\bar{B}\bar{C}$	$ABC + A\bar{B}\bar{C} + \bar{A}\bar{B}\bar{C}$
0	0	0	0	0	1	1
0	0	1	0	0	0	0
0	1	0	0	0	0	0
0	1	1	0	0	0	0
1	0	0	0	1	0	1
1	0	1	0	0	0	0
1	1	0	0	0	0	0
1	1	1	1	0	0	1

(c)

A	B	C	$B\bar{C}$	$\bar{B}C$	$B\bar{C} + \bar{B}C$	$A(B\bar{C} + \bar{B}C)$
0	0	0	0	0	0	0
0	0	1	0	1	1	0
0	1	0	1	0	1	0
0	1	1	0	0	0	0
1	0	0	0	0	0	0
1	0	1	0	1	1	1
1	1	0	1	0	1	1
1	1	1	0	0	0	0

(d)

A	B	C	A + B	A + C	$\bar{A} + \bar{B}$	$(A + B)(A + C)(\bar{A} + \bar{B})$
0	0	0	0	0	1	0
0	0	1	0	1	1	0
0	1	0	1	0	1	0
0	1	1	1	1	1	1
1	0	0	1	1	1	1
1	0	1	1	1	1	1
1	1	0	1	1	0	0
1	1	1	1	1	0	0

5. Only the values of the expressions are listed:

(a)

A	B	$A\bar{B} + \bar{A}B$
0	0	0
0	1	1
1	0	1
1	1	0

(b)

A	B	C	$A\bar{B} + B\bar{C}$
0	0	0	0
0	0	1	0
0	1	0	1
0	1	1	0
1	0	0	1
1	0	1	1
1	1	0	1
1	1	1	0

(c)

A	C	$A\bar{C} + AC$
0	0	0
0	1	0
1	0	1
1	1	1

(d)

A	B	C	$\bar{A}\bar{B}C + AB\bar{C} + \bar{A}BC$
0	0	0	0
0	0	1	0
0	1	0	0
0	1	1	1
1	0	0	0
1	0	1	1
1	1	0	1
1	1	1	0

(e)

A	B	C	$A(\bar{A}\bar{B}C + AB\bar{C} + AB\bar{C})$
0	0	0	0
0	0	1	0
0	1	0	0
0	1	1	0
1	0	0	1
1	0	1	1
1	1	0	1
1	1	1	0

7. (a) $\overline{BC} + \overline{AC} + \overline{AB}$ (b) $\overline{C} + \overline{B} + \overline{A}$
   (c) $A(B + C)$ (d) A is a minimal expression.
9. (a) $ABC(A B \overline{C} + A \overline{B} C + \overline{A} B C) = 0$, for no assignment of binary values,
    will make this expression take the value 1.
   (b) $AB + A\overline{B} + \overline{A}C + \overline{A}\overline{C} = 1$, for every assignment of values, will give
    this expression the value 1.
   (c) $XY + XYZ + XY\overline{Z} + \overline{X}YZ = Y$
   (d) $XY(\overline{X}YZ + X\overline{Y}Z + XY\overline{Z}) = 0$
11. (a) $\overline{A}(\overline{B} + \overline{C})(\overline{A} + B) = \overline{A}B + \overline{A}\overline{C}$ or $\overline{A}(B + \overline{C})$
   (b) $\overline{A}B + \overline{B}C + \overline{A}C$
   (c) $(\overline{A} + B)(B + \overline{C})(\overline{C} + D) = \overline{A}B\overline{C} + \overline{A}C + \overline{A}BD + \overline{A}CD =$
    $\overline{A}\overline{C} + \overline{B}C + \overline{A}BD$
   (d) $(\overline{A} + \overline{B}) + (C + \overline{D})(B + \overline{C}) = \overline{A} + \overline{B} + BC + B\overline{D} + \overline{C}\overline{D} =$
    $\overline{A}\overline{B} + C + \overline{D}$
   (e) $\overline{A} + \overline{B}C + CD$
13. The important columns in these tables are as follows:

X	Y	Z	$\overline{(X+Y+Z)}$	$\overline{X}\,\overline{Y}\,\overline{Z}$
0	0	0	1	1
0	0	1	0	0
0	1	0	0	0
0	1	1	0	0
1	0	0	0	0
1	0	1	0	0
1	1	0	0	0
1	1	1	0	0

X	Y	Z	$\overline{(XYZ)}$	$\overline{X} + \overline{Y} + \overline{Z}$
0	0	0	1	1
0	0	1	1	1
0	1	0	1	1
0	1	1	1	1
1	0	0	1	1
1	0	1	1	1
1	1	0	1	1
1	1	1	0	0

15. (a) $\overline{A}BC + A\overline{B}C + AC + BC$
   (b) $A\overline{B} + A\overline{C} + ABC + AB\overline{C} + \overline{A}BC + BC$ (This can be simplified.)
   (c) $AB + ABC$
17. Rule 13
19. (a) $AB + AD + BC + CD$
   (b) $AB + AD + AC + BC + CD + C + BD + D + DC = C + D + AB$

(c) $ABC + ABD + AC + BC + DC + ADC + BDC + DC =$
   $AC + BC + DC + ABD$
(d) $A\overline{B}\overline{C} + ABC$

21. $\overline{X}\overline{Y}Z + XY\overline{Z}$

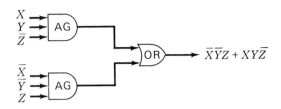

23. $(X + Y)(X + Z) = X + XZ + YZ$
$$= X + Z + YZ$$
$$= X + Z$$

25. $XY + X\overline{Z}$

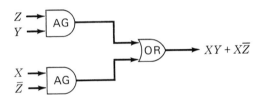

27.

X	Y	$X + \overline{X}Y$	$X + Y$
0	0	0	0
0	1	1	1
1	0	1	1
1	1	1	1

29. $Y\overline{Z} + \overline{Y}Z$ is the sum-of-products expression and $(Y + Z)(\overline{Y} + \overline{Z})$ is the product-of-sums expression.

35. (a)

	$\overline{X}$	X
$\overline{Y}$	1	
Y	1	

$\overline{X}\overline{Y} + \overline{X}Y$

(b)

	$\overline{X}\overline{Y}$	$\overline{X}Y$	XY	$X\overline{Y}$
$\overline{Z}$	1		1	
Z				

$\overline{X}\overline{Y}\overline{Z} + XY\overline{Z}$

(c)

	$\overline{X}\overline{Y}$	$\overline{X}Y$	XY	$X\overline{Y}$
$\overline{Z}$	1	1		
Z	1			

$\overline{X}Y\overline{Z} + \overline{X}\overline{Y}$

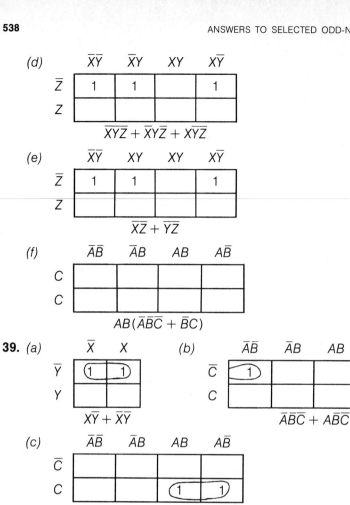

(d)

	$\bar{X}\bar{Y}$	$\bar{X}Y$	XY	$X\bar{Y}$
$\bar{Z}$	1	1		1
Z				

$$\bar{X}\bar{Y}\bar{Z} + \bar{X}Y\bar{Z} + X\bar{Y}\bar{Z}$$

(e)

	$\bar{X}\bar{Y}$	$\bar{X}Y$	XY	$X\bar{Y}$
$\bar{Z}$	1	1		1
Z				

$$\bar{X}\bar{Z} + \bar{Y}\bar{Z}$$

(f)

	$\bar{A}\bar{B}$	$\bar{A}B$	AB	$A\bar{B}$
$\bar{C}$				
C				

$$AB(\bar{A}\bar{B}C + \bar{B}C)$$

39. *(a)*

	$\bar{X}$	X
$\bar{Y}$	1	1
Y		

$$X\bar{Y} + \bar{X}\bar{Y}$$

(b)

	$\bar{A}\bar{B}$	$\bar{A}B$	AB	$A\bar{B}$
$\bar{C}$	1			1
C				

$$\bar{A}\bar{B}\bar{C} + A\bar{B}\bar{C}$$

(c)

	$\bar{A}\bar{B}$	$\bar{A}B$	AB	$A\bar{B}$
$\bar{C}$				
C			1	1

$$A\bar{B}C + ABC$$

(d)

	$\bar{A}\bar{B}$	$\bar{A}B$	AB	$A\bar{B}$
$\bar{C}$			1	1
C			1	1

$$ABC + AB\bar{C} + A\bar{B}C + A\bar{B}\bar{C}$$

(e)

	$\bar{A}\bar{B}$	$\bar{A}B$	AB	$A\bar{B}$
C				1
C			1	1

$$ABC + A\bar{B}\bar{C} + A\bar{B}C$$

(f)

	$\bar{A}\bar{B}$	$\bar{A}B$	AB	$A\bar{B}$
$\bar{C}$	1			
C		1	1	

$$ABC + \bar{A}BC + \bar{A}\bar{B}C$$

41. *(a)*   *(b)*

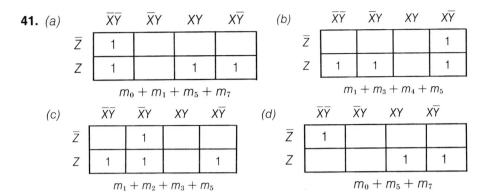

$m_0 + m_1 + m_5 + m_7$ (a)
$m_1 + m_3 + m_4 + m_5$ (b)
$m_1 + m_2 + m_3 + m_5$ (c)
$m_0 + m_5 + m_7$ (d)

45. *(b)*

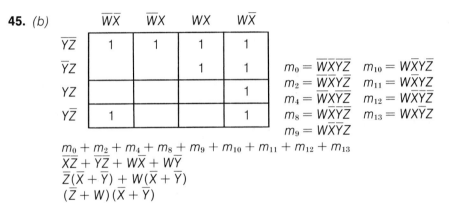

$m_0 = \overline{W}\overline{X}\overline{Y}\overline{Z}$ $m_{10} = W\overline{X}Y\overline{Z}$
$m_2 = \overline{W}\overline{X}Y\overline{Z}$ $m_{11} = W\overline{X}YZ$
$m_4 = \overline{W}X\overline{Y}\overline{Z}$ $m_{12} = WX\overline{Y}\overline{Z}$
$m_8 = W\overline{X}\overline{Y}\overline{Z}$ $m_{13} = WX\overline{Y}Z$
$m_9 = W\overline{X}\overline{Y}Z$

$m_0 + m_2 + m_4 + m_8 + m_9 + m_{10} + m_{11} + m_{12} + m_{13}$
$\overline{X}\overline{Z} + Y\overline{Z} + W\overline{X} + W\overline{Y}$
$\overline{Z}(\overline{X} + Y) + W(\overline{X} + \overline{Y})$
$(\overline{Z} + W)(\overline{X} + \overline{Y})$

47. *(a)* $m_1 + m_3 + m_5 + m_7 + m_{12} + m_{13} + m_8 + m_9$

Product-of-sums:

$\overline{(WY + W\overline{Z})} =$
$$(\overline{W} + \overline{Y})(W + Z)$$

Sum-of-products:

$W\overline{Y} + \overline{W}Z$

(b) $m_0 + m_5 + m_7 + m_8 + m_{11} + m_{13} + m_{15}$

Product-of-sums:

$\overline{(X\overline{Z} + Y\overline{Z} + \overline{W}XZ + \overline{X}YZ)} =$
$(\overline{X} + Z)(\overline{Y} + Z)(W + X + \overline{Z})$
$$(X + Y + \overline{Z})$$

don't-cares

49. *(a)* $\overline{A}\overline{B}\overline{C} + A\overline{B}\overline{C} + ABC + \overline{A}B\overline{C} + \overline{A}\overline{B}C = \overline{B}C$

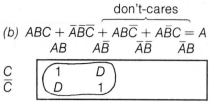

don't-cares

(b) $ABC + \overline{A}\overline{B}C + AB\overline{C} + A\overline{B}C = A$
    AB $\overline{A}\overline{B}$ $A\overline{B}$ $\overline{A}B$

don't-cares

(c) $ABCD + \overline{A}\overline{B}CD + \overline{A}BCD + A\overline{B}CD + \overline{A}\overline{B}C\overline{D} + ABC\overline{D}$
    AB $A\overline{B}$ $\overline{A}B$ $\overline{A}B$

$CD + \overline{A}\overline{B}D$

Chapter 4

1.

5.

9.

13.

15.

17.

CHAPTER 5

1.

	Ge	SI
(a)	$e_0 = 0.3$ V	0.7 V

(b) Approx. 2 mA

9.

(a) $e_0 = -2.75$ V

(b) Yes; the emitter-base junction is forward biased (*npn* base more positive than emitter).

13.

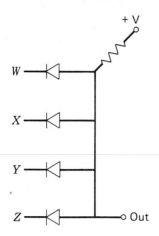

15. +0.1 V
25. T3 and T5
31. 8.333 mA max.
35. $\overline{X}$ will be a 1 when X is a 0 and a 0 when X is a 1.
41. Both will be 0s (at about ground).

43.

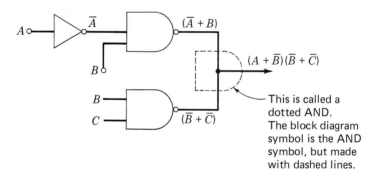

This is called a dotted AND. The block diagram symbol is the AND symbol, but made with dashed lines.

45.

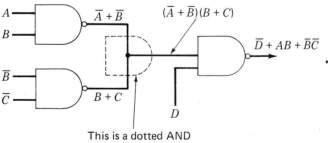

This is a dotted AND as in Question 43

49. 200 μA

CHAPTER 6

1.

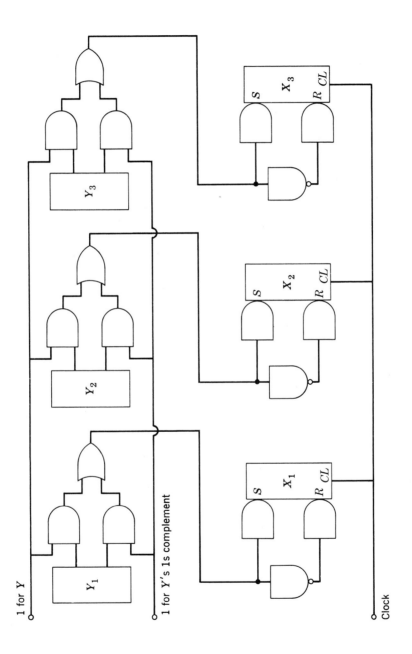

3. *(a)* 0.0110   *(b)* 0.1010   *(c)* 1.1100   *(d)* Not representable

5. −4 would be stored 1.0100 in the magnitude system, 1.1011 in the 1s complement system, and 1.1100 in the 2s complement system.

7. $s = 1$ and $c = 1$

9. −12 in 1s complement; −13 in 2s complement.

11. The sum will overflow the register and cause an incorrect addition. Most machines sense for this and turn on an "addition overflow" or indicate the overflow in some manner.

15.

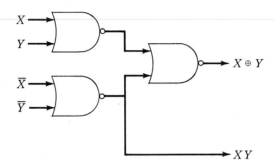

27. Logical addition, 0.111011
Logical multiplication, 0.100010
Exclusive OR, 0.011001

29. The logical MULTIPLY will clear those digits of X where 0s occur in Y, and the logical ADD will act 1s into the places in X where 1s occur in Y.

41.

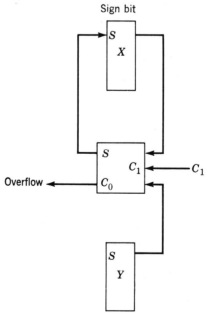

$$\text{Overflow} = (A > \emptyset) \cdot (B > \emptyset) \cdot (C_1 = 1) + (A < \emptyset) \cdot (B < 0) \cdot (C_1 = \emptyset)$$
$$\text{Overflow} = \overline{X}\overline{Y}C_1 + XY\overline{C_1}$$

43. The general scheme is:

Carry out = 1

53. (a) 0 0000 0000 0100 0010
    (b) 1 0000 0001 0010 0010
    (c) 0 0001 0000 0011 0100
    (d) 1 0001 0000 1001 0111
57. (a) 0 0000 0000 0100 0010
    (b) 1 1111 1110 1101 1110
    (c) 0 0001 0000 0011 0100
    (d) 1 1110 1111 0110 1001

CHAPTER 7

1. 143,360 cores
12 flip-flops for address register
35 flip-flops for memory buffer register
3. 147,456 cores; 36 sense amplifiers; 36 inhibit drivers; 64 X drivers, and
64 Y drivers; 36 planes and 4,096 cores per plane
5. False, because all the selected cores are set to the 0 state and 1s must
be rewritten.
7. X_2Y_2, X_2Y_3
9. (a) 1

11.

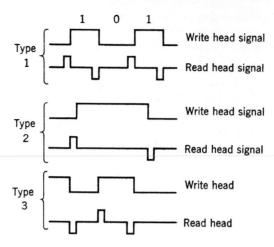

41. 40 μs, 20 μs
43. 3,600,000 bits/s
45. 262,500 bits/s

CHAPTER 8

3. 01100001
01100100
01100100
00010000
00010110
00000100
00000001
10000000   Carriage return is perhaps optional.
5. 27 holes in three cards. Easier to correct if cards are used, for erroneous cards may simply be replaced.
7. Nine holes

9.

DECIMAL	EXCESS 3 CODE	EVEN PARITY CHECK	ODD PARITY CHECK
0	0011	0	1
1	0100	1	0
2	0101	0	1
3	0110	0	1
4	0111	1	0
5	1000	1	0
6	1001	0	1
7	1010	0	1
8	1011	1	0
9	1100	0	1

11. (a) The errors are in the seventh, eighth, and ninth rows; the sixth digit in each row is in error, and the message is "that's right."

   (b) The error is the fourth digit in the sixth row, and the message is "don't stop."

13. 10 — One such code can be formed by adding a leading 0 to each of the 4-binary-digit Gray code groups listed in Chap. 8 and then adding another 16 rows with the 4 rightmost binary digits the same as those in Chap. 8 but with their order reversed and with a leading 1 added to each of these code rows.

15. (a) Errors are in the second, third, and fourth rows, the seventh digit in. The message is "that's fine."

   (b) Errors are in the second and third rows, the third digit in, and the message is "bad tapes." Notice that we corrected a double error in a column.

17. 0101 gives $+2\frac{2}{3}$ V.
   1010 gives $+5\frac{1}{3}$ V.
   1111 gives $+8$ V.

19. The code will detect but not correct errors occurring in two different columns. It will not detect or correct four errors occurring in two rows and two columns, i.e., two errors in each of two rows with errors in the same two columns in each row. There are many other patterns of these types, and analysis of these codes is very subtle.

23. The code in Question 15 will correct all the errors in Question 11. The code in Question 11 will correct the errors in Question 15(a) but only detect those in Question 15(b).

27. Double errors in a row lead to detection via the check digits. Since there are essentially no checks on the check digits, errors in these result in data loss.

CHAPTER 9

1.

S	OP code	Index register	Address
1 digit	5 digits	2 digits	14 digits

3.   Single address

OP code	Address
1	6 7 24

2^{18} different addresses

Double address

OP code	Address A	Address B
1	6 7 15	16 24

2^9 different addresses

5. Here is a possible program:

```
CLA   25
MUL   24
MUL   29
STO   30
CLA   25
MUL   28
ADD   30
ADD   27
STO   30
```

25 contains X
27 contairts C
28 contains B
29 contains A

7. Sign
bit $1 \longleftrightarrow 1112 \longleftrightarrow 151617 \longleftrightarrow 2324 \longleftrightarrow 30$

OP   Track   Sector
code   bits   bits

11.
```
CRA   302
MPX   302
ADD   301
DIV   303
STA   304
```

13. The SBM instruction subtracts the magnitude of the number stored in the location given by the address part of the instruction word from the number in the accumulator, and places this difference value in the accumulator. The instruction is indexable and indirectly addressable and can result in an overflow.

15. Change each AC_0 to $\overline{AC_0}$, each $\overline{AC_0}$ to AC_0, and BRM to BRP.

CHAPTER 10

1.

			Decimal digits		
S	OP code	1st address	2d address	3d address
1	2	3	3	3
binary digit	digits	digits	digits	digits

3. Four trips for an addition instruction

5.

ADDRESS	INDEX REGISTER	OP CODE	ADDRESS PART
0	01	SIR	39
1	01	CAD	200
2	00	ADD	300
3	00	STO	300
4	01	BRI	1
5	00	HLT	0
Location of data	200		
	239		
	300	contains 0 when program is started.	

INDEX

Page numbers in *italic* indicate illustrations or tables.

Abacus, 2, 48
Access time: of bipolar memories, 318
    defined, 20, 275, 328
    of magnetic drum storage, 322, 325
    of read-only memories, 318
    reading, 294
Accumulator: in arithmetic-logic unit, 220–221
    destination, 506
    flip-flop, 417–*418*
    function in a program of, *22, 24–26*
    instructions for, 409, 412, 425, 429–430, *476–478*
        branch, 427
        shift, 429–430
    logic operations and, 260–262
    minicomputers and, 452–455
    multiple, 445–446
    operation of, 22–23
    source, 506
Acoustic coupler, 389
Active transistor mode: in *npn* transistor, 172–174
    in *pnp* transistors, 175–177
Adders, binary: binary-coded-decimal, 237–*240*
    full, 223–224, 234–237
    half, 222–223
    parallel, 224–227
    quarter, 223
Adding machines, 2
Addition: arithmetic, 222–223
    binary, 51
    with floating-point numbers, 267–268
    logical, 75, 82, 260–262
    Modulo 2, 260–262
    in 9s complement system, 241–245
    in parallel element, 231–234

Address: buses and, 471, 473
    character addressable systems, 20*n.*, 500–501, 510
    construction of memory and, 20
    contents of, 277
    defined, 19
    instructions, 21–23, 408
        four-address, 446
        shift, 429–430
        stacks, 446–447
        three-address, 446
        two-address, 445–446
        zero-address, 446
    in magnetic drum memories, 325–326
    mode of, 454–455, *497*
    multiple-address computer and, 21*n.*, 445–447
    single-address computer and, 21*n.*
    storage devices: direct-access, 275*n.*
        random-access, 276–278
    symbolic referencing of storage, 35
    word addressable systems, 20*n.*
Address register, memory, 277–278, 289, *290*
        branch instructions and, 427
        indirect addressing and, 454–455
        instruction counter and, 415
        magnetic drum and, 326
        two-address computers and, 501
Addressing techniques, 449
    on IBM 360/370 computers, 508–513
    index registers, 449–451, 506
    indirect, 454–455
    paging, 451–454
Aiken, Howard, 5
Algebra, modern, 73
"Algebra of sets, the," 74

Algol language, 37
Alphanumeric codes, 369–372
 ASCII, 369, *371–372*
  oscilloscopes and, 382–383
 BCD, 369, *370*, 372
 Hallerith, 365
 two-address computers and, 500–501
 verifier and, 367
American National Standards Institute, 369, *376*
 protocols for digital systems, 465, 467
American Standard Code for Information Interchange
  (ASCII), 369, *371–372*
 8-bit coded character, 388, *389*
 oscilloscopes and, 382–383
Analog quantities, 16
Analog-to-digital converter, 16, 391
 electronic high-speed, 395–399
 shaft encoders, 392–394
 terminology, *399*
AND gates, 76–78, 178–179
 AND-to-OR, 232–*233*
 binary adders and, 227, 237–239
 buses and, *466*
 decoders and, 295
 diode, 179–180
  diode-transistor logic and, 189
 NAND and NOR gates and, 97–99
 positive and negative, 181
 RS flip-flops and, 135
 transfer circuits and, 127
AND operation, 260
Anode of the diode, 170
Arithmetic-logic unit (ALU), 219–273
 addition: 1s complement, 228–229
  2s complement, 229–231
 addition and subtraction: 9s complement, 241–245
  in a parallel element, 231–234
 basic operations of, 246–250
 binary adders: binary-coded-decimal, 237–239
  full, 223–224, 234–237
  half, 222–223
  parallel, 224–227
 complements: 9s addition and subtraction,
   241–245
  1s addition, 228–229
  2s addition, 229–231
 construction of, 220–221
 control unit, 219–220
 defined, 19
 division, 254–260
 floating-point number systems and, 262–267
  performing arithmetic with, 267–268
 integer representation, 221–222
 logical operations, 260–262
 microcomputers and, 470, *471*
 multiplication: binary, 250–253
  decimal, 253–254
 positive and negative numbers, 227
  binary-coded-decimal, 239–241
 questions, 268–273
 shift operation, 245–246
Arithmetic operations, controlling, *416–424*
 sequence of, 424–426
Assembler program, 21, 34
 uses of, 34–37
Assembly languages, 34–37
 address assignment and, 35
 convenient data representation and, 35
 error detection and, 35–36

Assembly languages: program listings and, 35
Associative laws of Boolean algebra, 76, 83
Asynchronous bus, 467*n*.
Asynchronous operation, 128, 388
Atlas computers, 452
Auxiliary memory, 274, 275
 instructions and, 407

B-box register, 449
Babbage, Charles, 4–5, 19
Backup store memory, 274
Balanced multiplicative decoder network, 297, *299*
Base of a number system, 48–49
Base register, 512–513
Basic language, 28*n.*, 31
 interpreters and, 34*n*.
 online systems and, 37
Batch processing, 11
Baudot code, *361*, 362
 parity checking, 386
Binary, 124
Binary adders (*see* Adders, binary)
Binary-coded-decimal (BCD) adders, 237–*240*
 alphanumeric code, 369, *370*, 372
 counters, 138–139
  in integrated circuits, 149, *151*
 9s complement system and, 241–245
 number representation, 58–61
 registers, 220
 two-address computers, 501, 503, 507
Binary counters, 132–137
 binary-coded-decimal, 138–139
  in integrated circuits, 149, *151*
 flip-flops and: *D* 136–137
  JK, 135–137
 four-stage, 135, 139
 gated-clocked, 135
 three-stage, 134
 up-down, 137
Binary number system, 49
 addition and subtraction, 51
 binary-coded-decimal number representation,
   58–61
 complements, 56–60
 conversion to: from decimal numbers, 53–54, *59*
  from hexadecimal numbers, 63–64
 counting in, 49–50
 digital computers and, 49
 Leibniz and, 49
 multiplication and division, 51–53
 negative numbers in, 55–56
Binary operations, 78
Binary-to-Gray code, 316–*318*
Bipolar logic, 143, 146, 202
Bipolar memories, 304–307
 static MOS devices compared to, 308–310
Bistable circuits, 49
 flip-flops as, 125
Bit winding, 300
Bits: in the arithmetic-logic unit, 220
 cost per, 274–276, 316
 density of, 333, 335
 link, 485
 magnetic core and, 279
 in minicomputers, 452–455
 page, 453
 sign, 55–56
  in binary division, 255–260

Bits: sign: in floating-point number representation, 263–267
  integer representation by, 221–222, 227, 239, 241
  tape cartridges and, 344
  two-address computers and, 506
  word length and, 276–278
Boole, George, 73–74
Boolean algebra and gate networks, 73–123
  basic duality of, 87
  basic laws of, 82–84
  complementation and inverters, 78–79
  De Morgan's theorems, 86–87
  derivation of expressions: Boolean, 87–90
    product-of-sums, 94–95
    three-input-variables, 95–97
  evaluation of expressions: containing parentheses, 80–82
    logical, 79–80
  fundamental concepts of, 74–75
  gates: combination of, 91
    NAND and NOR, 97–100
    OR and AND, 76–78
  logical multiplication, 75–76
  origin of, 73–74
  product-of-sums, 92–94
    derivation of, 94–95
    don't-cares, 108–110
  proof by perfect induction, 84–85
  questions, 110–123
  simplification of expressions, 86
    map method for, 100–103
  subcubes and covering, 103–108
  sum-of-products, 92–94
  three-input-variable expressions, 95–97
Branch instructions, 25–26, 426–429, 480
  branch on index code, 450, 451
  condition flags and, 488
Buffer register, memory, 277, 278, 289, 290
  associated circuitry and, 292–294
  branch instructions and, 427
  microprogramming and, 434–435
  OP-code and, 424–425
  two-address computers and, 501
Burroughs Corporation, 264, 448
Buses, 463–470
  asynchronous, 467n.
  data, 467
  defined, 456, 465n.
  general interface management, 467
  handshaking and, 467, 469–470
  international standard, 468
  microprocessors and, 470, 471, 473, 488
  minicomputers and, 486, 487
  names for, 470n.
  single-bus, 456–458, 465
    computer organization of, 464
  synchronous, 467n.
  three-state drivers and, 465, 466
Bytes: addressable, 510
  defined, 63
  on flexible disk, 334, 335
  hexadecimal systems and, 64
  microprocessors and, 471

Calculators, 2–4
Calculi, 2
"Calculus of propositions, the," 74

Calling program, 485–486
Canonical expansion, 88
Card punching machine, 28
  high-speed, 384–385
  operation of, 365–366
  quantity in use, 31
Carry-ripple problem, 237
Cash registers, 2
Cathode of the diode, 170
Cathode-ray-tube devices, 382–384
CDC computers, 460, 462–463
Central processing unit (CPU), 455–463
  buses for, 456–458, 470
  direct memory access and, 458
  interrupt lines and, 457–458
  multiprocessing: mode, 458–460
    systems, 462, 472–475
  peripheral processing units and, 460, 462
Channel program, 460
Character addressable systems, 20n., 500–501, 510
Character recognition, 374–376
Character transmission systems, 388–391
Characteristic, 263
Charactron tube, 384
Charge pumps, 316n.
Clock pulses, 128n.
  arithmetic operations and, 419
  magnetic drum memories and, 326
Clocks, 128–131
Cobol language, 28n., 37
Coding, 21
Coding forms, 28, 29
Coincident-current four-wire random-access core memory, 300
Coincident-current selection technique, 281–284
  core memory: characteristics of, 289
    semiconductor, 306
    writing into, 288
Collator, 367, 368
Collector, 171–176
  common, 177, 178
Combinational networks, 91, 99
Command and control systems, 17
Common collector, 177, 178
Commutative laws of Boolean algebra, 83–84
Compiler languages, 37–38
  defined, 34
  PL/1, 38–42
    questions concerning, 44–46
  programs, 34, 38
Complementer, 242–243
Complements, 78
  binary number, 56–60
  Boolean algebra rules of, 78, 82
  De Morgan's theorems and, 86–87
  flip-flops and, 125
  NAND and NOR gates and, 97–99
  9s, 56–57, 59–60
    addition and subtraction in, 241–245
    negative numbers and, 241
  1s, 58
    addition and subtraction in, 228–229, 231–232, 234n.
    positive and negative numbers and, 227
  product-of-sums and, 108–110
  radix-minus-one, 57
  to represent negative numbers, 56–57
  symbols indicating, 78

Complements: 10s, 56
    addition and subtraction in, *244*
    negative numbers and, 241
  true, 57
  2s, 57–58
    addition and subtraction in, *229–234*
    minicomputers and, 452
    positive and negative numbers and, 227
Computer architecture, 444
Computer operation, 20–46
  construction of memory, 20
  instructions, 20–23
    branch, skip or jump, 25–26
    multiplication, 23–24
  languages: assembly, 34–37
    compiler, 37–38
    PL/1, 38–42
  programming systems, 33–34
  questions, 42–46
    on PL/1, 44–46
  telephone communications, 14, 27
Computer organization, 443–519
  addresses, 444–448
    single-address, 481–499
    two-address, 500–506
  addressing techniques, 449
    index registers, 449–451
    paging and indirect, 451–455
  IBM 360/370, 506–513
  index registers, 449–451
  instruction word formats, 444–448
  interconnecting system components, 455–463
  interfacing-buses, 463–470
  microprocessors and microcomputers, 470–481,
    488–499
  questions, 513–519
  representation of instructions, 448–449
  single-address, 481–487
    microprocessor, 488–499
  two-address, 500–506
Computer terminals, 13–14
Computers, 1–20
  applications of: to business, 8–9
    to problems, 6–8
    to science, 9–11
  calculators and, 2–4
  computer industry, 1–2
  digital, 4–6
    basic components of, 18–20
    control systems of, 14–16
  general-purpose, 16–17
  questions, 42–44
  special purpose, 16–17
  types of systems, 11–14
  time-shared, 17–18
Condition code register, *481*
Condition flags, 488, *498*
Conditional instructions, 25
Conditional operations, 248
Control circuitry, 19, 259
Control memory, 434
Control systems, 14–16
Control unit, 405–442
  arithmetic operations, *416–424*
    sequence of, 424–426
  branch, skip or jump, 426–429
  defined, 406
  execution-cycle, 412–415

Control unit: instruction-cycle, 412–415
  instruction word, 406–412
  microprogramming and, 432–437
    variations in, 438–440
  operation of, 405–406
  questions, 440–442
  registers, 412–415
    sequence of operation, 415–417
  shift instruction, 429–432
Controller module, 467
Convenient data representation, 35
Conventional current, 170
Core (see Magnetic core memory)
Core-memory array, 289
Core-memory plane, 285, 286
Counter design, 157–161
Counter table, 142–143
Counters (*see* specific types of counters)
Current enhancement mode, 203
Current-mode logic, 198
Current-steering logic, 198
Cutoff transistor mode, 169
  in *npn* transistor, 172, 174–175
  in *pnp* transistors, 175–177
Cycle stealing, 458

D-type flip-flop, 136–137, 208–209
Darlington configuration, 192
Data bus, 467
Data General computers, 63, *265*, 454, 455
  two-address, 505–506
Datamatic Corporation, 446
DDP-24 computer, 408–*411*
Decade counter, *138*
Decimal number system, 48–49
  binary-coded-, 58–61
  conversion to: from binary numbers, 53–54, *59*
    from hexadecimal numbers, 64–65
Decoder matrix, 291, 295
Decoders, 295–299
  magnetic drum memories and, 326
Delay time, 131*n.*
  in read-only memory, 321
De Morgan's theorems, 86–87
Destination accumulator, 506
Dian series N printer, 379, *381*
Differential amplifier, 198
Digit winding, 300, *302*
Digital circuits, 168–218
  computer, 169
  diode: AND circuit, 179–180
    in switching, 169–177
  diode-transistor logic, 189–191
  emitter follower, 177–178
  gates: AND, 178–180
    NOR, 184–186
    OR, 180–181
  inverter, 181–184
  logic: CMOS, 206–209
    diode-transistor, 189–191
    emitter-coupled, 198–202
    resistor-transistor, 181–182, 184, 187–188
    transistor-transistor, 191–198
  metal-oxide semiconductor, 202–206
  questions, 209–218
  transistor: flip-flop, 186–187
    in switiching, 169–177
  transistor-diode logic, 189–191

Digital circuits: transistor-resistor logic, 187–188
transistor-transistor logic, 191–198
Digital computers, electronic, 4–6
basic components of, 18–20
binary system and, 49
control systems and, 14–16
differences between calculators and, 4
repetitious work and, 7
Digital Equipment Corporation computers, 63
bus for, 456–457
floating-point number systems and, 265
instruction repertoires of, 507
minicomputers, 481–487
paging and, 452–454
Digital recording techniques, 346
return-to-bias, 347–349
return-to-zero, 346–348
non-return-to-zero, 349–351
Digital-to-analog converter, 16, 391–392, 394–395
terminology, 399
Digital voltmeters, 399
Diode-transistor logic (DTL), 189–191
Diodes: closed and open, 171
gates: AND, 179–180, 295, 297
OR, 181
Schottky, 194–196, 307
semiconductor, 170, 195
silicon, 170, 171
in switching circuits, 169–177
Direct-access storage devices (DASD), 275n.
Direct addressing, 449
Direct memory access, 458
Disable input, 465, 466
Displacement, 506
Display device, 14
Distributive law of Boolean algebra, 83, 84
Division: binary, 51–53, 248–250, 254–260
with floating-point numbers, 267
Don't-care outputs, 109–110, 158
Dot matrix printers, 378
Dual inline package, 140, 141
Duodecimal number system, 49
Dynamic MOS memories, 305, 314–316
Dynamic storage devices, 276

E flip-flop, 415, 416, 419–424
control signals, 420–422
operation of, 424–425
Eckert, S. P., 5
Edsac computer, 5
Edvac computer, 5
Electromagnetic printers, 381
Electrostatic printers, 381
Emitter, 171–176
multiple, 191–192
Emitter-coupled logic (ECL), 198–202
characteristics of, 200
Fairchild, 200
generations of, 201
motorola, 200
speed of, 198
Emitter follower, 177–178
Eniac computer, 5
Erasable and reprogrammable memory, 321
Error detection, 35–36
codes, 385–387
Even-parity-bit checking, 385–386
Excess 3 code, 59–60

Execution cycle, 412–415
Exponent, 262–268
Expressions, Boolean: derivation of, 87–90
product-of-sums, 94–95
three-input-variable, 95–97
evaluation of: containing parentheses, 80–82
logical, 79–80
simplification of, 86
map method for, 100–103
Extract, 260

Falling edge clock signal, 129
Fan-in, fan-out, 182
Field effect transistor (FET), 143, 146, 202–206
in static MOS memories, 304–305
Field programmable ROM, 318n.
Firmware, 439
Fixed-head systems, 327, 329
Fixed-point arithmetic, 262
Flash converters, 398
Flexible disk storage systems, 332–335
Flip-flops, 125–127
accumulator, 417–418
binary counters and, 133–137
characteristics of, 125
D-type, 136–137, 208–209
decoders and, 295–298
matrix, 291
delay time of, 131n.
E, 415, 416, 419–425
in early computers, 140
edges of waveforms and, 129n.
gated, 152–154
I, 415, 416, 419–424
branch instructions and, 427–429
control signals, 420–422
operation of, 424–425
shift instructions, 430, 432
integer representation and, 222
in integrated circuits, 141–143, 146, 149
JK, 135–137, 141
BCD counters and, 139
clocked, 187–188
counter design and, 159–161
dual, 147
integrated circuits, 143
inverters and, 184
master-slave, 154–157
RS flip-flops and, 136, 189
logical operations and, 260–262
magnetic core memory and, 281
master-slave, 154–157, 190–191, 197–198
memory buffer registers and, 292–294
R, 415, 424–425
as random-access device, 275
recording techniques and, 350
registers, 128, 220, 246–248, 275, 290, 417–418
resistor-transistor logic and, 188
RS: AND gates and, 135
clocked, 129–131, 153–154
conventions of, 125–126
counter design and, 157–159
gated, 152–154
input rules of, 126
integrated circuits and, 140, 152
JK flip-flops and, 136, 189
logic circuits and, 186–187, 189–191, 201–202,
205

Flip-flops: *RS:* transfer circuits and, 127–128
  waveforms of, *127*
  "safety factor" in, 154
  semiconductor memories and, 304–307
  SET and RESET and, 186–*187*
  shift registers and, 131–132
  SR, 430–432
  as static storage device, 275–276
    MOS memories and, 308–310
  transistor, 186–187
  transistor-transistor logic, 196–197
  W, 415, 425
Floating-point number systems, 262–267
  in IBM 360/370 computers, 508–511
  performing arithmetic operations with, 267–268
Flowcharts/flow diagrams, 7
  of algebraic formula, *10*
  computer instructions and, 9
  of paycheck calculation, *8*
  programming procedure and, 21
Flying heads, 329
Formac language, 37
Fortran language, 37, 265, 507
Forward biased diode, 170, *171*
  saturated transistors and, 174
Four-address instructions, 446
Four-stage counter, 135
  BCD counters and, 139
Fraction, 264–267
Full adder, binary, 223–224, 234–237
  and half adder relationship, *225*
  in integrated circuit container, 236–237

Gated-clocked binary counter, 135, *137*
Gates: AND, 76–78, 178–179
  AND-to-OR, 232, *233*
  binary adders and, 227, 237–239
  buses and, *466*
  decoders and, 295
  diode, 179–180
  diode-transistor logic and, 189
  minicomputers and, 452
  NAND and NOR gates and, 97–99
  positive and negative, 181
  recording techniques and, 350
  RS flip-flops and, 135
  transfer circuits and, 127
  combination of, 91
  in early computers, 140
  flip-flops and, 135, 152–154, 260–262
    master-slave, 154–157, *190*–191
  integrated circuits and, 146, *147*
  NAND, 97–100
    gated flip-flops and, 152–157, *190*–191
    in integrated circuits, 140, *141*
    and logic circuits, 189, 191–*193, 205*
    NAND-to-, 143
  NMOS and, 205–206
  NOR, 97–100, 184–186
    CMOS and, 206–*207*
    flip-flops, 152
    MOS and, 205–206
    two-input, 184–185
  OR, 76–78, 180–181
    AND-to-, 232–*233*
    binary adder and, 237–239
    buses and, *466*
    diode, *181*

Gates: OR: exclusive, *242*
    FET logic and, *205*
    inclusive, 180
    integrated circuits and, 140
    minicomputers and, 452
    NAND and NOR gates and, 97–99
    positive and negative, 181
  transmission, *207*–208, 242
Gating networks, 91
  in read-only memories, 316–317
  (*See also* Boolean algebra and gate networks)
General-purpose digital computer, 17, 405–406
  input for, 19
General-purpose registers, 445–446, 508–510, 512
Gray code, *393, 394*
  binary-to-, 316–*318*

Half adder, binary, 222–223
  and full adder relationship, *225*
Harvard University, 59
Hewlett-Packard Corporation, 265, 448
Hex inverter, *147*
Hexadecimal number systems, 61–65
High-level languages, 37
High-speed memory, 274
Hollerith, Herman, 3*n.*
Hollerith code, 365
Horizontal microprogramming, 438–439
Hysteresis loop, 279–280, *282*
  in magnetic drum storage, 322

I flip-flop, 415, *416,* 419–424
  control signals, *420*–422
  instructions: branch, 427–429
    shift, 430, 432
  operation of, 424–425
IBM (International Business Machines), 3*n.*
  Aiken's machine and, 5
  alphanumeric codes, 369, 372
  early computers, 6
  floating-point number systems, 265
  full adder used by, 234–236
  instruction words, 448
  printers, 379, *380*
  third-generation computers, 6
  360/370 computer, 506–513
    bytes and, 63
    floating-point number systems, 265
    1400 series computer and, 500
    instruction words and, 448
    introduction of, 6
    organization of, 459
    peripheral processing units, 462
    two-address instructions and, 445
  two-address computers, 500
Index registers, 449–451
  instructions for, *479,* 506
Indirect addressing, 454–455
Inhibit winding, 285–287
  combined with sense windings, 300–*303*
  core memory: reading from, 288
    writing into, 288
  timing sequence and, 287–288
Ink jet printers, 381–382
Inner memory, 274, 407
In-phase output, 178
Input data, 11

Input devices, 357–376, 391–404
  alphanumeric codes of, 369–372
  business vs. scientific uses, 358
  character recognition, 374–376
  data preparation, 373–374
  defined, 19
  interconnecting components, 455–463
  operation of, 357–358
  perforated tape, 359–362
    readers, 362–364
  punched cards, 365–367
    readers, 367–369
  questions, 399–404
  reading the program, 26–33
  for systems with analog components, 391–392
    analog-to-digital converters, 392–398
    digital-to-analog converters, 394–395
Input winding, 279–281
  coincident-current technique and, 281–284
  core planes and, 285
  timing sequence and, 287–288
Institute for Advanced Study, 5
Instruction counter, 413, 415, 424
  branch instructions and, 427
  two-address computers and, 501
Instruction cycle, 412–415, 422
Instruction words (see Words, instruction)
Insulated gate n- (and p-) channel enhancement
    mode field effect transistors, 202
Integer part, 263
Integer representation, 221–222
Integrated circuits (IC), 139–148
  chips, 443, 470
  containers, 140, 141
  counter tables and, 142–143
  described, 6, 139–140
  feedback and, 140, 142
  lines, 143–145
  medium- and large-scale, 148–151
  memory, 276, 278
    bipolar, 305–307
  metal-oxide semiconductors and, 146
  resistor-transistor logic and, 147, 148
  three-state line drivers and, 465
  two full adders in, 236–237
Intel computers, 488–499
  addressing modes for, 497
  central processing unit of, 496
  flags used in, 498
  instructions for, 489–495
  interrupt servicing, 499
Interblock gap, 336
Interface messages, 467
Interfacing, 463–470
Internal storage (see Memory)
Interpreter, 34n.
Interrecord gap, 336
Interrupt lines, 457
  input-output devices and, 486–487
  microprocessors and, 488, 498
Interrupt mask bit, 474–475
Inverters: circuit, 181–184
  CMOS, 206
  complementation and, 78–79
  n-channel, 204–205
  transistor, 174, 175, 192–193
Investigation of the Laws of Thought, on Which Are
    Founded the Mathematical Theories of Logic
    and Probabilities, An (Boole), 73–74
Item-mark digit, 501, 503

JK flip-flops, 135–137, 141
  BCD counters and, 139
  clocked, 187–188
  counter design and, 159–161
  dual, 147
  integrated circuits, 143
  inverters and, 184
  master-slave, 154–157
  RS flip-flops and, 136, 189
Job (program and data cards), 11
Jovial language, 37
Jump instructions, 25–26, 426–429, 480
  condition flags and, 488
Junction transistors, 171

Karnaugh maps, 100–103
  don't-care outputs and, 109–110
Kelvin, Lord, 21
Keyboard, 27, 28
  ledger-card printer and, 33
  oscilloscopes and, 383, 387, 388, 390
  printer and oscilloscope display and, 32
  program entry and, 31
Keyboarding, 359, 361
Keyboard-to-magnetic-tape device, 373–374

Laplace, Marquis de, 47
Large-scale integration (LSI), 148–151, 219
  in read-only memory, 318, 321
Latch, 124
Latency, 328–329
Leading edge of square waves, 129
Ledger card, 33
Leibniz, Baron Gottfried Wilhelm von, 2, 49
Level-setting amplifiers, 395
Light-emitting diodes (LEDs), 149
Line-at-a-time printer, 379
Linear recurring sequence generator, 140n.
Linear selection, 300–304, 308, 313
Linear shift register, 140n.
Link bit, 485
Load instruction, 182, 220
Location in memory (see Address)
Lockheed Corporation computers, 454
Logic circuits: CMOS, 206–209
  diode-transistor, 189–191
  emitter-coupled, 198–202
  resistor-transistor, 181–182, 184, 187–188
  transistor-transistor, 191–198
  (See also Arithmetic-logic unit)
Logic networks, 91
Logical addition, 75, 82, 260–262
"Logical algebra," 74
Logical design, 124–167
  clocks, 128–131
  counters: BCD, 138–139
    binary, 132–137
    design of, 157–161
  flip-flops, 125–127
    gated, 152–154
    master-slave, 154–157
    transfer circuits and, 127–128
  integrated circuits, 139–148
    medium- and large-scale, 148–151
  questions, 161–167
  shift registers, 131–132
Logical expressions, 79–80
Logical multiplication, 75–76, 82, 260–262

Mad language, 37
Magnetic core memory, 278–281
  address register, 289
  arrays: characteristics of, 289
    storage in two-dimensional, 281–284
  buffer registers, 289, 292–294
  characteristics of, 294–*296*
  core planes and, 285–287
  dimensions, 289
  instructions and, 407, 412–415
  organization and wiring schemes, 300–304
  as random-access device, 278
  reading from, 288, 292–294
  registers, 289, 292–294
  as static storage device, 275–276
  storage in a two-dimensional array, 281–284
  timing sequence, 287–288
  writing into, 288, 294
  X/Y input lines, 282–284
    bipolar memory and, 307
    buffer register, 293–294
    core memory array and, 289
    core plane assembly and, 285–287
    driving, 290–292, 304
    timing sequence and, 287–288
Magnetic disk, 327–332
  flexible, 332–335
Magnetic drum memory, 321–325
  as auxiliary storage, 276
  characteristics of, *324*
  parallel and serial operation of, 325–326
  storage capacity of, 323, 325
  time unit for, 323
  track of, 322–323
Magnetic ink character reading (MICR), 375
Magnetic tape, 336–340
  as backup storage, 276
  cassettes and cartridges, 340–345
  drive, 336–339
  instructions and, 407
  interrupt lines and, 456–457
  keyboard-to-, 373–374
  layout of, *340*
  parts of, 336
  as sequential-access device, 275
    serial access and, 275*n.*
  speed of, 338–339
  tracks, *340*
Main memory, 274, 275
  random access devices and, 277, 278
Management control systems, 17
Mantissa, 262–268
Many-to-one decoder, 291, 295
Map methods for simplifying: don't-care outputs and,
      109–110
  expressions, 100–103
  subcubes and, 103–108
"Mark sense" reading device, 28, *31*
Masking, 260
Master-slave flip-flop, 154–157
  in circuits: DTL, *190*–191
    TTL, 197–198
Mauchly, J. W., 5
Maximal subcube, 105–108
Medium-scale integration (MSI), 148–*151*
  full adders in, 234–237
Memory, 274–356
  arithmetic-logic unit and, 220–221
  bipolar IC, 305–307
  categories of, 274–276

Memory: construction of, 20
  decoders and, 295–299
  defined, 19
  digital recording techniques, 346
  direct access, 458
  "dumps," 63
  dynamic, 314–316
  instructions for, 21–23, 407, *476–478*
  magnetic disk, 327–332
    floppy disk, 332–335
  magnetic drum, 321–325
    parallel and serial operation, 325–326
  magnetic tape, 336–340
    cassettes and cartridges, 340–345
  memory buffer register, 292–294
  questions, 351–356
  random-access, 276–278
    semiconductor, 304–305
  read-only, 316–321
  return-to-bias recording, *347–349*
  return-to-zero recording, 346–348
    non–return-to-zero, 349–351
  static MOS, 308–314
  storage devices, 274–276
  tape cassettes and cartridges, 340–345
Memory address register (*see* Address register,
      memory)
Memory buffer register (*see* Buffer register,
      memory)
Memory chip, 310–313
  in dynamic memories, 314
  microcomputers and, 470
  in read-only memories, 321
Memory cycle, 287–288
  registers and, 289
  times, 313
Memory reference instructions, 506
Memory registers: address, 277–278, 289, *290*
  buffer, 277, 278, 289, 290
    associated circuitry and, 292–294
  flip-flops and, 290
Metal-oxide semiconductor (MOS), 146, 202–206
  complementary, 206–209
  described, 148
  memories: access time of, 318
    dynamic, 305, 314–316
    read-only, 406
    static, 304–305, 308–314
  MOSFET, 202–*204, 206*
Microcomputers, 1, 6, 470–481
  buses and, 465
    synchronous, 467*n.*
  cost of, 451
  integrated circuit chips and, 443
  single-address computer organization, 481–487
    word, 408
  single bus and, 458
Microoperations, 432–434
Microprocessor, 406, 470–481
  addressing modes for, *475*
  chips, 443, 488
  single-address, 488–499
Microprogramming, 432–437
  variations in, 438–440
Minicomputers, 1, 6
  buses and, 465
    synchronous, 467*n.*
  cost of, 443–444, 451
  single-address word and, 408
  single bus and, 458

Minneapolis-Honeywell computers: alphanumeric codes and, 369
   instruction words and, 448, 513
   two-address computers, 445, 500–507
Mintern: defined, 100
   mapping of expressions and, 101–103
   subcubes and, 103–107
MIT (Massachusetts Institute of Technology), 74
Mnemonic operation codes, 34–35
   index registers and, 450, *451*
Modem, 13, 390–391
Modern algebra, 73
Modules, 331*n*.
Modulo 8 counter, 134
Modulo 15 counter, 135
Modulo 2 addition, 260–262
Monolithic integrated circuitry, 148
Moore School of Engineering, University of Pennsylvania, 5
Motorola corporation, 200, 473–474
Movable-head systems, 327, 329
   as auxiliary storage, 276
   as direct-access device, 275*n*.
Multiphase clock, 154
Multiple accumulators, 445–446, 505–506
Multiplication: binary, 51–53, 248–253
   decimal, 253–254
   with floating-point numbers, 267
   logical, 75–76, 82
Multiprocessing mode, 458–460
Multiprocessor systems, 462
Multiprogramming mode, 507–508

N-type semiconductor material, 170, 171
   in CMOS, 206–207
   in MOS, 202–205
      memories, 310
NAND gates, 97–100
   gated flip-flops and, 152–154
      master-slave, *155–157, 190*–191
   in integrated circuits, 140, *141*
   and logic circuits: DTL, 189
      FET, *205*
      TTL, 191–*193*
   NAND-to-, 143
National Bureau of Standards, 446
National Cash Register Company, 264
Negative-going edge clock signal, 129–131
   BCD counters and, 138–139, 149
   and flip-flops: *JK*, 188
      master-slave, 154–157
Negative numbers, 54–56
   complements to represent, 56–57, 227–231
   positive and, 227
      BCD, 239–241
Neumann, John Von, 5
Nondestructive read memory, 277
Nonimpact printers, 381–382
Nonrepresentable number, 226
Nonrestoring division, 255, 259–260
Nonsaturating logic, 198
NOR gates, 97–100, 184–186
   flip-flops and, 152
   metal-oxide semiconductors and, 205–206
      CMOS, 206–*207*
   two-input, 184–185
NOVA computer, 63, 505–506

Npn transistors: defined, 171
   emitter follower and, 177, *178*
   integrated circuits and, 148
   inverter, 205
   operation of, 172–175
Number systems, 47–72
   binary, 49
      addition and subtraction in, 51
      complements, 56–60
      converting decimal numbers to, 53–54, *59*
      counting in, 49–50
      multiplication and division in, 51–53
      negative numbers in, 55–56
   binary-coded-decimal number representation, 58–61
   complements, 56–57
      binary number, 56–60
   decimal, 48–49
      binary-coded-, 58–61
      conversion to binary, 53–54, *59*
   hexadecimal, 61–65
   negative, 54–56
      complements to represent, 56–57
   octal, 61–65
   origin, 47
   questions, 65–72

Object program, 34
Octal number systems, 61–65
Odd-parity check, 362, 385–386
Online interactive systems, 11–12
   program entry and, 28
Operand, 20*n.*, 31
   arithmetic-logic unit and, 220–221
   stacks instructions and, 446–447
Operation-code (OP code): arithmetic operations and, 424–425
   indirect addressing and, 454
   instruction words and, 21–23, 408–412, 445–448
   microprogramming and, 435, 488
   minicomputers and, 452
   register, 415, 422
   shift instructions and, 429–430
   shortening addresses and, 449
   two-address computers and, 501, 503–504
Operation registers, 274, 275
Optical character reading, 375, *376*
OR gates, 76–78, 180–181
   AND-to-, 232–*233*
   binary adder and, 237–239
   buses and, *466*
   diode, *181*
   exclusive, *242*
   field effect transistor logic and, 205
   inclusive, 180
   integrated circuits and, 140
   minicomputers and, 452
   NAND and NOR gates and, 97–99
   positive and negative, 181
Original equipment manufacturer (OEM) devices, 443
Oscilloscope, *13, 14,* 17, 31, *32*
   cathode-ray-tube devices and, 382
   terminals and, 387, 388, *390*
Output devices, 376–404
   cathode-ray-tube, 382–384
   defined, 19–20
   error-detecting/correcting codes, 385–387
   high-speed, 384–385

Output devices: interconnecting components and, 455–463
  operation of, 357–358
  parity checking, 385–387
  printers, 377–382
  questions, 399–404
  for systems with analog components, 391–392
    analog-to-digital converters, 392–398
    digital-to-analog converters, 394–395
  terminals, 387–391
Overflow sum, 226–227, 229
  defined, 234

P-type semiconductor material, 170, 171
  in CMOS, 206–207
  in MOS, 202–205
  memories, 310
Paging, 451–454
Paper tape, 359–362
  computer instructions and, 26–27
  as storage device, 275
    static, 276
Paper-tape-punching machine, 359, 361
  described, 26-27
  high-speed, 384–385
Paper-tape reader, 27, 362–*364*
  central processing unit and, 473
  speed of, 275
  tape-punch machines as, 361
Parallel adder, binary, 224–227
Parallel decoder, 297
Parentheses, evaluation of an expression containing, 80–82
Parity checking, 385–387, 503
Pascal, Blaise, 2
PDP computers, 63
  bits and, 448
  bus for, 456–*457*
  instruction repertoires of, 507
  minicomputers, 481–487
  paging, 452–454
Perfect induction, 82, 84–85
Perforated paper tape (*see* Paper tape)
Peripheral interface adapters, 470, *471*
Peripheral processing units (PPUs), 460, 462
Phase-encoded technique, 350
Pipeline computer, 462–463
Pnp transistors: defined, 171
  emitter follower and, 177, *178*
  integrated circuits and, 148
  operation of, 172, 175–177
Positional notation system, 48
Positive-going edge clock signal, 129–131
  binary counters and, 133–134
  race problem and, 132
Positive logic, 127, 198
Positive and negative numbers, 227
  binary-coded-decimal, 239–241
Prime implicant, 106
Printers, 377–382
Problem-oriented languages, 37
Product-of-sums, 92–94
  derivation of, 94–95
  don't-cares, 108–110
  three-input-variable and, 95–97
Product term, 88, 92
  minterm as, 100
  subcubes and, 106

Program listings, 35
Programmable ROM (PROM), 318–321
Programmers: assemblers and, 34–37
  compilers and, 34
  convenience of, 449
  error detection and, 35–36
  functions of, 4
  index registers and, 450
  instruction words and, 407
  interrupt lines and, 487
  systems, 38
Programming Language One (PL/1), 37–38
  introduction to, 38–42
  microprogramming and, 433
  questions concerning, 44–46
Programming languages, 33–34
Programs/programming, *22–26*
  applications, 507
  assembler, 34–37
  batch processing and, 11
  calling, 485–486
  channel, 460
  compiler, 37–38
  defined, 4
  iterative, 449–450
  multiprogramming, 507–508
  operating system, 507
  procedure for, 21
  reading into the computer, 26–33
  relocatable, 449, 507
  subprograms, 485
  systems, 33–34
  user, 507
Proof by perfect induction, 82, 84–85
Protocols, 465, 467
Punched-card-processing machines, 367, *368*
Punched-card punching machine, 28
  high-speed, 384–385
  operation of, 365–366
  quantity in use, 31
Punched-card reader, 28, 367–369
  speed of, 275
Punched cards, *29*, 365–367
  Aiken and, 5
  Babbage and, 5
  batch processing, 11
  card punching machine, *28*
  computer instructions and, 9, 26, 28
  "deck" of, 28
  development of, 3
  as storage device, 275
    static, 276
  time clocks and, 8

Quantizing, 391
Quarter adder, binary, 223

R flip-flop, 415, 424–425
Race problem, 132, 154
Radix-minus-one complement, 57–58
Radix of a number system, 48–49
Random-access memory (RAM), 276–278
  defined, 275
  microprocessors and, 471, 481
  semiconductor, 304–305
Random sequence generation, 140*n*.
Raytheon Manufacturing Company, 408–*409*, 446
RCA (Radio Corporation of America), 63, 446

Read-only memories (ROM), 277, 316–321
  microprogramming and, 406, 433–435, 439, 470, 481
Read time pulses, 288
Read-write memory, 277–278
Reading from memory, 288, 292–294
Reading access time, 294
Real-time control systems, 15–16
Recursive subprograms, 486
Refresh mechanisms, 316
"Region of ambiguity," 184*n*.
Registers: address, 277–278, 289, *290*
  branch instructions and, 427
  indirect addressing and, 454–455
  instruction counter and, 415
  magnetic drum and, 326
  two-address computers and, 501
  arithmetic-logic unit, 220
  B-box, 449
  base, 512–513
  basic operations of, 246–250
  buffer, 277, 278, 289, 290
    associated circuitry and, 292–294
    branch instructions and, 427
    microprogramming and, 434–435
    OP-code and, 424–425
    two-address computers and, 501
  condition code, *481*
  control, 412–415
    sequence of operation, 415–417
  defined, 55
  flip-flop, 128, 220, 246–248, 275, 290, 417–*418*
  floating point, 262–268, 508–511
  general-purpose, 445–446, 508–510, 512
  index, 449–451, 506
  length of, 220
  microprocessors and, 488, 498
  operation, 274, 275
  operation-code, 415, 422
  shift, 131–132, 430
    with feedback, 140, 142
    linear, 140*n*.
    operation, 245–246
    with parallel load ability, *247*
  stack pointer, 447
  as storage devices, 274–276
Relocatable programs, 449, 507
Remanent points, 280
Representable number, 226
Reprogrammable memory, 321
Resistor-transistor logic (RTL), 181–182, 187–188
  noise and, 184
  RS flip-flops in, 187
Restoring division, 255–258
Return-to-bias recording, *347*–349
Return-to-zero recording, 346–348
  non–return-to-zero, 349–351
Reverse biased diode, 170, *171*
  cutoff transistors and, 174
Ripple blanking, 149, *151*
Ripple counter, 135, *137*
Rising edge of square waves, 129
Rotational delay, 328–329
RS flip-flops, 125–*127*
  AND gates and, 135
  clocked, 129–131, 153–154
  conventions of, 125–126
  counter design and, 157–*159*
  gated, 152–154

RS flip-flops: input rules of, 126
  integrated circuits, 140, *152*
  JK flip-flops and, *136*, 189
  and logic circuits: DTL, 189–191
    ECL, 201–202
    FET, *205*
    RTL, 186–187
  transfer circuits and, 127–128
  waveforms of, *127*

SAGE Air Defense System, 14
Saturated transistor mode, 169, 174
  in *npn* transistor, 172, 174
  in *pnp* transistors, 175–177
Scaling the numbers, 262–263, 267–268
Schottky diode, *194–196*
  in bipolar IC memories, 307
Secondary memory, 274
Sector number, 325–326
Security, 508
Seek time, 328
Selection techniques, 281
Semiconductor junction, 170
Semiconductors, 169–170
  (*See also* Metal-oxide semiconductors)
Sense amplifier, 285
  reading from a core memory and, 288, 293, 300
Sense winding, 280–*282*
  coincident-current technique and, 284
  combined with inhibit windings, 300–*303*
  core planes and, 285
  reading from a core memory and, 288
Sequential-access storage device, defined, 275
Serial-access storage devices, defined, 275*n*.
Series-parallel, 244–245
Set index registers (SIR) code, 450, *451*
Seven-segment decoder, 149, *151*
Shaft encoders, 392–394
Shannon, Claude E., 74
Shift operation, 245–246, 429–432
Shift registers, 131–132
  with feedback, 140, 142
  linear, 140*n*.
  operation, 245–246
  with a parallel ability, *247*
Sign bit, 55–56
  in binary division, 255–260
  in floating-point number systems, 263–267
  integer representation by, 221–222, 227, 239, 241
Signed integer binary system, 222
Signed magnitude binary integer system, 222
Simplication of expressions, 86
  map method for, 100–103
Simulation, 439
Simultaneous converters, 398
Single-address computer organization, 481–487
  instruction words, 408
  microprocessors, 488–499
Singulary operations, 78
Skip instructions, 25–26, 426–429
Smithsonian Institution, 6
Sorter, 367, *368*
Source accumulator, 506
Source program, 34
Special-purpose digital computer, 16, 405–406
Sperry Rand, 5
Square wave, 129–131
SR flip-flop, 430–432

Stack instructions, 446–447, *479*
Standard load input, 146, 148
State diagram, 467, *469–470*
Statement. *31*, 34
  number, *31*
Static storage devices: defined, 275–276
  MOS, 304–305, 308–314
Storage (*see* Memory)
Storage devices, 274–276
Storage scopes, 382
Storage time delay, 194–195, 198*n*.
Stored-program computer, 5, 405
Subcubes and covering, 103–108
Subprograms, 485–486
  microprocessors and, 488, 498
Subtraction: binary, 51
  with floating-point numbers, 267–268
  in the 9s complement system, 241–245
  in a parallel arithmetic element, 231–234
Successive approximation conversion, 396, 398
Sum modulo 2, 260–262
Sum-of-products, 88, 92–94
  three-input-variable and, 95–96
Sum term, 92
Supervisory mode instructions, 508
Switching algebra, 74*n*., 82*n*.
Switching circuits, 169–177
"Symbolic Analysis of Relay and Switching Circuits,
  A," 74
Symbolic reference of storage addresses, 35
Synchronous operation, 128, 388–389

Tables of combinations, 79
  read-only memories and, 316, *317*
Tape (*see* Magnetic tape; Paper tape)
Tape cassettes and cartridges, 340–345
Telephone-computer link, 14, 27, 389–391
Teletypes, 11–14, *27*, 387
  microcomputers and, 470, *471*
Terminals, 387–391
Thermal printers, 381
Three-address instructions, 446
Three-input-variable expression, 95–97
Three-stage counter, 134
Three-state line drivers, 465, *466*
Time-shared computer systems, 17–18
  defined, 14
Toggle, 124
Tracks: on magnetic disk memories, 327–329, *331*
  width of, 329
  on magnetic drum memories, 322–323
  parallel and serial operation of, 325–326
Transfer circuit, 127–128
Transfer operation, 128, 426*n*.
Transistor-transistor logic (TTL), 140, *141*, 191–198
  characteristics, *195*
  flip-flops, 196–198
  inverters and, 192–193
  multiple emitter and, 191–192
  NAND gates and, 191–*193*
  Schottky diodes and, *194–196*
  shift registers and, *146*, 246
  "spikes," 193–194
  storage time delay, 194–195
  two full adders using, 236–237

Transistors: field effect, 202–206
  flip-flop, 186–187
  isolation, 305
  logic circuits: diode-transistor, 189–191
    resistor-transistor, 181–182, 184, 187–188
    transistor-transistor, 191–198
  multiple emitter, 191
  npn, 148, 171–175, 177, *178*, 205
  pnp, 148, 171, 172, 175–177
  Schottky, *194–195*
  in switching circuits, 169–177
Translator programs, 34*n*., 109
Transmission gate, *207–208*, 242
Tree-type decoding network, 297, *298*
True complement, 57
True magnitude form, 227
Truth tables, 79, *243*, 316, *317*
Turnaround time, 17
Turn-off time, 198
Two-address computer organization, 500–506
  IBM 360/370, 506–513
  instructions, 445–446

Unary operations, 78
Unconditional instruction, 25
U.S. Bureau of the Census, 3
  Univac 1 and, 5
U.S. Department of Labor, 2
Univac 1, 5, *461*
  floating-point number systems and, 264
University of Manchester, 5
  index registers developed at, 449
  MU5 computer, 462
Up-down counter, 137
Upward compatible computers, 506–507
User mode instructions, 508

Vacuum tubes, 5, 6, 140
Varian computers, 454–455
Veitch diagrams, 100*n*.
Verifier, 367, *368*
Vertical microprogramming, 438–439

Waveforms: binary counter, *133*
  clock, *129*, *130*
  inverter circuit. *175*
  RS flip-flop, *127*
  shift register, *132*
Windings (*see* specific types of windings)
Word addressable systems, 20*n*.
Word length, 276–*278*, 407*n*.
  core planes and, 285
  minicomputers and, 452
Word lines, 300
Words, instruction: branch instructions and, 426–427
  construction of, 406–412
  formats, 444–448
  IBM 360/370 computers and, 511–513
  index registers and, 450–451
  minicomputer, 483, 485
  paging and, 452–454
  representation of, 448–449
  two-address computers and, 501–506
Writing into memory, 288, 294

Zero-address instructions, 446–447